THE NEW ISLAMIC CENTURY

THE BETRAYAL OF THE COVENANT OF ALLAH
THE LIBERATION THROUGH ALLAH'S GUIDANCE

MUNAWAR SABIR

Order this book online at www.trafford.com
or email orders@trafford.com

Most Trafford titles are also available at major online book retailers.

Print information available on the last page.

ISBN: 978-1-6987-0916-1 (sc)
ISBN: 978-1-6987-0918-5 (hc)
ISBN: 978-1-6987-0917-8 (e)

Library of Congress Control Number: 2021917395

Trafford rev. 09/03/2021

North America & international
toll-free: 844-688-6899 (USA & Canada)
fax: 812 355 4082

Contents

Introduction

﴿ وَٱلَّذِينَ يَنقُضُونَ عَهْدَ ٱللَّهِ مِنۢ بَعْدِ مِيثَٰقِهِۦ وَيَقْطَعُونَ مَآ أَمَرَ ٱللَّهُ بِهِۦٓ أَن يُوصَلَ وَيُفْسِدُونَ فِى ٱلْأَرْضِ

أُو۟لَٰٓئِكَ لَهُمُ ٱللَّعْنَةُ وَلَهُمْ سُوٓءُ ٱلدَّارِ ٢٥ ﴾

But those who break the Covenant of Allah, after
having pledged their word on it, and sever what
which Allah has commanded to be joined together,
and who work corruption on earth, on them
shall be the curse and theirs is the ugly abode.

—Ar-Ra'd 13:25, Koran

Allah, in His infinite wisdom, has given man some understanding of His creation. Allah is the Creator of everything that is. He wills, and it is. He is beyond human comprehension, and His divine systems do not conform to human concepts, creed, or dogma. Allah, God the Creator, has created the universe of galaxies, worlds, stars, sun, moon, little atoms, protons, neutrons, and tiny particles that show the complexity of His genius. Allah, the Lord of creation, sends water from the heavens for sustenance of life on the earth. He directs sunshine to the earth to provide warmth and light to sustain human, plant, and animal life. Allah formed the sun, moon, and stars to create equilibrium in the universe, with every object in its intended place, revolving in its fixed orbit in perfect harmony and balance. He created the secrets and the mysteries of the heavens and the earth, the so-called sciences, and the knowledge of particles, elements, cells, mitochondria, chromosomes, gravity, and black holes, only a minute portion of which he revealed to man. Allah clearly provided humankind with a mind to wonder at His infinitesimal wisdom.

Yet humans are conceited and arrogant if they believe that God is driven by man-created creed, testament, dogma, Sunna, and Sharia.

Allah does not require a shrine, temple, tent, or a talisman to live in. His presence is everywhere. He is present in the smallest particle and in the greatest expanse. He is accessible to each and every object He has created. Every object obeys Allah's will except for humankind, who has been given free will. The covenant of Allah presents us with the scope of the freedom of choice that humankind has in doing what is wholesome and beautiful or that which is corrupt or ugly in the human role among the creation. It reminds us of how the scales of Allah's justice—the two hands of Allah, His mercy and His wrath—are reflected in the human domain, where people have been appointed Allah's vicegerents. Deeds of goodness and wholesomeness are associated with mercy, paradise, and the beautiful. Evil and corruption is rewarded with wrath, hell, and the ugly.

Allah, the Divine, is open to the most miniscule of beings. From this little particle, the connection to Allah, the Cherisher and the Nourisher of the universe, extends into the vastest of expanse. Within this communion of the Divine with the creation passes the Spirit of Allah into His creatures. The human lays his heart and mind open to Allah in submission to receive His Spirit and guidance.

In the space and the emptiness of the universe, there flow currents and whispers of wind and energy. These winds of silence, light, and sound carry the divine whisper, and in this sound is Allah's message. This message descends into the believer's receptive heart in peace, silence, and tranquility. When the angels and the Spirit descend with Allah's guidance, the eyes perceive the most beautiful divine light, the ears hear the softest tinkle of the bell, the nose smells the fragrance of a thousand gardens, and the skin feels the most tranquil of the gentle breeze. When this happens, the soul has seen nirvana. This is the knowledge of Allah.

For thousands of years, humans have been confused and misled by priests leading them away from Allah's guidance. They have invented myths and stories of creation and gods. For instance, among the Hindu, although Brahman is the creator, his role as the creator is shared by his co-god Vishnu, the destroyer. There are other gods in the pantheon—Shiva; the elephant-headed Ganesha, also called Ganapati; Sarasvati; Lakshmi; Durga or Devi; Surya; Agni; Rama; Krishna; and the monkey god Hanuman. The common man is confused. The priest, the Brahman, sings hymns in Sanskrit, a long-dead language that no one understands, which leads to further confusion and ongoing ignorance of God the Creator. This provides the priestly Brahman more power, wealth, and status as the gods' spokesperson. To confuse the matter further, the priest has taken the name of the god Brahman.

However, in Hinduism, *sanatana dharma* consists of virtues such as honesty, refraining from injuring living beings, purity, goodwill, mercy, patience, forbearance, self-restraint, generosity, and ascetism. Islam has a similar obligation to the believer to perform beautiful deeds as the believer has the promise from Allah with the phrase *alladhina aaminu wa 'amilu al saalihaat,*[1]

ٱلَّذِينَ ءَامَنُوا۟ وَعَمِلُوا۟ ٱلصَّٰلِحَٰتِ

which refers to those who persist in striving to set things right, who restore harmony, peace, and balance. The other acts of good works recognized in the covenant of the Koran are to show compassion, to be merciful and forgive others, to be just, to protect the weak, to defend the oppressed, to be generous and charitable, to be truthful, to seek knowledge and wisdom, to be kind, to be peaceful, to love others,

1

and to perform beautiful deeds. However, the essential obligation is submission to Allah, the only Creator of universe.

Among the Christians, Jesus is God or, on occasion, son of God. The priests, bishops, and pope give sermons in Latin, again a long-dead language, confusing the followers. Vishnu, Shiva, Ganesha, Sarasvati, Lakshmi, Durga, Surya, Agni, Rama, Krishna, and Hanuman—none of them have created the universe of galaxies, worlds, stars, suns, moons, little atoms, protons, neutrons, and tiny particles that show the complexity of Allah's genius. None of the Hindu gods were the creators, nor do they deserve to be worshipped. Similarly, Jesus is not a creator, nor is he God or son of God. He was God's messenger like Abraham, Moses, and Muhammad. He was teacher par excellence worthy of following. The priests, bishops, and pope are misguiding the people. The growth of Christianity is the result of colonialism and the resulting missionary work and false message of Jesus being God and son of God. Only God the Creator should be worshipped.

Among Allah's many names are *Rahman* and *Rahim*, which stand for His mercy and beneficence. The root of these two words comes from the Arabic and Hebrew word *rahm*, which stands for "womb." Allah the Creator is the Mother and the Nurturer of the universe. Allah loves His creation and therefore nourishes and nurtures them. In this love, Allah has provided humans with an intellect and freedom of choice in their intentions and actions. The covenant of Allah presents us with the scope of the freedom of choice that humankind has in doing what is wholesome and beautiful or that which is corrupt or ugly. Because man is wayward, Allah guides man with a covenant, a code of conduct. The concept of the covenant also symbolizes the relationship between humans, among Allah's creatures, and between man and the rest of His creation. They all share one God, one set of guidance and commandments, the same submission and obedience to Him, and the same set of expectations in accordance with His promises. They can all, therefore, trust one another since they all have similar obligations and expectations.

Whereas Allah gives a code of conduct to humans in a book, to the animals, Allah has given instinct and genetic markers that enable the beasts and the birds to live among their herds and flocks in tranquility, to wander the earth from a watering hole to a pasture, and to migrate across the earth with the seasons.

All believers of God unite to form one community, the fellowship of Allah, in which every person, man or woman, is independent yet interdependent on one another as all believers grasp on to the same handhold—the rope that Allah has stretched out for them. In this filial tie of independence, interdependence, and bonding, each believer becomes responsible for the welfare of others. In this relationship, every man is a brother, and every woman is a sister. This relationship of love and bonding creates equality, respect, kindness, and goodness in the family of believers. There is no jealousy or envy among people. Everyone has the same rights and the same responsibilities. None is higher than the other unless he is higher in virtue. No distinctions among race, tribe, caste, and color exist. All Muslims are brethren. Women have rights over men, and men have similar rights over women.

In this fellowship, there should be no oppression. Allah has guaranteed every individual's rights. Every man, woman, and child has the right to freedom and the right to practice their faith in accordance with their beliefs as, in Islam, there is no compulsion in matters of religion. Every person has the right to life, which includes mental, physical, and emotional well-being; right to safeguard one's property; right to intellectual endeavors, acquisition of knowledge, and education; right to make a living; and right to free speech and action to enjoin good and forbid evil. In enjoying his freedoms, the individual ensures that his activities do not impinge on the similar rights of others. No one individual or group has the right to oppress a believing man or woman nor to usurp their rights endowed by Allah. In view of the Koran, humans, communities, nations, and civilizations will continue to live in harmony and peace so long as they continue to fulfill Allah's covenant.

The major issue with Islam today is illiteracy and lack of knowledge of the *din*. People lack understanding of the Koran and Allah's message. Islam is still strong, growing stronger, and vibrant. There are more believers in the world than ever in history. Yet there are many things that have gone wrong within Islam. Muslims are blinded by blinkers of self-deception and delusion, and they cannot see the *fitnah* among their own selves. Believers, in isolation and in unity, need to look within themselves, in their community, and in the *ummah* and take stock objectively of their place with Allah and in this world. In this unity of purpose and action, believers require self-cleansing to enable them to observe themselves clearly, free of delusion and self-deception. Such unity of purpose and action requires a clean *nafs* with *taqwa* of Allah and knowledge of Him.

Believers need to understand each word of Allah's message and each covenant they have made with Him and to obey it diligently. They need to read and learn the Koran in their own language. Devotional reciting of the Koran should be in Arabic but, for a clear understanding of Allah's word, should read be in their own language. Similarly, in personal salat and *du'a*, they may beseech Allah in the vernacular and say communal prayers in Arabic. Over a short time, each person will have mastery of Allah's word and understand their *din,* rights, and obligations. The Koran is the *din*, covenant, Sharia, and law.

The twenty-first century is the century of learning, understanding, and communication. Such knowledge requires understanding of Allah's word, the revelations. It requires Allah's *nur* within the believers' hearts. When the blessed *Nabi* died, the era of prophecy ended with him. There were to be no more prophets or en masse revelations by Allah. When the blessed *Nabi* died, he bequeathed each believer the Koran and the knowledge of Allah. With submission to Allah's will, each believer has Allah in the niche of his heart. Allah speaks to the believer through each *ayah* and through each word of the Koran. The *Nabi* was a beacon of Allah's *nur* on each believer's path to Him. The believer speaks to Allah through the Koran, salat, and *du'a*, and Allah responds in the believer's heart and mind. This gives the believer peace and tranquility.

Submission (*islam*) gives *iman*, which promotes beautiful deeds (*ihsan*). Beautiful deeds bring the believer closer to Allah. In this closeness, the believer is aware of Allah's presence, and he continues to perform wholesome deeds in the *taqwa* of Allah. *Taqwa* of Allah shines His *nur* on the believer's *nafs* that blows away the smoke of desire and craving from the *nafs*. And the *nafs* shines in the likeness of a mirror with Allah's *nur*. *Fitnah* is rooted in the cravings and greed of man. Desire and craving for the shiny goods of this world muddies the *nafs*, and man cannot see Allah's presence within him. Man slips, and he strays from the path of Allah. Man is then lost. And the Koran speaks of such people thus:

These are they who have bartered guidance
for error: but their traffic is profitless,
and they have lost true direction.

Their similitude is that of a man who kindled a fire;
when it lighted all around him, Allah took away
their light and left them in utter darkness. So,
they could not see. Deaf, dumb, and blind, they
will not return to the path. (Koran 2:15–18)

When people around the world see the wretched condition of Muslims today, they pose the question "What is wrong with Islam?" And Muslims themselves wonder why—after all the submission, prayer, and humility—Muslims continue to be mired in the dustheap of humanity. Muslims continue to be poor, ignorant, and disunited. They cannot extricate themselves from the *fitnah* and oppression in Palestine, Syria, Kashmir, India, Chechnya, Afghanistan, and Iraq.

Those with the *taqwa* of Allah, the *muttaqeen*, are conscious that *fitnah* is rooted in the cravings of man. Cleansing of the *muttaqeen* begins with the knowledge that *fitnah* is set in the covetousness and cravings of Muslims; is rooted in the body politics of Islam; is embedded in the social fabric of Islam; is implanted in the way Muslims treat their mothers, sisters, wives, and daughters; and has roots in the way Muslims treat one another. *Fitnah* is in the way Muslim nations undermine and subvert one another. *Fitnah* is in the ongoing sectarian Shia-Sunni split.

And above all, the priesthood of Islam, the mercenary armies of Muslim states, and the rulers of Muslim states are the greatest purveyor of *fitnah*. Muslim rulers and their mercenary armies are the instruments of occupation and *fitnah* over the *ummah*. Muslims and their rulers plunder their kin and the community without shame or embarrassment. Some "Muslims" lead a life of self-deception and delusion. When the people know their Koran, they will know their *din*. They will not be misguided by the ulema.

The battles for the succession of the blessed *Nabi* were the legacy of the pagan and priestly Quraish for the control of the center of the new faith and the Kaaba. These past struggles of the pagan Quraish are irrelevant in today's world. Total Koran is the total *din*. Men and priests do not intervene in the believer's relationship with Allah. The division of Islam into the Sunni and Shia sects was the result of infighting among the descendants of Qusayy for the control of Islam. This battle has continued to this day, with the priest class battling to control the pulpit and the throne of the Islamic state. Over the centuries, priests have raised the flag of *fitnah* with a claim to be God, a prophet, the Mahdi, an imam of the *din*, and a spokesperson of Allah. Their claims were for supremacy over the believers. True Muslims are believers of Allah. Believers of Allah and His *din* are not Shia, Sunni, nor any other sect. These sects are inventions and innovations of priests, the likes of the priests of the pagans, Sumerians, Israelites, and Christians. Such secrecy, deception, and hypocrisy drive a wedge among the *ummah*.

Evil and fitnah have companions, those who conspire and scheme, the ones who execute, and those who condone, and finally everyone who sees evil and does nothing to avert it. When Believers refuse to follow the evil- doers and unjust rulers, the evil-doers and unjust rulers cannot rule over the Ummah. Every Believer has the power and authority to speak out against fitnah, deceit, injustice, treason and evil amongst his community. The Believers in unity have the power to cast out fitnah deceit, injustice, treason and evil from amongst their community. This moral autonomy of the individual, when bound together with the will of the community formulates the doctrine of infallibility of the collective will of the community, Ummah, which is the doctrinal basis of consensus. This consensus is in good as opposed to evil. When the Islamic rulers and the State falls into degradation and depravity because of the actions of those in authority, the burden of preventing such perpetration of fitnah and evil rests with every individual Believer, and in unison the community of the Believers. When fitnah and evil occur in the Islamic society those who bear the ultimate responsibility are the Believers for not acting against it and letting it occur.

Till the Muslims fight the *fitnah* within their own selves, in their society, and in their countries; obey the covenant of Allah; and lead their lives in *taqwa* of Allah, only then will they achieve supremacy and control of their lives. Allah declares:

﴿ هَٰذَا بَيَانٌ لِّلنَّاسِ وَهُدًى وَمَوْعِظَةٌ لِّلْمُتَّقِينَ ﴿١٣٨﴾ ﴾

Here is a declaration to the human, a guidance and advice to those who live in awareness, *Taqwa*, of Allah!

﴿ وَلَا تَهِنُوا وَلَا تَحْزَنُوا وَأَنتُمُ الْأَعْلَوْنَ إِن كُنتُم مُّؤْمِنِينَ ﴿١٣٩﴾ ﴾

So, lose not hope nor shall you despair, for you shall achieve supremacy if you are true Believers.

The law is the Koran and the guidance of the blessed prophet in matters of the *din*. In the fifteenth-century hijra, one and a half billion believers wish to live daily in accordance with the decrees of the Koran and the teachings of the blessed prophet. The Koran is the ever-living word of Allah, the Truth for all times. The prophet said, "The Qur'an consists of five heads, things **lawful**, things **unlawful**, clear and positive **precepts, mysteries** and **examples.** Then consider that is **lawful** which is there declared to be so, and that which is forbidden as **unlawful**; obey the **precepts**, believe in the **mysteries** and take warning from the

examples." The Koran, in clear terms, addresses the believers about what is permissible and what is forbidden. And the Koran is plain:

> Betray not the trust of Allah and His Messenger.
> Nor knowingly misappropriate wealth entrusted to
> you, whether on behalf of an orphan or another
> party. Be honest in handling property, goods, credit,
> confidences, secrets of your fellow men and display
> integrity and honesty in using your skills and talent.
> Whenever you give your word speak truthfully
> and justly even if a near relative is concerned.

Similarly, the *amri minkum*—those entrusted with the administration of the affairs of the believers—should not betray the trust of Allah, the messenger, and the believers and knowingly misappropriate the wealth of the Muslims. The populations of the Islamic lands are akin to the orphans whose land and heritage has been forcibly sequestered by conquest, to be redeemed and accounted for from the those who seized it for every grain of sand and every grain of stolen gold. The dictators, the royals, and their circle of sycophants and cheerleaders in all Muslim nation-states have siphoned off the cream of their national wealth. Suharto, Asif Ali Zardari, Benazir Bhutto, Nawaz Shariff and his family, Reza Shah of Iran, the Saudi royal family, the sheikhs of the Gulf states and Oman, Saddam Hussein, Anwar Sadat, Hosni Mubarak, their families, and the inner circle of their regimes plundered their nations' treasuries of trillions of dollars over the years of their prolonged reign.

However, the greatest pillage and plunder in history took place systematically when the descendants of ten barefoot, camel-herding Bedouins took control of the Arabian Peninsula with the help of British money and arms. In the latter half of the twentieth century, over a short period of fifty years, they took a heist of tens of trillion of dollars. In the Arabian Peninsula, in the kingdoms of Oman, Kuwait, the United Arab Emirates, Qatar, Bahrain, and Saudi Arabia, there are now 6 kinglings, over 200 billionaires, and thousands of millionaires among this narrow circle of 10 clans. Over this short period, the tent dwellers who had never been inside the confines of four walls of a dwelling now own hundreds of palaces in Arabia, Europe, and America.

Yet the plunder goes on and on. Each lowly member of these clans receives an allowance of millions of dollars per year. The total amount of petty cash taken out by the thirty thousand "princes" in allowances, salaries, commissions, and expenses is to the tune of thirty to a hundred billion dollars annually, which is more than the total annual combined budget of nation-states of Pakistan, Afghanistan, Iran, Syria, and Jordan, with a population of 250 million people. The number of princes increases daily, requiring a special office of the state to keep track of their allowances. The cost of security of the royal families (90,000 troops) and the cost of maintenance of personal jets, helicopters, yachts, and private royal air terminals in Jeddah and Riyadh are an additional several billion dollars. Such decadence occurs when most of the Arabs and Muslims live under in conditions of utter poverty and deprivation.

Mohammed bin Salman, the Saudi crown prince, has recently acquired a pleasure yacht in the Red Sea for half a billion dollars and a portrait of Jesus Christ by Leonardo da Vinci for another half a billion to decorate his boat. There is a hazy distinction between the people's wealth and personal spending for pleasure. This is theft. Yet the only claim to this plunder is when the descendants of ten barefoot, camel-herding Bedouins took control of the Arabian Peninsula with the help of British money and arms.

The law is the Koran and the guidance of the blessed prophet in the matters of the *din*. In the fifteenth-century hijra, one and a half billion believers wish to lead their daily lives in accordance with the decrees of the Koran and the teachings of the blessed prophet. The Koran is the ever-living word of Allah, the Truth for all times. And the Koran is plain and clear on guidelines, principles, and the law (precepts). And on these matters, the blessed prophet said, "My sayings do not abrogate the Word of Allah, but the Word of Allah can abrogate my sayings."

The prophet also said, "Convey to other persons none of my words, except that you know of a surety."

The blessed prophet said:

> I am no more than a man; when I order you
> anything respecting religion, receive it, and
> when I tell you anything about the affairs of the
> world, and then I am nothing but a man.

Allah proclaims:

﴿ وَأَنزَلْنَآ إِلَيْكَ ٱلْكِتَٰبَ بِٱلْحَقِّ مُصَدِّقًا لِّمَا بَيْنَ يَدَيْهِ مِنَ ٱلْكِتَٰبِ وَمُهَيْمِنًا عَلَيْهِ ۖ فَٱحْكُم بَيْنَهُم بِمَآ

أَنزَلَ ٱللَّهُ ۖ وَلَا تَتَّبِعْ أَهْوَآءَهُمْ عَمَّا جَآءَكَ مِنَ ٱلْحَقِّ ۚ لِكُلٍّ جَعَلْنَا مِنكُمْ شِرْعَةً وَمِنْهَاجًا ۚ وَلَوْ شَآءَ ٱللَّهُ لَجَعَلَكُمْ أُمَّةً

وَٰحِدَةً وَلَٰكِن لِّيَبْلُوَكُمْ فِى مَآ ءَاتَىٰكُمْ ۖ فَٱسْتَبِقُوا۟ ٱلْخَيْرَٰتِ ۚ إِلَى ٱللَّهِ مَرْجِعُكُمْ جَمِيعًا فَيُنَبِّئُكُم بِمَا كُنتُمْ فِيهِ تَخْتَلِفُونَ

٤٨ ﴾

> To you We revealed the Book of Truth, confirming the
> Scripture that came before it, and guarding it in safety:
> so, judge between them by what Allah hath revealed,
> and follow not their vain desires, diverging from the

Truth that has come to you. To each among you We have prescribed a Law and an Open Way. If Allah had so willed, He would have made you a single People, but (His plan is) to test you in what He has given you, so strive as in a race in all virtues. The goal of you all is to Allah; it is He that will show you the truth of the matters in which you dispute. (Al-Ma'idah 5:48)

﴿ لَمْ يَكُنِ ٱلَّذِينَ كَفَرُوا۟ مِنْ أَهْلِ ٱلْكِتَٰبِ وَٱلْمُشْرِكِينَ مُنفَكِّينَ حَتَّىٰ تَأْتِيَهُمُ ٱلْبَيِّنَةُ ۝١ ﴾ ﴿ رَسُولٌ مِّنَ ٱللَّهِ يَتْلُوا۟
صُحُفًا مُّطَهَّرَةً ۝٢ ﴾ ﴿ فِيهَا كُتُبٌ قَيِّمَةٌ ۝٣ ﴾

Those who reject the Truth, among the People of the Book and among the kafiru, were not going to depart from their ways until there should come to them clear Evidence, a Messenger from Allah, rehearsing scriptures kept pure and holy: Wherein are laws right and straight. (Al-Bayyinah 98: 1-3, Koran)

In the above two *ayahs*, Allah proclaims that He sent the book of truth with purified pages. *In this book are laws, right and straight, from Allah.* The prophet says that the Koran contains clear and positive precepts, guidelines and laws, and what is lawful and what is unlawful.

Allah has made laws, permissions, and prohibitions lucid and clear in the covenant. The believers do not require a hierarchy of clergy, priests, and self-proclaimed ulema. Why do the believers need the imams and the *masha'ikh* of the *madhahib* to direct their lives when Allah is the Teacher and the Guide? And Allah is accessible to the believer at all times.

The precepts of the covenant of Allah ensure human dignity, equality, justice, consultative government, a state where there is realization of lawful benefits to people, prevention of harm, removal of hardship, and education of individuals by inculcating in them self-discipline, patience, restraint, and respect for rights of others. It is a system under which there is restitution of all wrongs and imbalances in society.

The Islamic society, as envisioned in the Koran and the Sunna, is a moral and a just society, a society in which every individual, man or woman, from the highest to the lowest, from the first to the last, has equal, unimpeded, and unquestionable rights.

For the last fourteen hundred years, the land of Islam had been usurped by traitors to Islam and Allah. The rulers of Islam took possession of people's vicegerency by conquest or force of arms. Islam is a religion of voluntary submission of a human to the will to Allah after a considered conviction that Allah is the only reality and that everything else springs out of that reality. Allah has given every human the freedom of choice to submit to His will. There is no compulsion in the matters of the *din.* Yet there are humans who, by force of arms, compel other humans to submit to their will. They demand obedience through imprisonment, torture, and murder. Every Muslim state in this day is a police state. Every Muslim ruler abuses his authority to plunder and debase the lands of Islam.

The covenant's criterion of consultative and participative government was lost within seventy years after the blessed *Nabi* died. It has not been restored yet. No person has the right to impose himself and his family and clan as the ruler above the believers. The believers are free humans answerable to Allah only and governed by His covenant. The believers, both men and women, are not subject to other humans.

Allah has granted each Believer a right to freedom, a right of freedom to practice his faith in accordance to his beliefs, as in Islam there is no compulsion in matters of religion; a right to life, which includes a mental and physical and emotional wellbeing; a safeguard of property; a right to intellectual endeavors, acquisition of knowledge and education, a right to make a living and a right to free speech and action to enjoin good and forbid evil. In enjoying his (her) freedoms, the individual ensures that his activities do not impinge upon on the similar rights of others.

The believers, however, from time to time choose people among themselves to administer their affairs and the affairs of their community. The administrator of affairs (*amri minkum*) and his bureaucracy should deal with every individual and his or her problems with empathy, sympathy, and compassion. The word *compassion* is commonly translated to mean "sympathy," which is not quite correct. One with compassion does have empathy or sympathy with a subject, but when an injustice is committed, his inner self will compel him to correct the injustice with an action as opposed to just a feeling of passive sympathy. There should be a restitution of all wrongs and imbalances in society.

O you who believe! Obey Allah, and obey the messenger, and those charged with authority among you. If you differ in anything among yourselves, refer to Allah and His Messenger. If you do believe in Allah and the last day: that is the best, and most suitable for final determination. (Koran 4:59)

The community, the *ummah*, as a whole, after consultation and consensus grants people among themselves with authority to manage its affairs (*ulil amri minkum*). Those charged with authority act in their capacity as the representative (*wakil*) of the people and are bound by the Koranic mandate to consult the community in public affairs, and general consensus is a binding source of the law. The community, by consultation and in consensus, has the authority to depose any person charged with authority, including the head of the state, in the event of gross violation of the law and disobedience of the covenant of the Koran.

Islam pursues its social objectives by reforming the individual. The ritual ablution before prayer, the five daily prayers, fasting during the month of Ramadan, and the obligatory giving of charity all encourage punctuality, self-discipline, and concern for the well-being of others. The individual is seen not just a member of the community and subservient to the community's will but also morally autonomous agent who plays a distinctive role in shaping the community's sense of direction and purpose. The Koran has attached to the individual's duty of obedience to the government a right of to simultaneously dispute with the rulers over government affairs. The individual obeys the ruler on the condition that the ruler obeys the Islamic law according to the Koran and the Sunna. This is reflected in the declaration of the Hadith that *"there is no obedience in transgression; obedience is only in the righteousness."* The citizen is entitled to disobey an oppressive command that is contrary to the Islamic law according to the covenant of the Koran.

Even though these laws are part of the commandments of the Koran, the ulema-jurist-priests who became the administrators of Sharia chose to ignore them. Thus, the true Sharia in practice had and has no authority over the governing structure of Muslim countries. This practice has become ingrained in the Islamic society, which became a society governed by state elites who patronized priests and religious leaders, who in turn legitimized the un-Koranic regimes. The collaboration of elites of state and religion and the cooperative relationship between these two institutions has, for many centuries, become the Muslim solution to the problem of state and religion. It totally bypassed the common person, the vicegerent of God. This arrangement continues to be perpetuated into today's Islamic society.

The ruler-mullah alliance continues to be above the Sharia law and the customary law. The Sharia does not have authority over governance. These two establishments are not accountable to the Islamic populace. The Sharia law is subject to manipulation and falsification and has therefore sadly failed.

The ulema in Saudi Arabia, Iran, Sudan, and Egypt continue to issue fatwa at the behest of the corrupt ruling class. In fact, the ruling class in Islam is the source of *fitnah*. The Sharia and *fiqh* have failed, and it collapsed in AH 665 when the gates to *ijtihad* were slammed shut, and it has not since revived. In Islam, there are no professional ruling classes, sultans, politicians, priests, nor mercenary generals. The believer is independent and free, answerable only to Allah. The believer, in consultation with other believers, employs administrators, civil servants, and soldiers to run his or her affairs. Such state functionaries are the employees of the believers and not the masters. The Muslim states acquired un-Islamic regal, political, economic, and ecumenical systems from the Romans, Persians, Hindus, Central Asian nomadic tribes, and imperial European colonists. Once the Mu'awiyah and Abbasi caliphs began to wear the Roman and the Persian crowns, the populace could never impose the Koranic and Shariah law on them. Since then, the same pre-Islamic injustice and oppression of the Roman, Persian, Mongol, Hindu, and European civilizations has continued to percolate in the un-Koranic ruling classes of Islam. It is the governance of the Islamic state that has gone wrong.

The most important theological point made by the Koran is that there is one God, Allah, who is universal and beyond comparison, who creates and sustains both the material world and the world of human experience. Allah is *Haqq*, the absolute truth. All other forms of so-called truth are either false in their initial premises or contingently true only in limited situations. The recognition of this fact is of paramount importance to all believers. That Allah is *Haqq* is undeniable. *Haqq* does not fall into the domain of human fancy nor human ideas, but it stands for beliefs that manifest in concrete form. These beliefs must be in harmony with changing needs of time and with Allah's laws of the universe. No belief relating to this world can be called *haqq* unless its truth is established by positive demonstration of Allah's reality. This truth is permanent and unchanging.

There is no priesthood in Islam. *Haqq* does not need priests. Yet there are people among the believers who talk, dress, and preach like priests. They are indeed priests. They preach dogma and creed to the believers in the name of Allah and His blessed prophet. Yet what they preach distances the believers from Allah, the Koran, and the blessed prophet. The priests spread hatred among the believers and discord in the *ummah*. They concern themselves with obscure *Hadith* and man-made Sharia and *fiqh* that do not constitute the *din* of Allah. Their teachings and fatwas often contradict the Koran and the spirit of the blessed prophet's teaching.

If miraculously one day all the mullahs, self-proclaimed ulema, ayatollahs, imams, and Wahhabi preachers were to disappear from the face of this earth, from that day on, there will be no Shia, no Sunni, nor any other sect in the world. Every Muslim will be a believer of Allah. The mullahs, self-proclaimed ulema, ayatollahs, imams, and the Wahhabi preachers sustain one another through their own inbred dogma and creed. In turn, the mullahs and priests sustain their sects through their man-made belief systems. It is a cycle in which the priests continue to perpetuate their creeds generation after generation with "quote and reference" to their earlier imams and priests, repeating distortions, misquotations, and misrepresentations. The believers cannot hear the gentle message of Allah over all the noise and commotion created by the mullahs and religious scholars in the world of Islam. In the same token, if there were no rabbis, Christian priests, ministers, clerics, preachers, pastors, bishops, popes, pundits, and mullahs, there will be no Judaism, Christianity, Hinduism, nor sectarian Islam. All those who believe in one God will then be the servants of the same Allah, the religion of Abraham, Moses, Jesus, and Muhammad.

Yet priests have been with us since the times when man attained civilization. The priesthood of the Sumerian civilization left a powerful legacy on the generations that followed. Within a short time, the priestly culture spread to all human civilizations—to the Indus valley, Babylon, Egypt, Greece, and Rome. Priesthood independently sprung up in the Americas.

Humans crave a belief in the supernatural. They seek comfort and security in the idea of supernatural protection from gods. Priesthood is ever present and ready to exploit this need. Sumerians and all other civilizations were served by many gods—gods of war, fertility goddesses, sun god, moon god, gods of rain, gods of death, and so on. Priests were at hand to provide the protection at a cost, an offering to gods. The cult of gods did not operate in isolation. Though communities had their own particular guardian gods, they did share other gods with other towns and villages. Devotees traveled to distant places to pay homage to their gods. There was considerable exchange and sharing of patronage, protection, and blessing of gods among varying communities. Priesthood became the original corporations and propaganda machine for their gods.

Such publicity also took advantage of the weaknesses and vulnerabilities of the people. The greater the insecurity among the population, the more the devotees of particular gods were, the greater the wealth and influence of the priests. There were festivals of all sorts involving seasons—planting of seed, harvest, fertility, human sacrifice, fire, light, and many others. The priests began to control commerce, levy tithe, lend money on interest, organize professional armies, and provide temple prostitutes, alcohol, and protection against calamities. What mattered in the end was power and wealth. Priesthood became a network of guilds connected through secret societies that began to control the affairs of the world for all times to come.

Thirty-eight hundred years ago, the blessed *Nabi* Ibrahim saw through the deceit and falsehood of the cult of false gods of Mesopotamia. He began to speak out. Being a danger to the cult of the priests, he was threatened to be silent or else. Thirty-two hundred years ago, when the blessed *Nabi* Moses spoke against the same false gods, the priesthood persistently undermined and frustrated his efforts by worshipping the golden calf. Two thousand years ago, Jesus found the cult of the rabbis thoroughly objectionable. When he persisted in speaking against godlessness and corruption of the temple, the priests, and the moneylenders, he was nailed to the cross. Fourteen hundred years ago, when Blessed Muhammad rebelled against the gods and priesthood of the Quraish, he was threatened with death and banished from his home. It was the same organism of priesthood developed by the Sumerians whose descendants fought tooth and nail to protect their conspiratorial privileges, threatened by Ibrahim, Moses, Jesus, and Muhammad.

Priesthood created a cult of gods, spoke for their gods, and then assumed the power and wealth of the same gods. The corporation of gods run by priests in the days of Nabi Ibrahim is the longest-living organism, with its neurons and synapses running through the worshippers of the golden calf and then the Pharisees down to our times—the descendants of the priesthood of the Quraish, the enemies of the blessed *Nabi* Muhammad. They appointed and directed kings. The ruling classes and the priest class successfully formed the system that controlled every Muslim's religion and exploited all Islamic societies. Priesthood offered protection, vice, alcohol, gambling, and women to attract adherents to their gods. Priests directed trade and commerce and were the beneficiaries of usury. Priests foretold fortune and future, and for this supernatural prophecy, they gained the influence and gratitude of their followers.

The organism of priesthood has kept up with the times. It never let its tricks of the trade get stale. The religions required periodic stimulation from wars, miracles, festivals, human sacrifice, and coronations. Whenever the true prophets won over adherents from the priesthood of gods, the counteroffensive was never far behind.

Abraham reformed the Sumerian traditions in the name of the one true merciful God. He left behind many followers with oral and perhaps written traditions, which were passed on to the coming generations. The priesthood distorted his teachings. After eight lifetimes of seventy years, put end to end, Nabi Moses taught his people the worship of one merciful God. Moses reformed the pagan Egyptian traditions of his people. He spoke with God on Mount Sinai through the smoke and haze of the burning bush and climbed down to the desert carrying the Ten Commandments of God inscribed on two stone slabs. After a lifetime of struggle with his people and their traditional priesthood, he left an oral and written tradition. His people continued to revert to the pagan calf worship and pervert Allah's commandments.

When disputes arose questioning the divinity of Jesus Christ, it was a difference of opinion among the priests of the fourth century. The priests assumed the prerogative of God and formulated a doctrine that defined the relationship between humanity and God. This relationship was to become so convoluted that no two Christians have the same understanding of their relationship to their Maker. The trinity of God has an incongruent understanding for each person and each sect. For the human of common understanding, Jesus is God. Jesus, in fact, became God on May 20, 325. On that day, Jesus became the Creator, the Word, the Judge, the Redeemer, and the only Way. In return, the priest class retained and augmented the special hierarchical status as it was among the Sumerians, Babylonians, Egyptians, Israelites, and Byzantines as the spokespeople of their God and gods. They retained the power to guide, legislate, teach, judge, excommunicate, and execute. The priests wore crowns, regalia, and jewels; they carried ornamental staffs to signify divine connection. Their processions into the places of worship in full regalia with pomp and circumstance resembled more a spectacle and entertainment for the common folk than a true act of worship of the Creator. The priests spoke in strange tongues and words incomprehensible to men and women.

Three hundred years after the blessed *Nabi* Muhammad died, movements similar to ones that occurred after the times of the blessed prophets Ibrahim, Musa, and Jesus came to pass in Islam. Three months before the blessed *Nabi* died, he performed the hajj. After midday prayers on the ninth day of *Zul-hajj* (March 632 CE) at Arafat, the blessed *Nabi* delivered the historic hajj khutbah that had come to be known as the farewell address. When the blessed *Nabi* delivered the hajj khutbah, he knew that he had completed his earthly mission and that his days in the world were numbered. The blessed Muhammad was aware that he was dying, yet he did not appoint a successor. He was a *Nabi* and a *rasul.*

Only Allah has the prerogative of appointing and sending His messengers to this world. When Blessed Muhammad died, he left in this world his mortal remains, the Koran, Allah's covenant, and the *din.* When Blessed Muhammad was taken up by Allah, every believer inherited the Koran, Allah's covenant, and His *din.* Every believer became the successor, inheritor, and custodian of the prophet's legacy till the end of time. It was the negligence and the inability of the believer to assume his authority as the custodian of the prophet's legacy and Allah's covenant that degraded the *ummah* for over fourteen centuries.

After the *Nabi* passed away, the succession to the blessed *Nabi* Muhammad's *presumed* temporal authority became a problem from the very beginning. The period of the first four caliphs is regarded by the Muslims as the ideal period of Islamic history, when Islam was practiced perfectly. This is far from obvious when one looks at the contemporary records. For one thing, three of the four caliphs were assassinated.

What is the source of the continuing strife amongst the Muslims? Pagan Priesthood.

Mecca in the pre-Islamic times was a pagan sanctuary with a cube-shaped shrine as the center of heathen worship. Kaaba housed over 360 gods, with the presiding god called Hubal. According to legend, in the fourth century of the Common Era, Amr ibn Luhayy, a descendant of Qahtan, a sheikh of Hejaz, placed an idol called Hubal inside the Kaaba after the Quraish group of tribes supplanted the Khuza'ah as the protectors of the holy ancient place. Luhayy had traveled to Hit in Mesopotamia and brought back with him the cult of the goddesses al-Uzza and Manat and combined it with the cult of Hubal, the god of the Khuza'ah. Hubal is considered to be of Aramaic origin, and its name is a variation of Baal, the Sumerian god (hu' Baal). Hubal was one of the deities of the Quraish before Islam. Some of the deities of Kaaba had a universal following in the fourth century CE when Christianity had not yet gained a popular following in the Middle East. Al-Uzza was Venus of the Greeks, Aphrodite of the Romans, and Isis of the Egyptians. *Al-Lat* was the Athena of the Greeks and *Manat* of the Arabs and represented the goddess of fate for the Persians and the Romans. Hubal was the Semitic Baal, Adonis of the Syrian and Greek Pantheon, and Tammuz, the consort of Ishtar, of the Babylonians. And a six-day "funeral" for this god was observed at the very door of the temple in Jerusalem, to the horror of the reformer Ezekiel. Temples for the worship of Baal, Adonis, Tammuz, Venus, Athena, Uzza, Aphrodite, and Isis were commonplace in the Byzantine and Roman Empires. These gods formed the pantheon of the known world before the advent of Islam.

Arab tribes from all over Arabia assembled once a year for mass worship of their gods. The occasion was also used by the visiting tribes for trade of goods and as a social gathering. The traders and their caravans plied between Arabia and destinations in the Byzantine and Persian Empires as well as Yemen. Over thousands of years, Arab traders had acquired the paramount position of intermediaries in the exchange of goods between the Indian and Mediterranean traders. The trade, maritime, and the pilgrim connection provided Meccans and the Arab tribes freedom, prosperity, affluence, and luxury that were not within the reach of people of other settled communities of the Middle East. The Meccans loved their luxury, wine, and revelry that wealth brought with it. To satisfy their passionate search for pleasure, they held their celebrations and drinking parties to find satisfaction in their slave girls in the center of the city right in front of the Kaaba. There in the proximity of more than 360 images of gods belonging to over 300 Arabian tribes, the sacred elders and the priests of the Quraish and their aristocracy held their salons and shared stories, wine, and pleasures of the flesh.

Pagan worship at the Kaaba gave rise to a number of offices assumed by the king or the head priest of Mecca. These offices were *hijabah, siqayah, rifadah, nadwah, liwa,* and *qiyadah. Hijabah* bequeathed maintenance of the house and guardianship over its keys. *Siqayah* was the provision of fresh water and wine to the pilgrims. *Rifadah* was the provision of food to the pilgrims. *Nadwah* was the chairmanship of all religious meetings and their arrangements. *Liwa* was one who carried the flag, and *qiyadah* was the commander and head of the army defending Mecca and its pilgrims. These offices claimed a tithe and levy on each pilgrim, trader, and inhabitant of Mecca, which made the Quraish priesthood very rich.

Qusayy ibn Kilab, a man who had been brought up in Syria in around 480 CE, dispossessed the reigning tribe of Mecca, the Khuza'ah, with the help of the Quraish and assumed all the offices associated with the Kaaba. Thereafter, his clan became the richest and the most influential family in Arabia. Wherever there is wealth, there is greed and craving. The descendants of Qusayy fell on one another to gain control over the guardianship, priesthood, and wealth earned by the gods of Kaaba. To avoid civil war and disintegration of the Quraish tribe, a peace treaty was worked out, and the offices of Kaaba were divided between the two contesting clans. The descendants of Abd Manaf (Hashim) were granted the *siqayah* and *rifadah*, and the descendants of Abd al-Dar (Abd Shams) kept the *hijabah*, the *liwa*, and the *nadwah*. This peace lasted till the advent of Islam. Hashim's descendants continued to provision water, wine, and food for the pilgrims. Abd Shams's descendants continued to administer the upkeep of the Kaaba and its defenses.

Most historians and Muslims do not recognize the relationship of pagan priesthood of the Quraish with Islam's later civil wars and its wars for acquisition of territory. After the blessed *Nabi* died, there was an immediate though subdued struggle to revive the priestly power that had been destroyed by the fall of Mecca and the destruction of its gods. Though the powers that be could not revive the gods of the Kaaba, they could, however, take over Islam and bide their time till an opportune moment. With the rise of Islam and the conquest of Syria and Egypt, the choicest jobs of the new empire were given to the Quraish and to other Meccans. Whereas the descendants of Hashim—the providers of water, food, and wine to the pilgrims—stayed back in Mecca and Medina, the descendants of Abd Shams, the standard bearers of the army, were sent to the conquered territories. Among them was Mu'awiyah, the son of Abu Sufyan, the sworn enemy of Islam and the prophet. Both the son and the father were pagans till the last moment, till they could be pagans no more.

When Uthman ibn Affan was elected the third caliph, he filled the bureaucracy of the new empire with his kin, who were the descendants of Abd Shams. The corruption in the governance of Syria and the accumulation of wealth in the hands of Mu'awiyah and his kin incensed some soldiers to kill the caliph, Uthman. The grabbing power and wealth by one branch of the priestly family of the Quraish led to the murder of the caliph and a civil war between the next caliph, Ali ibn Abi Talib, and his stepmother-in-law, A'ishah, the blessed *Nabi's* widow. li ibn Abi Talib, Nabi Muhammad's cousin and son-in-law (Hashmi), was elected caliph; but Mu'awiyah, son of Abu Sufyan of the clan of Abd Shams (Shamsi) who happened to be the governor of Syria at the time, refused to recognize him as the caliph. Five years of civil war resulted between Mu'awiyah, based in Damascus, and Ali ibn Abi Talib of Beni Hashim, based in Kufah.

This was a civil war among the descendants of Qusayy, who had earlier avoided a civil war and disintegration of the tribe of Quraish by dividing the spoils of their priestly inheritance. The gods of Mecca, who had provided power and wealth to the descendants of Qusayy, had been destroyed. This time, the war was fought for the control of wealth and power that the Islamic empire had garnered. Fighting among Muslims, bloodshed, and killing of Muslims are strictly forbidden. This was a civil war among the Quraish and also among the prophet's immediate family. They had been used to bloodshed in their priestly days. Historians tell us about the battles, but we do not know of the conspiracies and family intrigues among the Quraish that undermined the new Islam's order. What actually followed was totally against the teachings of Allah, the Koran, and the blessed *Nabi.* However, what did occur was a norm among the Quraish—a fight for the control and perpetuation of power of the priesthood.

In 661, Ali ibn Abi Talib was assassinated, and Mu'awiyah assumed the caliphate by force of arms and established the Umayyad dynasty, which ruled the Muslim world for ninety years, from 661 to 750. This was a victory of the dynasty of Abu Shams over the dynasty of Hashim. This war and struggle had nothing to do with the blessed *rasul* of Allah, the Koran, nor the *din* of Islam.

In 750 CE, there was another civil war among the Quraish; the descendants of Abbas, the blessed *nabi's* uncle, of the Hashim's clan rose in revolt and overthrew the Umayyad, the descendants of Abu Sufyan of the Abu Shams clan, with much bloodshed and killing of Muslims by Muslims. The Hashemite slaughtered every Umayyad they could find. Thereafter, the Abbasid dynasty ruled the Muslim empire until 861. Abandoning Damascus, the Umayyad capital, the Abbasids built Baghdad as their capital.

After the succession to the presumed *temporal* authority of the blessed *Nabi* had been usurped by different priestly branches of the Quraish, a descendent of Abbas began to coerce clerics and judges to present him the authority to change the Koran. When Al-Ma'mun came to the throne, difficulties to his rule were increasing. To deal with these, Al-Ma'mun set up the so-called inquisition (*minhah*). The judges and people in authority had to state publicly that they believed that the Koran was created and rejected the view that it was an uncreated word of Allah. This was not a piece of theological hairsplitting but an important sociopolitical and legal question.

Soon after Nabi Muhammad's death, some people had the belief that the caliph was or should be a divinely inspired person whose decisions should be binding on Muslims. In other words, they wanted the caliph to carry a priestly authority both in temporal and spiritual matters, and this was also the viewpoint of the caliph Al-Ma'mun. If the Koran, though it was Allah's word, was created, then a leader inspired by Allah could presumably change it.

The opposite point of view was that of scholar-jurists, who had become an important class in Islamic lands. This, in effect, was a battle for the control of Islam between the descendants of the priesthood of Quraish, Qusayy's descendants, and the newly formed priest class from among the people. Quite a large population of the empire could not speak or read Arabic and required the services of ulema to understand the complex issues in the Koran. The scholars insisted that the Koran was the uncreated word of Allah and therefore unchangeable and that they alone were the authorized interpreters of the Koran, and only they could pronounce how it was to be applied to contemporary situations. That implied that it was they and not the caliph who had the final word. In fact, the descendants of the priesthood of Hashim and Shams or the newfangled ulema had neither the wisdom nor the authority to change or interpret the Koran. Allah addresses the Koran to the *Nabi* and to those who believe. After the blessed *Nabi* died, every believer inherited the Koran. When Allah speaks to those who believe, will He not inspire those whom He addresses with the understanding of His message?

The policy of inquisition was finally discontinued in around 850 CE because the people refused to accept the caliph's demands. It was a power struggle for the right to use the scriptures for the control of the religion as it had occurred among the pagans, the Israelites, the Jews, and the Christians.

Lady Fatimah and Ali ibn Abi Talib's descendants are held in high esteem by Muslims because of they descended from the blessed prophet. Ali ibn Abi Talib, his sons Hassan and Hussein, and their descendants also deserve veneration and honor by every believer because of their beautiful character and honorable conduct. Over the last fourteen hundred years, the lines of descent and pedigree have been dimmed by time, diluted with outside genes, polygamy, concubinage, and false claims of prophetic blood. The blessed *Nabi* said in his farewell address, "None is higher than the other unless he is higher in virtue."

In matters of the *din*, every believer received the prophet's heritage, the Koran, and the *din*. Every believer receives Allah in his heart according to his virtue. The battles for the succession of the blessed *Nabi* were the legacy of the pagan and priestly Quraish for the control of center of the new faith and the Kaaba. These past struggles of the Quraish are irrelevant in today's world. Total Koran is the total *din*. Men and priests do not intervene in the believer's relationship with Allah. The division of Islam into the Sunni and Shia sects was the result of infighting among the descendants of Qusayy for the control of Islam. This battle has continued to this day, with the priest class battling to control the pulpit and the throne of the Islamic state. Over the centuries, priests have raised the flag of *fitnah* with a claim to be God, a prophet, the Mahdi, an imam of the *din*, and a spokesperson of Allah. Their claims were for supremacy over the believers. True Muslims are believers of Allah. Believers of Allah and His *din* are not Shia, Sunni, nor any other sect, which are inventions and innovations of priests of the pagans, Sumerians, Israelites, and Christians.

Every Muslim today is enslaved by an infidel international diplomatic and financial system run through a network of secretive and deceitful treaties and clauses. Every Muslim carries the burden on his shoulder of four monkeys that direct his daily life. The monkeys of the secret international finance, diplomacy, crime, and intelligence syndicates sit on the back of every Muslim through the connivance and ignorance of Muslim rulers, mercenary armies, and religious leaders.

The Betrayal of the Covenant of Allah: The Circle of Evil

There is a satanic circle, the *circle of evil*, composing of shadowy, faceless people who all know one another and are in control of the world's wealth. This group comprising some of the world's richest men, Jewish moneylenders, Western royals, aristocrats, and business magnates manipulates and controls politicians, news media, universities, and the intelligence services of the Western democracies. These faceless conspirators are above the law, and their activities almost never hit the newsstands. Between them, they create circumstances in the Western and the Islamic worlds that allow them to place their puppets on the throne. These willing puppets—for instance, in Egypt, Jordan, Pakistan, Arabian Peninsula, and Central Asia—provide the faceless controllers reign over the Islamic lands. The circle of evil is composed of the Western world's richest men, both Jews and Christians; the Western world's corrupt political, military, and intelligence elite; and the Eastern world's corrupt Muslim rulers and greedy aristocracy.

The circle of evil deprives human kind of Allah's benevolence by diverting it to themselves. Of the total wealth and resources of the world, the circle of evil owns over 80 percent while six billion people subsist on the remaining 20 percent. The prosperity of the un-Koranic Western world is an illusion, and this illusion has become the focus of inspiration for educated Muslim economists, planners, students, and businesspeople. Underneath the facade of prosperity and boundless riches of the West lies the bottomless pit of debt. The commerce, trade, industry, shipping, highways, spacious homes, office towers, boulevards, and automobiles are all run by the engine of massive debt. People's homes, household appliances, automobiles, holidays, and college education are all financed by money borrowed from the moneylenders of the circle of evil.

Ibn Sa'ud afforded Britain the comfort of keeping the Arabs and Muslims divided and protected its commercial and political interests, which opposed a unified Muslim state. Shariff Hussein and his sons Faisal and Abdullah continued to be clients and servants of the British. For a paltry few thousand pounds and personal glory, they and their descendants sold the honor of Islam for the next one hundred years. 'Abd-al-'Aziz's sons and descendants inherited their father's debauchery and treason to Islam for their personal gain. This has now gone on for over ninety years. It should not be allowed to continue.

Treason runs deep in the veins of the descendants of Shariff Hussein and 'Abd-al-'Aziz (Ibn Sa'ud). They are *Munafiqeen* who have taken *awliya* from among the *kafireen*. According to Allah's covenant, they are of the *kafireen*. This circle of evil—the coalition of the *Yahudi*, *Salibi*, and the *Munafiqeen*—triumphed over Islam for over one hundred years. The Jewish money in London, New York, Berlin, and Paris along with the Christian powers of Europe and America collaborated with the *Munafiqeen*, Enver Pasha, Cemal Pasha, Talat Pasha, Shariff Hussein and sons, and Ibn Sa'ud and sons to defeat the Islamic Empire and fragment it into scores of impoverished mini-client-states for political and economic exploitation by the *Yahudi-Salibi-Munafiqeen* coalition.

Anwar Sadat and the Egyptian Army won partial victory over the Jewish state of Israel in 1973. The victory made Sadat a hero in the eyes of many Arabs, if not equal to then almost comparable to the great Arab hero Gamal Abdel Nasser. Puffed up by success and sycophancy from the likes of Henry Kissinger, Sadat forgot his own roots and began to take advice and comfort from Kissinger and the Israeli lobby in Washington. Against the advice of his closest advisers and the leaders of other Arab countries, he made a secret trip to Israel and addressed the Knesset, the Israeli parliament. Under the American tutelage and patronage, he abandoned his Arab allies, negotiated, and signed a peace treaty with many secret appendices with Israel at the expense of the Palestinians, Syrians, and Muslims in general. As a consequence, all Palestine and the Golan Heights are under Israeli occupation. The Arabs are disunited and in disarray. Sadat sold out Egyptian sovereignty, the Islamic nation, and the holy Islamic places in Jerusalem for four billion dollars a year. Sadat took Jews and Christians as *awliya* and willfully disobeyed the covenant that every Muslim, if he was a believer, has pledged to obey. He also disobeyed the provisions of the covenant of Yathrib and the prophet's teaching:

> Just as the bond to Allah is indivisible, all the believers shall stand behind the commitment of the least of them. All believers are bonded one to another to the exclusion of other men.
>
> This Pax Islamica is one and indivisible. No believer shall enter a separate peace without all other believers whenever there is fighting in the cause of God but will do so only on the basis of equality and justice to all others. In every expedition for the cause of God we undertake, all parties to the covenant shall fight shoulder to shoulder as one man. All believers shall avenge the blood of one another when anyone falls fighting in the cause of God.
>
> Hajj. And proclaim the Pilgrimage to mankind:
>
> And proclaim the Pilgrimage to mankind; they will come to thee on foot and mounted on every kind of camel, lean on account of journeys through deep and distant mountain highways; that they may witness the benefits provided for them and celebrate the

name of Allah, through the Days Appointed, over the cattle which He has provided for them for sacrifice: then eat you thereof and feed the distressed ones in want. Then let them complete the rites prescribed for them, perform their vows and again circumambulate the Ancient House. Such is the Pilgrimage: whoever honors the sacred rites of Allah, for him it is good in the sight of his Lord. Lawful to you for food in Pilgrimage are cattle, except those mentioned to you as exceptions: but shun the abomination of idols and shun the word that is false. (Al-Hajj 22:27–30, Koran)

Violate not the sanctity of the Symbols of Allah, or of the sacred month, or of the animals brought for sacrifice, nor the garlands that mark out such animals, nor the people coming to the Sacred House, seeking the bounty and good pleasure of their Lord. Help one another in virtue and piety but help not one another in sin and acrimony. Be in Taqwa of Allah, fear Allah, for Allah is swift in reckoning. (Al-Ma'idah 5:2, Koran)

When people and the rulers of Muslim lands indulge in shameful deeds (*Fahishah*), they do indeed follow Satan's footsteps and lose *furqan*, the criterion to distinguish right from wrong. Shameful actions open the gates to the world of iniquity, where there are no inhibitions nor shame. One licentious act leads to another till all thoughts of Allah are lost in a haze of debauchery and decadence. Intoxication leads to loss of inhibitions, licentiousness, and indecent acts against oneself and others. Inequity trespasses boundaries of self-control until there are trespasses against oneself, other people, the community, the state, and above all the commandments of Allah.

When Allah's gifts and grace are deemed inadequate, there begins a struggle for acquisition of wealth. Wealth condones *Fahasha*, and it facilitates the activities of lewdness, debauchery, and indecency. Under every pile of wealth lies the sweat and blood of its victims. Wealth is the engine of *Fahasha*, and wealth and power are begotten through foul means. The covenant of Allah forbids shameful deeds, dishonesty, and deceit. To sustain the incumbent royals and dictators in riches and power, the conscientious and those who fight for decency and truth are taken into custody, tortured, or imprisoned. Some simply disappear, never to be heard of again. The *Fahasha* and the powerful are not accountable to Allah, and they thrive in the company of Satan. Their acts of shame and profanity are perpetrated in the open and obvious to those who surround them in the circles of power.

Enter into submission to the will of Allah,
enter Islam whole-heartedly and follow not
the footsteps of Satan, for he is a sworn enemy
to you! (Al-Baqarah 2:208, Koran)

Do not follow Satan's footsteps: if any will follow
the footsteps of Satan, he will command to what is
shameful (Fahasha) and wrong (Munkar): and were
it not for the grace of Allah and His mercy on you,
not one of you would have been unblemished: but
Allah does purify whom He pleases: and Allah is all
Hearer and all Knower. (An-Nur 24:21–23, Koran)

Come not near to shameful deeds (fornication,
adultery and shameful activities) whether open
or secret. (Al-An'am: 151–53, Koran)

Muslim societies have been plagued by *fitnah* and oppression since the death of the blessed *Nabi.* In Muslim countries, *fitnah* is the result of the combination of internal and external forces. Although the perpetrators of *fitnah* often proclaim Allah as their Savior, their actions always belie their faith in Him.

Most believers, men and women, are not aware that Allah has granted each believer rights and freedom. Most do not know that when the blessed Muhammad died, every believer inherited the Koran, Allah's covenant, His *din*, and the Dar es Salaam. Every believer became the successor, inheritor, and the custodian of the blessed *nabi's* legacy till the end of time. Consequently, in the twenty-first century, majority of believers are unaware of their rights granted by Allah. They are unaware that Allah commands them to fight the *fitnah* of tyranny and oppression perpetrated by their self-appointed rulers, kings, military dictators, and infidel *awliya*, their Euro-Christian patrons.

The prophet proclaimed in Medina:

> All believers shall rise as one man against anyone who seeks to commit injustice, aggression, crime, or spread mutual enmity amongst the Muslims. All believers are bonded one to another to the exclusion of other men. The believers shall leave none of their members in destitution without giving him in kindness that he needs by the way of his liberty.

However, this fight for unity, equality, and justice did not occur in the lands of Islam; the army of God and the army of Islam did not arise to fight in the cause of Allah to defend against *fitnah*, tyranny, and oppression and to seek retribution against injustice. The absolute loyalty of the army of Islam is to God, the Koran, and the *ummah.* The army of Islam defends the believers, their faith, their land, their wealth, and their honor and fights only against *fitnah* for truth and justice. In case of injury to the believers, their faith, their land, their wealth, and their honor, the believers are obliged to exact retribution.

> No Believer shall side with an unbeliever against a Believer. Whosoever is convicted of killing a believer without a righteous cause shall be liable to the relatives of the killed. The killers shall be subject to retaliation by each believer until the relatives of the victim are satisfied with the retribution.

Had the Muslim communities stood united as one to avenge the blood of every fallen Muslim and rejected a separate peace with the pagans without all the Muslims participating in it, there would have been no *fitnah* and massacres in Algeria, Palestine, India, Afghanistan, Iraq, Bosnia, Chechnya, Kosovo, and Darfur. This unity demands revenge, retribution, and reprisal for every act of murder and injury in Dayr Yasin, Sabra, Shatila, Srebrenica, Jenin, Sarajevo, Falluja, Kosovo, Chechnya, Gujarat, Kashmir, Iraq, Guantanamo Bay, and Abu Ghraib. Had the Muslims stood up for one another and fought those who perpetrated *fitnah*, they would not have been groveling in the dustheap of humanity today.

Contrary to the stipulations of the covenant of Allah, the present six-million-man mercenary armies of Muslim states serve to bolster illegal regimes of *Munafiqeen*, the traitors to the cause of Islam. Instead of relieving the believers from *fitnah* and oppression, they cause them. They are the source of dichotomy and division in Islam; they are the defenders of the foreign hegemony over Islam. The armies of the sultans of the previous centuries and the rulers of modern times are the perpetrators of *fitnah*, and they are the enemies of Islam. They are the defenders of the borders created by the Western colonial powers that divide Islam today. They are the *fitnah.* Every Muslim state today is the source of *fitnah* that is eating into the heart and the soul of Islam.

Two hundred years ago, the circle of evil began its control of the world's wealth through conspiracy, subterfuge, and secrecy by undermining the stability of countries through war, strife, and discord and by undermining governments through the creation of confusion in the financial markets. The Western armies and intelligence services are the foot soldiers of the circle of evil, and the rulers both of the East and the West are their pawns and puppets to be manipulated at will for the purpose of control of the power and wealth of the world.

The circle of evil is the external *fitnah* whose intent is to destroy Islam. Its intent has always been to corrupt, divide, and control the wealth of the Islamic land through the manipulation of its rulers who were initially placed in positions of power by the circle with the help of Western armies, intelligence, and diplomacy. The weakness of the nation-state mercenary armies of the modern Islamic states clearly arises from the nonfulfillment of Allah's injunctions in the covenant. Faith in Allah's promise and His power, unity of the *ummah,* justice, and struggle to end *fitnah* and tyranny are essential actions ordained in the covenant. When an individual believer reneges in the fulfillment of his covenant with Allah, he only does it to the detriment to his own soul. However, such an action on the part of the community and its appointed leaders leads to the undermining, enslavement, and impoverishment of the whole Islamic community for many generations.

The foundation of the regimes of the imperial families of the Arabian Peninsula, Jordan, Brunei, and Morocco and the imperial occupation governments of Hosni Mubarak of Egypt and the generals of Pakistan are supported by the external *fitnah*—the British, US, and NATO armed forces, intelligence, and diplomatic services in opposition to the aspirations of their own people. In return, these regimes provide services to the circle of evil to subvert, undermine, and weaken the neighboring Islamic and Arab countries of Iran, Afghanistan, Iraq, Syria, Libya, Algeria, Sudan, and Mauritania. The *ummah* is saddled with the curse and the *fitnah* of priesthood, mercenary armies of Muslim states, their corrupt rulers, and the foreign masters of their rulers.

What went wrong? The Muslim army of the twentieth and twenty-first centuries has its guns pointed inward toward its own people, whereas the external borders of Islam are guarded and patrolled by the naval fleets of America and United Europe. The Muslim state armies should be fighting the treachery and oppression by enemies of Allah and Islam—the *kafirun*, the *mushrikun*, the *Munafiqeen*, and the *zalimun*, who have usurped and plundered the resources of the believers for the last two hundred years. Instead, the Muslim armies and security forces are themselves the source of oppression and treachery to the *momineen*, resisting the tyranny of the circle of evil of the *Munafiqeen* and the *Mutaffifeen*. Clear examples are the armed and security forces of Reza Shah Pahlavi of Iran, the mullahs of Iran, Saddam Hussein of Iraq, the Taliban, Pakistani governments, the Saudi family, Suharto, Syria, Anwar Sadat, Hosni Mubarak, al-Sisi, Gaddhafi, the Algerian military, and Morocco's royalty. This is a clear testimony that the believers of the covenant of Allah and those who control the so-called armies of Islam have not surrendered to the will of the same Allah and do not strive in His path.

The obligations assigned to the individual believer in the covenant of Allah are the same for the community of Islam and for the leaders the believers appoint to look after and to protect their individual and communal interests. The covenant is specific in pointing out the responsibilities of the individual, the community, and its appointed leaders.

Jihad is the internal struggle of the believer to cleanse oneself of the temptations of the evil that surrounds him or her. It is also a constant external struggle to rid the community of the treachery and oppression by the enemy of the covenant and *din*. The enemy may be obvious and visible and easily overpowered. The web of intrigue and conspiracies of the *kafirun*, the *mushrikun*, the *Munafiqeen*, and the *zalimun* is hard to detect and overcome. The deception may come from familiar people working from within the community for the circle of evil whose motive is to tempt you away from Allah's path, take control of your land and wealth, and in the process enslave you.

Each Believer has an obligation. Believers must take back their din, iman and signs and symbols of Allah from the kafaru, the Mushrikun, the munafiqeen, the fasiq, the mutaffifeen and the zalimun and take back the sacred rites of the Hajj from the filth. It is time for each Believer in Allah to realize that the booted foot of fitnah is slowly squeezing down their neck and it is time to free themselves.

The rites of hajj are sacred. The Saudis and the Wahhabis, in their ignorance and with their abominable personal conduct, have carried out atrocities and sacrilege to the holy sites of Mecca and Medina. This family secretly and in collaboration with Christian powers and Judaism has devastated Iraq, Syria, Lebanon, Yemen, and Libya and kept the Muslim world disunited. They are not fit to oversee the rites of hajj. The sovereignty of Mecca and Medina with Hejaz should be taken away from the corrupt Saudis and administered by an organization of Islamic states. The Saudi royal family's indulgence in drugs, alcohol, gambling, prostitution, murder, and profiteering from hajj finances is not compatible with the requirements as the overseers of the rites of hajj nor the covenant of Allah. They have breached each and every covenant they have made with Allah dealing with the unity of Islam and greeting and accepting *kafireen*, Christian and Jews, as their *awliya* by secretly destroying the unity of Islam and willfully decimating Muslim states.

One and a half billion believers must demand their removal and threaten to boycott hajj for five to ten years till the corrupt Saudi royal family, the *kafirun*, the *mushrikun*, the *Munafiqeen*, and the *zalimun* are evicted. For the first five years, only those whose life expectancy is less than five to seven years should go for hajj, but there is no obligatory requirement for *umrah* in Islam during this period. Let the believers take back their *din*, *iman*, and *islam* from the *kafirun*, the *mushrikun*, the *Munafiqeen*, and the *zalimun* under the guidance of Allah through the covenant that they have made with Him. The time has arrived. It is NOW.

Chapter One

The Covenant of Allah: Islam and the Believer

Religion, or the *din* of Islam, has a multi spatial influence on the individual believer in which he is aware of its three-dimensional impact on his intellectual, emotional, and physical being encompassing his total world of awareness and subconsciousness. The three dimensions are *islam* (total submission to the will of Allah, the one God, the Creator), *iman* (faith), and *ihsan* (doing what is beautiful and wholesome). The synthesis of three dimensions of *din* (religion) is what links the true believer to the Divine through total submission and faith in the reality of the Creator and performance of virtuous and wholesome deeds in devotion and service of Allah and His creation. These three dimensions are illustrated in Al-Baqarah in the description of a God-fearing person following his salutary obligations in the love of Allah and of his fellow humans in the form of *islam*, *iman*, and *ihsan* (submission, faith, and performance of virtuous deeds); all are acts interconnected yet separate.

۞ لَّيْسَ ٱلْبِرَّ أَن تُوَلُّوا۟ وُجُوهَكُمْ قِبَلَ ٱلْمَشْرِقِ وَٱلْمَغْرِبِ وَلَـٰكِنَّ ٱلْبِرَّ مَنْ ءَامَنَ بِٱللَّهِ وَٱلْيَوْمِ ٱلْـَٔاخِرِ وَٱلْمَلَـٰٓئِكَةِ وَٱلْكِتَـٰبِ وَٱلنَّبِيِّـۧنَ وَءَاتَى
ٱلْمَالَ عَلَىٰ حُبِّهِۦ ذَوِى ٱلْقُرْبَىٰ وَٱلْيَتَـٰمَىٰ وَٱلْمَسَـٰكِينَ وَٱبْنَ ٱلسَّبِيلِ وَٱلسَّآئِلِينَ وَفِى ٱلرِّقَابِ وَأَقَامَ ٱلصَّلَوٰةَ وَءَاتَى ٱلزَّكَوٰةَ وَٱلْمُوفُونَ بِعَهْدِهِمْ
إِذَا عَـٰهَدُوا۟ ۖ وَٱلصَّـٰبِرِينَ فِى ٱلْبَأْسَآءِ وَٱلضَّرَّآءِ وَحِينَ ٱلْبَأْسِ ۗ أُو۟لَـٰٓئِكَ ٱلَّذِينَ صَدَقُوا۟ ۖ وَأُو۟لَـٰٓئِكَ هُمُ ٱلْمُتَّقُونَ ﴿١٧٧﴾

It is not righteousness that you turn your faces
towards East or West; but it is righteousness to believe
in Allah and the Last Day, and the Angels, and the
Book, and the Rasools (messengers); to spend of
your substance, out of love for Him, for your kin,
for orphans, for the needy, for the wayfarer, for those

who ask, and for the ransom of slaves; to be steadfast in prayer, and practice regular charity, to fulfill the *covenants* which you have made; and to be firm and patient, in pain (or suffering) and adversity, and throughout all periods of panic. Such are the people of truth, the God-fearing. (Qur'an2; 177 Al Baqarah).

Islam: The Arabic word *islam* means "to resign oneself to, or to submit oneself," and in religious terminology, it means submission or surrender of oneself to Allah or to His will. Allah is the only true reality, and everything else in the universe is dependent on Allah for its reality and existence. Since Allah created the universe, all things in the universe are therefore totally dependent on Him and therefore are totally "submitted" to Allah. The Koran uses the term *islam* and its derivatives more than seventy times, in its broadest sense, that true religion is established by Allah alone and that everything in the universe praises and glorifies Him. All creatures, simply by existing, demonstrate the Creator's glory and perform acts that acknowledge Allah's mastery over them.

أَفَغَيْرَ دِينِ ٱللَّهِ يَبْغُونَ وَلَهُۥٓ أَسْلَمَ مَن فِى ٱلسَّمَـٰوَٰتِ وَٱلْأَرْضِ طَوْعًا وَكَرْهًا وَإِلَيْهِ يُرْجَعُونَ

Do they seek for other than the religion of Allah? While all creatures in the heavens and on earth have, willing or unwilling, bowed to His Will (accepted Islam), and to Him shall they all be brought back. (Ali 'Imran 3:83, Koran)

أَلَمْ تَرَ أَنَّ ٱللَّهَ يُسَبِّحُ لَهُۥ مَن فِى ٱلسَّمَـٰوَٰتِ وَٱلْأَرْضِ وَٱلطَّيْرُ صَـٰٓفَّـٰتٍ ۖ كُلٌّ قَدْ عَلِمَ صَلَاتَهُۥ وَتَسْبِيحَهُۥ ۗ وَٱللَّهُ عَلِيمٌۢ بِمَا يَفْعَلُونَ ﴿٤١﴾

Don't you see that to Allah bow down in worship all things that are in the heavens and on earth, the sun, the

> moon, the stars, the hills, the trees, the animals, and a great number among mankind? But a great number are (also) such as are fit for punishment: and such as Allah shall disgrace, none can rise to honor: for Allah carries out all that He wills. (Al-Hajj 22:18, Koran)

All the prophets have submitted themselves to Allah's will and hence have been called Muslims in the Koran. In the same way, their followers who have submitted to Allah's will are believers (Muslims); however, the ones who have received earlier revelations but later changed them and confined themselves to partial truth, and in their pride, closed their minds to the whole truth have lost the way. There are some people of the book who bow down in prayer, have faith in Allah, and in the last day perform virtuous deeds and who are among the righteous.

لَيْسُواْ سَوَآءً ۗ مِّنْ أَهْلِ ٱلْكِتَـٰبِ أُمَّةٌ قَآئِمَةٌ يَتْلُونَ ءَايَـٰتِ ٱللَّهِ ءَانَآءَ ٱلَّيْلِ وَهُمْ يَسْجُدُونَ ﴿١١٣﴾

> Not all of them are alike: of the People of the Book are a portion that stand (for the right); they rehearse the Signs of Allah all night long, and they prostrate themselves in adoration.

أَلَمْ تَرَ أَنَّ ٱللَّهَ يُسَبِّحُ لَهُۥ مَن فِى ٱلسَّمَـٰوَٰتِ وَٱلْأَرْضِ وَٱلطَّيْرُ صَـٰٓفَّـٰتٍ ۖ كُلٌّ قَدْ عَلِمَ صَلَاتَهُۥ وَتَسْبِيحَهُۥ ۗ وَٱللَّهُ عَلِيمٌۢ بِمَا يَفْعَلُونَ ﴿٤١﴾

> They believe in Allah and the Last Day; they enjoin what is right and forbid what is wrong; and they hasten (in emulation) in (all) good works: they are in the ranks of the righteous.

وَمَا يَفْعَلُوا۟ مِنْ خَيْرٍ فَلَن يُكْفَرُوهُ ۗ وَٱللَّهُ عَلِيمٌۢ بِٱلْمُتَّقِينَ ﴿١١٥﴾

Of the good that they do, nothing will be rejected of them; for Allah knows well those that do right. (Ali 'Imran 3:113–15, Koran)

إِنَّ ٱلدِّينَ عِندَ ٱللَّهِ ٱلْإِسْلَٰمُ ۗ وَمَا ٱخْتَلَفَ ٱلَّذِينَ أُوتُوا۟ ٱلْكِتَٰبَ إِلَّا مِنۢ بَعْدِ مَا جَآءَهُمُ ٱلْعِلْمُ بَغْيًۢا بَيْنَهُمْ ۗ وَمَن يَكْفُرْ بِـَٔايَٰتِ ٱللَّهِ

فَإِنَّ ٱللَّهَ سَرِيعُ ٱلْحِسَابِ ﴿١٩﴾

The religion before Allah is Islam (submission to His Will): nor did the people of the Book dissent there from except through envy of each other, after knowledge had come to them. But if any deny the Signs of Allah, Allah is swift in calling to account. (Ali 'Imran 3:19, Koran)

The true religion in the sight of Allah is only through submission to Him, and those who reject it will be in the ranks of the unguided.

وَمَن يَبْتَغِ غَيْرَ ٱلْإِسْلَٰمِ دِينًا فَلَن يُقْبَلَ مِنْهُ وَهُوَ فِى ٱلْءَاخِرَةِ مِنَ ٱلْخَٰسِرِينَ ﴿٨٥﴾

If anyone desires a religion other than Islam (submission to Allah), never will it be accepted of him; and in the Hereafter he will be in the ranks of those who have lost (all spiritual good). (Ali 'Imran 3:85, Koran)

Iman: Faith in Islam is not blind. Although belief in the unseen is important, there comes a point when the believer, as a spiritual human being, transcends the level of simple faith to a spiritual consciousness that penetrates the fog of the unseen, leading to knowledge of the true nature of things, the reality of Allah. The Koran speaks of this progression from *faith* to *knowledge* as an inward metamorphosis in which belief (*iman*) is transformed into certainty (*yaqin*). This certainty is expressed in the Koran in terms of the three types of knowledge of Allah.

The basic and fundamental knowledge is the *knowledge of certainty* (*ilm al-yaqin*, Koran 102:5). This type of certainty refers to the knowledge that results from human capacity for logical reasoning and the appraisal of what the Koran calls "clear evidence" (*bayyinat*) of Allah's presence in the world. The knowledge of certainty is rational and discursive, a point that the Koran acknowledges when it admonishes human beings to

قُلْ سِيرُوا۟ فِى ٱلْأَرْضِ فَٱنظُرُوا۟ كَيْفَ بَدَأَ ٱلْخَلْقَ ۚ ثُمَّ ٱللَّهُ يُنشِئُ ٱلنَّشْأَةَ ٱلْءَاخِرَةَ ۚ إِنَّ ٱللَّهَ عَلَىٰ كُلِّ شَىْءٍ قَدِيرٌ

Say: "Travel through the earth and see how Allah did originate creation; so, will Allah produce a later creation: for Allah has power over all things. (Al-'Ankabut 29:20, Koran)

وَهُوَ ٱلَّذِى يُحْىِۦ وَيُمِيتُ وَلَهُ ٱخْتِلَٰفُ ٱلَّيْلِ وَٱلنَّهَارِ ۚ أَفَلَا تَعْقِلُونَ ﴿٨٠﴾

It is He Who gives life and death, and to Him (is due) the alternation of Night and Day: will you not then understand? (Al-Mu'minun 23:80, Koran)

Over time and under the influence of contemplation and spiritual practice, the knowledge of certainty may be transformed into a higher form of knowledge of Allah, which the Qur'an calls the *eye of certainty* (*ain al-yaqin*, Koran 102:7). This term refers to the knowledge that is acquired by spiritual intelligence, which the believers locate metaphorically in the heart. Before attaining this type of knowledge, the heart of the believer must first be *opened to Islam*.

﴿ أَفَمَن شَرَحَ ٱللَّهُ صَدْرَهُۥ لِلْإِسْلَـٰمِ فَهُوَ عَلَىٰ نُورٍ مِّن رَّبِّهِۦ ۚ فَوَيْلٌ لِّلْقَـٰسِيَةِ قُلُوبُهُم مِّن ذِكْرِ ٱللَّهِ ۚ أُو۟لَـٰٓئِكَ فِى ضَلَـٰلٍ مُّبِينٍ

Is one whose heart Allah has opened to Islam, so
that he has received enlightenment from Allah.
Woe to those whose hearts are hardened against
celebrating the praises of Allah! They are manifestly
wandering (in error)! (Az-Zumar 39:22, Koran)

Once opened, the heart receives knowledge of the divine *light*, the illumination or the *nur* of Allah.

Just as with the knowledge of certainty, with the eye of certainty, the believer sees Allah's existence through His presence in this world, the signs of Allah. With the eye of certainty, what leads the believer to the knowledge of Allah are not the arguments to be understood by the rational intellect but by theophanic appearances (*bayyinat*) that strip away the veils of worldly phenomenon to reveal the divine reality underneath.

From the spiritual perspective, the one who perceives reality through the knowledge of Allah is a true *intellectual*. Unlike the scholar, who develops his or her skills through years of formal study, the spiritual intellectual does not need book learning to understand the divine light. A spiritual intellectual can be anyone, scholarly or otherwise, whose knowledge extends *outward* to take in the physical world, *upward* to realize his ultimate transcendence of the world through his link with the Absolute, and then *inward* to reconcile all that with his intellectual and emotional self. *Without such a vertical dimension of spirit, the scholar's knowledge, whatever its extent in academic terms, is of little worth.*

The third and most advanced type of knowledge builds on transcendent nature of knowledge itself. The highest level of consciousness is called the *truth of certainty* (*haqq al-yaqin*).

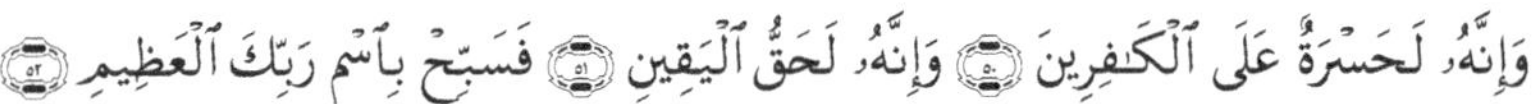

But truly (Revelation) is a cause of sorrow for the Unbelievers. But verily it is Truth of assured certainty. So, glorify the name of thy Lord Most High. (Al-Haqqah 69:50–52, Koran)

It is also known as *ilm ladduni* (knowledge by presence). This form of knowledge partakes directly of the divine reality and leaps off directly across the synapses of human mind to transcend both cognitive reasoning and intellectual vision at the same time. The "truth of certainty" refers to a state of consciousness in which a person knows the Real through direct participation in it without resorting to logical proofs. This type of knowledge characterizes God's prophets and *rasuls*, whose consciousness of the truth is both immediate and participatory as what it is based on comes from direct inspiration.

According to the Koran, faith in Islam has as much to do with *theoretical and empirical* knowledge as it does with simple belief. This multidimensional concept of knowledge comprehends a reality that lies hidden within the unique world yet can be revealed to the human mind and vision of spiritual intellect through the signs of Allah that are present in the world. In the Koran, Allah calls humanity:

فَلَآ أُقۡسِمُ بِمَا تُبۡصِرُونَ ۝٣٨ وَمَا لَا تُبۡصِرُونَ ۝٣٩

So, I do call to witness what you
see, and what you see not,

تَنزِيلٌ مِّن رَّبِّ ٱلۡعَٰلَمِينَ

(This is) a Message sent down from
the Lord of the Worlds.

وَإِنَّهُۥ لَحَقُّ ٱلۡيَقِينِ

But verily it is Truth of assured certainty.
(Al-Haqqah 69:38–39, 43, 51, Koran)

The Koranic notion of *iman* as dependent on knowledge is actualized in practice in the term *islam*. The term *islam* signifies the idea of surrender or submission. Islam is a religion of self-surrender; it is the conscious and rational submission of a dependent and limited human will to the absolute and omnipotent will of Allah. The type of surrender Islam requires is a deliberate, conscious, and rational act made by a person who knows with both intellectual certainty and spiritual vision that Allah is the reality.

The knower of God is a *Muslim*, one who submits to the divine truth and whose relationship with God is governed by *taqwa*, the consciousness of humankind's responsibility toward its Creator. However, consciousness of God alone is not sufficient to make a person a Muslim. Neither is it enough to be merely born a Muslim or to be raised in an Islamic cultural context. The concept of *taqwa* implies that the believer has the added responsibility of acting in accordance with three types of knowledge: *ilm al-yaqin*, *ain al-yaqin*, and *haqq al-yaqin* (knowledge of certainty, eye of certainty, and the truth of certainty). By doing so, the believer attains the honored title of "slave of Allah" (*abd Allah*, fem. *amat Allah*), for he recognizes that all power and all agency belongs to God alone:

وَلَوْلَآ إِذْ دَخَلْتَ جَنَّتَكَ قُلْتَ مَا شَآءَ ٱللَّهُ لَا قُوَّةَ إِلَّا بِٱللَّهِ ۚ إِن تَرَنِ أَنَا۠ أَقَلَّ مِنكَ مَالًا وَوَلَدًا ﴿٣٩﴾

Allah has willed it. There is no power but
Allah's. (Al-Kahf 18:39, Koran)

Trusting in the merciful Allah, his divine Master, yet fearing his Master's wrath, the slave of Allah walks the road of life in careful steps, making his actions deliberate so that he will not stray from the path that God has laid out for him:

إِيَّاكَ نَعْبُدُ وَإِيَّاكَ نَسْتَعِينُ ﴿٥﴾ ٱهْدِنَا ٱلصِّرَٰطَ ٱلْمُسْتَقِيمَ ﴿٦﴾ صِرَٰطَ ٱلَّذِينَ أَنْعَمْتَ عَلَيْهِمْ غَيْرِ ٱلْمَغْضُوبِ عَلَيْهِمْ وَلَا ٱلضَّآلِّينَ

Thee do we worship, and Thine aid we seek,
Show us the straight Path, The Path of those
on whom Thou hast bestowed Thy Grace,
those whose (portion) is not wrath, and who
go not astray. (Al-Fatihah 1:5–7, Koran)

It is a comprehensive and highly personal type of commitment that has little in common with academic understanding of Islam as a civilization or a cultural system. The universality of religious experience is an important premise of the Koran's argument against profane or secular life. The Koran is not concerned with defining creedal boundaries but with affirming the universal obligation to believe in one God. The Koran speaks of broad varieties of religious experience to which every human being can relate. When dealing with religious practices, the Koran is less concerned with details of the ritual than with the meaning that lies behind the rituals it prescribes. The detail of the ritual practice, which serves to define Islam to most believers, is usually left for the tradition to define.

By speaking in a transcendental voice and presenting a discourse that is relevant to human experience in general, the Koran overcomes the cultural limitations of the western Arabian civilization, in which it was originally revealed, and makes it accessible to peoples of different cultural backgrounds throughout the world. This universalism has never been more important than it is in the present, when the majority of the believers do not speak Arabic. Such transcendence of culture is necessary for the Koran, as the vehicle of the word of God, to overcome linguistic and cultural differences and express itself in a metalanguage that can be understood even when its original Arabic is translated into a non-Semitic language such as English, Mandarin, Hindi, or Malay. An example of this metalanguage is found in the three types of knowledge already discussed. Most people, whatever their experiences and cultural background, think in similar ways and have similar wants and needs. The Koran seeks to establish a common foundation for belief that is based on such shared perceptions and experiences.

Over and over again, the Koran reminds the reader to think about the truths that lie behind the familiar or mundane things of the world, such as signs of God in nature, the practical value of virtue, and the cross-cultural validity of moral principles. What is good for Muslims is meant to be good for all human beings, regardless of gender, color, or origin. The Koran, therefore, appeals to both reason and experience in determining the criterion for distinguishing between truth and falsehood.

The most important theological point made by the Koran is that there is one God, Allah, universal and beyond comparison, the Creator, who sustains both the material world and the world of human experience.

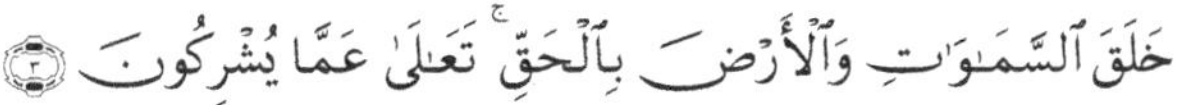

He has created the heavens and the earth for just ends, far is He above having the partners they ascribe to Him! (An-Nahl 16:3, Koran)

All other forms of so-called truth are either false in their initial premises or contingently true only in limited situations. The recognition of this fact produces a profound effect on the human soul that has forever drawn humans in the search for the divine, which forever transforms the outlook of the believer.

The faith of Islam is based on knowledge, which is both a liberation and a limitation. The certainty of the divine reality liberates the human spirit to expand outward, upward, and then inward to transform the human's emotional and intellectual self so that consciousness becomes three dimensional. This knowledge is also a limitation because with the knowledge of God comes a concomitant awareness of the limits and responsibility imposed on a person as a created being. Unlike a secular humanist, a true Muslim who submits to God cannot delude himself by claiming that he is the sole author of his destiny as he knows that a person's fate is controlled by factors beyond his control.

Ihsan: The third dimension of *din* is *ihsan*. The word *ihsan* is derived from the word *husn*, which designates the quality of being good, beautiful, virtuous, pleasing, harmonious, or wholesome. The Koran employs the word *hasana*, from the same root as *husn*, to mean "a good or a beautiful deed." For example:

مَّآ أَصَابَكَ مِنْ حَسَنَةٍ فَمِنَ ٱللَّهِ ۖ وَمَآ أَصَابَكَ مِن سَيِّئَةٍ فَمِن نَّفْسِكَ ۚ وَأَرْسَلْنَٰكَ لِلنَّاسِ رَسُولًا ۚ وَكَفَىٰ بِٱللَّهِ شَهِيدًا

Whatever beautiful touches you, it is from Allah, and whatever ugly thing touches you, it is from yourself. And We have sent thee as a Rasool to (instruct) humanity. And enough is Allah for a witness. (An-Nisa 4:79, Koran)

مَن جَآءَ بِٱلْحَسَنَةِ فَلَهُۥ خَيْرٌ مِّنْهَا ۖ وَمَن جَآءَ بِٱلسَّيِّئَةِ فَلَا يُجْزَى ٱلَّذِينَ عَمِلُوا۟ ٱلسَّيِّـَٔاتِ إِلَّا مَا كَانُوا۟ يَعْمَلُونَ

If any does beautiful deeds, the reward to him is better than his deed; but if anyone does evil, the doers of evil are only punished (to the extent) of their deeds. (Al-Qasas 28: 84, Koran)

The most significant Koranic usage of the word derived from *husn* is found in the adjective *husna*, most beautiful, which is applied to Allah's names. The Koran mentions Allah's most beautiful names in four verses. This means that Allah's attributes are more beautiful, more attractive, and more praiseworthy than attributes of anything else. Each divine name designates a superlative quality possessed by Allah alone. Allah is beautiful, and none is beautiful but Allah. Allah is majestic, and none is majestic but Allah. All of Allah's beautiful names can be placed in the formula of tawhid.

The Koran also uses the word *husna* as a noun, meaning "the best, the most beautiful," that which comprises all goodness, beauty, and desirability. *Husna* is the reward given to the devout and the faithful.

By following the straight path of Allah and the teachings of the prophets and living up to the faith, human beings actualize Allah's most beautiful names in themselves and finally come to participate in everything that is most beautiful. The word *husna* is thus used to designate both the attributes of Allah and the ultimate goal of human beings, the reward that they experience in the next world.

وَأَمَّا مَنْ ءَامَنَ وَعَمِلَ صَـٰلِحًا فَلَهُۥ جَزَآءً ٱلْحُسْنَىٰ ۖ وَسَنَقُولُ لَهُۥ مِنْ أَمْرِنَا يُسْرًا ۝

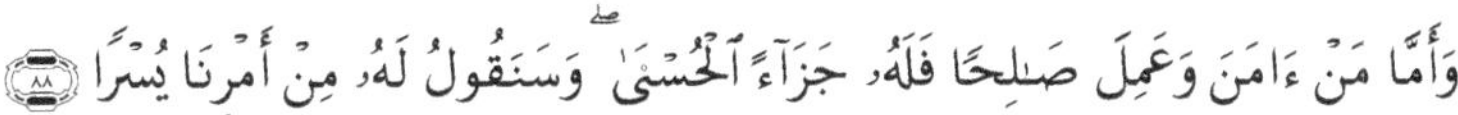

And for him who has faith and does
wholesome works, his recompense shall be
most beautiful. (Al-Kahf 18:88, Koran)

لِلَّذِينَ ٱسْتَجَابُوا۟ لِرَبِّهِمُ ٱلْحُسْنَىٰ ۚ وَٱلَّذِينَ لَمْ يَسْتَجِيبُوا۟ لَهُۥ لَوْ أَنَّ لَهُم مَّا فِى ٱلْأَرْضِ جَمِيعًا وَمِثْلَهُۥ مَعَهُۥ لَٱفْتَدَوْا۟ بِهِۦٓ ۚ أُو۟لَـٰٓئِكَ لَهُمْ سُوٓءُ ٱلْحِسَابِ وَمَأْوَىٰهُمْ جَهَنَّمُ ۖ وَبِئْسَ ٱلْمِهَادُ ۝

For those who answer their Lord, are the most
beautiful things and those who answer Him not-
theirs shall be an ugly reckoning, and their refuge
shall be in Gehenna. (Ar-Ra'd 13:18, Koran)

The word *ihsan* is a verb that means "to establish or to perform what is good and beautiful." The Koran employs the word *ihsan* and its active particle *muhsin* (the one who does what is beautiful and good) in seventy verses. The Koran often designates Allah as the One who does what is beautiful, and *al-Muhsin* is one of Allah's divine names. Allah created the universe of galaxies, stars, suns, and moons all in their ordained orbits, destined in their paths by Allah's mysterious forces, all shining and luminescent with Allah's blessed light (*nur*) that provides life and vigor to billions of His creatures.

ذَٰلِكَ عَٰلِمُ ٱلْغَيْبِ وَٱلشَّهَٰدَةِ ٱلْعَزِيزُ ٱلرَّحِيمُ ﴿٦﴾ ٱلَّذِىٓ أَحْسَنَ كُلَّ شَىْءٍ خَلَقَهُۥ ۖ وَبَدَأَ خَلْقَ ٱلْإِنسَٰنِ مِن طِينٍ ﴿٧﴾ ثُمَّ جَعَلَ نَسْلَهُۥ مِن
سُلَٰلَةٍ مِّن مَّآءٍ مَّهِينٍ ﴿٨﴾ ثُمَّ سَوَّىٰهُ وَنَفَخَ فِيهِ مِن رُّوحِهِۦ ۖ وَجَعَلَ لَكُمُ ٱلسَّمْعَ وَٱلْأَبْصَٰرَ وَٱلْأَفْـِٔدَةَ ۚ قَلِيلًا مَّا تَشْكُرُونَ ﴿٩﴾

He is the Knower of the unseen and the visible, and the Mighty, the Compassionate, who made beautiful everything that He created. And He created the human being from clay and made his progeny an extraction of mean water. Then he proportioned him and blew into him of His own spirit. (Al-Sajdah 32:6–9, Koran)

ٱللَّهُ ٱلَّذِى جَعَلَ لَكُمُ ٱلْأَرْضَ قَرَارًا وَٱلسَّمَآءَ بِنَآءً وَصَوَّرَكُمْ فَأَحْسَنَ صُوَرَكُمْ وَرَزَقَكُم مِّنَ ٱلطَّيِّبَٰتِ ۚ ذَٰلِكُمُ ٱللَّهُ رَبُّكُمْ ۖ
فَتَبَارَكَ ٱللَّهُ رَبُّ ٱلْعَٰلَمِينَ ﴿٦٤﴾

It is Allah who has made the earth as the resting place for you, and heaven a canopy, and He formed you, made your forms beautiful, and provided you sustenance of things pure and good. Such is your Lord. So, glory to Allah, the Lord of the Worlds. (Ghafir 40:64, Koran)

خَلَقَ ٱلسَّمَٰوَٰتِ وَٱلْأَرْضَ بِٱلْحَقِّ وَصَوَّرَكُمْ فَأَحْسَنَ صُوَرَكُمْ ۖ وَإِلَيْهِ ٱلْمَصِيرُ

He created heavens and the earth with His Reality (Haqq), formed you and made your forms beautiful and to Him is the homecoming. (At-Taghabun 64:3, Koran)

Love (Hubb): The Koran ascribes the love of Allah in about fifteen verses. The emotion most closely associated with *ihsan* is *hubb*. To have *ihsan* is to do what is beautiful. Five verses of the Koran mention that Allah loves those who have *ihsan* because by doing what is beautiful, they have developed beautiful traits that are worthy of Allah's love. In every verse of the Koran where Allah is said to love something, the object of this love is those human beings whose traits and activities are beautiful:

And spend of your substance in the cause of Allah and make not your own hands contribute to your destruction. Do what is beautiful. Surely Allah loves those who do what is beautiful. (Al-Baqarah 2:195, Koran)

۞ وَسَارِعُوٓاْ إِلَىٰ مَغۡفِرَةٖ مِّن رَّبِّكُمۡ وَجَنَّةٍ عَرۡضُهَا ٱلسَّمَٰوَٰتُ وَٱلۡأَرۡضُ أُعِدَّتۡ لِلۡمُتَّقِينَ ١٣٣ ٱلَّذِينَ يُنفِقُونَ فِي ٱلسَّرَّآءِ وَٱلضَّرَّآءِ

وَٱلۡكَٰظِمِينَ ٱلۡغَيۡظَ وَٱلۡعَافِينَ عَنِ ٱلنَّاسِۗ وَٱللَّهُ يُحِبُّ ٱلۡمُحۡسِنِينَ

Vie with one another, hastening to forgiveness from your Lord and to a Garden whose breadth is heavens and the earth, prepared for the god-wary, who give alms in both ease and in adversity and who restrain their anger and pardon people. Allah loves those who do what is beautiful. (Ali 'Imran 3:133–34)

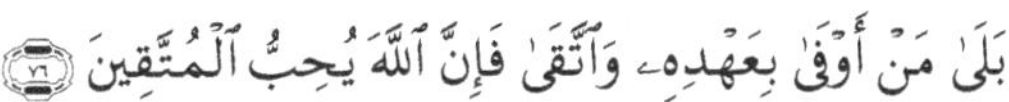

Whosoever fulfils his Covenant and has Taqwa of Allah, surely Allah loves those with Taqwa. (Ali 'Imran 3:76, Koran)

لَيۡسَ عَلَى ٱلَّذِينَ ءَامَنُواْ وَعَمِلُواْ ٱلصَّٰلِحَٰتِ جُنَاحٌ فِيمَا طَعِمُوٓاْ إِذَا مَا ٱتَّقَواْ وَّءَامَنُواْ وَعَمِلُواْ ٱلصَّٰلِحَٰتِ ثُمَّ ٱتَّقَواْ وَّءَامَنُواْ ثُمَّ ٱتَّقَواْ

وَّأَحۡسَنُواْۗ وَٱللَّهُ يُحِبُّ ٱلۡمُحۡسِنِينَ ﴿٩٣﴾

There is no fault in those who have faith and do wholesome deeds in what they eat, if they are with Taqwa, have faith do wholesome deeds, and then have Taqwa, have faith and then are with Taqwa and do what is beautiful. Allah loves those who do what is beautiful. (Al-Ma'idah 5:93, Koran)

إِنَّ ٱللَّهَ يُحِبُّ ٱلتَّوَّٰبِينَ وَيُحِبُّ ٱلۡمُتَطَهِّرِينَ ﴿٢٢٢﴾

Truly Allah loves those who repent, and He loves those who cleanse themselves. (Al-Baqarah 2:222, Koran)

فَبِمَا رَحۡمَةٖ مِّنَ ٱللَّهِ لِنتَ لَهُمۡۖ وَلَوۡ كُنتَ فَظًّا غَلِيظَ ٱلۡقَلۡبِ لَٱنفَضُّواْ مِنۡ حَوۡلِكَۖ فَٱعۡفُ عَنۡهُمۡ وَٱسۡتَغۡفِرۡ لَهُمۡ وَشَاوِرۡهُمۡ فِي ٱلۡأَمۡرِۖ فَإِذَا

عَزَمۡتَ فَتَوَكَّلۡ عَلَى ٱللَّهِۚ إِنَّ ٱللَّهَ يُحِبُّ ٱلۡمُتَوَكِّلِينَ ﴿١٥٩﴾

It is part of Allah's Mercy that that you deal gently with them. Had you been severe or harsh hearted, they would have broken away from you: so, pass over their faults and ask for forgiveness for them; and consult them in the affairs. Then, when you have taken a decision, put your trust in Allah. Allah loves those who have trust. (Ali 'Imran 3:159, Koran)

ۚ فَإِن فَآءَتْ فَأَصْلِحُوا۟ بَيْنَهُمَا بِٱلْعَدْلِ وَأَقْسِطُوٓا۟ ۖ إِنَّ ٱللَّهَ يُحِبُّ ٱلْمُقْسِطِينَ ﴿٩﴾

Make things wholesome among them
equitably and be just. Surely Allah loves
the just. (Al-Hujurat 49:9, Koran)

Such verses reveal that Allah loves humans who do what is beautiful; who have *taqwa* and are God-wary; who repent, ask for forgiveness, and cleanse themselves; who have trust in Allah; and who are just and fair. Twenty-three verses in the Koran mention traits in humans that Allah does not love: the truth concealers (*Munafiqeen*), the wrongdoers (*zalimun*), workers of corruption (*mufsidun*), the transgressors (*ta'adda*), the immoderate, the proud, and the boastful.

In the Koran, Allah's love is always directed at humans, and such a love designates the special relationship between Allah and human beings, the special trust in the form of vicegerency only given to mankind. However, Allah does not love human beings whose love is not directed at Him. How can humans love Allah, about whom they know nothing? Once people come to know that Allah is lovable and the first spark for love of Allah lights up, according to the Koran, the person must follow the *Nabi* by moving toward Allah through right practice, right faith, and doing what is beautiful. Through Allah's love, they will reach salvation. Allah commands the *Nabi* to utter these words:

قُلْ إِن كُنتُمْ تُحِبُّونَ ٱللَّهَ فَٱتَّبِعُونِى يُحْبِبْكُمُ ٱللَّهُ وَيَغْفِرْ لَكُمْ ذُنُوبَكُمْ ۗ وَٱللَّهُ غَفُورٌ رَّحِيمٌ ﴿٣١﴾ قُلْ أَطِيعُوا۟ ٱللَّهَ وَٱلرَّسُولَ ۖ فَإِن تَوَلَّوْا۟ فَإِنَّ
ٱللَّهَ لَا يُحِبُّ ٱلْكَٰفِرِينَ ﴿٣٢﴾

Say, if you love Allah, follow me and Allah will
love you and forgive your sins. Allah is Forgiving,

Compassionate. Say, "Obey Allah and the Rasool."
But if they turn their backs, Allah loves not those
who reject faith. (Ali 'Imran 3:31–32, Koran)

Allah wants people to love Him, and their love for Him follows His love for them. Human love precedes divine love. It is Allah who, in His mercy and bounty, kindles the spark of love for Him in the human heart. How is it possible for anyone to love Allah unless it has been instigated by Him through His mercy, compassion, and guidance? How could a human exist without His mercy and love?

يَـٰٓأَيُّهَا ٱلَّذِينَ ءَامَنُوا۟ مَن يَرْتَدَّ مِنكُمْ عَن دِينِهِۦ فَسَوْفَ يَأْتِى ٱللَّهُ بِقَوْمٍ يُحِبُّهُمْ وَيُحِبُّونَهُۥٓ أَذِلَّةٍ عَلَى ٱلْمُؤْمِنِينَ أَعِزَّةٍ عَلَى ٱلْكَـٰفِرِينَ

يُجَـٰهِدُونَ فِى سَبِيلِ ٱللَّهِ وَلَا يَخَافُونَ لَوْمَةَ لَآئِمٍ ۚ ذَٰلِكَ فَضْلُ ٱللَّهِ يُؤْتِيهِ مَن يَشَآءُ ۚ وَٱللَّهُ وَٰسِعٌ عَلِيمٌ ﴿٥٤﴾

O you who have faith, should any of you turn your
back on your religion, Allah will bring a people whom
He loves and who love Him, who are humble towards
the faithful and disdainful towards the disbelievers,
who struggle in the path of Allah and fear not the
reproaches of any blamer. That is Allah's bounty,
He bestows on whom so ever He will. Allah is all-
embracing and all Knowing. (Al-Ma'idah 5:54, Koran)

Wholesomeness: صَّـٰلِحَـٰت

According to the Koran, doing wholesome deeds, along with faith *iman*, will yield paradise.

وَمَنْ عَمِلَ صَٰلِحًا مِّن ذَكَرٍ أَوْ أُنثَىٰ وَهُوَ مُؤْمِنٌ فَأُوْلَٰٓئِكَ يَدْخُلُونَ ٱلْجَنَّةَ يُرْزَقُونَ فِيهَا بِغَيْرِ حِسَابٍ

Whoso does wholesome deeds, be it male or female, and has faith, shall enter the garden, therein provided for without reckoning. (Ghafir 40:40, Koran)

وَٱلَّذِينَ ءَامَنُوا۟ وَعَمِلُوا۟ ٱلصَّٰلِحَٰتِ سَنُدْخِلُهُمْ جَنَّٰتٍ تَجْرِى مِن تَحْتِهَا ٱلْأَنْهَٰرُ خَٰلِدِينَ فِيهَآ أَبَدًا ۖ لَّهُمْ فِيهَآ أَزْوَٰجٌ مُّطَهَّرَةٌ ۖ وَنُدْخِلُهُمْ ظِلاً

ظَلِيلاً ٥٧

Those who have faith and do wholesome deeds, them we shall admit to gardens through which rivers flow. (An-Nisa 4:57, 122, Koran)

Another fifty verses in the Koran mention that people who perform wholesome deeds and have faith shall inherit the garden. The Koran uses the word *saalihaat* for wholesome deeds and the word *salihun* for wholesome people. The root word for both means "to be sound, wholesome, right, proper, good."

Another word used in the Koran, about thirty times, is *islah*, which means "establishing wholesomeness." In modern times, the word *islah* has been used to mean "reform." The word *sulh* is used in the Koran once to mean peace and harmony in family relationship. In modern times, the word *sulh* has come to mean "peace in the political sense."

While the Koran calls the wholesome people as *salihun*, it employs the opposite, *fasid*, for the corrupt, ruined, evil, and wrong. The wholesome are the ones who live in harmony with the Real (*Haqq*) and establish wholesomeness (*saalihaat*) through their words and deeds throughout the world. In contrast, the corrupt (*mufsidun*) destroy the proper balance and relationship with Allah and His creation. *Fasid* means "corrupt, evil, wrong."

Allah measures out the good and the evil, the wholesome and the corrupt. Humans have enough freedom to make their own choices; if they make the choice to do beautiful and wholesome deeds motivated by faith and god-wariness, they please Allah and bring harmony and wholesomeness to the world, resulting in peace, justice, mercy, compassion, honor, equity, well-being, freedom, and many other gifts through Allah's grace. Others choose to do evil and work corruption (*mufsidun*) to destroy the right relationship among the creation, causing hunger, disease, oppression, pollution, and other afflictions. In the universal order, corruption is the prerogative of humans, and vicegerency gives them the freedom to work against the Creator and His creation. Only misapplied trust can explain how moral evil can appear in the world. Modern technology; scientific advancement; nuclear, chemical, and biological weapons of mass destruction; genetic engineering of plants, animals, and humans; and exploitation of nonrenewable resources of the earth had made self-destruction of the human race and all life on the planet a distinct and imminent possibility.

ظَهَرَ ٱلْفَسَادُ فِى ٱلْبَرِّ وَٱلْبَحْرِ بِمَا كَسَبَتْ أَيْدِى ٱلنَّاسِ لِيُذِيقَهُم بَعْضَ ٱلَّذِى عَمِلُوا۟ لَعَلَّهُمْ يَرْجِعُونَ

Corruption has appeared on the land and
in the sea because what people's hands have
earned, so that He may let them taste some of
their deeds, in order that they may turn back
from their evils. (Ar-Rum 30:41, Koran)

When humans choose wrong and corrupt actions, they displease Allah. Allah loves those who do what is beautiful, not those who do what is ugly:

وَإِذَا تَوَلَّىٰ سَعَىٰ فِي ٱلْأَرْضِ لِيُفْسِدَ فِيهَا وَيُهْلِكَ ٱلْحَرْثَ وَٱلنَّسْلَ ۗ وَٱللَّهُ لَا يُحِبُّ ٱلْفَسَادَ ﴿٢٠٥﴾

When he turns his back, he hurries about the earth to work corruption there and destroy the tillage and the stock. Allah loves not corruption. (Al-Baqarah 2:205, Koran)

Allah loves doing what is beautiful, and because of His love for those who do the beautiful, He brings them near to Himself, and His nearness is called Allah's Mercy:

وَلَا تُفْسِدُوا فِي ٱلْأَرْضِ بَعْدَ إِصْلَٰحِهَا وَٱدْعُوهُ خَوْفًا وَطَمَعًا ۚ إِنَّ رَحْمَتَ ٱللَّهِ قَرِيبٌ مِّنَ ٱلْمُحْسِنِينَ

Work not corruption in this world after it has made wholesome and call upon Allah in fear and hope. Surely the mercy of Allah is near to those who do what is beautiful. (Al-A'raf 7:56, Koran)

The Covenant of Allah: Islam, Iman, Ihsan

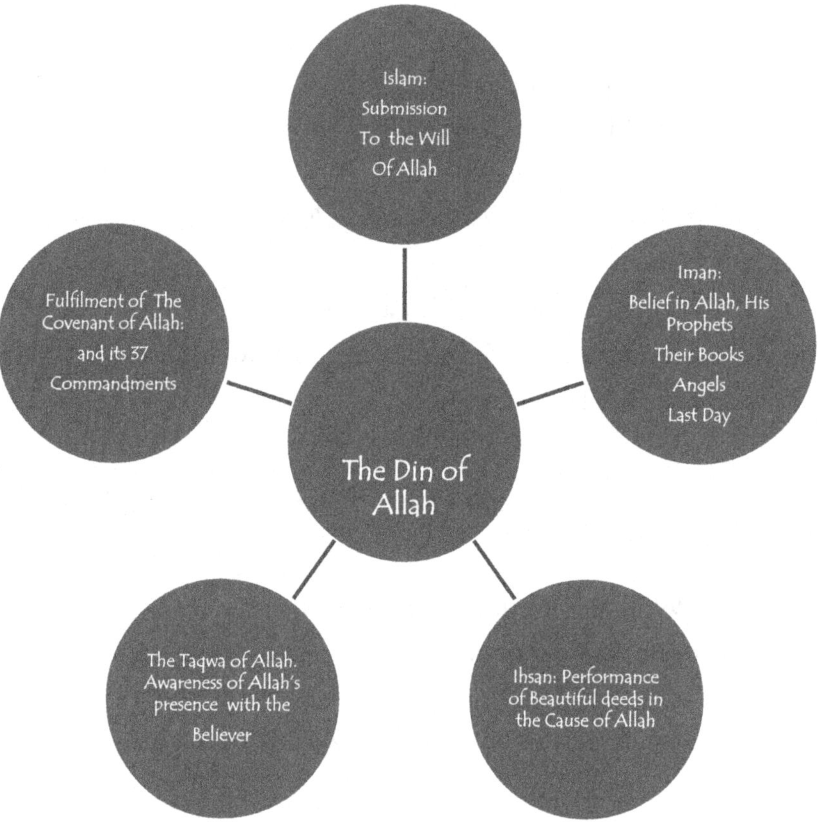

إِنَّنِيٓ أَنَا ٱللَّهُ لَآ إِلَٰهَ إِلَّآ أَنَا۠ فَٱعۡبُدۡنِي وَأَقِمِ ٱلصَّلَوٰةَ لِذِكۡرِيٓ ﴿١٤﴾

Verily I am Allah. There is no god but I, so worship Me, and perform salaat in remembrance of Me. (Taha 20:14, Koran)

Long time ago, humankind was unaware of the Creator of the universe. The Creator God, Allah, sent His prophets to every community to enlighten humanity about the Creator and His creation. The prophets taught humans of the obligations of humankind to their Creator and to His creation.

Islam is the continuation of the message of Allah that Nabi Ibrahim (Abraham) began to spread around the Middle East in the fog of time. Ibrahim, who had lived in the mists of time in Urfa along the Euphrates River, believed in one God, who created the universe and everything in it. Ibrahim taught that God the Creator sustains every object, living and nonliving. Ibrahim placed his total trust in the universal God, Allah. He faithfully obeyed Allah's commandments and did Allah's bidding, and one momentous occasion, Ibrahim was prepared to offer his most beloved son, Ishmael, in sacrifice at Allah's bidding. As it turned out, Allah was only testing Abraham's faith, and the child was miraculously saved by an angel. This test of faith became the foundation of belief and the *din* for mankind for all times to come.

Those who unquestioningly followed Blessed Nabi Ibrahim's example submitted their self to Allah and placed their trust in Allah were the *Muslims*, those people who bow down and submit their total *self* to the Creator and do the His bidding. With time, Nabi Ibrahim's life story became an oral folklore; and by the time it came to be written in testaments, it had changed a great deal. Other prophets, thousands in number, followed Ibrahim, giving the same message as he did to all mankind. In return for this unconditional surrender to God, the believers are promised peace, security, and well-being in this world and the hereafter.

Submission to God sealed a covenant between God and His believers. Some communities forgot the message, and their prophet became their lord and master. In their minds, their lord became their tribal deity to be worshipped at an altar or in a shrine. Their god became their tribal and personal savior. Priesthood took over the guardianship of their god and began to prescribe dogma and creed for the worshippers. The gods and their devotees became subject of creed and dogma crafted by rabbis, priests, and pundits of the temples, churches, and synagogues.

At the time of the birth of Nabi Muhammad, people found themselves drawn into several conflicting ideologies concerning God and gods separately and, occasionally, simultaneously. Each cult, tribe, or guild had its own god, and they also shared in specialized gods of seasons, fertility, prosperity, and abundance. Such proliferation of gods required temples and keepers to maintain order, organize festivals, and define creed and dogma for their gods. Wealth and power emanating from the organization of gods' affairs produced the first corporations of the world. Such wealth and power also produced competition and hence monopolies of control of influence and wealth. Jews had their own deity. The Roman Church became a monopoly and a corporation of hierarchical priesthood that persecuted dissenting views and fought competition. Their god shared some characteristics with Sol Invictus of the pagan Roman pantheon. Although competition prevailed among the pagans, tolerance of one another's gods was paramount as they all shared common avenues for festivals, and the wealth trickled down through the priests to the tribes and occasionally to the common man. Muhammad's own pagan family of the Quraish officiated as the priesthood of god Hubal and controlled the venue of worship for the pantheon of 360 other gods.

Even in paganism, every living being connects to its source of sustenance, be it Mother Earth, the sun, and ultimately the Creator. The innate human yearning, the *fitra*, is for the thoughts of the Creator. Even though early thoughts link the child to the heavens, clouds, stars, and sun, eventually, the child turns to the thoughts of God. Despite the innate thoughts of God or *fitra,* early environment and culture decides the structure of the faith, but the innate spirituality in man persists.

The culture of priesthood hierarchy and man-made dogma and creed overpower the instinctive spirituality of humans.

Tawhid: The Koran laid the foundation of the idea of one universal God, and from this fount arose all that is known and all that will ever be known. This foundation had been laid in the first twelve years of Blessed Nabi Muhammad's prophecy, and it took another ten years to establish the precepts of truth, justice, covenant, equality, good, and evil. The Koran laid out these principles in clarity for all times to come.

In the sixth-century Arabia, at the time of the birth of the blessed *Nabi,* the Arabian Peninsula was steeped in ignorance, superstition, spirit, and idol worship. There was no concept of one universal God. The people did not possess the know-how to grasp the concepts and precepts of knowledge of unity of Allah, the *taqwa* of Allah, and the criterion to distinguish between good and evil, *husna* and *Fahasha*. The distinction between good and evil was fuzzy.

The blessed *Nabi* Muhammad taught that everything in the universe originates from the one and the only reality of Allah and that man's ultimate salvation rests with the recognition of his total dependence on Him. This entails conscious submission to the will and the law of Allah. Muhammad received the revelation of the word of Allah, and Allah commanded Muhammad to spread the word to mankind. Today we believe that the universal God is the center of the belief of all the three monotheistic religions—Judaism, Christianity, and Islam. Nothing could be farther from the truth; for the Jews, God continues to be a tribal deity with His favorite children, and those who call themselves Christians, can only access God through His favorite son, Jesus. Yet God the Creator of the universe is the God of every particle and organism that was ever created. God, Allah, through the act and sustenance of His creation, is connected to each particle, every cell, and every soul. God is within the reach of every bit of His Creation.

Islam (Submission to the Will of Allah

Most Muslims today do not internalize and thus do not appreciate the implications of the term *islam* (submission). Submission, in religious terms, begins with a participatory understanding of God's will, followed by meaningful and purposeful actions of obedience to the will of Allah. Thus, submission to Allah is an ongoing process that begins with the acceptance of His greatness and magnificence and the minuteness of the human, the daily ritual of bowing down to Allah's majesty in submission during salat, and the continuing awareness of Allah's presence with the believer. Thus, the act of submission is participatory, in which the believer connects with Allah, which brings about communion between man and the Creator. Man accepts Allah in his heart, and Allah draws His believer closer to Himself.

Iman (Faith)

Faith in Islam is not blind. Although belief in the unseen is important, there comes a point when the believer, as a spiritual human being, transcends the level of simple faith to a spiritual consciousness that penetrates the fog of the unseen, leading to knowledge of the true nature of things, the reality of Allah. The Koran speaks of this progression from faith to knowledge as an inward metamorphosis in which belief (*iman*) is transformed into certainty *yaqin*. This certainty (*yaqin*) is expressed in the Koran in terms of three types of knowledge of Allah.

The basic and fundamental knowledge is the *knowledge of certainty* (*ilm al-yaqin*, Koran 102:5). This type of certainty refers to the knowledge that results from human capacity for logical reasoning and the appraisal of what the Koran calls "clear evidence" (*bayyinat*) of Allah's presence in the world. The knowledge of certainty is rational and discursive, a point that the Koran acknowledges when it admonishes human beings to

قُلْ سِيرُوا۟ فِى ٱلْأَرْضِ فَٱنظُرُوا۟ كَيْفَ بَدَأَ ٱلْخَلْقَ ۚ ثُمَّ ٱللَّهُ يُنشِئُ ٱلنَّشْأَةَ ٱلْءَاخِرَةَ ۚ إِنَّ ٱللَّهَ عَلَىٰ كُلِّ شَىْءٍ قَدِيرٌ

Say: "Travel through the earth and see how Allah did originate creation; so, will Allah produce a later creation: for Allah has power over all things. (Al-'Ankabut: 29:20, Koran)

وَهُوَ ٱلَّذِى يُحْىِۦ وَيُمِيتُ وَلَهُ ٱخْتِلَٰفُ ٱلَّيْلِ وَٱلنَّهَارِ ۚ أَفَلَا تَعْقِلُونَ ﴿٨٠﴾

It is He Who gives life and death, and to Him (is due) the alternation of Night and Day: will you not then understand? (Al-Mu'minun 23:80, Koran)

Over time and under the influence of contemplation and spiritual practice, the knowledge of certainty may be transformed into a higher form of knowledge of Allah, which the Qur'an calls the *eye of certainty* (*ain al-yaqin*, Koran 102:7). This term refers to the knowledge that is acquired by spiritual intelligence, which the believers locate metaphorically in the heart. Before attaining this type of knowledge, the heart of the believer must first be *opened to Islam.*

﴿ أَفَمَن شَرَحَ ٱللَّهُ صَدْرَهُۥ لِلْإِسْلَٰمِ فَهُوَ عَلَىٰ نُورٍ مِّن رَّبِّهِۦ ۚ فَوَيْلٌ لِّلْقَٰسِيَةِ قُلُوبُهُم مِّن ذِكْرِ ٱللَّهِ ۚ أُو۟لَٰٓئِكَ فِى ضَلَٰلٍ مُّبِينٍ

Is one whose heart Allah has opened to Islam, so that he has received enlightenment from Allah. Woe to those whose hearts are hardened against celebrating the praises of Allah! They are manifestly wandering (in error)! (Az-Zumar 39:22, Koran)

Once opened, the heart receives knowledge of the divine *light,* the illumination or the *nur* of Allah.

Just as with the knowledge of certainty, with the eye of certainty, the believer sees Allah's existence through His presence in this world, the signs of Allah. With the eye of certainty, what leads the believer to the knowledge of Allah are not the arguments to be understood by the rational intellect but by theophanic appearances (*bayyinat*) that strip away the veils of worldly phenomenon to reveal the divine reality underneath.

From the spiritual perspective, the one who perceives reality through the knowledge of Allah is a true *intellectual.* Unlike the scholar, who develops his or her skills through years of formal study, the spiritual intellectual does not need book learning to understand the divine light. A spiritual intellectual can be anyone, scholarly or otherwise, whose knowledge extends *outward* to take in the physical world, *upward* to realize his ultimate transcendence of the world through his link with the Absolute, and then *inward* to reconcile all that with his intellectual and emotional self. *Without such a vertical dimension of spirit, the scholar's knowledge, whatever its extent in academic terms, is of little worth.*

The third and most advanced type of knowledge builds on transcendent nature of knowledge itself. The highest level of consciousness is called the *truth of certainty* (*haqq al-yaqin*).

وَإِنَّهُۥ لَحَسْرَةٌ عَلَى ٱلْكَـٰفِرِينَ ﴿٥٠﴾ وَإِنَّهُۥ لَحَقُّ ٱلْيَقِينِ ﴿٥١﴾ فَسَبِّحْ بِٱسْمِ رَبِّكَ ٱلْعَظِيمِ ﴿٥٢﴾

But truly (Revelation) is a cause of sorrow for the Unbelievers. But verily it is Truth of assured

certainty. So, glorify the name of thy Lord
Most High. (Al-Haqqah 69:50–52, Koran)

It is also known as *ilm ladduni* (knowledge by presence). This form of knowledge partakes directly of the divine reality and leaps off directly across the synapses of human mind to transcend both cognitive reasoning and intellectual vision at the same time. The "truth of certainty" refers to a state of consciousness in which a person knows the Real through direct participation in it without resorting to logical proofs. This type of knowledge characterizes God's prophets and *Rasul's*, whose consciousness of the truth is both immediate and participatory as what it is based on comes from direct inspiration.

According to the Koran, faith in Islam has as much to do with *theoretical and empirical* knowledge as it does with simple belief. This multidimensional concept of knowledge comprehends a reality that lies hidden within the unique world yet can be revealed to the human mind and vision of spiritual intellect through the signs of Allah that are present in the world. In the Koran, Allah calls humanity:

So, I do call to witness what you
see, and what you see not,

تَنزِيلٌ مِّن رَّبِّ ٱلْعَٰلَمِينَ

(This is) a Message sent down from
the Lord of the Worlds.

وَإِنَّهُۥ لَحَقُّ ٱلْيَقِينِ

But verily it is Truth of assured certainty.
(Al-Haqqah 69:38-39, 43, 51, Koran)

The Koranic notion of *iman* as dependent on knowledge is actualized in practice in the term *islam*. The term *islam* signifies the idea of surrender or submission. Islam is a religion of self-surrender; it is the conscious and rational submission of a dependent and limited human will to the absolute and omnipotent will of Allah. The type of surrender Islam requires is a deliberate, conscious, and rational act made by a person who knows with both intellectual certainty and spiritual vision that Allah is the reality.

The knower of God is a *Muslim*, one who submits to the divine truth and whose relationship with God is governed by *taqwa*, the consciousness of humankind's responsibility toward its Creator. However, consciousness of God alone is not sufficient to make a person a Muslim. Neither is it enough to be merely born a Muslim or to be raised in an Islamic cultural context. The concept of *taqwa* implies that the believer has the added responsibility of acting in accordance with three types of knowledge: *ilm al-yaqin*, *ain al-yaqin*, and *haqq al-yaqin* (knowledge of certainty, eye of certainty, and the truth of certainty). By doing so, the believer attains the honored title of "slave of Allah" (*abd Allah*, fem. *amat Allah*), for he recognizes that all power and all agency belongs to God alone:

وَلَوْلَآ إِذْ دَخَلْتَ جَنَّتَكَ قُلْتَ مَا شَآءَ ٱللَّهُ لَا قُوَّةَ إِلَّا بِٱللَّهِ ۚ إِن تَرَنِ أَنَا۠ أَقَلَّ مِنكَ مَالًا وَوَلَدًا ﴿٣٩﴾

Allah has willed it. There is no power but
Allah's (Al-Kahf 18:39, Koran)

Trusting in the merciful Allah, his divine Master, yet fearing his Master's wrath, the slave of Allah walks the road of life in careful steps, making his actions deliberate so that he will not stray from the path that God has laid out for him:

إِيَّاكَ نَعْبُدُ وَإِيَّاكَ نَسْتَعِينُ ﴿٥﴾ ٱهْدِنَا ٱلصِّرَاطَ ٱلْمُسْتَقِيمَ ﴿٦﴾ صِرَاطَ ٱلَّذِينَ أَنْعَمْتَ عَلَيْهِمْ غَيْرِ ٱلْمَغْضُوبِ عَلَيْهِمْ وَلَا ٱلضَّآلِّينَ

Thee do we worship, and Thine aid we seek,
Show us the straight Path, The Path of those
on whom Thou hast bestowed Thy Grace,
those whose (portion) is not wrath, and who
go not astray. (Al-Fatihah 1:5-7, Koran)

It is a comprehensive and highly personal type of commitment that has little in common with academic understanding of Islam as a civilization or a cultural system. The universality of religious experience is an important premise of the Koran's argument against profane or secular life. The Koran is not concerned with defining creedal boundaries but with affirming the universal obligation to believe in one God. The Koran speaks of broad varieties of religious experience to which every human being can relate. When dealing with religious practices, the Koran is less concerned with details of the ritual than with the meaning that lies behind the rituals it prescribes. The detail of the ritual practice, which serves to define Islam to most believers, is usually left for the tradition of the *Rasul.* to define.

By speaking in inspirational and moving voice and presenting a discourse that is relevant to human experience, the Koran overcomes the cultural limitations of the western Arabian civilization, in which it was originally revealed, and makes it accessible to peoples of different cultural backgrounds throughout the world. This universalism has never been more important than it is in the present, when the majority of the believers do not speak Arabic. Such transcendence of culture is necessary for the Koran, as the vehicle of the word of God, to overcome linguistic and cultural differences and express itself in a metalanguage that can be understood even when its original Arabic is translated into a non-Semitic language such as English, Mandarin, Hindi, or Malay. An example of this metalanguage is found in the three types of knowledge already discussed. Most people, whatever their experiences and cultural background, think in similar ways and have similar wants and needs. The Koran seeks to establish a common foundation for belief that is based on such shared perceptions and experiences.

Over and over again the Qur'an reminds the reader to think about the truths that lay behind the familiar or mundane things of the world, such as *Signs of God* in nature, the practical value of virtue, and the cross-cultural validity of moral principles. What is good for Muslims is meant to be good for all human beings, regardless of gender, color, or origin. The Qur'an therefore appeals to both to reason and experience in determining the criterion for distinguishing between truth and falsehood.

The most important theological point made by the Qur'an is that there is one God: Allah, Universal and beyond comparison, the Creator who sustains both the material world and the world of human experience.

خَلَقَ ٱلسَّمَٰوَٰتِ وَٱلْأَرْضَ بِٱلْحَقِّ ۚ تَعَٰلَىٰ عَمَّا يُشْرِكُونَ ﴿٣﴾

He has created the heavens and the earth for just ends far is He above having the partners they ascribe to Him! (An-Nahl 16:3, Koran)

Nafs (the Self) and *Taqwa* of Allah

Allah is the only truth. All other forms of so-called truth are either false in their initial premise or contingently true only in limited situations. The recognition of this fact produces a profound effect on the human soul that has forever drawn humans in the search for the divine, which forever transforms the outlook of the believer.

Allah's *din* is divine. Allah is *Haqq*, and all truth emanates from Him. The Koran is Allah's word on the earth and the expression of *haqq*.

Haqq is the reality and the truth; *batil* refers to something that is imaginary and false. Those who believe in Allah only speak the truth. When humans add dogma and creed to Allah's *din*, it is not *haqq*. In matters of *din*, what is not absolute truth is not *haqq*. What is not *haqq* is *batil* (false or fabricated). What is not truthful cannot be a witness over Allah's word and *din*. Therefore, all human additions to the *din* of Allah do not constitute the truth, and every human fabrication to the *din* after the completion of *wahiy* is *batil* or falsehood.

۞ ٱللَّهُ نُورُ ٱلسَّمَٰوَٰتِ وَٱلۡأَرۡضِۚ مَثَلُ نُورِهِۦ كَمِشۡكَوٰةٖ فِيهَا مِصۡبَاحٌۖ ٱلۡمِصۡبَاحُ فِي زُجَاجَةٍۖ ٱلزُّجَاجَةُ كَأَنَّهَا كَوۡكَبٞ دُرِّيّٞ يُوقَدُ مِن
شَجَرَةٖ مُّبَٰرَكَةٖ زَيۡتُونَةٖ لَّا شَرۡقِيَّةٖ وَلَا غَرۡبِيَّةٖ يَكَادُ زَيۡتُهَا يُضِيٓءُ وَلَوۡ لَمۡ تَمۡسَسۡهُ نَارٞۚ نُّورٌ عَلَىٰ نُورٖۚ يَهۡدِي ٱللَّهُ لِنُورِهِۦ مَن يَشَآءُۚ وَيَضۡرِبُ ٱللَّهُ
ٱلۡأَمۡثَٰلَ لِلنَّاسِۗ وَٱللَّهُ بِكُلِّ شَيۡءٍ عَلِيمٞ ﴿٣٥﴾ ۞ فِي بُيُوتٍ أَذِنَ ٱللَّهُ أَن تُرۡفَعَ وَيُذۡكَرَ فِيهَا ٱسۡمُهُۥ يُسَبِّحُ لَهُۥ فِيهَا بِٱلۡغُدُوِّ وَٱلۡأٓصَالِ

Allah is the Light of the heavens and the earth. The parable of His Light is as if there were a Niche and within it a Lamp: the Lamp enclosed in Glass; the glass as it were a brilliant star: lit from a blessed Tree, an Olive, neither of the East nor of the West, whose Oil is well-nigh luminous, though fire scarce touched it: Light upon Light! Allah doth guide whom He will to His Light: Allah doth set forth Parables for men: and Allah

> doth know all things. (Lit is such a light) in houses, which Allah hath permitted to be raised to honor; for the celebration, in them, of His name: in them is He glorified in the mornings and in the evenings, (again and again). (An-Nur 24: 35-36, Koran)

Allah created His beings with love, and He nurtures His creation with love. His light illuminates the hearts of those who love Him, place their trust in Him, and submit to Him. Once their heart is open to Allah in submission, Allah's *nur* glows in the niche of the believer's heart, where the divine light, Spirit, and wisdom of Allah shines in man. The glow of the Spirit and wisdom shines with the brilliance of a star lit from divine wisdom, the tree of knowledge—the knowledge of Allah's signs. Allah is within those who believe. The believer's self, his *nafs*, is aglow with Allah's radiance—light upon light. The dwellings where Allah is praised and glorified in the mornings and in the evenings are aglow with Allah's *nur* and His knowledge.

When man is stripped of his raiment, veils of skin, flesh and bones, viscera, and circulating fluids, what is left over is nothing but his soul, his *self* (*nafs*). Removing the veils of self-admiration, self-image, and pride; wiping away covers of makeup and couture; removing masks and marks of social status; and stripping him of scars and years of greed and gluttony expose a tiny particle, the *nuqta,* that represents the self of man. This self is perhaps no greater than a little dot, the *nuqta.* The combined self of the entire human race, all the *nuqtas* combined, will perhaps not fill a small cup. Yet the ego of the human race through this minuteness of pride and arrogance has controlled the destiny of Allah's creation for thousands of years.

The *nafs,* unlike the Freudian ego, is capable of both good and evil. The *nuqta* of the *nafs* magnified a million times reveals a shiny disk, the mirror of the soul. The nature (*fitra*) of the *nafs* is to shine as a mirror with Allah's *nur.* When man walks the path of Allah in *taqwa of* Him with the knowledge that Allah is with him, watching him and guiding him, Allah's *nur* shines on the *nafs,* keeping it pure and safe. Once the heart is open to Allah in submission, Allah's *nur* glows in the niche of the believer's heart, where the divine light, Spirit, and wisdom of Allah shine in the human. For those who believe, Allah is within. The believer's self is aglow with Allah's radiance, light upon light.

However, when the human's desires, cravings, and ego overpower his love and obedience for Allah, the shiny mirror of the *nafs* becomes obscured by the smoke of his desires, and he loses sight of the *nur* of Allah; and in this darkness, man trips into error and decadence. The effort required to keep focus on Allah's *nur* and the *taqwa* of Allah is jihad. And this jihad is the obedience of Allah's commandments when Allah calls on His believers with the words,

يَٰٓأَيُّهَا ٱلَّذِينَ ءَامَنُوا

O you who Believe,

And He commands them to do acts of faith and goodness in seventy-five verses of the Koran. Obedience of every such command is jihad. The expression *in the Path of Allah*, of course, is the path of right conduct that Allah has set down in the Koran. Jihad is simply the complement to Islam, the surrender to the will of Allah. The surrender takes place to Allah's will, and it is Allah's will that people should struggle in His path. Hence, submission and surrender to Allah's will demands struggle in His path. Submission to Allah's command requires the believers to struggle against all negative tendencies in their self. Salat, zakat, fasting, and hajj are all struggles in the path of Allah. The greatest obstacles that people face in submitting themselves to

Allah are their desires and cravings for the temptations of this world. It is the *nafs* that directs intentions and actions of man to the good and the bad.

Nafs is the seat of the qualities of self-admiration, arrogance, pride, hardheartedness, suppression of Allah's love, pointing to faults of others, lying, gossiping, cheating, backbiting, envy, jealousy, criticism of others, self-praise, bitterness, covetousness of the belongings of others even when one possesses what is better, lack of contentment, constant complaining, lack of gratitude, blindness to one's blessings, wishing for increase without effort, selfishness, greed and covetousness that knows no bounds, love of control, love of self and its desires, hatred for those who criticize even if it is for one's own good, love for those who praise even if it is in hypocrisy, rejection of advice and counsel, and the habit of talking about oneself.

The same *nafs*, on the other hand, has a good side. When the human heart is open to Allah's *nur,* man becomes aware of Allah's presence with him, and all his actions become governed by the *taqwa* of Allah. The human becomes a believer, and all his intentions and actions are guided by Allah's presence in him.

Islam is a relationship between Allah and His believers. The *din* of Allah is an all-encompassing and highly personal type of relationship in which Allah's *nur,* or light resides in the believer's heart. The believer is conscious of Allah's closeness and mercy. The believer obeys trusts and loves Allah, and Allah in return loves those who love Him and perform beautiful deeds.

Allah has granted knowledge and the wisdom of *furqan* and *taqwa* to the believers who have opened their hearts and minds to Him. Man has been granted the freedom of choice in doing what is wholesome and beautiful or what is corrupt or ugly. This knowledge reminds the human of the scales of Allah's justice; the two hands of Allah,

His mercy and His wrath, are reflected in the human domain, where people have been appointed Allah's vicegerents. Deeds of goodness and wholesomeness are associated with Allah's mercy, paradise, and what is beautiful. Evil and corruption is rewarded with Allah's wrath, hell, and what is ugly.

In the *nafs*, the *taqwa* of Allah drives away man's cravings for wealth, his inclination toward disobedience of Allah's commandments, and the unwholesome qualities of arrogance, pride, lying, gossiping, cheating, backbiting, envy, jealousy, self-praise, bitterness, covetousness of the belongings of others, ingratitude, blindness to one's blessings, selfishness, greed, covetousness, love of control, and love of self.

The Covenant of Allah

There is an implicit assumption in the Koran that there exists an agreement between Allah and His creation, portrayed as a covenant, a mutual understanding in which Allah proposes a system of regulations for the guidance of humans. This guidance is presented in the form of commandments to be accepted and implemented by people. Allah then makes promise of what He will do in the event that man willingly abides by these commands and regulates his life in accordance with them. The concept of promise is clearly conditional on the human's obedience and submission (*islam*). The covenant of Allah symbolizes the relationship between Allah and man; man becomes His steward, vicegerent, or custodian on the earth through submission and obedience to His will (*islam*) as expressed in His commands and is able to take the advantage of Allah's promises and favors. The commandments of Allah, addressed to believers (men and women), are fundamental principles of the covenant between Allah and man that become obligatory to man when the fire of love for Allah is kindled in his heart, and he submits to His will and becomes His servant (believer) and steward on the earth.

The covenant of Allah forms the basis of the practice of the *din*. The principles of the *din* written down, proclaimed, and stored on a shelf do not have any merit. It is only the practice of the principles that brings the *din* to life. It is the practice of the *din* that unites the believer to Allah and through Him to other believers. The believer understands his obligations to his *din*. To believe is to obey the covenant. Those who do not fulfill the covenant of Allah are not His believers. Islam, the *din*, is a divine call that stems from Allah's *wahiy* through the blessed *Nabi* Muhammad. Allah's *wahiy* is the word from Him and constitutes the Koran. The blessed *Nabi* Muhammad was the walking Koran, and he carried Allah's word in his heart. The Koran, the word from Allah through *wahiy*, is the divine commandment. The word from Allah and the *wahiy* cannot be confused with human calls and systems. The prophets convey Allah's word. Prophets, as humans, also speak their own minds. Muhammad, the blessed *Nabi* of Allah, was careful not to mix his own words with those of Allah. The blessed *Nabi* said:

I am no more than a man; when I order you anything respecting religion, receive it, and when I tell you anything about the affairs of the world, and then I am nothing but a man.

No human has the prerogative to speak on behalf of Allah. Priests, imams, scholars, bishops, popes, and ayatollahs are all men like other men; some are more knowledgeable than the others. None, however, can represent Allah. They can represent their personal views on the meaning of scriptures; their opinions remain within the human domain.

Humans connect with Allah upon submission and accept Him in their hearts, and Allah is with them. Allah proposes a covenant, and the believer pledges on it with his submission to Allah. Allah speaks to the believers in seventy-five verses of the Koran and, in a clear language, tells them all that is lawful and what is forbidden and unlawful. And Allah calls on His believers with the words,

O you who Believe.

And He commands them to do acts of faith and goodness in seventy-five verses of the Koran.

Obedience of every such command is jihad. The individual is taught to obey the precepts of Allah's law in the Koran. Allah proclaims His law in the covenant to the believers in a simple lucid language. He addresses the believers in the Koran and shows them the right way to follow Him. The observance of the covenant of Allah is the total belief system based on unity of one's personality in communion with Him in total awareness and *taqwa* of Allah and observance of the thirty-seven commandments of the covenant. This communion is not only with Allah but also through Him with other believers and with the rest of Allah's creation, both alive and inanimate. The phrase *amilu al saalihaat* (to do good, to perform wholesome deeds) refers to those who persist in striving to set things right, who restore harmony, peace, justice, and balance. The individual believer, man and woman, is then guided by Allah and His *Nabi* through the covenant to show compassion, to be merciful and forgive others, to be just, to protect the weak, to defend the oppressed, to be generous and charitable, to be truthful, to seek knowledge and wisdom, to be kind, to be peaceful, to love others, and to perform beautiful deeds.

This is Islam. In this communion between Allah and His believer, there are no priests, no imams, no scholars, nor any ulema. The believer does not need a book nor a university degree to know God.

The believer does not need to know whether her folded hands should be above or below her navel or his pant legs should reach above or below his ankles. In the believers' communion with Allah, it does not matter if the prayers are led by a blind man or a lame woman so long as the person leading the prayer is with the *taqwa* of Allah. The believer, a man or a woman, reaches out to Allah in sincerity and bows down to Him in submission. Allah blesses him, and the believer praises Allah, who draws him closer. The believer asks for mercy, and Allah touches His devotee in love. The believer asks for forgiveness, and Allah pours His mercy on the believer. The believer loves Allah; in return, He promises the believer *Jannat*. When Allah bestows on the believer divine mercy, grace, and guidance, why will a believer burden himself with the baggage of human systems? Systems made up of laws, creed, and dogma fashioned by men?

Allah speaks to those men and women who believe in Him and guides them to the *din* of goodness, truth, unity, brotherhood, and justice. This guidance from Allah is summarized in seventy-five verses of the Koran, where Allah speaks to those who have submitted to Him and guides them to a way of life. Upon submission to the will of Allah, the believer affirms his covenant with Allah in which the believer pledges to live his life in accordance with His *din*.

Allah is the only reality, and it is through this reality that everything in the universe exists. Allah sustains and protects all that He has created. Everything that Allah has created is connected to Him through this act of creation. Allah sustains and protects His creation when those He created praise and thank Him for His beneficence. And Allah reassures His believers that He is aware of all that is hidden and all that is manifest. To Allah belongs all that is in the heavens and on the earth. Allah is the *Rahman* (the Most Gracious) and the *Rahim* (the Most Merciful). All of Allah's creatures in the heavens and the on earth praise and glorify Him with His most beautiful names. Allah is the Lord of everything that has ever existed or will ever exist. He alone is worthy of praise and worship. Joining anything in worship with Him is *shirk*, which upsets the human's relationship with Allah. Allah reminds His faithful:

> Believe in Allah, His Rasool, the Book that He has sent to His Rasool and the Scriptures that He sent to the Rasools before him. And those who deny Allah, His Angels, His Books, His Rasools, and the Day of Judgment have gone astray. Allah also says, "Verily, this is My Way leading straight, follow it, follow not other paths for they will separate you from My path".

> Verily those who pledge their allegiance unto you, (O Muhammad) pledge it unto none but Allah; the Hand of Allah is over their hands. Thereafter whosoever breaks his Covenant does so to the harm of his own soul, and whosoever fulfils his Covenant with Allah, Allah will grant him an immense Reward. (Al-Fath 48: 10, Koran)

In the journey in this world, man is presented with Allah's covenant as his guide, *taqwa* of Allah as his shield against evil, and *furqan* (the criterion to distinguish between good and evil) as Allah's compass to the straight path of righteousness. If man accepts the path of Allah and follows Allah's covenant as his guide, *taqwa* of Allah as his shield against evil, and *furqan* as Allah's compass to the straight path, he becomes a believer and of the righteous. The way to righteousness is through Allah's guidance and in the covenant of Allah in the Koran. Every little bit of devotion makes the *nur* of Allah glow in the heart till the believer is connected with Allah and begins to follow His path. This communion between the believer and Allah becomes exclusive.

Submission establishes the link between the believer and Allah. The believer asks, and Allah gives. The believer loves Allah, and Allah loves him in return. The believer asks for the straight path, and Allah shows him the way. The believer praises Allah, and Allah showers His mercy and grace upon him. The believer remembers Allah, and Allah responds to those who praise Him, thank Him, and ask Him.

Obedience to the commandments of the covenant of Allah brings the believer closer to Him. By establishing regular salat, giving zakat, fasting, and traveling for the pilgrimage to the Kaaba, the believer holds on to Allah. Through this relationship with Allah, he becomes conscious of Allah's closeness and knows with certainty that Allah is aware of his intentions and actions. The believer is conscious that Allah is his *Mawla* or Protector. The believer is in *taqwa* of Allah.

Verily, this is My Way leading straight: follow it:
follow not (other) paths for they will separate you
from His path. This He commands you that you
may remember. (Qur'an: 151-153. Al An' am).

And fulfill the Covenant of Allah. Thus, He
commands you that you may remember.
(Qur'an 6: 151-153. Al An 'am).

Believers! Fulfill your Covenants.
(Qur'an 5:1 Al Ma'idah).

Verily those who pledge their allegiance unto you
(O Muhammad), pledge it unto none but Allah;
the Hand of Allah is over their hands. Thereafter
whosoever breaks his Covenant, does so to the
harm of his own soul, and whosoever fulfils his

Covenant with Allah, Allah will grant him an immense Reward. (Al-Fath 48: 10, Koran)

﴿ ٱلَّذِينَ يَنقُضُونَ عَهْدَ ٱللَّهِ مِنۢ بَعْدِ مِيثَٰقِهِۦ وَيَقْطَعُونَ مَآ أَمَرَ ٱللَّهُ بِهِۦٓ أَن يُوصَلَ وَيُفْسِدُونَ فِى ٱلْأَرْضِ ۚ أُو۟لَٰٓئِكَ هُمُ

ٱلْخَٰسِرُونَ ﴿٢٧﴾ ﴾

Those who break Allah's Covenant after it is ratified, and who sunder what Allah has ordered to be joined and do mischief on earth: these cause losses (only) to themselves. (Al-Baqarah 2:27, Koran)

﴿ ٱلَّذِينَ يُوفُونَ بِعَهْدِ ٱللَّهِ وَلَا يَنقُضُونَ ٱلْمِيثَٰقَ ﴿٢٠﴾ ﴾ وَٱلَّذِينَ يَصِلُونَ مَآ أَمَرَ ٱللَّهُ بِهِۦٓ أَن يُوصَلَ وَيَخْشَوْنَ رَبَّهُمْ وَيَخَافُونَ سُوٓءَ

ٱلْحِسَابِ ﴿٢١﴾ ﴾

Those who fulfill the Covenant of Allah and fail not in their pledged word; Those who join together those things which Allah hath commanded to be joined, hold their Lord in awe, and fear the terrible reckoning. (Ar-Ra'd 13:20-21, Koran)

بَلَىٰ مَنْ أَوْفَىٰ بِعَهْدِهِۦ وَٱتَّقَىٰ فَإِنَّ ٱللَّهَ يُحِبُّ ٱلْمُتَّقِينَ ﴿٧٦﴾

Whosoever fulfils his Covenant and has Taqwa of Allah, surely Allah loves those with Taqwa. (Ali 'Imran 3:76, Koran)

Islam is a way of life in the straight path to Allah. It is Allah's guidance in which He proposes a system of regulations for the guidance of humans. This guidance is presented in the form of commandments to be accepted and implemented by people.

The concept of covenant also symbolizes the relationship between humans, amongst Allah's creatures, and between man and the rest of His creation. They all share one God, one set of guidance and commandments, the same submission and obedience to Him, and the same set of expectations in accordance with His promises. They can all, therefore, trust one another since they all have similar obligations and expectations. In view of the Koran, humans, communities, nations, and civilizations will continue to live in harmony and peace so long as they continue to fulfill Allah's covenant.

Economics plays a significant role in the social structure of Islam, so significant that Allah did not leave the economic aspect of life to be solely determined by human intellect, experience, caprice, and lust. Allah made it subject to revelation. Thus, Muslims prosper when they follow Allah's laws and subject themselves to scarcity when they turn to human systems. The Koran promises peace and plenty for those who obey their covenant with Him, and for those who turn away from Allah's covenant, the Koran portends a life of need, scarcity, and want.

وَمَنْ أَعْرَضَ عَن ذِكْرِى فَإِنَّ لَهُۥ مَعِيشَةً ضَنكًا وَنَحْشُرُهُۥ يَوْمَ ٱلْقِيَٰمَةِ أَعْمَىٰ ﴿١٢٤﴾ وَكَذَٰلِكَ نَجْزِى مَنْ أَسْرَفَ وَلَمْ يُؤْمِنۢ بِـَٔايَٰتِ رَبِّهِۦ ۚ
وَلَعَذَابُ ٱلْءَاخِرَةِ أَشَدُّ وَأَبْقَىٰٓ ﴿١٢٧﴾ أَفَلَمْ يَهْدِ لَهُمْ كَمْ أَهْلَكْنَا قَبْلَهُم مِّنَ ٱلْقُرُونِ يَمْشُونَ فِى مَسَٰكِنِهِمْ ۗ إِنَّ فِى ذَٰلِكَ لَءَايَٰتٍ لِّأُو۟لِى ٱلنُّهَىٰ ﴿١٢٨﴾

"But whosoever turns away from My Message,
verily for him is a life narrowed down, and We shall
raise him up blind on the Day of Judgment."

And thus, do We recompense him who transgresses
beyond bounds and believes not in the Signs

> of his Lord: and the Penalty of the Hereafter
> is far more grievous and more enduring.
>
> It is not a warning to such men (to call to
> mind) how many generations before them We
> destroyed, in whose haunts they (now) move?
> Verily, in this are Signs for men endued with
> understanding. (Taha 20:124, 127–28, Koran)

In the above *ayah* of the Koran, the word *ma'eeshat* comes from the word *ma'ashiyyat,* which is the recognized meaning of the word *economics.* The consequences of rejection of Allah's covenant and guidance are clearly portrayed. A life narrowed down or constricted is a miserable one, one of need, scarcity, unhappiness, poverty, hunger, disease, pestilence, and famine all at the same time or separately.

The Koran's covenant does not put off the realization of the fruits of obeying or ignoring Allah's guidance until after death, nor does it hide it in spiritual abstractness. Observance of the covenant makes life on the earth economically, physically, and spiritually rich and happy. Nonobservance of the covenant makes life on the earth economically miserable and physically and spiritually depressing. In fact, the economic, physical, and spiritual condition of a people provides a pragmatic test of the soundness of the revealed guidance.

Furthermore, the Koran declares that the people who transgress Allah's guidance and are economically deprived in this world will also be worse off in the hereafter.

> Verily for him is a life narrowed down, and We
> shall raise him up blind on the Day of Judgment.

According to the Koran, the economics and the observance of the moral code of Allah's covenant goes hand in hand, and they cannot be separated from each other.

بِسْمِ ٱللَّهِ ٱلرَّحْمَٰنِ ٱلرَّحِيمِ

﴿ خَلَقَ ٱلسَّمَٰوَٰتِ وَٱلْأَرْضَ بِٱلْحَقِّ ۚ تَعَٰلَىٰ عَمَّا يُشْرِكُونَ (٣) خَلَقَ ٱلْإِنسَٰنَ مِن نُّطْفَةٍ فَإِذَا هُوَ خَصِيمٌ مُّبِينٌ (٤) وَٱلْأَنْعَٰمَ خَلَقَهَا ۗ
لَكُمْ فِيهَا دِفْءٌ وَمَنَٰفِعُ وَمِنْهَا تَأْكُلُونَ (٥) وَلَكُمْ فِيهَا جَمَالٌ حِينَ تُرِيحُونَ وَحِينَ تَسْرَحُونَ (٦) وَتَحْمِلُ أَثْقَالَكُمْ إِلَىٰ بَلَدٍ لَّمْ تَكُونُوا۟
بَٰلِغِيهِ إِلَّا بِشِقِّ ٱلْأَنفُسِ ۚ إِنَّ رَبَّكُمْ لَرَءُوفٌ رَّحِيمٌ (٧) وَٱلْخَيْلَ وَٱلْبِغَالَ وَٱلْحَمِيرَ لِتَرْكَبُوهَا وَزِينَةً ۚ وَيَخْلُقُ مَا لَا تَعْلَمُونَ (٨) وَعَلَى ٱللَّهِ
قَصْدُ ٱلسَّبِيلِ وَمِنْهَا جَآئِرٌ ۚ وَلَوْ شَآءَ لَهَدَىٰكُمْ أَجْمَعِينَ (٩) هُوَ ٱلَّذِىٓ أَنزَلَ مِنَ ٱلسَّمَآءِ مَآءً ۖ لَّكُم مِّنْهُ شَرَابٌ وَمِنْهُ شَجَرٌ فِيهِ تُسِيمُونَ
(١٠) يُنۢبِتُ لَكُم بِهِ ٱلزَّرْعَ وَٱلزَّيْتُونَ وَٱلنَّخِيلَ وَٱلْأَعْنَٰبَ وَمِن كُلِّ ٱلثَّمَرَٰتِ ۗ إِنَّ فِى ذَٰلِكَ لَءَايَةً لِّقَوْمٍ يَتَفَكَّرُونَ (١١) وَسَخَّرَ لَكُمُ ٱلَّيْلَ
وَٱلنَّهَارَ وَٱلشَّمْسَ وَٱلْقَمَرَ ۖ وَٱلنُّجُومُ مُسَخَّرَٰتٌۢ بِأَمْرِهِۦٓ ۗ إِنَّ فِى ذَٰلِكَ لَءَايَٰتٍ لِّقَوْمٍ يَعْقِلُونَ (١٢) وَمَا ذَرَأَ لَكُمْ فِى ٱلْأَرْضِ مُخْتَلِفًا أَلْوَٰنُهُۥٓ ۗ
إِنَّ فِى ذَٰلِكَ لَءَايَةً لِّقَوْمٍ يَذَّكَّرُونَ (١٣) وَهُوَ ٱلَّذِى سَخَّرَ ٱلْبَحْرَ لِتَأْكُلُوا۟ مِنْهُ لَحْمًا طَرِيًّا وَتَسْتَخْرِجُوا۟ مِنْهُ حِلْيَةً تَلْبَسُونَهَا وَتَرَى
ٱلْفُلْكَ مَوَاخِرَ فِيهِ وَلِتَبْتَغُوا۟ مِن فَضْلِهِۦ وَلَعَلَّكُمْ تَشْكُرُونَ (١٤) وَأَلْقَىٰ فِى ٱلْأَرْضِ رَوَٰسِىَ أَن تَمِيدَ بِكُمْ وَأَنْهَٰرًا وَسُبُلًا لَّعَلَّكُمْ تَهْتَدُونَ
(١٥) وَعَلَٰمَٰتٍ ۚ وَبِٱلنَّجْمِ هُمْ يَهْتَدُونَ (١٦) أَفَمَن يَخْلُقُ كَمَن لَّا يَخْلُقُ ۗ أَفَلَا تَذَكَّرُونَ (١٧) وَإِن تَعُدُّوا۟ نِعْمَةَ ٱللَّهِ لَا تُحْصُوهَآ ۗ إِنَّ ٱللَّهَ لَغَفُورٌ
رَّحِيمٌ (١٨) ﴾

He has created the heavens and the earth for just ends
far is He above having the partners they ascribe to Him!

He has created man from a sperm-drop; and behold
this same (man) becomes an open disputer!

And cattle He has created for you (men):
from them you derive warmth, and numerous
benefits, and of their (meat) you eat.

And you have a sense of pride and beauty in them
as you drive them home in the evening, and as
you lead them forth to pasture in the morning.

And they carry your heavy loads to lands
that you could not (otherwise) reach
except with souls distressed: for your Lord
is indeed Most Kind, Most Merciful.

And (He has created) horses, mules, and donkeys,
for you to ride and use for show; and He has created
(other) things of which you have no knowledge.

And unto Allah leads straight the Way, but
there are ways that turn aside: if Allah had
willed, He could have guided all of you.

It is He Who sends down rain from the sky.
From it you drink, and out of it (grows) the
vegetation on which you feed your cattle.

With it He produces for you corn, olives, date
palms, grapes, and every kind of fruit: verily in
this is a Sign for those who give thought.

He has made subject to you the Night and
the Day; the Sun and the Moon; and the Stars
are in subjection by His Command: verily
in this are Signs for men who are wise.

And the things on this earth which He has multiplied in varying colors (and qualities): verily in this a Sign for men who celebrate the praises of Allah (in gratitude).

It is He Who has made the sea subject, that you may eat thereof flesh that is fresh and tender, and that you may extract there from ornaments to wear, and You see the ships therein that plough the waves, that you may seek (thus) of the bounty of Allah and that you may be grateful.

And He has set up on the earth mountains standing firm, lest it should shake with you; and rivers and roads; that you may guide yourselves.

And marks and signposts; and by the stars (Men) guide themselves.

Is then He Who creates like one that creates not? Will you not receive admonition?

If you would count the favors of Allah, never would you be able to number them; for Allah is Oft-Forgiving, Most Merciful. (An-Nahl 16:3–18, Koran)

Sama in the Koran signifies the universe and *Ardh* man's domain on earth pertaining to his social and economic world. Allah is the Lord of the heavens and the earth and all that comes forth from them. The divine laws under which the universe functions so meticulously and smoothly should also apply to the economic life of man so that he might achieve a balanced, predictable, equitable, and just financial life. *Sama* is the source of Allah's benevolence to mankind and of

His universal laws that govern human subsistence and sustenance on the earth (*ardh*), controlling man's economic life in this world. Allah's kingdom over the heavens and the earth sustains man's economic life and directly affects man's conduct and his obedience to Allah's covenant.

The covenant of Allah presents us with the scope of the freedom of choice that the humans have in doing what is wholesome and beautiful or what is corrupt and ugly in the human role among the creation that distinguishes right activity, right thought, and right intention from their opposites. It reminds us of how the scales of Allah's justice—the two hands of Allah, His mercy and His wrath—are reflected in the human domain, where people have been appointed Allah's vicegerents. Deeds of goodness and wholesomeness are associated with mercy, paradise, and the beautiful. Evil and corruption is rewarded with wrath, hell, and the ugly.

Chapter Three

The Covenant of Allah in the Present Times: The Thirty-Seven Commandments

بِسْمِ ٱللَّهِ ٱلرَّحْمَـٰنِ ٱلرَّحِيمِ

The verses or *ayahs* in this chapter contain thirty-seven commandments of Allah[2]. The essence of the Koran is in the seventy-five verses in which Allah addresses the believers directly with the words

يَـٰٓأَيُّهَا ٱلَّذِينَ ءَامَنُوا

O you who believe!

They form the core of this belief of the believer and the nucleus of his *din*.

The synthesis of the three dimensions of *din* (religion)—*islam* (submission), *iman* (faith), and *ihsan* (performance of good deeds)—is what links the true believer to the divine through total submission and faith in the reality of the Creator, in addition to performance of virtuous and wholesome actions of devotion and worship of the Sublime and through beautiful deeds in the service of Allah and His creation. With this practice, the polarity between faith and actions is reversed; instead of faith being the prerequisite for practice, practice defines faith. This reverse polarity is a reminder that Islam is defined not only as a set of beliefs but also as a body of actions that reveal

[2] For the *ayahs* and the suras, please refer to the thirty-seven commandments in chapter 1. In chapter 2, the *ayahs* from different suras have been combined according to subject matter.

the inner convictions of the believer. This practice-oriented picture of Islam is dependent on the commandments of Allah in the verses of the Koran, and the traditions provide explanatory statements that act as a complement to the Koran. In this relationship, the Koran's word-centered approach to Islam in which the divine word arouses knowledge of Allah in the human consciousness, in contrast the Hadith (tradition) expresses a law-centered perspective on Islam, in which the knowledge of spiritual realities is less important than performance of appropriate actions.

1. The Covenant of Allah: Believe in Allah

He is Allah, there is no Deity but He, Knower of
the hidden and the manifest. He is the Rahman
the Most Gracious, the Rahim, Most Merciful.

The Sovereign, The Pure and The
Hallowed, Serene and Perfect,

The Custodian of Faith, the Protector, the
Almighty, the Irresistible, the Supreme,

He is Allah, the Creator, the Sculptor, the
Adorner of color and form. To Him belong
the Most Beautiful Names, whatever so is in
the heavens and on earth, Praise and Glorify
Him; and He is the Almighty and All Wise.

There is no god but He, the Ever Living, the One
Who sustains and protects all that exists.

His are all things in the heavens and on earth. Who is
there to intercede in His presence except as He permits?

He knows what happens to His creatures in this world
and in the hereafter. Nor do His creatures know
the scope of His knowledge except as He wills.

His Throne extends over the heavens and the earth, and
He feels no fatigue in guarding and protecting them.

He is the Most High, Most Great.

Believe in Allah, His Messenger, and the Book that
He has sent to His Messenger and the Scriptures that
He sent to those before him. Any who deny Allah,
His angels, His Books, His Messengers, and the Day of
Judgment has gone astray. (An-Nisa 4:136, Koran)

Verily, this is My Way leading straight: follow it:
follow not (other) paths for they will separate you
from His path. This He commands you that you
may remember. (Al-An'am 6: 151–53, Koran)

Islam: The Arabic word *islam* means "to resign oneself to or to submit oneself." In religious terminology, it means submission or surrender of oneself to Allah or to Allah's will. Allah is the only true reality, and everything else in the universe is dependent on Him for its reality and existence. Since Allah created the universe, all things in the universe are, as a result, totally dependent on Allah and thus are totally "submissive" to Him. Allah, being the Creator of all things, is the *Rabb*, the Sustainer of the whole creation. Thus God the Creator is the universal God.

The Koranic notion of religious belief *iman* as dependent on knowledge is actualized in practice in the term *islam*. This term signifies the idea of surrender or submission. The type of surrender

Islam requires is a deliberate, conscious, and rational act made by a person who knows with both intellectual certainty and spiritual vision that Allah, who is the subject of Koranic discourse, is the reality.

A *Muslim* (fem. *Muslimah*) is "one who submits" to the divine truth and whose relationship with God is governed by *taqwa*, the consciousness of humankind's responsibility toward its Creator. However, consciousness of God alone is not sufficient to make a person a Muslim. Neither is it enough to be merely born a Muslim or to be raised in an Islamic cultural context. The concept of *taqwa* implies the consciousness of humankind's responsibility toward its Creator. However, consciousness of God alone is not sufficient to make a person a Muslim. Neither is it enough to be merely born a Muslim or to be raised in an Islamic cultural context. The concept of *taqwa* implies that the believer has the added responsibility of acting in a way that is in accordance with three types of knowledge: *ilm al-yaqin*, *ain al-yaqin*, and *haqq al-yaqin* (knowledge of certainty, eye of certainty, and the truth of certainty). The believer must endeavor at all times to maintain himself in a constant state of submission to Allah. Trusting in the divine mercy of his divine Master yet fearing Allah's wrath, the slave of Allah walks the road of life with careful steps, making his actions deliberate so that he will not stray from the straight path that Allah has laid out for him. It is an all-encompassing and highly personal type of commitment that has little in common with academic understanding of Islam as a civilization or a cultural system.[3]

The universality of religious experience is an important premise of the Koran's argument against a profane or secular life. This universalism has never been more important than it is in the present time when the majority of the believers do not speak Arabic. Such transcendence of culture is necessary for the Koran, as the vehicle of the word of God,

3 Vincent Cornell, "Fruit of Tree of Knowledge," in *Oxford History of Islam*, ed. John L. Esposito (Oxford University Press).

to overcome linguistic and cultural differences and express itself in a metalanguage that can be understood even when its original Arabic is translated into a non-Semitic language such as English, Mandarin, or Hindi. Most people, whatever their experiences and cultural background, think in similar ways and have similar wants and needs. The Koran seeks to establish a common foundation for belief that is based on such shared perceptions and experiences. Over and over again, the Koran reminds the reader to think about the truths that lie behind the familiar or mundane things of the world, such as signs of God in nature, the practical value of virtue, and the cross-cultural validity of moral principles. The Koran, therefore, appeals to both reason and experience in determining the criterion for distinguishing between truth and falsehood.

The most important theological point made by the Qur'an is that there is one God, Allah, Universal and beyond comparison, the Creator, who creates and sustains both the material world and the world of human experience. All other forms of so-called truth are either false in their initial premises or contingently true only in limited situations. The recognition of this fact produces a profound effect on the human soul that it forever transforms the outlook of the believer.

Imən: Faith of Islam is based on certain knowledge that is both a liberation and a limitation. It is a liberation in the sense that certainty of divine reality allows the human spirit to expand inward, outward, and upward so that consciousness becomes three dimensional. Nevertheless, it is also a limitation because with the knowledge of Allah comes a concomitant awareness of the limits and responsibility imposed on a person as a created being. Unlike a secular humanist, a true Muslim believer who submits to Allah cannot delude himself by claiming that he is the sole author of his destiny as he knows that a person's fate is routinely controlled by factors beyond his control.

Ihsan: This means doing good, virtuous, and wholesome deeds. The third dimension of *din* is *ihsan*. The word *ihsan* is derived from the word *husn*, which designates the quality of being good, beautiful, virtuous, pleasing, harmonious, or wholesome. The Koran employs the word *hasana*, from the same root as *husn*, to mean a good or a beautiful deed. For example:

مَّآ أَصَابَكَ مِنْ حَسَنَةٍ فَمِنَ ٱللَّهِ ۖ وَمَآ أَصَابَكَ مِن سَيِّئَةٍ فَمِن نَّفْسِكَ ۚ وَأَرْسَلْنَٰكَ لِلنَّاسِ رَسُولًا ۚ وَكَفَىٰ بِٱللَّهِ شَهِيدًا

Whatever beautiful touches you, it is from Allah, and whatever ugly touches you, it is from yourself. And We have sent thee as a Rasool to instruct humanity. And enough is Allah for a witness. (An-Nisa 4:79, Koran)

مَن جَآءَ بِٱلْحَسَنَةِ فَلَهُۥ خَيْرٌ مِّنْهَا ۖ وَمَن جَآءَ بِٱلسَّيِّئَةِ فَلَا يُجْزَى ٱلَّذِينَ عَمِلُوا۟ ٱلسَّيِّـَٔاتِ إِلَّا مَا كَانُوا۟ يَعْمَلُونَ

If any does beautiful deeds, the reward to him is better than his deed; but if any one does evil, the doers of evil are only punished (to the extent) of their deeds. (Al-Qasas 28:84, Koran)

وَأَمَّا مَنْ ءَامَنَ وَعَمِلَ صَٰلِحًا فَلَهُۥ جَزَآءً ٱلْحُسْنَىٰ ۖ وَسَنَقُولُ لَهُۥ مِنْ أَمْرِنَا يُسْرًا ﴿٨٨﴾

And for him who has faith and does wholesome works, his recompense shall be most beautiful. (Al-Kahf 18:88, Koran)

The word *ihsan* is a verb that means "to establish or to perform what is good and beautiful." The Koran employs the word *ihsan* and its active particle *muhsin* (the one who does what is beautiful and good)

in seventy verses. The Koran often designates Allah as the One who does what is beautiful, and *al-Muhsin* is one of Allah's divine names. Allah's beautiful work is the creation of the universe of galaxies, stars, sun, and moon, all in their ordained orbits, destined in their paths by Allah's mysterious forces. All are shining and luminescent with Allah's blessed light (*nur*), providing life and vigor to billions of Allah's creatures so that they may acknowledge and praise their Creator, who made this beautiful and wholesome universe.

The Koran ascribes the love of Allah in about fifteen verses. One of the emotions most closely associated with *ihsan* is *hubb*. To have *ihsan* is to do what is beautiful. According to the Koran in five verses, Allah loves those who have *ihsan* because, by doing what is beautiful, they themselves have developed beautiful character traits and are worthy of Allah's love. In every Koranic verse where Allah is said to love something, the object is of this love are human beings, not the human species, whose traits and activities are beautiful.

The phrase *amilu al saalihaat* (to do good, to perform wholesome deeds) refers to those who persist in striving to set things right, who restore harmony, peace, and balance. The other acts of good works recognized in the covenant of the Koran are to show humility, to be generous and charitable, to be truthful, to seek knowledge and wisdom, to be kind, to be peaceful, to love others, and to perform beautiful deeds.

The following commandments of Allah comprise thirty-seven steps or pillars that embrace the essence of the believer's faith. The synthesis of three dimensions of *din* (religion)—*islam, iman*, and *ihsan,*—is what links the true believer to the divine through total submission and faith in the reality of the Creator in addition to performance of virtuous and wholesome acts of devotion and worship of the Sublime and through wholesome deeds in the service of the Creator and His creation. The type of surrender Islam requires is a deliberate, conscious, and rational act made by a person who knows with both intellectual certainty and spiritual vision that Allah is the reality. The believer's relationship with God is governed by *taqwa*, the consciousness of humankind's responsibility toward its Creator. The believer, upon his submission to Allah's will and mercy, enters into a covenant with Allah, portrayed as a mutual understanding in which Allah proposes a system of regulations for the guidance of humans. This guidance is presented in the form of commandments to be accepted and implemented by people. Allah then makes promise of what He will when man willingly abides by these commands and regulates his life according to them. The concept of promise is clearly conditional on human obedience. The covenant of the Koran symbolizes the relationship between Allah and man; man becomes His steward, vicegerent, or custodian on the earth through submission and obedience to His will (*islam*) as expressed in His commands and is able to take the advantage of Allah's promises and favors.

Allah addresses those who believe in Him in seventy-five verses of the Koran, giving them guidance and advice and a promise of rewards in this world and the hereafter. Those who do not believe in Him—the infidels, the *kafirun*—are promised a place in hellfire forever. A similar reward is promised to those who submit to Allah according to their word but not in their deeds. Such people are the hypocrites or the *Munafiqeen*.

The concept of covenant also symbolizes the relationship between humans and the rest of His creation. They all share in one Allah, one set of guidance and commandments, the same submission and obedience to Him, and the same set of expectations in accordance with His promises. They all can therefore trust one another since they all have similar obligations and expectations. In view of the Koran, humans, communities, nations, and civilizations will continue in harmony and peace so long as they continue to fulfill Allah's covenant.

The essence of the Koran is in seventy-five verses in which Allah addresses the believers directly with the words:

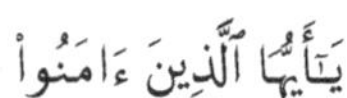

O you who believe!

In the following section, these seventy-five verses of the Koran have been arranged in thirty-seven commandments of Allah according to the subject matter of the commandment. The thirty-seven steps, pillars, or commandments form the core of the believer's faith; they are his *din*. Religion, as practiced by followers of different faiths, comprises set rituals and prayers individually or in congregation and celebrations of rituals in communal and family settings. The *din*, as envisaged in the covenant of Allah, is a three-dimensional belief system based on total submission and communion of oneself to Allah in constant awareness of Him (*taqwa*) through the fulfillment of these thirty-seven commandments. This communion is not only with Allah but also through Him with other humans and Allah's other creation.

Those who submit to Allah must believe in Allah,
His blessed Messenger, and the Book that Allah has
sent to His Messenger, the Qur'an and the Scriptures
that He sent to those Prophets before him.

Anyone who denies Allah, His angels, His Books,
His Messengers, and the Day of Judgment has
gone astray. Verily, this is Allah's Way leading
straight, follow it, and do not follow other paths

for they will separate you from Allah's path. Do
not join any other being in worship with Allah.

This He commands that you may remember.

Celebrate the Praises of Allah often, and Glorify
Him in the morning and in the night.

It is Allah and His Angels who send their
blessings upon you, that Allah may lead you
out of the depths of darkness into light.
Allah is full of mercy to the believers!

On the Day they meet Him with the greeting
Salaam, He has for them a generous reward.

Be quick in race to forgiveness from your Lord for
He has prepared for the righteous a garden whose
measurement is that of the heavens and of the earth.

Allah loves those who do beautiful deeds, those
who give freely in charity whether in prosperity
or in adversity, and those who restrain anger and
pardon all humans. (Koran, various *ayahs*)

Allah made a covenant with all the peoples of the book—the children of Israel, those who call themselves Christians, and then the Muslims—as an essential observation of their religion. Those who chose to ignore their obligations to Allah therefore suffered from dire consequences.

۞ وَلَقَدْ أَخَذَ ٱللَّهُ مِيثَٰقَ بَنِىٓ إِسْرَٰٓءِيلَ وَبَعَثْنَا مِنْهُمُ ٱثْنَىْ عَشَرَ نَقِيبًا ۖ وَقَالَ ٱللَّهُ إِنِّى مَعَكُمْ ۖ لَئِنْ أَقَمْتُمُ ٱلصَّلَوٰةَ
ءَاتَيْتُمُ ٱلزَّكَوٰةَ وَءَامَنتُم بِرُسُلِى وَعَزَّرْتُمُوهُمْ وَأَقْرَضْتُمُ ٱللَّهَ قَرْضًا حَسَنًا لَّأُكَفِّرَنَّ عَنكُمْ سَيِّـَٔاتِكُمْ وَلَأُدْخِلَنَّكُمْ جَنَّٰتٍ
تَجْرِى مِن تَحْتِهَا ٱلْأَنْهَٰرُ ۚ فَمَن كَفَرَ بَعْدَ ذَٰلِكَ مِنكُمْ فَقَدْ ضَلَّ سَوَآءَ ٱلسَّبِيلِ ﴿١٢﴾ فَبِمَا نَقْضِهِم مِّيثَٰقَهُمْ لَعَنَّٰهُمْ
جَعَلْنَا قُلُوبَهُمْ قَٰسِيَةً ۖ يُحَرِّفُونَ ٱلْكَلِمَ عَن مَّوَاضِعِهِۦ ۙ وَنَسُوا۟ حَظًّا مِّمَّا ذُكِّرُوا۟ بِهِۦ ۚ وَلَا تَزَالُ تَطَّلِعُ عَلَىٰ خَآئِنَةٍ مِّنْهُمْ إِلَّا
قَلِيلًا مِّنْهُمْ ۖ فَٱعْفُ عَنْهُمْ وَٱصْفَحْ ۚ إِنَّ ٱللَّهَ يُحِبُّ ٱلْمُحْسِنِينَ ﴿١٣﴾ وَمِنَ ٱلَّذِينَ قَالُوٓا۟ إِنَّا نَصَٰرَىٰٓ أَخَذْنَا مِيثَٰقَهُمْ
فَنَسُوا۟ حَظًّا مِّمَّا ذُكِّرُوا۟ بِهِۦ فَأَغْرَيْنَا بَيْنَهُمُ ٱلْعَدَاوَةَ وَٱلْبَغْضَآءَ إِلَىٰ يَوْمِ ٱلْقِيَٰمَةِ ۚ وَسَوْفَ يُنَبِّئُهُمُ ٱللَّهُ بِمَا كَانُوا۟
يَصْنَعُونَ ﴿١٤﴾ يَٰٓأَهْلَ ٱلْكِتَٰبِ قَدْ جَآءَكُمْ رَسُولُنَا يُبَيِّنُ لَكُمْ كَثِيرًا مِّمَّا كُنتُمْ تُخْفُونَ مِنَ ٱلْكِتَٰبِ
وَيَعْفُوا۟ عَن كَثِيرٍ ۚ قَدْ جَآءَكُم مِّنَ ٱللَّهِ نُورٌ وَكِتَٰبٌ مُّبِينٌ ﴿١٥﴾ يَهْدِى بِهِ ٱللَّهُ مَنِ ٱتَّبَعَ رِضْوَٰنَهُۥ سُبُلَ
ٱلسَّلَٰمِ وَيُخْرِجُهُم مِّنَ ٱلظُّلُمَٰتِ إِلَى ٱلنُّورِ بِإِذْنِهِۦ وَيَهْدِيهِمْ إِلَىٰ صِرَٰطٍ مُّسْتَقِيمٍ ﴿١٦﴾

Allah took a covenant from the Children of Israel, and We appointed twelve leaders from among them. And Allah said "I am with you if you establish salaat, practice regular charity, believe in my messengers, honor and assist them and loan to Allah a beautiful loan, Verily I will wipe out from you your evils and admit you to Gardens with rivers flowing beneath. But if any of you after this disbelieved, he has truly wandered from the path of rectitude.

Therefore, because of breach of their covenant, We were annoyed with them and made their hearts grow hard. They perverted words from their meaning an abandoned a greater part of the message that was sent them. Thou will not cease to discover treachery from them barring a few. Nevertheless, bear with them and pardon them. Verily Allah loves those who are wholesome.

> Moreover, We took the Covenant from those who call themselves Christians, but they have abandoned a good part of the Message that was sent to them. Therefore, We have stirred up enmity and hatred amongst them until the Day of Resurrection, when Allah will inform them of their handiwork.
>
> O People of the Book! There has come to you Our Messenger, revealing to you much that ye used to hide in the Scripture and passing over much. Indeed, there has come to you from Allah a light and a plain Book, in which Allah guides all those who seek His good pleasure to the path of peace. He brings them out of darkness into light by His will and guides them to a straight path". (Al-Ma'idah 5:12–16, Koran)

The verses in the above sura show the importance of the Koran:

> A light and plain Book from Allah where Allah guides all those who seek His good pleasure to the path of peace. He brings them out of darkness into light by His will and guides them to a straight path.

The Koran is a guide and Allah's covenant, a code of conduct for all humans to trust and believe in the Creator, the one universal God, Allah. Allah leads all those people who believe in Him to His straight path and to the path of peace. The children of Israel disobeyed Allah, and they lost His favor. As for those who called themselves Christians, Allah took their covenant, but they abandoned a large part of the message Allah sent them, to trust and believe in the Creator, the one God of the universe. Thereafter, Allah stirred up hatred and enmity among them because of their transgressions. Having split into sects and nations, they have continuously battled among themselves for two thousand years over doctrine, gold, wealth, and possessions. Allah has left every human ways open to His straight path through His covenant. Allah's covenant guides the believers to His way through its thirty-seven commandments.

Therefore, a believer is one who has submitted of his own free will to the will and command of the one universal God (*islam*), maintains his faith (*iman*) in God in constant awareness of Allah's presence with him (*taqwa* of Allah), fulfills his covenant with Allah, and performs wholesome and beautiful deeds (*ihsan*) in the service of God and His creation.

Believe in Allah:

He is Allah, there is no Deity but Him, Knower of
the hidden and the manifest. He is the Rahman, the
Most Gracious, the Rahim and Most Merciful.

He is Allah, there is no Deity but He, Knower of
the hidden and the manifest. He is the Rahman
the Most Gracious, the Rahim, Most Merciful.

He is Allah; there is no Deity but Him,

The Sovereign, the Pure and the Hallowed,

Serene and Perfect,

The Custodian of Faith, the Protector, the Almighty,

The Irresistible, the Supreme,

Glory be to Allah; He is above all
they associate with Him.

He is Allah, the Creator, the Sculptor,
the Adorner of color and form. To Him
belong the most beautiful names.

All that is in the heavens and on earth, praise
and glorify Him; and He is the Almighty and
All-Wise. (Al-Hashr 59:18–24, Koran)

Allah is truly the only reality, and everything else in the universe is dependent on Him for its reality and existence. Since Allah created the universe, all things in the universe are therefore totally dependent on Allah and hence totally "submitted" to Him. The Koran uses the term *submission* (*islam*) and its derivatives more than seventy times in its broadest sense—that true religion is established by Allah alone and that everything in the universe praises and glorifies Him. All creatures, simply by existing, demonstrate the Creator's glory and perform acts that acknowledge Allah's mastery over them.

إِنَّنِىٓ أَنَا ٱللَّهُ لَآ إِلَٰهَ إِلَّآ أَنَا۠ فَٱعْبُدْنِى وَأَقِمِ ٱلصَّلَوٰةَ لِذِكْرِىٓ ﴿١٤﴾

Verily I am Allah. There is no god but
I, so worship Me and perform salaat in
remembrance of Me. (Taha 20:14, Koran)

Shirk: Only Allah is worthy of worship. Those who worship other divinities and associate them with Allah have fallen into *shirk*. Other gods associated with Allah by some "Muslims" and non-Muslims are their caprice, wealth and material possessions, and power and influence over others. Absolute power corrupts. Religious figures, royals, and dictators in Islamic countries have lost track of their mortality and settled themselves on an elevated status ("I am divine, I am real, and others cannot have the same rights as I do"), leading them to serve their own egos in place of Allah. This leads to *shirk*, loss of *tawhid.* Sycophancy and blind subservience of self-serving courtiers leads these dictators into actions inimical to the community of Islam. People who claim to be kings and others who become dictators with the might of arms and take life and wealth on a whim commit act of *shirk* by misappropriating Allah's prerogative. Acts of worship, supplication, and remembrance (*dhikr*) have a specific ritual and devotional nature in which the worshipper orients himself to Allah and obeys His commands and prohibitions. To worship is to orient one's life and existence to Allah (*Haqq*), to beseech Allah (*Rahman* and *Rahim*) for guidance and help, and to show gratitude for the blessings already received. Such humility precludes a man's superiority over others.

Allah's guidance to mankind is through divine revelation through His prophets, who were charged with the task of communicating His word. Allah's blessed *Rasul* Muhammad took precautions to prevent Allah's guidance to humanity from becoming tainted with his own or with anyone else's expressions. Scholars in Iran, two and a half centuries after the *Nabi's* death, resurrected sayings and parables attributed to the blessed *Nabi* and circulated them in the Muslim world. These collections of sayings and the parables attributed to the blessed *Nabi* Muhammad were in the speech and expressions of the narrators of these stories. Over the next one thousand years, these Hadith collections began to take the divine role of Allah and His *rasul* in the minds of the common man through the teachings of Muslim ulema. Only Allah is worthy of worship. Those who give a divine status to the Hadith collections of the third century and equate them with Allah's word have lost their way. This is *shirk*, which leads to loss of *tawhid* and *furqan* (Allah's guidance).

Tawhid: The oneness, the reality of Allah, demands that human beings recognize the greatness of Allah and the minuteness of man; the reality of the Real and the unreality of the unreal place people in their correct relationship with Allah, and it allows them to understand that they are servants of Allah and that they must act in submission (*islam*). They must therefore recognize human failings and follow divine guidance brought by the prophets and their scriptures.

Verily, this is My Way leading straight: follow it:
follow not (other) paths for they will separate you
from His path. This He commands you that you
may remember. (Al-An'am: 151–53, Koran)

Join not anything in worship with Him.
(Al-An'am 6: 151–53, Koran)

Believe in Allah, His Messenger and the Book that
He has sent to His Rasool and the Scriptures that He
sent to those before him. Any who deny Allah, His
angels, His Books, His Messengers and the Day of
Judgment has gone astray. (An-Nisa 4:136, Koran)

Celebrate the Praises of Allah often and Glorify Him
in the morning and at night. It is Allah and His Angels
Who send their blessings upon you, that He may lead
you out of the depths of darkness into light. Allah is
full of mercy to the believers! On the Day they meet
Him with the salutation: Salaam, He has prepared for
them a generous Reward. (Al-Ahzab 33:41–48, Koran)

2. The Covenant of Allah: The Nabi, the *Rasul*

O Nabi, We have sent thee as a witness, a
bearer of glad tidings, as a Warner and as one
who invites to Allah's Grace by His leave and
as an inspiration and beacon of light.

O Nabi, We have sent thee as a witness, a bearer of glad tidings, as a Warner and as one who invites to Allah's Grace by His leave and as an inspiration and beacon of light. Give glad tidings to the believers that they shall have from Allah bounty in abundance. Moreover, obey not the command of the unbelievers (kafireen) and the hypocrites (munafiqeen), heed not their annoyances and put your trust in Allah, for enough is Allah as Disposer of affairs. (Al-Ahzab 33:41–48, Koran)

Believe in Allah, His Messenger and the Book that He has sent to His Rasool and the Scriptures that He sent to those before him. Any who deny Allah, His angels, His Books, His Messengers and the Day of Judgment has gone astray. (An-Nisa 4:136, Koran)

Allah in His mercy, grace, and love for His creation has from the beginning of time communicated with humans and taught them all that they know about His workings, His universe, and His creation. Humans have always been resistant to accepting Allah's guidance regarding worship of Him and their relationship with other humans in matters of truth, justice, peace, equality, and sharing of their resources. Man's ego, selfishness, and greed always come in the way of his salvation. Allah inspired truthful men (prophets) with *taqwa* of Allah, humility, spiritual purity, and knowledge to convey His teaching and commandments to man so that he may continue to exist in the world during his short life in submission to Allah and in love, peace, and harmony with his fellow humans. To follow Allah's wisdom, man has to first submit himself unquestioningly to the mercy and will of Allah with the knowledge that, on an appointed day, he will meet his Maker to be questioned and judged on his conduct during his life on the earth.

وَٱلَّذِينَ ءَامَنُوا۟ وَعَمِلُوا۟ ٱلصَّٰلِحَٰتِ سَنُدْخِلُهُمْ جَنَّٰتٍ تَجْرِى مِن تَحْتِهَا ٱلْأَنْهَٰرُ خَٰلِدِينَ فِيهَآ أَبَدًا ۖ لَّهُمْ فِيهَآ أَزْوَٰجٌ مُّطَهَّرَةٌ ۖ وَنُدْخِلُهُمْ ظِلًّا

ظَلِيلًا ﴿٥٧﴾

Those who have faith and do wholesome deeds,
them we shall admit to gardens through which
rivers flow. (An-Nisa 4:57, 122, Koran)

Allah will measure out the good and the evil, the wholesome and the corrupt deeds that humans carried out in their lifetime. Humans have enough freedom to make their own choices. If they make the choice to do beautiful and wholesome deeds (*saalihaat*) motivated by faith (*iman*)and god-wariness (*taqwa*), they please Allah and bring harmony and wholesomeness to the world, resulting in peace, justice, mercy, compassion, honor, equity, well-being, freedom, and many other gifts through Allah's grace. While others choose to do evil and corruption (*mufsidun*), destroying the right relationship among the creation, causing hunger, disease, oppression, pollution, and other afflictions. In the universal order, corruption is the prerogative of humans, and vicegerency gives them the freedom to work against the Creator and His creation. When humans choose wrong and corrupt actions, they displease Allah. Allah loves those who do what is beautiful, not those who do what is ugly:

وَإِذَا تَوَلَّىٰ سَعَىٰ فِي ٱلْأَرْضِ لِيُفْسِدَ فِيهَا وَيُهْلِكَ ٱلْحَرْثَ وَٱلنَّسْلَ ۗ وَٱللَّهُ لَا يُحِبُّ ٱلْفَسَادَ ﴿٢٠٥﴾

When he turns his back, he hurries about the earth to work corruption there and destroy the tillage and the stock. Allah loves not corruption. (Al-Baqarah 2:205, Koran)

Obey Allah and His Messenger and turn not to others when you should hear him speak. For the worst of creatures in the sight of Allah are those who neither listen, nor look or try to comprehend. (Al-Anfal 8:20, Koran)

And how could you deny Faith when you learn the Signs of Allah and amongst you lives the Messenger? Whoever holds firmly to Allah will be shown a Way that is straight. (Ali 'Imran 3:100-101, Koran)

3. The Covenant with Allah

And fulfill the Covenant of Allah. Thus, He commands you that you may remember. (Al-An'am 6:151-53, Koran)

Believers! Fulfill your Covenant. (Al-Ma'idah 5:1, Koran)

Verily those who pledge their allegiance unto you (O Muhammad), pledge it unto none but Allah; the Hand of Allah is over their hands. Thereafter whosoever breaks his Covenant, does so to the harm of his own soul and whosoever fulfils his

Covenant with Allah, Allah will grant him an immense Reward. (Al-Fath 48:10, Koran)

Islam is a way of life in the straight path to Allah. There is an implicit assumption in the Koran that there exists an agreement between Allah and His creation portrayed as a mutual understanding in which Allah proposes a system of regulations for the guidance of the humans. This guidance is presented in the form of commandments to be accepted and implemented by people. Allah then makes promise of what He will do in the event that man willingly abides by these commands and regulates his life in accordance with them. The concept of promise is clearly conditional on man's obedience. The covenant of the Koran symbolizes the relationship between Allah and man; man becomes His steward, vicegerent, or custodian on the earth through submission and obedience to His will (*islam*) as expressed in His commands and is able to take the advantage of Allah's promises and favors.

The concept of covenant also symbolizes the relationship between humans and among Allah's creatures and the rest of His creation. They all share in one God, one set of guidance and commandments, the same submission and obedience to Him, and the same set of expectations in accordance with His promises. They all can, therefore, trust one another since they all have similar obligations and expectations. In view of the Koran, humans, communities, nations, and civilizations will continue to live in harmony and peace so long as they continue to fulfill Allah's covenant.

Economics plays a significant role in the social structure of Islam, so significant that Allah has not let the economic aspect of life to be solely determined by human intellect, experience, caprice, and lust. Allah has made it subject to revelation. Thus, Muslims prosper when they follow Allah's laws but subject themselves to scarcity when they turn to human systems. The Koran promises peace and plenty for those who obey their covenant with Him, and for those who turn away from Allah's covenant, the Koran portends a life of need, scarcity, and want.

وَمَنْ أَعْرَضَ عَن ذِكْرِى فَإِنَّ لَهُۥ مَعِيشَةً ضَنكًا وَنَحْشُرُهُۥ يَوْمَ ٱلْقِيَٰمَةِ أَعْمَىٰ ﴿١٢٤﴾ وَكَذَٰلِكَ نَجْزِى مَنْ أَسْرَفَ وَلَمْ يُؤْمِنۢ بِـَٔايَٰتِ رَبِّهِۦ ۚ

وَلَعَذَابُ ٱلْـَٔاخِرَةِ أَشَدُّ وَأَبْقَىٰٓ ﴿١٢٧﴾ أَفَلَمْ يَهْدِ لَهُمْ كَمْ أَهْلَكْنَا قَبْلَهُم مِّنَ ٱلْقُرُونِ يَمْشُونَ فِى مَسَٰكِنِهِمْ ۗ إِنَّ فِى ذَٰلِكَ لَءَايَٰتٍ لِّأُو۟لِى ٱلنُّهَىٰ ﴿١٢٨﴾

"But whosoever turns away from My Message,
verily for him is a life narrowed down and We shall
raise him up blind on the Day of Judgment."

And thus, do We recompense him who transgresses
beyond bounds and believes not in the Signs
of his Lord: and the Penalty of the Hereafter
is far more grievous and more enduring.

It is not a warning to such men (to call to
mind) how many generations before them We
destroyed, in whose haunts they (now) move?
Verily, in this are Signs for men endued with
understanding. (Taha 20:124, 127–28, Koran)

In the above *ayah* of the Koran, the word *ma'eeshat* comes from the word *ma'ashiyyat,* which is the recognized meaning of the word *economics.* The consequences of rejection of Allah's covenant and guidance are clearly portrayed. A life narrowed down or constricted is a miserable one, one of need, scarcity, unhappiness, poverty, hunger, disease, pestilence, and famine all at the same time or separately.

The Koran's covenant does not put off the realization of the fruits of obeying or ignoring Allah's guidance until after death, nor does it hide it in spiritual abstractness. Observance of the covenant makes life on the earth economically, physically, and spiritually rich and happy.

Nonobservance of the covenant makes life on the earth economically miserable and physically and spiritually depressing. In fact, the economic, physical, and spiritual condition of a people provides a pragmatic test of the soundness of the revealed guidance.

Furthermore, the Koran declares that the people who transgress Allah's guidance and are economically deprived in this world will also be worse off in the hereafter.

Verily for him is a life narrowed down and We shall raise him up blind on the Day of Judgment.

According to the Koran, the economics and the observance of the moral code of Allah's covenant goes hand in hand, and they cannot be separated from each other.

بِسْمِ ٱللَّهِ ٱلرَّحْمَٰنِ ٱلرَّحِيمِ

﴿ خَلَقَ ٱلسَّمَٰوَٰتِ وَٱلْأَرْضَ بِٱلْحَقِّ ۚ تَعَٰلَىٰ عَمَّا يُشْرِكُونَ (٣) خَلَقَ ٱلْإِنسَٰنَ مِن نُّطْفَةٍ فَإِذَا هُوَ خَصِيمٌ مُّبِينٌ (٤) وَٱلْأَنْعَٰمَ خَلَقَهَا ۗ
لَكُمْ فِيهَا دِفْءٌ وَمَنَٰفِعُ وَمِنْهَا تَأْكُلُونَ (٥) وَلَكُمْ فِيهَا جَمَالٌ حِينَ تُرِيحُونَ وَحِينَ تَسْرَحُونَ (٦) وَتَحْمِلُ أَثْقَالَكُمْ إِلَىٰ بَلَدٍ لَّمْ تَكُونُوا۟
بَٰلِغِيهِ إِلَّا بِشِقِّ ٱلْأَنفُسِ ۚ إِنَّ رَبَّكُمْ لَرَءُوفٌ رَّحِيمٌ (٧) وَٱلْخَيْلَ وَٱلْبِغَالَ وَٱلْحَمِيرَ لِتَرْكَبُوهَا وَزِينَةً ۚ وَيَخْلُقُ مَا لَا تَعْلَمُونَ (٨) وَعَلَى ٱللَّهِ
قَصْدُ ٱلسَّبِيلِ وَمِنْهَا جَآئِرٌ ۚ وَلَوْ شَآءَ لَهَدَىٰكُمْ أَجْمَعِينَ (٩) هُوَ ٱلَّذِىٓ أَنزَلَ مِنَ ٱلسَّمَآءِ مَآءً ۖ لَّكُم مِّنْهُ شَرَابٌ وَمِنْهُ شَجَرٌ فِيهِ تُسِيمُونَ
(١٠) يُنۢبِتُ لَكُم بِهِ ٱلزَّرْعَ وَٱلزَّيْتُونَ وَٱلنَّخِيلَ وَٱلْأَعْنَٰبَ وَمِن كُلِّ ٱلثَّمَرَٰتِ ۗ إِنَّ فِى ذَٰلِكَ لَءَايَةً لِّقَوْمٍ يَتَفَكَّرُونَ (١١) وَسَخَّرَ لَكُمُ ٱلَّيْلَ
وَٱلنَّهَارَ وَٱلشَّمْسَ وَٱلْقَمَرَ ۖ وَٱلنُّجُومُ مُسَخَّرَٰتٌۢ بِأَمْرِهِۦٓ ۗ إِنَّ فِى ذَٰلِكَ لَءَايَٰتٍ لِّقَوْمٍ يَعْقِلُونَ (١٢) وَمَا ذَرَأَ لَكُمْ فِى ٱلْأَرْضِ مُخْتَلِفًا أَلْوَٰنُهُۥٓ ۗ
إِنَّ فِى ذَٰلِكَ لَءَايَةً لِّقَوْمٍ يَذَّكَّرُونَ (١٣) وَهُوَ ٱلَّذِى سَخَّرَ ٱلْبَحْرَ لِتَأْكُلُوا۟ مِنْهُ لَحْمًا طَرِيًّا وَتَسْتَخْرِجُوا۟ مِنْهُ حِلْيَةً تَلْبَسُونَهَا وَتَرَى
ٱلْفُلْكَ مَوَاخِرَ فِيهِ وَلِتَبْتَغُوا۟ مِن فَضْلِهِۦ وَلَعَلَّكُمْ تَشْكُرُونَ (١٤) وَأَلْقَىٰ فِى ٱلْأَرْضِ رَوَٰسِىَ أَن تَمِيدَ بِكُمْ وَأَنْهَٰرًا وَسُبُلًا لَّعَلَّكُمْ تَهْتَدُونَ
(١٥) وَعَلَٰمَٰتٍ ۚ وَبِٱلنَّجْمِ هُمْ يَهْتَدُونَ (١٦) أَفَمَن يَخْلُقُ كَمَن لَّا يَخْلُقُ ۗ أَفَلَا تَذَكَّرُونَ (١٧) وَإِن تَعُدُّوا۟ نِعْمَةَ ٱللَّهِ لَا تُحْصُوهَآ ۗ إِنَّ ٱللَّهَ لَغَفُورٌ
رَّحِيمٌ (١٨) ﴾

He has created the heavens and the earth for just ends:
far is He above having the partners they ascribe to Him!

He has created man from a sperm-drop; and behold
this same (man) becomes an open disputer!

And cattle He has created for you (men):
from them you derive warmth and numerous
benefits and of their (meat) you eat.

And you have a sense of pride and beauty in them
as you drive them home in the evening and as
you lead them forth to pasture in the morning.

And they carry your heavy loads to lands
that you could not (otherwise) reach
except with souls distressed: for your Lord
is indeed Most Kind, Most Merciful.

And (He has created) horses, mules and donkeys,
for you to ride and use for show; and He has created
(other) things of which you have no knowledge.

And unto Allah leads straight the Way, but
there are ways that turn aside: if Allah had
willed, He could have guided all of you.

It is He Who sends down rain from the sky.
From it you drink and out of it (grows) the
vegetation on which you feed your cattle.

With it He produces for you corn, olives, date
palms, grapes and every kind of fruit: verily in
this is a Sign for those who give thought.

He has made subject to you the Night and
the Day; the Sun and the Moon; and the Stars
are in subjection by His Command: verily
in this are Signs for men who are wise.

And the things on this earth which He has multiplied
in varying colors (and qualities): verily in this a Sign for
men who celebrate the praises of Allah (in gratitude).

It is He Who has made the sea subject, that you
may eat thereof flesh that is fresh and tender and
that you may extract there from ornaments to
wear and You see the ships therein that plough
the waves, that you may seek (thus) of the
bounty of Allah and that you may be grateful.

And He has set up on the Earth mountains
standing firm, lest it should shake with you; and
rivers and roads; that you may guide yourselves.

And marks and sign-posts; and by the
stars (Men) guide themselves.

Is then He Who creates like one that creates
not? Will you not receive admonition?

If you would count up the favors of Allah,
never would you be able to number

> them; for Allah is Oft-Forgiving, Most Merciful. (An-Nahl 16:3–18, Koran)

Sama in the Koran signifies the universe, and *ardh* is man's domain on the earth pertaining to his social and economic world. Allah is the Lord of the heavens and the earth and all that comes forth from them. The divine laws under which the universe functions so meticulously and smoothly should also apply to the economic life of man so that he might achieve a balanced, predictable, equitable, and just financial life. *Sama* is the source of Allah's benevolence to mankind and of His universal laws that govern human subsistence and sustenance on the earth (*ardh*), controlling man's economic life in this world. Allah's kingdom over the heavens and the earth sustains man's economic life and directly affects man's conduct and his obedience to Allah's covenant.

4. The Covenant of Allah: *Taqwa* of Allah

The word *taqwa* means "to be dutiful to Allah, to be wary of Allah, to be conscious of Allah, to be pious toward Allah, and to fear Allah." A person with *taqwa* always has Allah in mind with every action and word spoken, "as if Allah sees you and you see Him."

> Be in Taqwa of Allah and fear Allah and let every soul judge as to the provision he has sent forth for the morrow. Yes, be in Taqwa of Allah and fear Allah: for Allah is well acquainted with all that you do. (Al-Hashr 59:18–24, Koran)

> So be in Taqwa of Allah and fear Allah as much as you can; listen and obey; and spend in charity for the benefit of your own souls. And those saved from their own greed are the ones that prosper. If ye loan

to Allah a beautiful loan, He will double it for you and He will forgive you: for Allah is both Appreciative (Shakoor) and Magnanimous (Haleem), Knower of what is hidden and what is manifest, Exalted in Might, Full of Wisdom. (At-Taghabun 64:14–18, Koran)

Humankind! We created you from a single pair of a male and a female and made you into nations and tribes, that ye may know each other. Verily the most honored of you in the sight of Allah is the one with taqwa of Allah, the most righteous of you. And Allah is All Knowing, All-Aware. (Al-Hadid 57:28-29, Koran)

Be in Taqwa of Allah, Fear Allah and believe in His Messenger and He will bestow on you the double portion of His Mercy: He will provide for you a Light by which ye shall walk straight in your path and He will forgive you ; for Allah is Most Forgiving, Most Merciful. That the People of the Book may know that they have no power whatever over the Grace of Allah, that His Grace is entirely in His Hand to bestow on whomsoever He wills. For Allah is the Lord of Grace abounding. (Al-Hadid 57:28–29, Koran).

Be in Taqwa of Allah and be with those who are true in word and deed. (At-Tawbah 9:11, Koran).

Be not presumptuous and impudent before Allah and His Messenger; be in taqwa of Allah, fear Allah: for Allah is He Who hears and knows all things. (Al-Hujurat 49:2, Koran)

The believer protects himself by always keeping Allah in view with every action and thought, ensuring that his every action is in accord with Allah's way. Perform every act and utter every word as if you see Allah, and if you do not see Him, be aware that Allah not only sees your deeds but also knows your thoughts. To ensure that one is dutiful to Allah, conscious of His presence, and God fearing, the believer with every action recites:

In the name of Allah, Most Gracious, Most Merciful.

There is a distinction between two types of divine mercy. In the broader sense, mercy refers to Allah's gentleness and kindness to all His creation, for He brings into existence, nurtures, and protects it to its destination. In a narrower sense, Allah's mercy refers to closeness to Allah that is given to those with *taqwa* in contrast to the chastisement inflicted on those who have chosen to stay distant from Him. Their distance from Allah in itself is chastisement because to be distant from the wholeness and harmony of the Real (Truth) is to be overcome by the turmoil and chaos of the unreal (falsehood). Allah's mercy is achieved by *taqwa* of Allah, which itself demands both submission (*islam*) and faith (*iman*).

وَرَحْمَتِي . وَسِعَتْ كُلَّ شَيْءٍ ۚ فَسَأَكْتُبُهَا لِلَّذِينَ يَتَّقُونَ وَيُؤْتُونَ ٱلزَّكَوٰةَ وَٱلَّذِينَ هُم بِـَٔايَٰتِنَا يُؤْمِنُونَ ﴿١٥٦﴾ ٱلَّذِينَ يَتَّبِعُونَ
ٱلرَّسُولَ ٱلنَّبِيَّ ٱلْأُمِّيَّ ٱلَّذِي يَجِدُونَهُۥ مَكْتُوبًا عِندَهُمْ فِي ٱلتَّوْرَىٰةِ وَٱلْإِنجِيلِ يَأْمُرُهُم بِٱلْمَعْرُوفِ وَيَنْهَىٰهُمْ عَنِ ٱلْمُنكَرِ وَيُحِلُّ لَهُمُ ٱلطَّيِّبَٰتِ
وَيُحَرِّمُ عَلَيْهِمُ ٱلْخَبَٰٓئِثَ وَيَضَعُ عَنْهُمْ إِصْرَهُمْ وَٱلْأَغْلَٰلَ ٱلَّتِي كَانَتْ عَلَيْهِمْ ۚ فَٱلَّذِينَ ءَامَنُوا۟ بِهِۦ وَعَزَّرُوهُ وَنَصَرُوهُ وَٱتَّبَعُوا۟ ٱلنُّورَ ٱلَّذِيٓ أُنزِلَ
مَعَهُۥٓ ۙ أُو۟لَٰٓئِكَ هُمُ ٱلْمُفْلِحُونَ ﴿١٥٧﴾

> My Chastisement I mete out to whomsoever I will; but My Mercy extends to all things. That Mercy I shall ordain for those who are muttaqun, those who have *Taqwa* and practice regular charity and those who believe in Our Signs.
>
> Those who follow the Rasool, the Nabi of the unlettered, about whom they find mentioned in the Taurat (Torah) and the Injeel (Gospel). He bids them what is just and forbids them what is evil; he allows them as lawful what is good and pure and prohibits them from what is bad and impure; he relieves them of their heavy burdens and from the fetters that are on them. So it is those who believe in him, honor him, help him and follow the Light, which is sent down with him, it is they who will prosper. (Al-A'raf 7:156–57, Koran)

5. The Covenant of Allah: Worship of Allah: Bow down, Prostrate Yourself, and Serve Your Lord

> Establish regular Salaat, give regular charity and hold fast to Allah. He is your Mawla, Protector, the best of Protectors and the best Helper. (Al-Hajj 22:77–78, Koran)
>
> Those who do wholesome deeds, establish regular prayers and regular charity have rewards with their Lord. On them shall be no fear, nor shall they grieve. (Al-Baqarah 2:227–80)

Seek help with patience, perseverance and prayer. Allah is with those who patiently persevere. (Al-Baqarah 2:153, Koran)

When you arise for salaat, purify yourself by washing your faces, your hands to the elbows, wipe your heads and wash your feet to the ankles. If you are unclean purify yourself. Allah does not wish that you should be burdened, but to make you clean and to bestow His blessings on you, that you may be grateful. (Al-Ma'idah 5:6, Koran)

Approach not prayers with a mind befogged until you understand all that you utter, nor come up to prayers in a state of un-cleanliness, till you have bathed. (An-Nisa 4:43, Koran)

Bow down, prostrate yourself and serve your Lord and do wholesome deeds that you may prosper. Perform Jihad; strive to your utmost in Allah's cause as striving (jihad) is His due. He has chosen you and Allah has imposed no hardship in your endeavor to His cause. You are the inheritors of the faith of your father Abraham. He has named you Muslims of the times before and now, so that Allah's Rasool may be an example to you and that you are an example to humankind. (Al-Hajj 22:77-78, Koran)

When the call is proclaimed to prayer on Friday, the day of assembly, hasten earnestly to the Remembrance of Allah and leave off business and everything else: that is best for you if ye but knew! And when the Prayer is finished, then may ye

> disperse through the land and seek of the Grace of Allah: remember and praise Allah a great deal: that ye may prosper. (Al-Jumu'ah 62:9–10, Koran)

The Koran, Allah's word, is the fundamental source of the believers' spiritual well-being. Recitation of the Koran imparts peace, tranquility, and closeness to Allah and also renews the believers' vows to obey Allah's covenant. All believers memorize some parts of the Koran, particularly Sura Al-Fatihah, and certain other verses to recite the salat. The salat is the daily renewal of the Koran in the believer, a daily rejuvenation of his or her covenant with Allah and communion with Him.

The blessed *Nabi* said, "*Iman is* knowledge in the heart, a voicing with the tongue and activity with the limbs." The term *heart*, often used in the Koran, refers to a specific faculty or a spiritual organ that provides humans with intellect and rationality. Therefore, *iman* means confidence in the reality and truth of things and commitment to act on the basis of the truth that they know. Thus, *iman* involves knowledge and words and actions on the basis of that knowledge. The Koran is Allah's speech to the believers, and it is the foundation of everything Islamic. Thus, humans connect with Allah by speaking to Him. The believer speaks to Allah through daily salat and supplication (*du'a*). The words are accompanied by action of the body and limbs, symbolizing subservience, respect, and humility. The salat consists of cyclic movements of standing in humility in the presence of Allah, bowing down to Him, going down in prostration in the Lord's presence, sitting in humility, reciting verses from the Koran, and praising Allah. Recitation of the Koran serves to embody the Koran within the person reciting salat. Allah is the light, and His word, the Koran, is His luminosity. To embody the Koran through faith and practice is to become transformed by this divine light that permeates through the believer in his closeness to Allah. Such proximity to Allah's presence gives the worshipper a "luminous presence."

6. The Covenant of Allah: Fasting Is Prescribed to You in the Month of Ramadan

> Fasting is prescribed to you, in the month of Ramadan as it was prescribed to those before you, that you may practice self-restraint. The Qur'an was revealed in the month of Ramadan, guidance to humankind for judgment between right and wrong. For everyone except those ill or on a journey, this month should spend it in fasting. Allah intends to make it easy on you so that you may complete the prescribed period of fasting and to glorify Him to express your gratitude for His Guidance (Al-Baqarah 2:178–79, Koran)

The month of fasting during Ramadan is a month of self-reflection, self-discipline, prayer, and remembrance of Allah. This is a month of renewal of a believer's commitment to Allah's covenant and a vow to follow His guidance. During this month, there is heightened attention to the rules of right conduct, which helps the believer in his commitment to follow Allah's straight path during the following year. This month is a reminder to the believers of their obligation to Allah's creatures in need of sustenance, shelter, protection, peace, and other help.

7. The Covenant of Allah: Zakat: Spend out of Bounties of Allah in Charity and Wholesome Deeds

> And the likeness of those who give generously, seeking to please Allah and to strengthen their souls, is as a garden, high and fertile where heavy rain falls on it and makes it yield a double the amount of harvest and if it receives not heavy rain, light moisture suffices it.

The parable of those who spend their substance in the way of Allah is that of a grain of corn: it grows seven ears and each ear has a hundred grains. Allah gives plentiful return to whom He pleases, Allah cares for all and He knows all things. Those who give generously in the cause of Allah and follow not up their gifts with reminders of their generosity or with injury, for them their reward is with their Lord; on them shall be no fear, nor shall they grieve. Kind words and the covering of faults are better than charity followed by injury. Allah is Free of all wants and He is Most Merciful. (Al-Baqarah 2:261–63, Koran)

Let not those among you who are blessed with grace and ample means hold back from helping their relatives, the poor and those who have left their homes in Allah's cause. Let them forgive and overlook, do you not wish that Allah should forgive you? And Allah is Oft Forgiving, Most Merciful. (An-Nur 24:21–23, Koran)

Spend out of bounties of Allah in charity and wholesome deeds before the Day comes when there will be neither bargaining, friendship nor intercession. Those who reject faith are the wrongdoers. (Al-Baqarah 2:254–57, Koran)

Void not your charity by boast, conceit and insult, by reminders of your generosity like those who want their generosity to be noted by all men but they believe neither in Allah nor in the Last Day. Theirs is a parable of a hard-barren rock, on which there is a little soil, washed by heavy rain, which leaves it just a bare stone. And Allah guides not those who reject Faith. And the likeness of those who give generously, seeking to please Allah and to strengthen their souls, is as a garden, high and fertile where heavy rain falls on it and makes it yield a double the amount of harvest and if it receives not heavy rain, light moisture suffices it. Allah notices whatever you do. (Al-Baqarah 2:264–65, Koran)

۞ إِنَّمَا ٱلصَّدَقَٰتُ لِلْفُقَرَآءِ وَٱلْمَسَٰكِينِ وَٱلْعَٰمِلِينَ عَلَيْهَا وَٱلْمُؤَلَّفَةِ قُلُوبُهُمْ وَفِى ٱلرِّقَابِ وَٱلْغَٰرِمِينَ وَفِى سَبِيلِ ٱللَّهِ وَٱبْنِ ٱلسَّبِيلِ ۖ

فَرِيضَةً مِّنَ ٱللَّهِ ۗ وَٱللَّهُ عَلِيمٌ حَكِيمٌ ﴿٦٠﴾

Alms are for the poor and the needy and those employed to administer the funds; for those whose hearts have been recently reconciled to the truth ; for those in bondage and in debt; in the cause of Allah; and for the wayfarer: thus is it ordained by Allah and Allah is full of knowledge and wisdom. (At-Tawbah 9:60, Koran).

In the above verses, the clear indication is that a human is given bounty by Allah. In return, his obligation is to distribute the surplus after his needs have been met to the needy. The Koran specifies that the zakat be distributed to the *fuqara* (the poor who ask), to *al-masakin* (the poor and the needy who do not ask), to zakat administrators, to those who spread the light of Islam to those inclined, for freedom of those in bondage, to those in debt, for the cause of Allah, and for the wayfarer who treads the path for Allah's service.

In the covenant, the individual surrenders to Allah his life and belongings in return for His guidance, a place in paradise in the hereafter, and peace with prosperity in this world. Every believer according to his or her covenant with Allah has the obligation to extend the benefits that He has provided him or her to those who did not receive the same. Such acts of generosity will be rewarded by Allah with a place in *Jannat* (place of peace and plenty) in the afterlife. Life of *Jannat* is to be attained in this world also, provided the compact with Allah is adhered to. The believer is Allah's instrument in fulfilling His promise to Adam that, among his progeny,

> None will remain without food or clothes and none
> will suffer from heat or thirst. (Koran 20:118)

In the verses below, Allah has promised those who believe and obey His covenant a reward for their acts of charity. He will double the harvest of their labors, forgive their sins, and provide them with His bounties, and they shall not grieve. Fear and grief arise from misfortunes, which cause anxiety, depression, and panic. Allah promises to safeguard the believers from misfortune.

And to those devouring usury, Allah will deprive them of all blessings. Obeying Allah's covenant provides *Jannat* in the hereafter and a life of *Jannat*, peace, and plenty in this world. It also brings balance, harmony, and stability to the economic life of the world in that it meets the necessities of each individual and eliminates unnecessary suffering.

يَٰٓأَيُّهَا ٱلَّذِينَ ءَامَنُوٓاْ أَنفِقُواْ مِن طَيِّبَٰتِ مَا كَسَبْتُمْ وَمِمَّآ أَخْرَجْنَا لَكُم مِّنَ ٱلْأَرْضِ ۖ وَلَا تَيَمَّمُواْ ٱلْخَبِيثَ مِنْهُ تُنفِقُونَ وَلَسْتُم
بِـَٔاخِذِيهِ إِلَّآ أَن تُغْمِضُواْ فِيهِ ۚ وَٱعْلَمُوٓاْ أَنَّ ٱللَّهَ غَنِىٌّ حَمِيدٌ ﴿٢٦٧﴾ ٱلشَّيْطَٰنُ يَعِدُكُمُ ٱلْفَقْرَ وَيَأْمُرُكُم بِٱلْفَحْشَآءِ ۖ وَٱللَّهُ يَعِدُكُم مَّغْفِرَةً مِّنْهُ
وَفَضْلًا ۗ وَٱللَّهُ وَٰسِعٌ عَلِيمٌ ﴿٢٦٨﴾ يُؤْتِى ٱلْحِكْمَةَ مَن يَشَآءُ ۚ وَمَن يُؤْتَ ٱلْحِكْمَةَ فَقَدْ أُوتِىَ خَيْرًا كَثِيرًا ۗ وَمَا يَذَّكَّرُ إِلَّآ أُوْلُواْ ٱلْأَلْبَٰبِ
﴿٢٦٩﴾ وَمَآ أَنفَقْتُم مِّن نَّفَقَةٍ أَوْ نَذَرْتُم مِّن نَّذْرٍ فَإِنَّ ٱللَّهَ يَعْلَمُهُۥ ۗ وَمَا لِلظَّٰلِمِينَ مِنْ أَنصَارٍ ﴿٢٧٠﴾

> O you who believe! Give of the good things that you
> have honorably earned and of the fruits of the earth

that We have produced for you and do not even aim
at giving anything which is bad, that you would not
receive yourself except with closed eyes. And know
that Allah is free of all wants and worthy of all praise.

The Satan threatens you with poverty and
bids you to unseemly actions. Allah promises
you His forgiveness and bounties. And Allah
cares for all and He knows all things.

He grants wisdom to whom He pleases; and
those who are granted wisdom receive indeed a
magnificent benefit, but none will grasp the Message
but men of knowledge and understanding.

And whatever you spend in charity or devotion,
be sure Allah knows it all. But the wrongdoers
have no helpers. (Al-Baqarah 2: 267–70)

The covenant of Allah has laid down principles and guidelines for the well-being of the economic life of the believers. Obeying the principles will bring peace, harmony, spiritual enlightenment, and economic prosperity. Disobeying means misery, ruin, and Allah's wrath.

Land and sources of production are not the personal property of individuals. *Ardh* is the source of life and means of sustenance and production of food and resources and therefore must remain available to the community of Islam, the *ummah.*

Every Muslim, man and woman, who at the end of the year is in possession of about fifteen dollars or more in cash or articles of trade must give zakat at the minimum rate of 2.5 percent. Zakat is incumbent on all liquid, visible, movable, and immovable properties belonging to Muslims. Two and a half percent of all the liquid assets of a Muslim adult after deduction of reasonable amount of expenses for the maintenance of the person's family and other dependents is not an excessive amount of money. Allah constantly reminds the believers to practice regular charity. Giving to the needy with love and respect out of love of Allah is a profound act of spiritual cleaning. The more one gives in wealth and in kindness, the higher is his status with Allah.

In the united Muslim lands of the Dar es Salaam, if every adult man and woman gives minimum of *$15* in zakat, the total collected will amount to *$12 billion.*

- If every one of the two thousand billionaires and two million millionaires in the Islamic world contributes a minimum of 2.5 percent of their liquid wealth in the way of Allah, the total collected will be to the tune of another *$100 billion.*
- If we approach another twenty million prosperous businesspeople with liquid assets of five hundred thousand dollars to pay their minimum zakat, the sum collected from them will amount to another *$250 billion.*
- The total sum thus collected amounts to *$362 billion.*
- Now we appeal to the same population that in this twenty-first century that 2.5 percent is not really enough to feed and house the large disadvantaged population of the *ummah* and ask for 5 percent of their liquid assets. The total collected will amount to *$724 billion.* Half this sum may then be used to feed, clothe, house, and educate the poor and needy population and the remaining half to create industries and jobs and job training for the people who have not been able to exit the cycle of poverty.
- If we approach Hosni Mubarak, Mu'ammar Gaddhafi, Ben Ali, Saddam Hussein, Saudi and Gulf sheikhs, and other Arab

royal families for 5 percent of their three-trillion-dollar stash, we will have another *$150 billion* annually.

- There is an estimated forty-five thousand tons of accumulated gold hoardings in the Islamic countries in the form of jewelry, gold bricks, gold bars, gold artifacts, and national treasures in museums of an estimated value of $1.8 trillion. Five percent in zakat will amount to *$85 billion* annually.
- In addition, there is a hoard of precious stones worth another two trillion dollars, 5 percent of which will yield another *one hundred billion dollars* in zakat money.

The total zakat owed to the Muslim community is over *1.1 trillion dollars annually.*

Even though the Islamic states have been milked dry by our elite and their colonial cohorts, the *ummah* acting in accordance with Allah's covenant shall be able to eradicate all poverty and destitution within the Dar es Salaam within *three years* with the resources from within the community of believers. The remedy lies within the *ummah* with zakat amounting to *$3.3 trillion* over three years without ever touching any of the government revenues. So why is the *ummah* so destitute? Fewer than five thousand families in the Islamic state are hoarding the wealth of the *ummah.*

Were the precepts of the covenant of Allah applied to the rest of humanity, all poverty, deprivation, and disease will disappear from the world in one year. Less than 10 percent of the world's population owns 80 percent of its wealth. This disparity is caused by unbridled feudalism and capitalism in man's history.

The total wealth of the world is estimated to be three hundred trillion dollars. If every human gave away 2.5 to 5.0 percent of their surplus income in zakat to eradicate poverty, disease, and hunger in the global village, *$7.5 to $15.0 trillion* will become available, half of which can be used to eradicate hunger, illiteracy, unemployment, and disease annually and the remaining amount to build the world's infrastructure for environmentally sustainable agriculture and industrial production to sustain mankind. In no time, the world will be a stable place, eradicating wars, famines, epidemics, ignorance, and hunger.

The solution to the ills of humanity lies in Allah's word:

> And the likeness of those who give generously, seeking to please Allah and to strengthen their souls, is as a garden, high and fertile where heavy rain falls on it and makes it yield a double the amount of harvest and if it receives not heavy rain, light moisture suffices it.

> The parable of those who spend their substance in the way of Allah is that of a grain of corn: it grows seven ears and each ear has a hundred grains. Allah gives plentiful return to whom He pleases, Allah cares for all and He knows all things. Those who give generously in the cause of Allah and follow not up their gifts with reminders of their generosity or with injury, for them their reward is with their Lord; on them shall be no fear, nor shall they grieve.

8. The Covenant of Allah: Hajj: And Proclaim the Pilgrimage to Mankind

> And proclaim the Pilgrimage to mankind; they will come to thee on foot and mounted on every kind of camel, lean on account of journeys through deep and distant mountain highways; that they may witness the benefits provided for them and celebrate the name of Allah, through the Days Appointed, over the

> cattle which He has provided for them for sacrifice: then eat you thereof and feed the distressed ones in want. Then let them complete the rites prescribed for them, perform their vows and again circumambulate the Ancient House. Such is the Pilgrimage: whoever honors the sacred rites of Allah, for him it is good in the sight of his Lord. Lawful to you for food in Pilgrimage are cattle, except those mentioned to you as exceptions: but shun the abomination of idols and shun the word that is false. (Al-Hajj 22:27-30, Koran).

> Violate not the sanctity of the Symbols of Allah, or of the sacred month, or of the animals brought for sacrifice, nor the garlands that mark out such animals, nor the people coming to the Sacred House, seeking the bounty and good pleasure of their Lord. Help one another in virtue and piety but help not one another in sin and acrimony. Be in Taqwa of Allah, fear Allah, for Allah is swift in reckoning. (Al-Ma'idah 5:2, Koran)

For thirteen hundred years, Muslims have traveled to Mecca on foot, on horse, and on camelback, taking more than a year to complete the rituals of the hajj. This slow pace helps the believer in his spiritual pursuit and his worldly quest to get acquainted with Muslims of other lands that have kept the *ummah* united. The hajj since then has been seen as a grand rite of passage from the life of this world to a communion with Allah in a grand festival of worship in devotion to Him. Hajjis have been treated as models of piety and blessedness. With modern air travel, hajj has become accessible to a larger population, bringing the Islamic world closer. To the large number of children and young adults performing hajj, the rituals at the house inspire the renewal of their vows to the covenant of Allah, and they carry forward their passion to inspire others to perform the good works in the path of Allah.

9. The Covenant of Allah: Truth: Speak Always the Truth

يَـٰٓأَيُّهَا ٱلَّذِينَ ءَامَنُوا۟ ٱتَّقُوا۟ ٱللَّهَ وَقُولُوا۟ قَوْلًا سَدِيدًا ﴿٧٠﴾ يُصْلِحْ لَكُمْ أَعْمَـٰلَكُمْ وَيَغْفِرْ لَكُمْ ذُنُوبَكُمْ ۗ وَمَن يُطِعِ ٱللَّهَ وَرَسُولَهُۥ فَقَدْ فَازَ
فَوْزًا عَظِيمًا ﴿٧١﴾ إِنَّا عَرَضْنَا ٱلْأَمَانَةَ عَلَى ٱلسَّمَـٰوَٰتِ وَٱلْأَرْضِ وَٱلْجِبَالِ فَأَبَيْنَ أَن يَحْمِلْنَهَا وَأَشْفَقْنَ مِنْهَا وَحَمَلَهَا ٱلْإِنسَـٰنُ ۖ إِنَّهُۥ كَانَ
ظَلُومًا جَهُولًا ﴿٧٢﴾ لِّيُعَذِّبَ ٱللَّهُ ٱلْمُنَـٰفِقِينَ وَٱلْمُنَـٰفِقَـٰتِ وَٱلْمُشْرِكِينَ وَٱلْمُشْرِكَـٰتِ وَيَتُوبَ ٱللَّهُ عَلَى ٱلْمُؤْمِنِينَ وَٱلْمُؤْمِنَـٰتِ ۗ وَكَانَ ٱللَّهُ
غَفُورًا رَّحِيمًۢا ﴿٧٣﴾

O you who believe! Have Taqwa of Allah, fear Allah and always speak the truth, that He may direct you to deeds of righteousness and forgive your sins: he that obeys Allah and His Rasool have already attained the highest achievement.

We did indeed offer al-Amanah, the Trust to the Heavens and the Earth and the Mountains; but they shrank from the burden, being afraid of it, but man assumed it and has proved to be a tyrant and a fool, with the result that Allah has to punish the Munafiqeen, truth concealers, men and women and the Mushrikun, unbelievers, men and women and Allah turns in Mercy to the Believers, men and women; for Allah is Forgiving, Most Merciful. (Al-Ahzab 33:69–73, Koran)

To live up to the trust of Allah, the vicegerent—the human—has to distinguish between good and evil, truth and falsehood, *adl* and *zulm*. Falsehood is the abomination that corrupts the very basis of Allah's vicegerency and His covenant with man. The Koran discredits workers of corruption, the worst among them being the *Munafiqeen* (truth concealers), the hypocrites who claim to do good deeds but whose intentions are vile and harmful to others. Good deeds are based on truth and are therefore motivated by *iman* and *taqwa*. Corruption, dishonesty, and falsehood arise when humans—Allah's vicegerents on the earth—turn away from the covenant of Allah and forget the message of the prophets::

﴿ وَٱلَّذِينَ يَنقُضُونَ عَهْدَ ٱللَّهِ مِنۢ بَعْدِ مِيثَـٰقِهِۦ وَيَقْطَعُونَ مَآ أَمَرَ ٱللَّهُ بِهِۦٓ أَن يُوصَلَ وَيُفْسِدُونَ فِى ٱلْأَرْضِ أُو۟لَـٰٓئِكَ لَهُمُ ٱللَّعْنَةُ وَلَهُمْ

سُوٓءُ ٱلدَّارِ ﴿٢٥﴾ ﴾

But those who break the Covenant of Allah, after having pledged their word on it and sever that Allah has commanded to be joined together and who work corruption on earth, on them shall be the curse and theirs is the ugly abode. (Ar-Ra'd 13:25, Koran)

10. The Covenant of Allah: *Fahasha*: Avoid Indecency, Iniquity, Abomination, Shameful Deeds, and Scandalous Acts

Allah's covenant forbids the believers from shameful deeds—adultery, fornication, sodomy, deception, treason, lying, cheating, stealing, and murder—whether in open or in secret. People who commit such deeds are not immune from other abominations against their community and humankind.

A believer's life and soul is akin to a dew pond of crystal-clear spring from which a fountain gushes forth pure and refreshing; in the same manner, beautiful deeds of the believers quench the thirst of humanity and bring peace and satisfaction. Acts of indecency and shame sully the dew pond with water so foul that the believers and humanity fall prey to plague, pestilence, and diseases of the body and spirit and lose Allah's grace.

When people and the rulers of Muslim lands indulge in shameful deeds (*Fahasha*), they do indeed follow Satan's footsteps and lose *furqan*, the criterion to distinguish right from wrong. Shameful actions open the gates to the world of iniquity, where there are no inhibitions nor shame. One licentious act leads to another till all thoughts of Allah are lost in a haze of debauchery and decadence. Intoxication leads to loss of inhibitions, licentiousness, and indecent acts against oneself and others. Inequity trespasses boundaries of self-control until there are trespasses against oneself, other people, the community, the state, and above all the commandments of Allah.

When Allah's gifts and grace are deemed inadequate, there begins a struggle for acquisition of wealth. Wealth condones *Fahasha* and facilitates the activities of lewdness, debauchery, and indecency. Under every pile of wealth lies the sweat and blood of its victims. Wealth is the engine of *Fahasha* and wealth and power are begotten through foul means. The covenant of Allah forbids shameful deeds, dishonesty, and deceit. To sustain the incumbent royals and dictators in riches and power, the conscientious and those who fight for decency and truth are taken into custody, tortured, or imprisoned. Some simply disappear, never to be heard of again. The *Fahasha* and the powerful are not accountable to Allah, and they thrive in the company of Satan. Their acts of shame and profanity are perpetrated in the open and obvious to those who surround them in the circles of power.

Enter into submission to the will of Allah,
enter Islam whole-heartedly and follow not
the footsteps of Satan, for he is a sworn enemy
to you! (Al-Baqarah 2:208, Koran)

Do not follow Satan's footsteps: if any will follow
the footsteps of Satan, he will command to what is

shameful (Fahasha) and wrong (Munkar): and were it not for the grace of Allah and His mercy on you, not one of you would have been unblemished: but Allah does purify whom He pleases: and Allah is all Hearer and all Knower. (An-Nur 24:21–23, Koran).

Come not near to shameful deeds (fornication, adultery and shameful activities) whether open or secret. (Al-An'am: 151–53, Koran)

11. The Covenant of Allah: Unity of the *Ummah*

And hold fast, all together, by the Rope, which Allah stretches out for you and be not divided among yourselves; and remember with gratitude Allah's favor on you; you were enemies and He joined your hearts in love, so that by His Grace, you became brethren and a community. You were on the brink of the pit of fire and He saved you from it. Thus, does Allah make His Signs clear to you that you may be guided. Let there arise out of you a band of people inviting to all that is good, enjoining what is right and forbidding that is wrong. They are the ones to attain happiness.

Be not like those who are divided amongst themselves and fall into disputations after receiving clear signs: for them is a dreadful penalty. (Ali 'Imran 3:103–5, Koran)

Persevere in patience and constancy; vie in such perseverance; strengthen each other; and be in Taqwa of Allah, fear Allah that you may prosper. (Ali 'Imran 3:200, Koran)

> This is a grace from Allah and a favor; and Allah is All Knowing and All Wise. If two parties among the Believers fall into a quarrel, make peace between them: but if one of them transgresses beyond bounds against the other, then fight you all against the one who transgresses until he complies with the Command of Allah; but if he complies, then make peace between them with justice and fairness: for Allah loves those who are fair and just. The Believers are but a single Brotherhood: so make peace and reconciliation between your two brothers; and fear Allah, that you may receive Mercy. (Al-Hujurat 49:6–10, Koran)

> Just as the bond to Allah is indivisible, all the Believers shall stand behind the commitment of the least of them. All the Believers are bonded one to another to the exclusion of other men. (The Covenant of Muhammad)

The Divide of Islam

All Muslims are one brotherhood, one *ummah*, all servants of one Allah, the First and the Last, fulfilling His covenant, witnessed over by Allah's messenger, an *ummah* that is witness over other nations. After the peace conference at the Palace of Versailles, the French and the British met quietly in San Remo in Italy to carve up the former possessions of the Ottoman Empire. France was given Syria and Lebanon; Persia became a British protectorate, and Mesopotamia and Palestine came under British possession.

The map of modern Middle East was conceived by a young Englishman drunk with power and alcohol. Winston Churchill traveled to Cairo in March 1921. Winston Churchill and Thomas

Edward Lawrence had reviewed the aspirants of the Arabian thrones at the Ship restaurant in London over dinner and, after dinner, brandy and liqueurs. The two likeliest candidates were Shariff Hussein's sons Faisal and Abdullah. On March 21, 1921, the Cairo Conference opened with thirty-eight participants, out of whom thirty-six were British. Churchill wrote afterward a description of this meeting: "Lawrence suggested that Feisal be crowned head of Iraq, not only because of his personal knowledge and friendship of the individual, but also on the ground that in order to counteract the claims of rival candidates and in order to pull together the scattered elements of a backward and half civilized country it was essential that the first ruler should be an active and inspiring personality."[4]

His motion with Churchill's approval carried without dissent. Abdullah, in Lawrence's view, was "lazy and by no means dominating," but though unfit to rule Iraq, he would be permitted to rule over Transjordan under the watchful eye of a British high commissioner. Churchill announced his intention to appoint Abdullah in Palestine. Years later, Churchill would say, "Emir Abdullah is in Transjordania where I put him one Sunday afternoon in Jerusalem."

Zionism's hopes were honored. Sir Herbert Samuel—a Jew, Winston Churchill's cabinet colleague—was appointed high commissioner in Palestine and instructed to foster a Jewish homeland in Palestine. An Englishwoman who attended the conference remembers, "Winston going around the hotel followed by an Arab carrying a pail and a bottle of wine. When things got boring at the conference everyone would cheer when Winston came in."

On March 23, 1921, Winston Churchill, Sir Herbert Samuel, and Lawrence left Cairo Station by rail for Jerusalem. Between them, they

---

[4] William Manchester, *The Last Lion* (Bantam Double Day Publishing Group Ltd), 700.

drew the boundaries of the British-mandated territory. What was once one land for hundreds of years became Syria, Lebanon, Palestine, Iraq, Kuwait, and Hejaz. Hejaz was soon occupied with British encouragement by Ibn Sa'ud. Israel was carved out of Palestine. Little desert domains of desert Bedouins, following treaties with Britain, became the Trucial States with further hinterland added to their territories for exploitation and exploration of oil by the British. The Arabian Peninsula was further carved into Oman, Muscat, and the South and North Yemen.

The borders between the Muslim communities and the kingdoms of Islam are Western innovation for division, exploitation, and control of Muslim lands, the Dar es Salaam. This divide was carried out and maintained by the West with the connivance of the rulers of Islam against the commandments of the covenant between Allah and His people.

12. The Covenant of Allah: Perseverance and Patience

يَٰٓأَيُّهَا ٱلَّذِينَ ءَامَنُوا۟ ﴿ تُفْلِحُونَ لَعَلَّكُمْ ٱللَّهَ وَٱتَّقُوا۟ وَرَابِطُوا۟ وَصَابِرُوا۟ ٱصْبِرُوا۟ ﴾

O ye who believe! persevere in patience and
constancy; vie in such perseverance; strengthen
each other; and fear Allah; that ye may prosper.

Ṣabr, *ṣābir*, *ṣabbār*, and *ṣābara* denote the quality of patience and steadfastness, self-restraint, forbearance, endurance, and perseverance. One of Allah's ninety-nine names is *al-Ṣabur*, the Patient. It is one who does not precipitate an act before it's time but decides matters according to a specific plan and brings them to fruition in a predefined manner, neither procrastinating nor hastening matters before their time but disposing each matter in its appropriate time in the way of its needs and requirements and doing all that without being subjected to a force opposing Allah's will. *Ṣabr*, *ṣābir*, *ṣabbār*, and *ṣābara* are mentioned in the Koran sixty-nine times. Allah reassures the believers:

> O Believers, be patient and vie you with patience. (3:200)
>
> Pray for succor to Allah and be patient. (7:128)
>
> Be thou patient, Allah will not leave to waste
> the wage of good –doers. (11:115)
>
> Be thou patient; Surely Allah's promise is true. (30:60)
>
> Bear patiently whatever may befall you. (31:17)
>
> So be thou patient with a sweet patience. (70:5)
>
> And be patient unto your Lord. (74:7)
>
> O Believers, seek you help in patience and prayer. (21:153)
>
> But come sweet patience. (12:18, 83)
>
> Surely Allah is with the is with the patient. (2:153, 249)
>
> Allah loves the patient. (3:146)

For a man and a woman to be patient (*ṣabr*) requires endurance and discipline to affirm a rational resolve in opposing the impulses of passion or anger. It involves balancing two opposing desires. The believer has to overcome the impulse leading to rashness and haste and at the same time lean toward the inclination to delay the act. To be patient, one has to resolve the conflict between acts, anger and rashness on one hand and procrastination and delay on the other. Lack of *ṣabr*, self-restraint, patience, and self-discipline has overwhelmed the Muslim world at the beginning of the twenty-first century. The

Muslim world has been rudderless and leaderless over one hundred years and poorly led during the previous one thousand years. The result is 1.5 billion individuals following their own instincts for the sake of mere survival.

Şabr teaches self-restraint in the matters of need and giving precedence to others over oneself in matters of need. Islam teaches that the elders, the sick, the needy, the women, and the children take precedence in matters of care, shelter, and food and that spirituality takes precedence over one's daily needs. Consideration and the well-being of the kin, the neighbor, and the fellow man requires a thought before fulfilling one's own requirements. The state of *şabr* in the Muslim world is obvious when one looks at the lineups at the bus and rail stations. People are being trampled at the holy sites. Old men, women, and the disabled were pushed and trampled during the holiest act of circumambulation of the Kaaba, at Safa and Marwah, and during the ritual stoning of the devil. The same is true in the shopping centers, down the streets, and bus lineups.

The extreme desire for immediate gratification of desires and cravings leads to small and major crimes. Lying, theft, and robbery are common acts involved in the impulse of possession of the unreachable. Military revolutions, palace coups, conspiracies, and conquests bring power in the hands of the unjust and ambitious and people of vast ambitions but without a capacity for hard work, honesty, and *şabr* or patience.

> Persevere in patience and constancy; vie in
> such perseverance; strengthen each other;
> and be in Taqwa of Allah, fear Allah that you
> may prosper. (Ali 'Imran 3:200, Koran)

13. The Covenant of Allah: Theft, Deception, Fraud, Honesty, and Justice

Betray not the trust of Allah and His *rasul.* Nor knowingly misappropriate wealth entrusted to you, whether on behalf of an orphan or another party. Be honest in handling property, goods, credit, confidences, and secrets of your fellow men and display integrity and honesty in using your skills and talents. Whenever you give your word, speak truthfully and justly, even if a near relative is concerned. Similarly, the *amri minkum*—those entrusted with the administration of the affairs of the believers—should not betray the trust of Allah, the *rasul*, and the believers and knowingly misappropriate the wealth of the Muslims. The populations of the Islamic lands are akin to the orphans whose land and heritage has been forcibly sequestered by conquest, soon to be redeemed and accounted for from the those who ceased it, who will on the appointed day be asked to account for every grain of sand and every grain of stolen gold. The Arabian Peninsula and other Muslim lands have been the plundering fields of the royal families and their kin for one hundred years in partnership with the circle of evil.

The rulers of the Arabian Peninsula and their royal relatives regularly skim off the cream and top third of the wealth of the *ummah* for their personal benefit. The dictators, the royals, and their circle of sycophants and cheerleaders in all Muslim nation-states have siphoned off the cream of their national wealth. Suharto, Benazir Bhutto, Nawaz Sharif, Reza Shah of Iran, Saddam Hussein, Anwar Sadat, Hosni Mubarak, Gaddhafi, Ben Ali, kings of Arabian Peninsula, their families, and the inner circle of their regimes have plundered their nation's treasuries of trillions of dollars over the years of their prolonged rein on power. The greatest pillage and plunder in history took place systematically when the descendants of ten barefoot, camel-herding Bedouins took control of the Arabian Peninsula with the help of British money and arms. In the second half of the twentieth century, over a short period of forty-five years, they took a heist of $4.5 trillion. In the Arabian Peninsula, in the kingdoms of Oman, Kuwait, the United Arab Emirates, Qatar, Bahrain, and Saudi Arabia, there are now six kings and over five hundred billionaires and thousands of millionaires among this narrow circle of ten clans. Over this short period, these tent dwellers who had never been inside the confines of a dwelling now own hundreds of palaces in Arabia, Europe, and America. Yet the plunder is ongoing. The total amount of petty cash taken out by the ever-increasing progeny of these Bedouin sheikhs in allowances, salaries, commissions, and expenses is so immense that their take of fifty billion dollars annually is more than the total combined annual budget of nation-states of Pakistan, Afghanistan, Iran, Syria, and Jordan, with a population of 250 million people. The cost of security of these "royals" (90,000 troops), personal jets, helicopters, yachts, travel, and private air terminals in Jeddah, Riyadh, Dubai, and Doha is an additional twenty billion dollars. This is going on when most Arabs and Muslims live in conditions of utter poverty and deprivation.

Two fundamental terms used in the Koran are *haqq* (right and honest means of income) and *batil* (wrongful and dishonest way of making money). The ways of making money approved by the Koran are halal, and those forbidden are haram.

Muslims the world over follow the verses about fasting in Sura Al-Baqarah 2:183–87 but very conveniently ignore the following verse (188):

> And do not devour each other's wealth
> dishonestly, nor use it as bait for the judges,
> with intent that ye may devour dishonestly and
> knowingly a little of (other) people's wealth.

﴿ يَٰٓأَيُّهَا ٱلَّذِينَ ءَامَنُواْ كُتِبَ عَلَيۡكُمُ ٱلصِّيَامُ كَمَا كُتِبَ عَلَى ٱلَّذِينَ مِن قَبۡلِكُمۡ لَعَلَّكُمۡ تَتَّقُونَ ١٨٣ أَيَّامٗا مَّعۡدُودَٰتٖۚ فَمَن كَانَ
مِنكُم مَّرِيضًا أَوۡ عَلَىٰ سَفَرٖ فَعِدَّةٞ مِّنۡ أَيَّامٍ أُخَرَۚ وَعَلَى ٱلَّذِينَ يُطِيقُونَهُۥ فِدۡيَةٞ طَعَامُ مِسۡكِينٖۖ فَمَن تَطَوَّعَ خَيۡرٗا فَهُوَ خَيۡرٞ لَّهُۥۚ وَأَن تَصُومُواْ خَيۡرٞ
لَّكُمۡ إِن كُنتُمۡ تَعۡلَمُونَ ١٨٤ شَهۡرُ رَمَضَانَ ٱلَّذِيٓ أُنزِلَ فِيهِ ٱلۡقُرۡءَانُ هُدٗى لِّلنَّاسِ وَبَيِّنَٰتٖ مِّنَ ٱلۡهُدَىٰ وَٱلۡفُرۡقَانِۚ فَمَن شَهِدَ مِنكُمُ ٱلشَّهۡرَ
فَلۡيَصُمۡهُۖ وَمَن كَانَ مَرِيضًا أَوۡ عَلَىٰ سَفَرٖ فَعِدَّةٞ مِّنۡ أَيَّامٍ أُخَرَۗ يُرِيدُ ٱللَّهُ بِكُمُ ٱلۡيُسۡرَ وَلَا يُرِيدُ بِكُمُ ٱلۡعُسۡرَ وَلِتُكۡمِلُواْ ٱلۡعِدَّةَ وَلِتُكَبِّرُواْ ٱللَّهَ
عَلَىٰ مَا هَدَىٰكُمۡ وَلَعَلَّكُمۡ تَشۡكُرُونَ ١٨٥ وَإِذَا سَأَلَكَ عِبَادِي عَنِّي فَإِنِّي قَرِيبٌۖ أُجِيبُ دَعۡوَةَ ٱلدَّاعِ إِذَا دَعَانِۖ فَلۡيَسۡتَجِيبُواْ لِي وَلۡيُؤۡمِنُواْ بِي
لَعَلَّهُمۡ يَرۡشُدُونَ ١٨٦ أُحِلَّ لَكُمۡ لَيۡلَةَ ٱلصِّيَامِ ٱلرَّفَثُ إِلَىٰ نِسَآئِكُمۡۚ هُنَّ لِبَاسٞ لَّكُمۡ وَأَنتُمۡ لِبَاسٞ لَّهُنَّۗ عَلِمَ ٱللَّهُ أَنَّكُمۡ كُنتُمۡ تَخۡتَانُونَ
أَنفُسَكُمۡ فَتَابَ عَلَيۡكُمۡ وَعَفَا عَنكُمۡۖ فَٱلۡـَٰٔنَ بَٰشِرُوهُنَّ وَٱبۡتَغُواْ مَا كَتَبَ ٱللَّهُ لَكُمۡۚ وَكُلُواْ وَٱشۡرَبُواْ حَتَّىٰ يَتَبَيَّنَ لَكُمُ ٱلۡخَيۡطُ ٱلۡأَبۡيَضُ مِنَ ٱلۡخَيۡطِ
ٱلۡأَسۡوَدِ مِنَ ٱلۡفَجۡرِۖ ثُمَّ أَتِمُّواْ ٱلصِّيَامَ إِلَى ٱلَّيۡلِۚ وَلَا تُبَٰشِرُوهُنَّ وَأَنتُمۡ عَٰكِفُونَ فِي ٱلۡمَسَٰجِدِۗ تِلۡكَ حُدُودُ ٱللَّهِ فَلَا تَقۡرَبُوهَاۗ كَذَٰلِكَ يُبَيِّنُ
ٱللَّهُ ءَايَٰتِهِۦ لِلنَّاسِ لَعَلَّهُمۡ يَتَّقُونَ

O you who believe! Fasting is prescribed to you as it was prescribed to those before you, that ye may (learn) self-restraint,

(Fasting) for a fixed number of days; but if any of you is ill, or on a journey, the prescribed number (should be made up) from days later. For those who can do it (with hardship), is a ransom, the feeding of one that is indigent but he that will give more, of his own free will, it is better for him. And it is better for you that ye fast, if ye only knew.

Ramadan is the (month) in which was sent down the Qur'an, as a guide to mankind, also Clear (Signs) for guidance and judgment (between right and wrong). So, every one of you who is present (at his home) during that month should spend it in fasting, but if anyone is ill, or on a journey, the prescribed period (should be made up) by days later. Allah intends every facility for you; He does not want to put you to difficulties. (He wants you) to complete the prescribed period and to glorify Him in that He has guided you; and perchance ye shall be grateful.

When My servants ask thee concerning Me, I am indeed close (to them): I listen to the prayer of every suppliant when he calls on Me: let them also, with a will, listen to My call and believe in Me: that they may walk in the right way.

Permitted to you, on the night of the fasts, is the approach to your wives. They are your garments and ye are their garments. Allah knows what you used to do secretly among yourselves; but He turned to you and forgave you; so now associate with them and seek what Allah hath ordained for you and eat and drink until the white thread of dawn appear to you distinct from its black thread; then complete your fast till the night appears; but do not associate with your wives while ye are in retreat in the mosques. Those are limits (set by) Allah: approach not nigh thereto. Thus, doth Allah make clear His Signs to men: that they may learn self-restraint.

﴿ وَلَا تَأْكُلُوٓا۟ أَمْوَٰلَكُم بَيْنَكُم بِٱلْبَٰطِلِ وَتُدْلُوا۟ بِهَآ إِلَى ٱلْحُكَّامِ لِتَأْكُلُوا۟ فَرِيقًا مِّنْ أَمْوَٰلِ ٱلنَّاسِ بِٱلْإِثْمِ وَأَنتُمْ تَعْلَمُونَ ١٨٨ ﴾

And do not devour each other's wealth dishonestly, nor use it as bait for the judges, with intent that ye may devour dishonestly and knowingly a little of (other) people's wealth. (Al Baqarah 2:183–88, Koran)

There are several dishonest financial practices, cheating, bribery, stealing, embezzlement, hoarding, and swindling, but one mentioned specifically in the Koran is often overlooked. That is the one practiced by the aristocrats, clergy, clerics, and claimants of spiritual leadership all across the world:

﴿ ۞ يَٰٓأَيُّهَا ٱلَّذِينَ ءَامَنُوٓاْ إِنَّ كَثِيرٗا مِّنَ ٱلۡأَحۡبَارِ وَٱلرُّهۡبَانِ لَيَأۡكُلُونَ أَمۡوَٰلَ ٱلنَّاسِ بِٱلۡبَٰطِلِ وَيَصُدُّونَ عَن سَبِيلِ ٱللَّهِۗ وَٱلَّذِينَ
يَكۡنِزُونَ ٱلذَّهَبَ وَٱلۡفِضَّةَ وَلَا يُنفِقُونَهَا فِي سَبِيلِ ٱللَّهِ فَبَشِّرۡهُم بِعَذَابٍ أَلِيمٖ ﴿٣٤﴾

O you who believe! There are indeed many among the leaders, priests and clerics, who in falsehood devour the substance of men and hinder (them) from the Way of Allah. And there are those who bury gold and silver and spend it not in the Way of Allah: announce unto them a most grievous penalty. (At-Tawbah 9:34, Koran)

Like the politicians and dictators, these priests and spiritual leaders deceive the unlettered masses with false doctrines and fallacies to keep them entrapped in their web to safeguard their own power over people and wealth.

14. The Covenant of Allah: Obey Allah and His *Rasul* and Those Charged with Authority among You

Obey Allah and obey the Messenger and those charged amongst you with authority in the settlement of your affairs. If you differ in anything among yourselves, refer it to Allah and His Rasool (The Qur'an and the Prophet's teachings). If you do believe in Allah and the last Day that is best and the most beautiful conduct in the final determination. (An-Nisa 4:43, Koran)

The Koran teaches that all affairs of the individuals and of the Muslim community should be conducted through mutual consultation (*ijma*) and decisions arrived at through consensus. Furthermore, the Koran proclaims consultation as a principle of government and a method that must be applied in the administration of public affairs. The sovereignty of the Islamic state belongs exclusively to Allah, whose will and command binds the community and state. The dignified designation in the Koran of the community as vicegerent of Allah on the earth makes the Muslim community, the *ummah,* a repository of what is known as "executive sovereignty" of the Islamic state. The community as a whole, after consultation and consensus, grants people among themselves with authority to manage its affairs (*ulil amri minkum*). Those charged with authority act in their capacity as the representative (*wakil*) of the people and are bound by the Koranic mandate to consult the community in public affairs, and consensus is the binding source of the law. The community by consultation and in consensus has the authority to depose any person charged with authority, including the head of state, in the event of gross violation of Allah's law.

وَٱلَّذِينَ ٱسْتَجَابُواْ لِرَبِّهِمْ وَأَقَامُواْ ٱلصَّلَوٰةَ وَأَمْرُهُمْ شُورَىٰ بَيْنَهُمْ وَمِمَّا رَزَقْنَٰهُمْ يُنفِقُونَ ﴿٣٨﴾ وَٱلَّذِينَ إِذَآ أَصَابَهُمُ ٱلْبَغْىُ هُمْ يَنتَصِرُونَ ﴿٣٩﴾

Those who hearken to their Lord and establish regular prayer; who (conduct) their affairs by mutual Consultation; who spend out of what We bestow on them for Sustenance; And those who, when an oppressive wrong is inflicted on them do not flinch and courageously defend themselves. (Ash-Shura 42:38–39, Koran)

Islam pursues its social objectives by reforming the individual. The ritual ablution before prayer, the five daily prayers, fasting during the month of Ramadan, and the obligatory giving of charity all encourage punctuality, self-discipline, and concern for the well-being of others. The individual is seen not just as a member of the community and subservient to the community's will but also as a morally autonomous agent who plays a distinctive role in shaping the community's sense of direction and purpose. The Koran has attached to the individual's duty of obedience to the government a right to simultaneously dispute with rulers over government affairs. The individual obeys the ruler on the condition that the ruler obeys the covenant of the Koran and Allah's commandments, which are obligatory to all Muslims regardless of their status in the social hierarchy. This is reflected in the declaration of the blessed *Nabi* that *"There is no obedience in transgression; obedience is only in the righteousness."*

The citizen is entitled to disobey an oppressive command that is contrary to the covenant of the Koran. The blessed *Nabi,* Allah's emissary, brought His word to the world and disseminated it to the populations of all the continents. Thus, it is essential to obey the commandments that Blessed Muhammad brought from Allah for mankind.

يَٰٓأَيُّهَا ٱلَّذِينَ ءَامَنُوٓاْ أَطِيعُواْ ٱللَّهَ وَأَطِيعُواْ ٱلرَّسُولَ وَأُوْلِي ٱلۡأَمۡرِ مِنكُمۡۖ فَإِن تَنَٰزَعۡتُمۡ فِي شَيۡءٖ فَرُدُّوهُ إِلَى ٱللَّهِ وَٱلرَّسُولِ إِن كُنتُمۡ تُؤۡمِنُونَ بِٱللَّهِ وَٱلۡيَوۡمِ ٱلۡأٓخِرِۚ

ذَٰلِكَ خَيۡرٞ وَأَحۡسَنُ تَأۡوِيلًا

O you who believe! Obey Allah and obey the Messenger and those charged with authority among you. If ye differ in anything among yourselves, refer it to Allah and His Messenger, if ye do believe in Allah and the Last Day: that is best and most suitable for final determination. (An-Nisa 4:59, Koran)

15. The Covenant of Allah: Freedom of Religion: Let There Be No Compulsion in Religion

> Let there be no compulsion in religion: Truth stands out clear from Error: whoever rejects Evil and believes in Allah hath grasped the most trustworthy handhold that never breaks. And Allah hears and knows all things. (Al-Baqarah 2:254–57, Koran)

The Koranic notion of religious belief (*iman*) is dependent on knowledge that is actualized in practice in the term *islam*. The term *islam* signifies the idea of surrender or submission. Islam is a religion of self-surrender; it is the conscious and rational submission of dependent and limited human will to the absolute and omnipotent will of Allah. The type of surrender Islam requires is a deliberate, conscious, and rational act made by a person who knows with both intellectual certainty and spiritual vision that Allah, who is the subject of Koranic discourse, is the only reality.

The knower of God is a Muslim (fem. *Muslimah*), "one who submits" to the divine truth and whose relationship with God is governed by *taqwa*, the consciousness of humankind's responsibility toward its Creator. However, consciousness of God alone is not sufficient to make a person a Muslim. Neither is it enough to be merely born a Muslim or to be raised in an Islamic cultural context. The concept of *taqwa* implies that the believer has the added responsibility of acting in accordance with the three types of knowledge—*ilm al-yaqin, ain al-yaqin* and *haqq al-yaqin* (knowledge of certainty, eye of certainty, and the truth of certainty). The believer must endeavor at all times to maintain himself or herself in a constant state of submission to Allah. By doing so, the believer attains the honored title of "slave of Allah" (*abd Allah,* feminine: *amat Allah*), for he recognizes that all power and all agency belongs to God alone. Thus, the believer surrenders to the will of Allah through his own deliberate, conscious, and rational act, and he knows with both intellectual certainty and spiritual vision that Allah is the reality. No one can compel anyone to undergo that submission without his will and understanding.

16. The Covenant of Allah: *Awliya*: Allah Is the *Waliy*, Protector of Those Who Have Faith

> Do not take the Kafirun (infidels), Jews
> and Christians as your awliya

> Waliy: O you who believe! Allah is the Waliy
> and the protector of the Believers.

Allah commands:

> Believers not to take people outside their
> ranks in closeness and confidence, who in their
> loathing for them wish them destruction.

Allah, in His covenant, reminds the believers repeatedly:

> Not to take the Kafirun (infidels), Jews and Christians
> as their awliya, (friends and protectors) in place
> of Believers. They are friends and protectors unto
> each other. He who amongst Believers turns to
> them is one of them. Allah does not guide those
> who are unjust and evil doers (zalimun). He that
> from amongst the Believers turns to them is from
> amongst the Kafirun, Mushrikun and the zalimun.

> Take not for Awliya, friends and protectors,
> from amongst your kin who are Kafirun.

Allah also admonishes believers

> Not to take My enemies and yours as Awliya (friends and protectors), offering them love and regard, even though they have rejected the Truth bestowed on you. You have come out to strive in My Cause and to seek My favor, take them not as friends, holding in secret regard and friendship for them, for I know full well all that you conceal and all that you reveal. And any of you that do this, has strayed from the Straight Path.
>
> Befriend not people who have incurred Allah's wrath.

There is a recurring cycle in Islamic history of destruction and humiliation of Islam by the manipulations of the circle of evil. The story starts with a scheming Jew who spins a web, planning meticulously to amass the world's wealth, and uses the power and the organization of the strongest Christian monarch by tempting him with acquisition of a world empire and its fabulous wealth. Then meticulous planning begins; the execution of such an expedition may take several years in which intelligence services, diplomats, and armed services play a role, while only the top select echelon is aware of all the moves on the chessboard. A willing victim, a weak Muslim—a *Munafiq*—with propensity toward greed and lust for power and endowed with overwhelming vanity and conceit is picked up, trained, and slowly eased into a position of power to be used at the opportune moment.

Ottoman Empire

The plan to destabilize the Ottoman Empire was hatched by the Jewish Rothschild cousins in Berlin, Paris, and London. Each branch of the family collaborated with their favorite governments in those cities. The

German chancellor von Bethmann Hollweg, a Jew and a Rothschild cousin, won the day, and the kaiser began to make overtures to the Young Turks and assisted their revolution against the sultan. Enver Pasha was the Turkish *Munafiq* who joined the circle of evil, the *Yahudi, Salibi,* and *Munafiq* coalition. Talat, Cemal, and Enver *presided* over the dissolution of the Ottoman Empire, subjugating the Middle East to the West for the next one hundred years.

State of Israel

The history of the creation of the State of Israel tells us that Theodor Herzl and Chaim Weizmann were the founding fathers of Israel. The hidden hand that helped create the Jewish state is seldom mentioned. The actual creators of Israel were a group of English and Jewish conspirators in the British cabinet. David Lloyd George appointed Alfred Milner, a Jew, to his war cabinet in 1916 as secretary of war. After becoming the secretary of war, he brought in Leo Amery, another Jew, albeit a secret one, as secretary of the war cabinet. Milner had close contacts with the Rothschilds; in 1912, he had helped Natty Rothschild unify the divided Jewish community of London under one spiritual head, Chief Rabbi Joseph Herman Hertz.[5]

Another Jew, a cabinet minister, Herbert Samuel, convinced the cabinet in 1915—when Palestine was still a Turkish possession—that Palestine should become a British protectorate, "into which the scattered Jews in time swarm back from all quarters of the globe, in due course obtain home rule and form a Jewish Commonwealth like that of Canada and Australia." Lord Walter Rothschild, as the leader of the British Jews, twisted the ears of the prime minister Lloyd George and his foreign secretary for a declaration about Palestine. Lloyd George had previously served as the legal counsel for the British Zionist Federation. Balfour

---

[5] The House of Rothschild. Niall Ferguson Penguin Books. Page 259.

suggested that "they submit a declaration for the cabinet to consider." The declaration was written by Milner and revised several times. The final version was drafted by Leo Amery, which read,

His Majesty's Government view with favor the establishment in Palestine a national home for the Jewish people and will use their best endeavors to facilitate the achievement of this object, it being clearly understood that nothing shall be done which may prejudice the civil and religious rights of existing non-Jewish communities in Palestine, or the rights and political status enjoyed in any other country.

This declaration was approved by the British cabinet and was addressed to Lord Walter Rothschild and signed by the foreign secretary Balfour. The Balfour Declaration—as this Jewish Magna Carta came to be known, the document that gave the illegitimate birth to the state of Israel—was written by Lord Alfred Milner, a Jew, revised and finalized by Leo Amery, another Jew, at the behest of and addressed to Lord Walter Rothschild, the leader of the Jews in London, for the purpose of the creation of a Jewish state in the name of the British government on a land that did not belong to either the Jews or the British. In fact, this was an agreement among a group of conspiring *Yahudi-Salibi* conspirators belonging to a secret organization that had a long history of fraud and extortion to grab the world's wealth.

In this case, the plotters made a full circle in their relationship. Lord George Joachim Goschen, a German Jew, patronized Alfred Milner, another German Jew, and brought him into the English establishment and introduced him to the Rothschilds. Milner, in turn, brought Leo Amery, a secret Jew, into the war cabinet; and together, they wrote the Balfour Declaration for the Lord Rothschild. To complete the circle, George Goschen's daughter Phyllis Evelyn Goschen married Francis Cecil Balfour, Foreign Secretary Balfour's son, on August 31, 1920.

Herbert Samuel to guide and control King Abdullah of Jordan to facilitate the Jewish migration to Palestine. Arthur Hirtzel, a Jew, was appointed as head of the British India Office, which also controlled the British governance of Iraq and Arabia. Hirtzel, at that time, expressed the need for Ibn Sa'ud to establish himself in Mecca. Rufus Isaacs, Lord Reading, another Jew, was appointed as the British viceroy of India. Isaacs directed the British policy in Iraq, Palestine, and Arabia. He used 'Abd al-'Aziz to remove Sharif Hussein's son Ali from Hejaz. He had a free hand in Arabia and Iraq. He used British Indian troops to quell uprisings in Iraq. Isaacs also facilitated the massacres and repression in At Ta'if, Bureida, and Huda by providing 'Abd al-'Aziz with money, artillery, rifles, ammunition, training, and transport.

From this time onward, Zionists were considered an ally of the British government, and every help and assistance was forthcoming from each government department. Space was provided for the Zionists in Mark Sykes's office with liaison to each government department. The British government provided financial, communication, and travel facilities to those working in the Zionist office. Mark Sykes, who had negotiated the Sykes-Picot Agreement giving Syria to the French, was now working for the Zionists, offering them a part of the same territory.

Partition of the Land of Islam in the Middle East

To complete the circle of evil, Sharif Hussein and his sons—hungry for power, fame, and gold—were the willing recruits of the British to destabilize the Ottoman Empire and carve out a Jewish state in Palestine. Hussein led a revolt against his caliph, sultan, country, and coreligionists under the protection of an alien, *kafir*, colonial, expansionist power under the full knowledge that parts of the Islamic state—including Syria, Lebanon, Palestine, and Iraq—would pass from Islamic rule to an economic and colonial serfdom of a non-Muslim, *kafir* power. While the British set out to expedite the war against the Turks, they also began to lay the groundwork for an indirect postwar British political control of Arabia.

June 1916 was a historical moment when, for the first time in the history of Islam since the Battle of Badr in the first year of hijra, combined forces of the *kafireen* and *Munafiqeen* and British and Hussein's armies attacked the city of the *Nabi* of Islam, though unsuccessfully; this attack introduced the combined evil dominion of the *Mutaffifeen*, *kafireen*, and *Munafiqeen* over the heartlands of Islam for the century to come.

For his treachery, Sharif Hussein received his first reward in gold sovereigns in March 1916, a shipment amounting to £53,000, three months before he announced his revolt. Commencing on August 8, 1916, the official allowance was set at £125,000 a month, a sum that was frequently exceeded on Hussein's demand; for example, in November 1916, £375,000 in gold sovereigns was dispatched to Hussein by the British for hajj expenses. The payments were broken down into five categories representing the four armies under the command of Hussein's sons and an allotment for the upkeep of the mosque at Kaaba and for hajj facilities as well as for the operation of Hussein's government in Mecca and Jeddah. Forty thousand pounds was allotted to Faisal, £30,000 to Abdullah, £20,000 each for Ali and Zeid, and £15,000 for expenses at Mecca and Jeddah.

The year 1916 must have been the lowest point in the history of Islam, when it was surrounded by powerful enemies around the world; and inside, it was being destroyed by self-serving traitors at the very heart of the faith, the Kaaba. For the first time in the history of Islam, the very upkeep of the holy mosque of Mecca and the Kaaba and hajj expenses were being paid for by the *kafireen*, at the behest of the *Munafiqeen*, under the claim of their lineage from the holy prophet. While claiming the bloodline, they forgot the teachings of the Koran and the example of the prophet.

'Abd al-'Aziz was picked as a willing tool by British scouts in around 1902 and was kept on a short leash with small handouts to keep him available and above starvation level. 'Abd al-'Aziz set out to conquer Arabia with the financial and military assistance of the British. Sir Percy Cox, a British resident in the Persian Gulf, wrote, "With Ibn-Saud in Hasa (the Gulf Coast of Arabia) our position is very much strengthened." Percy Cox openly encouraged Ibn Sa'ud to attack the remaining territory of the Ibn Rashids to divert them from reinforcing Turkish troops against the British. Ibn Sa'ud had constant British financial aid, arms, and advisers, initially William Shakespeare and Percy Cox and later Harry St. John Philby.

After they helped him master eastern Arabia in 1917, the British found another use for Ibn Sa'ud. In 1924, Hussein declared himself caliph of Islam without the consent of the British. Ibn Sa'ud, with British encouragement, started his thrust to Hejaz; although the British ostensibly cut off the arms supplies to both sides, they continued to supply small but crucial amounts of money and arms to Ibn Sa'ud and his merciless Ikhwan. Some of the military equipment used by Ibn Sa'ud was expensive and could only have been obtained from the British and used with the help of British instructors. At the time, statements by British officials did point to the British hand in Ibn Sa'ud's attack on Mecca. Arthur Hirtzel—a Jew, head of the British India Office at that time—expressed the need for Ibn Sa'ud to establish himself in Mecca. The British viceroy of India at that time, another Jew, Rufus Isaacs, Lord Reading, directed the British policy in Arabia. He used 'Abd al-'Aziz to remove Sharif Hussein's son Ali from Hejaz.

Ibn Sa'ud afforded Britain the comfort of keeping the Arabs and Muslims divided and protected its commercial and political interests, which opposed a unified Muslim state. Sharif Hussein and his sons Faisal and Abdullah continued to be clients and servants of the British. For a few thousand pounds and personal glory, they and their descendants, Faisal, Abdullah, Hussein, and Abdullah sold the honor of Islam for the next one hundred years. 'Abd al-'Aziz's sons inherited their father's debauchery and treason against Islam for their personal gain.

Treason runs deep in the veins of the descendants of Sharif Hussein and 'Abd al-'Aziz. They are *Munafiqeen* who have taken their *awliya* from among the *kafireen*. According to the covenant, they are of the *kafireen*. This circle of evil, the coalition of the *Yahudi, Salibi*, and *Munafiqeen* triumphed over Islam for over one hundred years. The Jewish money in London, New York, Berlin, and Paris collaborated with the Christian powers of Europe and America and the *Munafiqeen*—Enver Pasha, Cemal Pasha, Talat Pasha, Sharif Hussein and sons, and Ibn Sa'ud and sons—to defeat the Islamic Empire and fragment it into scores of impoverished mini-client-states for political and economic exploitation by the *Yahudi*, *Salibi*, *Munafiq* coalition.

Egypt and the Slavery in Palestine

Anwar Sadat and the Egyptian Army won partial victory over the Jewish state of Israel in 1973. The victory made Sadat a hero in the eyes of many Arabs—if not equal to, then almost comparable to the great Arab hero Gamal Abdel Nasser. Puffed up by success and sycophancy from the likes of Henry Kissinger, Sadat forgot his own roots and began to take advice and comfort from Kissinger and Israeli lobbyists in Washington. Against the advice of his closest advisers and the leaders of other Arab countries, Sadat offered himself as a servant and a tool of the circle of evil, the *Yahudi-Salibi* confederation. He made a trip to Israel and addressed the Knesset, the Israeli Parliament. Under American tutelage and patronage, he abandoned his Arab allies, negotiated, and signed a peace treaty with many secret appendices with Israel at the expense of the Palestinians, Syrians, and Muslims in general.

As a consequence, all Palestine and the Golan Heights are under Israeli occupation. The Arabs are disunited and in disarray. Sadat sold the Egyptian sovereignty, the Islamic nation, and the holy Islamic places in Jerusalem for three billion dollars a year. Sadat took Jews and Christians as *awliya* and willfully disobeyed the covenant that every Muslim has pledged to obey. He also disobeyed the provisions of the covenant of Yathrib and the blessed *nabi's* teaching:

> Just as the bond to Allah is indivisible, all the believers shall stand behind the commitment of the least of them. All believers are bonded one to another to the exclusion of other men.
>
> This Pax Islamica is one and indivisible. No believer shall enter a separate peace without all other believers whenever there is fighting in the cause of God but will do so only on the basis of equality and justice to all others. In every expedition for the cause of God we undertake, all parties to the covenant shall fight shoulder to shoulder as one man. All believers shall avenge the blood of one another when anyone falls fighting in the cause of God.

Once again, the *Yahudi-Salibi* ingenuity used a *Munafiq* to grow the seeds of discord in the Islamic world.

The Ruin of Iraq

Saddam Hussein replaced al-Bakr as president of Iraq in July 1979. The bloodbath that followed eliminated all potential opposition to him. Saddam was now the master of Iraq with no one around him daring to question his actions. Two actions that he initiated led the

Islamic community to disastrous disunity and debt. He attacked fellow Muslims, Iran in 1980 and Kuwait in 1990.

The Iran-Iraq War turned out to be a battle between two egomaniac personalities with a Messiah complex, neither of them willing to call a truce to the hostilities. The result was emaciation and bleeding of both countries to near bankruptcy. The Iraqi troops launched a full-scale invasion of Iran on September 22, 1980. France supplied high-tech weapons to Iraq, and the Soviet Union was Iraq's largest weapon supplier. Israel provided arms to Iran, hoping to bleed both the nations by prolonging the war. At least ten nations sold arms to both the warring nations to profit from the conflict. The United States followed a more duplicitous policy toward both warring parties to prolong the war and cause maximum damage to both.

The Iran-Iraq War was not between good and evil. Islam forbids fighting among the Muslims, murder, and taking of life unless it is in the cause of justice. Saddam Hussein launched a murderous war to regain a few square miles of territory that his country had relinquished freely in the 1975 border negotiations. There were one and a half million Muslim casualties in this senseless fraternal war. The war ended in a ceasefire that essentially left prewar borders unchanged. The Covenant of Allah not only forbids such an internecine war but also provides a mechanism for dispute resolution.

Instead of condemning the aggressor, the Arab states sided with Saddam Hussein, providing him with funds for further bloodletting. Saddam Hussein used banned chemical weapons against fellow Muslims, Iranians, and Kurds. The eight-year-long war exhausted both countries. Primary responsibility for the prolonged bloodletting must rest with the governments of the two countries, the ruthless military regime of Saddam Hussein and the ruthless clerical regime of Ayatollah Khomeini in Iran. Whatever his religious convictions were,

Khomeini had no qualms about sending his followers, including young boys, to their deaths for his own greater glory. This callous disregard for human life was no less characteristic of Saddam Hussein. Saudi Arabia gave $25.7 billion and Kuwait $10 billion to Iraq to fuel the war and the killings. Saddam also owed the Soviets, the USA, and Europe $40 billion for the purchase of arms. The cost of war to the Iranians was even greater. The world community sold arms for eight and a half years and watched the bloodletting. The USA sold arms and information to both sides to prolong the war strategically and to profit and gain influence and bases in Gulf countries. Ayatollah Khomeini, in particular, was a hypocrite in dealing with Israel in secret when his public pronouncements were venomously anti-Israel.

Iran, Iraq, and all the Arab states of the Persian Gulf took the Western countries, the Soviet Union, and Israel as their *awliya*, in contradiction to the commandments of the covenant. The ayatollah and his clerics should have known and understood their obligations to Allah and to their people as spelled out in Allah's covenant. The uncontrolled Arab-Iranian hostility left a deep, festering wound in the body of the nation of Islam. The West made gains by setting up permanent bases in Saudi Arabia, Oman, the United Arab Emirates, Bahrain, Qatar, and Kuwait. This is the land that Muhammad, the blessed *rasul* of Allah, freed from infidels, only to be handed over to infidels by the *Munafiqeen.*

After the Kuwait war, at the invitation of King Fahd, the USA has continued to maintain large operational army and air force bases and command and control facilities that enable them to monitor air and sea traffic and civilian and military communications in the Middle East. Bahrain became the headquarters of a US naval fleet. The Middle East, at the beginning of the twenty-first century, is under the absolute military and economic control of the USA and NATO. The circle of evil—the *Yahudi*, *Salibi*, and *Munafiqeen*—continue to dominate the lives of Muslims.

17. The Covenant of Allah: Jihad: Fight the Infidel Until There Is No More Treachery and Oppression

> Fight the infidel until there is no more treachery and oppression and there prevails Justice and Faith in Allah altogether and everywhere. If they cease, then Allah is seer of what they do. If they refuse, be sure that Allah is your Protector, the Best to protect and the Best to help. And why should you not fight in the cause of Allah and for those men, women and children, who are weak, abused and oppressed, those who beseech their Lord to deliver protectors and helpers.

The Koranic use of the term *jihad* means "struggle." The Koran commonly uses the verb along with the expression *in the path of Allah*. The path of Allah, of course, is the path of right conduct that Allah has set down in the Koran. Jihad is simply the complement to *islam*, the surrender to the will of Allah. The surrender takes place in Allah's will, and it is Allah's will that people struggle in His path. Submission to Allah's command requires the believers to struggle against all negative tendencies in themselves and in the society that draw them away from Allah's path. Salat, zakat, fasting, and hajj are all struggles in the path of Allah. The greatest obstacles that people face in submitting themselves to Allah are their laziness, lack of imagination, and currents of contemporary opinion. These weaknesses and events carry them along without resisting. It takes an enormous struggle to submit to an authority that breaks one's likes and dislikes of current trends and pressures of society to conform to the crowd.

The jihad, which is normally a daily struggle within oneself against temptations and evil, will sometimes take an outward form against the enemies of Islam. Such a war is permitted strictly in the path of Allah in today's contemporary world to enforce truth, justice, and freedom.

> And why should you not fight in the cause of Allah and for those men, women and children, who are weak, abused and oppressed, those who beseech their Lord to deliver them from their oppressors and those who ask Allah to send for them protectors and helpers. (An-Nisa 4:71–75, Koran)

The oft-repeated phrase in the Koran to proclaim jihad is to fight *fitnah*, tyranny, and oppression. Yet most of the wars in the Muslim world were civil wars, with Muslims killing Muslims for the sake of territory, wealth, and power.

Life is a chain of emotions, intentions, and actions. Before each deed, the human stops to intend an action. Each intention is the product of an emotion that acts on the human's self, the *nafs*. The *nafs* may intend to act on its animal instincts of craving and lust, or in situations where the self is sufficiently refined with *taqwa* of Allah, the human will follow His path as commanded by the covenant. The self is in a continuous battle whether to follow its base cravings or to perform wholesome deeds. Such ongoing fluctuation of intent between the base and the honorable is stressful. Such stress leads to anxiety, anger, and depression, which in the end will cause an emotional turmoil and breakdown. When the human intends to do his deeds with the knowledge that Allah is with him, that Allah is aware of his intent, and that Allah guides him to the right objective and action, there is peace and satisfaction.

When the believer is in *taqwa* of Allah, the *nur* of Allah cleans his *nafs* and aids him in obeying His covenant. Jihad is this struggle that prepares the believer in following and obeying Allah's commandments without question. Jihad is the struggle of the human from the path of ignorance to the path of Allah. The human hears Allah's call amid the noise and commotion of the world and, through the eye of his soul, lets the *nur* of Allah into the niche of his heart. Allah's call is about obedience, goodness, and selflessness. The human bows down his head on the earth in submission to his Lord and in humility. The Lord guides, and the believer follows; the believer has faith in Allah, and Allah holds his hand. Allah shows His believer the way to goodness, and the believer performs wholesome deeds. The *nur* of Allah glows in the believer's heart, and the believer accepts Allah in his heart.

This communion between the believer and Allah becomes exclusive. Submission establishes a link between the believer and Allah. Allah commands, and the believer follows. The believer asks, and Allah gives. The believer loves Allah, and Allah loves him in return. The believer asks for the straight path, and Allah shows him the way. The believer praises Allah, and Allah showers His mercy and grace upon him. The believer remembers Allah, and Allah responds to those who praise Him.

The *nafs*, unlike the Freudian ego, is capable of both good and bad. The *nuqta* of the *nafs*, when magnified a million times, becomes visible as a shiny disk, a mirror. The inherent nature (*fitra*) of the *nafs* is to shine like a mirror with Allah's *nur*. When the human walks the path of Allah in *taqwa* of Him with the knowledge that Allah is with him, watching him and guiding him, Allah's *nur* shines on the *nafs*, keeping it pure and safe. However, when the human's desires, cravings, and ego overpower his love and obedience of Allah, the shiny mirror of his *nafs* becomes obscured by the dirt and smoke of his desires, and he loses sight of the *nur* of Allah and trips into error and decadence.

The effort required to keep focusing on Allah's *nur* and *taqwa* of Him is the inner jihad. And this jihad is obedience to Allah's commandments when He calls on His believers with the words,

يَـٰٓأَيُّهَا ٱلَّذِينَ ءَامَنُوا۟

O you who Believe.

And He commands them to do acts of faith and goodness in the *seventy-five* verses of the Koran. Obedience to every such command is jihad. Jihad, foremost, is the struggle to fulfill the commandments of Allah in the covenant. The *taqwa* of Allah shines His light (*nur*) into the core of man, in the self, that clears the smoke of evil and temptation from the *nafs*, allowing man to follow God.

Once the believer has purified his self with Allah's *nur*, he has prepared himself for the outer jihad. When the believer has purified his own *nafs* and soul with submission to Allah (*islam*) and faith (*iman*) in the only reality, the Lord, and by performance of wholesome deeds in the name of Allah, he is ready for the outer struggle for his *din*, to fight the *fitnah* of tyranny and oppression.

The blessed *Nabi* of Allah wrote the following covenant in the first year of hijra in Medina. This is the essential constitution of whole of the *ummah*. This is a covenant given by Muhammad to the believers.

1. They constitute one Ummah to the exclusion of all other men.
2. The believers shall leave none of their members in destitution without giving him in kindness that he needs by the way of his liberty.
3. No believer shall slay a believer in retaliation for an unbeliever, nor shall he assist an unbeliever against a believer.
4. All believers shall rise as one man against anyone who seeks to commit injustice, aggression, crime, or spread mutual enmity amongst the Muslims even if such a person is their kin.
5. Just as the bond to Allah is indivisible, all the believers shall stand behind the commitment of the least of them. All believers are bonded one to another to the exclusion of other men.

6. This Pax Islamica is one and indivisible. No believer shall enter a separate peace without all other believers whenever there is fighting in the cause of God but will do so only on the basis of equality and justice to all others. In every expedition for the cause of God we undertake, all parties to the covenant shall fight shoulder to shoulder as one man. All believers shall avenge the blood of one another when anyone falls fighting in the Way of Allah.
7. The pious believers follow the best and the most upright guidance. Whoever is convicted of killing a believer deliberatively but without righteous cause shall be liable to the relatives of the killed. Until the latter are satisfied, the killer shall be subject to retaliation by each and every believer.

Allah speaks to the believers thus about the struggle in His way:

﴿ وَقَٰتِلُوا۟ فِى سَبِيلِ ٱللَّهِ ٱلَّذِينَ يُقَٰتِلُونَكُمْ وَلَا تَعْتَدُوٓا۟ ۚ إِنَّ ٱللَّهَ لَا يُحِبُّ ٱلْمُعْتَدِينَ ١٩٠ ﴾

Fight in the cause of Allah those who fight you, but do
not transgress limits; for Allah loves not transgressors.

﴿ وَٱقْتُلُوهُمْ حَيْثُ ثَقِفْتُمُوهُمْ وَأَخْرِجُوهُم مِّنْ حَيْثُ أَخْرَجُوكُمْ ۚ وَٱلْفِتْنَةُ أَشَدُّ مِنَ ٱلْقَتْلِ ۚ وَلَا تُقَٰتِلُوهُمْ عِندَ ٱلْمَسْجِدِ ٱلْحَرَامِ حَتَّىٰ
يُقَٰتِلُوكُمْ فِيهِ ۖ فَإِن قَٰتَلُوكُمْ فَٱقْتُلُوهُمْ ۗ كَذَٰلِكَ جَزَآءُ ٱلْكَٰفِرِينَ

١٩١

And slay them wherever you catch them and turn
them out from where they have turned you out; for
Fitnah, tumult and oppression are worse than slaughter;
but fight them not at the Sacred Mosque, unless they
fight you there first ; but if they fight you, slay them.
Such is the reward of those who suppress faith.

﴿ فَإِنِ ٱنتَهَوْا۟ فَإِنَّ ٱللَّهَ غَفُورٌ رَّحِيمٌ ﴿١٩٢﴾

﴾ But if they cease, Allah is Oft-
Forgiving, Most Merciful.

﴿ وَقَـٰتِلُوهُمْ حَتَّىٰ لَا تَكُونَ فِتْنَةٌ وَيَكُونَ ٱلدِّينُ لِلَّهِ ۖ فَإِنِ ٱنتَهَوْا۟ فَلَا عُدْوَٰنَ إِلَّا عَلَى ٱلظَّـٰلِمِينَ ﴿١٩٣﴾

And fight them on until there is no more Fitnah, tumult or oppression and there prevail justice and faith in Allah; but if they cease, let there be no hostility except to those who practice oppression. (Al-Baqarah. 2:190–93, Koran)

وَمَا لَكُمْ لَا تُقَـٰتِلُونَ فِى سَبِيلِ ٱللَّهِ وَٱلْمُسْتَضْعَفِينَ مِنَ ٱلرِّجَالِ وَٱلنِّسَآءِ وَٱلْوِلْدَٰنِ ٱلَّذِينَ يَقُولُونَ رَبَّنَآ أَخْرِجْنَا مِنْ هَـٰذِهِ ٱلْقَرْيَةِ

ٱلظَّالِمِ أَهْلُهَا وَٱجْعَل لَّنَا مِن لَّدُنكَ وَلِيًّا وَٱجْعَل لَّنَا مِن لَّدُنكَ نَصِيرًا ﴿٧٥﴾ ﴾

And why should you not fight in the cause of Allah and for those men, women and children, who are weak, abused and oppressed, those who beseech their Lord to deliver them from their oppressors and those who ask Allah to send for them protectors and helpers.

﴿ ٱلَّذِينَ ءَامَنُوا۟ يُقَـٰتِلُونَ فِى سَبِيلِ ٱللَّهِ ۖ وَٱلَّذِينَ كَفَرُوا۟ يُقَـٰتِلُونَ فِى سَبِيلِ ٱلطَّـٰغُوتِ فَقَـٰتِلُوٓا۟ أَوْلِيَآءَ ٱلشَّيْطَـٰنِ ۖ إِنَّ كَيْدَ ٱلشَّيْطَـٰنِ كَانَ

ضَعِيفًا ﴿٧٦﴾ ﴾

Those who believe fight in the cause of Allah and those who reject Faith fight in the cause of Evil: so fight you against the friends of Satan: feeble indeed is the cunning of Satan. (An-Nisa 4:75–76, Koran)

﴿ وَلَا تَهِنُوا۟ فِى ٱبْتِغَآءِ ٱلْقَوْمِ ۖ إِن تَكُونُوا۟ تَأْلَمُونَ فَإِنَّهُمْ يَأْلَمُونَ كَمَا تَأْلَمُونَ ۖ وَتَرْجُونَ مِنَ ٱللَّهِ مَا لَا يَرْجُونَ ۗ وَكَانَ ٱللَّهُ

عَلِيمًا حَكِيمًا ﴿١٠٤﴾ ﴾

And slacken not in following up the enemy; if you are suffering hardships, they are suffering similar hardships; but you have hope from Allah, while they have none. And Allah is full of Knowledge and Wisdom. (An-Nisa 4:104, Koran)

﴿ إِن يَنصُرْكُمُ ٱللَّهُ فَلَا غَالِبَ لَكُمْ ۖ وَإِن يَخْذُلْكُمْ فَمَن ذَا ٱلَّذِى يَنصُرُكُم مِّنۢ بَعْدِهِۦ ۗ وَعَلَى ٱللَّهِ فَلْيَتَوَكَّلِ

ٱلْمُؤْمِنُونَ

If Allah helps you none can overcome you: if He forsakes you, who is there, after that, that can help you? In Allah, then, let Believers put their trust. (Ali 'Imran 3: 160, Koran)

﴿ وَلَقَدْ أَرْسَلْنَا مِن قَبْلِكَ رُسُلًا إِلَىٰ قَوْمِهِمْ فَجَآءُوهُم بِٱلْبَيِّنَٰتِ فَٱنتَقَمْنَا مِنَ ٱلَّذِينَ أَجْرَمُوا۟ ۖ وَكَانَ حَقًّا عَلَيْنَا نَصْرُ ٱلْمُؤْمِنِينَ ﴿٤٧﴾ ﴾

We did indeed send, before you Rasools to their respective peoples, with Clear Signs: To those who transgressed, We meted out Retribution: and as a right those who earned from us, We helped those who believed. (Ar-Rum 30:47, Koran)

﴿ هَٰذَا بَيَانٌ لِّلنَّاسِ وَهُدًى وَمَوْعِظَةٌ لِّلْمُتَّقِينَ ﴿١٣٨﴾ ﴾

Here is a declaration to the human, a guidance and advice to those who live in awareness, Taqwa of Allah!

﴿ وَلَا تَهِنُوا وَلَا تَحْزَنُوا وَأَنتُمُ الْأَعْلَوْنَ إِن كُنتُم مُّؤْمِنِينَ ﴿١٣٩﴾ ﴾

So, lose not hope nor shall you despair, for you shall achieve supremacy, if you are true in Faith.

﴿ إِن يَمْسَسْكُمْ قَرْحٌ فَقَدْ مَسَّ الْقَوْمَ قَرْحٌ مِّثْلُهُ ۚ وَتِلْكَ الْأَيَّامُ نُدَاوِلُهَا بَيْنَ النَّاسِ وَلِيَعْلَمَ اللَّهُ الَّذِينَ آمَنُوا وَيَتَّخِذَ مِنكُمْ شُهَدَاءَ ۗ

وَاللَّهُ لَا يُحِبُّ الظَّالِمِينَ ﴿١٤٠﴾ ﴾

If you have suffered a setback, verily a setback has been there for the other party too. We make such days of adversity go around amongst the humans so that Allah may distinguish those who believe and choose His witnesses from amongst them. And Allah loves not the evil doers.

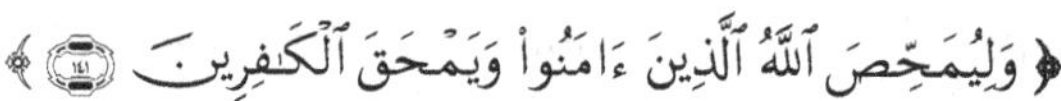

Allah's objective is to distinguish the True Believers from those who reject Faith.
(Ali 'Imran 3:138–41, Koran)

Wars and slaughter are abhorrent to Allah. Allah says:

If anyone slew a person, unless it is in retribution for murder or for spreading mischief, fasaad in the land it would be as if he slew the whole people. And if anyone saved a life, it would be as if he saved the life of the whole people. Take not life, which Allah has made sacred, except by the way of justice or law. This He commands you, that you may learn wisdom.

And then Allah declares to the believers that *fitnah,* treachery, and oppression are worse than slaughter. They are so vile and repugnant to Allah that He commands the believers to fight those who assail them and inflict oppression:

> And slay them wherever you catch them and turn them out from where they have turned you out; for Fitnah, tyranny and oppression are worse than slaughter; And fight them on until there is no more Fitnah, tumult or oppression and there prevail justice and faith in Allah; but if they cease, let there be no hostility except to those who practice'. oppression. (Al-Baqarah 2:190–93, Koran)

Allah's command to fight *fitnah*, however, is conditional:

> If the oppressors cease, let there be no further hostility except to those who practice oppression. Do not transgress limits. Allah does not love transgressors. (Al-Baqarah 2:190–93, Koran)

> When the Believers fight against Fitnah and oppression, they fight in the cause of Allah. Those who reject faith in Allah, they fight in the cause of evil. (An-Nisa 4:75–76, Koran)

18. The Covenant of Allah: *Fitnah,* Tyranny, and Oppression Are So Vile and Repugnant that Allah Commands the Believers to Fight Those Who Assail Them

Fitnah: Allah has granted each believer the freedom to practice his or her *din* in accordance with his or her beliefs since, in Islam, there is no compulsion in matters of religion; the right to life, which includes mental, physical, and emotional well-being; the right to intellectual endeavors, acquisition of knowledge, and education; the right to make a living; and the right to free speech and action to enjoin good and forbid evil. In enjoying his freedoms, a person should ensure that his activities do not impinge on the similar rights of others. Oppression and tyranny—which deprives a believer, a community of believers, or their nation (the *ummah*) of their God-given rights and freedom—is *fitnah* as described in the Koran. The tyrants and oppressors cannot belong to the fellowship of Allah, of His Covenant, nor of the blessed *Nabi* of Allah.

In the above *ayahs*, Allah commands the believers to fight such infidels until there is no more *fitnah*, treachery, and oppression and until there prevails justice and faith in Allah everywhere. He orders them to slay them wherever they catch them and turn them out from where they have turned them out, for *fitnah*, tumult, and oppression are worse than slaughter. Allah has forbidden the taking of life. "Take not life, which Allah has made sacred, except by the way of justice or law." *Fitnah*, tyranny, and oppression are so vile and repugnant that Allah commands the believers to fight those who assail them and inflict oppression. "Go forth, advance! Whether equipped well or lightly, perform *jihad* strive your utmost and struggle with your wealth and your persons in the cause of Allah." Allah loves those who fight for His cause in unison and solidarity. *Fitnah*, tyranny, and oppression not only afflict those who perpetrate it but also affect everyone, guilty and innocent alike. Allah's command to fight *fitnah* is conditional however: if the oppressors cease, let there be no further hostility except to those who practice *fitnah*. Do not transgress limits. Allah does not love transgressors.

In the twenty-first century, weakness, poverty, disunity, and fragmentation of the *ummah* arise from lack of appreciation of the immense understanding and knowledge in the Koran. Muslims look at the word of Allah but do not see it. They listen to the word but do not hear it. Allah's *nur* (His light) is with them, but they do not let it enter their hearts. The mirror of their *nafs* is covered with the smoke of their greed and craving of worldly wealth. They cannot see Allah's *nur* through the smoky darkness in their heart. *Fitnah*, treachery, and oppression are by-products of darkened hearts, causing blindness to the *nur* of Allah. Without His *nur*, there cannot be *taqwa* of Allah; and in the absence of the consciousness of the reality of Allah, the darkened soul is open to the evil of Satan.

Muslim societies have been plagued by *fitnah* and oppression since the death of the blessed *Nabi*. In Muslim countries, *fitnah* is the result of the combination of internal and external forces. Although the perpetrators of *fitnah* often proclaim Allah as their Savior, their actions always belie their faith in Him.

Most believers do not know that when the blessed Muhammad died, every believer inherited the Koran, Allah's covenant, His *din*, and the Dar es Salaam. Every believer became the successor, inheritor, and custodian of the blessed *Nabi*'s legacy till the end of time. Consequently, in the twenty-first century, majority of believers are unaware of their rights granted by Allah. They are unaware that Allah commands them to fight the *fitnah* of tyranny and oppression perpetrated by their self-appointed rulers, kings, military dictators, and infidel *awliya*, the Euro-Christian patrons.

Internal *Fitnah:* Hundreds of years of rule of sultans and later of the Western colonial masters produced three unique sources of internal *fitnah* that rules the roost in the Muslim societies of our day.

1. Priesthood. There is no priesthood in Islam; the believer has a highly personal and exclusive relationship with Allah. Such relationship does not permit the intervention of another human being. When the blessed Muhammad was taken up by Allah, the priests and clerics of Islam assumed the legacy of the pagan

priesthood and began to speak on behalf of Allah. Through distortion and misrepresentation of the word of Allah and the pronouncements of His *Nabi,* over the last fourteen hundred years, the priests and imams of Islam have created divisions and schisms in Islam to generate hundreds of self-righteous sects and subsects among the Muslims. Each sect is the enemy of the other. Every group has the dagger in the back of the other. This gradually smoldering *fitnah* of the priesthood is slowly consuming the body of the *ummah.*

2. Mercenary Armies of Islam: The blessed *Nabi* said,

> All believers shall rise as one man against anyone who seeks to commit injustice, aggression, crime, or spread mutual enmity amongst the Muslims. All believers are bonded one to another to the exclusion of other men. The believers shall leave none of their members in destitution without giving him in kindness that he needs by the way of his liberty.

However, this fight for unity, equality, and justice did not occur in the lands of Islam; the army of God and of Islam did not arise to fight in the cause of Allah to defend against *fitnah*, tyranny, and oppression and to seek retribution against injustice. The absolute loyalty of the army of Islam is to God, the Koran, and the *ummah.* The army of Islam defends the believers, their faith, their land, their wealth, and their honor and fights only against *fitnah* for truth and justice. In case of injury to the believers, their faith, their land, their wealth, and their honor, the believers are obliged to exact retribution. No believer shall side with an unbeliever against a believer. Whosoever is convicted of killing a believer without a righteous cause shall be liable to the relatives of the killed. The killers shall be subject to retaliation by each believer until the relatives of the victim are satisfied with the retribution.

Had the Muslim communities stood united as one to avenge the blood of every fallen Muslim and rejected a separate peace with the pagans without all the Muslims participating in it, there would have been no *fitnah* and massacres in Algeria, Palestine, India, Afghanistan, Iraq, Bosnia, Chechnya, Kosovo, and Darfur. This unity demands revenge, retribution, and reprisal for every act of murder and injury in Dayr Yasin, Sabra, Shatila, Srebrenica, Janin, Sarajevo, Fallujah, Kosovo, Chechnya, Gujarat, Kashmir, Iraq, Guantanamo Bay, and Abu Ghraib. Had the Muslims stood up for one another and fought those who perpetrated the *fitnah*, they would not have been groveling in the dustheap of humanity today.

Contrary to the stipulations of the covenant of Allah, the present six-million-man mercenary armies of Muslim states serve to bolster illegal regimes of *Munafiqeen, the* traitors to the cause of Islam. Instead of relieving the believers of *fitnah* and oppression, they cause them. They are the source of dichotomy and division in Islam; they are the defenders of the foreign hegemony over Islam. The armies of the sultans of the previous centuries and the rulers of modern times are the perpetrators of *fitnah* and the enemies of Islam. They are the defenders of the borders created by the Western colonial powers that divide Islam today. They are the *fitnah*.

3. Rulers of Islam. Islam is a religion of voluntary submission of a human to the will of Allah after a considered conviction that Allah is the only reality and that everything else springs out of that reality. Allah has given every human the freedom of choice to submit or not to His will. There is no compulsion in matters of the *din*. And yet there are humans who, by force of arms, compel other humans to submit to their will. They demand obedience through imprisonment, torture, and murder. Every Muslim state in this day is a police state. Every Muslim ruler abuses his authority to plunder and debase the lands of Islam. Every Muslim state today is the source of *fitnah* that is eating into the heart and the soul of Islam.

The External *Fitnah* of the Circle of Evil: Two hundred years ago, the circle of evil began its control of the world's wealth through conspiracy, subterfuge, and secrecy by undermining the stability of countries through war, strife, and discord and by weakening governments through creation of confusion in financial markets. The Western armies and intelligence services are the foot soldiers of the circle of evil, and the rulers of both the East and the West are their pawns and puppets to be manipulated at will to control the power and wealth of the world. The circle of evil is the external *fitnah* whose intent is to destroy Islam. It has always been its intention to corrupt, divide, and control the wealth of the Islamic land through the manipulation of its rulers, who were initially placed in positions of power by the circle with the help of the Western armies, intelligence, and diplomacy.

The weakness of the mercenary armies of the modern Islamic states clearly arises from the nonfulfillment of Allah's injunctions in the covenant. Faith in Allah's promise and power, unity of the *ummah*, justice, and the struggle to end *fitnah* and tyranny are essential actions ordained in the covenant. When a believer reneges on his covenant with Allah, he only does it to the detriment to his own soul. However, such an action on the part of the community and its appointed leaders leads to the undermining, enslavement, and impoverishment of the whole Islamic community for many generations.

The foundation of the regimes of the imperial families of the Arabian Peninsula, Jordan, Brunei, and Morocco and the imperial occupation governments of Hosni Mubarak of Egypt and the generals of Pakistan are supported by the external *fitnah*—the British, US, and NATO armed forces, intelligence, and diplomatic services—in opposition to the aspirations of their own people. In return, these regimes provide services to the circle of evil to subvert, undermine, and weaken the neighboring Islamic and Arab countries of Iran, Afghanistan, Iraq, Syria, Libya, Algeria, Sudan, and Mauritania. The *ummah* is saddled with the curse and the *fitnah* of the priesthood, the mercenary armies of Muslim states, their corrupt rulers, and the foreign masters of their rulers.

Imagine a country with the largest land base, with coasts rimmed by thousands of miles of blue oceans, and with a vast number of rivers flowing from hundreds of snowcapped mountains through its deserts, grasslands, fertile valleys, and plains into rich deltas, lakes, and oceans bursting with marine life and other resources—a land blessed by Allah with resources never equaled in history, peopled with a devout, hardworking population with the knowledge of how to utilize such resources in the service of Allah and His creatures. Again, see in your mind's eye an army, the largest in history of mankind, keeping this land, its borders and resources, its oceans and skies, and its people and wealth secure from marauders who have traditionally raided other lands for their resources. These defense forces compose of an army of six million men in about 300 infantry and mechanized divisions equipped with 30,000 tanks and armored vehicles, an air force of 3,580 aircraft of varying models, and a naval force equipped with 230 coastal and oceangoing ships equipped with armaments bought from the West and Russia. There are also 60 submarines in the armada. These armed forces are also equipped with short- and medium-range missiles tipped with about sixty nuclear bombs. The country has a budding arms-manufacturing industry producing low- and medium-technology arms. The annual budget of the combined forces is $150 billion, of which $50 billion annually goes to Western countries to purchase their discarded and obsolete weaponry. The West then uses these funds to refurbish its own arsenal with the latest, high-tech weapons.

You might have guessed that we are talking about the combined might of the Islamic world at the onset of the twenty-first century. This army has never won any battle of significance since the war for the Gallipoli Peninsula about a century ago. These armed forces have not defended in any significant manner the Islamic world since the disintegration of the Ottoman Empire. The wars of independence of Islamic lands from the colonial rule in India, Iran, Iraq, Syria, Egypt, Morocco, and Algeria were fought by the masses with civil disobedience and guerrilla warfare. The state-organized armies of Islam have failed to safeguard the freedom of the people of Palestine, Iraq, Kashmir, Sinkiang, Iraq, Kosovo, Bosnia, Mindanao, Chechnya, and Russia.

What went wrong? The Muslim army of the twentieth and the twenty-first centuries has its guns pointed toward its own people, whereas the external borders of Islam are guarded and patrolled by the naval fleets of America and Europe. The Muslim state armies should be fighting the treachery and oppression by enemies of Allah and Islam—the *kafaru*, *mushrikun*, *Munafiqeen*, and *zalimun*, who have usurped and plundered resources of the believers for the last two hundred years. Instead, the Muslim armies and security services are themselves the source of oppression and treachery to the *momineen*, resisting tyranny of the circle of evil of the *Munafiqun* and the *Mutaffifeen*. The clear examples are the armed and security forces of Reza Shah Pahlavi, the mullahs of Iran, Saddam Hussein of Iraq, the Taliban, the Pakistani governments, the Saudi family, Suharto, Syria, Anwar Sadat, Hosni Mubarak, Gaddhafi, the Algerian military, and Morocco's royalty.

This is a clear testimony that the believers of the covenant of Allah and those who control the so-called armies of Islam have not surrendered to the will of Allah and do not strive in His path. The obligations assigned to the individual believer in the covenant of Allah are the same for the community of Islam and for the leaders whom the believers appoint to look after and to protect their individual and communal interests. The covenant is specific in pointing out the responsibilities of the individual, the community, and its appointed leaders.

Jihad is the internal struggle of the believer to cleanse oneself of the temptations of the evil that surrounds him or her. It is also a constant external struggle to rid the community of the treachery and oppression by the enemy of the covenant and *din*. The enemy may be obvious, visible, and easily overpowered. The web of intrigues and conspiracies of the *kafaru*, *mushrikun*, *Munafiqeen*, and *zalimun* is hard to detect and overcome. The deception may come from familiar people working from within the community for the circle of evil whose motive is to tempt you away from Allah's path and also take control of your land and wealth, enslaving you in the process. The following four principles should guide the believers in their striving for Allah's cause.

a) Faith in Allah's Covenant and Promise. Join not anything in worship with Him. Allah is the *Waliy* (Friend and Defender) of the believers who obey His covenant. Allah promises His strength and power (*al-qawiyy al-Aziz*) to aid the believer and promises victory in his striving for Allah's *din*. Therefore, the believer shall maintain his faith in Allah's promise always. Trust in Allah's promise endows the believer with the greatest strength from Allah's might in his determination to struggle and fight for Allah's cause. All strength belongs to Allah. All physical, worldly, political, and cosmic strength is nothing before the infinite strength of Allah.

إِنَّ رَبَّكَ هُوَ ٱلْقَوِىُّ ٱلْعَزِيزُ ﴿٦٦﴾

Allah is the All-powerful the Almighty, Al-qawiyy al-Aziz. (Hud 11:66, Koran)

لَا قُوَّةَ إِلَّا بِٱللَّهِ

There is no Power except in Allah.
(Al-Kahf 18:39, Koran)

﴿ كَتَبَ ٱللَّهُ لَأَغْلِبَنَّ أَنَا۠ وَرُسُلِىٓ ۚ إِنَّ ٱللَّهَ قَوِىٌّ عَزِيزٌ ﴿٢١﴾

Verily it is I and My Messengers who will be victorious Verily Allah is All-powerful, All-mighty. (Al-Mujadila 58:21, Koran).

b) Unity. The believers constitute one *ummah* to the exclusion of all other men. Just as the bond with Allah is indivisible, all believers shall stand in commitment with the least of them. All believers are bonded to one another to the exclusion of other men. The believers shall leave none of their members in destitution and give them in kindness and liberty what they need. The pious believers follow the best and the most upright guidance of Allah's covenant.

c) Jihad. All believers shall rise as one against anyone who seeks to commit injustice, aggression, or crime or spread mutual enmity among the Muslims. This Pax Islamica is one and indivisible. No believer shall enter a separate peace without all other believers whenever there is fighting in the cause of Allah but will do so only on the basis of equality and justice to all others. In every expedition for the cause of Allah, all parties to the covenant shall fight shoulder to shoulder as one man. All believers shall avenge the blood of one another when anyone falls while fighting for the cause of Allah.

d) Murder. No believer shall slay a believer in retaliation for an unbeliever, nor shall he assist an unbeliever against a believer. Whoever is convicted of killing a believer deliberately but without righteous cause shall be liable to the relatives of the killed. Until the latter are satisfied, the killer shall be subject to retaliation by each and every believer.

e) Justice. Justice (*'adl*) is a divine attribute defined as "putting in the right place." The opposite of *'adl* is *zulm*, which in Koranic terms means "wrongdoing." Wrongdoing is a human attribute defined as "putting things in the wrong place." *Zulm* (wrongdoing) is one of the common terms used in the Koran to refer to the negative acts employed by human beings. Wrongdoing is the opposite of justice, putting everything in its right place, and every act of humans as prescribed by Allah. Wrongdoing is to put things where they do not belong. Hence, wrongdoing is injustice, for example, associating others with Allah; others do not belong in the place for the divine. It is to place false words in place of the truth and to put someone else's property in place of your own. Other examples are taking a life against the divine commandments, replacing people's liberty with oppression, waging war instead of peace, and usurping people's right to govern themselves. The Koran repeatedly stigmatizes men of wrongdoing.

The Koran, when it points out who is harmed by injustice and wrongdoing, always mentions the word *nafs* (self). People cannot harm Allah. By being unjust or by putting things in the wrong place, people harm themselves. They distort their own natures, and they lead themselves astray. Who can one wrong? It is impossible to wrong or do injustice against Allah since all things are His creatures and do His work. Hence, wrongdoing and injustice is an activity against people and Allah's creation. Allah had prescribed His covenant to the humans for the good of human beings. People, tribes, and nations are being helped since Allah leads them into accord, harmony, and justice, which in turn create peace in the world. Allah has laid out all the basic principles for justice in His covenant for the humans to live in harmony. Those who refuse to follow His commandments are therefore ungrateful and hence *kafirs*. Thus, they are wrongdoers (*zalimun*) and only harm themselves. Therefore, there can be no jihad unless it is for justice and against wrongdoing.

There is a clear reason for the glaring weakness of the state-run armies of the Muslim nation-states. The Muslim states are governed by self-appointed kings, dictators, and politicians who are divorced from their *din* and their people. They belong to and serve the interests of the circle of evil.

> Make careful preparations and take precautions.
> Then go forth in groups or all together to the
> endeavor. There amongst you is he who will
> linger behind, if misfortune befalls you, he will
> say, "Allah did favor him as he was not with you."
> When good fortune comes to you from Allah,
> he would wish that he had been with you.
>
> Those who swap the life of this world for the hereafter
> let them fight in the cause of Allah. Whosoever fights
> in the cause of Allah, whether he is slain or he is
> victorious, there is a great award for him from Allah.
>
> And why should you not fight in the cause of
> Allah and for those men, women and children,
> who are weak, abused and oppressed, those who
> beseech their Lord to deliver them from their
> oppressors and those who ask Allah to send for them
> protectors and helpers. (An-Nisa 4:71–75, Koran)
>
> Remember Allah's blessings on you. When a people
> planned to stretch out their hands against you and
> Allah did hold back their hands from you to protect

you from your enemies. Be in taqwa of Allah, fear Allah and place your trust in Allah. (Al-Ma'idah 5:11, Koran)

Be in taqwa of Allah, fear Allah. Perform Jihad and strive your utmost in Allah's Cause and approach Him so that you may prosper. (Al-Ma'idah 3:35, Koran).

If any among you turn back on his faith Allah will bring a people whom He loves and who love Him and who are humble towards the believers and stern towards unbelievers, who perform jihad and strive in the cause of Allah and fear not reproaches of any blamer. Such is the Grace of Allah that He bestows on whom He wills. Allah is All-Sufficient for His Creatures and all Knowing. (Al-Ma'idah 5:54, Koran).

When you meet the infidels rank upon rank, in conflict never turn your backs to them. (Al-Anfal 8:15, Koran)

Respond to Allah and His Rasool when He calls you to that gives you life. And know that Allah intervenes in the tussle between man and his heart, and it is to Allah that you shall return. Fear treachery or oppression that afflicts not only those who perpetrate it but affects guilty and innocent alike. Know that Allah is strict in punishment. (Al-Anfal 8:24–25, Koran)

Fight the infidel until there is no more treachery and oppression and there prevails Justice and Faith in Allah altogether and everywhere. If they cease, then Allah is seer of what they do. If they refuse, be sure that Allah is your Protector, the Best to protect and the Best to help. (Al-Anfal 8:39–40, Koran)

When you meet the enemy force, stand steadfast against them and remember the name of Allah much, so that you may be successful. And obey Allah and His Messenger and do not dispute with one another lest you lose courage and your strength departs and be patient. Allah is with those who patiently persevere. (Al-Anfal 8:45–46, Koran)

Whether you do or do not help Allah's Messenger, your leader, Allah strengthens him with His Peace and with forces that you do not see. The words of the infidels He humbled into the dirt but Allah's word is Exalted, High. Allah is Mighty, Wise. Go forth, advance! Whether equipped well or lightly, perform jihad strive your utmost and struggle with your wealth and your persons in the cause of Allah. That is best for you, if you knew. (At-Tawbah 9:38–41, Koran)

Fight the unbelievers who surround you. Let them find you firm and know Allah is always with those who have taqwa, who are Allah-wary. (At-Tawbah 9:123, Koran)

Remember the Grace of Allah, bestowed upon you, when there came down hordes to overpower you: We sent against them a hurricane and forces that that you did not see but Allah sees all that ye do.

Behold! They came on you from above you and from below you, your eyes became dim, and the hearts gaped up to the throats and you imagined various vain thoughts about Allah! (Al-Ahzab 33:9, Koran)

If ye will aid (the cause of) Allah, He will aid you and make your foothold firm. But those who reject Allah, for them is destruction and Allah will render their deeds vain. That is because they hate the Revelation of Allah; so, He has made their deeds fruitless. Do they not travel through the earth and see what was the end of those before their times, who did evil? Allah brought utter destruction on them and similar fates await those who reject Allah. That is because Allah is the Protector of those who believe, but those who reject Allah have no protector. (Muhammad 47:7–11, Koran)

Be not weak and ask for peace, while you are having an upper hand: for Allah is with you and will never decrease the reward of your good deeds.

The life of this world is but play and amusement: and if ye believe, fear Allah and guard against evil, He will grant you your recompense and will not ask you (to give up) your possessions.

Behold, you are those invited to spend of your wealth in the Way of Allah: but among you are some that are parsimonious. But any who are miserly are so at the expense of their own souls. But Allah is free of all wants and it is ye that are needy. If ye turn back (from the Path), He will substitute in your stead another people; then they would not be like you! (Muhammad 47:33–38, Koran)

When ye are told to make room in the assemblies, spread out and make room: ample room will Allah provide for you. And when ye are told to rise up, for prayers, Jihad or other good deeds rise up: Allah will exalt in rank those of you who believe and who have been granted Knowledge. And Allah is well acquainted with all you do. (Al-Mujadila 58:11, Koran)

Why do you promise what you do not carry out? Hateful is indeed to Allah that you say what you do not act upon. Allah loves those who fight in His cause in array of unison and solidarity. (As-Saf 61:2–4, Koran)

Shall I guide you to a bargain that will save you from a painful torment? That you believe in Allah and His Messenger and that you perform Jihad (strive to your utmost) in the way of Allah, with all that you own and in all earnestness: that will be best for you, if you but knew! He will forgive you your sins and admit you to Gardens beneath which rivers flow and to beautiful dwellings in Jannat of adn (Gardens of Eternity): that is indeed the supreme blessing. And another favor will He bestow, which you will cherish; help from Allah and a speedy victory. So, give the glad tidings to the believers. (As-Saf 61:10–13, Koran)

19. The Covenant of Allah: Forgiveness: Be Quick in the Race for Forgiveness from Your Lord, Restrain Anger, and Pardon All Humans

O you who believe! Be quick in the race for forgiveness from your Lord. Those who give freely whether in prosperity, or in adversity, those who restrain anger and pardon all humans, for Allah loves those who

do beautiful deeds. Fear the Fire, which is prepared
for those who reject Faith; And obey Allah and the
Messenger; that ye may obtain mercy. Be quick in
the race for forgiveness from your Lord and for a
Garden whose measurement is that of the heavens
and of the earth, prepared for the righteous.

Those who give freely whether in prosperity,
or in adversity, those who restrain anger and
pardon all humans, for Allah loves those who do
beautiful deeds. (Ali 'Imran 3:130–34, Koran)

Among Allah's names are *ar-Rahman* (the Beneficent), *ar-Rahim* (the Merciful), and *al-Ghafoor* (the Forgiving). His mercy overtakes His punishment and anger.

﴿ ۞ قُلْ يَٰعِبَادِىَ ٱلَّذِينَ أَسْرَفُوا۟ عَلَىٰٓ أَنفُسِهِمْ لَا تَقْنَطُوا۟ مِن رَّحْمَةِ ٱللَّهِ ۚ إِنَّ ٱللَّهَ يَغْفِرُ ٱلذُّنُوبَ جَمِيعًا ۚ إِنَّهُۥ هُوَ ٱلْغَفُورُ ٱلرَّحِيمُ ۝٥٣ ﴾

Say: "O my Servants who have transgressed against
their souls! Despair not of the Mercy of Allah: for Allah
forgives all sins: for He is Oft-Forgiving, Most Merciful.

Every human action in daily life reaches back into the divine reality that everything in the universe is governed by tawhid, yet Allah has granted humans a freedom of choice, which can upset the balance in the creation, the balance of justice, and the balance of atmospheric elements and lead to environmental pollution, destruction of animal species, and destruction of populations, cities, and agriculture through human actions. The covenant tells people why they should be Allah's servants and explains which path they should follow to become His vicegerents.

It makes it clear that human activity is deeply rooted in the Real, and this has everlasting repercussions in this world and in the hereafter.

The wholesome (*salihun*) are the ones who live in harmony with the Real (*Haqq*) and establish wholesomeness (*saalihaat*) through their words and deeds throughout the world. In contrast, the corrupt (*mufsidun*) destroy the proper balance and relationship with Allah and His creation. *Fasid* means "corrupt, evil, wrong."

Allah measures out good and evil, the wholesome and the corrupt. Humans have enough freedom to make their own choices; if they make the choice to do beautiful and wholesome deeds(*saalihaat*) motivated by faith (*iman*) and god-wariness (*taqwa*), they please Allah and bring harmony and wholesomeness to the world, resulting in peace, justice, mercy, compassion, honor, equity, well-being, freedom, and many other gifts through Allah's grace. Others choose to do evil and work with corruption (*mufsidun*), destroying the right relationship among the creation, causing hunger, disease, oppression, pollution, and other afflictions. In the universal order, corruption is the prerogative of humans, and vicegerency gives humans the freedom to work against the Creator and His creation. Only misapplied trust can explain how moral evil can appear in the world. When humans choose wrong and corrupt actions, they displease Allah. Allah loves those who do what is beautiful, not those who do what is ugly:

$$\text{وَإِذَا تَوَلَّىٰ سَعَىٰ فِى ٱلْأَرْضِ لِيُفْسِدَ فِيهَا وَيُهْلِكَ ٱلْحَرْثَ وَٱلنَّسْلَ ۗ وَٱللَّهُ لَا يُحِبُّ ٱلْفَسَادَ}$$

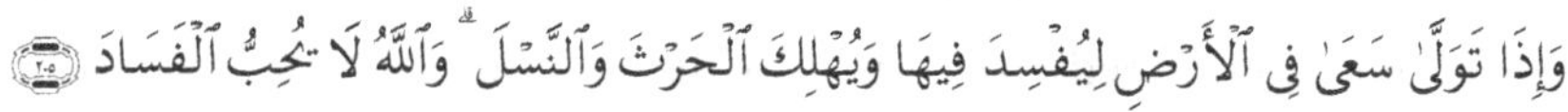

When he turns his back, he hurries about the
earth to work corruption there and destroy
the tillage and the stock. Allah loves not
corruption. (Al-Baqarah 2:205, Koran)

Allah loves doing what is beautiful, and because of His love for those who do the beautiful, He brings them near to Himself, and His nearness is called Allah's mercy:

وَلَا تُفْسِدُوا۟ فِى ٱلْأَرْضِ بَعْدَ إِصْلَـٰحِهَا وَٱدْعُوهُ خَوْفًا وَطَمَعًا ۚ إِنَّ رَحْمَتَ ٱللَّهِ قَرِيبٌ مِّنَ ٱلْمُحْسِنِينَ ﴿٥٦﴾

> Work not corruption in this world after it has made wholesome and call upon Allah in fear and hope. Surely the mercy of Allah is near to those who do what is beautiful. (Al-A'raf 7:56, Koran)

The covenant of the Koran presents us the scope of the freedom of choice that humans have in doing what is wholesome and beautiful or what is corrupt or ugly. The human's role among the creation distinguishes right activity, right thought, and right intention from their opposites. It reminds us of how the scales of Allah's justice, the two hands of Allah—His mercy and His wrath—are reflected in the human domain, where people have been appointed Allah's vicegerents. Deeds of goodness and wholesomeness are associated with mercy, paradise, and the beautiful. Evil and corruption is rewarded with wrath, hell, and the ugly.

To err is human. Allah is most forgiving to those who have erred and repented. Above all, Allah's mercy knows no bounds. The Koran and the teaching of the blessed *Nabi* guide those who seek the path of Allah. Allah says:

> O my Servants who have transgressed against their souls! Despair not of the Mercy of Allah: for Allah forgives all sins: for He is Oft-Forgiving, Most Merciful.

> Turn ye to your Lord (in repentance) and bow to His (Will), before the Penalty comes on you: after that ye shall not be helped. (Az-Zumar 39:53, Koran)

Allah, in His mercy, has laid down guidelines for punishment of the transgressors. For transgressors and sinners, there is Allah's wrath in this world and the next. If they repent, however, Allah forgives them. The Koran constantly emphasizes repentance and reform of a person and Allah's mercy and grace. Allah's mercy knows no bounds. Justice (*'adl*) is a divine attribute defined as "putting every object in the right place." When the transgressor repents, mends his ways, and does not repeat the wrongdoing, evil has been replaced with good. Allah bestows His mercy.

The community's obligation is to pardon and help educate and reform an individual. Allah advises every human to restrain from anger and resentment. Anger is a smoldering volcano quietly burning the human from the inside, robbing his tranquility and peace. Forgiving others restores peace and brings nearness to Allah. For the unrepentant transgressor, the penalty is prescribed in the Koran. Never is the gate to Allah's mercy closed. The key to this gate is repentance and a walk in Allah's path.

20. The Covenant of Allah: If Anyone Slew a Person, It Would Be as If He Slew the Whole People

> If anyone slew a person, unless it be for punishment for murder or for spreading mischief in the land, it would be as if he slew the whole people: and if anyone saved a life, it would be as if he saved the life of all the people.

Life is sacred. Allah forbids the taking of life unless it is by the way of justice (jihad against tyranny and oppression) or when ordained by the law of equality or punishment for murder, where the Koran recommends clemency. As the covenant forbids the believers and the community of Islam to take a life and murder, the same injunction applies to the ruler or the *amri minkum* appointed by the believers. War against Muslims and others for acquisition of territory and wealth is forbidden, and anyone waging such a war blatantly disobeys Allah's covenant and is not of the believers. Persecution, punishment, imprisonment, and murder of the citizens of the Islamic state who strive for the cause of Allah is a heinous crime. Rulers and their bureaucracy responsible for such crimes are unfit to discharge their responsibility and liable for punishment for their crime according to the law of the Koran.

> If anyone slew a person - unless it be for murder or for spreading mischief in the land - it would be as if he slew the whole people: and if anyone saved a life, it would be as if he saved the life of the whole people. (Al-Ma'idah 5:32, Koran)

> Take not life, which Allah hath made sacred, except by the way of justice or law: This He commands you, that you may learn wisdom. (Al-An'am: 151–53)

21. The Covenant of Allah: Usury and Hoarding of Wealth

> Devour not usury, doubled and multiplied; Be in *taqwa* of Allah (fear Allah) that ye may prosper.

Forbidden is the practice of usury to the Muslims. Also forbidden is making money from money. Money in its present form is only a medium of exchange, a way of defining the value of an item, but in itself has no value and therefore should not give rise to more money by earning interest through deposit in a bank or loaning it to someone else. The human endeavor, initiative, and risk involved in a productive venture are much more important than the money used to finance it. Money deposited in a bank or hoarded is potential capital rather than capital. Money becomes capital only when it is invested in a venture. Accordingly, money loaned to a business is regarded as a debt and is not capital; and as such, it is not entitled to any return, such as interest.

Muslims are encouraged to spend (purchase necessities or spend in the way of Allah) or invest their money and are discouraged from keeping their money idle. Hoarding money is unacceptable. Allah's commandments in His covenant with the believers in the following three *ayahs* exhort Muslims to (a) spend in charity after their needs are met, (b) devour not in usury, and (c) hoard not gold and silver.

وَيَسْـَٔلُونَكَ مَاذَا يُنفِقُونَ قُلِ ٱلْعَفْوَ ۗ كَذَٰلِكَ يُبَيِّنُ ٱللَّهُ لَكُمُ ٱلْـَٔايَـٰتِ لَعَلَّكُمْ تَتَفَكَّرُونَ

They ask thee how much they are to spend (in charity); say: "What is beyond your needs." Thus, doth Allah make clear to you His Signs: in order that ye may consider. (Al-Baqarah 2:222, Koran)

يَمْحَقُ ٱللَّهُ ٱلرِّبَوٰا۟ وَيُرْبِى ٱلصَّدَقَـٰتِ ۗ وَٱللَّهُ لَا يُحِبُّ كُلَّ كَفَّارٍ أَثِيمٍ ﴿٢٧٦﴾

Allah will deprive usury of all blessing but will give increase for deeds of charity; for He loves not creatures ungrateful and wicked. (Al-Baqarah 2:275–76, Koran)

ٱللَّهِ ۗ وَٱلَّذِينَ يَكْنِزُونَ ٱلذَّهَبَ وَٱلْفِضَّةَ وَلَا يُنفِقُونَهَا فِى سَبِيلِ ٱللَّهِ فَبَشِّرْهُم بِعَذَابٍ أَلِيمٍ ﴿٣٤﴾

And there are those who hoard gold and silver and spend it not in the Way of Allah: announce unto them a most grievous penalty. (Al-A'raf 9:34, Koran)

Gharar (uncertainty, risk, or speculation) is forbidden. Any transaction entered into should be free from uncertainty, risk, and speculation. The parties cannot predetermine a granted profit, and this does not allow an undertaking from the borrower or the customer to repay the borrowed principal, plus an amount to consider inflation. Therefore, options and futures are regarded as un-Islamic; so are foreign exchange transactions because rates are determined by interest differentials.

An Islamic government is forbidden to lend or borrow money from institutions such as international banks, the World Bank, or the International Monetary Fund on interest as both usury and interest are expressly forbidden. Banking based on fiat money is also forbidden. The value of money is diluted by the creation of new money out of nothing; the property rights of savers and those who have been promised future payments, such as pensioners, are violated. This is stealing. The trappings of the money and banking system have been compared to that of a cult; only those who profit from it understand its inner workings. They work hard to keep it that way. The central banks print notes adorned with signatures, seals, and pictures of a president or that of a queen; counterfeiters are severely punished; governments pay their expenses with them; and populations are forced to accept them. They are printed like newspapers in such vast quantity, representing an equal worth to all the treasures of this world, all the resources above and under the ground, all assets of populations, and their work and labor to fabricate every item that has ever been manufactured. And yet these notes cost nothing to make. In truth, this has been the greatest hoax, the worst crime against humanity, a swindle of proportions never seen by humanity before.

As we have found, the Koran forbids usury, gambling, speculation, and hoarding of gold and silver. The Koran does advocate trade; spending on good things in life, kith, and kin; and giving wealth for the cause of Allah. The modern economic system is entirely alien to the teachings of the Koran and full of pitfalls and trappings laid down by Satan. The Dar es Salaam has slid downhill, submerged into the quicksand of make-believe economy. Every successful businessman and trader is forced to operate in the pagan, sinful system of economy. Here is the solution for a successful economic system as laid down in the covenant of the Koran:

1. Elimination of usury and interest in Dar es Salaam.
2. Elimination of fiat money and of banking based on money created out of nothing with a printing press. There will be no more creation and lending of capital nine times that of the bank deposits. It is dishonest and forbidden because it is based on institutionalized theft, supported by the state and international institutions.
3. Creation of a single currency for the united Islamic state, such as gold dinars and silver dirhams based on the measures established by Umar ibn al-Khattab, the second caliph. A currency bureau, an arm of the state of Dar es Salaam, will supervise the minting and circulation of the currency.
4. Drastic changes to Dar es Salaam's trading relations with the rest of the world. All goods utilized within the state—whether industrial, agricultural, manufactured, or raw—will be produced within the country so that the *ummah* is self-sufficient and independent of foreign trading systems. The goods for export—oil, minerals, raw and manufactured

goods—shall be sold against gold and gold-based currency as well as barter. Paper and printed money will not be acceptable. Pricing for international trade will use an index of equal value to human labor internationally.

Those that spend of their goods in charity
by night and by day, in secret and in public,
have their reward with their Lord: on them
shall be no fear, nor shall they grieve.

Those who devour usury will not stand except
stands the one whom the Satan by his touch has
driven to madness. That is because they say: "Trade
is like usury," but Allah hath permitted trade
and forbidden usury. Those who after receiving
direction from their Lord, desist, shall be pardoned
for the past; their case is for Allah to judge; but
those who repeat (the offence) are Companions
of the Fire; they will abide therein (forever).

Allah will deprive usury of all blessing but
will give increase for deeds of charity; for
He does not love ungrateful and wicked
creatures. (Al-Baqarah 2:274–76, Koran)

Those who believe and perform wholesome
deeds, establish regular prayers and regular
charity have rewards with their Lord. On them
shall be no fear, nor shall they grieve.

Fear Allah and give up what remains of your demand
for usury, if you are indeed believers. If you do it not,

take notice of war from Allah and His Messenger: but if you turn back, you will still have your capital sums.

Deal not unjustly and ye shall not be dealt with unjustly.

If the debtor is in a difficulty, grant him time until it is easy for him to repay. But if ye remit it by way of charity, that is best for you. (Al-Baqarah 2:277–80, Koran)

Devour not usury, doubled and multiplied; Be in taqwa of Allah (fear Allah) that ye may prosper.

Fear the Fire, which is prepared for those who reject Faith; and obey Allah and the Messenger; that ye may obtain mercy.

Be quick in the race for forgiveness from your Lord and for a Garden whose measurement is that of the heavens and of the earth, prepared for the righteous.

Those who give freely whether in prosperity, or in adversity; those who restrain anger and pardon all humans; for Allah loves those who do beautiful deeds (Al-Muhsinun). (Ali 'Imran 3:130–34, Koran)

There are indeed many among the priests and clerics who in falsehood devour the substance of men and hinder them from the way of Allah. And there are those who bury gold and silver and spend it not in the way of Allah: announce unto them a most grievous penalty.

On the Day when heat will be produced out of
that wealth in the fire of Hell and with it will be
branded their foreheads, their flanks and their
backs, "This is the treasure which you buried
for yourselves: taste then, the treasures which
you buried!" (At-Tawbah 9:34–35, Koran)

22. The Covenant of Allah: Be Good to Your Parents; Allah Forbids Infanticide and Abortion

The Koran repeatedly commands the believers to do what is beautiful to be brought under the sway of Allah's gentle, merciful, and beautiful names. Human qualities gain their reality from the most beautiful divine qualities. When humans turn to Allah, their beautiful qualities become indistinguishable from Allah's own.

﴿ وَلِلَّهِ مَا فِي ٱلسَّمَٰوَٰتِ وَمَا فِي ٱلْأَرْضِ لِيَجْزِيَ ٱلَّذِينَ أَسَٰٓـُٔوا۟ بِمَا عَمِلُوا۟ وَيَجْزِيَ ٱلَّذِينَ أَحْسَنُوا۟ بِٱلْحُسْنَى ﴿٣١﴾ ﴾

To Allah belongs all that is in the heavens and
on earth; so that He rewards those who do ugly,
according for what they have done and He rewards
those who do beautiful with the most beautiful.

The first beautiful act that believers perform after tawhid is to do what is beautiful and do good to their parents, those who brought them into existence. It is parents who provide means that Allah employs in creating people, nurturing, educating, and making them beautiful and God fearing. Allah takes credit for His creation, which is the requirement of tawhid. Allah expects his creatures to act appropriately toward His intermediaries of creation. Only in this manner can humans expect other creatures, including their own children, to act beautifully toward them.

Respect and care for the parents is the fundamental act in the Islamic society to maintain the cohesion of the family structure. The family is the underlying unit of the community that forms the support group for children, adults, the elderly, the relatives, the neighborhood, the kin, and the communal structure around the mosque and schools.

Infanticide and its modern version, abortion, and the taking of life of both humans and animals are forbidden by the Koran. Allah has made life sacred. And avoid *Fahasha*, the shameful deeds that set the human down a slippery slope of the ugly and evil.

لَا تَعْبُدُونَ إِلَّا ٱللَّهَ وَبِٱلْوَٰلِدَيْنِ إِحْسَانًا وَذِى ٱلْقُرْبَىٰ وَٱلْيَتَٰمَىٰ وَٱلْمَسَٰكِينِ وَقُولُوا۟ لِلنَّاسِ حُسْنًا وَأَقِيمُوا۟ ٱلصَّلَوٰةَ وَءَاتُوا۟
ٱلزَّكَوٰةَ

Worship none but Allah; treat with kindness your parents and kindred and orphans and those in need; speak fair to the people; be steadfast in prayer; And practice regular charity. (Al-Baqarah 2:82, Koran)

﴿ ۞ قُلْ تَعَالَوْا۟ أَتْلُ مَا حَرَّمَ رَبُّكُمْ عَلَيْكُمْ ۖ أَلَّا تُشْرِكُوا۟ بِهِۦ شَيْـًٔا ۖ وَبِٱلْوَٰلِدَيْنِ إِحْسَٰنًا ۖ وَلَا تَقْتُلُوٓا۟ أَوْلَٰدَكُم مِّنْ إِمْلَٰقٍ ۖ نَّحْنُ
نَرْزُقُكُمْ وَإِيَّاهُمْ ۖ وَلَا تَقْرَبُوا۟ ٱلْفَوَٰحِشَ مَا ظَهَرَ مِنْهَا وَمَا بَطَنَ ۖ وَلَا تَقْتُلُوا۟ ٱلنَّفْسَ ٱلَّتِى حَرَّمَ ٱللَّهُ إِلَّا بِٱلْحَقِّ ۚ ذَٰلِكُمْ وَصَّىٰكُم بِهِۦ لَعَلَّكُمْ
تَعْقِلُونَ ﴿١٥١﴾

Say: "Come, I will rehearse what Allah hath (really) prohibited you from": join not anything as equal with Him; be good to your parents; kill not your children on a plea of want - We provide sustenance for you and for them - come not nigh to shameful deeds, whether open or secret; take not life, which Allah hath made sacred, except by way of justice and law: thus doth He command you, that ye may learn wisdom. (Al-An' am 6:151, Koran)

﴿ لَّا تَجْعَلْ مَعَ ٱللَّهِ إِلَٰهًا ءَاخَرَ فَتَقْعُدَ مَذْمُومًا مَّخْذُولًا ﴿٢٢﴾ ۞ وَقَضَىٰ رَبُّكَ أَلَّا تَعْبُدُوٓا۟ إِلَّآ إِيَّاهُ وَبِٱلْوَٰلِدَيْنِ إِحْسَٰنًا ۚ إِمَّا يَبْلُغَنَّ عِندَكَ
ٱلْكِبَرَ أَحَدُهُمَآ أَوْ كِلَاهُمَا فَلَا تَقُل لَّهُمَآ أُفٍّ وَلَا تَنْهَرْهُمَا وَقُل لَّهُمَا قَوْلًا كَرِيمًا ﴿٢٣﴾ وَٱخْفِضْ لَهُمَا جَنَاحَ ٱلذُّلِّ مِنَ ٱلرَّحْمَةِ وَقُل رَّبِّ
ٱرْحَمْهُمَا كَمَا رَبَّيَانِى صَغِيرًا ﴿٢٤﴾ ﴾

Take not with Allah another object of worship; or thou wilt sit in disgrace and destitution Thy Lord hath decreed that ye worship none but Him and that ye be kind to parents. Whether one or both of them attain old age in thy life, say not to them a word of contempt, nor repel them, but address them in terms of honor. And out of kindness, lower to them the wing of humility and say: "My Lord! Bestow on them thy Mercy even as they cherished me in childhood." (Al-Isra 17:22, 24, Koran)

﴿ وَوَصَّيْنَا ٱلْإِنسَٰنَ بِوَٰلِدَيْهِ إِحْسَٰنًا ۖ حَمَلَتْهُ أُمُّهُۥ كُرْهًا وَوَضَعَتْهُ كُرْهًا ۖ وَحَمْلُهُۥ وَفِصَٰلُهُۥ ثَلَٰثُونَ شَهْرًا ۚ حَتَّىٰٓ إِذَا بَلَغَ أَشُدَّهُۥ وَبَلَغَ أَرْبَعِينَ
سَنَةً قَالَ رَبِّ أَوْزِعْنِىٓ أَنْ أَشْكُرَ نِعْمَتَكَ ٱلَّتِىٓ أَنْعَمْتَ عَلَىَّ وَعَلَىٰ وَٰلِدَىَّ وَأَنْ أَعْمَلَ صَٰلِحًا تَرْضَىٰهُ وَأَصْلِحْ لِى فِى ذُرِّيَّتِىٓ ۖ إِنِّى تُبْتُ إِلَيْكَ وَإِنِّى مِنَ
ٱلْمُسْلِمِينَ ﴿١٥﴾ ﴾

We have enjoined on man kindness to his parents: in pain did his mother bear him and in pain did she give him birth. The carrying of the (child) to his weaning is (a period of) thirty months. At length, when he reaches the age of full strength and attains forty years, he says: "O my Lord! grant me that I may be grateful for Thy favor which Thou hast bestowed upon me and upon both my parents and that I may work righteousness

> such as Thou may approve; and be gracious to me in my issue. Truly have I turned to Thee and truly do I bow (to Thee) in Islam." (Al-Ahqaf 46:15, Koran)

23. The Covenant of Allah: Women and Equality

> You are forbidden to take women against their will. Nor should you treat them with harshness, on the contrary treat them with them on a footing of equality kindness and honor.

Fifty percent of the population of the believers, the women, has been excluded from the mainstream Islam by the mullahs, jurist-scholars, and the Hadith scholars against the commandments of the Koran. Women were regarded as inferior beings in most pre-Islamic cultures, including among the Arabs, Persians, Greeks, and Romans as well as the Hindus. Their status was not any higher among the Turkish and the Mongol tribes of Central Asia. In Judaism, women were forbidden from the inner sanctuary of the temple; and in the early Pauline Christianity, their position was relegated to the entrance of or outside the church at prayer time.

Islam brought dignity and grace to the status of women—the mothers, wives, and daughters. Women had their rights established and their social status elevated as equal to that of men. They attended prayer services at the Prophet's Mosque; they held regular and frequent discourse with the *Nabi* of Allah on religious, women's, and family issues. They participated in battles alongside their men. Women worked outside their homes. The first person to convert to Islam, Khadijah, was a successful international trader and owned an import and export business, dealing goods from India, Persia, Africa, Yemen, and the Byzantine Empire. She employed several men to assist her in her business. Other women memorized the Koran and taught other

Muslims. A'ishah gave regular talks and discourses on religious matters. Other women led the ritual prayers and *dhikr-e-Allah* gatherings.

The ulema and other followers of the *Hadith collections* over the last one thousand years have totally excluded women from congregation prayers, businesses, public and social affairs, and most importantly education. The Muslim communities have betrayed Allah and His *Rasul* concerning their obligations to the women—their mothers, wives, sisters, and daughters. Allah's covenant provides equality to every individual within the community, both men and women. Allah has elevated the rank and dignity of the children of Adam, both men and women, with special favors above that of most of his creation, including the angels. The dignity and favors promised by Allah include six special values: faith, life, intellect (education), property, lineage, and freedom of speech and action.

Equality of Men and Women: The Koran addresses men and women who submit to Allah, who believe, who are devout, who speak the truth, who are righteous, who are humble, who are charitable, who fast and deny themselves, who guard their chastity, and who remember Allah and promises them a great reward and forgiveness for their transgressions. In this address, Allah treats men and women equitably with the promise of a similar reward for their good acts. In Allah's eyes, all men and women who do good deeds carry an equal favor with Him.

Allah admonishes believing men and women to lower their gaze and guard their chastity. Allah is well acquainted with what men did. Allah also admonishes women to dress modestly and not display their adornments outside their immediate family environment. Allah commands believers, men and women, to turn *all together* toward Allah so that they may prosper. This can happen only when the believers, men and women, turn to Allah collectively as a community in a mosque as was customary during the lifetime of the *Nabi* of Allah.

According to the Koran, men and women are autonomous and answerable to Allah for their own deeds and actions, and only they as individuals are rewarded or punished for their deeds. In a community, men as a group or the state has no authority from the Koran to enforce any restrictions on the freedom of righteous and believing women. To every man and woman, Allah has bestowed rights to *faith, life, intellect, property, education, and freedom of action and speech.* The authority of a ruler who denies these basic freedoms to men or to women is openly disputable. A person obeys the ruler on the condition that the ruler obeys the Koran and Allah's covenant.

For men and women who surrender unto Allah,

For men and women who believe,

For men and women who are devout

For men and women who speak the truth,

For men and women who persevere in righteousness,

For men and women who are humble,

For men and women who are charitable,

For men and women who fast and deny them selves

For men and women who guard their chastity,

For men and women who remember Allah much,

For them Allah has forgiveness and a great reward.

Say to the

Believing men that they should lower
their gaze and guard their modesty:

That will make for greater purity for them:

And Allah is acquainted with all that they do.

And say to the

Believing women that they should lower
their gaze and guard their modesty.

That they should not display their adornments
except what is ordinarily obvious,

That they should draw a veil over

Their bosom and not display their adornments

(Except to the immediate family)

And that they should not strike their feet

In order to draw attention

To their hidden adornments.

and O ye Believers!

Turn ye all together Toward Allah that ye may prosper.

The believer's men and women are
protectors one of another.

They enjoin what is just and forbid what is evil.

They observe regular prayers, practice regular
charity and obey Allah and His messenger.

On them will Allah pour His mercy, for
Allah is exalted in power, wise.

O ye who believe! Guard your souls,

If ye follow [right] guidance,

No hurt can come to you from those who stray.

The goal of you all is to Allah,

It is He who will show you the truth of all that ye do.

The Koran, as in the sura above, addresses men and women equally, subjecting them together to similar obligations of submission to Allah, regular prayer, giving in charity, modesty in dress and behavior, righteousness, humility, chastity, worship, truthfulness, remembrance of Allah, and being kind and just. Allah blessed mankind (*insan*), both men and women, with dignity, justice, and equality. He promised them the same rewards and gave them the same obligations. *Be steadfast in prayer and practice regular charity* is an ongoing and repetitive theme in the Koran. Allah calls those who believe, both men and women, to hasten to the congregation prayer on Friday, the day of assembly.

يَٰٓأَيُّهَا ٱلَّذِينَ ءَامَنُوٓاْ إِذَا نُودِيَ لِلصَّلَوٰةِ مِن يَوۡمِ ٱلۡجُمُعَةِ فَٱسۡعَوۡاْ إِلَىٰ ذِكۡرِ ٱللَّهِ وَذَرُواْ ٱلۡبَيۡعَۚ ذَٰلِكُمۡ خَيۡرٞ لَّكُمۡ إِن كُنتُمۡ تَعۡلَمُونَ ٩ فَإِذَا
قُضِيَتِ ٱلصَّلَوٰةُ فَٱنتَشِرُواْ فِي ٱلۡأَرۡضِ وَٱبۡتَغُواْ مِن فَضۡلِ ٱللَّهِ وَٱذۡكُرُواْ ٱللَّهَ كَثِيرٗا لَّعَلَّكُمۡ تُفۡلِحُونَ ١٠

O ye who believe! (Men and women) When the call is proclaimed to prayer on Friday (the Day of Assembly), hasten earnestly to the Remembrance of Allah and leave off business (and traffic): that is best for you if ye but knew!

and when the Prayer is finished, then may ye disperse through the land and seek of the Bounty of Allah: and celebrate the Praises of Allah often (and without stint): that ye may prosper. (Al-Mumtahanah 62:9–10, Koran)

Women attended obligatory prayers, *jum'ah* prayers, and Eid prayers in the Prophet's Mosque. Whenever the apostle of Allah finished his prayers with *Taslim*, the women would get up first, and he would stay in his place for a while before getting up. The purpose of staying was that the women might leave before the men who had finished their prayer.

Soon after the *Nabi* died, there occurred an enormous expansion of the Islamic domain. Women, for a while, enjoyed their newly won freedom and dignity given by Islam and proclaimed by the blessed *Nabi*

Muhammad. Soon afterward, the Arabs reached an unprecedented level of prosperity and began to accumulate large harems of wives, concubines, and female slaves and servants. These women were increasingly confined to their quarters and not allowed to go out unchaperoned. Subsequently, the architecture of the Middle East dwellings changed to suit the new circumstances. The courtyard of the house had high walls, and the only entrance was where the master of the house sat. The master of the harem was so jealous of the chastity of his women that he only employed eunuchs as his servants and guards at his house. The institution of eunuchs was a peculiar Middle Eastern practice related to the institution of the harems of the elite.

The trampling of women's rights was and is a betrayal of the blessed *Nabi* Muhammad's emancipation of women. As more Arabs, Romans, Persians, Hindus, Turks, and Mongols embraced Islam, they brought with them their peculiar bias against women and female infants. The Islamic emancipation of women was ignored; women were confined within their houses, covered head to foot in cloth, denied spiritual growth, and denied access to education and to places of worship. Shamefully, the scholars and the ulema encouraged this state of affairs. Women were gradually discouraged from praying in the mosque and were excluded from congregational worship. Thus, the Muslims for centuries have betrayed the *Nabi* of Allah and disobeyed Allah's covenant.

Pre-Islamic Arab and other cultures regarded women as their chattel and possession. Abduction and rape of opponents' women was a favored pastime of those victorious in battle to humiliate the vanquished. Thus, the birth of a female child was regarded as a matter of shame, which led to the practice of infanticide. This practice was forbidden earlier on during the prophet's mission. However, the primordial masculine instinct resurfaced in the new Muslim. His subconscious shame and embarrassment of the female in his household was sublimated into gentler and more socially acceptable alternative. As the Koran points out, he chose to retain the female child on sufferance and contempt rather than bury her in the dust. And the Koran says, "*What an evil choice they decide on!*" The shame and cultural burden in some of the Muslim societies is so intense that the female infant is buried in the coffin of yashmak (burka) in the confines of her brick house. She is not killed off physically but intellectually and spiritually by withholding the intellectual and spiritual sustenance that Allah had provided for her.

قَدْ خَسِرَ ٱلَّذِينَ قَتَلُوٓا۟ أَوْلَٰدَهُمْ سَفَهًۢا بِغَيْرِ عِلْمٍ وَحَرَّمُوا۟ مَا رَزَقَهُمُ ٱللَّهُ ٱفْتِرَآءً عَلَى ٱللَّهِ ۚ قَدْ ضَلُّوا۟ وَمَا كَانُوا۟
مُهْتَدِينَ ﴿١٤٠﴾

Indeed, Lost are those who slay their children, foolishly and without knowledge and have forbidden that which Allah has provided for them and inventing lies against Allah. They have indeed gone astray and heeded no guidance. (Al-An' am 6:140, Koran)

وَإِذَا بُشِّرَ أَحَدُهُم بِٱلْأُنثَىٰ ظَلَّ وَجْهُهُۥ مُسْوَدًّا وَهُوَ كَظِيمٌ ﴿٥٨﴾ يَتَوَٰرَىٰ مِنَ ٱلْقَوْمِ مِن سُوٓءِ مَا بُشِّرَ بِهِۦٓ ۚ أَيُمْسِكُهُۥ عَلَىٰ هُونٍ أَمْ
يَدُسُّهُۥ فِى ٱلتُّرَابِ ۗ أَلَا سَآءَ مَا يَحْكُمُونَ ﴿٥٩﴾

When news is brought to one of them, of the birth of a female child, his face darkens, and he is filled with inward grief! With shame does he hide himself from his people, because of the bad news he has had! Shall he retain it on sufferance and contempt, or bury it in the dust? Ah! What an evil choice they decide on? (An-Nahl 16:58-59, Koran)

Women have their freedoms, bestowed by the covenant of Allah. Women can achieve their God-given equality and respect only when they stand up to men to demand equality and respect in all the spheres of life in Muslim societies. This will occur only when women have an intellectual awakening to understand and assert their rights. The dignity and favors promised by Allah include six special values: faith, life, intellect (education), property, lineage, and freedom of speech and action.

Until Muslim men do not eliminate their *fitnah* against 50 percent of believers—their mothers, wives, sisters, and daughters—they will continue to be mired in the pit of ignorance, poverty, and *Fahasha.* To arise out of the pit of decadence, they will have to swallow their ego and pride and learn to respect and honor their women. To every man and woman, Allah has bestowed equal rights to faith, life, intellect, property, education, and freedom of speech and action, enjoining what is right and forbidding what is wrong.

> You are forbidden to take women against their will.
> Nor should you treat them with harshness, so that
> you may renounce of the dower you have given
> them and that is only permitted where they have
> been guilty of open lewdness. On the contrary live
> with them on a footing of kindness and honor.
> If ye take a dislike to them it may be that you
> dislike a thing, through which Allah brings about
> a great deal of good. (An-Nisa 4:19, Koran)

> Truly, among your wives and your children are some
> that are contenders to your obligations so beware!
> If ye forgive them and overlook their faults, verily
> Allah is Most -Forgiving, Most Merciful. Your
> riches and your children may be but a temptation:
> Whereas Allah! With Him is an immense reward.

> So be in taqwa of Allah and fear Allah as much as you can; listen and obey; and spend in charity for the benefit of your own souls. And those saved from their own greed are the ones that prosper. If ye loan to Allah a beautiful loan, He will double it for you and He will forgive you: for Allah is both Appreciative (Shakoor) and Magnanimous (Haleem), Knower of what is hidden and what is manifest, Exalted in Might, Full of Wisdom. (At-Taghabun 64:14–18, Koran)

> Those who slander decent women, thoughtless but believing, are cursed in this life and in the Hereafter: for them is a grievous Penalty. (An-Nur 24:21–23, Koran)

24. The Covenant of Allah: Wealth

> Crave not those things of what Allah has bestowed His gifts more freely on some than others, men are assigned what they earn and women that they earn.

Allah created the earth and then bestowed on man His favors to extract sustenance from it. He also created the sun, moon, and stars to create a just equilibrium and harmony in the universe. The sun provides energy for the growth, sustenance, and well-being of humans, plants, and animals. Gradually, man began to extract more than his personal needs from the earth; and the boom of economics, trade, and commerce started, creating cycles of imbalance, disharmony, wars, poverty, and injustice throughout the globe. Not only did this disharmony caused by greed blemish humans but animal life also suffered by the disappearance of whole species. Pollution and contamination of the environment resulted from the race trying to accumulate and hoard the world's wealth in a few hands. Man disobeyed Allah's universal laws and covenant.

In return for all of Allah's favors, Allah commands the following:

- Justice (a*l*-*'adl*). Justice, fairness, honesty, integrity, and evenhanded dealings are a prerequisite of every Muslim's conduct when dealing with others whether socially or in a business transaction.
- Doing what is good and beautiful (*al-ihsan*). This attribute includes every positive quality such as goodness, beauty, and harmony. Human beings have an obligation to do what is wholesome and beautiful in their relationship with Allah and His creatures.
- Providing for those near you (*qurba*) and your kith and kin. Help them with wealth, kindness, compassion, humanity, and sympathy.

Allah forbids *Fahasha*—all evil deeds, lies, false testimony, fornication, selfishness, ingratitude, greed, and false belief. One must fulfill the covenant of Allah and whosoever does beautiful and righteous deeds will be given a new life and rewarded with greater wages by Allah.

۞ إِنَّ ٱللَّهَ يَأْمُرُ بِٱلْعَدْلِ وَٱلْإِحْسَٰنِ وَإِيتَآيِٕ ذِى ٱلْقُرْبَىٰ وَيَنْهَىٰ عَنِ ٱلْفَحْشَآءِ وَٱلْمُنكَرِ وَٱلْبَغْىِ ۚ يَعِظُكُمْ لَعَلَّكُمْ تَذَكَّرُونَ ﴿٩٠﴾ وَأَوْفُوا۟ بِعَهْدِ ٱللَّهِ

إِذَا عَٰهَدتُّمْ وَلَا تَنقُضُوا۟ ٱلْأَيْمَٰنَ بَعْدَ تَوْكِيدِهَا وَقَدْ جَعَلْتُمُ ٱللَّهَ عَلَيْكُمْ كَفِيلًا ۚ إِنَّ ٱللَّهَ يَعْلَمُ مَا تَفْعَلُونَ ﴿٩١﴾

Allah commands justice, the doing of good and liberality to kith and kin and He forbids all shameful deeds and injustice and rebellion: He instructs you, that ye may receive admonition.

Fulfill the Covenant of Allah when ye have entered into it and break not your covenants

after ye have confirmed them: indeed, ye
have made Allah your surety; for Allah knows
all that you do. (Koran 16:90–91)

مَنْ عَمِلَ صَٰلِحًا مِّن ذَكَرٍ أَوْ أُنثَىٰ وَهُوَ مُؤْمِنٌ فَلَنُحْيِيَنَّهُۥ حَيَوٰةً طَيِّبَةً ۖ وَلَنَجْزِيَنَّهُمْ أَجْرَهُم بِأَحْسَنِ مَا كَانُوا۟ يَعْمَلُونَ

Whoever works righteousness, man or woman and has
Faith, verily, to him will We give a new Life, a life that is
good and pure and We will bestow on such their reward
according to the best their actions. (Koran 16:97)

Tawhid, the main pillar of Islam, signifies that man's economic life depends wholly on Allah's laws of the universe and that their relationship to those who believe is through the obedience to the covenant of Allah. Allah maintains in the Koran that there is no creature on the earth whose sustenance is not provided by Allah.

۞ وَمَا مِن دَآبَّةٍ فِى ٱلْأَرْضِ إِلَّا عَلَى ٱللَّهِ رِزْقُهَا وَيَعْلَمُ مُسْتَقَرَّهَا وَمُسْتَوْدَعَهَا ۚ كُلٌّ فِى كِتَٰبٍ مُّبِينٍ ۝٦

No creature crawls on earth that Allah does
not nourish. He knows its essential nature
and its varying forms; every detail has its
place in the obvious plan. (Koran 11:6)

How are the people in need provided for their
sustenance and needs of daily lives?

All wealth belongs to Allah, who bestows it on some people more than others. This wealth is given in trust, whereby the possessor is obliged to give the surplus for Allah's cause, to his kin, to the widows and orphans, and to the needy first in his community and then in the other communities around him. Wealth is to be shared so that not a single individual of the *ummah*, or indeed in the world, should go hungry or be without education and shelter.

۞ لَّيْسَ ٱلْبِرَّ أَن تُوَلُّوا۟ وُجُوهَكُمْ قِبَلَ ٱلْمَشْرِقِ وَٱلْمَغْرِبِ وَلَـٰكِنَّ ٱلْبِرَّ مَنْ ءَامَنَ بِٱللَّهِ وَٱلْيَوْمِ ٱلْـَٔاخِرِ وَٱلْمَلَـٰٓئِكَةِ وَٱلْكِتَـٰبِ وَٱلنَّبِيِّـۧنَ
وَءَاتَى ٱلْمَالَ عَلَىٰ حُبِّهِۦ ذَوِى ٱلْقُرْبَىٰ وَٱلْيَتَـٰمَىٰ وَٱلْمَسَـٰكِينَ وَٱبْنَ ٱلسَّبِيلِ وَٱلسَّآئِلِينَ وَفِى ٱلرِّقَابِ وَأَقَامَ ٱلصَّلَوٰةَ وَءَاتَى ٱلزَّكَوٰةَ وَٱلْمُوفُونَ
بِعَهْدِهِمْ إِذَا عَـٰهَدُوا۟ ۖ وَٱلصَّـٰبِرِينَ فِى ٱلْبَأْسَآءِ وَٱلضَّرَّآءِ وَحِينَ ٱلْبَأْسِ ۗ أُو۟لَـٰٓئِكَ ٱلَّذِينَ صَدَقُوا۟ ۖ وَأُو۟لَـٰٓئِكَ هُمُ ٱلْمُتَّقُونَ ﴿١٧٧﴾

It is not righteousness that ye turn your faces towards
East or West; but it is righteousness to believe in
Allah and the Last Day and the Angels and the Book
and the Messengers; to spend of your substance,
out of love for Him, for your kin, for orphans, for
the needy, for the wayfarer, for those who ask and
for the ransom of slaves; to be steadfast in prayer
and practice regular charity, to fulfill the contracts
which you have made; and to be firm and patient,
in pain (or suffering) and adversity and throughout
all periods of panic. Such are the people of truth,
the God-fearing. (Al-Baqarah 2:177, Koran)

وَإِذَا قِيلَ لَهُمْ أَنفِقُوا۟ مِمَّا رَزَقَكُمُ ٱللَّهُ قَالَ ٱلَّذِينَ كَفَرُوا۟ لِلَّذِينَ ءَامَنُوٓا۟ أَنُطْعِمُ مَن لَّوْ يَشَآءُ ٱللَّهُ أَطْعَمَهُۥٓ إِنْ أَنتُمْ إِلَّا فِى ضَلَـٰلٍ مُّبِينٍ

And when they are told, "Spend you of (the bounties)
with which Allah has provided you," The Unbelievers say
to those who believe: "Shall we then feed those whom,
if Allah had so willed, He would have fed, Himself?
Ye are in nothing but manifest error. (Koran 36:47)

۞ إِنَّمَا ٱلصَّدَقَٰتُ لِلْفُقَرَآءِ وَٱلْمَسَٰكِينِ وَٱلْعَٰمِلِينَ عَلَيْهَا وَٱلْمُؤَلَّفَةِ قُلُوبُهُمْ وَفِى ٱلرِّقَابِ وَٱلْغَٰرِمِينَ وَفِى سَبِيلِ ٱللَّهِ وَٱبْنِ ٱلسَّبِيلِ ۖ

فَرِيضَةً مِّنَ ٱللَّهِ ۗ وَٱللَّهُ عَلِيمٌ حَكِيمٌ ﴿٦٠﴾

Alms are for the poor and the needy and those employed to administer the funds; for those whose hearts have been (recently) reconciled (to the truth); for those in bondage and in debt; in the cause of Allah; and for the wayfarer: (thus is it) ordained by Allah and Allah is full of knowledge and wisdom. (At-Tawbah 9:60, Koran).

In the above verses, the clear indication is that a human is given bounty by Allah. In return, his obligation is to distribute the surplus after his needs have been met to the needy. The Koran specifies that the zakat be distributed to the *fuqara* (the poor who ask), to *al-masakin* (the poor and the needy who do not ask), to zakat administrators, to those who spread the light of Islam to those inclined, for freedom of those in bondage, to those in debt, for the cause of Allah, and for the wayfarer who treads the path for Allah's service.

In the covenant, the believer surrenders to Allah his life and belongings in return for His guidance, a place in paradise in the hereafter, and peace with prosperity in this world. Every believer according to his or her covenant with Allah has the obligation to extend the benefits that He has provided him or her to those who did not receive the same. Such acts of generosity will be rewarded by Allah with a place in *Jannat* (place of peace and plenty) in the afterlife. Life of *Jannat* is to be attained in this world also, provided the compact with Allah is adhered to. The believer is Allah's instrument in fulfilling His promise to Adam that,

none will remain without food or clothes, and none
will suffer from heat or thirst. (Koran 20:118)

In the verses below, Allah has promised those who believe and obey His covenant that, as the reward for their acts of charity, He will double the harvest of their labors, forgive their sins, and provide them of His bounties; nor shall they have fear or grieve. Fear and grief arise from misfortunes, which cause anxiety and depression. Allah's promise, therefore, is to safeguard the believers from misfortunes. And to those devouring usury, Allah will deprive them of all blessings. Obeying of Allah's covenant provides *Jannat* in the hereafter and in this world. It also brings balance, harmony, and stability to the economic life of the world in that it meets the necessities of each person and eliminates unnecessary suffering.

يَٰٓأَيُّهَا ٱلَّذِينَ ءَامَنُوا۟ لَا تُبْطِلُوا۟ صَدَقَٰتِكُم بِٱلْمَنِّ وَٱلْأَذَىٰ كَٱلَّذِى يُنفِقُ مَالَهُۥ رِئَآءَ ٱلنَّاسِ وَلَا يُؤْمِنُ بِٱللَّهِ وَٱلْيَوْمِ ٱلْءَاخِرِ ۖ فَمَثَلُهُۥ كَمَثَلِ
صَفْوَانٍ عَلَيْهِ تُرَابٌ فَأَصَابَهُۥ وَابِلٌ فَتَرَكَهُۥ صَلْدًا ۖ لَّا يَقْدِرُونَ عَلَىٰ شَىْءٍ مِّمَّا كَسَبُوا۟ ۗ وَٱللَّهُ لَا يَهْدِى ٱلْقَوْمَ ٱلْكَٰفِرِينَ ﴿٢٦٤﴾ وَمَثَلُ ٱلَّذِينَ
يُنفِقُونَ أَمْوَٰلَهُمُ ٱبْتِغَآءَ مَرْضَاتِ ٱللَّهِ وَتَثْبِيتًا مِّنْ أَنفُسِهِمْ كَمَثَلِ جَنَّةٍۭ بِرَبْوَةٍ أَصَابَهَا وَابِلٌ فَـَٔاتَتْ أُكُلَهَا ضِعْفَيْنِ فَإِن لَّمْ يُصِبْهَا وَابِلٌ
فَطَلٌّ ۗ وَٱللَّهُ بِمَا تَعْمَلُونَ بَصِيرٌ ﴿٢٦٥﴾

O you who believe! Do no render in vain your charity
by reminders of your generosity or by injury, like him
who spends his wealth to be seen of men, but he does
not believe in Allah nor in the Last Day. His likeness is
the likeness of a smooth rock on which is a little soil;
on it falls heavy rain, which leaves it bare. They will not
be able to do anything with what they have earned.
And Allah does not guide the disbelieving people.

And the he likeness of those who spend their substance, seeking to please Allah and to strengthen their souls, is as a garden, high and fertile; heavy rain falls on it but makes it yield a double increase of harvest and if it receives not heavy rain, light moisture suffices it. And Allah is seer of what you do. (Al-Baqarah 2:264–65, Koran)

يَٰٓأَيُّهَا ٱلَّذِينَ ءَامَنُوٓاْ أَنفِقُواْ مِن طَيِّبَٰتِ مَا كَسَبْتُمْ وَمِمَّآ أَخْرَجْنَا لَكُم مِّنَ ٱلْأَرْضِ ۖ وَلَا تَيَمَّمُواْ ٱلْخَبِيثَ مِنْهُ تُنفِقُونَ وَلَسْتُم
بِـَٔاخِذِيهِ إِلَّآ أَن تُغْمِضُواْ فِيهِ ۚ وَٱعْلَمُوٓاْ أَنَّ ٱللَّهَ غَنِىٌّ حَمِيدٌ ﴿٢٦٧﴾ ٱلشَّيْطَٰنُ يَعِدُكُمُ ٱلْفَقْرَ وَيَأْمُرُكُم بِٱلْفَحْشَآءِ ۖ وَٱللَّهُ يَعِدُكُم مَّغْفِرَةً مِّنْهُ وَفَضْلًا
ۗ وَٱللَّهُ وَٰسِعٌ عَلِيمٌ ﴿٢٦٨﴾ يُؤْتِى ٱلْحِكْمَةَ مَن يَشَآءُ ۚ وَمَن يُؤْتَ ٱلْحِكْمَةَ فَقَدْ أُوتِىَ خَيْرًا كَثِيرًا ۗ وَمَا يَذَّكَّرُ إِلَّآ أُوْلُواْ ٱلْأَلْبَٰبِ ﴿٢٦٩﴾ وَمَآ
أَنفَقْتُم مِّن نَّفَقَةٍ أَوْ نَذَرْتُم مِّن نَّذْرٍ فَإِنَّ ٱللَّهَ يَعْلَمُهُۥ ۗ وَمَا لِلظَّٰلِمِينَ مِنْ أَنصَارٍ ﴿٢٧٠﴾

O ye who believe! Give of the good things that ye have (honorably) earned and of the fruits of the earth that We have produced for you and do not even aim at getting anything which is bad, in order that out of it ye may give away something, when ye yourselves would not receive it except with closed eyes. And know that Allah is free of all wants and worthy of all praise.

The Evil One threatens you with poverty and bids you to conduct unseemly. Allah promises you His forgiveness and bounties. And Allah cares for all and He knows all things.

He grants wisdom to whom He pleases; and he to whom wisdom is granted receives indeed a benefit overflowing; but none will grasp the Message but men of understanding.

And whatever ye spend in charity or devotion, be
sure Allah knows it all. But the wrongdoers have
no helpers. (Al-Baqarah 2:267–70, Koran)

ٱلَّذِينَ يُنفِقُونَ أَمْوَٰلَهُم بِٱلَّيْلِ وَٱلنَّهَارِ سِرًّا وَعَلَانِيَةً فَلَهُمْ أَجْرُهُمْ عِندَ رَبِّهِمْ وَلَا خَوْفٌ عَلَيْهِمْ وَلَا هُمْ يَحْزَنُونَ ﴿٢٧٤﴾

ٱلَّذِينَ يَأْكُلُونَ ٱلرِّبَوٰا۟ لَا يَقُومُونَ إِلَّا كَمَا يَقُومُ ٱلَّذِى يَتَخَبَّطُهُ ٱلشَّيْطَٰنُ مِنَ ٱلْمَسِّ ۚ ذَٰلِكَ بِأَنَّهُمْ قَالُوٓا۟ إِنَّمَا ٱلْبَيْعُ مِثْلُ ٱلرِّبَوٰا۟ ۗ وَأَحَلَّ ٱللَّهُ

ٱلْبَيْعَ وَحَرَّمَ ٱلرِّبَوٰا۟ ۚ فَمَن جَآءَهُۥ مَوْعِظَةٌ مِّن رَّبِّهِۦ فَٱنتَهَىٰ فَلَهُۥ مَا سَلَفَ وَأَمْرُهُۥٓ إِلَى ٱللَّهِ ۖ وَمَنْ عَادَ فَأُو۟لَٰٓئِكَ أَصْحَٰبُ ٱلنَّارِ ۖ هُمْ فِيهَا

خَٰلِدُونَ ﴿٢٧٥﴾ يَمْحَقُ ٱللَّهُ ٱلرِّبَوٰا۟ وَيُرْبِى ٱلصَّدَقَٰتِ ۗ وَٱللَّهُ لَا يُحِبُّ كُلَّ كَفَّارٍ أَثِيمٍ ﴿٢٧٦﴾

Those who (in charity) spend of their goods
by night and by day, in secret and in public,
have their reward with their Lord: on them
shall be no fear, nor shall they grieve.

Those who devour usury will not stand except
as stands one whom the Satan by his touch hath
driven to madness. That is because they say: "Trade
is like usury," but Allah hath permitted trade
and forbidden usury. Those who after receiving
direction from their Lord, desist, shall be pardoned
for the past; their case is for Allah (to judge); but
those who repeat (the offence) are Companions
of the Fire; they will abide therein (forever.)

Allah will deprive usury of all blessing but will give
increase for deeds of charity; for He loves not creatures
ungrateful and wicked. (Al-Baqarah 2:274–76, Koran)

Economic Principles of the Covenant of Allah

The covenant of Allah in the Koran has laid down principles and guidelines for the well-being of the economic life of the believers. Obeying the principles will bring peace, harmony, spiritual enlightenment, and economic prosperity. Disobeying means misery, ruin, and Allah's wrath.

First Principle: Land and sources of production are not the personal property of individuals. *Ardh* is the source of life and means of sustenance and production of food and resources and therefore must remain available to the community, the *ummah.*

Allah created *Ardh* and *sama* and has power over everything in and between them. To Allah belong the heaven and the earth and what is in between them. *Sama* in the Koran signifies the universe and *Ardh* man's domain on the earth pertaining to his social and economic world. Allah is the Lord of the heavens and the earth. The divine laws under which the universe functions so meticulously and smoothly should also apply to the economic life of man so that he might achieve a balanced, predictable, equitable, and just financial life. *Sama* is the source of Allah's benevolence to mankind and of His universal laws that govern the human subsistence and sustenance on the earth, controlling man's economic life. Allah's kingdom over the heavens and the earth sustains man's economic life and directly affects man's conduct and his obedience to Allah's covenant.

Ayahs in Sura An-Nahl are explicit. Allah created the heavens and the earth for just ends—to bring peace, harmony, equilibrium, and justice to the universe. He is Allah, the One, Lord of creation. He sends water from the heavens for the sustenance of life on the earth—humans, plants, and animals. Allah sends sunshine to the earth to provide warmth and light to sustain human, plant, and animal life. Allah created the moon and the stars to create equilibrium in the universe, with every object in its intended place revolving in its fixed orbit in perfect harmony and balance. Allah has the secrets and mysteries of the heavens and the earth, the so-called sciences, and the knowledge of particles, elements, cells, mitochondria, chromosomes, gravity, and black holes, only an infinitesimal portion of which he revealed to man.

In other *ayahs* of Sura An-Nahl, Allah clearly mentions all the comforts He has provided man for the sustenance of life and for his economic well-being. Allah created cattle for humans for warmth, food, and transport and horses, mules, and donkeys for riding and to show. With the moisture from the skies, He produces for man corn, olives, date palms, grapes, and every type of fruit. Allah made good things for humans in different colors and quantities so that man can celebrate and praise Allah in gratitude. Allah made the sea subject to humans so that they may eat fresh and tender seafood, obtain beautiful ornaments from the ocean, sail their ships, and plow the oceans around the world. From the cattle, Allah produces milk, pure and wholesome to drink; and from the fruit of the date palm and vine, you get food and drink. And from the bees, there is honey of varying colors that heals ailments.

Historically, land was there for man and the beasts to roam around freely and spread through the world. Later, tribes and communities laid claims on pieces of land they needed for their needs with some extra surrounding area for their security. At the beginning of the Islamic era, productive land and water resources were owned by tribes for the use of their clan members. After the message of the Koran was established, the clans, tribes, former kingdoms, and nations amalgamated to form the community of Islam, the *ummah,* which in principle owned the title to the land and resources with theoretical tenancy. The owner ship of land by the *ummah* began to change with the downfall of the Abbasid caliphate.

From 1040 to 1200, with the collapse of the central authority, there were many regional power struggles that allowed for the breakdown of the eastern Iranian frontiers against nomadic invasions. Central Asian nomads searching for pasturage in the tenth, eleventh, and the twelfth centuries spilled over into the region north of the Aral Sea and into Transoxania and Afghanistan. From contact with settled peoples, trade, and the activities of the missionaries, these Turkish peoples began to convert to Islam. Their chieftains became acquainted in the ways of agriculture, trade, city administration, and imperial conception of rule and order. Most of the useful land in the Islamic states was taken over by the Turkish chiefs and soldiers for their own use and for the advancement of their own political power.

The Seljuk decline opened the way for the third phase in the history of the region from 1150 to 1350. This was a period of further nomadic invasion from inner Asia, culminating in the devastating Mongol invasions and the establishment of Mongol regimes over most of the Middle East. With every change of the ruling class, the land and resources shifted from the peasantry to the tribal chiefs and the soldiery. To the west, the slave military forces in Egypt and Syria consolidated the Mamluk regime, with land being distributed among the new elite.

The final phase was the Timurid period, 1400–1500. The Mongol period was succeeded by new times of troubles and conquest by Timur, also known as Tamerlane. This era of repeated nomadic invasions brought demographic changes in the ethnic and religious identity of populations. A new Turkic-speaking population migrated into Transoxania, the Hindu Kush mountain range, Iran, the Caucasus, Anatolia, and Mesopotamia. Turkish settlement led to the Islamization of northeastern Iran, Armenia, and Anatolia both by settlement of newcomers and by the conversion of existing populations.

To consolidate their power, control of provinces was delegated to the family members and the nomadic chieftains. *Iqtas* lands were assigned to the military leaders. The result was usurpation of power at both the provincial and local levels, with the formation of micro- regimes funded by the resources of the land and heavy taxation of the peasants.

The Ottoman cavalry were recruited from among Turkish warriors. They were not garrisoned as a regular army, but they were provided with land grants and *timars* (Arabic equivalent of *iqtas*) throughout the empire. The timar holders provided local security and served in Ottoman campaigns. The *timar* system was based on an old-fashioned feudal pattern. The Ottomans also used the resources of the land to maintain their control over the empire and toward their new conquests. The timar holders exploited the peasants and the subject population.

The subject population belonged to a lesser order of existence. All commoners, Muslim and non-Muslim, were considered the *reava* (flocks) to be shorn in the interests of the political elite. The Ottomans operated on the principle that the subjects should serve the interests of the state; the economy was organized to ensure the flow of tax revenues, goods in kind, and the services needed by the government and the elites. The populace was systematically taxed by maintaining a record of the population, households, property, and livestock.

All the lands in the empire were owned by the ruler; some lands (*tapulu*) were on perpetual lease to the peasants who had the right to assign that right to their male descendants, and *mukatalu* lands were leased to a tax collector in return for a fixed payment for a lease. In the fifteenth century, the Ottomans had conceded to Turkish military rulers and Muslim religious rulers the ownership right to the land. In the course of the next century and a half, the sultans dispossessed the local notables and reassigned the tax rights to the *timar* holders appointed by the sultan. Ottoman policies were inimical to accumulation of private property. Large private fortunes were regularly confiscated by the state. The Ottoman economic policy on taxation and trade was based on fiscalism that was aimed at accumulation of as much bullion as possible in the state treasury, which was primarily used for the expenditure of running the Topkapi court and the ongoing wars in the West.

The ownership of land in the Islamic world is not owned or distributed according to the covenant of the Koran, causing the present unequal distribution of wealth, poverty, deprivation, and degradation of a large part of the Islamic society. Land, therefore, belongs to Allah, who bestowed it to man and woman, His regents on the earth. The covenant expects man to take care of the land for all of Allah's creatures—men and beasts—as well as conserve its resources for future generations. Whatever is left over after his own needs are met goes to the necessities of the rest of humanity, starting with his *qurba* (near and dear) and then his community, followed by the surrounding communities. The land does not belong to the states, governments, tribal chiefs, military, aristocracy, timars, or *iqt'at.* Land cannot be owned by individuals or families nor inherited.

Men and women live in small communities. These form a fellowship and a brotherhood that looks after its own who are in need, and such a need may be of sustenance, clothing, shelter, knowledge, well-being, spirituality, understanding, protection, justice, or simple reassurance. And such assistance is extended to the surrounding communities till it reaches the far-flung communities of the *ummah.* Each basic community owns the land in its surrounds, tilled and administered by the community as a whole for its well-being in justice and harmony according to the covenant of Allah. The Islamic economic system is based on capitalism in the production of wealth and communism in its expenditure, with the difference being that individuals are free and able to make wealth but are responsible for the needs of kith and kin and their neighbor. The state has little role in the welfare system. The land owned by the community may be assigned to individuals or may be tilled communally for the mutual benefit of the whole community, producing food and paying for schools, hospitals, roadways, municipal services, and so. on. The community is meant to be self-sufficient economically and responsible for each and every individual's welfare, health, schooling, and old-age pensions.

Second principle: All surplus money and resources should not remain with individuals. How much is enough for one's needs? A hundred? A thousand? A hundred thousand? A million? A billion? How much is enough? After accumulation of a certain amount of money, any further hoarding becomes an act of obscenity and evil. All surplus money and resources shall be used for the benefit and uplift of the community and humanity.

۞ وَيَسْـَٔلُونَكَ مَاذَا يُنفِقُونَ قُلِ ٱلْعَفْوَ ۗ كَذَٰلِكَ يُبَيِّنُ ٱللَّهُ لَكُمُ ٱلْـَٔايَٰتِ لَعَلَّكُمْ تَتَفَكَّرُونَ

They ask thee how much they are to spend (in charity); say: "What is beyond your needs". Thus, doth Allah make clear to you His Signs: in order that ye may consider. (Al-Baqarah 2:222, Koran)

Third Principle: Wealth and commodities should not be hoarded. Surplus wealth is to be spent for the needs of the community as prescribed by Allah.

۞ يَٰٓأَيُّهَا ٱلَّذِينَ ءَامَنُوٓا۟ إِنَّ كَثِيرًا مِّنَ ٱلْأَحْبَارِ وَٱلرُّهْبَانِ لَيَأْكُلُونَ أَمْوَٰلَ ٱلنَّاسِ بِٱلْبَٰطِلِ وَيَصُدُّونَ عَن سَبِيلِ ٱللَّهِ ۗ

وَٱلَّذِينَ يَكْنِزُونَ ٱلذَّهَبَ وَٱلْفِضَّةَ وَلَا يُنفِقُونَهَا فِى سَبِيلِ ٱللَّهِ فَبَشِّرْهُم بِعَذَابٍ أَلِيمٍ ﴿٣٤﴾

O you who believe! There are indeed many among the priests and anchorites, who in falsehood devour the substance of men and hinder (them) from the Way of Allah. And there are those who bury gold and silver and

spend it not in the Way of Allah: announce unto them
a most grievous penalty. (At-Tawbah 9:34, Koran).

Fourth Principle: Wealth shall be spread throughout the community, the *ummah*, and shall not be impounded, stolen, and looted by conquerors, tribes, rulers, classes, and the *Mutaffifeen* (dealers in fraud) as practiced in un-Koranic societies, Muslim and Non-Muslim.

مَّآ أَفَآءَ ٱللَّهُ عَلَىٰ رَسُولِهِۦ مِنْ أَهْلِ ٱلْقُرَىٰ فَلِلَّهِ وَلِلرَّسُولِ وَلِذِى ٱلْقُرْبَىٰ وَٱلْيَتَـٰمَىٰ وَٱلْمَسَـٰكِينِ وَٱبْنِ ٱلسَّبِيلِ كَىْ لَا

يَكُونَ دُولَةًۢ بَيْنَ ٱلْأَغْنِيَآءِ مِنكُمْ ۚ وَمَآ ءَاتَىٰكُمُ ٱلرَّسُولُ فَخُذُوهُ وَمَا نَهَىٰكُمْ عَنْهُ فَٱنتَهُوا۟ ۚ وَٱتَّقُوا۟ ٱللَّهَ ۖ إِنَّ ٱللَّهَ شَدِيدُ ٱلْعِقَابِ

٧

What Allah has bestowed on His Rasool from
the people of the townships, belongs to Allah, to
His Rasool and to the near of kin and orphans,
the poor and the homeless, in order that it
may not (merely) make a circuit between the
wealthy among you. So, take what the Rasool
assigns to you and deny yourselves that which he
withholds from you. And fear Allah, for Allah is
strict in Punishment. (Al-Hashr 59:7, Koran)

Fifth Principle: No one shall subsist on the earnings of another, and except for those who are incapacitated, everyone shall work. Everyone—man and woman—shall also contribute their labor and sweat toward community well-being.

The Koran calls the people who stint *Mutaffifeen*, those who get the full measure from others but stint when measuring for others. They lead an easy life from the earnings of others. The Koran mentions three such groups. One group consists of people who "take with an even balance and give less than what is due."

وَيْلٌ لِّلْمُطَفِّفِينَ ﴿١﴾ ٱلَّذِينَ إِذَا ٱكْتَالُوا۟ عَلَى ٱلنَّاسِ يَسْتَوْفُونَ ﴿٢﴾ وَإِذَا كَالُوهُمْ أَو وَّزَنُوهُمْ يُخْسِرُونَ ﴿٣﴾ أَلَا يَظُنُّ أُو۟لَٰٓئِكَ أَنَّهُم مَّبْعُوثُونَ
﴿٤﴾ لِيَوْمٍ عَظِيمٍ ﴿٥﴾ يَوْمَ يَقُومُ ٱلنَّاسُ لِرَبِّ ٱلْعَٰلَمِينَ ﴿٦﴾

Woe to those that deal in fraud, those
who, from others exact full measure,

But when measuring or weighing for
others, give less than due.

Do they not think that they will be called
to account, on a Mighty Day,

A Day when (all) mankind will stand before the
Lord of the Worlds? (Mutaffifeen 83:1–6, Koran)

Another group comprises those who inherit money, land, and property, and they use that wealth to accumulate more and more without ever giving back to the needy. The third group gobbles up the earnings of others:

۞ يَٰٓأَيُّهَا ٱلَّذِينَ ءَامَنُوٓا۟ إِنَّ كَثِيرًا مِّنَ ٱلْأَحْبَارِ وَٱلرُّهْبَانِ لَيَأْكُلُونَ أَمْوَٰلَ ٱلنَّاسِ بِٱلْبَٰطِلِ وَيَصُدُّونَ عَن سَبِيلِ ٱللَّهِ ۗ وَٱلَّذِينَ
يَكْنِزُونَ ٱلذَّهَبَ وَٱلْفِضَّةَ وَلَا يُنفِقُونَهَا فِى سَبِيلِ ٱللَّهِ فَبَشِّرْهُم بِعَذَابٍ أَلِيمٍ ﴿٣٤﴾

O ye who believe! There are indeed many among
the priests and clerics, who in falsehood devour the
substance of men and hinder (them) from the Way of
Allah. And there are those who bury gold and silver

and spend it not in the Way of Allah: announce unto them a most grievous penalty. (Qur'an 9:34 Al A'raf).

Squander not your wealth among yourselves in egotism and conceit: Let there be trade and traffic amongst you with mutual goodwill nor kill or destroy yourselves: for verily Allah hath been Most Merciful to you. If any do that in rancor and injustice, soon shall We cast them into the fire: and easy it is for Allah. If you abstain from all the odious and the forbidden, Allah shall expel out of you all evil in you and admit you to a Gate of great honor.

And crave not those things of what Allah has bestowed His gifts more freely on some than others, men are assigned what they earn and women that they earn. But ask Allah of His bounty. Surely Allah is knower of everything

O you who believe! Let not your riches or your children divert you from the remembrance of Allah. If any act thus, the loss is their own. And spend something (in charity) out of the substance which We have bestowed on you, before Death should come to any of you and he should say, "O my Lord! Why didst Thou not give me respite for a little while? I should then have given (largely) in charity and I should have been one of the doers of good." (Al-Munafiqun 63:9–11, Koran)

25. The Covenant of Allah: Justice and Truth

Stand firmly for Allah as a witness of fair dealing. Let not the malice of people lead you to iniquity. Be just, that is next to worship. Be with taqwa of Allah, fear Allah.

O you who believe! Fear Allah and speak always the truth that He may direct you to righteous deeds and forgive you your sins: he that obeys Allah and His Rasool have already attained the highest achievement. (Al-Ahzab 33:69-73,Koran)

Stand firm for justice as witness to Allah be it against yourself, your parents, or your family, whether it is against rich or poor, both are nearer to Allah than they are to you. Follow not your caprice lest you distort your testimony. If you prevaricate and evade justice Allah is well aware what you do. (An-Nisa 4:135, Koran)

O you who believe! Stand firmly for Allah as a witness of fair dealing. Let not the malice of people lead you to iniquity. Be just, that is next to worship. Be with taqwa of Allah, fear Allah. Allah is well aware with what you do. (Al-Ma'idah 5:8, Koran)

Betray not the trust of Allah and His Messenger. Nor knowingly misappropriate things entrusted to you. (Al-Anfal 8:27, Koran)

If you have taqwa of Allah and fear Allah, He will grant you a Criterion to judge between right and wrong and remove from you all misfortunes and evil and forgive your sins. Allah is the bestower of grace in abundance. (Al-Anfal 8:29, Koran)

Be in taqwa of Allah, fear Allah and be with those who are true in word and deed. (At-Tawbah 9:119, Koran)

Deal not unjustly and ye shall not be dealt with unjustly. (Al-Baqarah 2:277–80, Koran)

Whenever you give your word speak honestly even if a near relative is concerned.

And come not near the orphan's property, except to improve it, until he attains the age of full strength,

And give full measure and full weight with justice. No burden We place on any soul but that which it can bear. (Al-An'am 6:151–52, Koran)

If an impostor (fasiq) comes to you with any news, ascertain the truth, lest you harm people unsuspectingly and afterwards become full of remorse for what you have done. And know that amongst you is Allah's Messenger: were he in many matters to follow your desires, you would certainly fall into misfortune: but Allah has bestowed on you the love of iman (faith) and has made it beautiful in your hearts and he has made abhorrent to you disbelief, wickedness and disobedience to Allah: such indeed are those who are righteous (rashidun). (Al-Hujurat 49:6–10, Koran)

Justice (*'adl*) is a divine attribute defined as "putting in the right place." The opposite of *'adl* is *zulm*, which in Koranic terms means "wrongdoing." Wrongdoing is a human attribute defined as "putting things in the wrong place." *Zulm* is one of the common terms used in the Koran to refer to the negative acts employed by human beings. Wrongdoing is the opposite of justice. Of the 250 verses where the Koran mentions *zulm* (wrongdoing) or *zalimun* (wrongdoers), it mentions the object of wrongdoing in only twenty-five verses. In one verse, the object of wrongdoing are people:

﴿ إِنَّمَا ٱلسَّبِيلُ عَلَى ٱلَّذِينَ يَظْلِمُونَ ٱلنَّاسَ وَيَبْغُونَ فِى ٱلْأَرْضِ بِغَيْرِ ٱلْحَقِّ ۚ أُو۟لَٰٓئِكَ لَهُمْ عَذَابٌ أَلِيمٌ ﴿٤٢﴾ ﴾

The blame is only against those who oppress
men with wrongdoing and insolently transgress
beyond bounds through the land defying right
and justice: for such there will be a Penalty
grievous. (Ash-Shura 42:42, Koran)

In another verse, the object of wrongdoing and injustice is the signs of Allah:

﴿ وَٱلْوَزْنُ يَوْمَئِذٍ ٱلْحَقُّ ۚ فَمَن ثَقُلَتْ مَوَٰزِينُهُۥ فَأُو۟لَٰٓئِكَ هُمُ ٱلْمُفْلِحُونَ ﴿٨﴾ وَمَنْ خَفَّتْ مَوَٰزِينُهُۥ فَأُو۟لَٰٓئِكَ ٱلَّذِينَ خَسِرُوٓا۟ أَنفُسَهُم بِمَا

كَانُوا۟ بِـَٔايَٰتِنَا يَظْلِمُونَ ﴿٩﴾ ﴾

The weighing that day will be true. He whose
scales are heavy, are the prosperous. Those whose
scale are light they have lost themselves for
wronging Our Signs. (Al-A'raf 7:8–9, Koran)

Allah reveals His signs in nature and in scriptures so that the people may be guided. By disobeying these signs, they wrong only themselves.

In the remaining twenty-three verses in which the object of wrongdoing is mentioned, the wrongdoers are said to only wrong themselves.

﴿ وَظَلَّلْنَا عَلَيْكُمُ ٱلْغَمَامَ وَأَنزَلْنَا عَلَيْكُمُ ٱلْمَنَّ وَٱلسَّلْوَىٰ ۖ كُلُوا۟ مِن طَيِّبَٰتِ مَا رَزَقْنَٰكُمْ ۖ وَمَا ظَلَمُونَا وَلَٰكِن كَانُوٓا۟ أَنفُسَهُمْ يَظْلِمُونَ ﴿٥٧﴾ ﴾

And We gave you the shade of clouds and sent down
to you Manna and quails, saying: "Eat of the good
things We have provided for you:" (but they rebelled);
to Us they did no harm, but they wronged their own
souls. (Al-Baqarah 2:57, Al-A'raf 7:160, Koran)

﴿ إِنَّ ٱللَّهَ لَا يَظْلِمُ ٱلنَّاسَ شَيْـًٔا وَلَٰكِنَّ ٱلنَّاسَ أَنفُسَهُمْ يَظْلِمُونَ ﴿٤٤﴾ ﴾

Verily Allah will not deal unjustly with humans
in anything: it is the human who wrongs
his own soul. (Yunus 10:44, Koran)

﴿ وَمَا ظَلَمْنَٰهُمْ وَلَٰكِن ظَلَمُوٓا۟ أَنفُسَهُمْ ۖ

And We wronged them not, but they
wronged themselves. (Hud 11:101, Koran)

﴿ وَمَن يَعْمَلْ سُوٓءًا أَوْ يَظْلِمْ نَفْسَهُۥ ثُمَّ يَسْتَغْفِرِ ٱللَّهَ يَجِدِ ٱللَّهَ غَفُورًا رَّحِيمًا ﴿١١٠﴾ ﴾

If anyone does evil or wrongs his own soul but
afterwards seeks Allah's forgiveness, he will find Allah
Oft-Forgiving, Most Merciful. (An-Nisa 4:110, Koran)

The Koran admonishes:

Deal not unjustly and you shall not be dealt with unjustly. (Al-Baqarah 2:278, Koran)

26. The Covenant of Allah: Knowledge

O you who believe! Allah will exalt in rank those of you who believe and who have been granted Knowledge. Proclaim! And thy Lord is Most Bountiful, He Who taught (the use of) the Pen, Taught man that which he knew not. O my Lord! Enrich me in knowledge.

When ye are told to make room in the assemblies, spread out and make room: ample room will Allah provide for you. And when ye are told to rise up, for prayers, Jihad or other good deeds rise up: Allah will exalt in rank those of you who believe and who have been granted Knowledge. And Allah is well acquainted with all you do. (Al-Mujadila 58:11, Koran)

﴿ ٱقْرَأْ بِٱسْمِ رَبِّكَ ٱلَّذِى خَلَقَ ﴿١﴾ خَلَقَ ٱلْإِنسَـٰنَ مِنْ عَلَقٍ ﴿٢﴾ ٱقْرَأْ وَرَبُّكَ ٱلْأَكْرَمُ ﴿٣﴾ ٱلَّذِى عَلَّمَ بِٱلْقَلَمِ ﴿٤﴾ عَلَّمَ ٱلْإِنسَـٰنَ مَا لَمْ يَعْلَمْ ﴿٥﴾

﴿ Proclaim! In the name of thy Lord and Cherisher, Who created, Created man, out of a (mere) clot of congealed blood: Proclaim! And thy Lord is Most Bountiful, He Who taught (the use of) the Pen, Taught man that which he knew not. (Iqra 96:1–5, Koran)

﴿ وَٱلَّذِى جَآءَ بِٱلصِّدْقِ وَصَدَّقَ بِهِۦٓ ۙ أُو۟لَـٰٓئِكَ هُمُ ٱلْمُتَّقُونَ ﴿٣٣﴾ ﴾

And he who brings the Truth and believes therein, such are the men who do right. (Az-Zumar 39:33, Koran)

﴿ فَتَعَٰلَى ٱللَّهُ ٱلْمَلِكُ ٱلْحَقُّ ۗ وَلَا تَعْجَلْ بِٱلْقُرْءَانِ مِن قَبْلِ أَن يُقْضَىٰٓ إِلَيْكَ وَحْيُهُۥ ۖ وَقُل رَّبِّ زِدْنِى عِلْمًا

High above all is Allah, the King and the Truth! Be not in haste with the Qur'an before its revelation to thee is completed, but say, "O my Lord! Enrich me in knowledge." (Taha 20:114, Koran)

﴿ أَمَّنْ هُوَ قَٰنِتٌ ءَانَآءَ ٱلَّيْلِ سَاجِدًا وَقَآئِمًا يَحْذَرُ ٱلْءَاخِرَةَ وَيَرْجُوا۟ رَحْمَةَ رَبِّهِۦ ۗ قُلْ هَلْ يَسْتَوِى ٱلَّذِينَ يَعْلَمُونَ وَٱلَّذِينَ

لَا يَعْلَمُونَ ۗ إِنَّمَا يَتَذَكَّرُ أُو۟لُوا۟ ٱلْأَلْبَٰبِ ﴿٩﴾ ﴾

Is one who worships devoutly during the hours of the night prostrating himself or standing (in adoration), who takes heed of the Hereafter and who places his hope in the Mercy of his Lord, (like one who does not)? Say: "Are those equal, those who know and those who do not know? It is those who are endued with understanding that receive admonition. (Az-Zumar 39:9, Koran)

Knowledge of God: Humans have always looked at God on two levels in two ways:

Emotionally: It is a personal and humanized god that is tribal. This god has favorite children whom he protects and rewards over and above others. He is readily accessible in a temple, shrine, mausoleum, or mosque and has priests in attendance as intermediaries. The priest class formulates dogma, creed, and rituals to appease the god. This god is unpredictable, loving, or demanding, subject to anger and joy in accord with the deeds and sacrifices of his devotees. He has a specially trained class of helpers who acts as cheerleaders and who perform crowd control for him. These helpers include the popes, bishops, priests, ayatollahs, rabbis, imams, ulema, pundits, and various classes of religious police. Proximity to their god provides this class's power over other men and women. This source of power naturally leads to competition and often wars between the devotees. Wars fought in the name of this god leads to injustice and usurpation of the rights of others.

The priest class, scholars, and writers introduced and interjected ideas that made their god dependent on creed and dogma invented by them. Writers of the Old and New Testaments fashioned Yahweh and Jesus according to their own caprice. Muslim scholars produced Hadith and interpreted Sharia that made Allah and Muhammad subject to their own fancy. Such collective manipulations at first divided humans and then splintered communities into factions. Marriages of Henry VII fragmented the Christian Europe, and non -succession of Imam Ali split the Muslim world. These mechanizations of men interrupted the message of the God of Abraham that Moses, Jesus, and Muhammad had come to teach. In the fundamental emotional nature of humans, there is an essence of paganism under the surface that wells over in times of stress, grief, and failing belief. The signs of disbelief, mistrust, and *shirk* lie in faith in astrology, horoscope, saint worship, and amulets and in the worship of gods of wealth, power, and politics.

Intellectually: Humans wholeheartedly accept the concept of God as the Creator of everything that is. He wills, and it is. He is beyond human comprehension, and His divine systems do not conform to the human concepts, creed, and dogma. Allah, God the Creator, created the galaxies, worlds, stars, sun, moon, little atoms, protons, neutrons, and tiny particles that show the complexity of His genius, and the Lord of creation sends water from the heavens and directs sunshine to the earth to provide warmth and light to sustain human, plant, and animal life. Allah formed the sun, moon, and stars to create equilibrium in the universe, every object in its intended place revolving in its fixed orbit in perfect harmony and balance. Allah created the secrets and mysteries of the heavens and the earth, the so-called sciences, and the knowledge of particles, elements, cells, mitochondria, chromosomes, gravity, and black holes, only a minute portion of which he revealed to man. Allah clearly provided humans a mind to wonder at His infinitesimal wisdom.

Yet man is conceited and arrogant enough to believe that God is driven by man-created creed, testament, dogma, Sunna, and Sharia. Allah does not require a shrine, a temple, a tent, or a talisman to live in. His presence is everywhere. He is present in the smallest particle (*nuqta*) and in the greatest expanse. He is accessible to each and every object He has created. Every object obeys Allah's will except for the human.

The human has been given free will. The covenant of the Koran presents us with the scope of man's freedom of choice in doing what is wholesome and beautiful or what is corrupt or ugly. It reminds us of how the scales of Allah's justice, the two hands of Allah—His mercy and His wrath—are reflected in the human domain, where people have been appointed His vicegerents. Deeds of goodness and wholesomeness are associated with mercy, paradise, and the beautiful. Evil and corruption is rewarded with wrath, hell, and the ugly.

Allah the Divine is open to the most miniscule of beings. From this little particle (*nuqta*), the connection to Allah, the Cherisher and the Nourisher of the universe, extends into the vastest of expanse. Within this communion of the divine with the creation passes the Spirit of Allah into His creatures. The human lays his heart and mind open to Allah in submission to receive Allah's Spirit and guidance. In the space and the emptiness of the universe, there flow currents and whispers of wind and energy. These winds of silence, light, and sound carry the divine whisper, and in this sound is Allah's message. This message descends into the believer's receptive heart in peace, silence, and tranquility. When the angels and the Spirit descend with Allah's guidance, the eyes perceive the most beautiful divine light, the ears hear the softest tinkle of the bell, the nose smells the fragrance of a thousand gardens, and the skin feels the most tranquil of the gentle breeze. When this happens, the soul has seen nirvana. This is the knowledge of Allah.

Allah sent thousands of prophets to mankind to teach the humanity precepts and principles to His straight path of unity, truth, and goodness. Over thousands of years, these precepts and principles spread around the world through civilizations till the mankind as a whole began to comprehend the message of one universal God, the Creator of every particle and every being in the whole universe. The human listened and occasionally regressed into his inherent paganism, greed, selfishness, and egotism. Allah bestowed on the human a vicegerency on the earth, a mind, free will, and a covenant. Allah then announced that there would be no more prophets; the era of prophecy had ended. The human, in stages, had received the knowledge required to live in submission to Allah's will in peace and harmony on the earth in accordance with the divine laws, which were sent down as guidance to every community for a life of truth, justice, goodness, and peace. Such knowledge consisted of the following:

- Unity: There is one absolute Being from which all stems. The galaxies and all the living things in the universe are all connected to one another and cannot be separated from that absolute Being. Everything alive—humans, animals, plants, and microorganisms—are created by the absolute Being, all nurtured with the same organic matter, all breathing the same air. And in turn, their physical self disintegrates into the same elements that then return to the earth and the universe. In this cycle of creation and disintegration, the only one permanent is the Real, the Absolute. All else is an illusion and a mirage. One moment you are here, and in the next, you are gone. Nothing is left behind—no riches, no honor, no ego, and no pride. What is left, however, is an account of your deeds, upon which one day you will be judged.

- Mind: The human is bestowed with a mind and free will. The mind has the ability to perceive ideas and knowledge from the divine and from the signs of Allah. The whisper of the divine, the rustle of the wind, the light of God, the fragrance of God's creation, and the sensation of the divine touch all inspire the human mind with the endless stream of ideas and knowledge. Man has been granted the ability to process his thoughts and gain knowledge with free will.

The verse of the light encompasses the totality of the message and guidance that God sent to man through His prophets. The pagan in the human confused God's message and began to worship the messenger. With the end of the era of the prophets, man has to open his heart to the light of Allah and learn to recognize the goodness of God within himself, in his own heart.

۞ ٱللَّهُ نُورُ ٱلسَّمَٰوَٰتِ وَٱلْأَرْضِ ۚ مَثَلُ نُورِهِۦ كَمِشْكَوٰةٍ فِيهَا مِصْبَاحٌ ۖ ٱلْمِصْبَاحُ فِى زُجَاجَةٍ ۖ ٱلزُّجَاجَةُ كَأَنَّهَا كَوْكَبٌ دُرِّىٌّ يُوقَدُ مِن
شَجَرَةٍ مُّبَٰرَكَةٍ زَيْتُونَةٍ لَّا شَرْقِيَّةٍ وَلَا غَرْبِيَّةٍ يَكَادُ زَيْتُهَا يُضِىٓءُ وَلَوْ لَمْ تَمْسَسْهُ نَارٌ ۚ نُّورٌ عَلَىٰ نُورٍ ۗ يَهْدِى ٱللَّهُ لِنُورِهِۦ مَن يَشَآءُ ۚ وَيَضْرِبُ ٱللَّهُ
ٱلْأَمْثَٰلَ لِلنَّاسِ ۗ وَٱللَّهُ بِكُلِّ شَىْءٍ عَلِيمٌ ﴿٣٥﴾ فِى بُيُوتٍ أَذِنَ ٱللَّهُ أَن تُرْفَعَ وَيُذْكَرَ فِيهَا ٱسْمُهُۥ يُسَبِّحُ لَهُۥ فِيهَا بِٱلْغُدُوِّ وَٱلْءَاصَالِ

Allah is the Light of the heavens and the earth. The parable of His Light is as if there were a Niche and within it a Lamp: the Lamp enclosed in Glass; the glass as it were a brilliant star: lit from a blessed Tree, an

> Olive, neither of the East nor of the West, whose Oil is well-nigh luminous, though fire scarce touched it: Light upon Light! Allah doth guide whom He will to His Light: Allah doth set forth Parables for men: and Allah doth know all things. (Lit is such a light) in houses, which Allah hath permitted to be raised to honor; for the celebration, in them, of His name: in them is He glorified in the mornings and in the evenings, (again and again). (An-Nur 24:35–36, Koran)

For mankind, the parable of the divine light is fundamental in the belief in one universal God. Allah is the light of heavens and the earth. Allah's love, mercy, and grace nurture His creation. The divine light illuminates the depths of the hearts of those who bow down in submission to, love for, and trust in Allah. Aglow is the lamp in their heart with the divine light that shines with the brightness of a star—a star lit from the light of divine wisdom, the tree of knowledge, the knowledge of Allah's signs. For those who believe, Allah is within. The believer is aglow with Allah's radiance—light upon light. The dwellings where Allah's name is praised and glorified in the mornings and evenings are luminous with Allah's light.

The fundamental knowledge is the "knowledge of certainty" (*ilm al-yaqin*, Koran 102:5). This type of certitude refers to knowledge that results from the human capacity for logic and reasoning and the appraisal of what the Koran calls "clear evidence" (*bayyinat*) of Allah's presence in the world. This knowledge also comes through the study of Koran, the teachings of the prophets, and the signs of Allah. The signs of Allah encompass the whole knowledge of the creation; man's scientific and philosophical disciplines include only a miniscule fragment of this knowledge. The knowledge of certainty is rational and discursive, a point that the Koran acknowledges when it admonishes human beings to

﴿ قُلْ سِيرُوا۟ فِى ٱلْأَرْضِ فَٱنظُرُوا۟ كَيْفَ بَدَأَ ٱلْخَلْقَ ۚ ثُمَّ ٱللَّهُ يُنشِئُ ٱلنَّشْأَةَ ٱلْـَٔاخِرَةَ ۚ إِنَّ ٱللَّهَ عَلَىٰ كُلِّ شَىْءٍ قَدِيرٌ ﴾

Say: "Travel through the earth and see how Allah did originate creation; so will Allah produce a later creation: for Allah has power over all things. (Al-'Ankabut 29:20, Koran)

﴿ وَهُوَ ٱلَّذِى يُحْىِۦ وَيُمِيتُ وَلَهُ ٱخْتِلَٰفُ ٱلَّيْلِ وَٱلنَّهَارِ ۚ أَفَلَا تَعْقِلُونَ ﴿٨٠﴾ ﴾

It is He Who gives life and death and to Him (is due) the alternation of Night and Day: will ye not then understand? (Al Mu'minun 23:80, Koran)

Over time and under the influence of contemplation and spiritual practice, the knowledge of certitude may be transformed into a higher form of knowledge of Allah, which the Koran calls the "eye of certitude" (*ain al-yaqin*, Koran 102:7). This term refers to the knowledge that is acquired by spiritual intelligence that believers in the East locate metaphorically in the heart. Before attaining this type of knowledge, the heart of the believer must first be "opened to Islam."

﴿ أَفَمَن شَرَحَ ٱللَّهُ صَدْرَهُۥ لِلْإِسْلَٰمِ فَهُوَ عَلَىٰ نُورٍ مِّن رَّبِّهِۦ ۚ فَوَيْلٌ لِّلْقَٰسِيَةِ قُلُوبُهُم مِّن ذِكْرِ ٱللَّهِ ۚ أُو۟لَٰٓئِكَ فِى ضَلَٰلٍ مُّبِينٍ ﴿٢٢﴾

Is one whose heart Allah has opened to Islam, so that he has received enlightenment from Allah. Woe to those whose hearts are hardened against celebrating the praises of Allah! They are manifestly wandering (in error)! (Az-Zumar 39:22, Koran)

Once opened, the heart receives knowledge as a type of divine light or illumination (*nur*) leads the believer toward the remembrance of Allah. Just as with the knowledge of certainty, with the eye of certainty, the believer sees Allah's existence through His presence in this world. With the eye of certainty, what lead the believer to the knowledge of Allah are not the arguments to be understood by the rational intellect but by theophanic appearances (*bayyinat*) that strip away the veil of worldly phenomenon to reveal the divine reality underneath.

From the spiritual perspective, the one who perceives reality through the knowledge of Allah is a true "intellectual." Unlike the scholar, who develops his or her skills through years of formal study, the spiritual intellectual does not need book learning to understand the divine light. A spiritual intellectual can be anyone, scholarly or otherwise, whose knowledge extends both outward to take in the physical world and upward to realize his or her ultimate transcendence of the world through his or her link with the absolute. Without such a vertical dimension of spirit, the scholar's knowledge, whatever its extent may be in academic terms, is of little worth.

The third and most advanced type of knowledge builds on transcendent nature of knowledge itself. The highest level of consciousness is called the "truth of certitude" (*haqq al-yaqin*).

﴿ وَإِنَّهُۥ لَحَسْرَةٌ عَلَى ٱلْكَٰفِرِينَ ﴿٥٠﴾ وَإِنَّهُۥ لَحَقُّ ٱلْيَقِينِ ﴿٥١﴾ فَسَبِّحْ بِٱسْمِ رَبِّكَ ٱلْعَظِيمِ ﴿٥٢﴾

But truly (Revelation) is a cause of sorrow for the Unbelievers. But verily it is Truth of assured

certainty. So, glorify the name of thy Lord
Most High. (Al-Haqqah 69:50–52, Koran)

It is also known as *ilm ladduni* (knowledge "by presence"). This form of knowledge partakes directly of the divine reality and leaps off directly across the synapses of human mind to transcend both cognitive reasoning and intellectual vision at the same time. The "truth of certainty" refers to a state of consciousness in which a person knows the Real through direct participation in it without resorting to logical proofs. This type of knowledge characterizes God's prophets and messengers, whose consciousness of the truth is both immediate and participatory as what it is based on comes from direct inspiration.

According to both the word of Allah as expressed in the Koran and the tradition of the blessed *Nabi* Muhammad, faith in Islam has as much to do with theoretical and empirical knowledge as it does with simple belief. This multidimensional conception of knowledge comprehends a reality that lies hidden within the unique world yet can be revealed by the human mind and the vision of the spiritual intellect through the signs of Allah that are present in the world itself. In the Koran, Allah calls humanity:

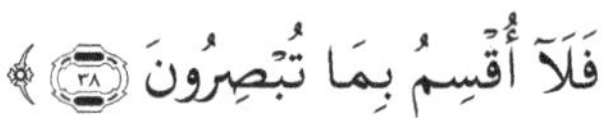

So, I do call to witness what you see.

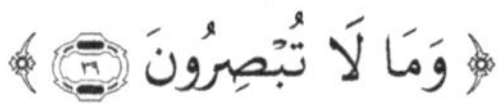

And what you see not,

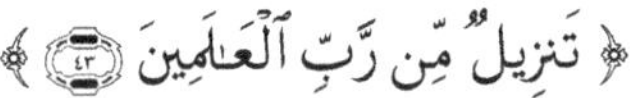

(This is) a Message sent down from
the Lord of the Worlds.

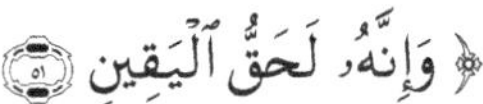

But verily it is Truth of assured certainty.
(Al-Haqqah 69:38–39, 43, 51)

أَلْهَىٰكُمُ ٱلتَّكَاثُرُ ﴿١﴾ حَتَّىٰ زُرْتُمُ ٱلْمَقَابِرَ ﴿٢﴾ كَلَّا سَوْفَ تَعْلَمُونَ ﴿٣﴾ ثُمَّ كَلَّا سَوْفَ تَعْلَمُونَ ﴿٤﴾ كَلَّا لَوْ تَعْلَمُونَ عِلْمَ ٱلْيَقِينِ
﴿٥﴾ لَتَرَوُنَّ ٱلْجَحِيمَ ﴿٦﴾ ثُمَّ لَتَرَوُنَّهَا عَيْنَ ٱلْيَقِينِ ﴿٧﴾ ثُمَّ لَتُسْـَٔلُنَّ يَوْمَئِذٍ عَنِ ٱلنَّعِيمِ ﴿٨﴾

The lure of abundance beguiles you, Until you reach the graves. But in the end, you will know. Soon you shall know! Nay were you to know with the knowledge of certainty. That you shall surely see the flaming fire. You shall see it with the eye of certainty. Then, you will be questioned on that Day about the pleasures you indulged in. (At-Takathur 102:1–8)

27. The Covenant of Allah: Inviting to All That Is Good and Right and Forbidding What Is Wrong

Let there arise out of you a band of people inviting to all that is good, enjoining what is right and forbidding what is wrong: they are the ones to attain happiness. (Ali 'Imran 3:103–5, Koran)

The Koranic principle of enjoining what is good and forbidding what is evil is supportive of the moral autonomy of the person, man and woman. This principle authorizes a person to act according to his or her best judgment in situations in which his or her intervention will advance a good purpose. The following saying of the blessed *Nabi* also supports individual action by a believer:

> If any one of you sees an evil, let him change it by his hand and if he is unable to do that, let him change by his words and if he is still unable to do that let him denounce it in his heart, but this is the weakest form of belief.

This principle assigns to the individual an active role in the community in which he or she lives. *The Koran annunciated the principle of free speech fourteen hundred years ago.* Believing men and women are reminded that they are the best of people, a witness over other nations. Such a responsibility carries with it a moral burden of an exemplary conduct of one who submits to the divine truth and whose relationship with Allah is governed is by *taqwa*, the consciousness of humankind's responsibility toward its Creator. The believer has the responsibility of acting in accordance with the three types of knowledge—the knowledge of certitude (*ilm al-yaqin*), the eye of certitude (*ain al-yaqin*), and the truth of certitude (*haqq al-yaqin*). With that knowledge and faith, the believer is well equipped to approach others to enjoin what is right and forbid what is wrong. This moral autonomy of the individual, when bound together with the will of the community, formulates the doctrine of infallibility of the collective will of the *ummah*, which is the doctrinal basis of consensus.

28. The Covenant of Allah: Do Not Say to Another Muslim, "You Are Not a Believer."

> When you go forth in the cause of Allah be careful to discriminate and say not to the one who greets you with alaikum o salaam, "Though art not a believer". Would you covet perishable goods of this life when there are immeasurable treasures with Allah? You were like the person who offered you salutation, before Allah conferred on you His favors. Therefore, carefully investigate for Allah is well aware of all that you do. (An-Nisa 4:94, Koran)

Every believer's journey into Islam cannot be the same and uniform. A lot depends on the cultural background, education, and intellectual biases of the person. The first principle of faith is tawhid, the assertion that God is one, that there is only a single worthy object of worship, Allah. All other objects of worship are false. To serve anything else is to fall into error, misguidance, and sin of *shirk*. The Koranic notion of religious belief (*iman*) as dependent on knowledge is actualized in practice in the term *islam*. The term *islam* signifies the idea of surrender or submission. Islam is a religion of self-surrender; it is the conscious and rational submission of a dependent and limited human will to the absolute and omnipotent will of Allah. The type of surrender Islam requires is a deliberate, conscious, and rational act made by a person who knows with both intellectual certainty and spiritual vision that Allah, who is the subject of Koranic discourse, is reality itself. The knower of God is a Muslim (fem. *Muslimah*), "one who submits" to the divine truth and whose relationship with God is governed by *taqwa*, the consciousness of humankind's responsibility toward its Creator.

However, consciousness of God alone is not sufficient to make a person a Muslim. Neither is it enough to be merely born a Muslim or to be raised in an Islamic cultural context. The believer must endeavor at all times to maintain himself or herself in a constant state of submission to Allah. By doing so, the believer attains the honored title of "slave of Allah" (*abd Allah*, feminine: *amat Allah*), for he recognizes that all power and agency belongs to God alone. After submission to the will of Allah, observation of the five pillars opens the way for the believer to understand *ihsan* and perform good deeds for humanity:

إِنَّ ٱلَّذِينَ ءَامَنُوا۟ وَعَمِلُوا۟ ٱلصَّٰلِحَٰتِ وَأَقَامُوا۟ ٱلصَّلَوٰةَ وَءَاتَوُا۟ ٱلزَّكَوٰةَ لَهُمْ أَجْرُهُمْ عِندَ رَبِّهِمْ وَلَا خَوْفٌ عَلَيْهِمْ وَلَا هُمْ يَحْزَنُونَ

> Those who believe, do deeds of righteousness and
> establish regular prayers and regular charity, will have
> their reward with their Lord: on them shall be no fear,
> nor shall they grieve. (Al-Baqarah 2:277, Koran)

Every individual is at a different stage of their life's journey. Only Allah is the judge and the knower of the hidden and the manifest. Only He knows what is in a person's heart.

29. The Covenant of Allah: Suspicion and Lack of Trust: Avoid Suspicion, for in Some Cases, It Is Sin, and Spy Not on Each Other nor Speak Ill of Each Other Behind One's Back

> Avoid suspicion, for suspicion in some cases is sin;
> and spy not on each other, nor speak ill of each other
> behind their backs. Would any of you eat the flesh
> of his dead brother? No, you would abhor it. Be in
> taqwa of Allah, fear Allah: for Allah is Forgiving,
> Most Merciful. (Al-Hujurat 49:12–13, Koran)

Allah gave humans the trust of vicegerency over the earth with the stipulation that they acknowledge Him as their Lord and worship and thank Him for His benevolence. As part of that trust, people are free to make their choices about their actions. Allah does not force them to make the correct choices without taking the trust away from them, and if He took the trust away, they no longer are humans.

With the abuse of vicegerency came selfish acquisition of wealth, land, and women. Acquisition of wealth breeds greed, covetousness, and hoarding of wealth. The prospect of loss of such acquisitions produces insecurity and constant watchfulness. Such paranoia in humans has had a forceful impact on the society of man that leads to assumptions, suspicions, and suppositions that result in quarrels among people and wars between nations, thus a breakdown of the world order. Suspicion among nations has produced expensive and intricate security and intelligence systems that use spying equipment on the ground, in the air, and in space to obtain information on other nations. People and police spy on other people; cities are full of cameras tracking the movement of citizens. Big Brother watches everyone. Mistrust and suspicion prevails over the world, suggesting sickness in society. The same insecurity of people's psyche gives rise to resentment, jealousy, anger, and mistrust, leading to feuds and social disruption.

30. The Covenant of Allah: Do Not Ridicule Other Believers or Revile Each Other with Wicked Names

> Let not some folk among you ridicule others: it may be that they are better than you are: nor let some women mock others: it may be that the others are better than them: nor defame or revile each other by offensive names: ill-seeming is wicked name calling for the one who has believed; and those who do not desist are indeed wrong-doers. (Al-Hujurat 49:11, Koran)

The covenant of Allah forbids suspicion, spying on each other, backbiting, and ridiculing other believers. The heart is like a shining mirror. Troublesome deeds are like smoke that will cover the mirror; you will not be able to see yourself, and you will be veiled from the reality of Allah. To understand the reality of Allah, you have to uncover ignorance and darkness so as to see the light and the reality. Some traits of this darkness are arrogance, ego, pride, envy, vengeance, lying, gossiping, backbiting, and other unwholesome characteristics. To be rid of these evils and odious traits, one has to clean and shine the mirror of the heart. This cleansing of the heart is done by acquiring knowledge and acting upon it to fight against one's ego by ridding oneself of multiplicity of being through unity. When the heart becomes alive with the light and *nur* of unity, the eye of the clean heart will see the reality of Allah's attributes.

31. The Covenant of Allah: Secret Counsels and Pacts: Secret Counsels Are Only inspired by Satan so That He May Cause Grief to the Believers

When you hold secret counsel, do it not for iniquity
and hostility and disobedience to the Messenger;
but do it for righteousness and self-restraint; and
fear Allah, to Whom ye shall be brought back.

Secret counsels are only inspired by the Satan,
in order that he may cause grief to the Believers;
but he cannot harm them in the least, except
as Allah permits; and on Allah let the Believers
put their trust. (Al Mujadila 58:9–10, Koran)

No believer, individual, community, or ruler shall make a compact on behalf of the *ummah* or part of it in secret with the unbelievers. Islam regards secret pacts with enemies and hostile actions against one's own people as treason. When the *Nabi* was in Medina, there were some people who professed Islam but at the same time conspired with the enemy, the *kafirun*, against fellow Muslims. The Koran has the following description of the fate of the *Munafiqeen*.

وَمِنَ ٱلنَّاسِ مَن يَقُولُ ءَامَنَّا بِٱللَّهِ وَبِٱلْيَوْمِ ٱلْأَخِرِ وَمَا هُم بِمُؤْمِنِينَ ﴿٨﴾ يُخَٰدِعُونَ ٱللَّهَ وَٱلَّذِينَ ءَامَنُواْ وَمَا يَخْدَعُونَ إِلَّآ أَنفُسَهُمْ
وَمَا يَشْعُرُونَ ﴿٩﴾ فِى قُلُوبِهِم مَّرَضٌ فَزَادَهُمُ ٱللَّهُ مَرَضًا ۖ وَلَهُمْ عَذَابٌ أَلِيمٌۢ بِمَا كَانُواْ يَكْذِبُونَ ﴿١٠﴾ وَإِذَا قِيلَ لَهُمْ لَا تُفْسِدُواْ فِى ٱلْأَرْضِ قَالُوٓاْ إِنَّمَا
نَحْنُ مُصْلِحُونَ ﴿١١﴾ أَلَآ إِنَّهُمْ هُمُ ٱلْمُفْسِدُونَ وَلَٰكِن لَّا يَشْعُرُونَ ﴿١٢﴾

Of the people there are some who say: "We believe in
Allah and the Last Day;" but they do not really believe.

Fain would they deceive Allah and those who believe,
but they only deceive themselves and realize it not!

In their hearts is a disease; and Allah has increased
their disease: and grievous is the penalty they
incur, because they are false to themselves.

When it is said to them: "Make not mischief on the
earth," they say: "Why, we only want to make peace!"

Of a surety, they are the ones who make
mischief, but they realize (it) not.

(Al-Baqarah 2:8–12, Koran)

ٱللَّهُ يَسْتَهْزِئُ بِهِمْ وَيَمُدُّهُمْ فِى طُغْيَـٰنِهِمْ يَعْمَهُونَ ﴿١٥﴾ أُو۟لَـٰٓئِكَ ٱلَّذِينَ ٱشْتَرَوُا۟ ٱلضَّلَـٰلَةَ بِٱلْهُدَىٰ فَمَا رَبِحَت تِّجَـٰرَتُهُمْ وَمَا كَانُوا۟ مُهْتَدِينَ ﴿١٦﴾
مَثَلُهُمْ كَمَثَلِ ٱلَّذِى ٱسْتَوْقَدَ نَارًا فَلَمَّآ أَضَآءَتْ مَا حَوْلَهُۥ ذَهَبَ ٱللَّهُ بِنُورِهِمْ وَتَرَكَهُمْ فِى ظُلُمَـٰتٍ لَّا يُبْصِرُونَ ﴿١٧﴾ صُمٌّۢ بُكْمٌ عُمْىٌ فَهُمْ لَا
يَرْجِعُونَ ﴿١٨﴾

Allah will throw back their mockery on them
and give them rope in their trespasses; so they
will wander like blind ones to and fro.

These are they who have bartered guidance
for error: but their traffic is profitless,
and they have lost true direction.

Their similitude is that of a man who kindled a fire;
when it lighted all around him, Allah took away
their light and left them in utter darkness. So, they
could not see. Deaf, dumb and blind, they will not
return to the path. (Al-Baqarah 2:15–18, Koran)

In our age, we have people who think that they can get the best of both worlds by compromising their nations and Islam's interests with the enemy. King Abdullah of Transjordan secretly met with Zionist leaders from 1922 onward, merely a year after the creation of Transjordan. These meetings continued during the Palestinian disturbances in 1932 and 1936. The amity between the two conspiring sides was so total that, in a meeting, Abdullah and the Jewish envoy discussed ways of eliminating the mufti of Jerusalem, the leader of Palestinians, and the enemy of both sides[6]. He secretly conspired with Chaim Weizmann for the partition of Palestine in 1947.

6 Avi Shlaim, *The Politics of Partition*, 203.

Abdullah's grandson Hussein started his secret contacts with Israeli leaders in 1957, and by 1963, meetings with the leaders became a regular occurrence. In 1963, Hussein made a secret visit to Tel Aviv[7]. In the period preceding 1967, Hussein performed several treasonable acts that were openly anti-Arab. In response to the creation of PLO, which wanted to replace him as the Palestinian representative, Hussein's intelligence service provided the names and location of the Palestinian fighters infiltrating and battling the Israelis[8]. Hussein did not stop here. His intelligence service also provided the Israelis information about other Arab countries[9]. From 1970 onward, there were several secret meetings between Hussein and the Israeli defense minister Moshe Dayan and with Israeli prime minister Golda Meir[10]. This extensive period of secret Jordanian-Israeli cooperation produced the most treasonable act of Hussein's life, informing Israel of the impending Egyptian-Syrian attack on October 1973[11].

The rulers of Islam who work against their own faith and their own people have a disease in their hearts. They make mischief on the earth against their own faith and nation in secret collusion with the enemies in return for personal gain, power, and wealth. Allah promises a grievous penalty for them because they are false to themselves and do not realize it. Every Muslim today is enslaved by an infidel international diplomatic and financial system run through a network of secretive and deceitful treaties and clauses. Every Muslim carries the burden of four monkeys that direct his daily life. The monkeys of secret international finance, diplomacy, crime, and intelligence

---

7 Dan Raviv and Yossi Melman, *Every Spy a Prince*, 213.

8 Ian Black and Benny Morris, *Israel's Secret Wars*, 238.

9 Raviv and Melman, *Every Spy*, 214.

10 *Secret Channels*, Mohamed Heikal, 310.

11 Morris and Black, *Israel's Secret Wars*, 265.

syndicates sit on the back of every Muslim through the connivance and ignorance of Muslim rulers, mercenary armies, and religious leaders.

32. The Covenant of Allah: Intoxicants and Gambling: Forbidden to You Are Intoxicants and Gambling

> Forbidden to you are intoxicants and gambling, dedication of stones and divination by arrows. These are an abomination and Satan's handiwork; they hinder you from prayer and remembrance of Allah and place enmity and hatred amongst you. Abstain from them so that you may prosper. (Al-Ma'idah 5:90–91, Koran)

Today the world is bedeviled with evils that consume people and deprive them of self-control and motivation to lead a life of purpose and usefulness for themselves, their families, and their fellow humans. The urge for immediate gratification and relief from the stresses of daily life sends people scurrying to alcohol and drugs. In the Western world, a tenth of the adult population is addicted to alcohol or drugs, and another half are habitual users of intoxicants. One in every three families carries the burden of an addicted dear one. In the Muslim world, although alcohol is the lesser substance of abuse, marijuana, cocaine, hashish, and *khat* use is rampant. Tobacco, a substance of extreme addiction but of mild intoxicant properties, is the weed of popular use. A fifth of the world's workforce is underproductive and disabled physically and intellectually because of intoxication and addiction.

The covenant of the Koran fourteen hundred years ago forbade humans from the use of intoxicants in an effort to save mankind from self-destruction. Gambling in all forms—including lotteries, slot machines, betting, card playing, and entertainment in casinos—is forbidden. The covenant says,

> These are an abomination and Satan's handiwork; they hinder you from prayer and remembrance of Allah and place enmity and hatred amongst you. Abstain from them so that you may prosper. (Al-Ma'idah 5:90–91, Koran)

33. The Covenant of Allah: Forbidden to You Are the Carrion, Blood, and Flesh of Swine and Any Other Food on Which Any Name Besides That of Allah Has Been Invoked

> Eat of good things provided to you by Allah and show your gratitude in worship of Him. Forbidden to you are the carrion, blood and flesh of swine and on any other food on which any name besides that of Allah has been invoked. If forced by necessity, without willful disobedience or transgressing due limits, one is guilt less. Allah is Most Forgiving and Most Merciful. (Al-Baqarah 2:172–73, Koran)

Allah, in His generosity and mercy, has permitted the believers to eat of all good things provided by Him. Expressly forbidden is to eat unclean food, which constitutes four things: carrion, blood, flesh of swine, and animals slaughtered in the name of any other than Allah.

During the last millennium, science has discovered harmful parasites and bacteria in the flesh of diseased animals, swine, and the blood of animals. Before the establishment of veterinarian and pathological sciences, the Koran had made a clear distinction between food that was clean and good and what was bad and harmful for humans.

34. The Covenant of Allah: Make Not Unlawful the Good Things That Allah Hath Made Lawful to You

> Make not unlawful the good things, which Allah hath made lawful to you. Commit no excess; Allah loves not people given to excess. Eat of things that Allah has provided for you, lawful and good. Be in taqwa of Allah, fear Allah in whom you believe. (Al-Ma'idah 5:87, Koran)

Allah has, in very explicit words, laid out in His covenant the acts forbidden to the believers:

1. *Shirk*: Join not anything as equal with Him. (Worship Allah and do not associate others with Him.)
2. Mistreatment of parents: Be good to your parents.
3. Infanticide and abortion: Kill not your children on a plea of want. We provide sustenance for you and for them.
4. *Fahasha*: Come not near shameful deeds, whether open or in secret.
5. Taking of life: Take not life, which Allah hath made sacred, except by way of justice and law.
6. Stealing: Come not near to the orphan's property, except to improve it, until he attains the age of full strength. The term *orphan* may also include other helpless citizens who may be subject to oppression.
7. Cheating: And give measure and weight with justice; (do not cheat) no burden do we place on any soul but that which it can bear.
8. Lying and falsification: Whenever you speak, speak the truth, even if a near relative is concerned.
9. Violation of Allah's Covenant: Fulfill the covenant of Allah: "Thus, does He command you that ye may remember. Verily,

this is My Way leading straight: follow it; follow not other paths: they will scatter you about from His Path; thus, doth He command you, that ye may be righteous" (Al-An'am 6:151–53, Koran).

10. Intoxicants.
11. Gambling.
12. Dedication of stones.
13. Divination by arrows: "These are an abomination and Satan's handiwork; they hinder you from prayer and remembrance of Allah and place enmity and hatred amongst you. Abstain from them so that you may prosper" (Al-Ma'idah 5:90–91, Koran).
14. Carrion.
15. Blood.
16. Flesh of swine.
17. "Any other food on which any name besides that of Allah has been invoked" (Al-Baqarah 2:172–73, Koran).
18. Usury (*riba*): "Devour not usury double and multiplied: Be in taqwa of Allah, that you may prosper" (Ali 'Imran 3:130, Koran).
19. Disrespect toward women: "It is not lawful for you to take women against their will, nor should you treat them with harshness. On the contrary treat then with honor and kindness" (An-Nisa 4:19, Koran).
20. Any actions that infringe on the unity of the *ummah* and the nation of Islam: "And hold fast, all together, by the Rope which Allah stretches out for you and be not divided among yourselves. You were enemies and He joined your hearts in love, so that by His Grace, you became brethren and a community. Thus, does Allah makes His Signs clear to you that you may be guided. Be not like those who are divided amongst themselves and fall into disputations after receiving clear signs; for them is a dreadful penalty."

These twenty actions have been forbidden (haram) by the covenant of Allah. At the same time, Allah commands:

> Make not unlawful the good things, which Allah hath made lawful to you. Commit no excess; Allah loves not people given to excess. Eat of things that Allah has provided for you, lawful and good. Be in taqwa of Allah, fear Allah in whom you believe. (Al-Ma'idah 5:57, Koran)

Islamic scholar-jurists frequently quote various Hadith and proclaim many aspects of the daily life of pious and observant believers as haram. Such actions include listening to music, women's education, women's role in congregational prayers, and other mundane activities such as kite flying, tourism, pursuit of Western education, and use of modern technology. Those are the personal views of the mullahs and do not have the divine sanction of the covenant between Allah and His believers.

1. **Music:** Music is part of the human soul. Every child, when happy, springs up to a melody and dance to the rhythm. When the blessed *Nabi* received the revelation from Allah, at times, it appeared in the form of a tinkle or the chimes of a bell, and the words of the revelation blossomed in Blessed Muhammad's mind. The Koran, when recited in rhythmic Arabic, produces a heavenly song of Allah's revelation. Singing Allah's *dhikr* with or without instrument or music has a powerful and profound effect on the listener's soul, which reflects divine beauty. Listening to mere wind chimes makes one aware of the divine origin of the sounds of the wind, the rustle of trees, and the sound of running water in rivers, falls, and oceans. Allah gave the human the ability to produce the most beautiful sounds in His remembrance, to celebrate life and happiness, and to enjoy Allah's other provisions to mankind.

Observation of Allah's covenant bestows peace and tranquility to the soul and hence happiness and contentment on the believer. Islam is not a religion of gloom, sorrow, and melancholia but that of celebration of Allah's blessings and of doing beautiful deeds. To show contentment, peace, harmony, happiness, and proper balance of things in life is to express *shukr*, gratitude to Allah for His mercy and grace. The human is asked to use all his senses—sight, hearing, smell, taste, and touch—to recognize Allah's truth and signs. They signify the perception of Allah's *nur* (light), resonance of the sound of Allah's harmonious music in nature, the fragrance of Allah's garden, the flavor of Allah's bounty, and the feel of Allah's creation around us. Allah does not forbid against His divine gift of harmony and song; on the contrary, He urged the recitation of the Koran in slow, rhythmic tones and the celebration and praising of Allah often, glorifying Him in the morning and at night. It is Allah and His angels who also send their blessings on the believers so "He may lead the Believers you out of the depths of darkness into light." Celebration of Allah's praises and glorifying Him means to rejoice, to be happy, and to be joyous. The word *celebrate*, therefore, has the connotation of a happy occasion, which includes song and music.

2. **Confinement of believing and devout women** is not a mandate of Allah's covenant nor is covering women from head to toe.
3. **Acquisition of knowledge:** Education is Allah's gift to humanity and is incumbent on every believer, man or woman. Scholars of Islam ignore the Koranic admonition,

> Make not unlawful the good things, which Allah
> hath made lawful to you. Commit no excess;
> Allah loves not people given to excess.

35. The Covenant of Allah: Contracts and Agreements: When You Make a Transaction Involving Future Obligations, Write It down in Presence of Witnesses

> When you make a transaction involving future obligations, write it down in presence of witnesses, or let a scribe write it down faithfully. Let the party incurring the liability dictate truthfully in the presence of two witnesses from among your own men and if two men are not available then a man and two women, so that if one of them errs then the other one, can remind him. Disregard not to put your contract in writing, whether it be small or large, it is more suitable in the eyes of Allah, more suitable as evidence and more convenient to prevent doubts in the future amongst yourselves. (Al-Baqarah 2:282–83, Koran)

Fourteen hundred years ago, the Koran laid out the basis of the modern legal system of written and witnessed agreements. Muslim jurists have used this *ayah* to curtail the rights of women as witnesses in the modern court system, where they consider the testimony of two women equivalent to the testimony of one man. The mullahs imply that women have an inferior memory and intellectual capacity. Although the Koran is silent on the reason for the need for two women witnesses, it is obvious that women carry the burden and the responsibilities of nurturing and taking care of their infants and families. Women are Allah's instruments of creation and the nurturer of mankind. The act of creation and nurture has precedence over worldly affairs of commerce. Women cannot neglect their divine obligation of creation to attend to the communal affairs as witnesses in the transactions of this world. The need for a second woman witness becomes necessary when one of them becomes preoccupied with her obligations of procreation and upbringing of a family.

There is abundant of scientific evidence that the intellectual capacity of both men and women is unique in their development. This uniqueness complements the intellect and memory of men and women in the functioning of mankind. This uniqueness is a gift of Allah to humankind.

The human memory is affected by the inbuilt nature and development of the brain and its environment. Adolescent brain development is different in boys and girls. Male's aged six to seventeen years display more prominent age-related reduction in gray matter (the part of the brain that allows us to think) and increases in white matter (which transfers information between distant regions) than females. These changes in brain composition are linked to developmental processes in which nerve cell connections are "pruned" in gray matter and made more efficient (myelinated) in white matter. The more dramatic changes seen in males may be related to the different effects of estrogen and testosterone on the brain[12]. Women have smaller brains than men and have smaller bodies; women have more gray matter, and men have more white matter. This finding may help explain why women are typically better than men at verbal tasks, while men are typically better than women at spatial tasks, as well as why the sexes perform equally well on intelligence tests in spite of males having larger brains[13].

Several studies have evaluated sex differences in the histology of the cerebral cortex. One study in humans detected higher neuronal density

---

12 De Bellis, MD, et al., "Sex Differences in Brain Maturation during Childhood and Adolescence," *Cereb. Cortex* 11, no. 6 (2001): 552–57.

13 R. C. Gur et al., "Sex Differences in Brain Gray and White Matter in Healthy Young Adults: Correlations with Cognitive Performance," *J. Neurosci.* 19, no, 10 (1999): 4065–72.

in the female cortex compared with males[14]. In contrast, other studies have shown that the number of neurons in the cerebral cortex is greater in males than in females. Studies by Rabinowicz et al. demonstrated that males have 15 percent more cortical neurons and 13 percent greater neuronal density than females[15]. Similarly, Pakkenberg et al. showed a 16 percent higher neuronal number in males, but sex differences in neuronal density were not present[16]. Although women have fewer neocortical neurons, certain anatomical and histological characteristics of female brains may allow for more extensive dendritic arborization and more neuronal connections among nerve cells[17]. Certain diseases that cause neuronal loss in the cerebral cortex may be more detrimental to women due to their lower number of cortical neurons compared with men[18].

The cerebellum, an area of the brain important for posture and balance, and the pons, a brain structure linked to the cerebellum that helps control consciousness, are larger in men than in women[19]. As the brain ages, the amount of tissue mass declines, and the amount of fluid

---

[14] H. Haug, "Brain Sizes, Surfaces and Neuronal Sizes of the Cortex Cerebri: A Stereological Investigation of Man and His Variability and a Comparison with Some Mammals (Primates, Whales, Marsupials, Insectivores and One Elephant)," *Am. J. Anat.* 180, no. 2 (1987): 126–42.

[15] T. Rabinowicz et al., "Gender Differences in the Human Cerebral Cortex: More Neurons in Males; More Processes in Females," *J. Child Neurol.* 14, no. 2 (1999): 98–107.

[16] B. S. Pakkenberg and H. J. Gundersen, "Neocortical Neuron Number in Humans: Effect of Sex and Age," *J. Comp. Neurol.* 384, no. 2 (1997): 312–20.

[17] G.M. de Courten-Myers, "The Human Cerebral Cortex: Gender Differences in Structure and Function," *J. Neuropathology Exp. Neurol.* 58, no. 3 (1999): 217–26.

[18] T. Rabinowicz et al., "Structure of the Cerebral Cortex in Men and Women," *J. Neuropathol. Exp. Neurol.* 61, no. 1 (2002): 46–57.

[19] N. Raz et al., "Age and Sex Differences in the Cerebellum and the Ventral Pons: A Prospective MR Study of Healthy Adults," *AJNR Am. J. Neuroradiology* 22, no. 6 (2001): 1161–67.

increases. This effect is less severe in women than in men, suggesting that women are somewhat less vulnerable to age-related changes in mental abilities[20–21]. However, women are more prone to dementia than men perhaps because of the potentially greater susceptibility to loss of neurons and neuronal connections.

Language Differences. Although men and women have been shown to process some language tasks similarly, in other aspects of language processing, there are significant sex differences[22]. Imaging studies of the living brain show that in women neurons on both sides of the brain are activated when they are listening, while in men neurons on only one side of the brain are activated. Men and women appear to process single words similarly, but in the interpretation of whole sentences, women use both sides of the brain, while men use one side[23]. Boys have a higher incidence than girls of developmental language disorders, such as developmental dyslexia. Despite these differences during childhood, it is not clear whether adult women have better verbal skills than men[21].

Spatial Information Differences. Men and women process spatial information differently[24]. When negotiating a virtual reality maze, both men and women use the right hippocampus to figure out how to exit. However, men also use the left hippocampus for this task,

---

20 R. C. Gur et al., "Gender Differences in Age Effect on Brain Atrophy Measured by Magnetic Resonance Imaging," *Proc. Natl Acad. Sci. USA* 88, no. 7 (1991): 2845–49.

21 S. F. Witelson, "Sex Differences in Neuroanatomical Changes with Aging," *N. Engl. J. Med.* 325, no. 3 (1991): 211–12.

22 Ibid.

23 K. Kansaku and S. Kitazawa, "Imaging Studies on Sex Differences in the Lateralization of Language," *Neurosci. Res.* 41, no. 4 (2001): 333–37.

24 J. D. Ragland et al., "Sex Differences in Brain-Behavior Relationships between Verbal Episodic Memory and Resting Regional Cerebral Blood Flow," *Neuropsychologia* 38, no. 4 (2000): 451–61.

while women do not. Women also use the right prefrontal cortex, while men do not[25]. In an imaging study, men were found to activate a distributed system of different brain regions on both sides of the brain while performing a spatial task. Women, however, activated these regions on only the right side of the brain. Women appear to rely on landmarks to navigate their environments, whereas men tend to use compass directions[26].

Memory Differences. Some functions of memory appear to be different in males and females[27]. Higher rates of blood flow in certain portions of the brain are associated with increased memory of verbal tasks in women but not in men[28]. Compared with men, women have been shown to be better at remembering faces[29]. A key part of the brain involved in processing emotionally influenced memories acts differently in men and women.

The amygdala, an almond-shaped structure found on both sides of the brain, behaves very differently in males and females while the subjects are at rest. In men, the right amygdala is more active and shows more connections with other regions of the brain. Conversely, in women, the left amygdala is more connected with other regions of the brain. In addition, the regions of the brain with which the amygdala communicates while a subject is at rest are different in men

---

[25] G. Gron et al., "Brain Activation during Human Navigation: Gender-Different Neural Networks as Substrate of Performance," *Nat. Neurosci.* 3, no. 4 (2000): 404–8.

[26] D. M. Saucier et al., "Are Sex Differences in Navigation Caused by Sexually Dimorphic Strategies or by Differences in the Ability to Use the Strategies?" *Behav. Neurosci.* 116, no. 3 (2002): 403–10.

[27] S. J. Duff and E. Hampson, "A Sex Difference on a Novel Spatial Working Memory Task in Humans," *Brain Cogn.* 47, no. 3 (2001): 470–93.

[28] Ragland et al., "Sex Differences," 451–61.

[29] R. C. Gur et al., "Computerized Neurocognitive Scanning: I. Methodology and Validation in Healthy People," *Neuropsychopharmacology* 25, no. 5 (2001).

and women. These findings suggest that the brain is wired differently in men and women. In men, the right-hemisphere amygdala showed more connectivity with brain regions such as the visual cortex and the striatum. In contrast, the left amygdala in women was more connected to regions such as the insular cortex and the hypothalamus.

Many brain areas communicating with the amygdala in men are engaged with and responding to the external environment. For example, the visual cortex is responsible for vision, while the striatum coordinates motor actions. Conversely, many regions connected to the left-hemisphere amygdala in women control aspects of the environment within the body. Both the insular cortex and the hypothalamus, for example, receive strong input from the sensors inside the body.

Throughout evolution, women have had to deal with a number of internal stressors, such as childbirth, that men have not had to experience. The brain seems to have evolved to be in tune with those different stressors. One of the brain areas communicating with the amygdala in women is implicated in disorders such as depression and irritable bowel syndrome, which predominantly affect women.

The sexes use different sides of their brains to process and store long-term memories. Another study in 2002 demonstrated how a particular drug, propranolol, can block memory differently in men and women. Differences between men and women in cognitive pattern are now well established. On average, men outperform women on a variety of spatial tasks, with the largest difference occurring on tests of spatial rotation and manipulation, where an object must be identified in an altered orientation, or after certain imaginary manipulations such as folding. Men also excel at tests of mathematical reasoning, with the differences between sexes especially marked at the higher end of the distribution. Women, in contrast, are generally better able to recall the spatial layout of an array of objects, to scan perceptual arrays quickly to find matching objects, and to recall verbal material, whether word lists or meaningful paragraphs.

Some of these differences are found early in development and last throughout the life span. The sex differences in verbal memory, spatial orientation, and mathematical reasoning have been found across cultures. These differences are due to our long evolutionary history as hunter-gatherers, in which the division of labor between men and women was quitc marked. Men more often traveled farther from the home base during hunting and scavenging, whereas women gathered food nearer home. In parallel with nonhuman studies, this would tend to show different navigational strategies, with men, for example, relying more on geometric cues and women more on landmark cues.

Summary. At present, when men and women have begun to perform similar tasks, each sex has certain specialization that, on the whole, complements the other sex's abilities. None is better, and none is inferior to the other. Mullahs will continue with their age-old prejudices to maintain women's lower status. Allah, in His infinitesimal wisdom, has bestowed on men and women unique strengths that complement each other for the benefit of humanity.

We digressed from the main topic of the written agreements because of an ongoing controversy in certain legal, scholastic Muslim circles about women's capacity as witnesses in the modern court system. This controversy about women's witnessing needed to be addressed in an informed and scientific manner. It is hoped that the above discussion will go a long way to contradict those mullahs who claim to be privy to Allah's intentions.

36. The Covenant of Allah: Respect Other People's Privacy: Enter Not Houses Other Than Yours until You Have Asked Permission and Invoked Peace on Those in Them

> Enter not houses other than yours until you have
> asked permission and invoked peace upon those
> in them. If you find none in the house whom
> you seek enter not unless permission is granted.
> If you asked to leave go back, it is best for you
> that makes for greater purity for you. Allah knows
> all that you do. (An-Nur 24:27, Koran)

The four walls of every person's home are his circle of privacy, within the confines of which he or she has freedom from intrusion by outsiders, be it the neighbor or the state. The residents of the home are protected from physical intrusion or intrusion with electronic devices. This dwelling is the basic autonomous unit of the Islamic state that amalgamates with other such units to form a community. The communities, with some complexity, join other communities to form the state. What is important is that the residents of each dwelling have their seclusion protected by the mandate of the covenant of the Koran. Importantly, each of the adult residents has a voice in the administration of the common affairs of the community. Each family is an independent, autonomous, basic unit of the *ummah*.

37. The Covenant of Allah: This Day I Have Perfected Your Religion for You

> This Day I have perfected your religion for you.
> We have made the (Qur'an) easy in your own
> tongue, that with it you may give glad tidings to
> the righteous and warnings to people given to
> contention. Therein is proclaimed every wise decree,

by command from Our Presence, for We are ever sending revelations, as a Mercy from your Lord. We have explained in detail in this Qur'an, for the benefit of mankind, every kind of similitude.

This day have those who reject faith (kafaru) given up all hope of compromising your faith, fear them not but only fear Me. This day have I perfected your religion for you, bestowed on you with My blessings and decreed Islam as your religion. (Al-Ma'idah 5:3, Koran)

Ha Mim. By the Book that makes matters lucid; We revealed it during the blessed night, verily We are always warning against Evil. Therein is proclaimed every wise decree, by command from Our Presence, for We are ever sending revelations, as a Mercy from your Lord: for He is the hearer and knower. The Lord of the heavens and the earth and all that is in between them, if you have an assured faith. There is no god but He: it is He who gives life and death, the Lord and Cherisher, your Lord and Lord of your forefathers. (Ad-Dukhan 44:1–8, Koran)

So have We made the (Qur'an) easy in your own tongue, that with it you may give glad tidings to the righteous and warnings to people given to contention. But how many (countless) generations before them have We destroyed? Canst, thou find a single one of them (now) or hear (so much as) a whisper of them? (Taha 19:97, Koran)

We have explained in detail in this Qur'an, for the benefit of mankind, every kind of similitude:

but man is, in most things, contentious. And
what is there to keep back men from believing,
now that guidance has come to them, nor from
praying for forgiveness from their Lord, but
that (they ask that) the ways of the ancients be
repeated with them, or the Wrath be brought to
them face to face? (Al-Kahf 18:54–55, Koran)

The blessed *Nabi* of Allah, Muhammad, proclaimed to the world on the mount of Arafat Allah's *wahiy* (message) on the last Friday, the ninth day of *Zul-hajj* in the tenth year of hijra (631CE).

This day have I perfected your religion for you.

ٱلْيَوْمَ يَئِسَ ٱلَّذِينَ كَفَرُوا۟ مِن دِينِكُمْ فَلَا تَخْشَوْهُمْ وَٱخْشَوْنِ ۚ ٱلْيَوْمَ أَكْمَلْتُ لَكُمْ دِينَكُمْ وَأَتْمَمْتُ عَلَيْكُمْ نِعْمَتِى وَرَضِيتُ لَكُمُ ٱلْإِسْلَٰمَ

دِينًا

This day have those who reject faith (kafaru) given up
all hope of compromising your faith, fear them not but
only fear Me. This day have I perfected your religion for
you, bestowed on you with My blessings and decreed
Islam as your religion. (Al-Ma'idah 5:3, Koran)

On that day, the *din* of Islam was complete, and all man-made innovations after that were just novelties; anyone indulging in such innovations was making a sport of his religion. Those believers who fulfill the commandments of the Koran, Allah's covenant, are the *muttaqeen*. From that day on, men and women who obey and keep their covenant with Allah are the believers (*muttaqeen*) of Allah and the Koran, the word that Allah revealed to the blessed *Nabi*, Muhammad. The Believers who follow the Qur'an and fulfill the

Covenant of Allah, for their din Allah only suffices them. They are not Shia or Sunni nor any other sect.

The Koran establishes a universal order based on the divinely ordained values of life. Were every human to fulfill the covenant of the Koran, the world shall be at peace forever, and justice will prevail. By following the *Hadith collections* of the third-century hijra, *Muslims* have relegated their faith from a divinely ordained order to a human set of values, misleading themselves and deviating others from Allah's path. According to the Koran, *iman* is not just belief but also, in fact, knowledge. *Iman* is the conviction that is based on reason and knowledge. The Koran does not recognize belief that involves blind acceptance. Islam does include acceptance of certain things that cannot be explained by perception through human senses. Our reason and thinking will compel us to recognize the existence of such things. *Iman*, according to the Koran, signifies conviction based on full mental acceptance and intellectual satisfaction. *Iman* gives a person inner contentment, a feeling of *amn* (same common root). Thus, *iman* means to believe in something and to testify to its truthfulness, to have confidence in that belief, and to bow down in obedience.

There are five fundamental facts stated in the Koran that a believer must accept: *iman* in Allah, the law of *mukafat* and the afterlife, angels (*malaika*), the revelations, and the messengers. Belief in Allah means not only to profess obedience to Him and His Covenant but also to show it in one's actions and to be always in *taqwa* of Allah. Belief in the law of *mukafat* means to have conviction that every action of the human has an inescapable consequence of reward or retribution. Angels are not the winged creatures depicted in children's literature. They are heavenly forces that carry out laws of Allah governing the universe. They bow to Allah since they follow his orders. They also bow to the humans because we are able to study, understand, and manipulate the laws of nature for the benefit of mankind. Belief in revelations and messengers implies that human intellect alone cannot safely reach the final destination without the divine guidance in the form of *wahiy*, revelation delivered by the messengers to mankind. This guidance is to whole humankind sent through many messengers. The Muslim tradition began with *Ibrahim*, our father (Abraham of the Bible). The believers have a belief system and a course of action to witness over and spread the message to mankind that began with *Ibrahim* and was completed with *Muhammad*. Whereas the message of *wahiy* is divine and universal for all human races, the message of Hadith collections of the third century are human and therefore subject to error and cannot be equated with the Koran.

38. The Covenant of Allah: Those Who Believe and Perform Beautiful Deeds Are Companions of the Garden; Therein Shall They Abide Forever

After his submission to the will and mercy of Allah, the believer is obliged to obey and fulfill the covenant he has made with Allah as part of the compact of submission and has to perform wholesome and good deeds. In the first thirty-seven covenants, Allah addresses the believer as

O you who believe!

The covenant of the Koran is a total belief system of an individual based upon total submersion of one's personality with Allah with total awareness and *taqwa* of Him at all times through observance of the thirty-seven commandments of Allah's covenant. This communion is not only with Allah but also, through Him, with other humans and Allah's creation, both alive and inanimate.

After the believer has completely understood and accepted the thirty-seven covenants, the believer has the obligation and the promise from Allah with the phrase

Alladhina aaminu wa 'amilu al saalihaat.[30]

الَّذِينَ ءَامَنُواْ وَعَمِلُواْ ٱلصَّـٰلِحَـٰتِ

It refers to those who persist in striving to set things right, who restore harmony, peace, and balance. The other acts of good works recognized in the covenant of the Koran are to show compassion, to be merciful and forgive others, to be just, to protect the weak, to defend the oppressed, to be generous and charitable, to be truthful, to seek knowledge and wisdom, to be kind, to be peaceful, to love others, and to perform beautiful deeds.

إِنَّ ٱلَّذِينَ ءَامَنُواْ وَعَمِلُواْ ٱلصَّـٰلِحَـٰتِ سَيَجْعَلُ لَهُمُ ٱلرَّحْمَـٰنُ وُدًّا ۝

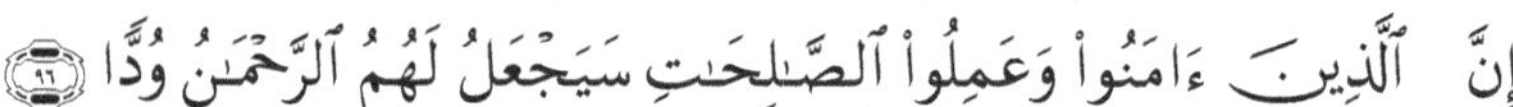

On those who believe and do good, will
[Allah] Most Gracious bestow love.

So this becomes the thirty-eighth covenant.

There are fifty such verses in the Koran that remind the believers of the rewards of righteous deeds. The following are some of the *ayahs* in the Koran mentioning the righteous deeds.

---

[30] Koran 2:25; 2:82, 277; 4:57, 122; 5:5; 7:42; 10:9; 11:23; 13:29; 14:23; 18:2, 88, 107; 19:60, 96; 20:75, 82, 112; 21:94; 22:14; 23:50, 56; 24:55; 25:70–71; 26:67; 28:80; 29:7, 9, 58; 30:15, 45; 31:8; 32:19; 34:4, 37; 38:24; 41:8; 42:22–23, 26; 45:21, 30; 47:2, 12; 48:29; 64:9; 65:11; 84:25; 85:11; 95:6; 98:7; 103:3.

Alladhina aaminu wa 'amilu al saalihaat.[31]

ٱلَّذِينَ ءَامَنُواْ وَعَمِلُواْ ٱلصَّـٰلِحَـٰتِ

وَٱلَّذِينَ ءَامَنُواْ وَعَمِلُواْ ٱلصَّـٰلِحَـٰتِ أُوْلَـٰٓئِكَ أَصْحَـٰبُ ٱلْجَنَّةِ ۖ هُمْ فِيهَا خَـٰلِدُونَ

But those who believe and work righteousness.
They are Companions of the Garden: therein shall
they abide (forever). (Al-Baqarah 2:82, Koran)

إِنَّ ٱلَّذِينَ ءَامَنُواْ وَعَمِلُواْ ٱلصَّـٰلِحَـٰتِ وَأَقَامُواْ ٱلصَّلَوٰةَ وَءَاتَوُاْ ٱلزَّكَوٰةَ لَهُمْ أَجْرُهُمْ عِندَ رَبِّهِمْ وَلَا خَوْفٌ عَلَيْهِمْ وَلَا هُمْ يَحْزَنُونَ

﴿٢٧٧﴾

Those who believe, do deeds of righteousness and
establish regular prayers and regular charity, will have
their reward with their Lord: on them shall be no fear,
nor shall they grieve. (Al-Baqarah 2:277, Koran)

وَأَمَّا ٱلَّذِينَ ءَامَنُواْ وَعَمِلُواْ ٱلصَّـٰلِحَـٰتِ فَيُوَفِّيهِمْ أُجُورَهُمْ ۗ وَٱللَّهُ لَا يُحِبُّ ٱلظَّـٰلِمِينَ ﴿٥٧﴾

"As to those who believe and work righteousness,
Allah will pay them in full their reward;
but Allah loves not those who do wrong
(zalimeen). (Ali 'Imran 3:57, Koran)

[31] Ibid.

وَٱلَّذِينَ ءَامَنُوا۟ وَعَمِلُوا۟ ٱلصَّـٰلِحَـٰتِ سَنُدْخِلُهُمْ جَنَّـٰتٍ تَجْرِى مِن تَحْتِهَا ٱلْأَنْهَـٰرُ خَـٰلِدِينَ فِيهَآ أَبَدًا ۖ لَّهُمْ فِيهَآ أَزْوَٰجٌ مُّطَهَّرَةٌ ۖ وَنُدْخِلُهُمْ ظِلًّا

ظَلِيلًا ﴿٥٧﴾

But those who believe and do deeds of righteousness, We shall soon admit to Gardens, with rivers flowing beneath, their eternal home and therein shall they have companions pure and holy: We shall admit them to shades, cool and ever deepening. (An-Nisa 4:57, Koran)

وَٱلَّذِينَ ءَامَنُوا۟ وَعَمِلُوا۟ ٱلصَّـٰلِحَـٰتِ سَنُدْخِلُهُمْ جَنَّـٰتٍ تَجْرِى مِن تَحْتِهَا ٱلْأَنْهَـٰرُ خَـٰلِدِينَ فِيهَآ أَبَدًا ۖ وَعْدَ ٱللَّهِ حَقًّا ۚ وَمَنْ أَصْدَقُ مِنَ

ٱللَّهِ قِيلًا ﴿١٢٢﴾

But those who believe and do deeds of righteousness, We shall soon admit them to Gardens - with rivers flowing beneath - to dwell therein forever. Allah's promise is the truth and whose word can be truer than Allah's?

Chapter Four

Hadith Collections of the Third-Century Hijra

Whenever an ayah (a verse) of the Koran was revealed to the blessed *Nabi* Muhammad, he dictated every letter and word of the revelation to his scribes, disciples, and followers. Thousands of disciples also memorized the revealed word of the Koran. During his last sermon on the ninth day of *Zul-hajj* in the tenth year of hijra, he asked Allah to be his witness that he had faithfully conveyed the revelations to the people in complete form as Allah had commanded. His audience in unison replied, "O Prophet of Allah, You have indeed delivered Allah's Revelation faithfully."

۞ يَـٰٓأَيُّهَا ٱلرَّسُولُ بَلِّغْ مَآ أُنزِلَ إِلَيْكَ مِن رَّبِّكَ

O Apostle! Proclaim the (Message) which hath been sent to thee from thy Lord. (Al-Ma'idah 5:67, Koran)

Allah revealed the Koran to His blessed *Nabi* in stages, and He promised the preservation of the Koran.

﴿ إِنَّا نَحْنُ نَزَّلْنَا ٱلذِّكْرَ وَإِنَّا لَهُۥ لَحَـٰفِظُونَ ۝٩ ﴾

We have, without doubt, revealed the Message and We will assuredly preserve it. (Al-Hijr 15:9, Koran)

Thus, the Holy Koran is the word of Allah, and it contains His covenant with the believers revealed to Muhammad, the *Rasul* of

Allah. Allah commanded the *Rasul* to proclaim the divine word to the world. When the blessed *Nabi* began his mission in Mecca in the sixth century, reading and writing skills around the world were limited. Literacy was perhaps limited to less than five percent of the population in the courtesan and clerical circles. Among the population, in general, knowledge was transmitted through oral tradition and was limited to practical matters of livelihood, trade, and religion. Books and scriptures were not accessible to the population at large. Therefore, concepts and principles were based on cultural experience that was hard to change. This situation caused diversity among neighborly communities. Unity of ideas occurred often through compulsion from above when conquerors pushed through the ideas of their culture to the subject people.

Had the blessed prophet Muhammad in the year 610 of the Common Era, at the beginning of his mission, opened an office across from the Kaaba and from there distributed printed and bound copies of the Koran to the pilgrims coming from all across Arabia, he would have made no impact on the psyche of that population. The people did not possess the know-how to grasp the concepts and precepts of knowledge of unity of Allah, tawhid, *taqwa* of Allah, and the criterion to distinguish between good and evil (*husna* and *Fahasha*) at that time. They lacked the concept of one universal God. The prophet began teaching every new believer the very basics of the precepts of the belief in accordance with the intellectual understanding and capability of each individual. He did not speak to anyone on matters beyond their comprehension. His tutelage of each new follower started with basic knowledge as if teaching a primer to a beginning class student and graduated to more complex issues. There were hardly any philosophers, scientists, or scholars at that time in the Meccan and the Medinan society who required a complex discourse on divinity.

While the prophet was laying the foundation for the understanding of the Koran, the Koran was gradually being revealed. The Koran laid the foundation of the idea of one universal God, and from this fount arose all that is known and all that will ever be known. It laid this foundation for the believers in the first twelve years of Blessed Muhammad's prophecy, and it took another ten years to establish the precepts of truth, justice, covenant, equality, good, and evil. The seventy-five *ayahs* beginning with the words *O you who Believe*, which contain the commandments of the covenant of Allah, were only revealed during the last three years of the blessed *nabi's* life. The Koran laid out these principles in clarity for all time to come.

It took twenty-three years for the entirety of the Koran to be revealed, lifting the veil from the knowledge of Allah layer by layer, until the believers could finally comprehend the whole of the revelation. In the meantime, the blessed prophet not only proclaimed the revelation and the word of Allah but he also gently paved the way for the sixth-century Bedouins, traders, and shepherds to understand the Koran. The Koran is the whole of the revelation and a complete exposition of the *din* of Allah. The prophecy ended for all times with the completion of the revelation. The blessed prophet's mission had been completed with the revelation of the Koran, and within three months, he passed away.

Muhammad—a man of wisdom, a prophet, and the blessed messenger of Allah—was aware that his worldly existence was approaching its end, yet he did not appoint a successor. It was because his prophetic task was only to deliver Allah's word, the Koran, to humanity. No other human was ever given such an authority. When the task of the delivery of the revelation had been completed, humanity had guidance from Allah for all times to come. The prophet had primed and prepared humanity in anticipation and then the actual revelation of the Koran. He nurtured his *ummah* with knowledge and guidance during the period the Koran was being revealed, and once the revelation had been completed, he left it to humanity as a total system of Allah's guidance.

The Koran is Allah's dialogue with the believer. Salat, *dhikr*, and *du'a* are man's response in this dialogue. The parable of divine light is the foundation of the belief in one universal God for the whole humankind. Allah is the light of the heavens and the earth. Allah loves His creation. His light illuminates the hearts and minds of those who love Him, place their trust in Him, and open their mind and soul in submission to Him. Once hearts and minds are open to Allah in submission, they form the niche in which the divine light, Spirit, and wisdom of Allah percolate and shine within us. The glow and luminescence of this Spirit and wisdom is of such brilliance that it glows with the brightness of a star. This star is lit from the light of divine wisdom, the tree of knowledge—the knowledge of Allah's signs. For those who believe, Allah is within. The believer is aglow with Allah's radiance—light upon light. The dwellings where Allah's name is praised and glorified in the mornings and evenings are aglow with Allah's light. When Allah is within, Allah's guidance is ever present with the believer. When Allah draws man close to Him, Allah's spiritual light (*nur*) is within man, and man is with Allah. And thus, the dialogue continues.

Allah has granted the knowledge and wisdom of *furqan* and *taqwa* to the believers who have opened their hearts and minds to Him. Man has been granted the freedom of choice in doing what is wholesome and beautiful or what is corrupt and ugly. It is only man among the creation that has been given the knowledge to distinguish right activity, right thought, and right intention from their opposites. This knowledge reminds man of the scales of Allah's justice; the two hands of Allah, His mercy and His wrath, are reflected in the human domain, where people have been appointed Allah's vicegerents. Deeds of goodness and wholesomeness are associated with mercy, paradise, and what is beautiful. Evil and corruption is rewarded with wrath, hell, and what is ugly.

In the sixth century, at the time of the birth of the blessed prophet, the Arabian Peninsula was steeped in ignorance, superstition, spirit, and idol worship. There was no belief or concept of one universal God. In the rest of the Middle East, the one God was a tribal deity of the Jews, and the God of Christians was accessible to man through the creed of the Trinity, in which God had incarnated into the human Jesus and Jesus into the divine God. So, what the blessed Muhammad taught the initiates to the faith of one Allah was the primer necessary for the transformation from the life of ignorance and paganism to the infinite wisdom and mercy of Allah.

The word of Allah, the Koran, was being revealed gradually, and its complete guidance was not yet available to the early believers. The prophet once said, "Speak to men according to their mental capacities, for if you speak all things to all men, some cannot understand you and fall into errors." The prophet paved the way of humankind to the straight path of Allah, gently and gradually imparting knowledge of Allah to the new initiates as if teaching primary school students and progressing to the understanding of higher grades. The prophet was the conduit for the humankind from paganism to the light of Allah. The prophet was mortal, and his role was a fleeting one, while Allah is forever.

The blessed Muhammad taught humankind to open their hearts and minds to the light of Allah. When the niche in the human heart is lit with Allah's *nur* (light), that person glows like a brilliant star with Allah's knowledge. Once that person has been initiated into Allah's light, Allah becomes his guide, and the covenant is the compass to his redemption. Salat, *dhikr*, recitation, fasting, and *taqwa* are the beams of light that maintain the believer's connection with the divine light. Islam is this direct link between the believer and the divine. The believer asks, and Allah gives. The believer loves Allah, and Allah loves him in return. The believer asks for the straight path, and Allah shows him the way. The believer praises Allah, and Allah showers His mercy and grace on him. The believer remembers Allah, and Allah responds to those who praise Him, thank Him, and ask of Him.

What the prophet left behind is the book for every human. The Koran, when recited and studied in sincerity, opens man's heart to the divine knowledge and mercy. All guidance that a person asks for is provided by Allah. Thc Blessed Nabi's teachings were the primer to the way of Allah and the Koran. The *Nabi* said, "The Qur'an consists of ***five heads:*** things ***lawful*** and things ***unlawful***, clear, and positive ***precepts, mysteries*** *and* ***examples***. The Prophet said, "*Consider that is* ***lawful*** *which has been declared to be so, and that which is forbidden as* ***unlawful***. *Obey the* **precepts**, *believe in* **mysteries**, *and take warnings from* **examples**."

During the period of revelation of the Qur'an, some of the disciples began to write down the blessed prophet's parables and sayings. Some of these sayings and parables were beautiful quotations of Muhammad's teachings, while the others were mundane answers to a disciple's questions simplified for the understanding of the common, unlettered Bedouin and shepherd. These sayings were later repeatedly quoted according to the understanding of the listener, passed from the mouths to the ears of ten generations over two hundred years. They were modified, embellished, or kept pure according to the intention, memory, and understanding of the converser.

The blessed prophet of Allah instructed his disciples:

> Do not have anything else dictated from me,
> save the Qur'an. If anyone has written any
> word other than the Qur'an, erase it.[32]

[32] Quoted in *Sahih Muslim*.

On another occasion, the prophet permitted one of the disciples (Abdullah ibn Umar) to write down some of his sayings. On the whole, Prophet Muhammad discouraged his disciples to write down his sayings in case they became confused with the writings in the Koran. One day the messenger appeared while some of his disciples were writing down his sayings. He was aghast when he interjected,

> What! Are you compiling another book
> along with the Book of Allah?

The prophet then commanded that the transcribing disciples should keep Allah's words pure and not to mix them up with any kinds of ambiguities. The disciples then made a bonfire of their notes and parables in an open field.[33]

The blessed *Nabi* left behind the following documents when he died:

1. The Koran.
2. A register of about 1,500 names of the disciples.
3. Copies of letters the prophet wrote to various kings and rulers.
4. Documents of various treatise and obligatory rules.

The blessed prophet did not leave behind a copy of his sayings, teachings, parables, or speeches. His sense of humility would have prevented him from doing so. He had wanted to keep Allah's words pure. It has been quoted from the prophet's wife A'ishah that her father, Abu Bakr, had a very restless night; and the following morning, he sent for his collection of hadith and a made a bonfire of it.[34] Umar ibn al-Khattab had similar misgivings about his collection of the hadith. For a whole month, he performed *istikhara* (fasting, meditation, and seclusion), at the end of which he swore in Allah's

[33] *Tadween-e-Hadith*, 249.

[34] Ibid., 285–88.

name that he would not let His words be amalgamated with other words. He said that,

> he thought of the people of previous generations
> who had passed before us, who wrote books
> and adhered to those books so strongly
> that they forgot the Book of Allah.[35]

During the caliphate of Umar ibn al-Khattab, two to twelve years after the prophet's death, there was an abundance of hadith circulating. Umar placed people under oath and ordered them that whatever hadith they had in their possession be brought before him. The public submitted whatever hadith were in their possession. Umar then ordered a public bonfire of those hadith.[36] He sent a circular to all cities to destroy any evidence of the hadith copies. It is documented that Umar had imprisoned Abdullah bin Ma'sood, Abu Durda, and Abu Ma'sood Ansari for illegally being in possession of hadith.[37]

There were some written hadith pertaining to the time of the prophet written by Abdullah ibn Umar, 'Ali ibn Abi Talib, and Unus on their own volition. There is no historical record documenting whether the prophet was aware of them. There is no record of any collected works of hadith approved or given by the prophet to the Muslims. These three *Sahaba* worked very closely with Caliph Umar in the administration of the caliphate; therefore, the hadith written by Abdullah ibn Umar, 'Ali ibn Abi Talib, and Unus would have become part of Caliph Umar's bonfire. Obviously then, the hadith of these three *Sahaba* that have come to us could not be in their original version.

---

[35] Ibid., 394.

[36] *Sahih Muslim*, vol. 5, p. 141.

[37] Quoted in *Tazkara ul Hafiz*.

According to al-Bukhari, when ibn al-'Abbas was asked what the prophet had left behind for the Muslims, he said, "The Messenger had left behind nothing save the Qur'an."[38] During the times of the first four caliphs who had been the messenger's conferees, not a single copy of hadith was compiled or completed under their supervision. Moreover, exceptional measures were taken to safeguard the purity of the Koran.

Whenever the blessed *Nabi* received a revelation, he would first memorize it and then proclaim it. He would then instruct his companions to memorize it. The prophet would immediately ask the scribes to write down the revelation he had received. He would then recheck and confirm it himself. Whenever a revelation was conveyed to his companions, the prophet would also mention in which sura (chapter) and after what *ayah* (verse) this new revelation should fit. Every Ramadan, the prophet would recite and reconfirm with Angel Gabriel the portion of the Koran that had thus far been revealed, including the order of the chapter and verse. The Koran was authenticated and confirmed by the prophet himself during his lifetime. The complete Koran with the correct sequences of the verses was present during the lifetime of the prophet.

According to the historians, the Koran was written on different materials. When the prophet passed away, Abu Bakr ordered that the Koran be written on a common material in the shape of sheets and bound together with a string so that pages did not get lost. During the time of Uthman, the third caliph, the companions had their own copies of the manuscript of the Koran that had not been authenticated by the prophet. To avoid any mistakes, Uthman borrowed the original manuscript of the Koran that had been authorized by the prophet from Hafsah, the prophet's wife. Uthman then ordered the four companions

---

[38] Al-Bukhari, *Fuzail ul Qur'an*, vol. 3.

who had been among the scribes who wrote the Koran when the prophet dictated it, led by Zaid ibn Thabit, to make several copies of Hafsah's manuscript. These copies were then sent to every capital of the state. He requested that all other manuscripts be destroyed. Two of the original manuscripts sent to the capitals exist today. One is in the Tashkent Museum and the other in the Topkapi Sarayi Museum in Istanbul. It is obvious that the hadith was never part of the *din* of the believers of Allah; otherwise, the same measures for the preservation of the hadith would have been taken after the demise of the prophet.

Modern scholars, after much searching for the earliest copies of the hadith, discovered a manuscript under the name of Imam Hamam ibn e Mamba. This manuscript was published by Dr. Hameed Ullah in Hyderabad, India. Hamam ibn e Mamba was a student of Abu Huraira. In ibn e Mamba's manuscript, there are 138 hadith, which the author claimed were compiled under the tutelage of his teacher, Abu Huraira. Abu Huraira died in hijra 58. These hadith were obviously written before hijra 58. Ibn e Mamba is believed to have died in hijra 131, seventy-three years after the death of his teacher. Abu Huraira and ibn e Mamba were able to compile only 138 hadith in Medina before hijra 58, whereas in hijra 300 Imam al-Bukhari compiled 600,000 hadith, and Imam Hanbal collected 1,000,000 hadith, out of which they gave Abu Huraira credit for 5,000. Abu Huraira's hadith had an incredible geometric growth of 360 percent over 250 years.

During the Abbasid period, as we noted earlier, there was a spectacular progress of scholarship in the fields of Islamic arts and sciences. At the same time, the number of hadith compilations increased. The basis of the development of the Islamic arts and sciences was an amalgamation of superior Byzantine, Persian, Chinese, and Hindu cultures under the banner of Islam. This amalgamation resulted in the absorption of the arts of history and mythology from these cultures into Islamic scholarship. After all, writers and scholars were new Muslims converted from the fellowship of Christianity, Judaism, Zoroastrianism, Hinduism, Buddhism, and Confucianism.

All the original hadith compilers and historians were Persians, while none were Arabs. Persians had the ancient tradition of both oral and written folklore and mythology. The hadith compilers were all born in Iran during the third Islamic century (hijra), and they collected the oral traditions of the hadith in Iraq and Iran. There were no written compilations of hadith before their collection except that of ibn e Mamba. From the hundreds of thousands of hadith that these scholars gathered, they chose some and discarded others. The criterion for their selection was their personal judgment as they had no decree from Allah (revelation), nor did they have the consent and approval of the messenger of Allah confirming the authenticity of the prophet's sayings and parables. There were no compiled records of the prophet's sayings from which they could borrow their material for collection. Their collections of the prophet's sayings were from word of mouth, gathered from various towns and villages in Iraq and Iran.

The Koran demands that any transaction, to bear authenticity, must be written down and be witnessed by two or three people.

> When you make a transaction involving future obligations, write it down in the presence of witnesses, or let a scribe write it down faithfully. Let the party incurring the liability dictate truthfully in the presence of two witnesses from among your own men and if two men are not available then a man and two women, so that if one of them errs, then the other one can remind him. Disregard not to put your contract in writing, whether it be small or large, it is more suitable in the eyes of Allah, more suitable as evidence, and

more convenient to prevent doubts in the future
amongst yourselves. (Al-Baqarah 2:282–83)

The same principle applies to corroboration of religious and historical documents. None of the hadith collections had been written down and witnessed. After giving their own verdict on the genuineness of the collected hadith, the religious scholars selected some and discredited others in accordance with their own opinion. No one can vouch for the truth of the hadith based on hearsay and prove that these were indeed the words of the prophet. How could one equate the words passed from mouth to ear through the mental synapses of generation after generation for 250 years with that of the Koran?

After the compilation of the hadith, the scholars pronounced the hadith collections as the inseparable part of the *din* of Islam. Six different editions of the hadith are now being pronounced as the most authentic by the Sunnis and are called the *Sihah Sitta.* The Shia have their own collection. Scholars of Sharia have gone as far as to call these hadith collections *wahiy*, the revelation at par with the Koran.

Although there are some profound parables and sayings of the blessed *Nabi* Muhammad in the hadith collections, there are indeed some that go against the blessed prophet's character and the spirit of the Koran. The prophet's person in some hadith has been relegated and disparaged, while others blemish his character. Whereas the language and the message of the Koran is divine and profound, the language of the hadith collections commonly diminishes the actions and the sayings of the blessed messenger. This makes the believer wonder how the same person, the blessed *Nabi,* could be the fount of wisdom of the Koran and also the source of the mundane hadith collections. The words of the hadith are not those of the *Nabi* but those of the common men of the third-century hijra who had attempted to create a concordance of sayings and parables of Allah's messenger from hearsay and memories passed through word of mouth from one generation to another over the course of 250 years. The result is a document of immense historical value for all generations to come. But it is not a divine document equating the word of Allah with the word of Blessed Nabi passed through the mental synapses of ordinary humans.

Therefore, the hadith collection does not embody the *din*, nor is it comparable to the Koran in authority and authenticity regarding the *din*. The most important theological point made by the Koran is that there is one God, Allah, universal and beyond comparison, who creates and sustains both the material world and the world of human experience. Allah is *Haqq*, the absolute Truth. All other forms of so-called truth are either false in their initial premises or contingently true only in limited situations. The recognition of this fact is of paramount importance to all believers. The concept that Allah is *Haqq* is undeniable. *Haqq*, the absolute Truth, does not fall into the domain of human fancy or ideas, but it stands for beliefs that manifest in concrete form. These beliefs must be in harmony with the changing needs of time and with Allah's laws of the universe. No belief relating to this world can be called *haqq* unless its truth is established by the positive demonstration of Allah's reality. This truth is permanent and unchanging. The hadith collections cannot be called *haqq*, nor can they be called the absolute truth. The reader of the hadith is constantly reminded by the authors of the various degrees of genuineness of the hadith and is advised to sift the truthful ones from the fabricated hadith.

Hadith collectors (the Persians referred to above) found that 99 percent of the hadith were spurious and discarded them. How can we be certain of the truthfulness of the remaining 1 percent of the hadith when our so-called Sunni and Shia scholars and imams continue to label each other's hadith collections as false and fabricated? Any hadith that do not have the precise words of the blessed *Nabi*, the context in which the words were uttered, the witnesses who had been present, the time context, the historical background, and the state of intellectual and moral capacity of the narrators is missing the absolute truth and is liable to mislead the listeners. None of the hadith are related to the blessed *Nabi* Muhammad's words. They are commentaries and interpretations of the words spoken by the prophet as understood by the narrator. Meanings change when words are substituted. And words were indeed substituted many times when the stories about the prophet passed through the memory synapses of more than twelve generations, from Arabic to Farsi and Turki and then back to Arabic, over 250 years.

While *haqq* is reality and truth, *batil* refers to something that is imaginary or false. In matters of *din,* what is not the absolute truth is not *haqq*. What is not *haqq* is *batil* (false or fabricated). What is not truthful cannot be a witness over Allah's word and *din.*

- Imam al-Bukhari (born in Bukhara 256 or 260H) collected 600,000 hadith and, after sifting through them, decided to retain 2,630 hadith and published them in book form under the title *Us'hal kitab baaduz kitab e Allah* (*The Purest Book after the Book of Allah*). The remaining hadith were declared spurious and discarded. *Thus, for his lifetime's labors, al-Bukhari's harvest of those hadith, which he regarded as truthful, was 0.43 percent.*
- Imam Muslim ibn al-Hajjaj (born in Nishapur, 209–261H) collected 300,000 hadith and, after discarding the spurious hadith, retained 4,348. *He regarded as truthful 1.43 percent of the total number of hadith investigated.*
- Imam Abu Isa Muhammad al-Tirmidhi (born in Termez, 209–279H) collected 300,000 hadith, retained 3,115, and discarded the remaining as spurious. *He regarded as truthful 1.5 percent of the total number of hadith investigated.*

- Abu Da'ud (born in Sistan, Iran, 202–275H), collected 500,000 hadith, retained 4,800, and discarded the rest as spurious. *He regarded as truthful 0.96 percent of the total number of hadith investigated.*
- Abu 'Abd Allah ibn Majah (born in Qazvin, Iran, 209–273H) collected 400,000 hadith. *He regarded as truthful 1 percent of the total number of hadith investigated.*
- Imam Abd ar-Rahman al-Nasa'i (born in Nisa, Khorasan, Iran, died 303H) collected 1,000,000 hadith and, after retaining 4,321, discarded the rest as spurious. *He regarded as truthful 0.43 percent of the total number of hadith investigated.*

The hadith collectors should have realized that, after a lifetime's efforts in collecting the parables and the sayings of the blessed *Nabi*, their harvest of the hadith that they regarded as *Sahih* or truthful was a miniscule 0.43 to 1.5 percent; the remaining 98.5 to 99.57 percent hadith, according to their own judgment, were spurious and deserved to be destroyed. You cannot base your *din* on 1 percent truth and 99 percent falsehood.

Yet this falsehood was equated with Allah's word, in spite of the fact that Allah proclaimed to the world on the last Friday, the ninth day of *Zul-hajj* in the tenth year of hijra (631CE), at Arafat:

ٱلْيَوْمَ يَئِسَ ٱلَّذِينَ كَفَرُوا۟ مِن دِينِكُمْ فَلَا تَخْشَوْهُمْ وَٱخْشَوْنِ ۚ ٱلْيَوْمَ أَكْمَلْتُ لَكُمْ دِينَكُمْ وَأَتْمَمْتُ عَلَيْكُمْ نِعْمَتِى وَرَضِيتُ لَكُمُ ٱلْإِسْلَٰمَ

دِينًا

This day have those who reject faith (kafaru)
given up all hope of compromising your faith,
fear them not, but only fear Me. This day have
I perfected your religion for you, bestowed

on you with My blessings, and decreed Islam
as your religion (Al-Ma'idah 5:3, Koran)

﴿ حمٓ ﴿١﴾ وَٱلۡكِتَٰبِ ٱلۡمُبِينِ ﴿٢﴾ إِنَّآ أَنزَلۡنَٰهُ فِي لَيۡلَةٖ مُّبَٰرَكَةٍۚ إِنَّا كُنَّا مُنذِرِينَ ﴿٣﴾ فِيهَا يُفۡرَقُ كُلُّ أَمۡرٍ حَكِيمٍ ﴿٤﴾ أَمۡرٗا مِّنۡ عِندِنَآۚ إِنَّا كُنَّا
مُرۡسِلِينَ ﴿٥﴾ رَحۡمَةٗ مِّن رَّبِّكَۚ إِنَّهُۥ هُوَ ٱلسَّمِيعُ ٱلۡعَلِيمُ ﴿٦﴾ رَبِّ ٱلسَّمَٰوَٰتِ وَٱلۡأَرۡضِ وَمَا بَيۡنَهُمَآۖ إِن كُنتُم مُّوقِنِينَ ﴿٧﴾ لَآ إِلَٰهَ إِلَّا هُوَ يُحۡيِۦ
وَيُمِيتُۖ رَبُّكُمۡ وَرَبُّ ءَابَآئِكُمُ ٱلۡأَوَّلِينَ

Ha Mim. By the Book, that makes matters lucid; We revealed it during the blessed night, verily We are always warning against Evil. Therein is proclaimed every wise decree, by command, from Our Presence, for We are ever sending revelations, as a Mercy from your Lord: for He is the hearer and knower. The Lord of the heavens and the earth and all that is in between them, if you have an assured faith. There is no god but He: it is He Who gives life and death, the Lord and Cherisher, your Lord and Lord of your forefathers. (Ad-Dukhan 44:1–8)

﴿ فَإِنَّمَا يَسَّرۡنَٰهُ بِلِسَانِكَ لِتُبَشِّرَ بِهِ ٱلۡمُتَّقِينَ وَتُنذِرَ بِهِۦ قَوۡمٗا لُّدّٗا ﴿٩٧﴾ وَكَمۡ أَهۡلَكۡنَا قَبۡلَهُم مِّن قَرۡنٍ هَلۡ تُحِسُّ مِنۡهُم مِّنۡ أَحَدٍ أَوۡ
تَسۡمَعُ لَهُمۡ رِكۡزَۢا ﴿٩٨﴾ ﴾

So, have We made the (Qur'an) easy in your own tongue, that with it you may give glad tidings to the righteous, and warnings to people given to contention. But how many (countless) generations before them have We destroyed? Canst thou find a single one of them (now) or hear (so much as) a whisper of them? (Taha 19:97, Koran)

﴿ وَلَقَدْ صَرَّفْنَا فِي هَٰذَا ٱلْقُرْءَانِ لِلنَّاسِ مِن كُلِّ مَثَلٍ ۚ وَكَانَ ٱلْإِنسَٰنُ أَكْثَرَ شَيْءٍ جَدَلًا ﴿٥٤﴾ وَمَا مَنَعَ ٱلنَّاسَ أَن يُؤْمِنُوٓا۟ إِذْ جَآءَهُمُ
ٱلْهُدَىٰ وَيَسْتَغْفِرُوا۟ رَبَّهُمْ إِلَّآ أَن تَأْتِيَهُمْ سُنَّةُ ٱلْأَوَّلِينَ أَوْ يَأْتِيَهُمُ ٱلْعَذَابُ قُبُلًا

We have explained in detail in this Qur-an, for the benefit of mankind, every kind of similitude: but man is, in most things, contentious. And what is there to keep back men from believing, now that guidance has come to them, nor from praying for forgiveness from their Lord, but that (they ask that) the ways of the ancients be repeated with them, or the Wrath be brought to them face to face? (Al-Kahf 18:54–55, Koran)

In the above four *ayahs*, Allah has amply explained to mankind that all that the believers need to know of their *din* is in the Koran:

This day have I perfected your religion for you. You have been given the Book that makes matters lucid. So, have We made the (Qur'an) easy in your own tongue, that with it you may give glad tidings to the righteous, and warnings to people given to contention. We have explained in detail in this Qur'an, for the benefit of mankind, every kind of similitude: but man is, in most things, contentious.

In the Koran, Allah has made it amply clear that the Koran is a perfect and complete book and guidance of the *din*. The Koran has been made simple for every person's understanding of their *din*.

- The Koran has described Islam as *ad-deen*, which is generally translated in English as "religion." Islam is not a religion and has never been described as such in the Koran. Islam is a way of life, a system, a code of law. *Islam signifies the divine order that governs life on the earth and its relationship to Allah's laws regulating the order of the universe.* The Koran establishes a universal order based on the divinely ordained values of life. Were every human to observe the covenant of the Koran, the world would be at peace forever, and justice would prevail. By following the hadith collection of the third-century hijra, *Muslims* have relegated their faith from a divinely ordained order to a human set of values, misleading themselves and causing others to deviate from Allah's path.

- The hadith collection of sayings, deeds, and ethos attributed to the messenger of Allah was collected by hadith scholars in book form in the third-century hijra. A part of the hadith collection is concerned with character traits of the prophet. Believers regard the character of the holy prophet as an embodiment of humanity. Unfortunately, the hadith collections blemish and stain his character.
- From historical evidence, it is apparent that the blessed *Nabi* Muhammad does not refer to the hadith as part of *din*, nor did his companions believe it to be so. The hadith collections passed down to us from the third-century hijra are not the original words of the messenger and do not carry the sanction of Allah or Blessed Muhammad. The contents of these hadith collections are mind boggling. When you read Imam al-Bukhari's hadith collection, you will find words and sentences that no believer will ever have the audacity to attribute to the holy prophet, a man whose vision and insight made him the greatest personality of the last fourteen hundred years. The imam also had the audacity to name his hadith collection *Us'hal kitab baaduz kitab e Allah* (*The Purest Book after the Book of Allah*). Considering that he had rejected and discarded *99.57*

percent of his source material as spurious, bogus, fake, forged, counterfeit, and unauthentic, how could one compare the purity of the remaining *0.43 percent* of the source material with the Koran, the word of Allah, the source of all *haqq*?

﴿ وَمِنَ ٱلنَّاسِ مَن يَشْتَرِى لَهْوَ ٱلْحَدِيثِ لِيُضِلَّ عَن سَبِيلِ ٱللَّهِ بِغَيْرِ عِلْمٍ وَيَتَّخِذَهَا هُزُوًا ۚ أُو۟لَـٰٓئِكَ لَهُمْ عَذَابٌ مُّهِينٌ ۝٦ ﴾

But there are those people who purchase the <u>occupation of hadith (telling of tales),</u> so that they may mislead others from the Path of Allah and throw ridicule (on the Path): for such there will be a humiliating Penalty. (Luqman 31: 6, Koran)

- The hadith collections are the words of narrators and Imams al-Bukhari, Muslim, al-Tirmidhi, Abu Da'ud, ibn Majah, and Abd ar-Rahman al-Nasa'i. They are not the words of Allah or the inspired word of the holy prophet. The hadith collectors undertook the task of their own volition and did not have the divine sanction of Allah or of his messenger, nor did they have the authority and guidance of the *ummah.* These hadith collections performed a valuable task of gathering historical data of the prophet's time in Medina and contributions of the companions. History carries the bias of the narrator, and as such, a historical document cannot become the foundation of the *din* of Islam. The hadith collections of the third century have done a great disservice to Islam by distracting the believers from the Koran and by causing dissension and conflict among the *ummah.*

According to the Koran, *iman* is not just belief but it is also, in fact, knowledge. *Iman* is conviction that is based on reason and knowledge. The Koran does not recognize belief that involves blind acceptance.

Islam does include acceptance of certain things that cannot be explained by perception through the human senses. Our reason and thinking will compel us to recognize the existence of such things. *Iman*, according to the Koran, signifies conviction based on full mental acceptance and intellectual satisfaction. *Iman* gives a person inner contentment, a feeling of *amn* or contentment (same common root). Thus, *iman* means to believe in Allah and to testify to His reality, to have confidence in that belief, and to bow down in obedience. There are five fundamental facts stated in the Koran that a believer must accept: (1) *iman* in Allah, (2) the law of *mukafat* and the afterlife, (3) the angels (*malaika*), (4) the revelations, and (5) the messengers.

Belief in Allah means to profess obedience to Him and His covenant but also to show it in one's actions and to be always in *taqwa* of Allah. Belief in the law of *mukafat* means to have conviction that every human action has an inescapable consequence of either reward or retribution. Angels are not the winged creatures depicted in children's literature. They are heavenly forces that carry out the laws of Allah governing the universe. They bow to Allah since they follow his orders. They also bow to mans because we are able to study, understand, and manipulate the laws of nature for the benefit of mankind. Belief in revelations and messengers implies that human intellect alone cannot safely reach the final destination without the divine guidance in the form of *wahiy* delivered by the messengers to mankind. This guidance is to the whole humankind sent through many messengers.

The Muslim tradition began with *Ibrahim*, our father. The believers have a belief system and a divine commandment to be the witness and to spread the message to mankind that began with Blessed Nabi *Ibrahim* and was completed with Blessed Nabi *Muhammad*. Whereas the message of *wahiy* is divine and calls humankind to Allah, the God of the universe, the message of the hadith collection of the third century is a human historical document, a product of the frail human mind, and as such cannot be a witness over the *din* of Allah.

During the first three centuries of Islam, there was untrammeled freedom of the pursuit of knowledge by men of learning, leading to the pushing of the boundaries of knowledge and learning in the fields of sciences, philosophy, literature, astronomy, mathematics, and music to such an extent that Arabic remained the major intellectual and scientific language of the world for over a thousand years. However, after the completion of the hadith collection by al-Bukhari, Muslim, al-Tirmidhi, Abu Da'ud, ibn Majah, and Abd ar-Rahman al-Nasa'i, there came a new culture to Islam.

During the Abbasid period of al-Ma'mun there was popular discontent, and difficulties to the throne were increasing. To deal with these, al-Ma'mun set up an inquisition (*minhah*). The judges and people in authority had to state publicly that they believed that the Koran was created and rejected the view that it was an uncreated word of Allah. This was not a piece of theological hairsplitting but an important sociopolitical and legal question.

Soon after Prophet Muhammad's death, some people had the belief that the caliph was or should be a divinely inspired person whose decisions should be binding on Muslims. In other words, they wanted the caliph to carry a priestly authority both in temporal and spiritual matters, and this was also the viewpoint of the caliph al-Ma'mun. If the Koran, though it was Allah's word, was created, then a leader inspired by Allah could presumably change it. If the Koran, though it was Allah's word, was created, then a leader inspired by Allah could presumably change it.

The opposite point of view was that of scholar-jurists, who had become an important class in Islamic lands. Quite a large population of the empire could not speak or read Arabic; to understand the complex issues in the Koran, they had to depend on these jurist-scholars. The scholars insisted that the Koran was the uncreated word of Allah and therefore unchangeable and that they alone were its authorized interpreters who could pronounce how it was to be applied to contemporary situations. Their contention was that it was them, and not the caliph, who had the final word.

The policy of the inquisition was finally discontinued in around 850 AD because it failed to reconcile the rival interests of the caliph and the scholar-jurists. The scholar-jurists in Persia and Iraq embraced the hadith collections wholeheartedly and made them the main teaching material of the *din*, relegating the Koran to a secondary place in their sermons (khutbahs) and the curriculum of the seminaries (madrassas). In Persia and in India, the Arabic language did not become popular with the masses; therefore, the masses had difficulty understanding the basic message of the Koran. Here, the hadith could readily be recited to the unlettered population, notwithstanding the fact that there were doubts of soundness and objectivity attached to various hadith. Moreover, in societies with an oral tradition, precision, exactness, and total truthfulness of the hadith became an insignificant issue. Mullahs became the purveyors of outlandish tales of the blessed *Nabi* and his companions that are prevalent in these societies to our day.

Nationalism had always kindled the hearts of Persians, and in the ninth and tenth centuries of the Common Era, there was a resurgence of Farsi, maintaining its traditional grammar, though incorporating a large number of Arabic words. The influence of Farsi and the Persian culture spilled over into Turkey, Central Asia, and India, influencing the literary traditions of both Turkish and Urdu. The result was that the vast populations of Turkey, Persia, India, and Central Asia were cut off from learning the Arabic language. Teachers, scholar-jurists, and other learned people lacked fluency and mastery of Arabic language, although they were skilled in the intricacies of the hadith collections. During the next one thousand years in Turkey, Persia, and India, almost every Muslim child was taught to recite the Arabic Koran without ever learning the meaning of the words. Children could recite the Koran in Arabic since the Farsi, Turki, and Urdu languages shared the alphabet with Arabic but could not comprehend the meaning of the holy book.

The Persians had a great tradition of oral history in epic accounts of their ancient kings and heroes. The same deep-seated tradition necessitated the hard and long search for the stories of their new hero, the blessed *Nabi* Muhammad. Around the same period when the imams of Persia were compiling their epic hadith collections, poet Daqiqi was writing thousands of couplets about Zoroaster and the ancient Persian kings. When Daqiqi died with his epic account partly finished, Firdawsi took over his mantle and wrote the remaining *Shahnameh*, although it took him another thirty-five years to complete it.

With the completion of the hadith collections, the standard of Islamic scholarship began a slow decline; and by the beginning of the twentieth century, less than 5 percent of the Islamic world had any literary skills, and no new discovery or knowledge had emanated from the Muslims for over three hundred years. The responsibility of imparting knowledge to the young and old was now totally in the hands of people who called themselves the ulema when their own skills were suspect. The scholar-jurists sought the elite circles and became the servants of the sultans and the aristocracy. They valued their privileged position and fought hard to keep it that way. Their secure positions depended on secure endowments, which gradually became hereditary. Over three hundred years with no new knowledge in sciences, philosophy, literature, or mechanical and industrial skills, the Islamic world began to languish in the stale hadith collections, Sharia, and *fiqh*.

The Koran has defined knowledge as

﴿أَلَمْ تَرَ أَنَّ ٱللَّهَ أَنزَلَ مِنَ ٱلسَّمَآءِ مَآءً فَأَخْرَجْنَا بِهِۦ ثَمَرَٰتٍ مُّخْتَلِفًا أَلْوَٰنُهَا ۚ وَمِنَ ٱلْجِبَالِ جُدَدٌۢ بِيضٌ وَحُمْرٌ مُّخْتَلِفٌ أَلْوَٰنُهَا وَغَرَابِيبُ
سُودٌ ﴿٢٧﴾ وَمِنَ ٱلنَّاسِ وَٱلدَّوَآبِّ وَٱلْأَنْعَٰمِ مُخْتَلِفٌ أَلْوَٰنُهُۥ كَذَٰلِكَ ۗ إِنَّمَا يَخْشَى ٱللَّهَ مِنْ عِبَادِهِ ٱلْعُلَمَٰٓؤُا۟ ۗ إِنَّ ٱللَّهَ عَزِيزٌ غَفُورٌ ﴿٢٨﴾

> Seest thou not that Allah sends down rain from the sky? With it, we then bring out produce of various colors. And in the mountains are tracts white and red, of various shades of color, and black intense in hue. And so, amongst men and crawling creatures and cattle, are they of various colors. Those truly fear Allah, among His Servants, who have knowledge: for Allah is exalted in Might, Oft-Forgiving. (Fatir 35:27–28, Koran)

The knowledge that Allah envisions is that of His universe, His creation, and His laws. In other words, humans are asked go abroad to seek knowledge—the knowledge of Allah's creation of atoms, neutrons, protons, structure of light and color, rays, particles chromosomes, mitochondria, DNA, quantum theory, neurons, axons, osteons, metallurgy, minerals, galaxies, electricity, forces of gravity, magnetism, black holes, animals, plants, and microbes; Allah's scriptures and His covenants; anthropology; ocean depths; outer space; and myriad other disciplines pertaining to the glory and wonders of the ever-unfolding and infinitesimal complexity of Allah's divine magnificence. Allah gave men and women a mind with infinite complexity to unravel Allah's laws for their benefit and that of His other creatures.

The Islamic thirst and yearning for knowledge was so intense that early Muslim scholars spearheaded the knowledge of arts and sciences for over three hundred years. The torch of knowledge extinguished when the torchbearers failed to remember that they were searching for the truth (*haqq*) of Allah's mysteries; instead, they became entangled in the web of the hadith collections, and the extent of their search remained entombed in these traditions for one thousand years. Then the foreigners came to the land of Islam and woke the "Muslims" from a deep slumber to show them the path to the truth. Absolute truth emanates from Allah and the Koran. All the sciences, scriptures, lexis, and every phase of creation are dependent on Allah's divine laws and signs. Every messenger of Allah carried out His commandments without any deviation. The blessed *Nabi* of Allah, Muhammad, proclaimed to the world on the mount of Arafat Allah's *wahiy* (message) on the last Friday, the ninth day of *Zul-hajj* in the tenth year of hijra (631 CE):

ٱلْيَوْمَ يَئِسَ ٱلَّذِينَ كَفَرُوا۟ مِن دِينِكُمْ فَلَا تَخْشَوْهُمْ وَٱخْشَوْنِ ۚ ٱلْيَوْمَ أَكْمَلْتُ لَكُمْ دِينَكُمْ وَأَتْمَمْتُ عَلَيْكُمْ نِعْمَتِى وَرَضِيتُ لَكُمُ ٱلْإِسْلَٰمَ

دِينًا

> This day have those who reject faith (kafaru) have given up all hope of compromising your faith, fear them not, but only fear Me. This day have I perfected your religion for you, bestowed on you with My blessings, and decreed Islam as your religion. (Al-Ma'idah 5:3, Koran)

On that day, the *din* of Islam was complete, and all man-made innovations after that are just novelties, and anyone indulging in that was making a sport of his religion. From that day onward, the people, men and women, who obey and keep their covenant with Allah are the believers, the *muttaqeen*. They are the believers of Allah and the Koran, revealed to the world through the prophethood of Muhammad. The believers follow the Koran and Allah's covenant. For their *din*, Allah alone is sufficient. They are not Shias or Sunnis, nor do they belong to any other sect; they are the believers of Allah, *muttaqeen*. They believe in the one universal Allah, and they place their trust in Him in the same way that our father Ibrahim did thousands of years ago.

Each believer is in direct communion with Allah. This connection is exclusive. In Islam, there is no priesthood. In mosques and madrassas in nations where illiteracy abounds, self-appointed clergy, imams, ulema, and mullahs spend 90 percent of their time expounding the virtues of various hadith from the hadith collections of the third century and a fraction of the time on the message of the Koran. It is easier to speak eloquently in their vernacular to the illiterate audience about folklore and the hadith rather than taking the time and skill to elucidate simple verses of the Koran in Arabic. Clerics, ulema, and Islamic priests lack the discipline of precision and exactness required in the teaching of the Koran. The hadith have been declared *Sahih* for their presumed authenticity by the hadith compilers, yet these hadith have given way to numerous contradictions. Placing such hadith next to the *din* has resulted in the disintegration of the solidarity of Islam's brotherhood, the *ummah*, dividing it into several factions. Both the Sunnis and the Shias have their own kind of hadith. Every faction and sect has embellished its religion with hadith of their own inclination, declaring every other sect as having false traditions.

The meaning of the Koran is sometimes misconstrued by trying to interpret it on the basis of some hadith. For instance, in one Koranic translation, a hadith from al-Bukhari has been used to translate verse Luqman 31:6, distorting the message altogether.[39]

[39] Dr. Muhammad Taqi-ud-din Al-Hilali and Dr. Muhammad Muhsin Khan, *Interpretation of the Meaning of the Noble Qur'an* (Islamic University, Al-Madinah Al-Munawara).

وَمِنَ ٱلنَّاسِ مَن يَشْتَرِى لَهْوَ ٱلْحَدِيثِ لِيُضِلَّ عَن سَبِيلِ ٱللَّهِ بِغَيْرِ عِلْمٍ وَيَتَّخِذَهَا هُزُوًا ۚ أُو۟لَـٰٓئِكَ لَهُمْ عَذَابٌ مُّهِينٌ

And of mankind is he who purchases idle talks (i.e. music, singing) to mislead (men) from the path of Allah without knowledge, and takes it (the Qur'an) by way of mockery. For such there will be a humiliating torment (in the Hellfire).

Whereas the word ٱلْحَدِيث *hadith* universally is accepted to mean "story, tale, talk, discourse, or tidings," the translators of this publication have inserted *music and singing* to elucidate the meaning of *hadith*. Such an interjection of words, based on hadith collections, into the Koran falsifies Allah's words. Allah's messenger forbade his companions from mixing his words with that of the Koran.

Fifty percent of the population of the believers, the women of Islam, have been excluded from mainstream Islam by the hadith scholars against the commandments of the Koran. Women were regarded as inferior beings in most pre-Islamic cultures, including the Arabs, Persians, Greeks, Romans, and Hindus. Their status was not any higher among the Turkish and the Mongol tribes of Central Asia. In Judaism, women were forbidden from the inner sanctuary of the temple; and in early Pauline Christianity, their position was relegated to the entrance or outside the church at prayer time.

Islam brought dignity and grace to the status of women—the mothers, wives, and daughters. Women had their rights established and their social status elevated as equal to that of men. They attended prayer services at the Prophet's Mosque; they held regular and frequent discourse with Prophet's Mosque; they held regular and frequent discourse with the prophet of Allah on religious, women's, and family issues. They participated in battles alongside their men. Women worked outside their homes. The first person to convert to Islam, Khadijah, was a successful international trader and owned an import and export business, dealing in goods from India, Persia, Africa, Yemen, and the Byzantine Empire. She employed several men to assist her in her business. Other women memorized the Koran and taught other Muslims. A'ishah gave regular talks and discourses on religious matters. Other women led the ritual prayers and *dhikr-e-Allah* gatherings. The ulema and other followers of the hadith collections of the third century over the last one thousand years have betrayed Allah and His messenger in their obligations to their women—their mothers, wives, sisters, and daughters.

Whereas every believer has absolute faith that Allah's word is the absolute truth and obeys Allah's covenant, the followers of the hadith collections have anchored their understanding of the Holy Koran to the third-century hadith, thus fossilizing their thinking and rationality to the mindset of hadith narrators of that period. Accordingly, in their cultural setting, every believer must act and behave as the third-century Iranians and Arabs did. As most of the Sharia was based on the Persian collection of the hadith, the modern world must live up to the norm and behavior of that age. A tremendous amount of knowledge gleaned through Allah's revelation by the believers of different ages is expected to be moored to the third century also. Since the Koran is the absolute truth, why would one want to measure its authority and authenticity through the eyes of hadith collections whose veracity has been questioned by the believers over the last one thousand years.

Every Muslim claims that his way of salat is the true and genuine method of the prophet Muhammad; every sect claims to pray the same way as the prophet did. The principle of the *wudhu* stated in the Koran is that we must wash our face and hands up to the elbows. If a person washes to the elbows and another one to the wrists only, will both of them be correct or the one that follows the Koran? Similarly, if anyone lifted his hands to the ears or not, another folded his arms on his chest or below his navel, and someone let his arms hang by his side, who is correct? The space between his legs while standing for prayers, was it too little or too much? Did he recite Sura Al-Fatihah after the imam or not, or did he say *amen* after the Sura Al-Fatihah in a loud voice or not? Did he recite *tarawih* prayers in eight or twenty cycles? How did the messenger pray? If everyone is following the hadith in manner of the messenger's prayer, then who is wrong? As every sect has its own hadith, which hadith is correct? Thus, where is the unity of Islam among the hadith followers?

The only answer is that the messenger of Allah prayed only one way, his own way, and the hadith narrators were inaccurate in their reporting. If there can be such a disparity in the hadith narration of the most important function of the prayers that the messenger led five times day, day after day, for over ten years in Medina, how can we rely on the veracity of the remaining hadith collections? This points to the fact that they do not form the basis of the *din* because they are neither inspired by Allah nor the word of the messenger. The hadith collections are a historical document with some narrations that are compatible with the Koran, while others are in conflict with the covenant of Allah and should be discarded altogether. There are some hadith that are insulting to the dignity of the blessed prophet and therefore should be condemned.

Overall, the hadith collections have been used by *Shaitan* (Satan) to mislead and split the Muslim community into factions. Some "Muslims" manipulated by Satan rely mostly or exclusively on the hadith collections for their faith, beliefs, and actions, to the exclusion of the Koran. They act as Mohammedans, just as the Christians, Zoroastrians, and Buddhists follow their teachers and leaders. In contrast, the believers of Allah serve their covenant with Allah. The *din*, as envisaged in the covenant of Allah, is a total belief system of a person based on total submersion of one's personality with Allah with total awareness and *taqwa* of Allah at all times through observance of all the thirty-seven commandments of His covenant. This message, given by Allah through His blessed *Nabi,* is a communion not only with Allah but also through Him with other humans and the rest of Allah's creation, both alive and inanimate.

The phrase *amilu al saalihaat* (to do good, to perform wholesome deeds) refers to those who persist in striving to set things right, who restore harmony, peace, and balance. The other acts of good works recognized in the covenant of the Koran are to show compassion, to be merciful and forgive others, to be just, to protect the weak, to defend the oppressed, to be generous and charitable, to be truthful, to seek knowledge and wisdom, to be kind, to be peaceful, to love others, and to perform beautiful deeds.

Chapter Five

Covenant of Allah: Sharia and Fiqh

The blessed prophet said, "Do you know what saps the foundation of Islam, and ruins it?"

> *The errors of the learned destroy it, and the disputations of the hypocrite and the orders of the kings who have lost the way.*

The political upheavals of the post-Abbasid period caused a profound transformation of social organization of the Middle Eastern populations. The population was exposed to tremendous dangers to their lives and property and suffered extraordinary economic hardships caused by marauding armies. There were rapid changes of political overlords, a decline in older landowning and bureaucratic elite, and the imposition of new foreign rulers. With every new army, there was a period of massacres, looting, destruction, and confiscation of property. Agricultural lands were assigned to the new military elite, causing further instability in the region. In response, the people throughout the region drew together in defensive movements and created a new communal structure. This was, in fact, the first defensive movement of the Muslim peoples to take control of their lives.

The Abbasid Empire, in many ways, delayed the diffusion of Islam to the mass of Middle Eastern populations. Although the empire was the official sponsor and protector of Islam, the new religion remained a religion of the minority. The Abbasid Empire accepted the existing Christian, Jewish, and Zoroastrian communities and the authority of their religious institutions.

With the breakup of the Abbasid Empire, the old social elites were swept away. Churches could no longer protect their members, landowning families were dispossessed, and the administration crumbled. The result was a vacuum of leadership into which the only surviving elite element was drawn—Muslim scholars, teachers, preachers, and holy men. The *Karramiya*—a religious movement that combined theological principles, Sufi practices, and social mission—established networks of khanqahs (Sufi hospices) that eventually became the basis of community organizations and conversion to Islam. Town quarters became organized under the auspices of Islamic schools of law, Shia communities, or Sufi or other religious leadership. By the twelfth century, the majority of the Middle Eastern populations were identified with Islam. Communal leaders were Muslim ulema and Sufis. Christians, Jews, and Zoroastrians had become minorities everywhere. The newly Islamized populations of newly converted Christians, Jews, and Zoroastrians of differing backgrounds coalesced to form new community organizations, which form today's *ummah.*

As early as AD 660, Muslims had begun to divide into two camps: the Sunnis or the supporters of the existing Umayyad and later Abbasid caliphates and the Shiites, who opposed the established regimes and insisted that only the descendants of Ali had the right to the leadership of Muslims. In the tenth century, the Shiites—then deprived of living imams—codified their tradition in the books of hadith, law, and theology and elaborated a ritual calendar focused on the veneration of tombs of Ali at Najaf and his son Husayn at Karbala.

Among the Sunnis, a variety of small communities took form as people gathered around readers of the Koran, reciters of hadith, scholars of law, and theologians and mystics to whom they looked for inspiration and guidance. The legal schools evolved from the informal discussion of scholars, students, and judges into quasi-administrative bodies producing codes of law, staffing the judiciary, carrying on legal instruction, and providing informal leadership and instruction for the common people.

With the breakup of the Abbasid Empire, the legal schools were modified to become the basis of a mass Islamic society. Provided with endowments, the schools created permanent institutions known as madrassas, teaching colleges and residences, as the basis of their activities. The colleges provided buildings for classes, residences, kitchens, and stipends for both teachers and students. The ulema (scholars) also assumed a larger role in the communities by organizing groups, lodges, and sectarian associations under their leadership. The ulema also represented the urban populations to the conquerors; provided local administration and justice; and arranged for local security, public works, taxation, charities, and other services. With the expansion of the madrassas and religious education, the Koran became the focus of recitation and personal piety, while the hadith became the focal point for the study of the Sharia and the science of jurisprudence. While there was little dissension in the discussion of the intricacies of the Koran, the scholar-jurists became locked in arguments on the merits of various hadith. For the elucidation of the truth of the Koran, the logic and convoluted debates became moored to the elusive hadith.

At the same time, a new form of Islamic communal organization under Sufi auspices came into being. Sufis, for centuries, had gathered under charismatic, holy men in khanqahs for meetings, worship, and instruction. In the twelfth century, Sufi organizations under the influence of the legal schools and state support became more formal. Soon Sufis became organized into brotherhoods. The transmission of *dhikr,* the meditational method of concentrating the soul on the veneration of Allah, became the defining quality of fellowship. As Sufi organizations became more organized, they took on important roles in the towns and villages. In towns and villages throughout the Islamic lands, lay Muslims came to the Sufis for supplementary worship, spiritual consolation, healing, and charity. The Sufi brotherhoods also adopted the role of mediators of problems between the peoples and the governments and between factional and tribal rivals. Alongside the legal schools, Sufi communities emerged as a basic organizing social force among the Muslims.

For the Muslims, the prophet himself embodied both religious and political authority. He revealed Allah's will and law for the people. He was the ruler of the community who also collected taxes, waged wars, and arbitrated disputes. The early caliphs also claimed the prophet's religious authority to make pronouncements on religious laws and beliefs and claimed the political prerogatives of emperors. In the evolution of the caliphate, the new rulers such as the conquerors and emperors increasingly became political leaders with only symbolic religious authority. The caliphs maintained only nominal religious authority. By the time of the collapse of the Abbasid Empire, the authority to promulgate or discover law, to make judgments on religious belief, and to instruct ordinary Muslims devolved on the ulema and the holy men.

This became a defining moment in the history of Islam. The scholars and jurists assumed the role of the priesthood of their pre-Islamic ancestors. From then on, the priests of Islam assumed the role of custodianship of Allah on the earth. Like their pre-Islamic priestly models, they began to wear expensive robes and headgear resembling crowns and assumed fancy titles like maulana, *allama*, and ayatollah that presented them as the signs of Allah on the earth. This was the beginning of the downfall of Islam.

The Turkish invasions and the establishment of nomadic or slave military regimes made acute the question of religious or state authority functions. Nomads and slaves were foreigners in origin and culture, warriors imposed on civilian populations; their allegiance to Islam were often suspect, while the town and village elites were Muslim religious leaders. Turkish nomadic and slave military authorities were eager to establish internal order, to facilitate taxation, and to minimize resistance from their subject populations. They needed legitimatization and recognition, which only the holders of religious hierarchy could supply. The military elites thus sought the support of the religious elite by underwriting their activities. They provided endowments of mosques and khankahs and stipends for teachers, jurists, clerics, and students. Seljuk rulers endowed madrassas in every major city of their empire. They endowed Sufi khankahs to foster holy men who served as missionaries of Islam. In return, the religious leaders accepted Seljuk states, recognized their legitimacy, justified them to their subjects, and taught the necessity of obedience.

The Muslim society became, in practice, governed by state elites who patronized the ulema, who in return legitimized un-Koranic rulers. The collaboration of elites of state and religion and the cooperative relationship between these two institutions would, in future centuries, become the Middle Eastern Muslim solution to the problem of state and religion. The problem with this system of government was that it totally bypassed the common person, the vicegerent of Allah.

Not all Middle Eastern peoples accepted the governing collaboration of the elites of state (kings) and religion (priest class). Many people looked back to the image of the prophet as the embodiment of both religious and political authorities. And many a community ruled according to the laws laid out in the Koran. To unite disparate small communities and to organize and justify resistance to state control, such groups looked to holy Sufi men for a unified *religious-political* leadership in opposition to established states.

Islamic law originates from two major sources, the divine revelation (*wahiy*) and human reasoning (*aql*). The divine revelation is designated as Sharia, the path to righteousness, whereas *fiqh* refers to human understanding—knowledge and reasoning. Scholars include, along with the Koran, the teachings of the blessed prophet as the source of Sharia. Injunctions of the Koran and Sunna provide the core of the Sharia and are collectively called the *nusus*. The Sharia comprises the totality of guidance that Allah revealed to His blessed messenger relating to the dogma of Islam, its moral values, and its practical legal rules. Sharia thus comprises in its scope not only the law but also theology and the moral teachings of Islam. The dogma of theology (*ilm al kalam*) is primarily concerned with liberating a person from superstition and providing him or her with an enlightened conviction in the belief in Allah and the values of Islam. Morality (*ilm al akhlaq*) educates the person in moral virtue, the exercise of self-discipline, and restraint in the fulfillment of natural desires. Sharia provides clear rulings on the fundamentals of Islam, its basic moral values, and practical duties such as prayers, fasting, zakat, hajj, and other devotional matters. It also pronounces on what is lawful (halal) and unlawful (haram). Sharia is generally flexible with regard to matters such as civil transactions, criminal law, government policy, constitution, fiscal policy, and taxation.

Fiqh is concerned with the practical legal rules related to a person's conduct; it is the knowledge of the practical rules of the Sharia derived from the Koran and the Sunna. The practicalities of conduct of a. person are evaluated on a scale of five values: obligatory, recommended, permissible, reprehensible, and forbidden. *Fiqh* requires independent reasoning and intellectual exertion (*ijtihad*). To exercise *ijtihad*, a jurist will require knowledge of the Koran and the hadith and the ability to deduce the rules of Sharia from its source. The jurist qualified to exercise such judgments are called the *mujtahid*.

The history of the development of the Sharia is a short one; its development took two decades during the prophet's mission in Mecca and Medina. There are *350 legal verses* in the Koran (*ayat al ahkam*), with *140* related to dogma and devotional matters (salat, zakat), other charities, fasting, and hajj. *Seventy* verses are devoted to marriage, divorce, paternity, child custody, inheritance, and bequests. Rules concerning commercial transactions—such as sales, lease, loan, usury, and mortgage—constitute the subject of another seventy verses. There are about thirty verses on crimes and penalties, and thirty verses are on justice, equality, evidence, citizen's rights and duties, and consultation in government affairs. Ten verses focus on economic matters.

Fiqh, or the concern with legal practices, was rudimentary during the prophetic mission. *The development of* fiqh *was stimulated by the documentation of hadith by the third-century hijra. Extensive hadith material, both authentic and spurious, became available for fresh inquiry and research.* Therefore, *fiqh* is entirely human in origin as opposed to the Sharia, which is partly based on revelation (*wahiy*) and partly on hadith collections. Though the scholar-jurists regard hadith as *wahiy*, at par with the Koran, this assumption cannot be the truth. The Koran was revealed by Allah through Angel Gabriel and Allah's messenger, and Allah has promised its purity, truth, and sanctity. The Koran is Allah's word. The genuine hadith is the word of the blessed prophet inspired by Allah, but it is not a revelation. The Koran and other scriptures are the revealed books of Allah.

The *mutawatir* hadith are the word-for-word transmission of what the prophet said, and there are no more than ten such hadith. Another kind of hadith is known as *conceptual mutawatir*, in which the concept is taken from the prophet, but the words are that of the narrator. This kind of conceptual *mutawatir* occurs frequently. These are the sayings and the acts of the blessed prophet that explain the essentials of faith, the rituals of worship, the rules that regulate reward and punishment, and the description of the lawful and the unlawful. The companions of the prophet and the generations of Muslims during the last fourteen hundred years have faithfully adhered to these teachings. These explain and supplement the injunctions of the Koran.

The Sunna relates to the Sharia in various capacities. It may merely corroborate the Koran, it may clarify its ambiguous parts, or it may qualify and specify the general ruling of the Koran. The Sunna may contain sayings on matters on which the Koran is silent. However, some scholars and Muslims forget what the prophet said:

I am no more than a man; when I order you anything respecting religion, receive it, and when I tell you anything about the affairs of the world, and then I am nothing but a man.

During the time of the blessed prophet, he was readily accessible to answer everyone's inquiry about his or her new faith. Those who believed in Allah and His prophet accepted his guidance, and those who did not turned away. After the prophet passed away, the first controversy arose in Islam on the issue of caliph and *wilayah.* Most of the Muslims believed that the blessed prophet did not make a will regarding his successor and that they were free to choose anyone from among them as the caliph. Those who later came to be called the Shia believed that the blessed prophet had nominated Ali as his successor. However, neither Ali nor Fatimah pressed such a claim. As the prophet Muhammad did not nominate a specific person in authority in the matters of law in Islam, the responsibility of dealing with matters of religion and law fell on his contemporaries, some of whom possessed the quality of *adalah* (credibility) and had capacity for *ijtihad* (formulation of ideas to solve the problems of the contemporary Muslim world).

After the death of the prophet, the companions dispersed to different lands, and only a few remained in Mecca and Medina. The companions used to adjudicate on the basis of what they knew of the Koran and the Sunna, and when they had nothing to lean on, they referred to other companions who were present. If the companions were unaware of the situation in question, the adjudicator resorted to *ijtihad* for ascertaining the *hukm*[40]. Every companion who arrived in a particular town practiced *ijtihad* in matters he did not find in the Koran or the Sunna.

Because of the absence of the uniformity of knowledge and literacy, the companions (the *Sahaba*) naturally differed in their *ijtihad* and opinions.[41] Therefore, mere individual differences among the *Sahaba* resulted in the differences in their adjudications. These differences grew after the period of the *Sahaba*. The appointed governors (the *Tabi'un*) followed the fatwas of the *Sahaba* generally without opposing them.

For nearly two hundred years after the period of the *Sahaba* and the *Tabi'un*, matters rested with the faqihs, the jurists of various cities (for example, Abu Hanifah, Sufyan, and ibn Abi Layla at Kufah; ibn Jurayj in Mecca; Malik and ibn Majishun at Medina; Uthman al-Taymi and Siwar in Basra; al-Awza'i in Syria; and al-Layth ibn Sa'd in Egypt). These jurists either referred to the *Tabi'un* or practiced *ijtihad*.

The influence of most of these jurists increased gradually until they became the imams of their legal schools by which their followers came to be identified. However, before their popularity, the schools had no name, and no Muslim had ever identified with them at that time. The schools of law continued to multiply until, the beginning of the fourth century.

---

[40] In the Koran, *hukm* denotes arbitration, judgment, authority, and Allah's will. After the passing of the prophet Muhammad, with no central legal power in the post-Medina Muslim society, the noun acquired new meanings over time, with *hukm* coming to refer to temporal executive rule or to a court decision and the plural, *akham*, referring to specific Koranic rules, positive *fiqh* laws derived from Islamic legal methodology, and rules or edicts.

[41] Al Shaykh Taqi al-Din al-'Abbas Ahmad ibn Ali ibn 'Abd al-Qadir ibn Muhammad al-Bali al-Qahiri, also known as al-Maqrizi, *Al-Mawa'iz wa al-i'tibar fi dhikr al-khitat wa al-athar*, 766–845 hijra, AD 1364–1441.

Among the factors that were effectual in giving precedence to a particular school were the number of scholars associated with it, students, patrons, promoters, supporters, and the degree of their prestige, influence, and power in propagating it. Al-Maqrizi, in the fourth volume of his *al-Khutat*, states that,

"Al Qadi Abu Yusuf was appointed judge by Harun al-Rashid, and later after 170 hijra, he came to occupy the post of chief justice (*qadi al-qudat*). Since he was one of the closest disciples of Abu Hanifah, he did not appoint anyone to a judicial post unless they were followers of Abu Hanifah. He selected for the provincial judicial positions of Khurasan, Iraq, Syria, and other places only those who were followers of Abu Hanifah. Thus, it was he who was instrumental in propagating the madhab (school of law) of Abu Hanifah in different regions".

In the early stages of the propagation of the Hanafi madhab in the east, the Maliki school spread to West Africa and later to Egypt in 163 hijra. Al-Maqrizi says that the madhab of Idris al-Shafi'i arrived in Egypt in the year AH 198. The Hanbali and the Hanafi schools became popular in the areas surrounding Egypt in the seventh century.

According to al-Maqrizi, during the reign of Baybars al-Bunduqdari in AH 676, four judges were appointed in Egypt: a Shafi'i, a Maliki, a Hanafi, and a Hanbali. Henceforth, all the other madhabs were discouraged. Anyone who followed any other madhab except for those four in any Islamic town was regarded with hostility, disowned, and barred from judicial posts. The testimony of a person was not accepted unless he was an adherent of one of the four madhabs. The judges (*qadis*) issued decrees in these towns, ruling that it was obligatory to follow these madhabs and unlawful to adhere to any other.

Around the year 665 hijra, the jurists (faqihs) decreed that it was obligatory to follow one of the four madhabs and unlawful to adhere to any other. For nearly seven centuries since the advent of Islam, millions of Muslims had lived their lives following the Koran and the teachings of blessed prophet, content with their lives. Muslims had enjoyed complete freedom with respect to their religion and religious law; they were laymen following a mujtahid whom they had trusted. The mujtahid deduced the *ahkam* from the Koran on the jurisprudential principles upheld by them for acting on the teachings of the blessed prophet Muhammad. Most of the laymen had never heard of the names of these four madhabs.

Various causes for the restriction of the madhabs to four have been documented in the history of that period. During the reign of the caliphs, there was a vast divergence of madhab rulings on legal issues (*furu' al-deen*). This divergence of opinions and tendencies made it impossible to keep track of their rulings, considering that each one of the *Sahaba*, *Tabi'un*, and those who came after them had their own madhab and personal views in regard to the issues of Sharia and its practical laws. The caliphs resorted to curtailing the number of madhabs and were compelled to dissolve most of them.[42] Hence, they selected the four madhabs due to the large number of their followers and their abundant wealth. The widespread and never-ending differences in opinions and views resulting from the practice of *ijtihad* forced the caliphs to reduce the number of schools to only four, and they were powerless to set aside some of these four madhabs in view of the conflict that might result owing to the zealotry of their followers.

The immense bigotry of the four madhabs is noted in the *Mu'jam al-Buldan*[43] under the entry pertaining to Isfahan:

> *Destruction spread in Isfahan at this time and before it as a result of the prevalence of bigotry amongst the Shafi'i and the Hanafi and the unremitting*

[42] Al Sharif al-Murtada 'Alam al-Huda, *Riyad al-'ulama*, folio 350.

[43] *Mu'jam al-buldan*, vol. 1, p. 373.

> *wars between the two parties. Whereas one party gained ascendancy, it plundered the quarters of the other and burned down and destroyed them, and no bond or treaty would restrain them.*

These civil disturbances, strife, and bigotries were instrumental in shaping the policies of the caliphs and in compelling the faqihs to restrict themselves to the opinions of the *masha'ikh* as a mark of respect for them. The faqihs, on their part, accepted the caliph's orders restricting the madhab to four and invented reasons to justify it. Shah Wali Allah, in his book *Al-Insaf*, said:

> *After the period of Rashidun Caliphs, the Caliphate was taken over by a group of people who had no knowledge of the ahkam. Therefore, they needed the collaboration of the fuqaha'. Some of the top rank fled when accosted for service, while the others sought the nearness of the caliphs and wrote books on theology, polemics, and the differences between the different madhahib.*[44]

The restriction of following the four madhabs and the ban of adherence to any other madhab took place between seventh century and thirteenth century without any basis to justify it. It came as a policy of the caliphs and those ulema who sought nearness to the palace and to obtain the posts of judges, imams, scribes, and secretaries willingly complied with it.

Over the centuries, many scholars and laypeople did not submit to the restriction on madhabs and did not believe that any Koranic or Islamic precept made it obligatory on the Muslims to follow one of the four imams—Abu Hanifah (80–150), Malik ibn Anas (93–179), Idris al-Shafi'i (150–204), or Ahmad ibn Hanbal (164–241). None of the sources of Islamic law—the Koran, Sunna, consensus (*ijma*), nor reason (*aql*)—supported this restriction.

---

[44] *Al Insaf fi sabab al-ikhtilaf.*

The ability to deduce the *ahkam* from the Koran or the Sunna is not confined to any particular country nor limited to particular people to the exclusion of others. In other words, the field of inquiry into the *ahkam* is open to every believer with knowledge, belief, and understanding. Islam is not a *din* of compulsion, tyranny, and oppression, nor is its interpretation the monopoly of a particular class. Islam is the conscious submission of a person to the will and mercy of Allah.

The Koranic notion of religious belief (*iman*) is dependent on knowledge that is actualized in practice in the term *islam*. The term *islam* signifies the idea of surrender or submission. Islam is a religion of self-surrender. Islam is the conscious and rational submission of dependent and limited human will to the absolute and omnipotent will of Allah. The type of surrender Islam requires is a deliberate, conscious, and rational act made by a person who knows with both intellectual certainty and spiritual vision that Allah, who is the subject of Koranic discourse, is the reality.

The knower of God is a Muslim (fem. *Muslimah*), "one who submits" to the divine truth and whose relationship with God is governed by *taqwa*, the consciousness of humankind's responsibility toward its Creator. However, consciousness of God alone is not sufficient to make a person a Muslim. Neither is it enough to be merely born a Muslim or to be raised in an Islamic cultural context. The concept of *taqwa* implies that the believer has the added responsibility of acting in accordance with three types of knowledge—*ilm al-yaqin*, *ain al-yaqin*, *and haqq al-yaqin* (knowledge of certainty, eye of certainty, and truth of certainty). The believer must endeavor at all times to maintain himself or herself in a constant state of submission to Allah. By doing so, the believer attains the honored title of "slave of Allah" (masculine: *abd Allah,* feminine: *amat Allah*), for the believer recognizes that all power and agency belongs to Allah alone:

وَلَوْلَآ إِذْ دَخَلْتَ جَنَّتَكَ قُلْتَ مَا شَآءَ ٱللَّهُ لَا قُوَّةَ إِلَّا بِٱللَّهِ ۚ إِن تَرَنِ أَنَا۠ أَقَلَّ مِنكَ مَالًا وَوَلَدًا ﴿٣٩﴾

Allah has willed it. There is no power
but Allah's. (Koran 18:39)

Trusting in the divine mercy of his or her divine Master yet fearing Allah's wrath, the slave of Allah walks the road of life with careful steps, making his actions deliberate so that he will not stray from the path that Allah has laid out for him:

إِيَّاكَ نَعْبُدُ وَإِيَّاكَ نَسْتَعِينُ ﴿٥﴾ ٱهْدِنَا ٱلصِّرَٰطَ ٱلْمُسْتَقِيمَ ﴿٦﴾ صِرَٰطَ ٱلَّذِينَ أَنْعَمْتَ عَلَيْهِمْ غَيْرِ

ٱلْمَغْضُوبِ عَلَيْهِمْ وَلَا ٱلضَّآلِّينَ ﴿٧﴾

Thee do we worship, and Thine aid we seek, Show us
the straight way, The way of those on whom Thou
hast bestowed Thy Grace, those whose (portion) is
not wrath, and who go not astray. (Koran 1:5–7)

This is an all-encompassing and highly personal type of commitment that has little in common with the academic understanding of Islam as a civilization or a cultural system.

Those in search of Allah's covenant and His path, for the two hundred years after the blessed prophet passed away, sought guidance through contact with enlightened people from within their own community. These sages looked for the answers in the Koran, the teachings of the blessed prophet, or their own wisdom and experience and thus helped those seeking knowledge and wisdom. After this period, when the companions of the prophet and those who knew them had long gone, there arose scholars who sought to find the reason behind the injunctions of the Koran and the Sunna. They endeavored to formulate laws to govern the daily lives of Muslims in matters of worship, family life, personal relationships, business affairs, and settling disputes. Gradually, what was once a spontaneous act of worship out of love and obedience to Allah became an act of mechanical motions with a rigid, memorized prayer formula from the manuals of jurist-scholars.

- *The spontaneity of the act of praise, show of gratitude, beseeching, and supplication for Allah's mercy and grace taught by the prophet was lost. The Koran became relegated to recitation in the expression of a person's piety without any attempts to understand the depths of the wisdom of the Koran. Scholar-jurists became locked in arguments on the merits of various hadith. For the elucidation of the truth of the Koran, the logic and drawn-out debates became moored to the elusive hadith. Thus, the hadith and the Sharia overreached all other forms of acquisition of knowledge and wisdom. Whereas early on Islam had been within the sphere of the understanding of the common man, with the voluntary guidance of the neighborly sage, it now moved to the realm of the scholars cloistered in their ivory towers.*
- These scholars, or the ulema, were no longer of the people. They sought proximity to the palaces and were provided with endowments and teaching positions in educational institutions. The greater the number of followers and students, the higher was the prestige and income of the ulema from their supporters. The ulema also assumed a larger role in the communities by organizing groups, lodges, and sectarian associations under their leadership. The scholars also represented the urban populations to their conquerors, provided local administration and justice, and arranged for local security, public works, taxation, charities, and other services. Every scholar of any significance became the imam of his school of jurisprudence or the madhab. The most ambitious

scholar-jurists became the servants of the state and became an arm of the ruling class in controlling the masses. Such scholarship brought in a hierarchical, clerical, bureaucratic structure that necessitated the distinction of rank and order with titles and robes as in Christianity. In other words, the ulema, the jurist scholars, became the priests of Islam. What was meant to be a personal spiritual relationship between man and his Maker began to develop into an institutionalized hierarchy of priesthood in Islam.

- There were also teachers and holy men who chose to remain independent of the government. They chose humility and relative poverty and obscurity. They continued to teach from their front rooms, the courtyards of the mosques, and the khankahs.

The caliphs sought the support of the better-organized madhabs and the faqihs, who in return for the state sponsorship did the bidding of the caliphs. The result of such a close collaboration was an edict by the faqihs and the caliph to restrict the number of madhabs to four—the Hanafi, Maliki, Shafi'i, and the Hanbali. Thus, the judiciary and educational systems, as well as the control of the mosques and *wakf* (endowment properties) in the world of Islam, became the domain of leaders of these four schools. There is no priesthood or clergy in Islam.

Every believer has a direct relationship with Allah. The Koran is a simple book, within the understanding of the common man and woman in accordance with their intellectual and spiritual capacity. Allah says that He made the book easy for the believers. The scholars and the clerics, the priests, brought a new discipline to the world of Islam in the form of *fiqh* and jurisprudence. Thus, the new formalized form of Sharia and *fiqh* came to influence every phase of the daily life of Muslims. Whereas in the earlier times the *din* had been community driven on the basis of the covenant of Allah, it now became the prerogative of the mullah, the priest. The believers came to depend on

Muslim priests for advice and guidance concerning every phase of their daily life. Thus, the Christian, Jewish, Zoroastrian, and Hindu convert to Islam continued to depend on the priestly class as they had done before their conversion, except that this time the priest was a Muslim.

The priesthood introduced a new element of superstition—the use of amulets, worship at the graves of Sufis, the creation of sainthood among the priests, and lighting oil lamps on Thursday nights.

حمٓ ﴿١﴾ وَٱلْكِتَٰبِ ٱلْمُبِينِ ﴿٢﴾ إِنَّآ أَنزَلْنَٰهُ فِى لَيْلَةٍ مُّبَٰرَكَةٍ ۚ إِنَّا كُنَّا مُنذِرِينَ ﴿٣﴾ فِيهَا يُفْرَقُ كُلُّ أَمْرٍ حَكِيمٍ ﴿٤﴾ أَمْرًا مِّنْ عِندِنَآ ۚ إِنَّا كُنَّا
مُرْسِلِينَ ﴿٥﴾ رَحْمَةً مِّن رَّبِّكَ ۚ إِنَّهُۥ هُوَ ٱلسَّمِيعُ ٱلْعَلِيمُ ﴿٦﴾ رَبِّ ٱلسَّمَٰوَٰتِ وَٱلْأَرْضِ وَمَا بَيْنَهُمَآ ۖ إِن كُنتُم مُّوقِنِينَ ﴿٧﴾ لَآ إِلَٰهَ إِلَّا هُوَ يُحْىِۦ
وَيُمِيتُ ۖ رَبُّكُمْ وَرَبُّ ءَابَآئِكُمُ ٱلْأَوَّلِينَ ﴿٨﴾ ﴾

Ha Mim. By the Book, that makes matters lucid; We revealed it during the blessed night, verily We are always warning against Evil. Therein is proclaimed every wise decree, by command, from Our Presence, for We are ever sending revelations, as a Mercy from your Lord: for He is the hearer and knower. The Lord of the heavens and the earth and all that is in between them, if you have an assured faith. There is no god but He: it is He Who gives life and death, the Lord and Cherisher, your Lord and Lord of your forefathers. (Ad-Dukhan 44:1–8, Koran)

﴿ وَلَقَدْ صَرَّفْنَا فِى هَٰذَا ٱلْقُرْءَانِ لِلنَّاسِ مِن كُلِّ مَثَلٍ ۚ وَكَانَ ٱلْإِنسَٰنُ أَكْثَرَ شَىْءٍ جَدَلًا ﴿٥٤﴾ وَمَا مَنَعَ ٱلنَّاسَ أَن يُؤْمِنُوٓا۟ إِذْ جَآءَهُمُ
ٱلْهُدَىٰ وَيَسْتَغْفِرُوا۟ رَبَّهُمْ إِلَّآ أَن تَأْتِيَهُمْ سُنَّةُ ٱلْأَوَّلِينَ أَوْ يَأْتِيَهُمُ ٱلْعَذَابُ قُبُلًا ﴿٥٥﴾ ﴾

We have explained in detail in this Qur'an, for the benefit of humankind, every kind of similitude: but man is, in most things, contentious. And

> what is there to keep back men from believing,
> now that guidance has come to them, nor from
> praying for forgiveness from their Lord, but
> that (they ask that) the ways of the ancients be
> repeated with them, or the Wrath be brought to
> them face to face? (Al-Kahf 18:54–55, Koran)

Allah says the He has made the Koran easy to understand and that He has explained in detail for the benefit of humankind every kind of similitude. Moreover, Allah has in seventy-five commandments addressed the believer, outlining their obligations. The above *ayahs* make it clear that the completion of the Koran also completed the *din* of Allah.

At first, the caliphs and the *faqihs* decreed the restriction of interpretation of the divine laws to four madhabs in the whole of the Islamic world. The effect of this decree was decisive. The decree made the four madhabs stronger and more powerful. The other schools retreated until they were extinguished by the year 665/1266.

Ibn al-Fuwati[45], a distinguished Iraqi historian, states that in 645/1247, the four teachers charged with teaching *fiqh* of the four madhabs at the new college of al-Mustansiriyah in Baghdad were summoned and ordered not to mention their works to their students of *fiqh*. They were to confine themselves to the opinions of the early masters, the *masha'ikh*. Some of the teachers rejected the order, stating that the "*masha'ikh* were men, and so are we," implying that they were at par with the early *masha'ikh*. The teachers were then summoned to the house of the vizier Mu'ayyid al-Deen Muhammad ibn al-Alqami, who relayed to them the caliph al-Musta'sim's orders to restrict themselves to mentioning the statements of the *masha'ikh*. All the teachers then submitted their compliance.

[45] Ibn al-Fuwati, *Al-Hawadith al-Jami'ah*, 216, events of 645 hijra.

To reiterate, every believer's *din* is his submission to Allah, to have absolute faith in Him, and to perform wholesome and beautiful deeds in Allah's path. Devotion to any particular madhab or obedience to a particular *masha'ikh's* opinion does not form part of the *din.* The restriction of the discussion and debate on matters of law to the opinion of certain jurists, which is an ongoing process in Islam, is what finally led to the decay of the foundations of Islam as practiced by Muslims. It is not the same Islam as taught by the blessed prophet of Allah, and it is not the Islam of the Koran.

The closure of the doors of scholarship and research into the mysteries of the Koran and the signs of Allah was the greatest crime perpetrated against Islam. Only by discovering the reasoning and logic behind the Koran and the prophet's pronouncements could the Muslims promulgate new laws in accordance with the new circumstances they found themselves in during the coming centuries. The four imams were innovative and met the needs of their own times, but their proclamations were not divine and do not meet the expectations of the needs of the present day.

By fossilizing the life of the Muslims to the knowledge of the third century, hindered the accumulation of scientific knowledge and the knowledge of the physical world for the next one thousand years. Women became shackled to this fossilized *fiqh* for over a thousand years to bondage and ignorance, whereas at the time of the *Sahaba* women were educated and had the freedom to apply the principles of jurisprudence and legal rules and to conclude *ahkam* from the source. There were women who were full-fledged and respected *mujtahid.* By the seventh century, with the four madhabs in total control, the status of women as sanctified by the Koran was violated, and the accumulation of knowledge and wisdom became relegated to the study of the hadith, the Sharia, medicine, and astronomy. All scientific, philosophical, and religious inquiry became subject to the old decrees of the *masha'ikh* and imams of the four schools. The gates of knowledge and wisdom slammed shut when the doors to *ijtihad* closed, and they remained sealed for one thousand years.

The new believers were Arabs, Persians, Syrians, Greeks, Armenians, Turks, Christians, Jews, Hindus, animists, and of other denominations. All of them brought their own unique experiences to Islam. In this crucible of civilizations arose a single *ummah*, synthesized from diverse backgrounds. For a while, it appeared that all humankind would share a common civilization under one *Waliy*, Allah. There was a tremendous flowering of knowledge translated from ancient Greek, Farsi, Sanskrit, Mandarin, Hebrew, and a myriad of other dialect. This new knowledge coalesced in Arabic and once again spread around to other nations. With the jurist-scholars in control of education and institutions of learning, law, and religion, all serious inquiry gradually dwindled in the world of Islam. Literacy among the Muslims fell to below 5 percent at the beginning of modern times. The scholars restricted themselves to the learning of the hadith, the Sharia, logic, and astronomy and, in doing so, also actively discouraged others from seeking broader knowledge. The study of the Koran became relegated to recitation, and all serious inquiry into matters of Allah's commandments and the covenant came to lie outside the sway of the common man.

The influence of most of these jurists grew until they became the imams of their legal schools by which their followers came to be identified. However, before their popularity, the schools had no name, and no Muslim had ever identified with them at that time. The schools of law continued to multiply until the beginning of the fourth century.

Among the factors that were effectual in giving precedence to a particular school were the number of students, patrons, promoters, supporters, and the degree of their prestige, influence, and power in propagating it. The jurist-scholars maintained a close relationship with the caliphs and the palace officials, and they thus became the faqihs, the legislators of law, the judges, as well as the prosecutors of law. They also took over other positions on behalf of the caliph as the tax collectors, maintainers of law and order, and teachers in madrassas. As the administrators of mosques and prayer leaders, they were beginning to behave like priests and rabbis despite the fact that there is no priesthood in Islam. Every believer has a direct spiritual access to Allah without the intervention of a priest or a deceased saintly personality. Through their influence over the caliph, the faqihs of the four main madhabs had all the other madhabs abolished. The result of this grabbing of control over the *din* of Islam was that, by 665 hijra, no further decrees or fatwa were permitted unless they were in accordance with the teachings of the *masha'ikh* of the four recognized and organized madhabs. The gates of *ijtihad* were slammed shut, and no further dissension was permitted.

The early faqihs, after the period of the *Sahaba*, looked into the Koran and then into the Sunna to find the reasoning behind certain commandments of the Koran or the blessed prophet's decree. The Koran has no more than 350 legal verses. By the end of the era of the *Sahaba*, the number of the hadith verified to be true and accurate by the *Sahaba* was limited in number but was sufficient for a working Sharia.

They had fewer than eight hundred hadith, some duplicated, to anchor their arguments on. In the third and the fourth centuries, with the dramatic increase in jurisprudential activity, there was increasing reliance placed on the hadith in the proclamation of the law. The Koran was relegated to personal piety and recitation rather than inquiry. There was a frantic search for new and unknown hadith. The hadith on which the earlier madhabs had relied had been authenticated by the *Sahaba*, who had been present with the blessed prophet. In the third century, over a million hadith were circulating and growing in number by the month. This was a period when fabrication of the hadith was fashionable and prestigious.

Abu Huraira had converted to Islam after Khaybar. After his conversion, he spent considerable time in the company of the blessed *Nabi*. Nabi Muhammad had forbidden his companions from writing down his spoken words except for what was in the revelation. There are currently over 5,000 hadith attributed to Abu Huraira. His hadith are occasionally controversial and tend to be antifeminist. They also tend to be contradictory to what A'ishah is documented to have stated. Abu Huraira had spent three years in Medina by the time the blessed prophet passed away. That means that Abu Huraira's companionship with the prophet had lasted about one thousand days. During this period, Abu Huraira is said to have recorded 5,000 hadith, which amounts to five hadith every day. Had Abu Huraira been the blessed messenger's private secretary, recording every event in the prophet's life and every revelation as it was revealed, he could not have possibly recorded five events and sayings of the prophet day after day for the next one thousand days.

During the last three years of the blessed *Nabi's* life, at least eighteen suras of the Koran were revealed. The Prophet dictated the revelations to his scribes and helped his companions memorize these suras. One would presume that the blessed prophet Muhammad would have discussed the contents of all these suras with his companions. These suras are: *Al-Baqarah, Ali 'Imran, An-Nisa, Al-Ma'idah, Al-Anfal, At-Tawbah, Al-Hajj, Al-Ahzab, Muhammad, Al-Hujurat, Al-Hadid, Al-Mujadila, Al-Hashr, Al-Mumtahinah, As-Saf, Al-Jumu'ah, Al-Munafiqun, and At-Taghabun.* Abu Huraira spent all this time with the prophet, yet in the hadith attributed to him, there is almost no mention of these revelations or their contents. These suras contain all the *ayahs* in which Allah has addressed the believers directly and granted them His covenant. Many of the hadith attributed to Abu Huraira contradict the spirit of Allah's message in those suras.

Abu Huraira was reputedly an upright man. It is obvious then that someone else related spurious hadith that were attributed to him, which were then included in the hadith collections of the third century. These hadith then formed the basis of some of the Sharia and *fiqh*.

The five imams—al-Bukhari, Muslim, al-Tirmidhi, Abu Da'ud, and al-Nasa'i—between them studied 600,000 to a million hadith and judged between 2,630 and 4,348 to have shades of validity of being truthful or weak. The imams, among themselves, were not able to agree about which hadith were the truthful ones. Consequently, the second-generation hadith collected by these five imams were added to the earlier ones cited by the imams and *masha'ikh* of the four madhabs—Abu Hanifah, Malik ibn Anas, Idris al-Shafi'i, and Ahmad ibn Hanbal—and thus both the collections became the core of the Islamic jurisprudence, the Sharia. Whereas Abu Hanifah, Malik, al-Shafi'i, and ibn Hanbal regarded the hadith to be *wahiy* (revelation), the word of Allah at par with Koran, the addition of spurious and false hadith to the bank of hadith for use in Islamic jurisprudence, Sharia, muddied the justice system for the next eleven hundred years. Today we are still entombed in the fossilized cocoon of an imperfect human system, considered by most jurist-scholars to be divine.

The Koran is the *haqq* and the *din* and is the purest word of Allah. If the purity of the Koran and the *din* is to be likened to the purest dinar of gold, then every day for fourteen hundred years jurist-scholars and the priests of Islam added a little bit of the impurity of their human vision—hadith collections, words of the Shia, and the Sunni heresy—to this purest gold coin. And after all the centuries, Allah has preserved the purity of the Koran, and it shines with the *nur* of Allah. And what has happened to the *din* of the Muslims, the Shias, and the Sunnis? Their dinar is like the coin of their world—impure, false, and tarnished with the addition of base metal, with barely any shine of *haqq* in it. Their salvation is to shed the falsehood of human systems in their *din* and embrace the word of Allah, the Koran, and the *nur* of the shiny *din* of the Koran.

Sharia—the right path, the path to water, the path to righteousness—leads to the *house of justice and righteousness.* It is a house of human dignity, equality, justice, and consultative government; it is a house where there is a realization of lawful benefits to people, the prevention of harm (*darar*), the removal of hardship (*haraj*), and the education of individuals by inculcating in them self-discipline, patience (*ṣabr*), restraint, and respect for the rights of others. It is a house where there is restitution of all wrongs and where all imbalances in society are put right.

1. The front portico of the house and its facade are the *Sharia*, representing Allah's laws; signifying human dignity and justice and the equality of all humans, both men and women; signifying the sanctity of life, property, and intellect and the removal of all harm from Allah's creation.
2. The back wall and the back part of the house of justice and righteousness represent the government and the individuals who manage the affairs of the *ummah* as the *wakil.*
3. The right wall and the right side of the house represent those jurist-scholars who interpret, legislate, and administer justice.
4. The left wall represents the *ummah* and the people.
5. Above, over the roof and in the heavens, is Allah and His mercy, magnanimity, and beneficence.

﴿ ۞ وَٱكْتُبْ لَنَا فِى هَٰذِهِ ٱلدُّنْيَا حَسَنَةً وَفِى ٱلْءَاخِرَةِ إِنَّا هُدْنَآ إِلَيْكَ ۚ قَالَ عَذَابِىٓ أُصِيبُ بِهِۦ مَنْ أَشَآءُ ۖ وَرَحْمَتِى وَسِعَتْ كُلَّ شَىْءٍ ۚ

فَسَأَكْتُبُهَا لِلَّذِينَ يَتَّقُونَ وَيُؤْتُونَ ٱلزَّكَوٰةَ وَٱلَّذِينَ هُم بِـَٔايَٰتِنَا يُؤْمِنُونَ

"And ordain for us that which is good, in this life and in the Hereafter: for we have turned unto Thee." He said: "With My Punishment I visit whom I will; but My

Mercy extends to all things. That (Mercy) I shall ordain for those who do right, and practice regular charity, and those who believe in Our Signs. (Al-A'raf 7:156, Koran)

﴿ ۞ قُلْ يَٰعِبَادِىَ ٱلَّذِينَ أَسْرَفُوا۟ عَلَىٰٓ أَنفُسِهِمْ لَا تَقْنَطُوا۟ مِن رَّحْمَةِ ٱللَّهِ ۚ إِنَّ ٱللَّهَ يَغْفِرُ ٱلذُّنُوبَ جَمِيعًا ۚ إِنَّهُۥ هُوَ ٱلْغَفُورُ ٱلرَّحِيمُ ﴿٥٣﴾ ﴾

Say: "O my Servants who have transgressed against their souls! Despair not of the Mercy of Allah: for Allah forgives all sins: for He is Oft-Forgiving, Most Merciful." (Az-Zumar 39:53, Koran)

If one is to assess the state of the house of justice and righteousness after fourteen centuries of Allah's mercy upon the believers, the following report will paint a different picture:

1. The plaster and the paint of the facade of the house of justice and righteousness have all but gone during the last fourteen centuries. On the path to the house, there are thousands of supplicants begging for justice and lawful benefits, but no one receives it. The whole Islamic world lives in utter poverty. Literacy rate is less than 30 percent. Health care is dismal. Police and security services, without any doubt, are corrupt and oppressive. Institutions of justice do not exist, and lawlessness prevails. Not a single institution of higher learning in the world of Islam is of world standard. Infrastructure of the land is poor. Islamic states have not established Islamic banking and institutions of trade and finance, and Muslims do not even have a standard currency. One percent of the Muslim society owns 90 percent of the wealth and power. Every institution of the Islamic lands is there to serve 1 percent of the population. The army, judiciary, financial institutions, universities, industry, and the police all serve that 1 percent, the elite.

Women are excluded from business, education, professions, even the mosque.

2. The back wall and the back part of the house is beautiful with shiny white marble walls and pillars. In the courtyard are manicured lawns and gardens. The ruler and his officials live in luxury and splendor in their gilded palaces, oblivious to the poverty and squalor around them. The armed forces, the police, and the justice system are geared to safeguard the regime and the corrupt elite.
3. Inside the right wall is the site of the weekly meeting of the jurist-scholars. On the agenda are two important subjects that have taken their precious time for several months. They have not come to a consensus yet. There is a difference of opinion whether a pregnant woman who is a victim of rape should be flogged with one hundred lashes, be stoned to death, or married off to the rapist. They are unable to find suitable references in the Koran or the hadith. So what to do now? The gates of *ijtihad* are shut, the *masha'ikhs* and the faqihs of the old have not left any instructions, and the present-day faqihs can't decide. Meanwhile, the subject of this debate, a frightened woman, is lingering in a squalid prison. The other pressing problem is that everlasting riddle of the crescent moon. An eminent aviator has invented a machine in which he can fly into the heavens and skim and scan the skies to see if the crescent moon has arisen. The problem is that the local ulema do not trust him without the evidence of three witnesses who have seen the crescent moon arise. This machine cannot carry three witnesses. The jurists do not trust the photographs of the crescent moon because there is no reference to photographs in the Koran nor in the hadith. And of course, the gates of *ijtihad* are shut. What to do?

4. The fourth wall and the house to the left have the *ummah.* They have been clamoring for justice, representative and consultative government, and human dignity. Alas, it is nowhere in sight. Yet the house of justice and righteousness was built to ensure human dignity, equality, justice, consultative government, realistic expectation of lawful benefits to people, the prevention of harm to people, the removal of hardship, and the education of individuals by inculcating in them self-discipline, patience, restraint, and respect for rights of others. It is a house where there should be restitution of all wrongs and imbalances in society. Instead, there is an ongoing debate on reform, revolution, and rebellion.

What did go wrong with the Sharia?

1. **Justice:** Justice (*'adl*) is a divine attribute defined as "putting in the right place." The opposite of *'adl* is *zulm*, which in Koranic terms means "wrongdoing." Wrongdoing is a human attribute defined as "putting things in the wrong place." *Zulm* (wrongdoing) is one of the common terms used in the Koran to refer to the negative acts employed by human beings. Wrongdoing is the opposite of justice, putting everything in its right place. Every act of a human being is to be performed as prescribed by Allah. Hence, wrongdoing is to put things where they do not belong. Hence wrongdoing or injustice (*zulm*) is, for example, to associate others with Allah. Wrongdoing is to put things where they do not belong. Hence, wrongdoing is injustice, for example, associating others with Allah; others do not belong in the place for the divine. It is to place false words in place of the truth and to put someone else's property in place of your own. Other examples are taking a life against the divine commandments, replacing people's liberty with

oppression, waging war instead of peace, and usurping people's right to govern themselves.

The Koran, when it points out who is harmed by injustice and wrongdoing, always mentions the word *nafs* (self). People cannot harm Allah. By being unjust or by putting things in the wrong place, people harm themselves. They distort their own natures, and they lead themselves astray. Who can one wrong? It is impossible to wrong or do injustice against Allah since all things are His creatures and do His work. Hence, wrongdoing and injustice is an activity against people and Allah's creation. Allah had prescribed His covenant to humans for the good of human beings. People, tribes, and nations are being helped since Allah leads them into accord, harmony, and justice, which in turn create peace in the world. Allah has laid out all the basic principles for justice in His covenant for the humans to live in harmony. Those who refuse to follow His commandments are therefore ungrateful and hence *kafirs*. Thus, they are wrongdoers (*zalimun*) and only harm themselves. Of the 250 verses where the Koran mentions *zulm* (wrongdoing) or *zalimun* (wrongdoers), it mentions the object of wrongdoing in only 25 verses. In one verse, the object of wrongdoing are people:

﴿ إِنَّمَا ٱلسَّبِيلُ عَلَى ٱلَّذِينَ يَظْلِمُونَ ٱلنَّاسَ وَيَبْغُونَ فِى ٱلْأَرْضِ بِغَيْرِ ٱلْحَقِّ ۚ أُو۟لَـٰٓئِكَ لَهُمْ عَذَابٌ أَلِيمٌ ﴿٤٢﴾ ﴾

The blame is only against those who oppress
men with wrongdoing and insolently transgress
beyond bounds through the land, defying right
and justice: for such there will be a Penalty
grievous. (Ash-Shura 42:42, Koran)

In a second verse, the object of wrong and injustice are the signs of Allah:

﴿ وَٱلْوَزْنُ يَوْمَئِذٍ ٱلْحَقُّ ۚ فَمَن ثَقُلَتْ مَوَٰزِينُهُۥ فَأُو۟لَٰٓئِكَ هُمُ ٱلْمُفْلِحُونَ ۝٨ وَمَنْ خَفَّتْ مَوَٰزِينُهُۥ فَأُو۟لَٰٓئِكَ ٱلَّذِينَ خَسِرُوٓا۟ أَنفُسَهُم
بِمَا كَانُوا۟ بِـَٔايَٰتِنَا يَظْلِمُونَ ۝٩ ﴾

The weighing that day will be true. He whose scales are heavy, are the prosperous. Those whose scale are light; they have lost themselves for wronging Our Signs. (Al-A'raf 7:8–9, Koran)

Allah reveals His signs in nature and in scriptures so that the people may be guided. By disobeying these signs, they are wronging only themselves. In the remaining 23 verses in which the object of wrongdoing is mentioned, the wrongdoers are said to be only wronging themselves.

﴿ وَظَلَّلْنَا عَلَيْكُمُ ٱلْغَمَامَ وَأَنزَلْنَا عَلَيْكُمُ ٱلْمَنَّ وَٱلسَّلْوَىٰ ۖ كُلُوا۟ مِن طَيِّبَٰتِ مَا رَزَقْنَٰكُمْ ۖ وَمَا ظَلَمُونَا وَلَٰكِن كَانُوٓا۟ أَنفُسَهُمْ يَظْلِمُونَ
۝٥٧ ﴾

And We gave you the shade of clouds and sent down to you Manna and quails, saying: "Eat of the good things We have provided for you" (but they rebelled); to Us they did no harm, but they wronged their own souls. (Al-Baqarah 2:57, Al-A'raf 7:160, Koran)

﴿ إِنَّ ٱللَّهَ لَا يَظْلِمُ ٱلنَّاسَ شَيْـًٔا وَلَٰكِنَّ ٱلنَّاسَ أَنفُسَهُمْ يَظْلِمُونَ ۝٤٤ ﴾

Verily Allah will not deal unjustly with humans in anything: it is the human who wrongs his own soul. (Yunus 10:44, Koran)

﴿ وَمَا ظَلَمْنَٰهُمْ وَلَٰكِن ظَلَمُوٓاْ أَنفُسَهُمْ ﴾

And We wronged them not, but they
wronged themselves. (Hud 11:101, Koran)

﴿ وَمَن يَعْمَلْ سُوٓءًا أَوْ يَظْلِمْ نَفْسَهُۥ ثُمَّ يَسْتَغْفِرِ ٱللَّهَ يَجِدِ ٱللَّهَ غَفُورًا رَّحِيمًا ﴿١١٠﴾ ﴾

If anyone does evil or wrongs his own soul but
afterwards seeks Allah's forgiveness, he will find Allah
Oft-Forgiving, Most Merciful. (An-Nisa 4:110, Koran)

The Koran admonishes:

'Deal not unjustly and you shall not be dealt
with unjustly.' (Al-Baqarah 2:278)

Allah proclaims His law in the covenant to the believers in a simple, lucid language. Allah then addresses the believers in the Koran and shows them the right way to follow Him. The fulfillment of the covenant of Allah is the total belief system based on unity of one's personality and communion with Allah in total awareness and *taqwa* of Allah and observance of all the thirty-seven commandments of the covenant. This communion is not only with Allah but also through Him with other believers and with the rest of Allah's creation, both alive and inanimate. The phrase *amilu al saalihaat* (to do good, to perform wholesome deeds) refers to those who persist in striving to set things right, who restore harmony, peace, justice, and balance. The other acts of good works recognized in the covenant of the Koran are to show compassion, to be merciful and forgive others, to be just, to protect the weak, to defend the oppressed, to be generous and charitable, to be truthful and to seek knowledge and wisdom, to be kind, to be peaceful, to love others, and to perform beautiful deeds.

Above all, Allah's mercy knows no bounds. The Koran and the teachings of the blessed prophet guide those who seek the path of Allah.

> Say: "O my Servants who have transgressed against their souls! Despair not of the Mercy of Allah: for Allah forgives all sins: for He is Oft-Forgiving, Most Merciful. (Az-Zumar 39:53, Koran)

True Sharia should lead to the path of the house of justice and righteousness. The only purpose of this house of Sharia is to ensure that justice is done. And those who administer justice should remember that Allah says:

> O my Servants who have transgressed against their souls! Despair not of the Mercy of Allah: for Allah forgives all sins: for He is Oft-Forgiving, Most Merciful.

2. **The Law:** The law is the Koran and the guidance of the blessed prophet in matters of the *din*. The blessed prophet said:

> I am no more than a man; when I order you anything respecting religion, receive it, and when I tell you anything about the affairs of the world, and then I am nothing but a man.

In the fifteenth-century hijra, one and a half billion believers wished to conduct their daily lives in accordance with the decrees of the Koran and the teachings of the blessed Nabi. The Koran is the ever-living word of Allah, the truth for all times. The prophet said, "The

Qur'an consists of five heads, things **lawful**, things **unlawful**, clear and positive **precepts**, **mysteries** and **examples.** Then consider that is **lawful** which is there declared to be so, and that which is forbidden as **unlawful**; obey the **precepts**, believe in the **mysteries** and take warning from the **examples.**" The Koran, in clear terms, addresses the believers about what is permissible and what is forbidden and is plain and clear on guidelines, principles, and the law (precepts). On these matters, the blessed prophet said, "My sayings do not abrogate the Word of Allah, but the Word of Allah can abrogate my sayings."

The prophet also said, "Convey to other persons none of my words, except that you know of a surety."

Allah proclaims:

﴿ وَأَنزَلْنَآ إِلَيْكَ ٱلْكِتَٰبَ بِٱلْحَقِّ مُصَدِّقًا لِّمَا بَيْنَ يَدَيْهِ مِنَ ٱلْكِتَٰبِ وَمُهَيْمِنًا عَلَيْهِ ۖ فَٱحْكُم بَيْنَهُم بِمَآ أَنزَلَ ٱللَّهُ ۖ وَلَا تَتَّبِعْ
أَهْوَآءَهُمْ عَمَّا جَآءَكَ مِنَ ٱلْحَقِّ ۚ لِكُلٍّ جَعَلْنَا مِنكُمْ شِرْعَةً وَمِنْهَاجًا ۚ وَلَوْ شَآءَ ٱللَّهُ لَجَعَلَكُمْ أُمَّةً وَٰحِدَةً وَلَٰكِن لِّيَبْلُوَكُمْ فِى مَآ ءَاتَىٰكُمْ ۖ فَٱسْتَبِقُوا۟
ٱلْخَيْرَٰتِ ۚ إِلَى ٱللَّهِ مَرْجِعُكُمْ جَمِيعًا فَيُنَبِّئُكُم بِمَا كُنتُمْ فِيهِ تَخْتَلِفُونَ ﴿٤٨﴾ ﴾

To you We revealed the Book of Truth, confirming the Scripture that came before it, and guarding it in safety: so, judge between them by what Allah hath revealed, and follow not their vain desires, diverging from the Truth that has come to you. To each among you We have prescribed a Law and an Open Way. If Allah had so willed, He would have made you a single People, but (His plan is) to test you in what He has given you, so strive as in a race in all virtues. The goal of you all is to Allah; it is He that will show you the truth of the matters in which you dispute. (Al-Ma'idah 5:48, Koran)

﴿ لَمْ يَكُنِ ٱلَّذِينَ كَفَرُوا۟ مِنْ أَهْلِ ٱلْكِتَـٰبِ وَٱلْمُشْرِكِينَ مُنفَكِّينَ حَتَّىٰ تَأْتِيَهُمُ ٱلْبَيِّنَةُ ۝١ ﴾ ﴿ رَسُولٌ مِّنَ ٱللَّهِ يَتْلُوا۟ صُحُفًا مُّطَهَّرَةً ۝٢ ﴾ ﴿ فِيهَا كُتُبٌ قَيِّمَةٌ ۝٣ ﴾

Those who reject the Truth, among the People of the Book and among the kafiru, were not going to depart from their ways until there should come to them clear Evidence, A Messenger from Allah, rehearsing scriptures kept pure and holy: Wherein are laws right and straight. (Al-Baiyina 98:1–3, Koran)

In the above two *ayahs*, Allah proclaims that He sent the book of truth with purified pages. In this book are laws, right and straight, from Allah. The prophet says that the Koran contains clear and positive precepts, guidelines and laws, and what is lawful and what is unlawful.

Allah has made the laws, permissions, and prohibitions lucid and clear in the covenant. The believers do not require a hierarchy of clergy, priests, and self-proclaimed ulema. Why do believers need imams and the *masha'ikh* of the *madhabs* to direct their lives when Allah is the Teacher and the Guide? And Allah is accessible to the believer at all times.

So, the front wall and the facade of the house of justice and righteousness are the greatest guide, the book of truth, and the Koran. The Islamic society as envisioned in the Koran and the Sunna is a moral and a just society in which every individual—man and woman, from the highest to the lowest, from the first to the last—has equal, unimpeded, and unquestionable right to freedom; right to practice his faith in accordance with his beliefs as, in Islam, there is no compulsion in matters of religion; right to life, which includes a mental, physical, and emotional well-being; right to safeguard one's property; right to intellectual endeavors, acquisition of knowledge, and education; right to make a living; and right to free speech and action to enjoin good and forbid evil. In enjoying his freedoms, the individual ensures that his activities do not impinge on the similar rights of others.

3. **The Ruler:** For the last fourteen hundred years, the back wall of the house of justice has been usurped by traitors to Islam and Allah. The rulers of Islam took possession of people's vicegerency by conquest or by force of arms. The covenant's criterion of consultative and participative government was lost and has not been restored. No person has the right to impose himself and his family and clan as the ruler of the believers. The believers are free humans governed by Allah's covenant and not subject to other humans. The believers, however, from time to time, choose people among themselves to administer their affairs and of their community.

The administrator of affairs, the *amri minkum,* and his bureaucracy should deal with every individual and his or her problems with empathy, sympathy, and compassion. The word *compassion* is commonly translated to mean "sympathy," which is not quite correct. One with compassion does have empathy or sympathy with a subject, but if an injustice is being committed, his inner self will compel him to actively endeavor to correct it with an action as opposed to solely feeling passive sympathy; there should be restitution of all wrongs and imbalances in society.

> O you who believe! Obey Allah, and obey the messenger, and those charged with authority among you. If you differ in anything among yourselves, refer to Allah and His Messenger. If you do believe in Allah and the last day: that is the best, and most suitable for final determination. (Koran 4:59)

The community as a whole, after consultation and consensus, grants people among themselves with authority to manage its affairs (*ulil amri minkum*). Those charged with authority act in their capacity as the representative (*wakil*) of the people and are bound by the Koranic mandate to consult the community in public affairs, and general consensus is a binding source of the law. The community, by consultation and in consensus, has the authority to depose any person charged with authority, including the head of the state, in the event of gross violation of the law and disobedience of the covenant of the Koran.

Islam pursues its social objectives by reforming the individual. The ritual ablution before prayer, the five daily prayers, fasting during the month of Ramadan, and the obligatory giving of charity all serve to encourage punctuality, self-discipline, and concern for the well-being of others. The individual is seen not just a member of the community and subservient to the community's will but also as a morally autonomous agent who plays a distinctive role in shaping the community's sense of direction and purpose. The Koran has attached to the individual's duty of obedience to the government a right of to simultaneously dispute with the rulers over government affairs. The individual obeys the ruler on the condition that the ruler obeys the Islamic law according to the Koran and the Sunna. This is reflected in the declaration of the blessed *Nabi*:

> There is no obedience in transgression;
> obedience is only in the righteousness.

The citizen is entitled to disobey an oppressive command that is contrary to the Islamic law according to the covenant of the Koran.

Even though this injunction is part of the commandments of the Koran, the jurist-priests who became the administrators of Sharia chose to ignore it. Despite this admonition of the Koran and the

Nabi, this practice has become ingrained in Islamic society. Muslim society became, in practice, a society governed by state elites who patronized priests and religious leaders who, in turn, legitimized un-Koranic regimes. The collaboration of elites of the state and religion and the cooperative relationship between these two institutions would become, for many centuries, the Middle Eastern Muslim solution to the problem of state and religion. It totally bypassed the common person, the vicegerent of God. This arrangement continues to be perpetuated into today's Islamic society. This arrangement continues to be perpetuated into today's Islamic society. The ruler-mullah alliance continues to be above the Sharia law. The Sharia does not have the authority over governance, the ruling elite. These two establishments are not accountable to the Islamic populace. The Sharia law is subject to manipulation and falsification and has therefore sadly failed. The ulema in Saudi Arabia, Iran, Sudan, and Egypt continue to issue fatwa at the behest of the corrupt ruling class. The Sharia and *fiqh* had failed and collapsed in AH 665 when the gates to *ijtihad* were slammed shut and have not since revived.

4. **The Faqihs:** When the blessed prophet passed away, there was no clergy and priest class in Islam. During the following two hundred years, there arose hundreds of madhabs, each with an imam. The Sharia of the early madhabs failed as a tool of jurisprudence and justice. However, the work of the earlier imams documented sources from the Koran and the teachings of the blessed prophet as the source of Sharia. Injunctions of the Koran and Sunna provide the core of Sharia and are collectively called the *nusus.* Sharia provides clear rulings on the fundamentals of Islam, its basic moral values, and practical duties such as prayers, fasting, zakat, hajj, and other devotional matters. It also pronounces on what is lawful (halal) and unlawful (haram). This was a documentation of all that

> the blessed *Nabi* had pronounced in his last years. The Koran provided the law. The covenant of Allah clearly states what is lawful and what is forbidden. It was not the law that Allah proclaimed that failed. What failed were the legal system, the jurisprudence, and the *fiqh* that man created. Man failed to follow the dictates of the Koran.

The blessed *rasul.* of Allah said,

> Do you know what saps the foundation of Islam, and ruins it? The errors of the learned destroy it, and the disputations of the hypocrite and the orders of the kings who have lost the road.

The words of the blessed *rasul.* of Allah were realized soon after his death. Islam became beset by the triple menace of the errors of scholars (jurist-mullahs), the malice of hypocrites, and the tyranny of rulers. The followers of earlier imams became a hierarchy of priestly bureaucracy. Muslim society became, in practice, a society governed by self-appointed rulers who patronized the religious hierarchy, the ulema, which in turn legitimized un-Koranic rulers. In between were the opportunists, the hypocrites, those who were Muslims in name only, those who caused dissension, and those who would benefit from disputes among Muslims.

The ruling elite supported the clerics and the jurist-mullahs, and in return, the scholars of Islam sanctioned the un-Islamic practices of the elite. The mullahs had endowments, allowances, and a position of power above their fellow men; and in return, they overlooked the oppression and tyranny of the elite over their people. The Sharia, based on the Koran, endowed the *ummah*, in theory, with human dignity, equality, justice, a consultative government, a state where there was realization of lawful benefits to peoples, the prevention of harm to people, the removal of hardship, and the education of individuals by inculcating in them self-discipline, patience, restraint, and respect for rights of others.

The Sharia was supposed to bring about the restitution of all wrongs and all imbalances in society. Under the reign of the caliphs and the clerics, none of the above happened. Even today in the states with the mullah-politician alliance, where Sharia is supposedly practiced, there is tyranny, injustice, and open corruption under the Taliban, ayatollahs, Saudi-Wahhabi alliance, and Pakistani politician-general-mullah rule. These are the most oppressive regimes in the world. The political mullahs, like other politicians, crave power; the only difference between the mullahs and other politicians is that the clerics have the advantage of religious sentiment as their weapon. When in power, the ayatollahs, mullahs, the Wahhabi, and the Taliban all unashamedly and frankly practice torture and torment on citizens and their political opponents alike. If Machiavelli were alive today, he would learn a thing or two from the priests of Islam.

5. **Education and Knowledge:** Whereas Allah and the blessed *Nabi* advocate knowledge and education, the mullahs—the self-appointed guardians of knowledge and wisdom—oppose the acquisition of knowledge and education, especially the pursuit of knowledge of literature, arts, and sciences by both men and women. The current situation of the Muslim world is akin to the dark ages of Christianity. After the Council of Nicaea in 325 CE, it became part of the doctrine of the church that the bishop of Rome and his hierarchical priests were God's representatives on the earth, and their pronouncements were made with divine approval. Those who disagreed with this edict were persecuted, tortured, or exiled. Legislation against such "heretics" debarred them from public

> office and conducted purges against them[46]. A large group of Greek classical scholars left Europe, taking their books and manuscripts with them. Thus, all learning, philosophy, mathematics, and science were wiped from the memory of the European man for many centuries as if they never existed. This vast body of learning was lost to Western civilization for centuries but was preserved in the later Islamic empire and, thanks to the efforts of Islamic scholars, eventually resurfaced in Europe a thousand years later in the Renaissance.

In the tolerant atmosphere of Muslim Spain, science found fertile ground, and important contributions were made in medicine, geography, and cosmology and development of instruments for measurement, cartography, and navigation. Translation of manuscripts was carried out from Greek to Arabic and from Arabic into Latin and into many other European languages. Gradually, the Muslim thought, and ideas crept into Europe. Ibn al-'Arabi's mysticism and sublime poetry profoundly influenced leading European scholars like Roger Bacon, Dante, Cervantes, Averroes, Saint Francis of Assisi, and Chaucer.

Muslim knowledge of geometry, algebra, and instruments of measurement based on works of al-Biruni, Avicenna's *Canon*, and Averroes's *Kulliyat* was added to the Latin corpus in the thirteenth century CE. Learning in Europe now grew away from the constricted atmosphere of the monasteries with their deep, dogmatic, and conservative syllabus concerned with the study of the Bible and the writings of the church fathers. Thirteenth-century scholars now studied and argued in the new universities at Paris, Bologna, and Oxford. These universities were free of church domination and equipped with libraries, lecture halls, and a vast new range of textbooks translated from the libraries of Islamic learning. A wide

46 Johnson Paul, *A History of Christianity*, 87.

range of Greek and Arab scholars had become available to the searchers of knowledge. The church was, at long last, losing its stifling stranglehold on education. It was the respected colleges in Al-Andalus that became the models on which Oxford and Cambridge Universities were established[47]. These independent centers of learning in Christian countries were now studying the ever-increasing flow of scholarly works emerging from the world of Islam that gave an impetus to the rapid development of Europe.

Exactly the converse took place in the world of Islam. While knowledge flourished in the fertile ground during the Umayyad and Abbasid periods, the freedom to acquire education and knowledge came to a sudden halt in the thirteenth century of the Common Era. When the sun was rising on Europe, darkness of ignorance was gradually taking over the scholarship of Islam. The influence of the mullah-jurists grew until they became the imams of their legal schools by which their followers came to be identified. However, before their popularity, the schools had no name, and no Muslim had ever identified with them at that time. The schools of law continued to multiply until the beginning of the eleventh century of the Common Era.

The mullah-jurist-scholars maintained a close relationship with the caliphs and the palace officials; they thus appointed the faqihs, the legislators of law, the judges, as well as the prosecutors of law. They also took over other positions on behalf of the caliphs as the tax collectors, maintainers of law and order, and teachers in madrassas. As the administrators of mosques and prayer leaders, they were beginning to behave like priests and rabbis despite the fact that there is no priesthood in Islam. Every believer has a direct spiritual access to Allah without the intervention of a priest or a deceased saintly personality. Through their influence over the caliph, the faqihs of

---

[47] Akbar S. W. Ahmed, *Discovering Islam*, 4.

the four main madhabs had all the other madhabs abolished, and every Muslim was forced to acquiesce to the dictates of one of these four schools. By the fourteenth century of the Common Era, the neighborhood priest/jurist had complete control on the upbringing, education, marriage, and livelihood of every person of his madhab from the cradle to the grave.

Islam is the *din* in which the simple believer connects to his Allah through his emotions, heart, and mind. In the new stratification of Islam, he was forced to join a madhab and follow a sheikh to learn from the collection of four thousand hadith to enable him to perform the correct *wudhu* and recognize the length of pant legs, the space between his feet while praying, the length of his mustache, and the number of pebbles to wipe his bottom before he could learn to pray to his Allah. Before the advent of the *masha'ikhs*, the believer knew his Koran that directed him to his covenant with Allah, the thirty-seven commandments that included everything that is to know about his *din*, family, truth, justice, humility, honesty, and good deeds. While learning the practicalities of the hadith, the believer forgot the simple precepts of Allah and His *rasul's* message in the Koran. The result of this grabbing of control over the *din* of Islam was that, by 665 hijra (fourteenth century CE), no further decrees or fatwa were permitted unless they were in accordance with the teachings of the *masha'ikh* of the four recognized madhabs. No further independent inquiry was permitted. Islam had now sunk to the intellectual level of inquiry that prevailed in pre-Renaissance Christianity. The priests of Islam strangled Islamic education and knowledge the way the Roman Catholic Church had destroyed European enlightenment for one thousand years. In Islam the gates of *ijtihad* were slammed shut, and no further dissension was permitted till the European intellectuals came in the twentieth century to repay their debt to Islam.

In the meantime, hardly any Muslim woman could read and write. Women's schools had been abolished. Most men were functionally illiterate, and at the turn of the twentieth century, there was not a single scientist of renown who had been trained through Islamic education. The flame of knowledge was barely flickering when personalities like Sayyid Ahmad in Aligarh tried to revive it; the mullahs of India doused it in water of ignorance.

6. **Women:** The Koran endowed women with equality and freedom, human dignity, justice, the right to free speech, the right to share in consultative government, the creation of a state where there is realization of lawful benefits to women, the prevention of harm to women, the removal of hardship, and the education of individuals by inculcating in them self-discipline, patience, restraint, and respect for rights of others—a system where there is restitution of all wrongs and imbalances in society. For thirteen hundred years, the mullahs undermined these freedoms granted to women by Allah.

Allah sent down his *din* to both men and women. He asked humankind to believe in Him and worship Him with daily salat. Today the priests and the mullahs make women unwelcome in Allah's house, the house of prostration, the mosque. They falsify hadith and misrepresent the Koran to keep women out of mainstream of Islam. Allah asks men to lower their gaze and avoid *Fahasha;* instead, men and mullahs chose to shut the women behind closed doors and windows rather than subdue their own lust. They insist on shrouding women in hijab by misrepresenting the Koran and the hadith.

The mullahs and the madhabs have no jurisdiction over God-fearing and upright women's right to worship, nor did they have any jurisdiction over the manner of their apparel. The worship of Allah and a believing woman's apparel is a matter of concern between Allah and the believer. Islam is a religion of self-surrender; it is the conscious and rational submission of dependent and limited human will to the absolute and omnipotent will of Allah. The type of surrender Islam requires is a deliberate, conscious, and rational act made by a person who knows with both intellectual certainty and spiritual vision that Allah, who is subject of Koranic discourse, is the reality. The knower of God is a Muslim, "one who submits" to the divine truth and whose relationship with God is governed by *taqwa*, the consciousness of humankind's responsibility toward its Creator. After submission, the believer develops a personal relationship with Allah.

Allah addresses women and men in His covenant about their conduct, worship, and dress. The mullah and the ulema have no part in this relationship. They have their own obligations to Allah for the benefit of their own souls. The believer has the right to approach any knowledgeable person to seek advice and spiritual discourse. There is no hierarchical priesthood in Islam. Therefore, there is no guardianship over the Sharia, nor is there any religious constabulary. Allah is the Seer and Knower of all things. He does not need spies and enforcers to run His *din*.

The blessed prophet said Allah is the best of judges and that the command (*hukm*) rests with Him. The prophet himself was the subject of Allah's command and was powerless to hurry, delay, or alter Allah's *hukm*.

﴿ قُلْ إِنِّي عَلَىٰ بَيِّنَةٍ مِّن رَّبِّي وَكَذَّبْتُم بِهِۦ ۚ مَا عِندِي مَا تَسْتَعْجِلُونَ بِهِۦٓ ۚ إِنِ ٱلْحُكْمُ إِلَّا لِلَّهِ ۖ يَقُصُّ ٱلْحَقَّ ۖ وَهُوَ خَيْرُ ٱلْفَٰصِلِينَ

Say: "For me, I work on a clear Sign from my Lord,
but you reject Him. What you would see hastened,
is not in my power. The Command, *Hukm*, rests
with none but Allah: He declares the Truth, and He
is the best of judges." (Al-An'am 6:57, Koran)

﴿ ٱتَّخَذُوٓاْ أَحْبَارَهُمْ وَرُهْبَٰنَهُمْ أَرْبَابًا مِّن دُونِ ٱللَّهِ وَٱلْمَسِيحَ ٱبْنَ مَرْيَمَ وَمَآ أُمِرُوٓاْ إِلَّا لِيَعْبُدُوٓاْ إِلَٰهًا وَٰحِدًا ۖ لَّآ إِلَٰهَ إِلَّا هُوَ ۚ

سُبْحَٰنَهُۥ عَمَّا يُشْرِكُونَ ﴿٣١﴾ ﴾

They take their priests and their rabbis their lords in derogation of Allah, and (they take as their Lord) Christ, the son of Mary; yet they were commanded to worship but One God: La Ilaha illa Huwa, none has right to be worshipped but He. Praise and glory to Him: (far is He) from having the partners they associate (with Him). (At-Tawbah 9: 31, Koran)

This *ayah* in At-Tawbah is reflective of the existence of a situation in the Muslim world, which is similar to the one alluded to the Koran. The Muslims began to take their imams, priests, and scholars as their lords. Although the priests do not pretend to be divine, they pretend to possess an aura of holiness, and they decree *ahkam*, which is the prerogative of Allah. Some elevate themselves with an aura of divinity by claiming a descent from the blessed prophet Muhammad. Yet the prophet said:

I am no more than a man; when I order you anything respecting religion, receive it, and when I tell you anything about the affairs of the world, and then I am nothing but a man.

Their commandments to their followers occasionally are in contradiction to the message of the Koran. Also, they interpret the Sharia, overriding the verses of the Koran with falsified sayings of the blessed *Nabi*. They also place greater weight to the hadith collections of the third century than to the word of Allah. The result is that, over the centuries, in practice, the *din* of Allah has become the *din* of Muhammad; whereas Allah is only worthy of worship, the blessed

Nabi cannot be worshipped, only to be adored, respected, and blessed. In fact, in the khutbah, the worshippers hear more about the blessed prophet, Ali, Hasan, Husayn, Abu Bakr, Umar, and Uthman than the name of Allah and the teachings of the Koran. The blessed prophet brought the message of one Creator, Allah, the God whom *Nabi* Ibrahim submitted to and placed all his trust in. Allah is the Real, the Supreme, and worthy of worship. Humankind, regardless of their lineage, is mortal and insignificant.

The Community of Islam: The *ummah* forms the fourth wall of the house of justice and righteousness. The *ummah* is united as one people and one nation, whose heart Allah has joined in love so that they are brethren to one another. The *ummah* enjoins good and forbids evil. It is committed to truth and administers justice on the basis of truth, and the *ummah* has been commanded by Allah to act justly to others and to one another and in its advocacy of truth; it is a witness over itself and over mankind. The *ummah* observes due balance of moderation in all its actions; it avoids extremism and does not transgress due bounds in anything. Men and women are straight and honest in all their dealings. Every believer maintains himself in a permanent state of surrender (*taqwa*) to Allah. The *ummah* is united in a single brotherhood not to be divided into sects, schisms, principalities, states, or kingdoms. Allah has promised *Azabu azeem*, a dreadful penalty, to those causing divisions among the *ummah*. This community looks after its own members in peace, tribulation, and adversity and in times of stress.

Although, the *ummah* is the sovereign and Allah's vicegerent on the earth, this sovereignty throughout the history of Islam has been undermined by the *Munafiq*, the tyrants and oppressors.

The pyramid of a just and moral society is based on the foundation of a community upon community that gradually tapers to an apex where the ultimate guardian of justice is represented by Allah's covenant, the Koran. The governance is based on open, transparent, honest, truthful statecraft where justice is practiced by the *ummah's wakil* at the top and is seen by whole of the *ummah* at the base. In the same context, the community at the base acts as the custodians of the covenant of Allah and ensures that there is honesty in its governance, and the community bureaucracy is free from moral and economic corruption.

The Sharia system of the early *madhabs* failed as a tool of jurisprudence and justice. However, the achievement of the work of the earlier imams was to document the Sharia based on the Koran, which the blessed prophet taught during his lifetime. The injunctions of the Koran and Sunna provide the core of Sharia, which is collectively called the *nusus*. The Sharia comprises the guidance that Allah revealed to the His blessed messenger, relating the system of the *din* of Islam, its moral values, and its practical legal rules. Morality (*ilm al akhlaq*) educates the person in moral virtue and the exercise of self-discipline and restraint against the cravings of the self. The Sharia pronounces on what is lawful (halal) and unlawful (haram). All this is documentation of what is in the Koran and that which the prophet had expounded in his lifetime. The Koran provides the law, and it was not the law that failed. What failed was the legal system, the administration of justice, the jurisprudence, and the *fiqh* that man had created. There was nothing wrong with the law of the covenant of Allah. What went wrong was the destruction of a perfect legal system by human ego and noncompliance and disobedience of the law by those who practiced the governance of the Islamic state.

Two walls of the house of justice and righteousness withstood the test of time and stood solidly on their foundations. The walls lost the paint and plaster and look somewhat dilapidated. The front facade representing law and justice is still standing. This is the law of the Koran and the covenant. The right wall representing the *ummah* of the believers is also intact as most of the members of the *ummah* have continued to observe their covenant with Allah.

The back wall representing the rulers continues to crumble to dust. It is continually being rebuilt with ever-changing facades and fasciae of granite and marble. Its foundations are on the sand of deceit and falsehood, threatening the continuation of the cycle of collapse and refurbishing.

The fourth wall representing scholar-jurists, faqihs, mujtahid, and mullahs is in utter ruin, confusion, and disarray. There are books, manuscripts, and parchments—some whole, others moth eaten—strewn everywhere, a scene of utter confusion. Strewn around are the modern tools at the mullahs' disposal: loudspeakers and sound systems that the mullahs use to shout at one another and at the people. The mullahs aggrandize themselves with grand names, regalia, and titles. All of them regard themselves as ulema, the holders of ultimate knowledge, but they refuse to broaden their horizons with the acquisition of broader knowledge of Allah's creation and signs required to live a life of survival and spirituality. They have failed to learn from the signs of Allah about decay and renewal of life.

The roof representing Allah's mercy and beneficence had long since fallen, yet Allah continues to be merciful and benevolent to the believers. Muslims are responsible for their own situation they are in.

The blessed *Nabi* had said,

> Do you know what saps the foundation of Islam, and ruins it? The errors of the learned destroy it, and the disputations of the hypocrite and the orders of the kings who have lost the road.

The truth of the blessed *Nabi* Muhammad's words was soon realized. The followers of earlier imams and the later scholars became a hierarchy of priestly bureaucracy. Muslim society became, in practice, a society governed by state elites who patronized the religious figures, and the priest-ulema, in turn, legitimized the un-Koranic rulers. This alliance of rulers and priestly hierarchy and the cooperative relationship between these two institutions would, for many centuries, degrade the justice system and the law prescribed by the Koran. The *din* of Allah was fragmented by the so-called imams in the futile fight for the succession for the blessed prophet's legacy. No one can inherit a prophecy nor can acquire messenger ship as a birthright or kinship. This dichotomy has pitted Sunnis against Shias for fourteen centuries. There is only one *din* of Allah, *Islam*. This dichotomy prevented the orderly development of a representative spiritual and consultative government representing the common man. Education, public services, and elimination of poverty and common suffering were not pursued by the rulers nor by the clerics. The mullahs had endowments, allowances, and positions of power above their fellow men; and in return, they overlooked the oppression and tyranny of the elite over the people.

The Sharia, based on the Koran, endowed the *ummah* with human dignity, equality, justice, and consultative government. The Sharia envisaged a state in which there was a realization of lawful benefits to peoples, the prevention of harm to people, the removal of hardship, and the education of individuals by inculcating in them self-discipline, patience, restraint, and respect for rights of other humans. The mullah-elite hegemony betrayed the covenant of Allah and debased the rule of the law that the blessed *Nabi* had taught.

Whereas Allah and the blessed Prophet advocated knowledge and education, the mullahs opposed the acquisition of knowledge and education, especially the knowledge of numbers and sciences, by both men and women. The sciences portraying the signs of Allah were deliberately betrayed by the ignorance of the arrogant ulema. The Koran endowed women with equality and freedom, human dignity, justice, rights to free speech, a share in consultative government, lawful benefits, education, prevention of harm to women, removal of hardship, and restitution of all wrongs and imbalances in society. For thirteen hundred years, the mullahs have opposed these freedoms granted to women by Allah.

In a just society, in the Dar es Salaam, the Sharia and the institution of justice will need to be administered differently. The house of justice and righteousness will be a pyramid with Allah's mercy and beneficence above.

The Sharia: The Law, the Believer, and His *Wakil*: The front wall will represent the law, the Sharia. The law will be based on the decrees of the Koran and the prophet's pronouncements on religion:

> I am no more than a man; when I order you
> anything respecting religion, receive it, and
> when I tell you anything about the affairs of the
> world, and then I am nothing but a man.

The term *islam* signifies the idea of surrender or submission. Islam is a religion of self-surrender; it is the conscious and rational submission of the dependent and limited human will to the absolute and omnipotent will of Allah. The knower of God, upon his surrender to Allah's will, accepts the covenant of Allah and consciously agrees to follow its commandments. The believer chooses Allah's path according to his own free will and choice. The knower of God is a Muslim, "one who submits" to the divine truth and whose relationship with God is governed by *taqwa*, the consciousness of humankind's responsibility toward its Creator. The act of submission and acceptance of Allah's covenant establishes a relationship between Allah and the believer, in which Allah is ever present in the conscious heart and mind of the believer.

However, consciousness of God alone is not sufficient to make a person a Muslim. The concept of *taqwa* implies that the believer has the added responsibility of acting in accordance with three types of knowledge—*ilm al-yaqin*, *ain al-yaqin*, and *haqq al-yaqin* (knowledge of certainty, eye of certainty, and truth of certainty). The believer must endeavor at all times to maintain and align himself or herself in a constant state of submission to Allah. By doing so, the believer attains the honored title of "slave of Allah" (*abd Allah*, fem.: *amat Allah*), for he recognizes that all power and all agency belongs to God alone:

وَلَوْلَآ إِذْ دَخَلْتَ جَنَّتَكَ قُلْتَ مَا شَآءَ ٱللَّهُ لَا قُوَّةَ إِلَّا بِٱللَّهِ ۚ إِن تَرَنِ أَنَا۠ أَقَلَّ مِنكَ مَالًا وَوَلَدًا

Allah has willed it. There is no power
but Allah's. (Koran 18:39)

Trusting in Allah's mercy and grace yet fearing God's wrath, the slave of Allah walks the road of life with careful steps, making his or her actions deliberate so that he or she will not stray from the path that God has laid out:

إِيَّاكَ نَعْبُدُ وَإِيَّاكَ نَسْتَعِينُ ۝٥ ٱهْدِنَا ٱلصِّرَٰطَ ٱلْمُسْتَقِيمَ ۝٦ صِرَٰطَ ٱلَّذِينَ أَنْعَمْتَ عَلَيْهِمْ غَيْرِ
ٱلْمَغْضُوبِ عَلَيْهِمْ وَلَا ٱلضَّآلِّينَ ۝٧

Thee do we worship, and Thine aid we seek, Show us
the straight way, The way of those on whom Thou
hast bestowed Thy Grace, those whose (portion) is
not wrath, and who go not astray. (Koran 1:5–7)

It is an all-encompassing and highly personal type of commitment and relationship in which Allah's light (*nur*) resides in the believer's heart The believer is conscious of Allah's closeness and mercy and obeys, trusts, and loves Allah. Allah in return loves those who love Him and perform beautiful deeds. The parable of divine light defines Allah's relationship with his servant, the believer.

Allah is the light of heavens and earth. Allah's light illuminates hearts and minds of those who love Him, place their trust in Him, and open their heart, mind, and soul in submission to Him. Once hearts and minds are open to Allah in submission, they form the niche in which the divine light, Spirit, and wisdom of Allah glows in man. The luminescence of the Spirit and wisdom shines with the brightness of a star. This star is lit from the light of divine wisdom, the tree of knowledge—the knowledge of Allah's signs. For those who believe, Allah is within. The believer is aglow with Allah's radiance—light upon light. The dwellings where Allah's name is praised and glorified in the mornings and evenings are lit with Allah's light.

Allah has granted the knowledge and the wisdom of *furqan* and *taqwa* to the believers who have opened their hearts and minds to Him. Man has been granted the freedom of choice in doing what is wholesome and beautiful or what is corrupt and ugly. It is only man among the creation who has been given the knowledge to distinguish right activity, right thought, and right intention from their opposites. This knowledge reminds the human of the scales of Allah's justice, the two hands of Allah—His mercy and His wrath—which are reflected in the human domain, where people have been appointed Allah's vicegerents. Deeds of goodness and wholesomeness are associated with mercy, paradise, and what is beautiful. Evil and corruption is rewarded with wrath, hell, and what is ugly.

On his journey, the believer has Allah within, Allah's covenant as his guide, the *taqwa* of Allah as shield against evil, and *furqan*, which is Allah's compass to the straight path of righteousness. The believer, on his chosen journey on the path of Allah, is well equipped. He has Allah's protection, guidance, and direction. Does he need a man-made Sharia and *fiqh* based on man-made hadith collection of the third century? Isn't Allah's word sufficient and clear enough? The covenant of Allah is the law.

Those who believe are connected to Allah and know the divine law. Those on their journey in Allah's path who have gone astray need guidance. There is no compulsion in religion. Allah has given man, among the creation, the knowledge to distinguish right activity, right thought, and right intention from their opposites. For those on Allah's path who go astray and seek forgiveness and guidance, Allah is the most merciful. Islam seeks to reform the individual. For those who go astray repeatedly and seek Allah's pardon, Allah's mercy knows no bounds. It is human to err. Among humans, there is an oft-repeated cycle of belief and error. Beseeching Allah's forgiveness and guidance reforms the individual, putting him back on track to faith and the performance of beautiful deeds. The Koran repeatedly reassures us that *"Allah is most Forgiving."* When Allah forgives those, who have erred and then repented and asked for forgiveness, why will then one man punish another who has erred and then asked for forgiveness? The return to faith is through reform and guidance and not through abuse and brutality.

The second wall of the house of justice and righteousness will represent the believers, and the third wall will represent the administrators of the affairs of the *ummah* who will be appointed by the *ummah*. The *ummah* will, from among themselves, choose believing men and women of wisdom and learning from all walks of life to put together laws based on the decrees and the spirit of the Koran and on what the prophet actually taught. Laws will be universal for the whole *ummah* to suit the circumstances of the present times.

Since the days of the blessed *Nabi,* the world has changed. Since then, there has been an industrial revolution. The darkness of the night has shrunk by six hours. Consequently, functional literacy and scholarship has expanded, and with this expanded knowledge the common believer has accumulated more knowledge of his *din* than the mullah or the scholar from older times. The precepts of the Koran are there for all times. The hadith collections of the third century have become fixed in the mores and knowledge of that time. The everlasting wisdom and knowledge of the Koran surpasses the tradition and stories of the old-time hadith related through the minds of people one thousand years ago. They do not always accurately represent what the blessed Prophet taught in his time.

Conclusion: The Sharia is the law of the Koran that is explained and supplemented by the practice and the teachings of the blessed prophet. Whereas the law of the Koran is the revelation and is mandatory, the Sunna is not a revelation, and only its parts dealing with matters of *din* constitute the mandatory part of law. The *mutawatir* hadith are the word-for-word transmission of what the prophet said. There are no more than *ten* such hadith. Another kind of hadith is known as *conceptual mutawatir*, in which the concept is taken from the prophet, but the words are that of the narrator. This kind of *mutawatir* is frequent. They are the sayings and the acts of the blessed prophet that explain the essentials of faith, the rituals of worship, the rules that regulate the punishments, and the description of the lawful and the unlawful. The blessed prophet said, "I am no more than a man; when I order you anything respecting religion, receive it, and when I tell you anything about the affairs of the world, and then I am nothing but a man." Therefore, the prophet's worldly deeds and sayings do not constitute to the *din* or the law.

The practice of *fiqh* and *ijtihad* was a human experiment in legislation of laws in the name of Allah and His *rasul. Fiqh* and *ijtihad* are imperfect results of our limited human understanding and have often been mutually contradictory; they form the law that is transient and contingent on local circumstances and the level of human development and always to be ordained on the principles of the covenant of the Koran. These laws are human and therefore are subject to change by humankind according to the changing needs of the people, nevertheless in accordance with the covenant of Allah.

The blessed *Nabi* said: "The Qur'an consists of five heads, things **lawful,** things **unlawful,** clear and positive **precept**s, **mysteries** and **example**s. Then consider which is lawful and that which is forbidden as unlawful; obey the precepts, believe in the mysteries and take warning from the examples." The only purpose of the Sharia is to ensure that the laws are just and that justice is done.

- Justice (*'adl*) is a divine attribute, defined as "putting every object in the right place."
- Wrongdoing is a human attribute defined as "putting things in the wrong place or negative acts employed by human beings."

Sharia should ensure human dignity, equality, justice, consultative government, a state where there is realization of lawful benefits to people, the prevention of harm, the removal of hardship, and the education of individuals by inculcating in them self-discipline, patience, restraint, and respect for the rights of others. Sharia is a system under which there is a restitution of all wrongs and imbalances in society. When the law and the justice system does not fulfill these requirements, it cannot be deemed to be according to Allah's laws and does not fulfill the requirements of Sharia.

The Islamic society as envisioned in the Koran and in the Sunna is a moral and just society—a society in which every individual, man and woman, from the highest to the lowest, has an equal and unimpeded right to freedom, a right to practice their faith in accordance to their beliefs. This is because, in Islam, there is no compulsion in matters of religion. Individuals should enjoy a right to life, which includes mental, physical, and emotional well-being; the safeguarding of their property; right to intellectual endeavors and the acquisition of knowledge and education; right to make a living; right to free speech; and right to action for the purpose of enjoining good and forbidding evil. In enjoying these freedoms, the individual ensures that their activities do not impinge on the similar rights of others.

The Sharia can be implemented justly only when the governance is just and moral and established in accordance with the laws of the Koran. It should have a participatory representative and a consultative structure based on a truthful and transparent justice system. The community as a whole, after consultation and consensus, grants people among themselves with the authority to manage its affairs. Those charged with authority act in their capacity as the representative (*wakil*) of the people and are bound by the Koranic mandate to consult the community in public affairs, and general consensus is the binding source of the law. The community, by consultation and in consensus, has the authority to depose any person charged with authority, including the head of state in the event of gross violation of the law and disobedience of the covenant of the Koran.

Islam pursues its social objectives by reforming the individual. Every individual is seen not just a member of the community and subservient to the community's will but also morally autonomous agent who plays a distinctive role in shaping the community's sense of direction and purpose. The Koran has attached to the individual's duty of obedience to the government a right of to simultaneously dispute with the rulers over government affairs. The individual obeys the ruler on the condition that the ruler obeys the Islamic law according to the Koran. This is reflected in the declaration of the blessed *Nabi* that,

> "there is no obedience in transgression;
> obedience is only in the righteousness."

The citizen is entitled to disobey an oppressive command that is contrary to the Islamic law in accordance with the covenant of the Koran.

- It is obligatory for every believer to observe his covenant with Allah. The Sharia is essentially derived from the seventy-five verses of the Koran that give the thirty-seven commandments of the covenant.
- The prophet said that the Koran consists of five heads: things that are lawful, things that are unlawful, clear and positive precepts, mysteries, and examples.
- The Sharia is the guidance that Allah revealed to the His blessed messenger relating the system of belief of Islam, its moral values, and its practical legal rules. The lessons in morality serve to educate the individual in moral virtue and in the exercise of self-discipline and to practice restraint to the human cravings of the self.
- The Sharia provides clear rulings on the fundamentals of Islam, its basic moral values, and practical duties such as prayers, fasting, zakat, hajj, and other devotional matters. It also pronounces on what is lawful and what is unlawful. All this is the documentation of what the prophet had expounded in his lifetime.
- The Koran provided the law, and the prophet gave the guidance.

- The individual is taught to obey the precepts of Allah's law in the Koran. Allah proclaims His law in the covenant to the believers in a simple, lucid language. Allah addresses the believers in the Koran and shows them the right way to follow Him. The observance of the covenant of Allah is the total belief system based on the unity of one's personality and communion with Allah in total awareness and *taqwa* of Allah and with the observance of all of the thirty-seven commandments of the covenant. This communion is not only with Allah but also through Him with other humans and with rest of Allah's creation, both alive and inanimate.
- The phrase *amilu al saalihaat* (to do good, to perform wholesome deeds) refers to those who persist in striving to set things right, who restore harmony, peace, justice, and balance. The believer is then guided by Allah and His prophet in the covenant to show compassion, to be merciful and forgive others, to be just, to protect the weak, to defend the oppressed, to be generous and charitable, to be truthful, to seek knowledge and wisdom, to be kind, to be peaceful, to love others, and to perform beautiful deeds.

Allah has in very explicit words laid out in His covenant the acts forbidden to the believers:

1. *Shirk*: Join not anything as equal with Him. (Worship Allah and do not associate others with Him.)
2. Mistreatment of parents: Be good to your parents.
3. Infanticide and abortion: Kill not your children on a plea of want. We provide sustenance for you and for them.
4. *Fahasha*: Come not near shameful deeds, whether open or in secret.
5. Taking of life: Take not life, which Allah hath made sacred, except by way of justice and law.

6. Stealing: Come not near to the orphan's property, except to improve it, until he attains the age of full strength. The term *orphan* may also include other helpless citizens who may be subject to oppression.
7. Cheating: And give measure and weight with justice; (do not cheat) no burden do we place on any soul but that which it can bear.
8. Lying and falsification: Whenever you speak, speak the truth, even if a near relative is concerned.
9. Violation of Allah's covenant: Fulfill the covenant of Allah: "Thus, does He command you that ye may remember. Verily, this is My Way leading straight: follow it; follow no other paths: they will scatter you about from His Path; thus, doth He command you, that ye may be righteous" (Al-An'am 6:151–53, Koran).
10. Intoxicants.
11. Gambling.
12. Dedication of stones.
13. Divination by arrows.

    These are an abomination and Satan's handiwork; they hinder you from prayer and remembrance of Allah and place enmity and hatred amongst you. Abstain from them so that you may prosper. (Al-Ma'idah 5:90–91, Koran)
14. Carrion.
15. Blood.
16. Flesh of swine.
17. "Any other food on which any name besides that of Allah has been invoked" (Al-Baqarah 2:172–73, Koran).
18. Usury (*riba*): "Devour not usury double and multiplied: Be in taqwa of Allah, that you may prosper" (Ali 'Imran 3:130, Koran).

19. Disrespect toward women: "It is not lawful for you to take women against their will, nor should you treat them with harshness. On the contrary treat then with honor and kindness" (An-Nisa 4:19, Koran).
20. Any actions that infringe on the unity of the *ummah* and the nation of Islam.
    And hold fast, all together, by the Rope which Allah stretches out for you and be not divided among yourselves. You were enemies and He joined your hearts in love, so that by His Grace, you became brethren and a community. Thus, does Allah makes His Signs clear to you that you may be guided. Be not like those who are divided amongst themselves and fall into disputations after receiving clear signs; for them is a dreadful penalty.

These twenty actions have been forbidden (haram) by the covenant of Allah. At the same time, Allah commands:

> Make not unlawful the good things, which Allah hath made lawful to you. Commit no excess; Allah loves not people given to excess. Eat of things that Allah has provided for you, lawful and good. Be in taqwa of Allah, fear Allah in whom you believe. (Al-Ma'idah 5:57, Koran)

Islamic scholar-jurists frequently quote various Hadith and proclaim many aspects of the daily life of pious and observant believers as haram. Such actions include listening to music, women's education, women's role in congregational prayers, and other mundane activities such as kite flying, tourism, pursuit of Western education, and use of modern technology. Those are the personal views of the mullahs and do not have the divine sanction of the covenant between Allah and His believers.

Music: Music is part of the human soul. Every child, when happy, springs up to a melody and dance to the rhythm. When the blessed *Nabi* received the revelation from Allah, at times, it appeared in the form of a tinkle or the chimes of a bell, and the words of the revelation blossomed in Blessed Muhammad's mind. The Koran, when recited in rhythmic Arabic, produces a heavenly song of Allah's revelation. Singing Allah's *dhikr* with or without instrument or music has a powerful and profound effect on the listener's soul, which reflects divine beauty. Listening to mere wind chimes makes one aware of the divine origin of the sounds of the wind, the rustle of trees, and the sound of running water in rivers, falls, and oceans. Allah gave the human the ability to produce the most beautiful sounds in His remembrance, to celebrate life and happiness, and to enjoy Allah's other provisions to mankind.

Observation of Allah's covenant bestows peace and tranquility to the soul and hence happiness and contentment on the believer. Islam is not a religion of gloom, sorrow, and melancholia but that of celebration of Allah's blessings and of doing beautiful deeds. To show contentment, peace, harmony, happiness, and proper balance of things in life is to express *shukr*, gratitude to Allah for His mercy and grace. The human is asked to use all his senses—sight, hearing, smell, taste, and touch—to recognize Allah's truth and signs. They signify the perception of Allah's *nur* (light), resonance of the sound of Allah's harmonious music in nature, the fragrance of Allah's garden, the flavor of Allah's bounty, and the feel of Allah's creation around us. Allah does not forbid against His divine gift of harmony and song; on the contrary, He urged the recitation of the Koran in slow, rhythmic tones and the celebration and praising of Allah often, glorifying Him in the morning and at night. It is Allah and His angels who also send their blessings on the believers so "He may lead the Believers you out of the depths of darkness into light." Celebration of Allah's praises and glorifying Him means to rejoice, to be happy, and to be joyous. The word *celebrate*, therefore, has the connotation of a happy occasion, which includes song and music.

Confinement of Believing and devout women: Believers do not have a mandate in Allah's covenant about the confinement of believing and devout women nor that of covering women from head to toe.

Acquisition of knowledge and education: It is Allah's gift to humanity and is incumbent on every believer, man or woman. Scholars who portray Islam ignore the Koranic admonition

> Make not unlawful the good things, which Allah
> hath made lawful to you. Commit no excess;
> Allah loves not people given to excess.

The Covenant of Allah: The Society and State

Allah is *Haqq*. He is the Real; there is nothing real but the Real. Everything other than Allah is unreal, ephemeral, illusory, transitory, vanishing, nothing. Everything derives its existence from Allah. Everything good, praiseworthy, permanent, and real belongs to Him. Allah is independent. Everything in the heavens and the earth depends utterly on Allah for its existence and subsistence. Allah's reality is permanent and unchanging, everything else is relative, and everything else other than Allah has to be understood in relation to Him.

The sovereignty of the heavens and the earth belongs exclusively to Allah, whose will and command binds the Muslim community and state.

وَلِلَّهِ مَا فِي ٱلسَّمَٰوَٰتِ وَمَا فِي ٱلْأَرْضِۚ وَإِلَى ٱللَّهِ تُرْجَعُ ٱلْأُمُورُ ﴿١٠٩﴾

To Allah belongs all that is in the heavens and on
earth; and with Allah is the ultimate determination
of all things. (Ali 'Imran 3:109, Koran)

وَإِذْ قَالَ رَبُّكَ لِلْمَلَٰٓئِكَةِ إِنِّي جَاعِلٌ فِي ٱلْأَرْضِ خَلِيفَةًۖ قَالُوٓاْ أَتَجْعَلُ فِيهَا مَن يُفْسِدُ فِيهَا وَيَسْفِكُ ٱلدِّمَآءَ وَنَحْنُ نُسَبِّحُ بِحَمْدِكَ وَنُقَدِّسُ
لَكَۖ قَالَ إِنِّيٓ أَعْلَمُ مَا لَا تَعْلَمُونَ ﴿٣٠﴾

Behold, your Lord said to the angels: "I will
create a vicegerent on earth." They said: "Would
You place there one who will make mischief and
shed blood? While we celebrate Your praises and

glorify Your holy (name)?" He said: "I know what
you know not." (Al-Baqarah 2:30, Koran)

The Koran declares that Allah has subjugated the earth and the entire created universe for the benefit of human beings.

۞ ٱللَّهُ ٱلَّذِى سَخَّرَ لَكُمُ ٱلْبَحْرَ لِتَجْرِىَ ٱلْفُلْكُ فِيهِ بِأَمْرِهِۦ وَلِتَبْتَغُوا۟ مِن فَضْلِهِۦ وَلَعَلَّكُمْ تَشْكُرُونَ ﴿١٢﴾

It is Allah who has subjected the sea to you,
that ship may sail through it by His command,
that you may seek of His bounty, and that you
may be grateful. (Al-Jathiya 45:12, Koran)

The sovereignty of the Muslim state belongs to Allah. The *ummah*, through its covenant with Allah, is the repository of what is known as the "executive sovereignty" through the *ummah's* submission to the will of Allah. The *ummah* has the moral responsibility that is implied in the covenant, referred to in the Koran as the vicegerency (Koran 2:30-33). Those who uphold the requirements of the covenant are known as Allah's vicegerents (*khulafa*) on the earth. In the covenant of Allah, they are described as

يَـٰٓأَيُّهَا ٱلَّذِينَ ءَامَنُوا۟ ٱتَّقُوا۟ ٱللَّهَ وَقُولُوا۟ قَوْلًا سَدِيدًا ﴿٧٠﴾ يُصْلِحْ لَكُمْ أَعْمَـٰلَكُمْ وَيَغْفِرْ لَكُمْ ذُنُوبَكُمْ ۗ وَمَن يُطِعِ ٱللَّهَ وَرَسُولَهُۥ فَقَدْ فَازَ فَوْزًا

عَظِيمًا ﴿٧١﴾

O you who believe! Fear Allah, and (always) say a word
directed to the Right: That He may make your conduct
whole and sound and forgive you your sins: he that
obeys Allah and His Rasool, has already attained the
highest Achievement. (Al-Ahzab 33:70–71, Koran)

The society that is made up of such God-fearing people (*muttaqeen*) constitutes a "middle nation" or axial community (*ummah wast*) whose collective responsibility is to bear witness to the truth and act as an example for the rest of the humanity—a nation of moderation that is averse to extremism:

وَكَذَٰلِكَ جَعَلْنَٰكُمْ أُمَّةً وَسَطًا لِّتَكُونُوا۟ شُهَدَآءَ عَلَى ٱلنَّاسِ وَيَكُونَ ٱلرَّسُولُ عَلَيْكُمْ شَهِيدًا ۗ وَمَا جَعَلْنَا ٱلْقِبْلَةَ ٱلَّتِى كُنتَ عَلَيْهَآ إِلَّا

لِنَعْلَمَ مَن يَتَّبِعُ ٱلرَّسُولَ مِمَّن يَنقَلِبُ عَلَىٰ عَقِبَيْهِ ۚ وَإِن كَانَتْ لَكَبِيرَةً إِلَّا عَلَى ٱلَّذِينَ هَدَى ٱللَّهُ ۗ وَمَا كَانَ ٱللَّهُ لِيُضِيعَ إِيمَٰنَكُمْ ۚ إِنَّ ٱللَّهَ بِٱلنَّاسِ

لَرَءُوفٌ رَّحِيمٌ

Thus have We made of you an Ummah justly balanced, that you might be witnesses over the nations, and the Rasool a witness over yourselves; and we appointed the Qibla to which thou were used, only to test those who followed the Rasool from those who would turn on their heels (from the Faith). Indeed, it was (a change) momentous, except to those guided by Allah. And never would Allah make your faith of no effect. For Allah is to all people most surely full of Kindness, Most Merciful. (Al-Baqarah 2:143, Koran)

The *ummah* is a community of believers *(Jamma)* that enjoins good and forbids evil, a community that in its advocacy of truth is a witness over itself and over humankind. This community maintains itself in a permanent state of surrender to Allah (*ummah Muslimah*) as exemplified by the blessed *Nabi* Muhammad and his followers in Medina.

وَمَن يُسْلِمْ وَجْهَهُۥٓ إِلَى ٱللَّهِ وَهُوَ مُحْسِنٌ فَقَدِ ٱسْتَمْسَكَ بِٱلْعُرْوَةِ ٱلْوُثْقَىٰ ۗ وَإِلَى ٱللَّهِ عَٰقِبَةُ ٱلْأُمُورِ

Whoever submits his whole self to Allah, and is a doer of good, has grasped indeed the most trustworthy handhold; and with Allah rests the End and Decision of (all) affairs. (Luqman 31:22, Koran)

كُنتُمْ خَيْرَ أُمَّةٍ أُخْرِجَتْ لِلنَّاسِ تَأْمُرُونَ بِٱلْمَعْرُوفِ وَتَنْهَوْنَ عَنِ ٱلْمُنكَرِ وَتُؤْمِنُونَ بِٱللَّهِ ۗ وَلَوْ ءَامَنَ أَهْلُ ٱلْكِتَـٰبِ لَكَانَ خَيْرًا
لَّهُم ۚ مِّنْهُمُ ٱلْمُؤْمِنُونَ وَأَكْثَرُهُمُ ٱلْفَـٰسِقُونَ ﴿١١٠﴾ لَن يَضُرُّوكُمْ إِلَّآ أَذًى ۖ وَإِن يُقَـٰتِلُوكُمْ يُوَلُّوكُمُ ٱلْأَدْبَارَ ثُمَّ لَا يُنصَرُونَ ﴿١١١﴾

You are the best of Peoples, evolved for mankind, enjoining what is right, forbidding what is wrong, and believing in Allah. If only the People of the Book had Faith, it was best for them: among them are some who have Faith, but most of them are perverted transgressors. They will do you no harm, barring a trifling annoyance; if they come out to fight you, they will show you their backs, and no help shall they get. (Ali 'Imran 3:110–11, Koran)

The Koran is emphatic on the solidarity of the community of believers, a community that advocates unity and shuns separation, a community whose hearts Allah has joined in love so that, by Allah's grace, they become brethren unto one another. Allah repeatedly commands believers to call for all that is good, enjoining what is right and forbidding what is wrong. In the covenant of the Koran, Allah promises a dreadful penalty (*Azabu azeem*) to those creating a schism and division in the community of Muslims. The Muslim community of one and a half billion people around the world is a single unified *ummah* whose hearts have been joined in love by Allah and who are brethren unto one another, never to be divided into schisms, sects, principalities, states, or kingdoms. The individuals within the community of goodwill, both men and women, are equal in status and enjoy the same rights. Those ulema, preachers, imams, politicians, kings, and presidents who cause divisions and disputes among the *ummah* have been promised a dreadful penalty by Allah. They have been warned.

وَٱعۡتَصِمُواْ بِحَبۡلِ ٱللَّهِ جَمِيعٗا وَلَا تَفَرَّقُواْۚ وَٱذۡكُرُواْ نِعۡمَتَ ٱللَّهِ عَلَيۡكُمۡ إِذۡ كُنتُمۡ أَعۡدَآءٗ فَأَلَّفَ بَيۡنَ قُلُوبِكُمۡ فَأَصۡبَحۡتُم بِنِعۡمَتِهِۦٓ إِخۡوَٰنٗا وَكُنتُمۡ
عَلَىٰ شَفَا حُفۡرَةٖ مِّنَ ٱلنَّارِ فَأَنقَذَكُم مِّنۡهَاۗ كَذَٰلِكَ يُبَيِّنُ ٱللَّهُ لَكُمۡ ءَايَٰتِهِۦ لَعَلَّكُمۡ تَهۡتَدُونَ ﴿١٠٣﴾ وَلۡتَكُن مِّنكُمۡ أُمَّةٞ يَدۡعُونَ إِلَى ٱلۡخَيۡرِ وَيَأۡمُرُونَ بِٱلۡمَعۡرُوفِ
وَيَنۡهَوۡنَ عَنِ ٱلۡمُنكَرِۚ وَأُوْلَٰٓئِكَ هُمُ ٱلۡمُفۡلِحُونَ ﴿١٠٤﴾ وَلَا تَكُونُواْ كَٱلَّذِينَ تَفَرَّقُواْ وَٱخۡتَلَفُواْ مِنۢ بَعۡدِ مَا جَآءَهُمُ ٱلۡبَيِّنَٰتُۚ وَأُوْلَٰٓئِكَ لَهُمۡ عَذَابٌ
عَظِيمٞ ﴿١٠٥﴾

And hold fast, all together, by the Rope which Allah (stretches out for you), and be not divided among yourselves; and remember with gratitude Allah's favor on you; for you were enemies and He joined your hearts in love, so that by His Grace, you became brethren; and you were on the brink of the Pit of Fire, and He saved you from it. Thus, doth Allah make His Signs clear to you: that you may be guided. Let, there arise out of you a band of people inviting to all that is good, enjoining what is right, and forbidding what is wrong: they are the ones to attain felicity. Be not like those who are divided amongst themselves and fall into disputations after receiving Clear Signs: for them is a dreadful Penalty. (Ali 'Imran 3:103–5, Koran)

إِنَّ هَٰذِهِۦٓ أُمَّتُكُمۡ أُمَّةٗ وَٰحِدَةٗ وَأَنَا۠ رَبُّكُمۡ فَٱعۡبُدُونِ ﴿٩٢﴾

Verily, this Brotherhood of yours is a single Brotherhood, and I am your Lord and Cherisher: therefore, serve Me (and no other). (Al-Anbiyaa 21:92, Koran)

The *ummah* is a community that is committed to truth and administers justice based on truth. The Muslim community is commanded by Allah to act justly to others and to one another and observe due balance in all their actions and follow a balanced path and not to transgress due bounds in anything. A human, man and woman, should be straight and honest in all his dealings.

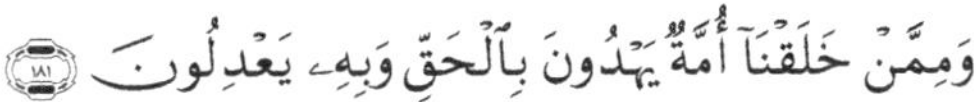

Of those We have created are people who
direct (others) with truth and dispense justice
therewith. (Al-A'raf 7:181, Koran)

وَٱلسَّمَآءَ رَفَعَهَا وَوَضَعَ ٱلْمِيزَانَ ﴿٧﴾ أَلَّا تَطْغَوْا۟ فِى ٱلْمِيزَانِ ﴿٨﴾ وَأَقِيمُوا۟ ٱلْوَزْنَ بِٱلْقِسْطِ وَلَا تُخْسِرُوا۟ ٱلْمِيزَانَ

And the Firmament has He raised high, and
He has set up the Balance (of Justice),In order
that you may not transgress (due) balance. So,
establish weight with justice and fall not short
in the balance. (Ar-Rahman 55:7-9, Koran)

The Koran teaches that affairs of the believers should be conducted through mutual consultation (*ijma*) and decisions reached through consensus. Furthermore, the Koran proclaims consultation as a principle of government and a method that must be applied in the administration of public affairs. The sovereignty of Islamic state belongs exclusively to Allah, whose will and command binds the community and state. The dignified designation of the community in the Koran as vicegerent of Allah on the earth makes the *ummah* a repository of executive sovereignty in the Islamic state. The community as a whole, after consultation and consensus, grants people among themselves with authority to manage its affairs (*ulil amri minkum*). Those charged with authority act in their capacity as the representative (*wakil*) of the people and are bound by the Koranic mandate to consult the community in public affairs, and consensus is the binding source of the law. The community, by consultation and in consensus, has the authority to depose any person charged with authority, including the head of state, in the event of gross violation of the law.

وَٱلَّذِينَ ٱسْتَجَابُوا۟ لِرَبِّهِمْ وَأَقَامُوا۟ ٱلصَّلَوٰةَ وَأَمْرُهُمْ شُورَىٰ بَيْنَهُمْ وَمِمَّا رَزَقْنَٰهُمْ يُنفِقُونَ ﴿٣٨﴾ وَٱلَّذِينَ إِذَآ أَصَابَهُمُ ٱلْبَغْىُ هُمْ يَنتَصِرُونَ ﴿٣٩﴾

> Those who hearken to their Lord and establish regular prayer; who (conduct) their affairs by mutual Consultation; who spend out of what We bestow on them for Sustenance; And those who, when an oppressive wrong is inflicted on them do not flinch and courageously defend themselves. (Ash-Shura 42:38–39, Koran)

Islam pursues its social objectives by reforming the individual. The ritual ablution before prayer, the five daily prayers, fasting during the month of Ramadan, the obligatory giving of charity all encourage punctuality, self-discipline, and concern for the well-being of others. The individual is seen not just a member of the community and subservient to the community's will but also as a morally autonomous agent who plays a distinctive role in shaping the community's sense of direction and purpose. The Koran has attached to the individual's duty of obedience to the government a right of to simultaneously dispute with rulers over government affairs. The individual obeys the ruler on the condition that the ruler obeys the covenant of the Koran and Allah's commandments, which are obligatory to all Muslims regardless of their status in the social hierarchy. This is reflected in the declaration of the blessed *Nabi* that *"there is no obedience in transgression; obedience is only in the righteousness."* The citizen is entitled to disobey an oppressive command that is contrary to the covenant of Allah.

يَٰٓأَيُّهَا ٱلَّذِينَ ءَامَنُوٓاْ أَطِيعُواْ ٱللَّهَ وَأَطِيعُواْ ٱلرَّسُولَ وَأُوْلِي ٱلۡأَمۡرِ مِنكُمۡۖ فَإِن تَنَٰزَعۡتُمۡ فِي شَيۡءٖ فَرُدُّوهُ إِلَى ٱللَّهِ وَٱلرَّسُولِ إِن كُنتُمۡ تُؤۡمِنُونَ بِٱللَّهِ
وَٱلۡيَوۡمِ ٱلۡأٓخِرِۚ ذَٰلِكَ خَيۡرٞ وَأَحۡسَنُ تَأۡوِيلًا

O you who believe! Obey Allah, and obey the Rasool, and those charged with authority among you. If you differ in anything among yourselves, refer it to Allah and His Rasool, if you do believe in Allah and the Last Day: that is best, and most suitable for final determination. (An-Nisa 4:59, Koran)

The dignity of the human being is a central concern of the Islamic law. Allah fashioned Adam in due proportion and breathed His Spirit into him, and Allah elevated Adam in rank above that of His angels. Allah bestowed dignity on the children of Adam, both men and women; gave them transport over land and oceans; gave them for the sustenance things, good and pure; and conferred on them special favors above a greater part of His creation. Allah elevated the children of Adam spiritually in rank above that of His angels. Allah breathed His spirit into Adam and elevated the rank and dignity of his children, both men and women, above that of most of His creation. Allah also appointed the children of Adam as his vicegerents on the earth and promised them special favors.

The dignity of human beings is considered to have five special values—faith, life, intellect, property, and lineage—that must be protected by the law as a matter of priority. *Although the basic interests of the community and those of the individual coincide within the structure of these values, the focus is nevertheless on the individual.* There is a clear message in Allah's proclamations in the Koran:

وَلَقَدْ كَرَّمْنَا بَنِيٓ ءَادَمَ وَحَمَلْنَٰهُمْ فِي ٱلْبَرِّ وَٱلْبَحْرِ وَرَزَقْنَٰهُم مِّنَ ٱلطَّيِّبَٰتِ وَفَضَّلْنَٰهُمْ عَلَىٰ كَثِيرٍ مِّمَّنْ خَلَقْنَا تَفْضِيلًا ﴿٧٠﴾

We have honored the progeny of Adam; provided them with transport on land and sea; given them for sustenance things good and pure; and conferred on them special favors, above a great part of Our Creation. (Al-Isra 17:70, Koran)

لَقَدْ خَلَقْنَا ٱلْإِنسَٰنَ فِيٓ أَحْسَنِ تَقْوِيمٍ ﴿٤﴾

We have indeed created man in the best of moulds. (At-Tin 95:4, Koran)

The Koranic principle of enjoining good and forbidding what is evil is supportive of the moral autonomy of the individual. This principle authorizes the individual to act according to his or her best judgment in situations in which his or her intervention will advance a good purpose. The following saying of the blessed *Nabi* also supports individual action by a believer:

If any one of you sees an evil, let him change it by his hand, and if he is unable to do that, let him change by his words, and if he is still unable to do that let him denounce it in his heart, but this is the weakest form of belief.

This principle assigns to the individual an active role in the community in which he or she lives. The Koran annunciated the principle of free speech fourteen hundred years ago. Believing men and women are reminded that they are the best of people, witnesses over other nations.

Such a responsibility carries with it a moral burden of an exemplary conduct of one who submits to the divine truth and whose relationship with Allah is governed is by *taqwa,* the consciousness of humankind's responsibility toward its Creator. The believer has the responsibility of acting in accordance with the three types of knowledge: the knowledge of certitude (*ilm al-yaqin*), the eye of certitude (*ain al-yaqin*), and the truth of certitude (*haqq al-yaqin*). With that knowledge and faith, the believer is well equipped to approach others to enjoin what is right and forbid what is wrong. *This moral autonomy of the individual, when bound together with the will of the community, formulates the doctrine of infallibility of the collective will of the* ummah, *which is the doctrinal basis of consensus.*

كُنتُمْ خَيْرَ أُمَّةٍ أُخْرِجَتْ لِلنَّاسِ تَأْمُرُونَ بِٱلْمَعْرُوفِ وَتَنْهَوْنَ عَنِ ٱلْمُنكَرِ وَتُؤْمِنُونَ بِٱللَّهِ ۗ وَلَوْ ءَامَنَ أَهْلُ ٱلْكِتَٰبِ لَكَانَ خَيْرًا
لَّهُم ۚ مِّنْهُمُ ٱلْمُؤْمِنُونَ وَأَكْثَرُهُمُ ٱلْفَٰسِقُونَ ﴿١١٠﴾

You are the best of Peoples, evolved for mankind,
enjoining what is right, forbidding that is wrong,
and believing in Allah. If only the People of the
Book had Faith, it was best for them: among them
are some who have Faith, but most of them are
perverted transgressors. (Ali 'Imran 3:110, Koran)

The Koran addresses men and women who submit to Allah, who believe, who are devout, who speak the truth, who are righteous, who are humble, who are charitable, who fast and deny themselves, who guard their chastity, and who always remember Allah, promising them great recompense and forgiveness for their transgressions. In this address, Allah treats individual men and women evenly with a promise of a similar reward for their good acts. In Allah's eyes, all men and all women who do good deeds carry an equal favor with Him.

Allah admonishes both believing men and women to restrain from lustful stares, lower their gaze, and guard their chastity. He is well acquainted with men's intentions and actions. Allah also reminds women to dress modestly and that they should not display their adornments outside of their immediate family environment.

Allah then tells believers, men and women, to turn *all together* in prayer toward Him so that they may prosper. This can happen only when the believers, men and women, turn to Allah collectively as a community in a mosque as was customary during the lifetime of His *Nabi*. According to the Koran, men and women are autonomous in their actions and deeds, are answerable to Allah for their own conduct and actions on the Day of Judgment and will be rewarded and punished according to their deeds.

In a community, men as a group or as rulers of the state have no sanction from the covenant of Allah to enforce restrictions on the freedom of righteous and believing women. Men as a group do not have any authority over women as a group. To every man and to every woman, Allah has bestowed rights to *faith, life, freedom, intellect, and property, which include freedom of action and speech as well as education.* The authority of a ruler who denies these basic freedoms to men or to women is openly disputable. The individual obeys the ruler on the condition that ruler obeys the covenant of the Koran.

إِنَّ ٱلْمُسْلِمِينَ وَٱلْمُسْلِمَٰتِ وَٱلْمُؤْمِنِينَ وَٱلْمُؤْمِنَٰتِ وَٱلْقَٰنِتِينَ وَٱلْقَٰنِتَٰتِ وَٱلصَّٰدِقِينَ وَٱلصَّٰدِقَٰتِ وَٱلصَّٰبِرِينَ وَٱلصَّٰبِرَٰتِ

وَٱلْخَٰشِعِينَ وَٱلْخَٰشِعَٰتِ وَٱلْمُتَصَدِّقِينَ وَٱلْمُتَصَدِّقَٰتِ وَٱلصَّٰٓئِمِينَ وَٱلصَّٰٓئِمَٰتِ وَٱلْحَٰفِظِينَ فُرُوجَهُمْ وَٱلْحَٰفِظَٰتِ وَٱلذَّٰكِرِينَ ٱللَّهَ كَثِيرًا

وَٱلذَّٰكِرَٰتِ أَعَدَّ ٱللَّهُ لَهُم مَّغْفِرَةً وَأَجْرًا عَظِيمًا

For Muslim men and women, for believing men and
women, for devout men and women, for true men
and women, for men and women who are patient and
constant, for men and women who humble themselves, for

men and women who give in charity, for men and women who fast (and deny themselves), for men and women who guard their chastity, and for men and women who engage much in Allah's praise, for them has Allah prepared forgiveness and great reward. (Al-Ahzab 33:35, Koran)

Absolute truth is only in Allah, universal and beyond comparison. All other so-called truths are either false in their initial premises or contingently true only in limited situations. The knower of Allah is a believer, a Muslim (one who submits to the divine truth and whose relationship with Allah is governed by *taqwa*). The seekers of truth are on a journey of discovery of knowledge, which extends outward to take in the physical world, upward through a link with the divine, and then inward to link with their emotions and the intellect, conscious and subconscious. The seekers are at various stages of their journey; their search takes them through differing intellectual pathways, through their diverse linguistic and cultural heritage, through their faith in God, and through their theoretical and empirical understanding of the faith. They comprehend the vision of divine reality through the signs of Allah that are present in the world itself. This multidimensional knowledge that comprehends the vision of the divine reality is unique to each human. This knowledge of the divine reality leaps directly across the synapses of human mind to transcend cognitive reasoning and occurs through direct participation and obedience of Allah and His covenant. This knowledge is not subject to creed or dogma. Therefore, the Koran admonishes:

لَآ إِكْرَاهَ فِى ٱلدِّينِ ۖ قَد تَّبَيَّنَ ٱلرُّشْدُ مِنَ ٱلْغَىِّ ۚ فَمَن يَكْفُرْ بِٱلطَّٰغُوتِ وَيُؤْمِنۢ بِٱللَّهِ فَقَدِ ٱسْتَمْسَكَ بِٱلْعُرْوَةِ ٱلْوُثْقَىٰ لَا ٱنفِصَامَ لَهَا ۗ وَٱللَّهُ

سَمِيعٌ عَلِيمٌ ﴿٢٥٦﴾

Let there be no compulsion in religion: Truth stands out clear from Error: whoever rejects Evil and believes in Allah hath grasped the most trustworthy handhold that never breaks. And Allah hears and knows all things. (Al-Baqarah 2:256, Koran)

Whosoever rejects evil and believes in Allah has His protection and guidance. The faith of the true believer as an individual is protected by Allah's promise in the Koran. No hurt will come to those who follow the right guidance:

يَٰٓأَيُّهَا ٱلَّذِينَ ءَامَنُواْ عَلَيْكُمْ أَنفُسَكُمْ ۖ لَا يَضُرُّكُم مَّن ضَلَّ إِذَا ٱهْتَدَيْتُمْ ۚ إِلَى ٱللَّهِ مَرْجِعُكُمْ جَمِيعًا فَيُنَبِّئُكُم بِمَا كُنتُمْ تَعْمَلُونَ ﴿١٠٥﴾

O you who believe! Guard your own souls; if you follow right guidance, no hurt can come to you from those who stray. The goal of you all is to Allah: it is He that will show you the truth of all that you do. (Al-Ma'idah 5:105, Koran)

Absolute truth is only with Allah. The seeker of the road to divine mercy may take one of the many pathways leading to Allah's beneficence, and Allah does show the right path to whom He will:

He doth guide whom He pleases to a Way that is straight. To those who do right is an abundant reward.

Therefore, it is not unto the ulema, the priests, the scholars, those in authority, and their religious police to criticize or restrain anyone from following a pathway different from theirs. The prerogative of judgment on anyone, a heretic or a believer, belongs only to Allah.

Chapter Seven

The Covenant of Allah in the Present Times: The Betrayal of the Covenant

Allah sent teachers, men of wisdom, holy men, and prophets to all parts of the world to guide humankind to a life of peace and faith. Allah's guidance to the people, communities, and nations came in the form of an agreement, a covenant. Those who believed in their Creator and followed their guidance from Allah were rewarded in this world and in the hereafter. Allah made a covenant with the peoples of the book, the children of Israel, those who call themselves Christians, and then the Muslims as an essential observation of their faith. This covenant calls mankind to belief and trust in the Creator, the one God of the universe, the Real. This covenant is an agreement between Allah and His creation, portrayed as a mutual understanding in which Allah proposes a system of regulations for the guidance of humans. This guidance is presented in the form of commandments to be accepted and implemented by people. Allah then makes a promise of what He will do in the event that man willingly abides by these commands and regulates his life according to them. The concept of promise is clearly conditional on human obedience. The covenant of Allah symbolizes the relationship between Allah and the human; the human becomes His steward, vicegerent, or custodian on the earth through submission and obedience to His will (*islam*) as expressed in His commands and is able to take the advantage of Allah's promises and favors.

Those who accepted the covenant and later failed to fulfill their part of the covenant suffered from dire consequences.

۞ وَلَقَدْ أَخَذَ ٱللَّهُ مِيثَٰقَ بَنِىٓ إِسْرَٰٓءِيلَ وَبَعَثْنَا مِنْهُمُ ٱثْنَىْ عَشَرَ نَقِيبًا ۖ وَقَالَ ٱللَّهُ إِنِّى مَعَكُمْ ۖ لَئِنْ أَقَمْتُمُ ٱلصَّلَوٰةَ وَءَاتَيْتُمُ ٱلزَّكَوٰةَ
وَءَامَنتُم بِرُسُلِى وَعَزَّرْتُمُوهُمْ وَأَقْرَضْتُمُ ٱللَّهَ قَرْضًا حَسَنًا لَّأُكَفِّرَنَّ عَنكُمْ سَيِّـَٔاتِكُمْ وَلَأُدْخِلَنَّكُمْ جَنَّٰتٍ تَجْرِى مِن تَحْتِهَا ٱلْأَنْهَٰرُ ۚ فَمَن
كَفَرَ بَعْدَ ذَٰلِكَ مِنكُمْ فَقَدْ ضَلَّ سَوَآءَ ٱلسَّبِيلِ ﴿١٢﴾ فَبِمَا نَقْضِهِم مِّيثَٰقَهُمْ لَعَنَّٰهُمْ وَجَعَلْنَا قُلُوبَهُمْ قَٰسِيَةً ۖ يُحَرِّفُونَ ٱلْكَلِمَ عَن
مَّوَاضِعِهِۦ ۙ وَنَسُوا۟ حَظًّا مِّمَّا ذُكِّرُوا۟ بِهِۦ ۚ وَلَا تَزَالُ تَطَّلِعُ عَلَىٰ خَآئِنَةٍ مِّنْهُمْ إِلَّا قَلِيلًا مِّنْهُمْ ۖ فَٱعْفُ عَنْهُمْ وَٱصْفَحْ ۚ إِنَّ ٱللَّهَ يُحِبُّ ٱلْمُحْسِنِينَ ﴿١٣﴾
وَمِنَ ٱلَّذِينَ قَالُوٓا۟ إِنَّا نَصَٰرَىٰٓ أَخَذْنَا مِيثَٰقَهُمْ فَنَسُوا۟ حَظًّا مِّمَّا ذُكِّرُوا۟ بِهِۦ فَأَغْرَيْنَا بَيْنَهُمُ ٱلْعَدَاوَةَ وَٱلْبَغْضَآءَ إِلَىٰ يَوْمِ ٱلْقِيَٰمَةِ ۚ وَسَوْفَ
يُنَبِّئُهُمُ ٱللَّهُ بِمَا كَانُوا۟ يَصْنَعُونَ ﴿١٤﴾ يَٰٓأَهْلَ ٱلْكِتَٰبِ قَدْ جَآءَكُمْ رَسُولُنَا يُبَيِّنُ لَكُمْ كَثِيرًا مِّمَّا كُنتُمْ تُخْفُونَ مِنَ ٱلْكِتَٰبِ
وَيَعْفُوا۟ عَن كَثِيرٍ ۚ قَدْ جَآءَكُم مِّنَ ٱللَّهِ نُورٌ وَكِتَٰبٌ مُّبِينٌ ﴿١٥﴾ يَهْدِى بِهِ ٱللَّهُ مَنِ ٱتَّبَعَ رِضْوَٰنَهُۥ سُبُلَ ٱلسَّلَٰمِ وَيُخْرِجُهُم مِّنَ
ٱلظُّلُمَٰتِ إِلَى ٱلنُّورِ بِإِذْنِهِۦ وَيَهْدِيهِمْ إِلَىٰ صِرَٰطٍ مُّسْتَقِيمٍ ﴿١٦﴾

Allah took a covenant from the Children of Israel and We appointed twelve leaders from among them. And Allah said "I am with you if you establish salaat, practice regular charity, believe in my messengers, honor and assist them, and loan to Allah a beautiful loan, Verily I will wipe out from you your evils, and admit you to Gardens with rivers flowing beneath. But if any of you after this disbelieved, he has truly wandered from the path of rectitude.

Therefore, because of breach of their covenant, We
cursed them and made their hearts grow hard. They
perverted words from their meaning an abandoned a
good part of the message that was sent them. Thou
will not cease to discover treachery from them barring
a few. Nevertheless, bear with them and pardon
them. Verily Allah loves those who are wholesome.

Moreover, from those who call themselves Christians,
We took their Covenant, but they have abandoned
a good part of the Message that was sent to them.
Therefore, We have stirred up enmity and hatred
among them until the Day of Resurrection, when
Allah will inform them of their handiwork.

O People of the Book! There has come to you Our Messenger, revealing to you much that you used to hide in the Scripture and passing over much. Indeed, there has come to you from Allah a light and a plain Book: Wherewith Allah guides all who seek His good pleasure to the path of peace. He brings them out of darkness unto light by His will and guides them unto a straight path.

(Al-Ma'idah 5:12–16, Koran)

The above sura and its verses show the importance of the Koran:

A light and plain Book from Allah where Allah guides all who seek His good pleasure to the path of peace. He brings them out of darkness into light by His will and guides them unto a straight path.

The Koran is a guide and Allah's covenant, a code of conduct for all humans to trust and believe in the Creator, the one universal God, Allah. Allah leads all those people who believe in Him to His straight path and to the path of peace. The children of Israel disobeyed Allah, and they lost His favor. As for those who called themselves Christians, Allah took their covenant, and they have abandoned a large part of the message that Allah sent them through Jesus, son of Mariam. Because of their refusal to fulfill their part of the bargain in the covenant, Allah has stirred up loathing and hatred among them because of their transgressions. Having split into sects and nations, they have battled among themselves in the last two thousand years over creed, gold, wealth, and possessions. Allah has left every human an open way to His straight path through His covenant and the Koran. Allah's covenant demands of the believers to be faithful to His covenant by fulfilling its commandments.

إِنَّ ٱلَّذِينَ يُبَايِعُونَكَ إِنَّمَا يُبَايِعُونَ ٱللَّهَ يَدُ ٱللَّهِ فَوْقَ أَيْدِيهِمْ ۚ فَمَن نَّكَثَ فَإِنَّمَا يَنكُثُ عَلَىٰ نَفْسِهِۦ ۖ وَمَنْ أَوْفَىٰ بِمَا عَٰهَدَ عَلَيْهُ ٱللَّهَ

فَسَيُؤْتِيهِ أَجْرًا عَظِيمًا ﴿١٠﴾

Verily those who pledge their allegiance unto you, (O Muhammad) pledge it unto none but Allah; the Hand of Allah is over their hands. Thereafter whosoever breaks his Covenant does so to the harm of his own soul, and whosoever fulfils his Covenant with Allah, Allah will grant him an immense Reward. (Al-Fath 48:10, Koran)

Allah addresses those who believe in Him directly in seventy-five verses of the Koran, giving them guidance, advice, and a promise of rewards in this world and the hereafter. Those who do not believe in Him, the infidels (the *kafirun*) are promised a place in hell forever. A similar penalty is promised to those who submit to Allah according to their word but not their deeds; such people are the hypocrites or the *Munafiqeen*. The concept of the covenant also symbolizes the relationship between man and Allah's creatures and the rest of His creation. They all share one God, one set of guidance and commandments, the same submission and obedience to Him, and the same set of expectations in accordance to His promises. They all can all, therefore, trust one another since they all have similar obligations and expectations. In view of the Koran, humans, communities, nations, and civilizations will continue in harmony and peace so long as they continue to fulfill Allah's covenant.

The *kafirun* are defined as the people who, in their arrogance, have drawn a veil over their minds and therefore cannot perceive the truth. The *Munafiqeen* are those who proclaim their belief according to their words but do not walk their talk. They are the chameleons who sit in to suit every occasion, but in their hearts is deception. They pretend to be of the faithful, but secretly, they do mischief against their faith. They are the enemies of faith.

Din. There are thirty-seven commandments in the covenant. Fulfillment of these pillars constitutes the *din* of the believer. Allah is above all *din*. Religion, as practiced by the followers of different faiths, comprises a set of rituals and prayers by individuals and congregations in communal and family settings. And *religion* is under the dictates of priests and clergy who define dogma, doctrine, and the role of God and worship in the religion. Islam, thus, is not a *religion* but a *din*. The *din*, on the other hand, is a belief system in which the believer acts his faith with unreserved submission to Allah and fulfillment of His covenant. With the fulfillment of the commandments of Allah, the believer achieves the unity of his person with Him when he lives his life in total awareness of Allah's presence with him. This is *taqwa* of Allah, in which the believer is aware that Allah is with him and watches over him. This communion is not only with Allah but through Him with other humans and with the rest of Allah's creation, both alive and inanimate.

The thirty-seven commandments of the covenant of Allah are three dimensional, comprising of *islam* (submission), *iman* (faith), and *ihsan* (the performance of beautiful deeds). These three dimensions constitute the *din* of the believer. The phrase *amilu al saalihaat* (to do good, to perform wholesome and beautiful deeds) refers to those who persist in striving to set things right, who restore harmony, peace, and balance. The other acts of good works recognized in the covenant of Allah are to show compassion, to be merciful and forgive others, to be just, to protect the weak, to defend the oppressed, to be generous and charitable, to be truthful, to seek knowledge and wisdom, to be kind, to be peaceful, to love others, and to perform beautiful deeds.

The covenant also symbolizes the relationship between man and Allah. Who is this Allah, and what do we know of Him? He does tell us a lot about Himself. Occasionally, He talks in the first person but mostly in the third person. In the Koran, He frequently calls on His blessed messenger, Muhammad, with guidance. He also speaks to His believers in seventy-five verses of the Koran. Some of the verses are directed at humans in general.

1. The Covenant of Allah in the Present Times: The Betrayal of the Covenant

> He is Allah; there is no Deity but He, The Sovereign, The Pure, and The Hallowed, Serene and Perfect, He is Allah, the Creator, the Sculptor, the Adorner of color and form. To Him belong the Most Beautiful Names: whatever so is in the heavens and on earth, Praise and Glorify Him; and He is the Almighty and All Wise. (Al-Hashr 59:18–24, Koran)

Allah describes Himself in the third person in the following verses:

- ALLAH! There is no god but He, the Ever Living, the One Who sustains and protects all that exists. No slumber can seize Him nor sleep. His are all things in the heavens and on earth. Who is there to intercede in His presence except as He permits? He knows what happens to His creatures in this world and in the hereafter. Nor do they know the scope of His knowledge except as He wills. His Throne extends over the heavens and the earth, and He feels no fatigue in guarding and protecting them. He is the Most High, Most Great. (Al-Baqarah 2:255, Koran)
- Join not anything in worship with Him. (Al-An'am 6:151–53, Koran)
- Believe in Allah, His Rasool, and the Book that He has sent to His Rasool and the Scriptures that He sent to those before him. Any

who deny Allah, His angels, His Books, His Rasools, and the Day of Judgment has gone astray. (An-Nisa 4:136, Koran)

- Verily, this is My Way leading straight: follow it: follow not (other) paths for they will separate you from His path. This He commands you that you may remember. (Al-An'am 6: 151–53, Koran)
- Celebrate the Praises of Allah often and Glorify Him in the morning and at night. It is Allah and His Angels who send their blessings upon you, that He may lead you out of the depths of darkness into light. Allah is full of mercy to the believers! On the Day, they meet Him with the salutation: Salaam, He has prepared for them a generous Reward. (Al-Ahzab 33:41–48, Koran)
- Be quick in race to forgiveness from your Lord for a garden whose measurement is that of the heavens and of the earth, prepared for the righteous.

Perfect, the Creator, the Sculptor, the Adorner of color and form. Whatsoever is in the heavens and on the earth belong to Him, and He is the Almighty and all-wise. We learn that Allah is the only reality, and everything else in the universe is dependent on Him for its reality and its existence. Since Allah is the Creator of the universe, all things are therefore totally dependent on Him and, hence, totally "submitted" to Allah. In the Koran, Allah uses the term *islam* and its derivatives more than seventy times; it says that true faith is established by Allah alone and that everything in the universe praises and glorifies Him. All creatures, simply by existing, demonstrate the Creator's glory and perform acts that acknowledge Allah's mastery over them.

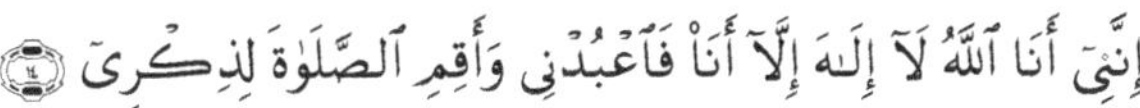

Verily I am Allah. There is no god but
I, so worship Me, and perform salaat in
remembrance of Me. (Taha 20:14, Koran)

Shirk: Allah demands total submission and loyalty to Him. Only Allah is worthy of worship. Those who worship other divinities and associate them with Allah have fallen into *shirk*. Other gods associated with Allah by some people are their caprice, wealth and possessions, and power and influence over others. Absolute power corrupts absolutely. Religious figures, royals, and politicians forget their mortality and settle themselves as being real—"I am divine, I am real, and others cannot have the same rights as I do"—leading them to serve their own egos in place of Allah. Religious figures, priests, mullahs, sheikhs, bishops, and popes elevate themselves as the spokespersons of God and dictate dogma and creed for their religion and cult. This leads to *shirk* or the loss of tawhid.

Tawhid, the oneness, and the reality of Allah, demands that human beings recognize the greatness of Allah and the minuteness of the human—the reality of the Real and the unreality of the unreal, which places people in their correct relationship with Allah and allows them to understand that they are His servants and that they must act in submission (*islam*). They must therefore recognize human failings and follow divine guidance brought by the prophets and their scriptures.

> Verily, this is My Way leading straight: follow it:
> follow not (other) paths for they will separate
> you from His path. This He commands you that
> you may remember. (Al-An'am 6: 151, Koran)

Allah, the Creator: Allah tells us about His creation and His mastery over everything in the universe. He tells us of His signs. It is these signs that provide humans with wisdom. Allah has bequeathed humans knowledge and insight that form wisdom. Through this knowledge, humans remove the veils of mystery from the galaxies and constellations and look into the depths of space and into the unknown world of the creation of the universe. Men and women have come to know the little cells in the human body and of the little particles of the atom. Through painstaking dedication, humans sit in their libraries, laboratories, and observatories to marvel at Allah's signs in His great works of the creation.

﴿ وَمِنْ ءَايَٰتِهِۦٓ أَنْ خَلَقَكُم مِّن تُرَابٍ ثُمَّ إِذَآ أَنتُم بَشَرٌ تَنتَشِرُونَ ﴿٢٠﴾ وَمِنْ ءَايَٰتِهِۦٓ أَنْ خَلَقَ لَكُم مِّنْ أَنفُسِكُمْ أَزْوَٰجًا لِّتَسْكُنُوٓا۟ إِلَيْهَا
وَجَعَلَ بَيْنَكُم مَّوَدَّةً وَرَحْمَةً ۚ إِنَّ فِى ذَٰلِكَ لَءَايَٰتٍ لِّقَوْمٍ يَتَفَكَّرُونَ ﴿٢١﴾ وَمِنْ ءَايَٰتِهِۦ خَلْقُ ٱلسَّمَٰوَٰتِ وَٱلْأَرْضِ وَٱخْتِلَٰفُ أَلْسِنَتِكُمْ وَأَلْوَٰنِكُمْ ۚ
إِنَّ فِى ذَٰلِكَ لَءَايَٰتٍ لِّلْعَٰلِمِينَ ﴿٢٢﴾ وَمِنْ ءَايَٰتِهِۦ مَنَامُكُم بِٱلَّيْلِ وَٱلنَّهَارِ وَٱبْتِغَآؤُكُم مِّن فَضْلِهِۦٓ ۚ إِنَّ فِى ذَٰلِكَ لَءَايَٰتٍ لِّقَوْمٍ يَسْمَعُونَ ﴿٢٣﴾ وَمِنْ
ءَايَٰتِهِۦ يُرِيكُمُ ٱلْبَرْقَ خَوْفًا وَطَمَعًا وَيُنَزِّلُ مِنَ ٱلسَّمَآءِ مَآءً فَيُحْىِۦ بِهِ ٱلْأَرْضَ بَعْدَ مَوْتِهَآ ۚ إِنَّ فِى ذَٰلِكَ لَءَايَٰتٍ لِّقَوْمٍ يَعْقِلُونَ ﴿٢٤﴾
وَمِنْ ءَايَٰتِهِۦٓ أَن تَقُومَ ٱلسَّمَآءُ وَٱلْأَرْضُ بِأَمْرِهِۦ ۚ ثُمَّ إِذَا دَعَاكُمْ دَعْوَةً مِّنَ ٱلْأَرْضِ إِذَآ أَنتُمْ تَخْرُجُونَ ﴿٢٥﴾ وَلَهُۥ مَن فِى ٱلسَّمَٰوَٰتِ وَٱلْأَرْضِ ۖ كُلٌّ
لَّهُۥ قَٰنِتُونَ ﴿٢٦﴾ وَهُوَ ٱلَّذِى يَبْدَؤُا۟ ٱلْخَلْقَ ثُمَّ يُعِيدُهُۥ وَهُوَ أَهْوَنُ عَلَيْهِ ۚ وَلَهُ ٱلْمَثَلُ ٱلْأَعْلَىٰ فِى ٱلسَّمَٰوَٰتِ وَٱلْأَرْضِ ۚ وَهُوَ ٱلْعَزِيزُ ٱلْحَكِيمُ ﴿٢٧﴾ ﴾

Among His Signs is this, He created you from dust; and then, behold, you are men scattered (far and wide)!

And among His Signs is this, He created for you mates from among yourselves, that you may dwell in tranquility with them, and He has put love and mercy between your (hearts): verily in that are Signs for those who reflect.

And among His Signs is the creation of the heavens and the earth, and the variations in your languages and your colours; verily in that are Signs for those who know.

And among His Signs is the sleep that you take by night and by day, and the quest that you (make for livelihood) out of His Bounty: verily in that are Signs for those who hearken.

And among His Signs, He shows you the lightning, by way both of fear and of hope, and He sends down rain from the sky and with it gives life to the earth after it is dead: verily in that are Signs for those who are wise.

And among His Signs is this: heaven and earth stand by His Command: then when He calls you, by a single call, from the earth, behold, you (straightway) come forth.

To Him belongs every being that is in the heavens and on earth: all are devoutly obedient to Him.

It is He Who begins (the process of) creation; then repeats it; and for Him it is most easy. To Him belongs the loftiest similitude (we can think of) in the heavens and the earth: for He is Exalted in Might, Full of Wisdom. (Al Rum 30:20-27, Koran)

Signs of Allah's Creation: Mars, Saturn, Neptune, Venus, Jupiter, and Earth

﴿ فَالِقُ ٱلْإِصْبَاحِ وَجَعَلَ ٱلَّيْلَ سَكَنًا وَٱلشَّمْسَ وَٱلْقَمَرَ حُسْبَانًا ۚ ذَٰلِكَ تَقْدِيرُ ٱلْعَزِيزِ ٱلْعَلِيمِ ﴿٩٦﴾ ﴾

He is the cleaver of the daybreak from the dark,
He makes the night for rest and tranquility, and
the sun and moon for the reckoning (of time),
[all] this is laid down by the Will of the Almighty,
the All-Knowing. (Al-An'am 6:96, Koran)

He is the cleaver of the daybreak from the dark.

﴿ هُوَ ٱلَّذِى جَعَلَ ٱلشَّمْسَ ضِيَآءً وَٱلْقَمَرَ نُورًا وَقَدَّرَهُۥ مَنَازِلَ لِتَعْلَمُوا۟ عَدَدَ ٱلسِّنِينَ وَٱلْحِسَابَ ۚ مَا خَلَقَ ٱللَّهُ ذَٰلِكَ إِلَّا بِٱلْحَقِّ ۚ يُفَصِّلُ
ٱلْءَايَٰتِ لِقَوْمٍ يَعْلَمُونَ ﴿٥﴾ ﴾

It is He Who made the sun to be a shining glory and
the moon to be a light (of beauty) and measured
out stages for it; that ye might know the number
of years and the count (of time). Nowise did
Allah create this but in truth and righteousness.
(Thus) doth He explain His Signs in detail, for
those who understand. (Yunus 10:5, Koran)

The Signs of Allah.

The waning moon.

﴿ ٱللَّهُ ٱلَّذِى خَلَقَ سَبْعَ سَمَـٰوَٰتٍ وَمِنَ ٱلْأَرْضِ مِثْلَهُنَّ يَتَنَزَّلُ ٱلْأَمْرُ بَيْنَهُنَّ لِتَعْلَمُوٓا۟

أَنَّ ٱللَّهَ عَلَىٰ كُلِّ شَىْءٍ قَدِيرٌ وَأَنَّ ٱللَّهَ قَدْ أَحَاطَ بِكُلِّ شَىْءٍ عِلْمًۢا ﴿١٢﴾ ﴾

Allah is He Who created seven heavens and of the earth a similar number. Through the midst of them (all) descends His command: that you may know that Allah has power over all things, and that Allah comprehends all things in (His) knowledge. (At-Talaq 65:12, Koran)

﴿ هُوَ ٱلَّذِىٓ أَنزَلَ مِنَ ٱلسَّمَآءِ مَآءً ۖ لَّكُم مِّنْهُ شَرَابٌ وَمِنْهُ شَجَرٌ فِيهِ تُسِيمُونَ ﴿١٠﴾

It is He Who sends down rain from the sky. From it ye drink, and out of it (grows) the vegetation on which ye feed your cattle.

﴿ يُنۢبِتُ لَكُم بِهِ ٱلزَّرْعَ وَٱلزَّيْتُونَ وَٱلنَّخِيلَ وَٱلْأَعْنَـٰبَ وَمِن كُلِّ ٱلثَّمَرَٰتِ ۗ إِنَّ فِى ذَٰلِكَ لَـَٔايَةً لِّقَوْمٍ

يَتَفَكَّرُونَ ﴿١١﴾ ﴾

With it He produces for you corn, olives, date palms, grapes, and every kind of fruit: verily in this is a Sign for those who give thought.

﴿ وَسَخَّرَ لَكُمُ ٱلَّيْلَ وَٱلنَّهَارَ وَٱلشَّمْسَ وَٱلْقَمَرَ ۖ وَٱلنُّجُومُ مُسَخَّرَٰتٌۢ بِأَمْرِهِۦٓ ۗ إِنَّ فِى ذَٰلِكَ لَءَايَـٰتٍ لِّقَوْمٍ يَعْقِلُونَ ﴿١٢﴾ ﴾

He has made subject to you the Night and the Day; the Sun and the Moon; and the Stars are in subjection by His Command: verily in this are Signs for men who are wise.

﴿ وَمَا ذَرَأَ لَكُمْ فِى ٱلْأَرْضِ مُخْتَلِفًا أَلْوَٰنُهُۥٓ ۗ إِنَّ فِى ذَٰلِكَ لَءَايَةً لِّقَوْمٍ يَذَّكَّرُونَ ﴿١٣﴾ ﴾

And the things on this earth which He has multiplied in varying colours (and qualities): verily in this a Sign for men who celebrate the praises of Allah (in gratitude).

﴿ وَهُوَ ٱلَّذِى سَخَّرَ ٱلْبَحْرَ لِتَأْكُلُوا۟ مِنْهُ لَحْمًا طَرِيًّا وَتَسْتَخْرِجُوا۟ مِنْهُ حِلْيَةً تَلْبَسُونَهَا وَتَرَى ٱلْفُلْكَ مَوَاخِرَ فِيهِ وَلِتَبْتَغُوا۟ مِن فَضْلِهِۦ وَلَعَلَّكُمْ تَشْكُرُونَ ﴿١٤﴾ ﴾

It is He Who has made the sea subject, that ye may eat thereof flesh that is fresh and tender, and that ye may extract therefrom ornaments to wear, and thou seest the ships therein that plough the waves, that ye may seek (thus) of the bounty of Allah and that ye may be grateful.

﴿ وَأَلْقَىٰ فِي ٱلْأَرْضِ رَوَٰسِيَ أَن تَمِيدَ بِكُمْ وَأَنْهَٰرًا وَسُبُلًا لَّعَلَّكُمْ تَهْتَدُونَ ﴿١٥﴾ ﴾

And He has set up on the earth mountains
standing firm, lest it should shake with you; and
rivers and roads; that ye may guide yourselves.

﴿ وَعَلَٰمَٰتٍ ۚ وَبِٱلنَّجْمِ هُمْ يَهْتَدُونَ ﴿١٦﴾ ﴾

And marks and signposts; and by the
stars (Men) guide themselves.

﴿ أَفَمَن يَخْلُقُ كَمَن لَّا يَخْلُقُ ۗ أَفَلَا تَذَكَّرُونَ ﴿١٧﴾ ﴾

Is then He Who creates like one that creates
not? Will you not receive admonition?
(An-Nahl 16:19–17, Koran)

Allah, in His infinite wisdom, has given man some understanding of His creation. Allah is the Creator of everything that is. He wills, and it is. He is beyond human comprehension, and His divine systems do not conform to the human concepts, creed, and dogma. Allah, God the Creator, created the galaxies, worlds, stars, sun, moon, little atoms, protons, neutrons, and tiny particles that show the complexity of His genius. Allah, the Lord of creation, sends water from the heavens for sustenance of life on the earth. Allah directs sunshine to the earth to provide warmth and light to sustain, human, plant, and animal life. Allah formed the sun, moon, and stars to create equilibrium in the universe, every object in its intended place revolving in its fixed orbit in perfect harmony and balance. Allah created the secrets and mysteries of the heavens and the earth, the so-called sciences, and the knowledge of particles, elements, cells, mitochondria, chromosomes, gravity, and black holes, only a minute portion of which he revealed to man.

Allah clearly provided humankind a mind to wonder at Allah's infinitesimal wisdom. Yet humans are conceited and arrogant to believe that God is driven by man-created creed, testament, dogma, Sunna, and Sharia. Allah does not require a shrine, temple, tent, or a talisman to live in. His presence is everywhere. He is present in the smallest particle and in the greatest expanse. He is accessible to each and every object He has created. Every object obeys Allah's will except for humankind, who has been given a free will. The covenant of Allah presents us with the scope of the freedom of choice that humankind has in doing what is wholesome and beautiful or what is corrupt and ugly in the human role among the creation. It reminds us of how the scales of Allah's justice, the two hands of Allah—His mercy and His wrath—are reflected in the human domain, where people have been appointed Allah's vicegerents. Deeds of goodness and wholesomeness are associated with mercy, paradise, and the beautiful. Evil and corruption is rewarded with wrath, hell, and the ugly.

Allah the Divine is open to the most miniscule of beings. From the vastest of the expanse to the minutest of the particle, there is a connection with Allah, the Cherisher and Nourisher of the universe. Within this communion of the divine with the creation passes the Spirit of Allah into His creatures. The human lays his heart and mind open to Allah in submission to receive His Spirit and guidance.

In the space and the emptiness of the universe, there flow currents and whispers of wind and energy. These winds of silence, light, and sound carry the divine whisper of Allah, and in this sound is Allah's knowledge. This knowledge descends into the believer's receptive heart in peace, silence, and tranquility. When the angels and the Spirit descend with Allah's guidance, the eyes perceive the most beautiful divine light, the ears hear the softest tinkle of the bell, the nose smells the fragrance of a thousand gardens, and the skin feels the most tranquil of the gentle breeze. When this happens, the soul has seen nirvana. This is the knowledge of Allah.

Amongst Allah's many names, *Rahman* and *Rahim* stand for His merry and beneficence. The root of these two words comes from the Arabic and Hebrew word *Rahm*, which means "womb." Allah the Creator is the Mother and the Nurturer of the universe. Allah loves His creation and therefore nourishes and nurtures it. In this love, Allah has provided humans with an intellect and a freedom of choice in their intentions and actions. Because human is wayward, Allah guides man with a covenant, a code of conduct. The concept of the covenant also symbolizes the relationship between humans, among Allah's creatures, and between man and the rest of His creation.

Whereas Allah gives a code of conduct the humans in a book, to the animals, Allah has given an instinct and genetic marker that enable the beasts and the birds to live among their herds and flocks in tranquility and to wander the earth from a watering hole to a pasture and to migrate across the earth with the seasons.

What is in the covenant?

The covenant of Allah is thousands of years old. Allah has—through the agency of His messengers, teachers, and men and women of wisdom—sent His guidance to human societies. The covenant revolves around the belief and obedience to the Creator, the one God. With the believer's submission and communion with God, there follows a communion of the believer with the rest of creation. Man has been given an independent will and thus has the freedom of intention and action to do what is good or evil. The belief and submission to God, in effect, demands the surrender of this free will in the straight path of

Allah. The believer surrenders the freedom of actions to do evil. Evil acts harm other believers and the rest of the creation of Allah.

Initially, the communion of a believer is with Allah, which expands into a communion of a group and a community with Allah and with one another. Such a communion has the capacity and potential to involve the whole humankind who believes in God and forsakes evil. Believers of God among this communion begin as a group of people who, with their independent will, intend to live in peace, tranquility, and justice according to a code of conduct based on righteousness and the will of Allah.

Jihad is the utmost struggle of man on his way from the path of ignorance to the path of Allah. Man hears Allah's call through the noise and the commotion of the world and, through the eye of his soul, lets the *nur* of Allah into the niche of his heart. Allah's call is to obedience, goodness, and selflessness. Man bows down his head on the earth in submission and in humility to his Lord. The Lord guides, and the believer follows; the believer has faith in his Allah, and Allah holds his hand. Allah shows His believer the way to goodness, and the believer performs wholesome deeds. The *nur* of Allah glows in the believer's heart, and the believer accepts Allah in his heart. Submission establishes a link between the believer and Allah. Allah commands, and the believer follows.

When a man is disrobed and then stripped of his flesh, bones, and body fluids, all that is left is his spirit, his self. This self is perhaps no bigger than a dot, a *nuqta*. If we collect all the dots, the *nuqta* of the whole humanity, they will perhaps not fill a cup. Yet what fills this one cup is what drives the human world, all its intentions and all its actions, both good and bad. The *nafs*, the inner self, of the human, unlike the Freudian ego, is capable of both good and bad. The *nuqta* of the *nafs*, when magnified a million times, becomes visible as a shiny disk, a mirror. The nature (*fitra*) of the *nafs* is to shine like a mirror with Allah's *nur*. When man walks the path of Allah in *taqwa* of Him with the knowledge that Allah is with him, watching him and guiding him, Allah's *nur* shines on the *nafs*, keeping it pure and safe. However, when man's desires, cravings, and ego overpower his love and obedience for Allah, the shiny mirror of his *nafs* becomes obscured by the smoke of his cravings. Man loses sight of the *nur* of Allah, and he falls into error and decadence.

The effort required to keep focus on Allah's *nur* and the *taqwa* of Him is the inner jihad. And this jihad is the effort involved in being conscious of Allah's commandments when Allah calls upon His believers with the words

يَـٰٓأَيُّهَا ٱلَّذِينَ ءَامَنُوا۟

O you who Believe.

And He commands them to do acts of faith and goodness in seventy-five verses of the Koran. Obedience to every such command is jihad. The expression in the path of Allah, of course, is the path of right conduct that Allah has set down in the Koran. Jihad is simply the complement to *islam*, the surrender to the will of Allah. The surrender takes place to Allah's will, and it is Allah's will that people struggle in His path. Hence, submission and surrender to Allah's will demands struggle in His path.

Acts of worship, supplication, and remembrance of Allah have a specific ritual and devotional nature in which the worshipper orients himself to Allah and obeys His commands and prohibitions. To worship is to orient one's life and existence to Allah (*Haqq*), to beseech Allah (*Rahman* and *Rahim*) for guidance and help, and to show gratitude for the blessings already received. Such humility precludes a man's superiority over others.

2. The Covenant of Allah: The Prophets of Allah

Allah's guidance to mankind is through the divine revelation to His prophets, who were charged with the task of communicating the word of Allah. Allah sent thousands of prophets to mankind to teach the humanity precepts and principles to His straight path of unity, truth, and goodness. Over thousands of years, these precepts and principles spread around the world through civilizations till the mankind as a whole began to comprehend the message of one universal God, the Creator of every particle and every being in the whole universe. Humankind listened and occasionally regressed into his inherent paganism, greed, selfishness, and egotism. Allah bestowed on the human a vicegerency on the earth, a mind, free will, and a covenant. Allah then announced that there would be no more prophets. The era of prophecy had ended. The human, in stages, had received the knowledge required to live in submission to Allah's will in peace and harmony on the earth in accordance with the divine laws, which were sent down as guidance to every community for a life of truth, justice, goodness, and peace. Such knowledge consisted of the following:

a) There is *one absolute Being* from whom all emanate; the universe of galaxies and all living things are all connected to one another and cannot be separated from that absolute Being. Everything alive—humans, animals, plants, and microorganisms—are created by the absolute Being; and all are nurtured in the same matter, all breathe the same air, and in turn, their physical selves disintegrate into the same elements that then return to the earth and the universe. In this cycle of creation and disintegration, the only permanence is of the Real, the Absolute. All else is an illusion and a mirage. One moment they exist, and in the next, they are gone, turned into dust, and then blown away by the wind into the expanse.

Nothing is left behind—no riches, no honor, no ego, and no pride. What is left, however, is an account of our deeds, upon which one day we will be judged.

b) Humankind has been bestowed with a *mind* and free will. The mind has the ability to perceive ideas and knowledge from the Divine, and from the Signs of Allah. The vibrations of the whisper of the divine, the rustle of the wind, the light of God, the fragrance of God's creation, and the sensation of the divine touch all inspire the human mind with the endless stream of ideas and knowledge. Man has been granted the ability to process his thoughts and gain knowledge with free will.

> Believe in Allah, His Messenger, and the Book that He has sent to His Messenger and the Scriptures that He sent to those before him. Any who deny Allah, His angels, His Books, His Messengers, and the Day of Judgment has gone astray. (An-Nisa 4:136, Koran)

> Celebrate the Praises of Allah often and glorify Him in the morning and at night. It is Allah and His Angels Who send their blessings upon you, that He may lead you out of the depths of darkness into light. Allah is full of mercy to the believers! On the Day they meet Him with the salutation: Salaam, He has prepared for them a generous Reward. (Al-Azhab 33:41–48, Koran)

The term *islam* signifies the idea of surrender or submission to the will of Allah. This act of self-surrender is the conscious and rational submission of the dependent and limited human will to the absolute and omnipotent will of Allah. The surrender that Islam requires is a deliberate, conscious, and rational act made by a person who knows with both intellectual certainty and spiritual vision that Allah, who is the subject of Koranic discourse, is reality itself.

3. The Covenant of Allah: The Covenant

The knower of God, upon his surrender to Allah's will, accepts the covenant of Allah and consciously agrees to follow its commandments. The believer chooses Allah's path according to his own free will and choice. The knower of God is a Muslim, "one who submits" to the divine truth and whose relationship with God is governed by *taqwa*, the consciousness of humankind's responsibility toward its Creator. The act of submission and the acceptance of Allah's covenant establishes a relationship between Allah and the believer in which Allah is ever present in the conscious, the heart, and the mind of the believer. However, consciousness of God alone is not sufficient to make a person a Muslim.

4. The Covenant of Allah: *Taqwa* of Allah

The concept of *taqwa* implies that the believer has the added responsibility of acting in accordance with three types of knowledge: *ilm al-yaqin, ain al-yaqin*, and *haqq al-yaqin* (knowledge of certainty, eye of certainty, and truth of certainty). The believer must endeavor at all times to maintain himself or herself in a constant state of submission to Allah. By doing so, the believer attains the honored title of "slave of Allah," for he recognizes that all power and all agency belongs to God alone:

وَلَوْلَآ إِذْ دَخَلْتَ جَنَّتَكَ قُلْتَ مَا شَآءَ ٱللَّهُ لَا قُوَّةَ إِلَّا بِٱللَّهِ ۚ إِن تَرَنِ أَنَا۠ أَقَلَّ مِنكَ مَالًا وَوَلَدًا

Allah has willed it. There is no power
but Allah's. (Koran 18:39)

It is an all-encompassing and highly personal type of commitment and relationship in which Allah's light (*nur*) resides in the believer's heart. The believer is conscious of Allah's closeness and mercy. The believer obeys trusts and loves Allah. Allah, in return, loves those who love Him and who perform beautiful deeds. The parable of divine light defines Allah's relationship with his servant, the believer.

Allah has granted knowledge and the wisdom of *furqan* and *taqwa* to the believers who have opened their hearts and minds to Him. Man has been granted the freedom of choice in doing what is wholesome and beautiful or what is corrupt and ugly. It is only the human, among all creation, who has been given the knowledge to distinguish right activity, right thought, and right intention from their opposites. This knowledge reminds man of the scales of Allah's justice; the two hands of Allah, His mercy and His wrath, are reflected in the human domain, where people have been appointed Allah's vicegerents. Deeds of goodness and wholesomeness are associated with mercy, paradise, and what is beautiful. Evil and corruption is rewarded with wrath, hell, and what is ugly.

On his journey, the believer has Allah within, Allah's covenant as his guide, the *taqwa* of Allah as shield against evil, and *furqan*, which is Allah's compass to the straight path of righteousness. The believer, on his chosen journey on the path of Allah, is well equipped. He has Allah's protection, guidance, and direction. Those who believe are connected to Allah and know the divine law. Those on their journey in Allah's path who have gone astray need guidance. There is no compulsion in religion. For those on Allah's path who go astray and seek forgiveness and guidance, Allah is the most merciful. Islam seeks to reform the individual. For those who go astray repeatedly and seek Allah's pardon, Allah's mercy knows no bounds. It is human to err. Among humans, there is an oft-repeated cycle of belief and error. Beseeching Allah's forgiveness and guidance reforms the individual, putting him back on track to faith and the performance of beautiful deeds. The Koran repeatedly reassures us that "Allah is most Forgiving."

The first four commandments of the covenant establish the relationship between the believer and his Creator. It is the relationship of the individual with Allah. This an exclusive relationship in which there are no intermediaries. The believer, through his *taqwa*, is with his Creator, and the Creator is in the believer's heart. The *Rabb*, the Lord, of the believer protects him and nurtures, repairs, and heals his body and spirit during each moment of the person's life. Allah takes care of the electrolytes, enzymes, cell structure, serotonin levels, emotional health, and each and every function of His believer's body. In return, Allah expects the believer's submission, devotion, and acknowledgment.

5. The Covenant of Allah: Salat

The word *salat* (*salâh*, plural *salawât*) means "prayer, worship, or oratories." The earliest mention of the word *salâh* in the Koran is in Suras Al-Ma'un, Al-Ma'arij, and Al-Muzzammil in the earliest Meccan suras. Suras Al-Ma'un and Al Ma'arij are addressed to humanity in general, and the third sura, Al-Muzzammil, speaks to the blessed *Nabi*. They summarize the obligations of a believer to the path of Allah. Sura Al-Ma'un and Sura Al-Ma'arij emphasize the steadfastness of *salâh*. The first commandment for the establishment of *salâh* prayers was given to the blessed Nabi in the early Meccan sura Al-Muzzammil:

> Read you, therefore, as much of the Qur'an as may be easy for you and establish regular salâh prayer and give regular Charity; and loan to Allah a Beautiful Loan.

And in this commandment, there is equal emphasis placed on reading the Koran, the establishment of *salậh*, and the giving of charity.

Early Meccan Suras

12: Al-Ma'un: 107

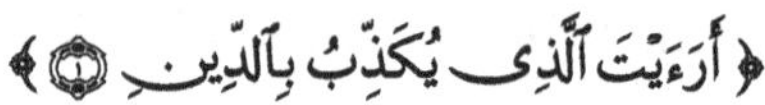

Do you see thou one who denies
the Judgment (to come)?

﴿ فَذَٰلِكَ ٱلَّذِى يَدُعُّ ٱلۡيَتِيمَ ٢ ﴾

Then such as the (man) who repulses
the orphan (with harshness),

﴿ وَلَا يَحُضُّ عَلَىٰ طَعَامِ ٱلۡمِسۡكِينِ ٣ ﴾

and encourages not the feeding of the indigent.

﴿ فَوَيۡلٌ لِّلۡمُصَلِّينَ ٤ ﴾

So, woe to the worshippers

﴿ ٱلَّذِينَ هُمۡ عَن صَلَاتِهِمۡ سَاهُونَ ٥ ﴾

Who are neglectful of their Prayers,

﴿ ٱلَّذِينَ هُمْ يُرَآءُونَ ٦ ﴾

Those who (want but) to be seen (of men),

﴿ وَيَمْنَعُونَ ٱلْمَاعُونَ ٧ ﴾

But refuse (to supply) (even) neighborly needs. (Al-Ma'un 107:1-7, Koran)

41: Al-Muzzammil: 73

﴿ ۞ إِنَّ رَبَّكَ يَعْلَمُ أَنَّكَ تَقُومُ أَدْنَىٰ مِن ثُلُثَيِ ٱلَّيْلِ وَنِصْفَهُۥ وَثُلُثَهُۥ وَطَآئِفَةٌ مِّنَ ٱلَّذِينَ مَعَكَ ۚ وَٱللَّهُ يُقَدِّرُ ٱلَّيْلَ وَٱلنَّهَارَ ۚ عَلِمَ أَن لَّن تُحْصُوهُ
فَتَابَ عَلَيْكُمْ ۖ فَٱقْرَءُوا مَا تَيَسَّرَ مِنَ ٱلْقُرْءَانِ ۚ عَلِمَ أَن سَيَكُونُ مِنكُم مَّرْضَىٰ ۙ وَءَاخَرُونَ يَضْرِبُونَ فِي ٱلْأَرْضِ يَبْتَغُونَ مِن فَضْلِ ٱللَّهِ ۙ وَءَاخَرُونَ
يُقَٰتِلُونَ فِي سَبِيلِ ٱللَّهِ ۖ فَٱقْرَءُوا مَا تَيَسَّرَ مِنْهُ ۚ وَأَقِيمُوا ٱلصَّلَوٰةَ وَءَاتُوا ٱلزَّكَوٰةَ وَأَقْرِضُوا ٱللَّهَ قَرْضًا حَسَنًا ۚ وَمَا تُقَدِّمُوا لِأَنفُسِكُم مِّنْ خَيْرٍ تَجِدُوهُ
عِندَ ٱللَّهِ هُوَ خَيْرًا وَأَعْظَمَ أَجْرًا ۚ وَٱسْتَغْفِرُوا ٱللَّهَ ۖ إِنَّ ٱللَّهَ غَفُورٌ رَّحِيمٌ ٢٠ ﴾

Your Lord does know that you (Muhammad) stand forth (to prayer) two-thirds of the night, or half the night, or a third of the night, and so does a party of those with you. But Allah does appoint Night and Day in due measure. He knows that ye are unable to keep count thereof. So, He hath turned to you (in mercy): read you, therefore, of the Qur'an as much as may be easy for you. He knows that there may be (some) among you in ill-health; others traveling through the land, seeking of Allah's bounty; yet others fighting in Allah's Cause. Read you, therefore, as much of the Qur'an as may be easy (for you); and establish regular Prayer and give regular Charity; and loan to Allah a Beautiful Loan. And whatever good you send forth for your souls, ye shall find it in Allah's Presence, yes, better and greater, in Reward, and seek you the Grace of Allah: for Allah is Oft-Forgiving, Most Merciful. (Al-Muzzammil 73:20, Koran)

44: Al-Ma'arij: 70

﴿ سَأَلَ سَآئِلُۢ بِعَذَابٖ وَاقِعٖ ١ ﴾

A questioner asked about a Penalty to befall,

﴿ لِّلۡكَٰفِرِينَ لَيۡسَ لَهُۥ دَافِعٞ ٢ ﴾

The Unbelievers, the which there is none to ward off,

﴿ مِّنَ ٱللَّهِ ذِي ٱلۡمَعَارِجِ ٣ ﴾

(a Penalty) from Allah, Lord of the Ways of Ascent.

﴿ تَعۡرُجُ ٱلۡمَلَٰٓئِكَةُ وَٱلرُّوحُ إِلَيۡهِ فِي يَوۡمٖ كَانَ مِقۡدَارُهُۥ خَمۡسِينَ أَلۡفَ سَنَةٖ ٤ ﴾

The angels and the Spirit ascend unto Him in a Day the measure whereof is (as) fifty thousand years:

﴿ فَٱصۡبِرۡ صَبۡرٗا جَمِيلًا ٥ ﴾

Therefore, do thou hold Patience, a Patience of beautiful (contentment).

﴿ إِنَّهُمْ يَرَوْنَهُۥ بَعِيدًا ۝٦ ﴾

They see the (Day) indeed as a far-off (event):

﴿ وَنَرَىٰهُ قَرِيبًا ۝٧ ﴾

But We see it (quite) near.

﴿ يَوْمَ تَكُونُ ٱلسَّمَآءُ كَٱلْمُهْلِ ۝٨ ﴾

The Day that the sky will be like molten brass,

﴿ وَتَكُونُ ٱلْجِبَالُ كَٱلْعِهْنِ ۝٩ ﴾

And the mountains will be like wool,

﴿ وَلَا يَسْـَٔلُ حَمِيمٌ حَمِيمًا ۝١٠ ﴾

And no friend will ask after a friend,

﴿ يُبَصَّرُونَهُمْ ۚ يَوَدُّ ٱلْمُجْرِمُ لَوْ يَفْتَدِى مِنْ عَذَابِ يَوْمِئِذٍۭ بِبَنِيهِ ۝١١ ﴾

Though they will be put in sight of each other, the sinner's desire will be: would that he could redeem himself from the Penalty of that Day by (sacrificing) his children,

﴿ وَصَٰحِبَتِهِۦ وَأَخِيهِ ١٢ ﴾

His wife and his brother,

﴿ وَفَصِيلَتِهِ ٱلَّتِى تُـْٔوِيهِ ١٣ ﴾

his kindred who sheltered him.

﴿ وَمَن فِى ٱلْأَرْضِ جَمِيعًا ثُمَّ يُنجِيهِ ١٤ ﴾

And all, all that is on earth, so it could deliver him:

﴿ كَلَّآ ۖ إِنَّهَا لَظَىٰ ١٥ ﴾

By no means! For it would be the Fire of Hell!

﴿ نَزَّاعَةً لِّلشَّوَىٰ ١٦ ﴾

Plucking out (his being) right to the skull!

﴿ تَدْعُوا۟ مَنْ أَدْبَرَ وَتَوَلَّىٰ ١٧ ﴾

Inviting (all) such as turn their backs and turn away their faces (from the Right),

﴿ وَجَمَعَ فَأَوْعَىٰٓ ﴿١٨﴾ ﴾

And collect (wealth) and hide it (from use)!

﴿ ۞ إِنَّ ٱلْإِنسَٰنَ خُلِقَ هَلُوعًا ﴿١٩﴾ ﴾

Truly man was created very impatient.

﴿ إِذَا مَسَّهُ ٱلشَّرُّ جَزُوعًا ﴿٢٠﴾ ﴾

Fretful when evil touches him.

﴿ وَإِذَا مَسَّهُ ٱلْخَيْرُ مَنُوعًا ﴿٢١﴾ ﴾

And stingy when good reaches him;

﴿ إِلَّا ٱلْمُصَلِّينَ ﴿٢٢﴾ ﴾

Not so those devoted to Prayer,

﴿ ٱلَّذِينَ هُمْ عَلَىٰ صَلَاتِهِمْ دَآئِمُونَ ﴿٢٣﴾ ﴾

Those who remain steadfast to their prayer;

﴿ وَٱلَّذِينَ فِىٓ أَمْوَٰلِهِمْ حَقٌّ مَّعْلُومٌ ﴿٢٤﴾ ﴾

And those in whose wealth is a recognized right

﴿ لِّلسَّآئِلِ وَٱلۡمَحۡرُومِ ٢٥ ﴾

For the (needy) who asks and him
who is prevented from asking;

﴿ وَٱلَّذِينَ يُصَدِّقُونَ بِيَوۡمِ ٱلدِّينِ ٢٦ ﴾

And those who hold to the truth
of the Day of Judgment;

﴿ وَٱلَّذِينَ هُم مِّنۡ عَذَابِ رَبِّهِم مُّشۡفِقُونَ ٢٧ ﴾

And those who fear the displeasure of their Lord,

﴿ إِنَّ عَذَابَ رَبِّهِمۡ غَيۡرُ مَأۡمُونٖ ٢٨ ﴾

For their Lord's displeasure is the opposite of

Peace and Tranquility.

﴿ وَٱلَّذِينَ هُمۡ لِفُرُوجِهِمۡ حَٰفِظُونَ ٢٩ ﴾

And those who guard their chastity,

﴿ إِلَّا عَلَىٰٓ أَزۡوَٰجِهِمۡ أَوۡ مَا مَلَكَتۡ أَيۡمَٰنُهُمۡ فَإِنَّهُمۡ غَيۡرُ مَلُومِينَ ٣٠ ﴾

Save with their wives and over whom
they have rights through custom,

They are not to be blamed,

﴿ فَمَنِ ٱبْتَغَىٰ وَرَآءَ ذَٰلِكَ فَأُو۟لَٰٓئِكَ هُمُ ٱلْعَادُونَ ﴿٣١﴾ ﴾

But those who trespass beyond this are transgressors;

﴿ وَٱلَّذِينَ هُمْ لِأَمَٰنَٰتِهِمْ وَعَهْدِهِمْ رَٰعُونَ ﴿٣٢﴾ ﴾

And those who respect their trusts and covenants;

﴿ وَٱلَّذِينَ هُم بِشَهَٰدَٰتِهِمْ قَآئِمُونَ ﴿٣٣﴾ ﴾

And those who stand firm in their testimonies;

﴿ وَٱلَّذِينَ هُمْ عَلَىٰ صَلَاتِهِمْ يُحَافِظُونَ ﴿٣٤﴾ ﴾

And those who guard (the sacredness) of their worship;

﴿ أُو۟لَٰٓئِكَ فِى جَنَّٰتٍ مُّكْرَمُونَ ﴿٣٥﴾ ﴾

Such will be the honored ones in the Gardens
(of Bliss). (Al-Ma'arij 70:1–35, Koran)

The Koran, very early in the blessed *Nabi's* mission to humanity, laid the foundation of principles of the *din of Allah*. Worship of Allah, deeds of charity, belief in the Day of Judgment, fear of displeasure of Allah, guarding of one's chastity, being truthful in testimonies, fulfillment of one's trusts and covenants, and guarding the sacredness of worship earn the Lord's pleasure and peace and tranquility.

The Koran states that the people who perform deeds of righteousness will be the honored ones in the gardens (of bliss):

- Those who remain steadfast to their prayer.
- Those with wealth who recognize the right of the needy who ask and the right of those who are prevented from asking.
- Those who hold to the truth of the Day of Judgment.
- Those who fear the displeasure of their Lord, which is the opposite of peace and tranquility.
- Those who guard their chastity and cohabit only with their wives and husbands.
- Those who respect their trusts and covenants.
- Those who stand firm in their testimonies.
- Those who guard (the sacredness) of their worship.

Worship of Allah and charity to fellow beings is the cornerstone of Islam. When we follow the revelations of the covenant of salat and zakat according to the sequence and the period of revelation, we find the following commandments to the believers:

Late Meccan Suras

60: Al Rum: 30

﴿ ضَرَبَ لَكُم مَّثَلًا مِّنْ أَنفُسِكُمْ ۖ هَل لَّكُم مِّن مَّا مَلَكَتْ أَيْمَٰنُكُم مِّن شُرَكَآءَ فِى مَا رَزَقْنَٰكُمْ فَأَنتُمْ فِيهِ سَوَآءٌ تَخَافُونَهُمْ

كَخِيفَتِكُمْ أَنفُسَكُمْ ۚ كَذَٰلِكَ نُفَصِّلُ ٱلْءَايَٰتِ لِقَوْمٍ يَعْقِلُونَ ﴿٢٨﴾ ﴾

He does propose to you a similitude from your own (experience): do you have partners among those whom your right hands possess, to share as equals in the wealth We have bestowed on you? Do ye fear

them as you fear each other? Thus, do We explain
the Signs in detail to a people that understand.

﴿ بَلِ ٱتَّبَعَ ٱلَّذِينَ ظَلَمُوٓاْ أَهْوَآءَهُم بِغَيْرِ عِلْمٍ ۖ فَمَن يَهْدِى مَنْ أَضَلَّ ٱللَّهُ ۖ وَمَا لَهُم مِّن نَّٰصِرِينَ ﴿٢٩﴾ ﴾

Nay, the wrong doers (merely) follow their
own lusts, being devoid of knowledge but
who will guide those whom Allah leaves
astray? To them there will be no helpers.

﴿ فَأَقِمْ وَجْهَكَ لِلدِّينِ حَنِيفًا ۚ فِطْرَتَ ٱللَّهِ ٱلَّتِى فَطَرَ ٱلنَّاسَ عَلَيْهَا ۚ لَا تَبْدِيلَ لِخَلْقِ ٱللَّهِ ۚ ذَٰلِكَ ٱلدِّينُ ٱلْقَيِّمُ وَلَٰكِنَّ أَكْثَرَ ٱلنَّاسِ
لَا يَعْلَمُونَ ﴿٣٠﴾ ﴾

So, set thou your face steadily and truly to the Faith:
Establish Allah's handiwork according to the pattern
on which He has made mankind: no change let there
be in the work wrought by Allah: that is the standard
Religion: but most among mankind understand not.

﴿ ۞ مُنِيبِينَ إِلَيْهِ وَٱتَّقُوهُ وَأَقِيمُواْ ٱلصَّلَوٰةَ وَلَا تَكُونُواْ مِنَ ٱلْمُشْرِكِينَ ﴿٣١﴾ ﴾

Turn you back in repentance to Him, and fear
Him: establish regular prayers, and be not be
among those who join gods with Allah,

﴿ مِنَ ٱلَّذِينَ فَرَّقُواْ دِينَهُمْ وَكَانُواْ شِيَعًا ۖ كُلُّ حِزْبٍۭ بِمَا لَدَيْهِمْ فَرِحُونَ ﴿٣٢﴾ ﴾

Those who split up their Religion, and become (mere)
sects, each party rejoicing in that which is with itself!

﴿ وَإِذَا مَسَّ ٱلنَّاسَ ضُرٌّ دَعَوْا۟ رَبَّهُم مُّنِيبِينَ إِلَيْهِ ثُمَّ إِذَآ أَذَاقَهُم مِّنْهُ رَحْمَةً إِذَا فَرِيقٌ مِّنْهُم بِرَبِّهِمْ يُشْرِكُونَ ٣٣ ﴾

When trouble touches men, they cry to their
Lord, turning back to Him in repentance: but
when He gives them a taste of Mercy as from
Himself. Behold, some of them pay part-
worship to other gods besides their Lord,

﴿ لِيَكْفُرُوا۟ بِمَآ ءَاتَيْنَٰهُمْ ۚ فَتَمَتَّعُوا۟ فَسَوْفَ تَعْلَمُونَ ٣٤ ﴾

As if to show their ingratitude for the favors
We have bestowed on them! Then enjoy (your
brief day); but soon will ye know (your folly).

﴿ أَمْ أَنزَلْنَا عَلَيْهِمْ سُلْطَٰنًا فَهُوَ يَتَكَلَّمُ بِمَا كَانُوا۟ بِهِۦ يُشْرِكُونَ ٣٥ ﴾

Or have We sent down authority to them, which points
out to them the things to which they pay part-worship?

﴿ وَإِذَآ أَذَقْنَا ٱلنَّاسَ رَحْمَةً فَرِحُوا۟ بِهَا ۖ وَإِن تُصِبْهُمْ سَيِّئَةٌۢ بِمَا قَدَّمَتْ أَيْدِيهِمْ إِذَا هُمْ يَقْنَطُونَ ٣٦ ﴾

When We give men a taste of Mercy, they
exult thereat: and when some evil afflicts
them because of what their (own) hands have
sent forth, behold, they are in despair!

﴿ أَوَلَمْ يَرَوْا أَنَّ ٱللَّهَ يَبْسُطُ ٱلرِّزْقَ لِمَن يَشَآءُ وَيَقْدِرُ إِنَّ فِى ذَٰلِكَ لَآيَٰتٍ لِّقَوْمٍ يُؤْمِنُونَ ۝ ﴾

See they not that Allah enlarges the provision
and restricts it, to whomsoever He pleases?
Verily in that are Signs for those who believe.

﴿ فَـَٔاتِ ذَا ٱلْقُرْبَىٰ حَقَّهُ وَٱلْمِسْكِينَ وَٱبْنَ ٱلسَّبِيلِ ذَٰلِكَ خَيْرٌ لِّلَّذِينَ يُرِيدُونَ وَجْهَ ٱللَّهِ وَأُوْلَٰٓئِكَ هُمُ ٱلْمُفْلِحُونَ ۝ ﴾

So, give what is due to kindred, the needy, and
the wayfarer. That is best for those who seek the
Countenance, of Allah, and it is they who will prosper.

﴿ وَمَآ ءَاتَيْتُم مِّن رِّبًا لِّيَرْبُوَا۟ فِىٓ أَمْوَٰلِ ٱلنَّاسِ فَلَا يَرْبُوا۟ عِندَ ٱللَّهِ وَمَآ ءَاتَيْتُم مِّن زَكَوٰةٍ تُرِيدُونَ وَجْهَ ٱللَّهِ فَأُوْلَٰٓئِكَ هُمُ ٱلْمُضْعِفُونَ

That which you lay out for increase through the
property of (other) people, will have no increase
with Allah: but that which you lay out for
charity, seeking the Countenance of Allah, (will
increase): it is these who will get a recompense
multiplied. (Ar-Rum 30:28–38, Koran)

61: Luqman: 31

﴿ وَوَصَّيْنَا ٱلْإِنسَٰنَ بِوَٰلِدَيْهِ حَمَلَتْهُ أُمُّهُ وَهْنًا عَلَىٰ وَهْنٍ وَفِصَٰلُهُ فِى عَامَيْنِ أَنِ ٱشْكُرْ لِى وَلِوَٰلِدَيْكَ إِلَىَّ ٱلْمَصِيرُ ۝ ﴾

And We have enjoined on man (To be good) to
his parents: in travail upon travail did his mother
bear him, and in years twain was his weaning:

(hear the command), "Show gratitude to Me and to your parents: to Me is (thy final) Goal.

﴿ وَإِن جَٰهَدَاكَ عَلَىٰٓ أَن تُشْرِكَ بِى مَا لَيْسَ لَكَ بِهِۦ عِلْمٌ فَلَا تُطِعْهُمَا ۖ وَصَاحِبْهُمَا فِى ٱلدُّنْيَا مَعْرُوفًا ۖ وَٱتَّبِعْ سَبِيلَ مَنْ أَنَابَ إِلَىَّ ۚ ثُمَّ
إِلَىَّ مَرْجِعُكُمْ فَأُنَبِّئُكُم بِمَا كُنتُمْ تَعْمَلُونَ ﴿١٥﴾ ﴾

"But if they strive to make thee join in worship with Me things of which thou hast no knowledge, obey them not; yet bear them company in this life with justice (And consideration), and follow the way of those who turn to Me (in love). In the End the return of you all is to Me, and I will tell you the truth (and meaning) of all that ye did."

﴿ يَٰبُنَىَّ إِنَّهَآ إِن تَكُ مِثْقَالَ حَبَّةٍ مِّنْ خَرْدَلٍ فَتَكُن فِى صَخْرَةٍ أَوْ فِى ٱلسَّمَٰوَٰتِ أَوْ فِى ٱلْأَرْضِ يَأْتِ بِهَا ٱللَّهُ ۚ إِنَّ ٱللَّهَ لَطِيفٌ خَبِيرٌ ﴿١٦﴾ ﴾

"O my son!" (Said Luqman), "If there be (but) the weight of a mustard-seed and it were (hidden) in a rock, or (anywhere) in the heavens or on earth, Allah will bring it forth: for Allah understands the finest mysteries, (and) is well-acquainted (with them).

﴿ يَٰبُنَىَّ أَقِمِ ٱلصَّلَوٰةَ وَأْمُرْ بِٱلْمَعْرُوفِ وَٱنْهَ عَنِ ٱلْمُنكَرِ وَٱصْبِرْ عَلَىٰ مَآ أَصَابَكَ ۖ إِنَّ ذَٰلِكَ مِنْ عَزْمِ ٱلْأُمُورِ ﴿١٧﴾ ﴾

"O my son! establish regular prayer, enjoin what is just, and forbid what is wrong; and bear with patient constancy whatever betide thee; for this is firmness (of purpose) in (the conduct of) affairs.

﴿ وَلَا تُصَعِّرْ خَدَّكَ لِلنَّاسِ وَلَا تَمْشِ فِي الْأَرْضِ مَرَحًا ۖ إِنَّ اللَّهَ لَا يُحِبُّ كُلَّ مُخْتَالٍ فَخُورٍ ﴿١٨﴾ ﴾

"And swell not thy cheek (For pride) at men,
nor walk in insolence through the earth: for
Allah loves not any arrogant boaster.

﴿ وَاقْصِدْ فِي مَشْيِكَ وَاغْضُضْ مِنْ صَوْتِكَ ۚ إِنَّ أَنْكَرَ الْأَصْوَاتِ لَصَوْتُ الْحَمِيرِ ﴿١٩﴾ ﴾

"And be moderate in thy pace and lower thy voice;
for the harshest of sounds without doubt is the
braying of the ass." (Luqman 31:14–19, Koran)

64: Fatir: 35

﴿ وَلَا تَزِرُ وَازِرَةٌ وِزْرَ أُخْرَىٰ ۚ وَإِنْ تَدْعُ مُثْقَلَةٌ إِلَىٰ حِمْلِهَا لَا يُحْمَلْ مِنْهُ شَيْءٌ وَلَوْ كَانَ ذَا قُرْبَىٰ ۗ إِنَّمَا تُنْذِرُ الَّذِينَ يَخْشَوْنَ رَبَّهُمْ بِالْغَيْبِ
وَأَقَامُوا الصَّلَاةَ ۚ وَمَنْ تَزَكَّىٰ فَإِنَّمَا يَتَزَكَّىٰ لِنَفْسِهِ ۚ وَإِلَى اللَّهِ الْمَصِيرُ ﴿١٨﴾ ﴾

Nor can a bearer of burdens bear another's burden.
If one heavily laden should call another to (bear) his
load, not the least portion of it can be carried (by
the other), even though he be nearly related. Thou
canst but admonish such as fear their Lord unseen
and establish regular Prayer. And whoever purifies
himself does so for the benefit of his own soul; and
the destination (of all) is to Allah. (Fatir 35:19, Koran)

﴿ إِنَّ ٱلَّذِينَ يَتۡلُونَ كِتَٰبَ ٱللَّهِ وَأَقَامُواْ ٱلصَّلَوٰةَ وَأَنفَقُواْ مِمَّا رَزَقۡنَٰهُمۡ سِرّٗا وَعَلَانِيَةٗ يَرۡجُونَ تِجَٰرَةٗ لَّن تَبُورَ ٢٩ ﴾

Those who read the Book of Allah, establish regular Prayer, and spend (in Charity) out of what We have provided for them, secretly and openly, hope for a Commerce that will never fail. (Fatir 35:29, Koran)

71: Ash-Shura: 42

﴿ وَٱلَّذِينَ يَجۡتَنِبُونَ كَبَٰٓئِرَ ٱلۡإِثۡمِ وَٱلۡفَوَٰحِشَ وَإِذَا مَا غَضِبُواْ هُمۡ يَغۡفِرُونَ ٣٧ ﴾

Those who avoid the greater crimes and shameful deeds, and, when they are angry even then forgive;

﴿ وَٱلَّذِينَ ٱسۡتَجَابُواْ لِرَبِّهِمۡ وَأَقَامُواْ ٱلصَّلَوٰةَ وَأَمۡرُهُمۡ شُورَىٰ بَيۡنَهُمۡ وَمِمَّا رَزَقۡنَٰهُمۡ يُنفِقُونَ ٣٨ ﴾

Those who hearken to their Lord, and establish regular prayer; who (conduct) their affairs by mutual Consultation; who spend out of what We bestow on them for Sustenance;

﴿ وَٱلَّذِينَ إِذَآ أَصَابَهُمُ ٱلۡبَغۡيُ هُمۡ يَنتَصِرُونَ ٣٩ ﴾

And those who, when an oppressive wrong is inflicted on them, (are not cowed but) help and defend themselves. (Ash-Shura 42:37-39, Koran)

76: Yunus: 10: Commandment to Nabi Musa

﴿ وَأَوْحَيْنَآ إِلَىٰ مُوسَىٰ وَأَخِيهِ أَن تَبَوَّءَا لِقَوْمِكُمَا بِمِصْرَ بُيُوتًا وَٱجْعَلُوا بُيُوتَكُمْ قِبْلَةً وَأَقِيمُوا ٱلصَّلَوٰةَ ۗ وَبَشِّرِ ٱلْمُؤْمِنِينَ ﴿٨٧﴾

We inspired Moses and his brother with this
Message: "Provide dwellings for your People in
Egypt, make your dwellings into places of worship,
and establish regular prayers: and give Glad Tidings
to those who believe!" (Yunus 10:87, Koran)

77: Hud: 11: Shu'ayb

﴿ قَالُوا يَٰشُعَيْبُ أَصَلَوٰتُكَ تَأْمُرُكَ أَن نَّتْرُكَ مَا يَعْبُدُ ءَابَآؤُنَآ أَوْ أَن نَّفْعَلَ فِىٓ أَمْوَٰلِنَا مَا نَشَٰٓؤُا ۖ إِنَّكَ لَأَنتَ ٱلْحَلِيمُ ٱلرَّشِيدُ ﴿٨٧﴾

They said: "O Shu'aib! Does your (religion of) prayer
command thee that we leave off the worship which
our fathers practiced, or that we leave off doing what
we like with our property? Truly, you are the one that
forbears faults and is right-minded!" (Hud 11:87, Koran)

﴿ وَلَا تَرْكَنُوٓا إِلَى ٱلَّذِينَ ظَلَمُوا فَتَمَسَّكُمُ ٱلنَّارُ وَمَا لَكُم مِّن دُونِ ٱللَّهِ مِنْ أَوْلِيَآءَ ثُمَّ لَا تُنصَرُونَ ﴿١١٣﴾ ﴾

And incline not to those who do wrong, or the
Fire will seize you; and ye have no protectors
other than Allah, nor shall ye be helped.

﴿ وَأَقِمِ ٱلصَّلَوٰةَ طَرَفَىِ ٱلنَّهَارِ وَزُلَفًا مِّنَ ٱلَّيْلِ ۚ إِنَّ ٱلْحَسَنَٰتِ يُذْهِبْنَ ٱلسَّيِّـَٔاتِ ۚ ذَٰلِكَ ذِكْرَىٰ لِلذَّٰكِرِينَ ﴿١١٤﴾ ﴾

And establish regular prayers at the two ends of the day
and at the approaches of the night: for those things that

are good remove those that are evil: be that the word
of remembrance to those who remember (their Lord):

﴿ وَٱصْبِرْ فَإِنَّ ٱللَّهَ لَا يُضِيعُ أَجْرَ ٱلْمُحْسِنِينَ ﴿١١٥﴾ ﴾

And be steadfast in patience; for verily Allah
will not suffer the reward of the righteous
to perish. (Hud 11:113–15, Koran)

79: Ar-Ra'd: 13

﴿ ٱلَّذِينَ يُوفُونَ بِعَهْدِ ٱللَّهِ وَلَا يَنقُضُونَ ٱلْمِيثَٰقَ ﴿٢٠﴾ ﴾

Those who fulfill the Covenant of Allah
and fail not in their plighted word;

﴿ وَٱلَّذِينَ يَصِلُونَ مَآ أَمَرَ ٱللَّهُ بِهِۦٓ أَن يُوصَلَ وَيَخْشَوْنَ رَبَّهُمْ وَيَخَافُونَ سُوٓءَ ٱلْحِسَابِ ﴿٢١﴾ ﴾

Those who join together those things which
Allah hath commanded to be joined, hold their
Lord in awe, and fear the terrible reckoning;

﴿ وَٱلَّذِينَ صَبَرُوا۟ ٱبْتِغَآءَ وَجْهِ رَبِّهِمْ وَأَقَامُوا۟ ٱلصَّلَوٰةَ وَأَنفَقُوا۟ مِمَّا رَزَقْنَٰهُمْ سِرًّا وَعَلَانِيَةً وَيَدْرَءُونَ بِٱلْحَسَنَةِ ٱلسَّيِّئَةَ أُو۟لَٰٓئِكَ لَهُمْ عُقْبَى
ٱلدَّارِ ﴿٢٢﴾ ﴾

Those who patiently persevere, seeking the
countenance of their Lord; establish regular
prayers; spend out of (the gifts) We have bestowed
for their sustenance, secretly and openly; and

turn off Evil with good: for such there is the
final attainment of the (Eternal) Home.

﴿ جَنَّٰتُ عَدْنٍ يَدْخُلُونَهَا وَمَن صَلَحَ مِنْ ءَابَآئِهِمْ وَأَزْوَٰجِهِمْ وَذُرِّيَّٰتِهِمْ ۖ وَٱلْمَلَٰٓئِكَةُ يَدْخُلُونَ عَلَيْهِم مِّن كُلِّ بَابٍ ﴿٢٣﴾ ﴾

Gardens of perpetual bliss: they shall enter there,
as well as the righteous among their fathers, their
spouses, and their offspring: and angels shall enter
unto them from every gate (with the salutation):

﴿ سَلَٰمٌ عَلَيْكُم بِمَا صَبَرْتُمْ ۚ فَنِعْمَ عُقْبَى ٱلدَّارِ ﴿٢٤﴾ ﴾

"Peace to you for that ye persevered in patience!
Now how excellent is the final Home!"

﴿ وَٱلَّذِينَ يَنقُضُونَ عَهْدَ ٱللَّهِ مِنۢ بَعْدِ مِيثَٰقِهِۦ وَيَقْطَعُونَ مَآ أَمَرَ ٱللَّهُ بِهِۦٓ أَن يُوصَلَ وَيُفْسِدُونَ فِى ٱلْأَرْضِ ۙ أُو۟لَٰٓئِكَ لَهُمُ ٱللَّعْنَةُ وَلَهُمْ سُوٓءُ ٱلدَّارِ ﴿٢٥﴾ ﴾

But those who break the Covenant of Allah, after
having pledged their word thereto, and cut asunder
those things which Allah has commanded to be
joined, and work mischief in the land, on them
is the Curse; for them is the terrible Home!

﴿ ٱللَّهُ يَبْسُطُ ٱلرِّزْقَ لِمَن يَشَآءُ وَيَقْدِرُ ۚ وَفَرِحُوا۟ بِٱلْحَيَوٰةِ ٱلدُّنْيَا وَمَا ٱلْحَيَوٰةُ ٱلدُّنْيَا فِى ٱلْءَاخِرَةِ إِلَّا مَتَٰعٌ ﴿٢٦﴾

Allah does enlarge or grant by (strict) measure,
the Sustenance (which He gives) to whom so He
pleases. The worldly rejoice in the life of this world:

but the life of this world is but little comfort in
the Hereafter. (Ar-Ra'd 13: 20-25, Koran)

80: Ibrahim: 14

Allah commands Nabi Ibrahim with the words:

﴿ قُل لِّعِبَادِىَ ٱلَّذِينَ ءَامَنُواْ يُقِيمُواْ ٱلصَّلَوٰةَ وَيُنفِقُواْ مِمَّا رَزَقْنَٰهُمْ سِرًّا وَعَلَانِيَةً مِّن قَبْلِ أَن يَأْتِىَ يَوْمٌ لَّا بَيْعٌ فِيهِ وَلَا خِلَٰلٌ

Speak to My servants who have believed that
they may establish regular prayers and spend (in
charity) out of the Sustenance We have given them,
secretly and openly, before the coming of a Day
in which there will be neither mutual bargaining
nor befriending. (Ibrahim 14:31, Koran)

And Ibrahim pleads to Allah:

﴿ رَّبَّنَآ إِنِّىٓ أَسْكَنتُ مِن ذُرِّيَّتِى بِوَادٍ غَيْرِ ذِى زَرْعٍ عِندَ بَيْتِكَ ٱلْمُحَرَّمِ رَبَّنَا لِيُقِيمُواْ ٱلصَّلَوٰةَ فَٱجْعَلْ أَفْـِٔدَةً مِّنَ ٱلنَّاسِ تَهْوِىٓ إِلَيْهِمْ

وَٱرْزُقْهُم مِّنَ ٱلثَّمَرَٰتِ لَعَلَّهُمْ يَشْكُرُونَ ﴿٣٧﴾ ﴾

O our Lord! I have made some of my offspring to
dwell in a valley without cultivation, by Thy Sacred
House; in order, O our Lord, that they may establish
regular Prayer: so, fill the hearts of some among men
with love towards them, and feed them with Fruits: so
that they may give thanks. (Ibrahim 14:37, Koran)

﴿ ٱلْحَمْدُ لِلَّهِ ٱلَّذِى وَهَبَ لِى عَلَى ٱلْكِبَرِ إِسْمَـٰعِيلَ وَإِسْحَـٰقَ ۚ إِنَّ رَبِّى لَسَمِيعُ ٱلدُّعَآءِ ٣٩ ﴾

Praise is to Allah. Who has granted me in old age Isma'il and Isaac: for truly my Lord is He, the Hearer of Prayer!

﴿ رَبِّ ٱجْعَلْنِى مُقِيمَ ٱلصَّلَوٰةِ وَمِن ذُرِّيَّتِى ۚ رَبَّنَا وَتَقَبَّلْ دُعَآءِ ٤٠ ﴾

O my Lord! Make me one who establishes regular Prayer, and also (raise such) among my offspring O our Lord! And accept Thou my Prayer. (Ibrahim 14:39–40, Koran)

83: Al-Isra: 17

﴿ أَقِمِ ٱلصَّلَوٰةَ لِدُلُوكِ ٱلشَّمْسِ إِلَىٰ غَسَقِ ٱلَّيْلِ وَقُرْءَانَ ٱلْفَجْرِ ۖ إِنَّ قُرْءَانَ ٱلْفَجْرِ كَانَ مَشْهُودًا ٧٨ ﴾

Establish regular prayers at the sun's decline till the darkness of the night, and the Morning Prayer and reading of the Qur'an: for Prayer and reading of the Qur'an in the morning carry their testimony.

﴿ وَمِنَ ٱلَّيْلِ فَتَهَجَّدْ بِهِۦ نَافِلَةً لَّكَ عَسَىٰٓ أَن يَبْعَثَكَ رَبُّكَ مَقَامًا مَّحْمُودًا ٧٩ ﴾

And pray in the small watches of the morning: (it would be) an additional prayer (or spiritual profit) for thee: soon will thy Lord raise thee to a Station of Praise and Glory! (Al-Isra 17:78–79, Koran)

﴿ وَبِٱلْحَقِّ أَنزَلْنَٰهُ وَبِٱلْحَقِّ نَزَلَ ۗ وَمَآ أَرْسَلْنَٰكَ إِلَّا مُبَشِّرًا وَنَذِيرًا ﴿١٠٥﴾ ﴾

We sent down the (Qur'an) in Truth, and in
Truth has it descended, and We sent thee but
to give Glad Tidings and to warn sinners.

﴿ وَقُرْءَانًا فَرَقْنَٰهُ لِتَقْرَأَهُۥ عَلَى ٱلنَّاسِ عَلَىٰ مُكْثٍ وَنَزَّلْنَٰهُ تَنزِيلًا ﴿١٠٦﴾ ﴾

(It is) a Qur'an which We have divided (into
parts), In order that thou might recite it to men
at intervals: We have revealed it by stages.

﴿ قُلْ ءَامِنُوا۟ بِهِۦٓ أَوْ لَا تُؤْمِنُوٓا۟ ۚ إِنَّ ٱلَّذِينَ أُوتُوا۟ ٱلْعِلْمَ مِن قَبْلِهِۦٓ إِذَا يُتْلَىٰ عَلَيْهِمْ يَخِرُّونَ لِلْأَذْقَانِ سُجَّدًا ﴿١٠٧﴾ ﴾

Say: "Whether ye believe in it or not, it is
true that those who were given knowledge
beforehand, when it is recited to them fall
down on their faces in humble prostration,

﴿ وَيَقُولُونَ سُبْحَٰنَ رَبِّنَآ إِن كَانَ وَعْدُ رَبِّنَا لَمَفْعُولًا ﴿١٠٨﴾ ﴾

And they say: "Glory to our Lord! Truly has
the promise of our Lord been fulfilled!"

﴿ وَيَخِرُّونَ لِلْأَذْقَانِ يَبْكُونَ وَيَزِيدُهُمْ خُشُوعًا ۩ ﴿١٠٩﴾ ﴾

They fall down on their faces in tears, and
it increases their (earnest) humility.

﴿ قُلِ ٱدْعُواْ ٱللَّهَ أَوِ ٱدْعُواْ ٱلرَّحْمَٰنَ ۖ أَيًّا مَّا تَدْعُواْ فَلَهُ ٱلْأَسْمَآءُ ٱلْحُسْنَىٰ ۚ وَلَا تَجْهَرْ بِصَلَاتِكَ وَلَا تُخَافِتْ بِهَا وَٱبْتَغِ بَيْنَ ذَٰلِكَ سَبِيلًا ﴿١١٠﴾

Say: "Call upon Allah or call upon Rahman: by whatever name ye call upon Him, (it is well): for to Him belong the Most Beautiful Names. Neither speak your Prayer aloud, nor speak it in a low tone, but seek a middle course between." (Al-Isra 17:105–10, Koran)

85: Maryam: 19

Jesus as a babe spoke from his mother's arms:

﴿ قَالَ إِنِّى عَبْدُ ٱللَّهِ ءَاتَىٰنِىَ ٱلْكِتَٰبَ وَجَعَلَنِى نَبِيًّا ﴿٣٠﴾ ﴾

He said: "I am indeed a servant of Allah: He hath given me revelation and made me a prophet;

﴿ وَجَعَلَنِى مُبَارَكًا أَيْنَ مَا كُنتُ وَأَوْصَٰنِى بِٱلصَّلَوٰةِ وَٱلزَّكَوٰةِ مَا دُمْتُ حَيًّا ﴿٣١﴾ ﴾

"And He hath made me blessed where so ever I be, and has enjoined on me Prayer and Charity as long as I live." (Maryam 19:30–31, Koran)

Isma'il

﴿ وَٱذْكُرْ فِى ٱلْكِتَٰبِ إِسْمَٰعِيلَ ۚ إِنَّهُۥ كَانَ صَادِقَ ٱلْوَعْدِ وَكَانَ رَسُولًا نَّبِيًّا ﴿٥٤﴾ ﴾

Also mention in the Book (the story of) Isma'il: he was true to what he promised, and he was a Messenger (and) a Prophet.

﴿ وَكَانَ يَأْمُرُ أَهْلَهُۥ بِٱلصَّلَوٰةِ وَٱلزَّكَوٰةِ وَكَانَ عِندَ رَبِّهِۦ مَرْضِيًّا ﴿٥٥﴾ ﴾

He used to enjoin on his people Prayer and Charity, and he was most acceptable in the sight of his Lord. (Maryam 19:54–55, Koran)

﴿ أُو۟لَٰٓئِكَ ٱلَّذِينَ أَنْعَمَ ٱللَّهُ عَلَيْهِم مِّنَ ٱلنَّبِيِّـۧنَ مِن ذُرِّيَّةِ ءَادَمَ وَمِمَّنْ حَمَلْنَا مَعَ نُوحٍ وَمِن ذُرِّيَّةِ إِبْرَٰهِيمَ وَإِسْرَٰٓءِيلَ وَمِمَّنْ هَدَيْنَا وَٱجْتَبَيْنَآ ۚ

إِذَا تُتْلَىٰ عَلَيْهِمْ ءَايَٰتُ ٱلرَّحْمَٰنِ خَرُّوا۟ سُجَّدًا وَبُكِيًّا ۩ ﴿٥٨﴾ ﴾

Those were some of the prophets on whom Allah did bestow His Grace, of the posterity of Adam, and of those whom We carried (in the Ark) with Noah, and of the posterity of Abraham and Israel, of those whom We guided and chose. Whenever the Signs of (Allah) Most Gracious were rehearsed to them, they would fall down in prostrate adoration and in tears,

﴿ ۞ فَخَلَفَ مِنۢ بَعْدِهِمْ خَلْفٌ أَضَاعُوا۟ ٱلصَّلَوٰةَ وَٱتَّبَعُوا۟ ٱلشَّهَوَٰتِ ۖ فَسَوْفَ يَلْقَوْنَ غَيًّا ﴿٥٩﴾ ﴾

But after them there followed a posterity who missed prayers and followed after lusts: soon then will they face Destruction. (Maryam 19:58–59, Koran)

86: Taha: 20: Moses

﴿ إِنِّيٓ أَنَا۠ رَبُّكَ فَٱخۡلَعۡ نَعۡلَيۡكَ إِنَّكَ بِٱلۡوَادِ ٱلۡمُقَدَّسِ طُوٗى ١٢ ﴾

Verily I am your Lord! (O Moses)Therefore
(in My presence) take off your shoes: you
are in the sacred valley of Tuwa.

﴿ وَأَنَا ٱخۡتَرۡتُكَ فَٱسۡتَمِعۡ لِمَا يُوحَىٰٓ ١٣ ﴾

I have chosen thee: listen, then to
the inspiration (sent to thee).

﴿ إِنَّنِيٓ أَنَا ٱللَّهُ لَآ إِلَٰهَ إِلَّآ أَنَا۠ فَٱعۡبُدۡنِي وَأَقِمِ ٱلصَّلَوٰةَ لِذِكۡرِيٓ ١٤ ﴾

Verily, I am Allah: there is no god but I: so,
serve Me only, and establish regular prayer for
celebrating My praise. (Taha 20:12–14, Koran)

Muhammad

﴿ فَٱصۡبِرۡ عَلَىٰ مَا يَقُولُونَ وَسَبِّحۡ بِحَمۡدِ رَبِّكَ قَبۡلَ طُلُوعِ ٱلشَّمۡسِ وَقَبۡلَ غُرُوبِهَاۖ وَمِنۡ ءَانَآيِٕ ٱلَّيۡلِ فَسَبِّحۡ وَأَطۡرَافَ ٱلنَّهَارِ لَعَلَّكَ تَرۡضَىٰ

 ﴾

Therefore, be patient with what they say, (Muhammad)
and celebrate constantly the praises of thy Lord,
before the rising of the sun, and before its setting; yes,
celebrate them for part of the hours of the night, and
at the sides of the day: that you will find comfort.

﴿ وَلَا تَمُدَّنَّ عَيْنَيْكَ إِلَىٰ مَا مَتَّعْنَا بِهِۦٓ أَزْوَٰجًا مِّنْهُمْ زَهْرَةَ ٱلْحَيَوٰةِ ٱلدُّنْيَا لِنَفْتِنَهُمْ فِيهِ ۚ وَرِزْقُ رَبِّكَ خَيْرٌ وَأَبْقَىٰ ١٣١ ﴾

Nor strain your eyes in longing for the things We have given for enjoyment to parties of them, the splendor of the life of this world, through which We test them: but the provision of thy Lord is better and more enduring.

﴿ وَأْمُرْ أَهْلَكَ بِٱلصَّلَوٰةِ وَٱصْطَبِرْ عَلَيْهَا ۖ لَا نَسْـَٔلُكَ رِزْقًا ۖ نَّحْنُ نَرْزُقُكَ ۗ وَٱلْعَٰقِبَةُ لِلتَّقْوَىٰ ١٣٢ ﴾

Enjoin prayer on your people and be constant therein. We ask you not to provide sustenance: We provide it for you. But the (fruit of) the Hereafter is for righteousness. (Taha 20:130–32, Koran)

87: Al-Anbiyaa: 21: Ishak/Yaqoob

﴿ وَوَهَبْنَا لَهُۥٓ إِسْحَٰقَ وَيَعْقُوبَ نَافِلَةً ۖ وَكُلًّا جَعَلْنَا صَٰلِحِينَ ٧٢ ﴾

And We bestowed on him Isaac and, as an additional gift, (a grandson), Jacob, and We made righteous men of everyone (of them).

﴿ وَجَعَلْنَٰهُمْ أَئِمَّةً يَهْدُونَ بِأَمْرِنَا وَأَوْحَيْنَآ إِلَيْهِمْ فِعْلَ ٱلْخَيْرَٰتِ وَإِقَامَ ٱلصَّلَوٰةِ وَإِيتَآءَ ٱلزَّكَوٰةِ ۖ وَكَانُوا۟ لَنَا عَٰبِدِينَ ٧٣ ﴾

And We made them leaders, guiding (men) by Our Command, and We sent them inspiration to do good deeds, to establish regular prayers, and to practice regular charity; and they constantly served Us (and Us only). (Al-Anbiyaa 21:72–73, Koran)

89: Al-An'am: 6

قُلْ إِنَّ هُدَى ٱللَّهِ هُوَ ٱلْهُدَىٰ ۖ وَأُمِرْنَا لِنُسْلِمَ لِرَبِّ ٱلْعَٰلَمِينَ ﴿٧١﴾

Say: "Allah's guidance is the (only) guidance,
and we have been directed to submit
ourselves to the Lord of the Worlds.

﴿ وَأَنْ أَقِيمُوا۟ ٱلصَّلَوٰةَ وَٱتَّقُوهُ ۚ وَهُوَ ٱلَّذِىٓ إِلَيْهِ تُحْشَرُونَ ﴿٧٢﴾ ﴾

"To establish regular prayers and to fear Allah: for
it is to Him that we shall be gathered together."

﴿ وَهُوَ ٱلَّذِى خَلَقَ ٱلسَّمَٰوَٰتِ وَٱلْأَرْضَ بِٱلْحَقِّ ۖ وَيَوْمَ يَقُولُ كُن فَيَكُونُ ۚ قَوْلُهُ ٱلْحَقُّ ۚ وَلَهُ ٱلْمُلْكُ يَوْمَ يُنفَخُ فِى ٱلصُّورِ ۚ عَٰلِمُ
ٱلْغَيْبِ وَٱلشَّهَٰدَةِ ۚ وَهُوَ ٱلْحَكِيمُ ٱلْخَبِيرُ ﴿٧٣﴾ ﴾

It is He Who created the heavens and the earth in true (proportions); the day He said, "Be," behold! It is. His Word is the Truth. His will be the dominion the day the trumpet will be blown. He knows the Unseen as well as that which is open. For He is the Wise, well-acquainted (with all things). (Al-An'am 6:71–73, Koran)

﴿ وَهَٰذَا كِتَٰبٌ أَنزَلْنَٰهُ مُبَارَكٌ مُّصَدِّقُ ٱلَّذِى بَيْنَ يَدَيْهِ وَلِتُنذِرَ أُمَّ ٱلْقُرَىٰ وَمَنْ حَوْلَهَا ۚ وَٱلَّذِينَ يُؤْمِنُونَ بِٱلْءَاخِرَةِ يُؤْمِنُونَ بِهِۦ ۖ وَهُمْ عَلَىٰ
صَلَاتِهِمْ يُحَافِظُونَ ﴿٩٢﴾ ﴾

And this is a Book which We have sent down, bringing blessings, and confirming (the revelations) which came before it: that you may warn the Mother of

Cities and all around her. Those who believe in the Hereafter believe in this (Book), and they are constant in guarding their Prayers. (Al-An'am 6:92, Koran)

﴿ قُلْ إِنَّنِي هَدَىٰنِي رَبِّيٓ إِلَىٰ صِرَٰطٍ مُّسْتَقِيمٍ دِينًا قِيَمًا مِّلَّةَ إِبْرَٰهِيمَ حَنِيفًاۚ وَمَا كَانَ مِنَ ٱلْمُشْرِكِينَ ﴿١٦١﴾ ﴾

Say: "Verily, my Lord hath guided me to a Way that is straight, a religion of right, the Path (trod) by Abraham the true in faith, and he (certainly) joined not gods with Allah."

﴿ قُلْ إِنَّ صَلَاتِي وَنُسُكِي وَمَحْيَايَ وَمَمَاتِي لِلَّهِ رَبِّ ٱلْعَٰلَمِينَ ﴿١٦٢﴾ ﴾

Say: "Truly, my prayer and my service of sacrifice, my life and my death, are (all) for Allah, the Cherisher of the Worlds." (Al-An'am 6:161–62, Koran)

90: Al-A'raf: 7

﴿ وَٱلَّذِينَ يُمَسِّكُونَ بِٱلْكِتَٰبِ وَأَقَامُوا۟ ٱلصَّلَوٰةَ إِنَّا لَا نُضِيعُ أَجْرَ ٱلْمُصْلِحِينَ ﴿١٧٠﴾ ﴾

As to those who hold fast by the Book and establish regular Prayer, never shall We suffer the reward of the righteous to perish. (Al-A'raf 7: 170, Koran)

Medina Suras

92: Al-Baqarah: 2: Addressed to Muslims

Alif Lam Mim.

﴿ ذَٰلِكَ ٱلْكِتَٰبُ لَا رَيْبَ ۛ فِيهِ ۛ هُدًى لِّلْمُتَّقِينَ ٢ ﴾

This is the book; in it is guidance, sure,
without doubt, to those who fear Allah;

﴿ ٱلَّذِينَ يُؤْمِنُونَ بِٱلْغَيْبِ وَيُقِيمُونَ ٱلصَّلَوٰةَ وَمِمَّا رَزَقْنَٰهُمْ يُنفِقُونَ ٣ ﴾

Who believe in the Unseen, are steadfast in prayer,
and spend out of what We have provided for them.

﴿ وَٱلَّذِينَ يُؤْمِنُونَ بِمَآ أُنزِلَ إِلَيْكَ وَمَآ أُنزِلَ مِن قَبْلِكَ وَبِٱلْءَاخِرَةِ هُمْ يُوقِنُونَ ٤ ﴾

And who believe in the Revelation sent to
thee, and sent before thy time, and (in their
hearts) have the assurance of the Hereafter.

﴿ أُو۟لَٰٓئِكَ عَلَىٰ هُدًى مِّن رَّبِّهِمْ ۖ وَأُو۟لَٰٓئِكَ هُمُ ٱلْمُفْلِحُونَ ٥ ﴾

They are on (true guidance), from their Lord, and it
is these who will prosper. (Al-Baqarah 2:1–5, Koran)

Addressed to the Children of Israel

﴿ وَلَا تَلْبِسُوا۟ ٱلْحَقَّ بِٱلْبَٰطِلِ وَتَكْتُمُوا۟ ٱلْحَقَّ وَأَنتُمْ تَعْلَمُونَ ٤٢ ﴾

And cover not Truth with falsehood, nor conceal the Truth when ye know (what it is).

﴿ وَأَقِيمُوا۟ ٱلصَّلَوٰةَ وَءَاتُوا۟ ٱلزَّكَوٰةَ وَٱرْكَعُوا۟ مَعَ ٱلرَّٰكِعِينَ ٤٣ ﴾

And be steadfast in prayer; practice regular charity; and bow down your heads with those who bow down (in worship).

﴿ ۞ أَتَأْمُرُونَ ٱلنَّاسَ بِٱلْبِرِّ وَتَنسَوْنَ أَنفُسَكُمْ وَأَنتُمْ تَتْلُونَ ٱلْكِتَٰبَ ۚ أَفَلَا تَعْقِلُونَ ٤٤ ﴾

Do ye enjoin right conduct on the people and forget (to practice it) yourselves. And yet you study the Scripture? Will ye not understand?

﴿ وَٱسْتَعِينُوا۟ بِٱلصَّبْرِ وَٱلصَّلَوٰةِ ۚ وَإِنَّهَا لَكَبِيرَةٌ إِلَّا عَلَى ٱلْخَٰشِعِينَ ٤٥ ﴾

Nay, seek (Allah's) help with patient perseverance and prayer: it is indeed hard, except to those who bring a lowly spirit,

﴿ ٱلَّذِينَ يَظُنُّونَ أَنَّهُم مُّلَٰقُوا۟ رَبِّهِمْ وَأَنَّهُمْ إِلَيْهِ رَٰجِعُونَ ٤٦ ﴾

Who bear in mind the certainty that they are to meet their Lord, and that they are to return to Him. (Al-Baqarah 2:42–46, Koran)

﴿ وَإِذْ أَخَذْنَا مِيثَٰقَ بَنِىٓ إِسْرَٰٓءِيلَ لَا تَعْبُدُونَ إِلَّا ٱللَّهَ وَبِٱلْوَٰلِدَيْنِ إِحْسَانًا وَذِى ٱلْقُرْبَىٰ وَٱلْيَتَٰمَىٰ وَٱلْمَسَٰكِينِ وَقُولُوا۟ لِلنَّاسِ حُسْنًا
وَأَقِيمُوا۟ ٱلصَّلَوٰةَ وَءَاتُوا۟ ٱلزَّكَوٰةَ ثُمَّ تَوَلَّيْتُمْ إِلَّا قَلِيلًا مِّنكُمْ وَأَنتُم مُّعْرِضُونَ ﴿٨٣﴾ ﴾

And remember We took a Covenant from the Children of Israel (to this effect): worship none but Allah; treat with kindness your parents and kindred, and orphans and those in need; speak fair to the people; be steadfast in prayer; And practice regular charity. Then did ye turn back, except a few among you, and ye backslide (even now).

﴿ وَإِذْ أَخَذْنَا مِيثَٰقَكُمْ لَا تَسْفِكُونَ دِمَآءَكُمْ وَلَا تُخْرِجُونَ أَنفُسَكُم مِّن دِيَٰرِكُمْ ثُمَّ أَقْرَرْتُمْ وَأَنتُمْ تَشْهَدُونَ ﴿٨٤﴾ ﴾

And remember We took your Covenant (to this effect): shed no blood amongst you, nor turn out your own people from your homes: and this ye solemnly ratified, and to this ye can bear witness.

﴿ ثُمَّ أَنتُمْ هَٰٓؤُلَآءِ تَقْتُلُونَ أَنفُسَكُمْ وَتُخْرِجُونَ فَرِيقًا مِّنكُم مِّن دِيَٰرِهِمْ تَظَٰهَرُونَ عَلَيْهِم بِٱلْإِثْمِ وَٱلْعُدْوَٰنِ وَإِن يَأْتُوكُمْ أُسَٰرَىٰ
تُفَٰدُوهُمْ وَهُوَ مُحَرَّمٌ عَلَيْكُمْ إِخْرَاجُهُمْ ۚ أَفَتُؤْمِنُونَ بِبَعْضِ ٱلْكِتَٰبِ وَتَكْفُرُونَ بِبَعْضٍ ۚ فَمَا جَزَآءُ مَن يَفْعَلُ ذَٰلِكَ مِنكُمْ إِلَّا خِزْىٌ فِى
ٱلْحَيَوٰةِ ٱلدُّنْيَا ۖ وَيَوْمَ ٱلْقِيَٰمَةِ يُرَدُّونَ إِلَىٰٓ أَشَدِّ ٱلْعَذَابِ ۗ وَمَا ٱللَّهُ بِغَٰفِلٍ عَمَّا تَعْمَلُونَ ﴿٨٥﴾ ﴾

After this it is you, the same people, who slay among yourselves, and banish a party of you from their homes; assist (their enemies) against them, in guilt and transgression; and if they come to you as captives, you ransom them, though it was not lawful for you to banish them. Then is it only a part of the Book that you believe in, and do you reject the rest?

But what is the reward for those among you who behave like this but disgrace in this life? And on the Day of Judgment, they shall be consigned to the most grievous penalty. For Allah is not unmindful of what you do. (Al-Baqarah 2:83–85, Koran)

Addressed to Muslims.

﴿ وَدَّ كَثِيرٌ مِّنْ أَهْلِ ٱلْكِتَٰبِ لَوْ يَرُدُّونَكُم مِّنۢ بَعْدِ إِيمَٰنِكُمْ كُفَّارًا حَسَدًا مِّنْ عِندِ أَنفُسِهِم مِّنۢ بَعْدِ مَا تَبَيَّنَ لَهُمُ ٱلْحَقُّ ۖ فَٱعْفُوا۟
وَٱصْفَحُوا۟ حَتَّىٰ يَأْتِىَ ٱللَّهُ بِأَمْرِهِۦٓ ۗ إِنَّ ٱللَّهَ عَلَىٰ كُلِّ شَىْءٍ قَدِيرٌ ﴿١٠٩﴾ ﴾

Quite a number of the People of the Book wish they could turn you (people) back to infidelity after you have believed. From selfish envy, after the Truth hath become manifest to them: but forgive and overlook, till Allah accomplishes His purpose: for Allah has power over all things.

﴿ وَأَقِيمُوا۟ ٱلصَّلَوٰةَ وَءَاتُوا۟ ٱلزَّكَوٰةَ ۚ وَمَا تُقَدِّمُوا۟ لِأَنفُسِكُم مِّنْ خَيْرٍ تَجِدُوهُ عِندَ ٱللَّهِ ۗ إِنَّ ٱللَّهَ بِمَا تَعْمَلُونَ بَصِيرٌ ﴿١١٠﴾ ﴾

And be steadfast in prayer and regular in charity: and whatever good you send forth for your souls before you, ye shall find it with Allah: for Allah sees well all that you do.

﴿ وَقَالُوا۟ لَن يَدْخُلَ ٱلْجَنَّةَ إِلَّا مَن كَانَ هُودًا أَوْ نَصَٰرَىٰ ۗ تِلْكَ أَمَانِيُّهُمْ ۗ قُلْ هَاتُوا۟ بُرْهَٰنَكُمْ إِن كُنتُمْ صَٰدِقِينَ ﴿١١١﴾ ﴾

And they say: "None shall enter Paradise unless he be a Jew or a Christian." Those are their (vain) desires. Say: "Produce your proof if you are truthful."

﴿ بَلَىٰ مَنْ أَسْلَمَ وَجْهَهُۥ لِلَّهِ وَهُوَ مُحْسِنٌ فَلَهُۥٓ أَجْرُهُۥ عِندَ رَبِّهِۦ وَلَا خَوْفٌ عَلَيْهِمْ وَلَا هُمْ يَحْزَنُونَ ١١٢ ﴾

Nay, whoever submits his whole self to Allah
and is a doer of good he will get his reward
with his Lord; on such shall be no fear, nor shall
they grieve. (Al-Baqarah 2:109–12, Koran)

﴿ يَـٰٓأَيُّهَا ٱلَّذِينَ ءَامَنُوا۟ ٱسْتَعِينُوا۟ بِٱلصَّبْرِ وَٱلصَّلَوٰةِ ۚ إِنَّ ٱللَّهَ مَعَ ٱلصَّـٰبِرِينَ ١٥٣ ﴾

O you who believe! Seek help with patient
Perseverance and Prayer: for Allah is with those who
patiently persevere. (Al-Baqarah 2:153, Koran)

﴿ ۞ لَّيْسَ ٱلْبِرَّ أَن تُوَلُّوا۟ وُجُوهَكُمْ قِبَلَ ٱلْمَشْرِقِ وَٱلْمَغْرِبِ وَلَـٰكِنَّ ٱلْبِرَّ مَنْ ءَامَنَ بِٱللَّهِ وَٱلْيَوْمِ ٱلْـَٔاخِرِ وَٱلْمَلَـٰٓئِكَةِ وَٱلْكِتَـٰبِ وَٱلنَّبِيِّـۧنَ
وَءَاتَى ٱلْمَالَ عَلَىٰ حُبِّهِۦ ذَوِى ٱلْقُرْبَىٰ وَٱلْيَتَـٰمَىٰ وَٱلْمَسَـٰكِينَ وَٱبْنَ ٱلسَّبِيلِ وَٱلسَّآئِلِينَ وَفِى ٱلرِّقَابِ وَأَقَامَ ٱلصَّلَوٰةَ وَءَاتَى ٱلزَّكَوٰةَ وَٱلْمُوفُونَ
بِعَهْدِهِمْ إِذَا عَـٰهَدُوا۟ ۖ وَٱلصَّـٰبِرِينَ فِى ٱلْبَأْسَآءِ وَٱلضَّرَّآءِ وَحِينَ ٱلْبَأْسِ ۗ أُو۟لَـٰٓئِكَ ٱلَّذِينَ صَدَقُوا۟ ۖ وَأُو۟لَـٰٓئِكَ هُمُ ٱلْمُتَّقُونَ ١٧٧ ﴾

It is not righteousness that ye turn your faces towards East or West; but it is righteousness to believe in Allah and the Last Day, and the Angels, and the Book, and the Messengers; to spend of your substance, out of love for Him, for your kin, for orphans, for the needy, for the wayfarer, for those who ask, and for the ransom of slaves; to be steadfast in prayer, and practice regular charity, to fulfill the contracts which you have made; and to be firm and patient, in pain (or suffering) and adversity, and throughout periods of panic. Such are the people of truth, the God-fearing. (Al-Baqarah 2:177, Koran)

﴿ حَٰفِظُواْ عَلَى ٱلصَّلَوَٰتِ وَٱلصَّلَوٰةِ ٱلۡوُسۡطَىٰ وَقُومُواْ لِلَّهِ قَٰنِتِينَ ٢٣٨ ﴾

Guard strictly your (habit of) prayers,
especially the Middle Prayer; and stand before
Allah in a devout (frame of mind).

﴿ فَإِنۡ خِفۡتُمۡ فَرِجَالًا أَوۡ رُكۡبَانٗاۖ فَإِذَآ أَمِنتُمۡ فَٱذۡكُرُواْ ٱللَّهَ كَمَا عَلَّمَكُم مَّا لَمۡ تَكُونُواْ تَعۡلَمُونَ ٢٣٩ ﴾

If ye fear (an enemy), pray on foot, or riding,
(as may be most convenient), but when you
are in security, celebrate Allah's praises in the
manner He has taught you, which ye knew not
(before). (Al-Baqarah 2:238–39, Koran)

﴿ إِنَّ ٱلَّذِينَ ءَامَنُواْ وَعَمِلُواْ ٱلصَّٰلِحَٰتِ وَأَقَامُواْ ٱلصَّلَوٰةَ وَءَاتَوُاْ ٱلزَّكَوٰةَ لَهُمۡ أَجۡرُهُمۡ عِندَ رَبِّهِمۡ وَلَا خَوۡفٌ عَلَيۡهِمۡ وَلَا هُمۡ
يَحۡزَنُونَ ٢٧٧ ﴾

Those who believe, and do deeds of righteousness,
and establish regular prayers and regular charity, will
have their reward with their Lord: on them shall be no
fear, nor shall they grieve. (Al-Baqarah 2:277, Koran)

94: An-Nisa: 4: Commandment of the Covenant of Allah with the Believers

﴿ يَٰٓأَيُّهَا ٱلَّذِينَ ءَامَنُوا۟ لَا تَقْرَبُوا۟ ٱلصَّلَوٰةَ وَأَنتُمْ سُكَٰرَىٰ حَتَّىٰ تَعْلَمُوا۟ مَا تَقُولُونَ وَلَا جُنُبًا إِلَّا عَابِرِى سَبِيلٍ حَتَّىٰ تَغْتَسِلُوا۟ ۚ وَإِن كُنتُم
مَّرْضَىٰٓ أَوْ عَلَىٰ سَفَرٍ أَوْ جَآءَ أَحَدٌ مِّنكُم مِّنَ ٱلْغَآئِطِ أَوْ لَٰمَسْتُمُ ٱلنِّسَآءَ فَلَمْ تَجِدُوا۟ مَآءً فَتَيَمَّمُوا۟ صَعِيدًا طَيِّبًا فَٱمْسَحُوا۟ بِوُجُوهِكُمْ وَأَيْدِيكُمْ ۗ إِنَّ
ٱللَّهَ كَانَ عَفُوًّا غَفُورًا ﴿٤٣﴾ ﴾

O you who believe!

Approach not prayers with a mind befogged, until ye can understand all that you say, nor in a state of ceremonial impurity (except when travelling on the road), until after washing your whole body. If ye are ill, or on a journey, or one of you cometh from offices of nature, or you have been in contact with women, and you find no water, then take for yourselves clean sand or earth, and rub therewith your faces and hands. For Allah doth blot out sins and forgive again and again. (An-Nisa 4:43, Koran)

Addressed to the Blessed Nabi and Muslims

﴿ أَلَمْ تَرَ إِلَى ٱلَّذِينَ قِيلَ لَهُمْ كُفُّوٓا۟ أَيْدِيَكُمْ وَأَقِيمُوا۟ ٱلصَّلَوٰةَ وَءَاتُوا۟ ٱلزَّكَوٰةَ فَلَمَّا كُتِبَ عَلَيْهِمُ ٱلْقِتَالُ إِذَا فَرِيقٌ مِّنْهُمْ يَخْشَوْنَ ٱلنَّاسَ كَخَشْيَةِ
ٱللَّهِ أَوْ أَشَدَّ خَشْيَةً ۚ وَقَالُوا۟ رَبَّنَا لِمَ كَتَبْتَ عَلَيْنَا ٱلْقِتَالَ لَوْلَآ أَخَّرْتَنَآ إِلَىٰٓ أَجَلٍ قَرِيبٍ ۗ قُلْ مَتَٰعُ ٱلدُّنْيَا قَلِيلٌ وَٱلْءَاخِرَةُ خَيْرٌ لِّمَنِ ٱتَّقَىٰ وَلَا تُظْلَمُونَ
فَتِيلًا ﴿٧٧﴾ ﴾

Hast thou not turned thy vision to those who were told to hold back their hands (from fight) but establish regular prayers and spend in regular Charity? When (at length) the order for fighting was issued to them, behold! a section of them feared men as - or even more than - they should have feared Allah; they said: "Our Lord! why hast Thou ordered us to fight? Wouldst Thou not grant us respite to our (natural) term, near (enough)?" Say: "Short is the enjoyment of this world: the Hereafter is the best for those who do right; never will you be dealt with unjustly in the very least! (An-Nisa 4:77, Koran)

﴿ وَإِذَا ضَرَبْتُمْ فِي ٱلْأَرْضِ فَلَيْسَ عَلَيْكُمْ جُنَاحٌ أَن تَقْصُرُوا۟ مِنَ ٱلصَّلَوٰةِ إِنْ خِفْتُمْ أَن يَفْتِنَكُمُ ٱلَّذِينَ كَفَرُوٓا۟ ۚ إِنَّ ٱلْكَٰفِرِينَ كَانُوا۟ لَكُمْ عَدُوًّا
مُّبِينًا ﴿١٠١﴾

When you travel through the earth, there is no blame on you if ye shorten your prayers, for fear the Unbelievers may attack you: for the Unbelievers are to you open enemies.

﴿ وَإِذَا كُنتَ فِيهِمْ فَأَقَمْتَ لَهُمُ ٱلصَّلَوٰةَ فَلْتَقُمْ طَآئِفَةٌ مِّنْهُم مَّعَكَ وَلْيَأْخُذُوٓا۟ أَسْلِحَتَهُمْ فَإِذَا سَجَدُوا۟ فَلْيَكُونُوا۟ مِن وَرَآئِكُمْ وَلْتَأْتِ
طَآئِفَةٌ أُخْرَىٰ لَمْ يُصَلُّوا۟ فَلْيُصَلُّوا۟ مَعَكَ وَلْيَأْخُذُوا۟ حِذْرَهُمْ وَأَسْلِحَتَهُمْ ۗ وَدَّ ٱلَّذِينَ كَفَرُوا۟ لَوْ تَغْفُلُونَ عَنْ أَسْلِحَتِكُمْ وَأَمْتِعَتِكُمْ فَيَمِيلُونَ
عَلَيْكُم مَّيْلَةً وَٰحِدَةً ۚ وَلَا جُنَاحَ عَلَيْكُمْ إِن كَانَ بِكُمْ أَذًى مِّن مَّطَرٍ أَوْ كُنتُم مَّرْضَىٰٓ أَن تَضَعُوٓا۟ أَسْلِحَتَكُمْ ۖ وَخُذُوا۟ حِذْرَكُمْ ۗ إِنَّ ٱللَّهَ أَعَدَّ
لِلْكَٰفِرِينَ عَذَابًا مُّهِينًا ﴿١٠٢﴾ ﴾

When you (O Messenger) are with them, and stand to lead them in prayer, let one party of them stand up (in prayer) with you, taking their arms with them; when they finish their prostrations, let them take their positions in the rear. And let the other party come up, which hath not yet prayed, and let them pray with you, taking all precautions, and bearing arms: the Unbelievers wish, if ye were negligent of your arms and your baggage, to assault you in a single rush. But there is no blame on you if you put away your arms because of the inconvenience of rain or because ye are ill; but take (every) precaution for yourselves. For the Unbelievers Allah hath prepared a humiliating punishment.

﴿ فَإِذَا قَضَيْتُمُ ٱلصَّلَوٰةَ فَٱذْكُرُوا۟ ٱللَّهَ قِيَـٰمًا وَقُعُودًا وَعَلَىٰ جُنُوبِكُمْ ۚ فَإِذَا ٱطْمَأْنَنتُمْ فَأَقِيمُوا۟ ٱلصَّلَوٰةَ ۚ إِنَّ ٱلصَّلَوٰةَ كَانَتْ عَلَى
ٱلْمُؤْمِنِينَ كِتَـٰبًا مَّوْقُوتًا ﴿١٠٣﴾ ﴾

When you pass (congregational) prayers, celebrate Allah's praises, standing, sitting down, or lying down on your sides; but when ye are free from danger, set up regular prayers: for such prayers are enjoined on Believers at stated times. (An-Nisa 4:101–3, Koran)

Reference to the Hypocrites

﴿ إِنَّ ٱلْمُنَـٰفِقِينَ يُخَـٰدِعُونَ ٱللَّهَ وَهُوَ خَـٰدِعُهُمْ وَإِذَا قَامُوٓا۟ إِلَى ٱلصَّلَوٰةِ قَامُوا۟ كُسَالَىٰ يُرَآءُونَ ٱلنَّاسَ وَلَا يَذْكُرُونَ ٱللَّهَ إِلَّا قَلِيلًا ﴿١٤٢﴾ ﴾

The Hypocrites, they think they are over-reaching Allah, but He will over-reach them: when they stand up to prayer, they stand without earnestness, to be seen of men, but little do they hold Allah in remembrance.

﴿ مُّذَبْذَبِينَ بَيْنَ ذَٰلِكَ لَآ إِلَىٰ هَـٰٓؤُلَآءِ وَلَآ إِلَىٰ هَـٰٓؤُلَآءِ ۚ وَمَن يُضْلِلِ ٱللَّهُ فَلَن تَجِدَ لَهُۥ سَبِيلًا ﴿١٤٣﴾ ﴾

(They are) distracted in mind even in the midst of it, being (sincerely) for neither one group nor for another. Whom Allah leaves straying, never wilt thou find for him the Way. (An-Nisa 4:142–43, Koran)

Reference to the Jews

﴿ فَبِظُلْمٍ مِّنَ ٱلَّذِينَ هَادُوا۟ حَرَّمْنَا عَلَيْهِمْ طَيِّبَٰتٍ أُحِلَّتْ لَهُمْ وَبِصَدِّهِمْ عَن سَبِيلِ ٱللَّهِ كَثِيرًا ﴿١٦٠﴾ ﴾

For the iniquity of the Jews We made unlawful for them certain (foods) good and wholesome which had been lawful for them; in that they hindered many from Allah's way.

﴿ وَأَخْذِهِمُ ٱلرِّبَوٰا۟ وَقَدْ نُهُوا۟ عَنْهُ وَأَكْلِهِمْ أَمْوَٰلَ ٱلنَّاسِ بِٱلْبَٰطِلِ ۚ وَأَعْتَدْنَا لِلْكَٰفِرِينَ مِنْهُمْ عَذَابًا أَلِيمًا ﴿١٦١﴾ ﴾

That they took usury, though they were forbidden; and that they devoured men's substance wrongfully; We have prepared for those among them who reject Faith a grievous punishment.

﴿ لَّٰكِنِ ٱلرَّٰسِخُونَ فِى ٱلْعِلْمِ مِنْهُمْ وَٱلْمُؤْمِنُونَ يُؤْمِنُونَ بِمَآ أُنزِلَ إِلَيْكَ وَمَآ أُنزِلَ مِن قَبْلِكَ ۚ وَٱلْمُقِيمِينَ ٱلصَّلَوٰةَ ۚ وَٱلْمُؤْتُونَ ٱلزَّكَوٰةَ
وَٱلْمُؤْمِنُونَ بِٱللَّهِ وَٱلْيَوْمِ ٱلْءَاخِرِ أُو۟لَٰٓئِكَ سَنُؤْتِيهِمْ أَجْرًا عَظِيمًا ﴿١٦٢﴾ ﴾

But those among them who are well-grounded in knowledge, and the Believers, believe in what hath been revealed to thee and what was revealed before thee; and (especially) those who establish regular prayer and practice regular charity and believe in Allah and in the Last Day: to them shall We soon give a great reward. (An-Nisa 4:160–62, Koran)

95: Al-Ma'idah: 5: Commandment of the Covenant of Allah with the Believers

﴿ يَٰٓأَيُّهَا ٱلَّذِينَ ءَامَنُوٓاْ إِذَا قُمۡتُمۡ إِلَى ٱلصَّلَوٰةِ فَٱغۡسِلُواْ وُجُوهَكُمۡ وَأَيۡدِيَكُمۡ إِلَى ٱلۡمَرَافِقِ وَٱمۡسَحُواْ بِرُءُوسِكُمۡ وَأَرۡجُلَكُمۡ إِلَى ٱلۡكَعۡبَيۡنِۚ
وَإِن كُنتُمۡ جُنُبٗا فَٱطَّهَّرُواْۚ وَإِن كُنتُم مَّرۡضَىٰٓ أَوۡ عَلَىٰ سَفَرٍ أَوۡ جَآءَ أَحَدٞ مِّنكُم مِّنَ ٱلۡغَآئِطِ أَوۡ لَٰمَسۡتُمُ ٱلنِّسَآءَ فَلَمۡ تَجِدُواْ مَآءٗ فَتَيَمَّمُواْ صَعِيدٗا
طَيِّبٗا فَٱمۡسَحُواْ بِوُجُوهِكُمۡ وَأَيۡدِيكُم مِّنۡهُۚ مَا يُرِيدُ ٱللَّهُ لِيَجۡعَلَ عَلَيۡكُم مِّنۡ حَرَجٖ وَلَٰكِن يُرِيدُ لِيُطَهِّرَكُمۡ وَلِيُتِمَّ نِعۡمَتَهُۥ عَلَيۡكُمۡ لَعَلَّكُمۡ
تَشۡكُرُونَ ﴿٦﴾ ﴾

O you who believe!

When ye prepare for prayer, wash your faces, and your hands (and arms) to the elbows; rub your heads (with water); and (wash) your feet to the ankles. If you are in a state of ceremonial impurity, bathe your whole body. But if ye are ill, or on a journey, or one of you comes from offices of nature, or you have been in contact with women, and you find no water, then take for yourselves clean sand or earth, and rub therewith your faces and hands. Allah does not wish to place you in a difficulty, but to make you clean, and to complete His favor to you, that ye may be grateful. (Al-Ma'idah 5:6, Koran)

Reference to Children of Israel and Christians

﴿ ۞ وَلَقَدْ أَخَذَ ٱللَّهُ مِيثَٰقَ بَنِىٓ إِسْرَٰٓءِيلَ وَبَعَثْنَا مِنْهُمُ ٱثْنَىْ عَشَرَ نَقِيبًا ۖ وَقَالَ ٱللَّهُ إِنِّى مَعَكُمْ ۖ لَئِنْ أَقَمْتُمُ ٱلصَّلَوٰةَ وَءَاتَيْتُمُ ٱلزَّكَوٰةَ
وَءَامَنتُم بِرُسُلِى وَعَزَّرْتُمُوهُمْ وَأَقْرَضْتُمُ ٱللَّهَ قَرْضًا حَسَنًا لَّأُكَفِّرَنَّ عَنكُمْ سَيِّـَٔاتِكُمْ وَلَأُدْخِلَنَّكُمْ جَنَّٰتٍ تَجْرِى مِن تَحْتِهَا ٱلْأَنْهَٰرُ ۚ فَمَن
كَفَرَ بَعْدَ ذَٰلِكَ مِنكُمْ فَقَدْ ضَلَّ سَوَآءَ ٱلسَّبِيلِ ﴿١٢﴾ ﴾

Allah did aforetime take a Covenant, from the children of Israel, and We appointed twelve captains among them. And Allah said: "I am with you: if ye (but) establish regular Prayers, practice regular Charity, believe in My Messengers, honor and assist them, and loan to Allah a beautiful loan, verily I will wipe out from you your evils, and admit you to Gardens with rivers flowing beneath; but if any of you, after this, resisted faith, he has truly wandered from the path of rectitude.

﴿ فَبِمَا نَقْضِهِم مِّيثَٰقَهُمْ لَعَنَّٰهُمْ وَجَعَلْنَا قُلُوبَهُمْ قَٰسِيَةً ۖ يُحَرِّفُونَ ٱلْكَلِمَ عَن مَّوَاضِعِهِۦ ۙ وَنَسُوا۟ حَظًّا مِّمَّا ذُكِّرُوا۟ بِهِۦ ۚ وَلَا تَزَالُ
تَطَّلِعُ عَلَىٰ خَآئِنَةٍ مِّنْهُمْ إِلَّا قَلِيلًا مِّنْهُمْ ۖ فَٱعْفُ عَنْهُمْ وَٱصْفَحْ ۚ إِنَّ ٱللَّهَ يُحِبُّ ٱلْمُحْسِنِينَ ﴿١٣﴾ ﴾

But because of the breach of their Covenant, We cursed them, and made their hearts grow hard: they change the words from their (right) places and forget a good part of the Message that was sent to them, nor will you cease to find them, barring a few, ever bent on (new) deceits: but forgive them, and overlook (their misdeeds): for Allah loves those who are kind.

﴿ وَمِنَ ٱلَّذِينَ قَالُوٓاْ إِنَّا نَصَٰرَىٰٓ أَخَذۡنَا مِيثَٰقَهُمۡ فَنَسُواْ حَظّٗا مِّمَّا ذُكِّرُواْ بِهِۦ فَأَغۡرَيۡنَا بَيۡنَهُمُ ٱلۡعَدَاوَةَ وَٱلۡبَغۡضَآءَ إِلَىٰ يَوۡمِ
ٱلۡقِيَٰمَةِۚ وَسَوۡفَ يُنَبِّئُهُمُ ٱللَّهُ بِمَا كَانُواْ يَصۡنَعُونَ ١٤ ﴾

From those, too, who call themselves Christians, We did take a Covenant, but they forgot a good part of the Message that was sent them: so, We estranged them, with enmity and hatred between the one and the other, to the Day of Judgment. And soon will Allah show them what it is they have done.

﴿ يَٰٓأَهۡلَ ٱلۡكِتَٰبِ قَدۡ جَآءَكُمۡ رَسُولُنَا يُبَيِّنُ لَكُمۡ كَثِيرٗا مِّمَّا كُنتُمۡ تُخۡفُونَ مِنَ ٱلۡكِتَٰبِ وَيَعۡفُواْ عَن كَثِيرٖۚ قَدۡ
جَآءَكُم مِّنَ ٱللَّهِ نُورٞ وَكِتَٰبٞ مُّبِينٞ ١٥ ﴾

O People of the Book! there has come to you Our Messenger, revealing to you much that ye used to hide in the Book, and passing over much (that is now unnecessary): There hath come to you from Allah a (new) light and a perspicuous Book.

﴿ يَهۡدِي بِهِ ٱللَّهُ مَنِ ٱتَّبَعَ رِضۡوَٰنَهُۥ سُبُلَ ٱلسَّلَٰمِ وَيُخۡرِجُهُم مِّنَ ٱلظُّلُمَٰتِ إِلَى ٱلنُّورِ بِإِذۡنِهِۦ وَيَهۡدِيهِمۡ إِلَىٰ صِرَٰطٖ مُّسۡتَقِيمٖ ١٦ ﴾

Wherewith Allah guides all who seek His good pleasure to ways of peace and safety, and leads them out of darkness, by His Will, unto the light, guides them to a Path that is Straight. (Al-Ma'idah 5:12–16, Koran)

Commandment of the Covenant
of Allah with the Believers

﴿ إِنَّمَا وَلِيُّكُمُ ٱللَّهُ وَرَسُولُهُۥ وَٱلَّذِينَ ءَامَنُوا۟ ٱلَّذِينَ يُقِيمُونَ ٱلصَّلَوٰةَ وَيُؤْتُونَ ٱلزَّكَوٰةَ وَهُمْ رَٰكِعُونَ ٥٥ ﴾

Your (real) friends are (no less than) Allah, His Messenger, and the (Fellowship of) Believers, those who establish regular prayers and regular charity, and they bow down humbly (in worship).

﴿ وَمَن يَتَوَلَّ ٱللَّهَ وَرَسُولَهُۥ وَٱلَّذِينَ ءَامَنُوا۟ فَإِنَّ حِزْبَ ٱللَّهِ هُمُ ٱلْغَٰلِبُونَ ٥٦ ﴾

As to those who turn (for friendship) to Allah, His Messenger, and the (Fellowship of) Believers, it is the Fellowship of Allah that must certainly triumph.

﴿ يَٰٓأَيُّهَا ٱلَّذِينَ ءَامَنُوا۟ لَا تَتَّخِذُوا۟ ٱلَّذِينَ ٱتَّخَذُوا۟ دِينَكُمْ هُزُوًا وَلَعِبًا مِّنَ ٱلَّذِينَ أُوتُوا۟ ٱلْكِتَٰبَ مِن قَبْلِكُمْ وَٱلْكُفَّارَ أَوْلِيَآءَ ۚ وَٱتَّقُوا۟ ٱللَّهَ
إِن كُنتُم مُّؤْمِنِينَ ٥٧ ﴾

O you who believe! Take not for friends and protectors those who take your religion for a mockery or sport, whether among those who received the Scripture before you, or among those who reject Faith; but fear you Allah if you have Faith (indeed).

﴿ وَإِذَا نَادَيْتُمْ إِلَى ٱلصَّلَوٰةِ ٱتَّخَذُوهَا هُزُوًا وَلَعِبًا ۚ ذَٰلِكَ بِأَنَّهُمْ قَوْمٌ لَّا يَعْقِلُونَ ٥٨ ﴾

When you proclaim your call to prayer, they take it (but) as mockery and sport; that is because they are a people without understanding. (Al-Ma'idah 5:55–58, Koran)

Commandment of the Covenant of Allah with the Believers

﴿ يَٰٓأَيُّهَا ٱلَّذِينَ ءَامَنُوٓاْ إِنَّمَا ٱلۡخَمۡرُ وَٱلۡمَيۡسِرُ وَٱلۡأَنصَابُ وَٱلۡأَزۡلَٰمُ رِجۡسٞ مِّنۡ عَمَلِ ٱلشَّيۡطَٰنِ فَٱجۡتَنِبُوهُ لَعَلَّكُمۡ تُفۡلِحُونَ ٩٠ ﴾

O you who believe! intoxicants and gambling, (dedication of) stones, and (divination by) arrows, are an abomination of Satan's handiwork: eschew such (abomination), that you may prosper.

﴿ إِنَّمَا يُرِيدُ ٱلشَّيۡطَٰنُ أَن يُوقِعَ بَيۡنَكُمُ ٱلۡعَدَٰوَةَ وَٱلۡبَغۡضَآءَ فِي ٱلۡخَمۡرِ وَٱلۡمَيۡسِرِ وَيَصُدَّكُمۡ عَن ذِكۡرِ ٱللَّهِ وَعَنِ ٱلصَّلَوٰةِۖ فَهَلۡ أَنتُم مُّنتَهُونَ ٩١
﴾

Satan's plan is to excite enmity and hatred between you, with intoxicants and gambling, and hinder you from the remembrance of Allah, and from prayer: will you not then abstain?

﴿ وَأَطِيعُواْ ٱللَّهَ وَأَطِيعُواْ ٱلرَّسُولَ وَٱحۡذَرُواْۚ فَإِن تَوَلَّيۡتُمۡ فَٱعۡلَمُوٓاْ أَنَّمَا عَلَىٰ رَسُولِنَا ٱلۡبَلَٰغُ ٱلۡمُبِينُ ٩٢ ﴾

Obey Allah, and obey the Messenger, and beware (of evil): if ye do turn back, know you that it is Our Messenger's duty to proclaim (the Message) in the clearest manner. (Al-Ma'idah 5:90–92, Koran)

96: Al-Bayyinah: 98: Reference to the People of the Book

﴿ لَمْ يَكُنِ ٱلَّذِينَ كَفَرُوا۟ مِنْ أَهْلِ ٱلْكِتَـٰبِ وَٱلْمُشْرِكِينَ مُنفَكِّينَ حَتَّىٰ تَأْتِيَهُمُ ٱلْبَيِّنَةُ ﴿١﴾ ﴾

Those who reject (Truth), among the People of the Book and among the Polytheists, were not going to depart (from their ways) until there should come to them clear Evidence,

﴿ رَسُولٌ مِّنَ ٱللَّهِ يَتْلُوا۟ صُحُفًا مُّطَهَّرَةً ﴿٢﴾ ﴾

A Messenger from Allah, rehearsing scriptures kept pure and holy:

﴿ فِيهَا كُتُبٌ قَيِّمَةٌ ﴿٣﴾ ﴾

Wherein are laws (or decrees) right and straight.

﴿ وَمَا تَفَرَّقَ ٱلَّذِينَ أُوتُوا۟ ٱلْكِتَـٰبَ إِلَّا مِنۢ بَعْدِ مَا جَآءَتْهُمُ ٱلْبَيِّنَةُ ﴿٤﴾ ﴾

Nor did the People of the Book make schisms, until after there came to them Clear Evidence.

﴿ وَمَآ أُمِرُوٓا۟ إِلَّا لِيَعْبُدُوا۟ ٱللَّهَ مُخْلِصِينَ لَهُ ٱلدِّينَ حُنَفَآءَ وَيُقِيمُوا۟ ٱلصَّلَوٰةَ وَيُؤْتُوا۟ ٱلزَّكَوٰةَ ۚ وَذَٰلِكَ دِينُ ٱلْقَيِّمَةِ ﴿٥﴾ ﴾

And they have been commanded no more than this: to worship Allah, offering Him sincere devotion, being True (in faith); to establish

regular Prayer; and to practice regular Charity;
and that is the Religion right and Straight.

﴿ إِنَّ ٱلَّذِينَ كَفَرُوا۟ مِنْ أَهْلِ ٱلْكِتَـٰبِ وَٱلْمُشْرِكِينَ فِى نَارِ جَهَنَّمَ خَـٰلِدِينَ فِيهَآ ۚ أُو۟لَـٰٓئِكَ هُمْ شَرُّ ٱلْبَرِيَّةِ ٦ ﴾

Those who reject (Truth), among the People of the Book and among the Polytheists, will be in Hellfire, to dwell therein (for aye). They are the worst of creatures.

﴿ إِنَّ ٱلَّذِينَ ءَامَنُوا۟ وَعَمِلُوا۟ ٱلصَّـٰلِحَـٰتِ أُو۟لَـٰٓئِكَ هُمْ خَيْرُ ٱلْبَرِيَّةِ ٧ ﴾

Those who have faith and do righteous deeds; They are the best of creatures. (Al-Bayyinah 98:1–7, Koran)

110: An-Nur: 24

﴿ رِجَالٌ لَّا تُلْهِيهِمْ تِجَـٰرَةٌ وَلَا بَيْعٌ عَن ذِكْرِ ٱللَّهِ وَإِقَامِ ٱلصَّلَوٰةِ وَإِيتَآءِ ٱلزَّكَوٰةِ ۙ يَخَافُونَ يَوْمًا تَتَقَلَّبُ فِيهِ ٱلْقُلُوبُ وَٱلْأَبْصَـٰرُ ٣٧

By men whom neither traffic nor merchandise can divert from the Remembrance of Allah, nor from regular Prayer, nor from the practice of regular Charity: their (only) fear is for the Day when hearts and eyes will be transformed (in a world wholly new),

﴿ لِيَجْزِيَهُمُ ٱللَّهُ أَحْسَنَ مَا عَمِلُوا۟ وَيَزِيدَهُم مِّن فَضْلِهِۦ ۗ وَٱللَّهُ يَرْزُقُ مَن يَشَآءُ بِغَيْرِ حِسَابٍ ٣٨ ﴾

That Allah may reward them according to the best of their deeds and add even more for them out of His Grace: for Allah doth provide for those whom He will, without measure.

﴿ وَٱلَّذِينَ كَفَرُوٓا۟ أَعْمَٰلُهُمْ كَسَرَابٍۭ بِقِيعَةٍ يَحْسَبُهُ ٱلظَّمْـَٔانُ مَآءً حَتَّىٰٓ إِذَا جَآءَهُۥ لَمْ يَجِدْهُ شَيْـًٔا وَوَجَدَ ٱللَّهَ عِندَهُۥ فَوَفَّىٰهُ حِسَابَهُۥ ۗ وَٱللَّهُ

سَرِيعُ ٱلْحِسَابِ ﴿٣٩﴾ ﴾

But the Unbelievers, their deeds are like a mirage in sandy deserts, which the man parched with thirst mistakes for water; until when he comes up to it, he finds it to be nothing: but he finds Allah (ever) with him, and Allah will pay him his account: and Allah is swift in taking account.

﴿ أَوْ كَظُلُمَٰتٍ فِى بَحْرٍ لُّجِّىٍّ يَغْشَىٰهُ مَوْجٌ مِّن فَوْقِهِۦ مَوْجٌ مِّن فَوْقِهِۦ سَحَابٌ ۚ ظُلُمَٰتٌۢ بَعْضُهَا فَوْقَ بَعْضٍ إِذَآ أَخْرَجَ يَدَهُۥ لَمْ يَكَدْ يَرَىٰهَا ۗ

وَمَن لَّمْ يَجْعَلِ ٱللَّهُ لَهُۥ نُورًا فَمَا لَهُۥ مِن نُّورٍ ﴿٤٠﴾ ﴾

Or (the Unbelievers' state) is like the depths of darkness in a vast deep ocean, overwhelmed with billow topped by billow, topped by (dark) clouds: depths of darkness, one above another: if a man stretches out his hand, he can hardly see it! For any to whom Allah gives not light, there is no light!

﴿ أَلَمْ تَرَ أَنَّ ٱللَّهَ يُسَبِّحُ لَهُۥ مَن فِى ٱلسَّمَٰوَٰتِ وَٱلْأَرْضِ وَٱلطَّيْرُ صَٰٓفَّٰتٍ ۖ كُلٌّ قَدْ عَلِمَ صَلَاتَهُۥ وَتَسْبِيحَهُۥ ۗ وَٱللَّهُ عَلِيمٌۢ بِمَا يَفْعَلُونَ ﴿٤١﴾

﴾

See you thou not that it is Allah Whose praises all beings in the heavens and on earth do celebrate, and the birds (of the air) with wings outspread? Each one knows its own (mode of) prayer and praise. And Allah knows well all that they do.

﴿ وَلِلَّهِ مُلْكُ ٱلسَّمَٰوَٰتِ وَٱلْأَرْضِ ۖ وَإِلَى ٱللَّهِ ٱلْمَصِيرُ ٤٢ ﴾

Yes, to Allah belongs the dominion of the heavens and the earth; and to Allah is the final goal (of all).

﴿ أَلَمْ تَرَ أَنَّ ٱللَّهَ يُزْجِى سَحَابًا ثُمَّ يُؤَلِّفُ بَيْنَهُۥ ثُمَّ يَجْعَلُهُۥ رُكَامًا فَتَرَى ٱلْوَدْقَ يَخْرُجُ مِنْ خِلَٰلِهِۦ وَيُنَزِّلُ مِنَ ٱلسَّمَآءِ مِن جِبَالٍ فِيهَا مِنۢ بَرَدٍ
فَيُصِيبُ بِهِۦ مَن يَشَآءُ وَيَصْرِفُهُۥ عَن مَّن يَشَآءُ ۖ يَكَادُ سَنَا بَرْقِهِۦ يَذْهَبُ بِٱلْأَبْصَٰرِ ٤٣ ﴾

See you not that Allah makes the clouds move gently, then joins them together, then makes them into a heap? then you will see rain issue forth from their midst. And He sends down from the sky mountain masses (of clouds) wherein is hail: He strikes there with whom He pleases, and He Turns it away from whom He pleases. The vivid flash of His lightning well-nigh blinds the sight.

﴿ يُقَلِّبُ ٱللَّهُ ٱلَّيْلَ وَٱلنَّهَارَ ۚ إِنَّ فِى ذَٰلِكَ لَعِبْرَةً لِّأُو۟لِى ٱلْأَبْصَٰرِ ٤٤ ﴾

It is Allah Who alternates the Night and the Day: verily in these things is an instructive example for those who have vision!

﴿ وَٱللَّهُ خَلَقَ كُلَّ دَآبَّةٍ مِّن مَّآءٍ ۖ فَمِنْهُم مَّن يَمْشِى عَلَىٰ بَطْنِهِۦ وَمِنْهُم مَّن يَمْشِى عَلَىٰ رِجْلَيْنِ وَمِنْهُم مَّن يَمْشِى عَلَىٰٓ أَرْبَعٍ ۚ يَخْلُقُ ٱللَّهُ مَا
يَشَآءُ ۚ إِنَّ ٱللَّهَ عَلَىٰ كُلِّ شَىْءٍ قَدِيرٌ ٤٥ ﴾

And Allah has created every animal from water: of them there are some that creep on their bellies; some that walk on two legs; and some

that walk on four. Allah creates what He wills:
for verily Allah has power over all things.

﴿ لَّقَدْ أَنزَلْنَآ ءَايَـٰتٍ مُّبَيِّنَـٰتٍ ۚ وَٱللَّهُ يَهْدِى مَن يَشَآءُ إِلَىٰ صِرَٰطٍ مُّسْتَقِيمٍ ﴿٤٦﴾ ﴾

We have indeed sent down Signs that make things manifest: and Allah guides whom He wills to a Way that is straight. (An-Nur 24:37–46, Koran)

﴿ وَعَدَ ٱللَّهُ ٱلَّذِينَ ءَامَنُوا۟ مِنكُمْ وَعَمِلُوا۟ ٱلصَّـٰلِحَـٰتِ لَيَسْتَخْلِفَنَّهُمْ فِى ٱلْأَرْضِ كَمَا ٱسْتَخْلَفَ ٱلَّذِينَ مِن قَبْلِهِمْ وَلَيُمَكِّنَنَّ لَهُمْ دِينَهُمُ
ٱلَّذِى ٱرْتَضَىٰ لَهُمْ وَلَيُبَدِّلَنَّهُم مِّنۢ بَعْدِ خَوْفِهِمْ أَمْنًا ۚ يَعْبُدُونَنِى لَا يُشْرِكُونَ بِى شَيْـًٔا ۚ وَمَن كَفَرَ بَعْدَ ذَٰلِكَ فَأُو۟لَـٰٓئِكَ هُمُ ٱلْفَـٰسِقُونَ ﴿٥٥﴾ ﴾

Allah has promised, to those among you who believe and work righteous deeds, that He will, of a surety, grant them in the land, inheritance (of power), as He granted it to those before them; that He will establish in authority their religion, the one which He has chosen for them; and that He will change (their state), after the fear in which they (lived), to one of security and peace: 'They will worship Me (alone) and not associate aught with Me.' If any do reject Faith after this, they are rebellious and wicked.

﴿ وَأَقِيمُوا۟ ٱلصَّلَوٰةَ وَءَاتُوا۟ ٱلزَّكَوٰةَ وَأَطِيعُوا۟ ٱلرَّسُولَ لَعَلَّكُمْ تُرْحَمُونَ ﴿٥٦﴾ ﴾

So, establish regular Prayer and give regular Charity; and obey the Messenger; that ye may receive mercy.

﴿ لَا تَحْسَبَنَّ ٱلَّذِينَ كَفَرُوا۟ مُعْجِزِينَ فِى ٱلْأَرْضِ ۚ وَمَأْوَىٰهُمُ ٱلنَّارُ ۖ وَلَبِئْسَ ٱلْمَصِيرُ ۝٥٧ ﴾

Never think thou that the Unbelievers are going
to frustrate (Allah's Plan) on earth: their abode
is the Fire, and it is indeed an evil refuge!

﴿ يَٰٓأَيُّهَا ٱلَّذِينَ ءَامَنُوا۟ لِيَسْتَـْٔذِنكُمُ ٱلَّذِينَ مَلَكَتْ أَيْمَٰنُكُمْ وَٱلَّذِينَ لَمْ يَبْلُغُوا۟ ٱلْحُلُمَ مِنكُمْ ثَلَٰثَ مَرَّٰتٍ ۚ مِّن قَبْلِ صَلَوٰةِ ٱلْفَجْرِ وَحِينَ
تَضَعُونَ ثِيَابَكُم مِّنَ ٱلظَّهِيرَةِ وَمِنۢ بَعْدِ صَلَوٰةِ ٱلْعِشَآءِ ۚ ثَلَٰثُ عَوْرَٰتٍ لَّكُمْ ۚ لَيْسَ عَلَيْكُمْ وَلَا عَلَيْهِمْ جُنَاحٌۢ بَعْدَهُنَّ ۚ طَوَّٰفُونَ عَلَيْكُم
بَعْضُكُمْ عَلَىٰ بَعْضٍ ۚ كَذَٰلِكَ يُبَيِّنُ ٱللَّهُ لَكُمُ ٱلْـَٔايَٰتِ ۗ وَٱللَّهُ عَلِيمٌ حَكِيمٌ ۝٥٨ ﴾

O ye who believe! let those whom your right hands
possess, and the (children) among you who have
not come of age ask your permission (before they
come to your presence), on three occasions, before
morning prayer; the while you doff your clothes for
the noonday heat; and after the late-night prayer:
these are your three times of undress: outside these
times it is not wrong for you or for them to move
about attending to each other: thus does Allah
make clear the Signs to you: for Allah is full of
knowledge and wisdom. (An-Nur 24:55–58, Koran)

112: Al-Hajj: 22

﴾ Those whose hearts, are filled with reverence,
when Allah's name is pronounced, they persevere
despite their limitations, and they keep up regular
prayer and spend in charity) out of what We have
bestowed upon them. (Al-Hajj 22:35–36, Koran)

وَلِكُلِّ أُمَّةٍ جَعَلْنَا مَنسَكًا لِّيَذْكُرُوا اسْمَ اللَّهِ عَلَىٰ مَا رَزَقَهُم مِّن بَهِيمَةِ الْأَنْعَامِ ۗ فَإِلَٰهُكُمْ إِلَٰهٌ وَاحِدٌ فَلَهُ أَسْلِمُوا ۗ وَبَشِّرِ الْمُخْبِتِينَ ﴿٣٤﴾

To every people did We appoint rites of sacrifice, that they might celebrate the name of Allah over the sustenance He gave them from animals for food, but your God is One God: submit then your wills to Him (in Islam): and give thou the good news to those who humble themselves,

﴿ الَّذِينَ إِذَا ذُكِرَ اللَّهُ وَجِلَتْ قُلُوبُهُمْ وَالصَّابِرِينَ عَلَىٰ مَا أَصَابَهُمْ وَالْمُقِيمِي الصَّلَاةِ وَمِمَّا رَزَقْنَاهُمْ يُنفِقُونَ ﴿٣٥﴾ ﴾

﴿ أُذِنَ لِلَّذِينَ يُقَاتَلُونَ بِأَنَّهُمْ ظُلِمُوا ۚ وَإِنَّ اللَّهَ عَلَىٰ نَصْرِهِمْ لَقَدِيرٌ ﴿٣٩﴾ ﴾

Sanction is given to those to fight because they have been wronged and Allah is indeed able to give them victory.

﴿ الَّذِينَ أُخْرِجُوا مِن دِيَارِهِم بِغَيْرِ حَقٍّ إِلَّا أَن يَقُولُوا رَبُّنَا اللَّهُ ۗ وَلَوْلَا دَفْعُ اللَّهِ النَّاسَ بَعْضَهُم بِبَعْضٍ لَّهُدِّمَتْ صَوَامِعُ وَبِيَعٌ وَصَلَوَاتٌ
وَمَسَاجِدُ يُذْكَرُ فِيهَا اسْمُ اللَّهِ كَثِيرًا ۗ وَلَيَنصُرَنَّ اللَّهُ مَن يَنصُرُهُ ۗ إِنَّ اللَّهَ لَقَوِيٌّ عَزِيزٌ ﴿٤٠﴾

Those who have been expelled from their homes unjustly because they said, "Our Lord is Allah." Had Allah's not deterred some men by means of others there would surely have been destruction of cloisters, churches, synagogues, and mosques, in which name of Allah is commemorated in abundant measure. Allah certainly aids those who help in His cause, for verily Allah Strong, Mighty.

﴿ ٱلَّذِينَ إِن مَّكَّنَّٰهُمْ فِى ٱلْأَرْضِ أَقَامُوا۟ ٱلصَّلَوٰةَ وَءَاتَوُا۟ ٱلزَّكَوٰةَ وَأَمَرُوا۟ بِٱلْمَعْرُوفِ وَنَهَوْا۟ عَنِ ٱلْمُنكَرِ ۗ وَلِلَّهِ عَٰقِبَةُ ٱلْأُمُورِ ﴿٤١﴾ ﴾

They are those whom if We give them power in the land, establish regular prayer and give regular charity, enjoin the right and forbid inequity. With Allah rests the sequel of all events. (Al-Hajj 22:39–41, Koran)

﴿ يَٰٓأَيُّهَا ٱلَّذِينَ ءَامَنُوا۟ ٱرْكَعُوا۟ وَٱسْجُدُوا۟ وَٱعْبُدُوا۟ رَبَّكُمْ وَٱفْعَلُوا۟ ٱلْخَيْرَ لَعَلَّكُمْ تُفْلِحُونَ ۩ ﴿٧٧﴾ ﴾

O you who believe!

Bow down, prostrate yourselves, and adore your Lord; and do good; that ye may prosper.

﴿ وَجَٰهِدُوا۟ فِى ٱللَّهِ حَقَّ جِهَادِهِۦ ۚ هُوَ ٱجْتَبَىٰكُمْ وَمَا جَعَلَ عَلَيْكُمْ فِى ٱلدِّينِ مِنْ حَرَجٍ ۚ مِّلَّةَ أَبِيكُمْ إِبْرَٰهِيمَ ۚ هُوَ سَمَّىٰكُمُ ٱلْمُسْلِمِينَ مِن
قَبْلُ وَفِى هَٰذَا لِيَكُونَ ٱلرَّسُولُ شَهِيدًا عَلَيْكُمْ وَتَكُونُوا۟ شُهَدَآءَ عَلَى ٱلنَّاسِ ۚ فَأَقِيمُوا۟ ٱلصَّلَوٰةَ وَءَاتُوا۟ ٱلزَّكَوٰةَ وَٱعْتَصِمُوا۟ بِٱللَّهِ هُوَ مَوْلَىٰكُمْ ۖ فَنِعْمَ
ٱلْمَوْلَىٰ وَنِعْمَ ٱلنَّصِيرُ ﴿٧٨﴾ ﴾

And strive in His cause as ye ought to strive, (with sincerity and under discipline). He has chosen you and has imposed no difficulties on you in religion; it is the cult of your father Abraham. It is He Who has named you Muslims, both before and in this (Revelation); that the Messenger may be a witness for you, and ye be witnesses for mankind! So, establish regular Prayer, give regular Charity, and hold fast to Allah! He is your Protector, the best to protect and the Best to help! (Al-Hajj 22:77–78, Koran)

113: Al-Anfal: 8

﴿ إِنَّمَا ٱلْمُؤْمِنُونَ ٱلَّذِينَ إِذَا ذُكِرَ ٱللَّهُ وَجِلَتْ قُلُوبُهُمْ وَإِذَا تُلِيَتْ عَلَيْهِمْ ءَايَٰتُهُۥ زَادَتْهُمْ إِيمَٰنًا وَعَلَىٰ رَبِّهِمْ يَتَوَكَّلُونَ ﴿٢﴾ ﴾

For, Believers are those who, when Allah is mentioned, feel a tremor in their hearts, and when they hear His Signs rehearsed, find their faith strengthened, and put all their trust in their Lord;

﴿ ٱلَّذِينَ يُقِيمُونَ ٱلصَّلَوٰةَ وَمِمَّا رَزَقْنَٰهُمْ يُنفِقُونَ ﴿٣﴾ ﴾

Who establish regular prayers and spend freely out of the gifts We have given them for sustenance:

﴿ أُو۟لَٰٓئِكَ هُمُ ٱلْمُؤْمِنُونَ حَقًّا ۚ لَّهُمْ دَرَجَٰتٌ عِندَ رَبِّهِمْ وَمَغْفِرَةٌ وَرِزْقٌ كَرِيمٌ ﴿٤﴾ ﴾

Such in truth are the Believers: they have grades of dignity with their Lord, and forgiveness, and bountiful provision. (Al-Anfal 8:2-4, Koran)

114: At-Tawbah: 9

﴿ فَإِذَا ٱنسَلَخَ ٱلْأَشْهُرُ ٱلْحُرُمُ فَٱقْتُلُوا۟ ٱلْمُشْرِكِينَ حَيْثُ وَجَدتُّمُوهُمْ وَخُذُوهُمْ وَٱحْصُرُوهُمْ وَٱقْعُدُوا۟ لَهُمْ كُلَّ مَرْصَدٍ ۚ فَإِن تَابُوا۟
وَأَقَامُوا۟ ٱلصَّلَوٰةَ وَءَاتَوُا۟ ٱلزَّكَوٰةَ فَخَلُّوا۟ سَبِيلَهُمْ ۚ إِنَّ ٱللَّهَ غَفُورٌ رَّحِيمٌ ﴿٥﴾ ﴾

But when the forbidden months are past, then fight and slay the Pagans wherever you find them, and seize them, beleaguer them, and lie in wait for them in every stratagem (of war); but if they repent, and establish regular prayers and practice regular charity, then open the way for them: for Allah is Oft-Forgiving, Most Merciful.

﴿ وَإِنْ أَحَدٌ مِّنَ ٱلْمُشْرِكِينَ ٱسْتَجَارَكَ فَأَجِرْهُ حَتَّىٰ يَسْمَعَ كَلَٰمَ ٱللَّهِ ثُمَّ أَبْلِغْهُ مَأْمَنَهُۥ ۚ ذَٰلِكَ بِأَنَّهُمْ قَوْمٌ لَّا يَعْلَمُونَ ﴿٦﴾

If one amongst the Pagans ask thee for protection, grant it to him, so that he may hear the word of Allah; and then escort him to where he can be secure. That is because they are men without knowledge. (At-Tawbah 9:5–6, Koran)

﴿ فَإِن تَابُوا۟ وَأَقَامُوا۟ ٱلصَّلَوٰةَ وَءَاتَوُا۟ ٱلزَّكَوٰةَ فَإِخْوَٰنُكُمْ فِى ٱلدِّينِ ۗ وَنُفَصِّلُ ٱلْءَايَٰتِ لِقَوْمٍ يَعْلَمُونَ ﴿١١﴾ ﴾

But (even so), if they repent, establish regular prayers, and practice regular charity, they are your brethren in Faith: (thus) do We explain the Signs in detail, for those who understand. (At-Tawbah 9:11, Koran)

﴿ مَا كَانَ لِلْمُشْرِكِينَ أَن يَعْمُرُوا۟ مَسَٰجِدَ ٱللَّهِ شَٰهِدِينَ عَلَىٰٓ أَنفُسِهِم بِٱلْكُفْرِ ۚ أُو۟لَٰٓئِكَ حَبِطَتْ أَعْمَٰلُهُمْ وَفِى ٱلنَّارِ هُمْ خَٰلِدُونَ ﴿١٧﴾ ﴾

It is not for the idolaters to tend the mosques of Allah while bearing witness against their own souls of disbelief. The works of such bear no fruit: in Fire shall they dwell.

﴿ إِنَّمَا يَعْمُرُ مَسَٰجِدَ ٱللَّهِ مَنْ ءَامَنَ بِٱللَّهِ وَٱلْيَوْمِ ٱلْءَاخِرِ وَأَقَامَ ٱلصَّلَوٰةَ وَءَاتَى ٱلزَّكَوٰةَ وَلَمْ يَخْشَ إِلَّا ٱللَّهَ ۖ فَعَسَىٰٓ أُو۟لَٰٓئِكَ أَن يَكُونُوا۟
مِنَ ٱلْمُهْتَدِينَ ﴿١٨﴾ ﴾

The mosques of Allah shall be maintained by those who believe in Allah and the Last Day, establish regular prayers, and practice regular charity, and fear none except Allah. It is only they who are on true guidance. (At-Tawbah 9: 17–18, Koran)

Reference to Hypocrites

﴿ قُلْ أَنفِقُوا طَوْعًا أَوْ كَرْهًا لَّن يُتَقَبَّلَ مِنكُمْ ۖ إِنَّكُمْ كُنتُمْ قَوْمًا فَاسِقِينَ ﴿٥٣﴾ ﴾

Say: "Spend for the Cause willingly or unwillingly: not from you will it be accepted: for you are indeed a people rebellious and wicked."

﴿ وَمَا مَنَعَهُمْ أَن تُقْبَلَ مِنْهُمْ نَفَقَاتُهُمْ إِلَّا أَنَّهُمْ كَفَرُوا بِاللَّهِ وَبِرَسُولِهِ وَلَا يَأْتُونَ الصَّلَاةَ إِلَّا وَهُمْ كُسَالَىٰ وَلَا يُنفِقُونَ إِلَّا وَهُمْ كَارِهُونَ ﴿٥٤﴾ ﴾

The only reasons why their contributions are not accepted are: that they reject Allah and His Messenger; that they come to prayer without earnestness; and that they offer contributions unwillingly.

﴿ فَلَا تُعْجِبْكَ أَمْوَالُهُمْ وَلَا أَوْلَادُهُمْ ۚ إِنَّمَا يُرِيدُ اللَّهُ لِيُعَذِّبَهُم بِهَا فِي الْحَيَاةِ الدُّنْيَا وَتَزْهَقَ أَنفُسُهُمْ وَهُمْ كَافِرُونَ ﴿٥٥﴾

Let not their wealth nor their (following in) sons dazzle thee: in reality Allah's Plan is to punish them with these things in this life, and that their souls may perish in their (very) denial of Allah.

﴿ وَيَحْلِفُونَ بِاللَّهِ إِنَّهُمْ لَمِنكُمْ وَمَا هُم مِّنكُمْ وَلَٰكِنَّهُمْ قَوْمٌ يَفْرَقُونَ ﴿٥٦﴾ ﴾

They swear by Allah that they are indeed of you; but they are not of you: yet they are afraid (to appear in their true colors). (At-Tawbah 9: 53–56, Koran)

﴿ وَالْمُؤْمِنُونَ وَالْمُؤْمِنَاتُ بَعْضُهُمْ أَوْلِيَاءُ بَعْضٍ ۚ يَأْمُرُونَ بِالْمَعْرُوفِ وَيَنْهَوْنَ عَنِ الْمُنكَرِ وَيُقِيمُونَ الصَّلَاةَ وَيُؤْتُونَ الزَّكَاةَ
وَيُطِيعُونَ اللَّهَ وَرَسُولَهُ ۚ أُولَٰئِكَ سَيَرْحَمُهُمُ اللَّهُ ۗ إِنَّ اللَّهَ عَزِيزٌ حَكِيمٌ ﴿٧١﴾ ﴾

The Believers, men and women, are protectors, one of another: they enjoin what is just, and forbid what is evil: they observe regular prayers, practice regular charity, and obey Allah and His Messenger. On them will Allah pour His Mercy: for Allah is Exalted in power, Wise. (At-Tawbah 9:71, Koran)

Allah says:

Establish regular Salaat, give regular charity, and hold fast to Allah. He is your Mawla, Protector, the best of Protectors and the best Helper. (Al-Hajj 22:77–78, Koran)

Those who do wholesome deeds, establish regular prayers and regular charity have rewards with their Lord. On them shall be no fear, nor shall they grieve. (Al-Baqarah 2:227–80, Koran)

Seek help with patience, perseverance and prayer. Allah is with those who patiently persevere. Qur'an 2:153 Al Baqarah

When you arise for salaat, purify yourself by washing your faces, your hands to the elbows, wipe your heads and wash your feet to the ankles. If you are unclean purify yourself. Allah does not wish that you should be burdened, but to make you clean, and to bestow His blessings on you, that you may be grateful. (Al-Ma'idah 5:6, Koran)

Approach not prayers with a mind befogged until you understand all that you utter, nor come up to prayers in a state of un-cleanliness, till you have bathed. (An-Nisa 4:43, Koran)

Bow down, prostrate yourself and serve your Lord, and do wholesome deeds that you may prosper. Perform Jihad; strive to your utmost in Allah's cause as striving (jihad) is His due. He has chosen you and Allah has imposed no hardship in your endeavor to His cause. You are the inheritors of the faith of your father Abraham. He has named you Muslims of the times before and now, so that Allah's Messenger may be an example to you and that you are an example to humankind. (Al-Hajj 22: 77–78, Koran)

When the call is proclaimed to prayer on Friday, the day of assembly, hasten earnestly to the Remembrance of Allah, and leave off business and everything else: that is best for you if ye but knew! And when the Prayer is finished, then may ye disperse through the land, and seek of the Grace of Allah: remember and praise Allah a great deal: that ye may prosper. (Al-Jumu'ah 62:9–10, Koran)

The prophet said, "*Iman is knowledge in the heart, a voicing with the tongue, and activity with the limbs.*" The term *heart* often used in the Koran refers to a specific faculty or a spiritual organ that provides humans intellect and rationality. Therefore, *iman* means confidence in the *reality* and *truth* of things and a commitment to act on the basis of the *truth* that you know. Thus, *iman* (faith) involves knowledge and words and actions on the basis of that knowledge.

The Koran, Allah's word, is the primary source of the believers' spiritual well-being. *Recitation of the Koran imparts peace, tranquility, and closeness to Allah.* Recitation of Allah's words also renews the believer's vows to obey Allah's covenant. All believers memorize *Sura Al-Fatihah* and certain other verses to recite the salat. The salat is the daily renewal of the Koran in the believer, a daily rejuvenation of his or her covenant with Allah and communion with Him. The Koran is Allah's speech with the believers, and it is the foundation of everything Islamic.

Humans connect with Allah by speaking to Him. The believer speaks to Allah through daily salat, *dhikr* (remembrance), and supplication (*du'a*). The words are accompanied by action of the body and limbs, symbolizing subservience, respect, and humility. The salat consists of cyclic movements of standing in humility in the presence of Allah, bowing down to Him, going down in prostration in the Lord's presence, and then sitting in humility, all the time reciting verses from the Koran and praising Allah. Recitation of the Koran serves to embody the Koran within the person reciting salat. Allah is light (*nur*), and His word, the Koran, is His luminosity. To embody the Koran through faith and practice is to become transformed by this divine light that permeates through the believer in his closeness to Allah. Such proximity to Allah's presence gives the worshipper a luminous presence.

The whole world is the place of prostration, and every place where Allah is remembered is aglow with Allah's *nur*. Every place of prostration and Allah's remembrance has His presence and light. The believing men and women approach the Lord in His *taqwa* in awe and gratitude, supplicating in His presence, aware that He is there and that they see Him. If they do not see Him, they are aware that He sees them and is sentient of their prayer, gratitude, and supplication. When Allah calls all believers, men and women, to salat, to remember and praise Him, the believers *purify* themselves by washing their faces and their hands to the elbows, wiping their heads, and washing their feet to the ankles. If they are unclean, they purify themselves by bathing. They then approach their Lord, submit to Him, and renew their covenant with Him. Salat, *dhikr*, recitation, fasting, *taqwa* of Allah, and *furqan* are the beams of light that maintain the believer's connection with the divine light.

Islam (submission, prostration) is the direct link between the believer and Allah. The believer asks, and Allah gives. The believer loves Allah, and Allah loves him in return. The believer asks for the straight path, and Allah shows him the way. The believer prays to Allah, and Allah showers His mercy and grace on him. The believer remembers Allah, and Allah responds to those who praise Him, thank Him, and ask Him. And Allah reassures them:

On you there shall be no fear, nor shall you grieve.
Seek help with patience, perseverance and prayer.
Allah is with those who patiently persevere.

The Masjid of Believers

﴿ وَٱلَّذِينَ ٱتَّخَذُوا۟ مَسْجِدًا ضِرَارًا وَكُفْرًا وَتَفْرِيقًۢا بَيْنَ ٱلْمُؤْمِنِينَ وَإِرْصَادًا لِّمَنْ حَارَبَ ٱللَّهَ وَرَسُولَهُۥ مِن قَبْلُ ۚ وَلَيَحْلِفُنَّ إِنْ
أَرَدْنَآ إِلَّا ٱلْحُسْنَىٰ ۖ وَٱللَّهُ يَشْهَدُ إِنَّهُمْ لَكَـٰذِبُونَ ﴿١٠٧﴾ ﴾

And there are those who would set up another Mosque with a view to create mischief, to mislead and divide the believers, to serve as a rendezvous for those who had contested Allah and His Messenger erstwhile. They swear that they have only the best intentions, but Allah bears witness that they lie.

﴿ لَا تَقُمْ فِيهِ أَبَدًا ۚ لَّمَسْجِدٌ أُسِّسَ عَلَى ٱلتَّقْوَىٰ مِنْ أَوَّلِ يَوْمٍ أَحَقُّ أَن تَقُومَ فِيهِ ۚ فِيهِ رِجَالٌ يُحِبُّونَ أَن يَتَطَهَّرُوا۟ ۚ وَٱللَّهُ يُحِبُّ
ٱلْمُطَّهِّرِينَ ﴿١٠٨﴾ ﴾

You shall not set foot in it. It is more fitting for you to pray in a mosque whose foundation was laid from the first day on piety (taqwa); There you will find persons who would keep pure, and Allah loves those who purify themselves.

﴿ أَفَمَنْ أَسَّسَ بُنْيَـٰنَهُۥ عَلَىٰ تَقْوَىٰ مِنَ ٱللَّهِ وَرِضْوَٰنٍ خَيْرٌ أَم مَّنْ أَسَّسَ بُنْيَـٰنَهُۥ عَلَىٰ شَفَا جُرُفٍ هَارٍ فَٱنْهَارَ بِهِۦ فِى نَارِ جَهَنَّمَ ۗ وَٱللَّهُ لَا
يَهْدِى ٱلْقَوْمَ ٱلظَّـٰلِمِينَ ﴿١٠٩﴾

Who then is more secure? The one who lays the foundation of his house on the fear (taqwa) of Allah and His Good Pleasure? Or the one who builds on a crumbling precipice so that the house will fall with him into the fire of Hell. And Allah does not guide people who do wrong.

﴿ لَا يَزَالُ بُنْيَٰنُهُمُ ٱلَّذِى بَنَوْا۟ رِيبَةً فِى قُلُوبِهِمْ إِلَّآ أَن تَقَطَّعَ قُلُوبُهُمْ ۗ وَٱللَّهُ عَلِيمٌ حَكِيمٌ

The edifice which they have built is never free from doubt and uncertainty in their hearts, until their hearts are cut to pieces. And Allah is All-Knowing, Wise.

﴿ ۞ إِنَّ ٱللَّهَ ٱشْتَرَىٰ مِنَ ٱلْمُؤْمِنِينَ أَنفُسَهُمْ وَأَمْوَٰلَهُم بِأَنَّ لَهُمُ ٱلْجَنَّةَ ۚ يُقَٰتِلُونَ فِى سَبِيلِ ٱللَّهِ فَيَقْتُلُونَ وَيُقْتَلُونَ ۖ وَعْدًا عَلَيْهِ
حَقًّا فِى ٱلتَّوْرَىٰةِ وَٱلْإِنجِيلِ وَٱلْقُرْءَانِ ۚ وَمَنْ أَوْفَىٰ بِعَهْدِهِۦ مِنَ ٱللَّهِ ۚ فَٱسْتَبْشِرُوا۟ بِبَيْعِكُمُ ٱلَّذِى بَايَعْتُم بِهِۦ ۚ وَذَٰلِكَ هُوَ ٱلْفَوْزُ ٱلْعَظِيمُ ﴿١١١﴾ ﴾

Allah has purchased of the Believers their lives and their worldly goods and in return has promised them the Garden (of Paradise): they will fight in His Cause, and slay and be slain: a pledge that is binding on Him in Truth, in the Torah, the Gospel, and the Qur'an: and who is more faithful to his Covenant than Allah? Then rejoice in the bargain which you have concluded: that is the achievement supreme.

﴿ ٱلتَّٰٓئِبُونَ ٱلْعَٰبِدُونَ ٱلْحَٰمِدُونَ ٱلسَّٰٓئِحُونَ ٱلرَّٰكِعُونَ ٱلسَّٰجِدُونَ ٱلْءَامِرُونَ بِٱلْمَعْرُوفِ وَٱلنَّاهُونَ عَنِ
ٱلْمُنكَرِ وَٱلْحَٰفِظُونَ لِحُدُودِ ٱللَّهِ ۗ وَبَشِّرِ ٱلْمُؤْمِنِينَ ﴿١١٢﴾ ﴾

Those who turn (to Allah) in repentance; those who serve Him and praise Him; that wander in devotion to the Cause of Allah; that bow down and prostrate themselves in prayer; that enjoin good and forbid evil; and observe the limits set by Allah; (these do rejoice). So, proclaim the glad tidings to the Believers. (At-Tawbah 9:107–12, Koran)

The Betrayal of the Covenant of Allah: The Masjid

Allah calls the believers to prayer; some believers are indeed afraid, and on some, there is indeed fear and grief. Places of prostration in the Islamic world are masculine preserves, men's clubs. Believing, upright women, if not totally forbidden, are indeed discouraged from praying in the mosques by men and those who control the mosques. The mosques that do permit women to pray have separate entrance for the women and a segregated and sometimes unclean, uncomfortable, unventilated prayer room for women and children. The khutbah and the prayers are inaudible. When Allah calls on the believers, He addresses both men and women together in unison.

Allah made tribes and nations from a single pair of male and female, men, and women, so that humans can communicate and come to know one another. Allah honors humans who have *taqwa* of Allah and are righteous. The acts of good works and righteousness recognized in the Koran are to show compassion, to be merciful and forgive others, to be just, to protect the weak, to defend the oppressed, to be generous and charitable, to be truthful, to seek knowledge and wisdom, to be kind, to be peaceful, to love others, and to perform beautiful deeds.

The earliest Muslims gathered for prayers in a makeshift mosque partly open to the elements. The prophet of Islam led the prayers for everyone to see and hear him. The men prayed behind the prophet, followed by rows of children and women occupying the back rows of the Prophet's Mosque, where they could be seen and heard by the rest of the congregation in the same small room. In between the prayers, men and women were able to mingle, and the blessed prophet was accessible to each person if they had a conversation and questions.

Direct contact between the prophet, as the imam who led the prayers, and those who seems to have been an important element in the Friday khutbah. The prophet preached the khutbah, leaning on a staff. And the people were in front of him, their faces raised toward him, and they listened as they watched him.

The idea that the mosque is a privileged place, a collective space where the community debates important matters before making decisions, is the key idea of Islam that provided the community autonomy and a voice. Everything passed through the mosque, which became the school for teaching new converts, ritual prayer, the principles of Islam, and how to behave toward others in places of worship and elsewhere. People came to know and bonded with one another. This is how the Ansar became the brethren of the Muhajirun.

The mosque became established as the place where dialogue between the leader and the people took place. The apparently simple decision to install a minbar in the mosque was treated by the prophet as a matter that concerned all Muslims. The prophet used to say the Friday prayers standing, leaning against a palm trunk. Not everyone could see the prophet clearly, and the believers urged the prophet to take his place on a platform at the time of prayer so that everybody could see him. Within a few months, the number of Muslims had grown considerably. "Why not build a pulpit like I have seen in Syria?" suggested a companion. The prophet asked those present for their advice on the question, and they agreed to the suggestion. A Medina carpenter cut a tree and built a pulpit with a seat and two steps up to the seat. Thus, all the congregation—men in front, children in the middle, and women at the back—were able to see and hear the blessed *Nabi* when he taught in the mosque.

The premise that women are discouraged from worshiping in the mosque because they "distract" men from their spiritual pursuit because women stimulate men's sexual urges rests on sham premise. Islam is a religion of reform and self-control. The covenant of Allah has established strict guidelines and boundaries over the believer's behavior both in private and in public. This argument operates from the premise that men's focus on self-control and self as human beings, as Muslims, is outside their control and that men cannot control their lust and urges since, upon seeing and listening to women, they are overcome by irresistible, uncontrollable sexual urges. By such reasoning, we imply that man is incapable of taking moral responsibility for their behavior and relationships.

The solution is to manipulate the external environment—women must be invisible—to keep men's responses in check. This raises important questions: What does this say about man's capacity to take full responsibility for his spirituality and sexuality? On what understanding of humanity are these arguments based?

For men and women who surrender unto Allah,
For men and women who believe, For men and
women who are devout For men and women who
speak the truth, For men and women who persevere
in righteousness, For men and women who are
humble, For men and women who are charitable,
For men and women who fast and deny themselves
<u>For men and women who guard their chastity,</u> For
men and women who remember Allah much, For
them Allah has forgiveness and a great reward.

Say to the Believing men that they should
lower their gaze and guard their modesty: That
will make for greater purity for them: And
Allah is acquainted with all that they do.

And say to the Believing women that they should
lower their gaze and guard their modesty; that
they should not display their adornments except

what is ordinarily obvious, That they should draw
a veil over their bosom and not display their
adornments(Except to the immediate family)And
that they should not strike their feet in order to
draw attention to their hidden adornments.

And O you Believers! (men and women)Turn you
all together Toward Allah that ye may prosper. The
believer's men and women are protectors one of
another; they enjoin what is just and forbid what is evil;
They observe regular prayers, practice regular charity,
and obey Allah and His messenger. On them will Allah
pour His mercy, for Allah is exalted in power, wise.

O ye who believe! Guard your souls, If ye follow
(right) guidance, No hurt can come to you from
those who stray; The goal of you all is to Allah, It is
He who will show you the truth of all that ye do.

The above *ayah* of the Koran has defined the boundaries of behavior for both men and women for all times to come. It tells men and women to lower their gaze in modesty. Could it be clearer? And then Allah tells both men and women:

O you Believers! Turn ye <u>all-together</u> toward Allah that ye may prosper. [And this could only occur in prayer in a place of prostration.] The believer's men and women are protectors one of another [meaning that men and women work as team to protect their mutual spiritual and earthly interests]; they enjoin what is just and forbid what is evil [*a clear indication that men and women together promote a just and moral community*]. They observe regular prayers, practice regular charity, and obey Allah and His messenger. *[Again, Allah urges both men and women to establish regular salat, practice regular charity, and obey His covenant as given to the blessed prophet in the Koran*] On them will Allah pour His mercy, for Allah is exalted in power, wise. [*The believers who turn to Allah together in prayer, work to protect one another, promote a just and moral society, establish regular prayer, give in charity, and obey Allah's covenant will bathe in His mercy.*]

Believing, God-conscious men and women should emerge from the pre-Islamic desert and the steppes of tribal societies to reclaim our humanity, our Islam, and we need to recognize our maleness and femaleness as a natural part of the communion of a common family of believers that honors its mothers, daughters, wives, and sisters. We must reject the idea of uncontrollable male sexuality and evil women.

The Betrayal of the Covenant of Allah: The Priesthood, the Mullah

There is no priesthood in Islam; the believer has a highly personal and exclusive relationship with Allah. Such relationship does not permit the intervention of another human being. When the blessed Muhammad was taken up by Allah, inherited the Koran, Allah's covenant, and His *din*. Every believer became the successor, inheritor, and custodian of the prophet's legacy till the end of time.

The priests and clerics of Islam assumed the legacy of the pagan priesthood and began to speak on behalf of Allah. Through distortion and misrepresentation of the word of Allah and the pronouncements of His *Nabi,* over the last fourteen hundred years, the priests and imams of Islam have created divisions and schisms in Islam to generate hundreds of self-righteous sects and subsects among Muslims. Each sect is the enemy of the other; every group has the dagger in the back of the other. This gradually smoldering *fitnah* of the priesthood is slowly consuming the body of the *ummah.*

Islam is a relationship between Allah and His believers. The *din* of Allah is an all-encompassing and highly personal type of relationship in which Allah's *nur* resides in the believer's heart. The believer is conscious of Allah's closeness and mercy and obeys, trusts, and loves Allah. Allah in return loves those who love Him and perform beautiful deeds.

Allah has granted knowledge and wisdom of *furqan* and *taqwa* to the believers who have opened their hearts and minds to Him. Man has been granted the freedom of choice in doing what is wholesome and beautiful or what is corrupt and ugly. This knowledge reminds the human of the scales of Allah's justice; the two hands of Allah—His mercy and His wrath—are reflected in the human domain, where people have been appointed His vicegerents. Deeds of goodness and wholesomeness are associated with mercy, paradise, and what is beautiful. Evil and corruption is rewarded with wrath, hell, and what is ugly.

Everything in the universe is connected to Allah through its creation, birth, sustenance, existence, demise, and death. Every particle and atom spins at the command of Allah's majesty; it has done so for billions of years and will continue to do so at Allah's command. They continue to spin in the cells of the living when they are alive and when the cells are devoid of life at Allah's command. Nothing ever happens without Allah's will and knowledge. No human, howsoever proud or strong, is independent of Him. The newborn is thus physically connected to Allah through His mercy. The particles and atoms in his cells spin at Allah's mercy in life and in death. Through Allah's mercy, his cells grow and multiply with sustenance from Allah.

Every man and woman in this journey is born alone and innocent. The individual leads his short life in this world, and when he dies, he leaves this world alone. In death, his cells disintegrate, yet the particles and atoms continue to spin at Allah's command forever. His life was a miracle and a mirage. Now the human was here, and in an instant, he was gone and all alone. The only reality is Allah. Every substance and relationship the human accumulated is left behind—parents, friends, wealth, children, priests, kings, human laws, honors, comforts, and so on. They all accompanied the human to the edge of his life and then parted to wait for their own demise one day.

In this journey, the human is presented with Allah's covenant as his guide, *taqwa* of Allah as his shield against evil, and *furqan*, the criterion to distinguish between the right and evil, as Allah's compass to the straight path of righteousness. If the human accepts these, he becomes a believer and among the righteous. The way to righteousness is in Allah's guidance and in His covenant in the Koran. Righteousness lies in the inspiration from the Koran through its recitation at leisure, at dawn, during the day, and under the glow of the lamp at night. Every little bit of devotion makes the *nur* of Allah glow in the heart till the believer is connected to Him and begins to follow His path. In this path, the believer does what is righteous and what is beautiful. Beautiful actions please Allah.

This communion between the believer and Allah is exclusive. Submission establishes the link between the believer and Allah. The believer asks, and Allah gives. The believer loves Allah, and Allah loves him in return. The believer asks for the straight path, and Allah shows him the way. The believer praises Allah, and Allah showers His mercy and grace on him. The believer remembers Allah, and Allah responds to those who praise Him, thank Him, and ask Him.

The believer on his chosen journey on the path of Allah is well equipped. He has Allah's protection, guidance, and direction. Does the believer need dogmas and laws based on human systems? Aren't Allah's word and the covenant sufficient as guidance? Allah is the absolute truth (*haqq*). All worldly, human, and priestly systems are not based on *haqq*. Allah is the only *Haqq*. What is not *haqq* is *batil*, the untruth. Those who let go of Allah's hand and clutch at the human priestly dogma and creed have fallen astray in Satan's footsteps.

The most important theological point made by the Koran is that there is one God, Allah, universal and beyond comparison, who creates and sustains both the material world and the world of human experience. Allah is *Haqq*, the absolute truth. All other forms of so-called truth are either false in their initial premises or contingently true only in limited situations. The recognition of this fact is of paramount importance to all believers. That Allah is *Haqq* is undeniable. *Haqq* does not fall into the domain of human fancy nor human ideas, but it stands for beliefs that manifest in concrete form. These beliefs must be in harmony with changing needs of time and with Allah's laws of the universe. No belief relating to this world can be called *haqq* unless its truth is established by positive demonstration of Allah's reality. This truth is permanent and unchanging.

There is no priesthood in Islam. *Haqq* does not need priests. Yet there are people among the believers who talk like priests, dress like priests, and preach like priests. They are indeed the priests. They preach dogma and creed to the believers in the name of Allah and His blessed *Nabi*. Yet what they preach distances the believers from Allah, the Koran, and the blessed prophet. The priests spread hatred among the believers and discord in the *ummah*. They concern themselves with obscure *Hadith* and man-made Sharia and *fiqh* that do not constitute the *din* of Allah. Their teachings and fatwas often contradict the Koran and the spirit of the blessed *Nabi's* teaching.

If miraculously one day all the mullahs, self-proclaimed ulema, ayatollahs, imams, and Wahhabi preachers were to disappear from the face of this earth, from that day on, there will be no Shia, no Sunni, nor any other sect in the world. Every Muslim will be a believer of Allah. The mullahs, self-proclaimed ulema, ayatollahs, imams, and

Wahhabi preachers sustain one another through their own inbred dogma and creed. In turn, the mullahs and priests sustain their sects through their man-made belief systems. It is a cycle in which the priests continue to perpetuate their creeds generation after generation with "quote and reference" to their earlier imams and priests, repeating distortions, misquotations, and misrepresentations. The believers cannot hear the gentle message of Allah over all the noise and commotion created by the mullahs and religious scholars in the world of Islam. In the same token, if there were no rabbis, Christian priests, ministers, clerics, preachers, pastors, bishops, popes, pundits, and mullahs, there will be no Judaism, Christianity, Hinduism, nor sectarian Islam. All those who believe in one God will then be servants of the same Allah, the religion of Abraham, Moses, Jesus, and Muhammad.

Yet priests have been with us since the times when man attained civilization. The priesthood of the Sumerian civilization left a powerful legacy on the generations to follow. Within a short time, the priestly culture spread to all human civilizations, to the Indus valley, Babylon, Egypt, Greece and Rome. Priesthood independently sprung up in the Americas.

Humans crave a belief in the supernatural. They seek comfort and security in the thought of supernatural protection from gods. Priesthood is ever present and ready to exploit this need. Sumerians and all other civilizations were served by many gods—gods of war, fertility goddesses, sun god, moon god, gods of rain, gods of death, and so on. Priests were at hand to provide the protection at a cost, an offering to gods. The cult of gods did not operate in isolation. Though communities had their own particular guardian gods, they did share other gods with other towns and villages. Devotees traveled to far, distant places to pay homage to their gods. There was considerable exchange and sharing of patronage, protection, and blessing of gods among varying communities. Priesthood became the original corporations and propaganda machine for their gods.

Such publicity also took advantage of the sense of weaknesses and vulnerabilities of the people. The greater the insecurity among the population, the more the devotees of particular gods were, the greater the wealth and influence of the priests. There were festivals of all sorts involving seasons, planting of seed, harvest, fertility, human sacrifice, fire, light, and many others. The priests began to control commerce, levy tithe, lend money on interest, organizc professional armies, and provide temple prostitutes, alcohol, and protection against calamities. What mattered in the end was the power and wealth. Priesthood became a network of guilds connected through secret societies that began to control the affairs of the world for all times to come.

6. The Covenant of Allah: Fasting during Ramadan

> Fasting is prescribed to you, in the month of Ramadan
> as it was prescribed to those before you, that you
> may practice self-restraint. The Qur'an was revealed
> in the month of Ramadan, guidance to humankind
> for judgment between right and wrong. For everyone
> except those ill or on a journey, this month should
> spend it in fasting. Allah intends to make it easy on
> you so that you may complete the prescribed period
> of fasting and to glorify Him to express your gratitude
> for His Guidance. (Al-Baqarah 2:178–79, Koran)

Fasting during Ramadan is a month of self-discipline, prayer, and remembrance of Allah. This is a month of renewal of a believer's commitment to Allah's covenant and a vow to follow His guidance. During this month, there is heightened attention to the rules of right conduct, which helps the believer follow Allah's straight path during the following year. This month is a reminder to the believers of their obligation to Allah's creatures in need of sustenance, shelter, protection, peace, and other help.

7. The Covenant of Allah: Hajj

And proclaim the Pilgrimage to mankind; they will come to thee on foot and mounted on every kind of camel, lean on account of journeys through deep and distant mountain highways; that they may witness the benefits provided for them, and celebrate the name of Allah, through the Days Appointed, over the cattle which He has provided for them for sacrifice: then eat you thereof and feed the distressed ones in want. Then let them complete the rites prescribed for them, perform their vows, and again circumambulate the Ancient House. Such is the Pilgrimage: whoever honors the sacred rites of Allah, for him it is good in the sight of his Lord. Lawful to you for food in Pilgrimage are cattle, except those mentioned to you as exceptions: but shun the abomination of idols and shun the word that is false. (Al-Hajj 22:27–30, Koran)

> Violate not the sanctity of the Symbols of Allah, or of the sacred month, or of the animals brought for sacrifice, nor the garlands that mark out such animals, nor the people coming to the Sacred House, seeking the bounty and good pleasure of their Lord. Help one another in virtue and piety but help not one another in sin and acrimony. Be in taqwa of Allah, fear Allah, for Allah is swift in reckoning. (Al-Ma'idah 5:2, Koran)

For thirteen hundred years, Muslims traveled to Mecca by foot or on horse- or camelback, taking more than a year to complete the rituals of the hajj. This slow pace helped the believer in his spiritual pursuit and his worldly quest to get acquainted with Muslims of other lands that kept the *ummah* united. The hajj since then has been seen as a grand rite of passage from this worldly life to a person's total devotion to Allah. Hajjis have been treated as models of piety and blessedness. With modern air travel, hajj has become accessible to a larger population, bringing the Islamic world closer. To the increasing numbers of younger generation performing hajj today, the rituals at the house inspire the renewal of their vows to the covenant of Allah.

8. The Covenant of Allah: Zakat

The covenant of Allah has laid down principles and guidelines for the wellbeing of the economic life of the believers. has laid down principles and guidelines for the well-being of the economic life of the believers. Obeying the principles will bring peace, harmony, spiritual enlightenment, and economic prosperity. Disobeying means misery, ruin, and Allah's wrath. According to Allah's laws:

- Land and sources of production do not become the personal property of individuals. *Ardh* is the source of life and means of sustenance and production of food and resources and therefore must remain available to the community, the *ummah.*
- Every Muslim, male and female, who at the end of the year is in possession of surplus wealth in cash or articles of trade must give zakat. Zakat is incumbent on all liquid, visible, movable, and immovable properties belonging to Muslims.

Two and a half percent of the liquid assets of a Muslim adult after deduction of reasonable expenses for the maintenance of the person's family and dependents, as prescribed by Shariah, is not an excessive amount of money. Allah constantly reminds believers to practice regular charity. Giving to the needy with love and respect out of love of Allah is a profound act of spiritual cleaning. *The more one gives in wealth and in kindness, the higher is his status with Allah.*

In the united Muslim lands of the Dar es Salaam, if every adult man and woman gives minimum of $15 in zakat, the total collected will amount to *$12 billion.* If everyone among a hundred billionaires and one million millionaires in the Islamic world contributed a minimum of 5 percent of their liquid wealth in the way of Allah, the total collected will be to the tune of another *$55 billion.* If we approach another five million prosperous businesspeople with liquid assets of five hundred thousand dollars to pay their zakat, the sum collected from them will amount to another *$125 billion*; the total sum thus collected amounts to *$192 billion.* And further generosity of, say, 10 percent will collect *$382 billion.* One-third of this amount may then be used to feed, clothe, house, and educate the poor and needy population and the remaining half to create industries and jobs and job training for the people who have not been able to exit the cycle of poverty.

There is an estimated *forty-five thousand tons* of accumulated gold hoardings in the Islamic countries, in the form of jewelry, gold bricks, gold bars, gold artifacts, and national treasures in museums with an estimated value of *$548 billion.* In addition, there is a hoard of precious stones worth another $100 billion. The zakat levy on the bullion and the precious stones will amount to another *$13 billion.* Even though the Islamic states have been milked dry by our elite and their colonial cohorts, the *ummah* acting in accordance with Allah's covenant shall be able to eradicate all poverty and destitution within the Dar es Salaam within five years with resources from within the community of believers amounting to *$1 trillion* without ever touching any of the government revenues.

And the likeness of those who give generously, seeking
to please Allah and to strengthen their souls, is as a

garden, high and fertile where heavy rain falls on it and makes it yield a double the amount of harvest, and if it receives not heavy rain, light moisture suffices it.

The parable of those who spend their substance in the way of Allah is that of a grain of corn: it grows seven ears, and each ear has a hundred grains. Allah gives plentiful return to whom He pleases, Allah cares for all, and He knows all things. Those who give generously in the cause of Allah and follow not up their gifts with reminders of their generosity or with injury, for them their reward is with their Lord; on them shall be no fear, nor shall they grieve. Kind words and the covering of faults are better than charity followed by injury. Allah is Free of all wants and He is Most Merciful. (Al-Baqarah 2:261–63, Koran)

Let not those among you who are blessed with grace and ample means hold back from helping their relatives, the poor, and those who have left their homes in Allah's cause. Let them forgive and overlook, do you not wish that Allah should forgive you? And Allah is Oft Forgiving, Most Merciful. (An-Nur 24:21–23, Koran)

Spend out of bounties of Allah in charity and wholesome deeds before the Day comes when there will be neither bargaining, friendship nor intercession. Those who reject faith are the wrongdoers. (Al-Baqarah 2:254–57, Koran)

Void not your charity by boast, conceit and insult, by
reminders of your generosity like those who want their
generosity to be noted by all men, but they believe
neither in Allah nor in the Last Day. Theirs is a parable
of a hard-barren rock, on which there is a little soil,
washed by heavy rain, which leaves it just a bare stone.
And Allah guides not those who reject Faith. And the
likeness of those who give generously, seeking to please
Allah and to strengthen their souls, is as a garden, high
and fertile where heavy rain falls on it and makes it
yield a double the amount of harvest, and if it receives
not heavy rain, light moisture suffices it. Allah notices
whatever you do. (Al-Baqarah 2:264–65, Koran)

۞ إِنَّمَا ٱلصَّدَقَٰتُ لِلْفُقَرَآءِ وَٱلْمَسَٰكِينِ وَٱلْعَٰمِلِينَ عَلَيْهَا وَٱلْمُؤَلَّفَةِ قُلُوبُهُمْ وَفِى ٱلرِّقَابِ وَٱلْغَٰرِمِينَ وَفِى سَبِيلِ ٱللَّهِ
وَٱبْنِ ٱلسَّبِيلِ ۖ فَرِيضَةً مِّنَ ٱللَّهِ ۗ وَٱللَّهُ عَلِيمٌ حَكِيمٌ ﴿٦٠﴾

Alms are for the poor and the needy, and those
employed to administer the (funds); for those
whose hearts have been (recently) reconciled (to
the truth); for those in bondage and in debt; in
the cause of Allah; and for the wayfarer: (thus is it)
ordained by Allah, and Allah is full of knowledge
and wisdom. (At-Tawbah 9:60, Koran)

In the above two verses, the clear indication is that man is given bounty by Allah. In return, his obligation is to distribute the surplus after his needs have been met to the needy. The Koran specifies that the charities be disbursed to the *fuqara* (the poor who ask), to *al masakin* (the poor and the needy who do not ask), to zakat administrators, to those who spread the light of Islam to those inclined, for the freedom of those in bondage, to those in debt, for the cause of Allah, and for the wayfarer who treads the path in Allah's service.

In the covenant between the individual believer and Allah, the individual surrenders to Allah his life and belongings in return for His guidance, a place in paradise in the hereafter, and peace with prosperity in this world. Every believer according to his or her covenant with Allah has the obligation to extend the benefits that Allah has provided them to those who did not receive the same benefits. Such acts of generosity will be rewarded by Allah with a place in *Jannat* (place of peace and plenty) in the afterlife. Life of *Jannat* is to be attained in this world also, provided the compact with Allah is adhered to. The believer is Allah's instrument who will fulfill His promise to Adam that, among his progeny,

> none will remain without food or clothes, and none
> will suffer from heat or thirst. (Koran 20:118)

In the verses below, Allah has promised those who believe and obey His covenant a reward for their acts of charity. He will double the harvest of their labors, forgive their sins, and provide them His bounties. And they shall not grieve. Fear and grief arise from misfortunes, which cause anxiety, depression, and panic. Allah promises to safeguard the believers from misfortunes.

And to those devouring usury, Allah will deprive them of all blessings. Obedience to Allah's covenant provides *Jannat* in the hereafter and a life of *Jannat*, peace, and plenty in this world. It also brings balance, harmony, and stability to the economic life of the world in that it meets the necessities of each individual and eliminates unnecessary suffering.

يَٰٓأَيُّهَا ٱلَّذِينَ ءَامَنُوٓاْ أَنفِقُواْ مِن طَيِّبَٰتِ مَا كَسَبۡتُمۡ وَمِمَّآ أَخۡرَجۡنَا لَكُم مِّنَ ٱلۡأَرۡضِۖ وَلَا تَيَمَّمُواْ
ٱلۡخَبِيثَ مِنۡهُ تُنفِقُونَ وَلَسۡتُم بِـَٔاخِذِيهِ إِلَّآ أَن تُغۡمِضُواْ فِيهِۚ وَٱعۡلَمُوٓاْ أَنَّ ٱللَّهَ غَنِيٌّ حَمِيدٌ ﴿٢٦٧﴾ ٱلشَّيۡطَٰنُ يَعِدُكُمُ
ٱلۡفَقۡرَ وَيَأۡمُرُكُم بِٱلۡفَحۡشَآءِۖ وَٱللَّهُ يَعِدُكُم مَّغۡفِرَةٗ مِّنۡهُ وَفَضۡلٗاۗ وَٱللَّهُ وَٰسِعٌ عَلِيمٞ ﴿٢٦٨﴾ يُؤۡتِي ٱلۡحِكۡمَةَ مَن يَشَآءُۚ
وَمَن يُؤۡتَ ٱلۡحِكۡمَةَ فَقَدۡ أُوتِيَ خَيۡرٗا كَثِيرٗاۗ وَمَا يَذَّكَّرُ إِلَّآ أُوْلُواْ ٱلۡأَلۡبَٰبِ ﴿٢٦٩﴾ وَمَآ أَنفَقۡتُم مِّن نَّفَقَةٍ أَوۡ
نَذَرۡتُم مِّن نَّذۡرٖ فَإِنَّ ٱللَّهَ يَعۡلَمُهُۥۗ وَمَا لِلظَّٰلِمِينَ مِنۡ أَنصَارٍ ﴿٢٧٠﴾

O you who believe! Give of the good things that ye have (honorably) earned, and of the fruits of the earth that We have produced for you, and do not even aim at getting anything which is bad, in order that out of it ye may give away something, when you yourselves would not receive it except with closed eyes. And know that Allah is free of all wants, and worthy of all praise.

The Evil One threatens you with poverty and bids you to conduct unseemly. Allah promises you His forgiveness and bounties. And Allah cares for all and He knows all things.

He grants wisdom to whom He pleases; and he to whom wisdom is granted receives indeed a benefit overflowing; but none will grasp the Message but men of understanding.

And whatever you spend in charity or devotion, be sure Allah knows it all. But the wrongdoers have no helpers. (Al-Baqarah 2:267–70, Koran)

The first eight commandments of Allah are concerned with the divine. The believer recognizes the greatness, power, magnificence, and mercy of the great Creator and bows down to him in humility and submission. The believer pledges to fulfill his covenant with the Almighty. The believer receives Allah in his heart and comes to recognize His constant presence with him. He recognizes the loftiness of Allah and the minuteness of his own self. Yet in this contrast of magnitude, Allah is approachable and draws the believer closer to Him in His love and mercy. In this *taqwa,* the believer calls Allah in his prayers. The believers fasts in gratitude for the gift of the Koran and for the guidance that Allah sent to humankind through His blessed prophet. And he thanks Allah for the gift of the prophet; the daily mercies of food, clothing, and warmth; and the pleasures of the family, neighbors, health, beauty of the creation, sun, flowers, and fresh air. And every day the believer thinks of his poor neighbor, the child without clothes, the sick woman across the street. He searches deep into his pocket and drops a coin for the neighbor and a shirt for the child and visits the sick woman.

The Betrayal of the Covenant of Allah: Zakat, the Stinginess of the *Ummah*

Allah gave mankind free will to wander the earth and freedom of action. In our time, there are men who in their pride force men and women against their free will. They are oppressors of mankind. Allah is the King. There are men who call themselves kings, and they rule countries. Unto themselves, they have taken the role of God; they think they are God.

Allah is the Knower and the Wise. There are men on the earth who feign to speak for Allah. They judge for Allah. Allah is the *Alim*. Yet these men drape themselves in magnificent robes and call themselves alims or ulema. They speak on behalf of Allah and His blessed *rasul.*

They deceive people. There are people who accumulate wealth. They steal and rob from people. When they see hungry and poor people, their hearts are rock hard. They have no pity.

Allah has bestowed immense wealth on the *ummah* and the land of Islam. Yet the Muslims are poor because they are poor in their *iman* and in spirit. In the lands of Islam, when each believer gives his obligatory zakat, each year *five hundred billion dollars* should become available to eradicate poverty, hunger, and disease. Yet the Muslim nations of Africa and South Asia are the perpetual carriers of the begging bowl. Their need and suffering showcases their stinginess and covetousness. The words of Allah fall on deaf ears:

> Void not your charity by boast, conceit, and insult, by reminders of your generosity like those who want their generosity to be noted by all men, but they believe neither in Allah nor in the Last Day. Theirs is a parable of a hard-barren rock, on which there is a little soil, washed by heavy rain, which leaves it just a bare stone. And Allah guides not those who reject Faith. And the likeness of those who give generously, seeking to please Allah and to strengthen their souls, is as a garden, high and fertile where heavy rain falls on it and makes it yield a double the amount of harvest, and if it receives not heavy rain, light moisture suffices it. Allah notices whatever you do. (Al-Baqarah 2:264–65, Koran)

9. The Covenant of Allah: Speak Always the Truth

﴿ يَٰٓأَيُّهَا ٱلَّذِينَ ءَامَنُواْ ٱتَّقُواْ ٱللَّهَ وَقُولُواْ قَوۡلٗا سَدِيدٗا ﴿٧٠﴾ يُصۡلِحۡ لَكُمۡ أَعۡمَٰلَكُمۡ وَيَغۡفِرۡ لَكُمۡ ذُنُوبَكُمۡۗ وَمَن يُطِعِ ٱللَّهَ وَرَسُولَهُۥ فَقَدۡ فَازَ
فَوۡزًا عَظِيمًا ﴿٧١﴾ إِنَّا عَرَضۡنَا ٱلۡأَمَانَةَ عَلَى ٱلسَّمَٰوَٰتِ وَٱلۡأَرۡضِ وَٱلۡجِبَالِ فَأَبَيۡنَ أَن يَحۡمِلۡنَهَا وَأَشۡفَقۡنَ مِنۡهَا وَحَمَلَهَا ٱلۡإِنسَٰنُۖ إِنَّهُۥ كَانَ ظَلُومٗا
جَهُولٗا ﴿٧٢﴾ لِّيُعَذِّبَ ٱللَّهُ ٱلۡمُنَٰفِقِينَ وَٱلۡمُنَٰفِقَٰتِ وَٱلۡمُشۡرِكِينَ وَٱلۡمُشۡرِكَٰتِ وَيَتُوبَ ٱللَّهُ عَلَى ٱلۡمُؤۡمِنِينَ وَٱلۡمُؤۡمِنَٰتِۗ وَكَانَ ٱللَّهُ غَفُورٗا
رَّحِيمَۢا ﴿٧٣﴾

O you who believe! Have taqwa of Allah, fear Allah, and always speak the truth, that He may direct you to deeds of righteousness and forgive your sins: he that obeys Allah and His Rasool, has already attained the highest achievement.

We did indeed offer al-Amanah, the Trust to the Heavens and the Earth and the Mountains; but they shrank from the burden, being afraid of it, but man assumed it, and has proved to be a tyrant and a fool, with the result that Allah has to punish the munafiqeen, truth concealers, men and women, and the mushrikeen, unbelievers, men and women, and Allah turns in Mercy to the Believers, men and women; for Allah is Forgiving, Most Merciful. (Al-Ahzab 33:69–73, Koran)

The very basis of Islam is truth (*haqq*). Every believer must always speak the truth. Allah guides the truthful to His path of righteousness. Without the truth, there is no *din* and no Islam. Allah's *din* is divine. Allah is *Haqq*, and all truth emanates from Him. The Koran is Allah's word on the earth and the expression of *haqq*. *Haqq* is the reality and the truth; *batil* refers to something that is imaginary and false. Those who believe in Allah only speak the truth. When humans add dogma and creed to Allah's *din*, it is not *haqq*. In matters of *din*, what is not absolute truth is not *haqq*. What is not *haqq* is *batil* (false or fabricated). What is not truthful cannot be a witness over Allah's word and *din*.

The Betrayal of the Covenant of Allah: Fabrication and Falsehood

All human additions to the *din* of Allah do not constitute the truth, and therefore, every human fabrication to the *din* after the completion of *wahiy* is *batil* (falsehood). The truth in the believer connects to Allah through *haqq*, the essence of Allah. In the same vein, it is falsehood that destroys the relationship between the human and his Lord, and the same untruth destroys the relationship among humans. Without truth, there is no *din*, and there is no Islam. And devoid of truth, the world of humans is barren, superficial, and false. Without truth, the Dar es Salaam cannot exist. All human transactions—whether personal, communal, national, or international—must always be based on the foundation of *haqq*.

All human transactions—whether personal, communal, national, or international—must always be based on the foundation of *haqq*. The statecraft, diplomacy, and international relations of the kings, sultans, autocrats, and so-called democracies have—from the beginning of time—been based on deception and mendacity. It is through secrecy, falsehood, and systematic deceit and propaganda that the modern nation-states exist and control their populations. Modern democracy, in effect, grants custody of nation-states to politicians whose sophistication belies their art of deception. The economy of modern nation-states is founded on falsehood, usury, and fake paper money. Justice means fairness, fairness means *haqq*, and *haqq* means the reality through Allah. Those who expect absolute truth from the adversarial system of the modern nation-state will not hear the truth (*haqq*). There will be peace, justice, and truth among the nation's only when the people will make their rulers accountable to the truth in a public square and humiliate those who cheat and lie. In the Islamic states, truth will triumph over falsehood. The core of the human values of the Dar es Salaam lies in truth and justice.

To live up to the trust of Allah, the vicegerency—man—has to distinguish between good and evil, truth and falsehood, *'adl* and *zulm*. Falsehood is the abomination that corrupts the very basis of Allah's vicegerency and His covenant with man. The Koran discredits workers of corruption, the worst among them being the *Munafiqeen*, truth concealers, and the hypocrites who claim to do good deeds, but their inner intentions are vile and harmful to others. Good deeds are based on truth and are therefore motivated by *iman* and *taqwa* of Allah. Corruption, dishonesty, and falsehood arise when humans—Allah's vicegerents on the earth—turn away from the covenant of Allah and forget the message of the prophets:

﴿ وَٱلَّذِينَ يَنقُضُونَ عَهْدَ ٱللَّهِ مِنۢ بَعْدِ مِيثَٰقِهِۦ وَيَقْطَعُونَ مَآ أَمَرَ ٱللَّهُ بِهِۦٓ أَن يُوصَلَ وَيُفْسِدُونَ فِى ٱلْأَرْضِ أُو۟لَٰٓئِكَ لَهُمُ ٱللَّعْنَةُ وَلَهُمْ

سُوٓءُ ٱلدَّارِ ﴿٢٥﴾ ﴾

But those who break the Covenant of Allah, after having pledged their word on it, and sever what which Allah has commanded to be joined together, and who work corruption on earth, on them shall be the curse and theirs is the ugly abode. (Ar-Ra'd 13:25, Koran)

10. The Covenant of Allah: *Fahasha*

Come not near shameful deeds, whether open or secret.

Fahishah: indecency, iniquity, abomination,
shameful deeds, scandalous acts.

Allah calls the believers not to follow in the footsteps of Satan. Satan leads them to shameful deeds (*Fahasha*) and what is wrong (*Munkar*). Allah commands the believers not to approach shameful deeds in open or in secret. Whoever rejects evil and believes in Allah has His handhold that never breaks. Allah expels all evil from those who abstain from the odious and the forbidden, and He will admit them through the gate of great honor. He will grant those with *taqwa* of Allah the criterion and ability to judge between right and wrong (*furqan*). Allah will save them from them misfortunes and evil and forgive their sins.

Man has been granted the freedom to choose the wholesome and beautiful or the corrupt and ugly. The core of the human—the *nafs*, the shiny mirror of the self—is tarnished by the dirt and the smoke of the evil and the corrupt. The *taqwa* and *nur* of Allah in man's heart blows away the dirt and smoke of evil and the ugly from the mirror of the human *nafs*. Allah promises those who perform good, reject evil, and believe in Him Allah's handhold that will never loosen. An *ummah* of one and a half billion believers in communion with Allah, surrounded in His *nur*, is a powerful force of good that will subdue all evil and ugly from the face of the earth.

A believer's life and soul akin to a dew pond of crystal-clear spring from which a fountain gushes forth pure and refreshing. In the same manner, the cascades of beautiful deeds of the believer quench the thirst of the community of believers. Acts of indecency and shame, fornication, deceit, oppression, theft, and murder contaminate the dew pond with water so foul that the believer and his community fall prey to plague, pestilence, and diseases of the body and spirit. And they all lose the grace of Allah.

The Betrayal of the Covenant of Allah: Shameful Deeds

Rulers of Muslim states indulge in shameful deeds *Fahasha*, follow Satan's footsteps, and have lost the *taqwa* of Allah and the *furqan*, the criterion to distinguish right from wrong. Through the corrupt rulers, Satan spins his web, he schemes, and he triumphs. The Muslim nation-states are the dens of inequity, ignorance, illiteracy, oppression, falsehood, injustice, corruption, and they are deeply indebted to usurious economic systems. Believers in the Muslim countries are taken into custody, tortured, and imprisoned in their struggle for justice as commanded by the covenant of Allah. Some simply disappear, while others are killed in extrajudicial executions. Such brutality maintains the incumbent royals and dictators in power. Those whose actions betray the covenant of Allah displease Him, and they walk in arrogance in the path of the devil, who leads them to a cycle of shame and iniquity.

Enter into submission to the will of Allah,
enter Islam whole-heartedly and follow not
the footsteps of Satan, for he is a sworn enemy
to you! (Al-Baqarah 2:208, Koran)

Do not follow Satan's footsteps: if any will follow
the footsteps of Satan, he will command to what is
shameful, Fahasha and wrong, Munkar: and were it
not for the Grace of Allah and His mercy on you,
not one of you would have been unblemished: but
Allah does purify whom He pleases: and Allah is
all Hearer and all Knower. (An-Nur 24:21-23)

Come not near to shameful deeds (fornication, adultery, and shameful activities) whether open or secret. (Al-An'am 6:151–53)

11. The Covenant of Allah: The Unity of *Ummah*

And hold fast, all together, by the Rope, which Allah stretches out for you, and be not divided among yourselves; and remember with gratitude Allah's favor on you; you were enemies and He joined your hearts in love, so that by His Grace, you became brethren and a community. You were on the brink of the pit of fire, and He saved you from it. Thus, does Allah make His Signs clear to you that you may be guided.

Let there arise out of you a band of people inviting to all that is good, enjoining what is right, and forbidding that is wrong. They are the ones to attain happiness.

Be not like those who are divided amongst themselves and fall into disputations after receiving clear signs: for them is a dreadful penalty. (Ali 'Imran 3:103–5, Koran)

Persevere in patience and constancy; vie in such perseverance; strengthen each other; and be in taqwa of Allah, fear Allah that you may prosper. (Ali 'Imran 3:200, Koran)

This is a grace from Allah, and a favor; and Allah is All Knowing and All Wise. If two parties among the Believers fall into a quarrel, make peace between them: but if one of them transgresses beyond bounds against

> the other, then fight you all against the one who transgresses until he complies with the Command of Allah; but if he complies, then make peace between them with justice, and fairness: for Allah loves those who are fair and just. The Believers are but a single Brotherhood: so make peace and reconciliation between your two brothers; and fear Allah, that you may receive Mercy. (Al-Hujurat 49:6–10, Koran)

> Just as the bond to Allah is indivisible, all the Believers shall stand behind the commitment of the least of them. All the Believers are bonded one to another to the exclusion of other men. (The Covenant of Muhammad)

The Communion of Believers: The believer's communion with Allah leads him to a communion with his fellow believers. In this relationship, the believers hold on to one another and to the rope that Allah has stretched to them. This rope is His covenant. The covenant of Allah thus becomes obligatory to each believer. After unity of Allah, tawhid—the unity of the *ummah* with Allah and the unity of the believers with one another—is the foremost commandment of Allah.

The Rope of Allah: Allah has ordained unity among the believers. He says to the believers,

> Hold fast, all together, the Rope, which Allah stretches out for you, and be not divided among yourselves. (Ali 'Imran 3:103–5, Koran)

When all the believers hold on to the rope that Allah casts to them, each believer connects to Allah and, through His mercy, to each and every believer. The Rope of Allah saves them from the turbulent waters of evil and falsehood. The rope of Allah saves them from the turbulent waters of evil and falsehood. The rope of Allah is His covenant, and those who pledge their allegiance to Allah, His hand is over their hands. In this communion, every believer who clasps onto the rope of Allah, His covenant, connects with the believers through unity, goodness, and truth.

> Verily those who pledge their allegiance unto you (O Muhammad), pledge it unto none but Allah; the Hand of Allah is over their hands. Thereafter whosoever breaks his Covenant, does so to the harm of his own soul, and whosoever fulfils his Covenant with Allah, Allah will grant him an immense Reward. (Al-Fath 48:10, Koran)

Thus, in this communion of each believer with Allah, there is a communion among all the believers. Allah tells the believers,

> Let there arise out of you a band of people inviting to all that is good, enjoining what is right, and forbidding that is wrong. They are the ones to attain happiness. (Ali 'Imran 3:103–5, Koran)

Upon his submission to Allah, the believer has His mercy and protection, and Allah's hand is on the believer's hands. Upon rejecting evil, the believer grasps Allah's handhold that never breaks. Allah expels all evil out of those who abstain from all that is forbidden.

> Allah holds the Believers hand upon the Believers submission to Allah and again Allah holds the Believer's hand when the Believer rejects all evil. In this condition of submission, faith, and performance

of wholesome deeds the Believers form a community that has Allah's protection and guidance.

In His call to unity of believers, Allah says to them:

> Be not like those who are divided amongst themselves and fall into disputations after receiving clear signs: for them is a dreadful penalty. (Ali 'Imran 3:103–105, Koran)

For those who lose their way and fight, Allah shows them a way to resolve their differences.

> The Believers are but a single Brotherhood: so make peace and reconciliation between your two brothers; and fear Allah, that you may receive Mercy. Persevere in patience and constancy; vie in such perseverance; strengthen each other; and be in taqwa of Allah, fear Allah that you may prosper." (Al-Hujurat 49:6–10, Koran)

Believers in communion with other believers form a living *ummah.* This *ummah* is akin to a beehive, the community of honeybees. Millions of bees work together in harmony to maintain the integrity and concord of their community. Individual bees work in cooperation to build their hive of a preordained design of hexagonal units, to maintain required environment within bee nurseries, and to raise their young. In cohesion and unity, they gather and store honey and make wax for the mutual good of all. When threatened, the bees swarm altogether and prepare to fight unto death to protect their community from intruders. All their activity is intended for the mutual benefit, survival, and prosperity of their bee community. No single bee is seen to rebel for its own selfish reasons, for enrichment nor aggrandizement of self. Muslims are ordained to act with the same unity of purpose, in the way of Allah, for mutual benefit of the *ummah.* Allah bequeathed the honeybee, in His mercy, a genetic cipher that guides their conduct that nurtures their hive and pollinates Allah's garden.

Upon man, Allah has bestowed freedom of choice, whereby he may choose to do good or follow his cravings to do evil. He has the choice to do good for his kin, community, and humanity or to let the greed and craving of his *nafs* satisfy his desires. For those who submit to Allah and have faith in Allah, the Koran and the covenant of Allah are their guide. The Koran ordains unity and actions for the common good to the believers. For those who forsake the *ummah* to satisfy their lust and cravings—the kings and politicians of Islam—they have forsaken their Allah and their *din.* Allah will change the condition of the Muslims when they believe in Him and His messengers and perform right and beautiful deeds.

﴿ مَّا كَانَ ٱللَّهُ لِيَذَرَ ٱلْمُؤْمِنِينَ عَلَىٰ مَآ أَنتُمْ عَلَيْهِ حَتَّىٰ يَمِيزَ ٱلْخَبِيثَ مِنَ ٱلطَّيِّبِ ۗ وَمَا كَانَ ٱللَّهُ لِيُطْلِعَكُمْ عَلَى ٱلْغَيْبِ وَلَٰكِنَّ ٱللَّهَ
يَجْتَبِى مِن رُّسُلِهِۦ مَن يَشَآءُ ۖ فَـَٔامِنُوا۟ بِٱللَّهِ وَرُسُلِهِۦ ۚ وَإِن تُؤْمِنُوا۟ وَتَتَّقُوا۟ فَلَكُمْ أَجْرٌ عَظِيمٌ

Allah will not leave the Believers in the state in which you are now, until He separates what is evil from what is good. Nor will Allah disclose to you the secrets of the Unseen, but He chooses of His Messengers (for the purpose) whom He pleases. So, believe in Allah and His Messengers; and if you believe and do right, you have a reward without measure. (Ali 'Imran 3:179, Koran)

The communion of individual believers with Allah and with one another translates into an *ummah* in which the critical mass of goodness on the earth outweighs evil. In this union, the Real is supreme, and His writ is the ultimate. With Allah's *nur* in every heart, there is *haqq* (truth) on the earth, and peace will reign. People will share their substance; there will be no want and therefore no greed. Wars will be abolished. Ultimately, there will be no religion as there will be no priests. Man will be with his Allah and Allah with His creation.

The *Ummah* and the World Order

Throughout the history of man, the route to power and control of people and their riches has been through a maze of secrecy, deceitful manipulation, subterfuge, and conspiracy. During and after the European crusades into the Islamic heartland, various Christian organizations from diverse lands of Europe began to band together into secret organizations to achieve their different agendas. In time, they began to control and influence the ruling houses of Europe, the papacy and the church, and the centers that controlled commerce and wealth. Wars between the kingdoms of Europe rarely had to do anything with the interest of people, justice, freedom, or human rights. Wars were fought to promote the interests of these secret organizations, which were the power behind the kings and the church.

All royal dynasties of the world originated from a band of robbers who invaded a land and came to control the centers of power and wealth. Their first act of governance was to eliminate all opposition (execution, massacres), control the population through brute force (army and secret services), and control the wealth of the land (rob the previous holders of their gold, precious stones, mansions, and estates through taxation of peasants and merchants). The rulers put on fancy garb and sat on a raised platform. The collaborators were given gaudy robes, high-sounding titles, and estates. To perpetuate the largesse from the rulers, the hangers-on supported the prolongation of the dynasty. Such was the beginning of the "establishment," a system of control of instruments of political and military power and acquisition of wealth in the hand of a select few.

With new invaders and the turnover of dynasties, the hangers-on, the courtiers, and the conspirators, the power behind the new rulers never changed. The clans behind the throne, the elite, the parasites, and the leeches honed their skills through greed and lechery, programmed their genes through marriage and social connections, and kept their power through secret organizations and conspiracy. The British Empire and the European royalty are a clear example of this inherited and aristocratic control lasting over a thousand years. The sovereigns of Europe sent their armies to the East and the West to loot and rob. The marauding armies presented the monarch with the pick of the robbed gold, diamonds, and treasures that had been hoarded by generations of Indians and other Asians over thousands of years. In return, the grateful sovereign rewarded his thugs with knighthoods, lordships, and earldoms of the realm. Thugs were ennobled over the meaner subjects to create nobility that would be the backbone of the dynasty. The nobility was presented with charters to fleece the subject nations around the world through constitutional pillage by taxation and unjust monopolistic trading practices.

After the Second World War, with the total economic ruin of European colonial powers, there occurred involuntary emancipation of the colonial subjects. The European heartland was in total ruins; with no military might to control the world's wealth, Europe faced further economic and industrial disaster. Nations of Europe and the United States then got together to establish a world order to maintain their hegemony over the rest of the world. The United Nations was created on the corrupted foundation of the League of Nations. Through a carefully crafted world order and a preordained power structure, the

United States, Russia, Britain, and France—through a veto power over the rest of the world—reigned supreme. The Security Council became the instrument of the big four to control the world. At that time, the only Islamic countries totally independent of foreign domination were Turkey and Afghanistan. Saudi Arabia, Iraq, Iran, Jordan, and Egypt were beholden to the British apron strings.

Other arrangements of control—the Bretton Woods Agreement, the International Monetary Fund, and the World Bank—were established to strengthen the Western grip over the world's resources. Toward the same end, the American Marshall Plan was inaugurated to rebuild and establish a united Europe with a single unified army, currency, and purpose meant for world domination. Such immaculate and secretive planning, coordination, and cooperation gave birth to the organization of the so-called G8 nations. The United States, Canada, Russia, Britain, France, Italy, Germany, and Japan formed the G8, a grouping of countries with a population of seven hundred million people dominating the world through superior technology, military power, economics, industrial manufacturing, trade, education, and transport. These countries are resource poor, and their economies will crumble if their access to cheap resources of the underdeveloped world is severed.

The greatest threat to the international and Islamic economy is the fiscal system designed at Bretton Woods that made the United States dollar the kingpin of the world's monetary order whereby the world has to acquire the dollar or the currency of G8 countries to buy the West's industrial goods or pay their debts. When Richard Nixon severed the link between gold and the dollar, the G8 countries began a bonanza of printing paper money twenty times their 1971 economic base. The United States Federal Reserve System, a privately owned banking system, was set up in the image of Bank of England to control the country's fiscal system. The USA, being the world's largest economy, influences the world's commercial base. The money supply of the USA and G8 countries is based on consumer demand. The money is printed by the Treasury and handed over to the central bank, or the Federal Reserve service, which in turn lends these notes created out of ink and paper at an interest rate determined by the Federal Reserve service. The commercial banks then loan out this "money made out of nothing" to the consumers at an additional interest rate generally calculated at prime rate fixed by the federal bank plus 1 to 5 percent, making a huge profit. The paper note printed by the treasury becomes *money* only when it is lent out to someone as the principal to be paid back with interest.

Almost all Western governments conduct business on deficit basis, meaning that they spent far greater money than they receive in revenue. The United States government had, by 1999, borrowed and accumulated a debt of $5.7 trillion. By 1997, the US government was paying out $350 billion in interest payments, amounting to the total revenues collected through personal income tax. The current US government debt is *$33 trillion*. The debt of the American people is another $33 trillion, while the total wealth of the whole world is estimated to be $333 trillion. With the printing of additional currency, the purchasing power of the dollar has continued to devalue by 5 percent each year since 1973. Therefore, the 2002 dollar has only 20 percent purchasing power of the 1972 dollar. In 2005, the third world farmers and workers had to labor fifteen hours to purchase industrial products produced by a European or American worker in one hour. In the same vein, the populations of the third world have to work five to seven times longer to service their international debt compared with what they did thirty years ago.

Islam and International Finance:

- The world's richest 1 percent of adults own more than half of the global household wealth, while 64 percent of the world's population own only 1.9 percent (Credit Suisse Global Wealth Report 2018). The total world wealth is US$317 trillion. There are thirty-six million millionaires in the world.
- The study finds wealth to be more unequally distributed than income across countries, Anthony Shorrocks, director of the Helsinki-based World Institute for Development Economics Research of the United Nations University (UNU-WIDER) that published the report, said at a press conference.
- To be among the most affluent, 10 percent of adults required $61,000 in assets, while over $1 million was needed to belong to the richest 1 percent. *This group of the most well off was made up of thirty-six million people.*
- Of these most well-off people, *9.25 million* live in the USA, *7.5 million* in Japan, *3.7 million* in Germany, *2.6 million* in Italy, *2.2 million* in Britain, *1.5 million* each in France and Spain, and *740,000* in Canada. *Eight million* are dispersed in the rest of the world.
- The concentration of wealth within countries was also found to vary significantly. "The share of the top 10 per cent (of wealth) ranges from around 40 per cent in China to 70 per cent in the United States, and higher still in other countries," the report authors said.
- In 2018, the year the data for the survey was collected, there were 499 dollar billionaires and 37 million millionaires throughout the world. These numbers were set to "rise fast in the next decade," the report said.

From the above report, it is clear that *1 percent* of the world's population owns more than 50 percent of world's wealth. More than

80 percent of these rich people live in the United States, Japan, Italy, Germany, Britain, Spain, France, Canada, and in other parts of the West, which comprise the G8 nations. More than 64 percent of the people of the world own less than 1.6 percent of the world's wealth.

The total wealth of the world is estimated to be *$330 trillion*. The world has three economic systems:

1. The international monetary system is based on usury and fake paper money. This system provides money for public, government, and commercial transactions. Its hub is the money printed by central banks, and it finances government expenditure, stocks and shares, commerce, industry, drug trade, currency transactions, and wars. Public and government debts are financed through this system. Most, if not all, real estate transactions are funded by debt; therefore, such wealth is illusory. The estimated fifty trillion debt accumulated by governments and people generates several layers of interest-bearing transactions. The interest on the illusory wealth of debt everyday siphons into secret caches that constitute real wealth. This system is haram and controls the life of every man under modern economies controlled by governments that, in turn, are regulated by the secret bureaucracy of the international monetary system and the World Bank.
2. A secret and concealed economic system is outside the jurisdiction of all the world's people and governments and outside the public glare. Every year three trillion dollars from gains of usury, a trillion dollars from drug trade, and other trillions in profits from the world's gas and minerals go to the purchase of a hoard of gold, diamonds, other precious minerals, mines, agricultural lands, and other resources by a secret group of people. There is no accounting nor any disclosure of such hidden treasure. A few thousand families

and secret societies hold this cache as a hedge against the day when all paper money and its illusory wealth will disappear with the shift of the decimal to the left. The black ciphers will fade into red, and the paper will disintegrate into ashes, only to be blown into oblivion as if it never existed. This system is based on secrecy, sorcery, covetousness, and greed. The holders of this wealth run the world.

3. The largest economy of the world involves four billion inhabitants of the world's poorest population who own almost nothing. It is the *gift* economy that has existed since man began his journey on the earth. Land and resources belong to Allah and will continue to belong to Him. The gift of knowledge and material things is passed on from one man to the next, generation after generation. Every man is connected to the other through their connection with Allah. Everyone helps the other till there is no need, no hunger, and no suffering. This system has been in existence for thousands of years till man, in his greed and covetousness, invaded other lands for more and destroyed the balance that Allah had established. Humans trade goods and services at a mutually agreed value system. Goods in barter or precious metals represent the value of the transaction in trade. And all other transactions are in the way of Allah (*fi sabilillah*) when goods and services are exchanged without any expectation of gain. They are merely given to please Allah.

The Ongoing Grabbing of the World's Resources: The modern economic system aims to control people and their economies by exploiting the weakness and insecurity of man. It controls the world by a few covetous and evil people. From the seventeenth century onward, bankers devised the fiat currency of *virtual* money that could be modified and manipulated by a few people to control agriculture and the mineral wealth of the world. He who made the rules of such economy also ruled the world.

The One-Thousand-Year War: November 25, 1095, is a milestone in the history of Europe and Christendom. On this day at the Council of Clermont, Pope Urban II—addressing a vast crowd of priests and knights and poor folk—declared a holy war against Islam. For Europe, this was a defining moment, and this event has ongoing repercussions until today in the Middle East. This holy war, begun in the twilight of the eleventh century, is still ongoing under various guises and forms into the beginning of the twenty-first century. NATO troops in Afghanistan, Kosovo, Bosnia, Libya, Somalia, and Iraq (the coalition) are the legacy of the Council of Clermont, now called the Council of Europe, and NATO.

The pope declared the race of Seljuk Turks who had recently converted to Islam to be barbarians. They had swept into Anatolia and seized lands from the Christian empire of Byzantium. The pope declared that the Turks were an accursed race that was utterly alienated from God who had not entrusted their spirit to God[48]. Killing these godless monsters was a holy act; it was a Christian duty to "exterminate this vile race from our lands."[49] Once they had purged Asia Minor of this Muslim filth, the knights would engage in a still holier task. They would then march to the holy city of Jerusalem and liberate it from the infidel. It was shameful that the tomb of Christ should be in the hands of Islam.

Since that time, there has been a constant onslaught against Islam by the West. When the Euro-Christian states were not fighting against

[48] Robert the Monk, *Historia Iherosolimitana*. Quoted by August C Krey, *The First Crusade: The Accounts of Eye Witnesses* (Princeton and London, 1921).

[49] Fulcher and Chartres, *History of the Expedition to Jerusalem, 1095–1127*, trans. Rita Ryan (Knoxville, 1969), 66.

one another, they grouped together in a pack to attack the Muslim states. On the surface for the public consumption, they fought for their religion to destroy the infidel, but the true motive underlying the thousand-year war was always economic exploitation of the East by the top echelons of the Euro-Christianity. The thousand-year incursions of exploitation have changed its stance every so often that the historians have lost the truth between the Crusades; Venetian trade; voyages of discovery; slave trade; colonialism; racism; economic subversion of the natives; piracy in the open seas; maritime ambushes and robbery of coastal cities; plunder of mineral, agriculture, and human resources; opium trade; capitalism; socialism; communism; world wars; globalization of world trade in the hands of few nations; and finally the control of oil.

When Damascus fell to the British troops in September 1918, Gen. Edmund Henry Allenby made it a point to visit the tomb of the great warrior Salah al-din Yusuf ibn Ayyub, the liberator of Jerusalem. Upon approaching the grave of the sultan, he kicked it with his riding boot and uttered, "*Finally, the Crusades have been avenged.*" Allenby, the Christian conqueror of Damascus, had remembered Pope Urban's one-thousand-year-old call to arms against Islam.

The G8 summitry and its move for globalization of the world's trade and economy aims to perpetuate the control of the resources and labor of the third world and the Islamic nations. The aim of the G8 and their elite who dictate their policies of the West is to prevent the unification of the Islamic world through internal subversion, military coups, and creation of discord among Muslim nations (Iran and Iraq, Iraq and Kuwait) and through the perpetuation of the Palestinian-Israeli conflict. Western support of incompetent and corrupt leaders of the Middle East—Reza Shah; Anwar Sadat; Hosni Mubarak; King Hussein of Jordan; Saddam Hussein; Saudi kings Fahd, Abdullah, and Salman; and Crown Prince Mohammed bin Salman—has muzzled the voice of the believer for the last three generations. For the price of a bit of flattery, a subtle threat, and a pocketful of money, Muslim generals, politicians, kings, and princes sold their countries' interests to the West. Musharraf put up for sale the sovereignty of Pakistan, Afghanistan, Central Asia, and Iraq to the Americans, renewing Western control over the resources and sovereignty of Islam for another century. Leaders of Islamic nations are watched for their vanity, submissiveness, megalomania, corruption, and lack of principles. Their weaknesses are scrutinized and analyzed. Accordingly, they are pampered with flattery, cash, and gifts and occasionally with blackmail and subtle threats till they singly or collectively become thoroughly emasculated, reminiscent of eunuchs prostrating in the presence of the king of the West in Washington. Before they know it, they have sold out their people's unity, sovereignty, resources, and dignity. All this does not occur accidentally. It is planned with care for years and executed by skillful players who have carefully studied the psyche and weaknesses of the Middle Eastern upstarts.

The Betrayal of the Covenant of Allah: The Circle of Evil: There is a satanic circle, the circle of evil, composing of shadowy, faceless people who all know one another and are in control of the world's wealth. This group comprising some of the world's richest men, Jewish moneylenders, Western royals, aristocrats, and business magnates manipulates and controls politicians, news media, universities, and the intelligence services of the Western democracies. These faceless conspirators are above the law, and their activities almost never hit the newsstands. Between them, they create circumstances in the Western and the Islamic worlds that allow them to place their puppets on the throne. These willing puppets—for instance, in Egypt, Jordan, Pakistan, Arabian Peninsula, and Central Asia—provide the faceless controllers reign over the Islamic lands. The circle of evil is composed of the Western world's richest men, both Jews and Christians; the Western world's corrupt political, military, and intelligence elite; and the Eastern world's corrupt Muslim rulers and greedy aristocracy.

The circle of evil deprives human kind of Allah's benevolence by diverting it to themselves. Of the total wealth and resources of the world, the circle of evil owns over 70 percent, while six billion people subsist on the remaining 30 percent. The prosperity of the un-Koranic Western world is an illusion, and this illusion has become the focus of inspiration for educated Muslim economists, planners, students, and businesspeople. Underneath the facade of prosperity and boundless riches of the West lies the bottomless pit of debt. The commerce, trade, industry, shipping, highways, spacious homes, office towers, boulevards, and automobiles are all run by the engine of massive debt. People's homes, household appliances, automobiles, holidays, and college education are all financed by money borrowed from the moneylenders of the circle of evil. The governments owe trillions of dollars to the circle as their budget deficits are financed by debt, whose interest amounts to a third of their national budgets. With the acquiescence of the people and their governments, the moneylenders create the illusion of immense wealth by printing money on fancy paper and then lending it to the governments and people. Further money is created by speculation on printed money and money trading. As if this was not enough, speculation on stocks generates further wealth through inside trading and fraudulent bookkeeping with the help of prestigious accounting firms. A major portion of the economies of world are run on usury, illicit drug and alcohol trade, and pharmaceuticals.

The Betrayal of the Covenant of Allah in Our Time: Muslim Complicity in the Invasion of Iran: In 1980, Iraq's Saddam Hussein was suddenly a big-time international "player" invited to the gaudy palaces of the Saudi Arabian monarchy. But there was an ulterior motive behind the flattering invitation. Saddam's army was the new protector of the Petro-rich against the Iranian hordes.[50]

In summer 1980, Iraq's wily president, Saddam Hussein, saw opportunities in the chaos sweeping the Persian Gulf. Iran's Islamic revolution had terrified the Saudi princes and other Arab royalty who feared uprisings against their own corrupt lifestyles. Saddam's help was sought too by CIA-backed Iranian exiles who wanted a base to challenge the fundamentalist regime of Ayatollah Ruhollah Khomeini. And as always, the Western powers were worried about the Middle East oil fields. Because of geography and his formidable Soviet-supplied army, Saddam was suddenly a popular fellow.

On August 5, 1980, the Saudi rulers welcomed Saddam to Riyadh for his first state visit to Saudi Arabia, the first for any Iraqi president. The Saudis obviously wanted something. At those fateful meetings, amid the luxury of the ornate palaces, the Saudi royal family encouraged Saddam Hussein to invade Iran. The Saudis also passed on a secret message about President Carter's geopolitical desires.

During that summer of 1980, President Carter's failure to free fifty-two American hostages held in Iran was threatening his political survival. This multisided political intrigue shaped the history from 1980 to the present day. Iraq's invasion of Iran in September 1980 deteriorated into eight years of bloody trench warfare that killed and maimed an estimated one million people. This war generated billions of dollars in profits for the West and their well-connected arms merchants.

Haig's Talking Points: Robert Parry in his article in the Consortium on December 31, 2002, states that he gained access to the Iran-Contra investigation documents, including papers marked secret and top secret, that apparently had been left behind by accident in a remote

---

[50] Robert Parry, Consortium, December 31, 2002.

Capitol Hill storage room. Those papers filled in twenty years of missing pieces of the intrigue that led to the Iraqi invasion of Iran. The papers clarified President Reagan's early strategy for a clandestine foreign policy hidden from Congress and the American people. One such document was two-page talking points prepared by Secretary of State Alexander Haig for a briefing of President Reagan. Marked top secret/sensitive, the paper recounted Haig's first trip to the Middle East in April 1981.

In the report, Haig wrote that he was impressed with bits of useful intelligence that he had learned. Both Egypt's Anwar Sadat and Saudi prince Fahd explained that Iran was receiving military spares for US equipment from Israel. This fact might have been less surprising to President Reagan, whose intermediaries allegedly collaborated with Israeli officials in 1980 to smuggle weapons to Iran behind President Carter's back.

But Haig followed that comment with another stunning assertion. It was also interesting to confirm that President Carter gave the Iraqis a green light to launch the war against Iran through Fahd. In other words, according to Haig's information, Saudi prince Fahd, later King Fahd, claimed that President Carter, apparently hoping to strengthen US hand in the Middle East and desperate to pressure Iran over the stalled hostage talks, gave clearance to Saddam's invasion of Iran. If true, Jimmy Carter, the peacemaker, had encouraged a war. Haig's written report contained no other details about the green light. The paper represented the first documented corroboration of Iran's long-held belief that the United States backed Iraq's 1980 invasion.

The Iraqi invasion did make Iran more desperate to get US spare parts for its air and ground forces. Yet the Carter administration continued to demand that the American hostages be freed before military shipments could resume. But according to house task force documents that Parry found in the storage room, the Republicans were more accommodating.

Secret FBI wiretaps revealed that an Iranian banker, the late Cyrus Hashemi who supposedly was helping President Carter on the hostage talks, was assisting Republicans with arms shipments to Iran and peculiar money transfers in fall 1980. Hashemi's elder brother, Jamshid, testified that the Iran arms shipments via Israel resulted from secret meetings in Madrid between the GOP campaign director William J. Casey and a radical Islamic mullah named Mehdi Karroubi.

For whatever reasons, on Election Day 1980, President Carter still had failed to free the hostages, and Ronald Reagan won in a landslide. Within minutes of President Reagan's inauguration on January 20, 1981, the hostages finally were freed. In the following weeks, the new Reagan administration put in place discreet channels to Middle East powers as Haig flew to the region for a round of high-level consultations. Haig met with Iraq's chief allies, Saudi Arabia and Egypt, and with Israel, which was continuing to support Iran as a counterweight to Iraq and the Arab states.

On April 8, 1981, Haig ended his first round of meetings in Riyadh. After Haig's return to Washington, his top-secret talking points fleshed out for President Reagan the actual agreements that were reached at the private sessions in Saudi Arabia, as well as at other meetings in Egypt and Israel. "As we discussed before my Middle East trip," Haig explained to President Reagan, "I proposed to President Sadat, Israel's Prime Minister Menachem Begin and Crown Prince Fahd that we establish a private channel for the consideration of particularly sensitive matters of concern to you. Each of the three picked up on the proposal and asked for early meetings."

Haig wrote that, upon his return, he immediately dispatched his counselor, Robert Bud McFarlane, to Cairo and Riyadh to formalize those channels. He held extremely useful meetings with both Sadat and Fahd, Haig boasted. These early contacts with Fahd, Sadat, and Begin solidified their three countries as the cornerstones of the administration's clandestine foreign policy of the 1980s: the Saudis as the moneymen, the Israelis as the middlemen, and the Egyptians as a ready source for Soviet-made equipment.

Although President Carter had brokered a historic peace treaty between Egypt and Israel, Sadat, Begin, and Fahd had all been alarmed at signs of US weakness, especially Washington's inability to protect the Shah of Iran from ouster in 1979. Haig's talking points captured that relief at President Carter's removal from office. "It is clear that your policies of firmness toward the Soviets have restored Saudi and Egyptian confidence in the leadership of the US," Haig wrote for the presentation to his boss.

Both Fahd and Sadat went much further than ever before in offering to be supportive. Haig said Sadat offered to host a forward headquarters for the rapid deployment force, including a full-time presence of US military personnel. Sadat also outlined his strategy for invading Libya to disrupt Mu'ammar al-Gaddhafi's intervention in Chad. Haig reported that Prince Fahd was also very enthusiastic about President Reagan's foreign policy. Fahd had agreed in principle to fund arms sales to the Pakistanis and other states in the region, Haig wrote. The Saudi leader was promising too to help the US economy by committing his oil-rich nation to a position of no drop in production of petroleum. "These channels promise to be extremely useful in forging compatible policies with the Saudis and Egyptians," Haig continued. "Both men value the 'special status' you have conferred on them and both value confidentiality."

In the following years, the Reagan administration would exploit the special status with all three countries to skirt constitutional restrictions on executive war-making powers. Secretly, the administration would tilt back and forth in the Iran-Iraq War between aiding the Iranians with missiles and spare parts and helping the Iraqis with intelligence and indirect military shipments. According to a sworn affidavit by a former Reagan national security staffer, Howard Teicher, the administration enlisted the Egyptians in a secret Bear Spares program that gave the United States access to Soviet-designed military equipment. Teicher asserted that the Reagan administration funneled some of those weapons to Iraq and also arranged other shipments of devastating cluster bombs that Saddam's air force dropped on Iranians troops.

In 1984, facing congressional rejection of continued CIA funding of the Nicaraguan contra rebels, President Reagan exploited the special status again. He tapped into the Saudi slush funds for money to support the Nicaraguan contra rebels in their war in Central America. The president also authorized secret weapons shipments to Iran in another arms-for-hostages scheme, with the profits going to off-the-shelf intelligence operations. That gambit, like the others, was protected by walls of deniability and outright lies.

When Parry interviewed Haig several years ago, he asked him if he was troubled by the pattern of deceit that had become the norm among international players in the 1980s. "Oh, no, no, no, no!" he boomed, shaking his head. "On that kind of thing? No. Come on. Jesus! God! You know, you'd better get out and read Machiavelli or somebody else because I think you are living in a dream world! People do what their national interest tells them to do and if it means lying to a friendly nation, they are going to lie through their teeth."

But sometimes the game playing did have unintended consequences. In 1990, a decade after Iraq's messy invasion of Iran, an embittered Saddam Hussein was looking for payback from the sheikhdoms that he felt had egged him into war. Saddam was especially furious with Kuwait for slant drilling into Iraq's oil fields and refusing to extend more credit. Again, Saddam was looking for a signal from the US president, this time George Bush. When Saddam explained his confrontation with Kuwait to US ambassador April Glaspie, he received an ambiguous reply, a reaction he apparently perceived as another green light. Eight days later, Saddam unleashed his army into Kuwait, an invasion that required five hundred thousand US troops and thousands more dead to reverse.

This document is a window into the workings of the circle of evil, the agents of Euro-Christianity, Zionism, and *Munafiqeen* that are out to destroy Islam. Saddam, Fahd, Sadat, Begin, and the agents of the West started a chain reaction in 1980 that set off the Iran-Iraq War, the Israeli invasion of Lebanon, the Iraqi invasion of Kuwait, the subsequent multination invasion of Iraq, the UN embargo of Iraq, the NATO invasion of Afghanistan, the ongoing occupation of Iraq, the second Israeli war against Lebanon, and the ongoing occupation and massacre of the Palestinians.

During the last forty-one years, the turmoil initiated by Saddam, Fahd and his Saudi clan, and Sadat in collaboration with the West and Israel has killed more than seven million Muslims—Arabs, Iranians, Afghans, Libyans, and Syrians. Many more millions have been made homeless. Five nations have been decimated and totally ruined. Millions have sought shelter in foreign lands. This circle of evil, in the last forty years, has prevented Islam from freeing itself from the clutches of slavery of the West. Once again, the *Yahudi-Salibi* ingenuity enrolled and used a *Munafiq* to sow the seeds of discord in the Islamic world.

1979 to 1991: Saddam, the Servant of the *Kafireen*, Traitor to Islam: Saddam Hussein replaced al-Bakr as president of Iraq in July 1979.

The bloodbath that followed eliminated all potential opposition to him. Saddam was now the master of Iraq with no one around him daring to question his actions. Two actions that he initiated led the Islamic community to disastrous disunity and debt. He attacked his fellow Muslims, Iran in 1980 and Kuwait in 1990.

The Iran-Iraq War turned out to be a battle between two egomaniac personalities, each with a Messiah complex, with neither of them willing to call a truce and a halt to the hostilities. The result was emaciation and bleeding of both countries to near bankruptcy. The Iraqi troops launched a full-scale invasion of Iran on September 22, 1980. France supplied high-tech weapons to Iraq, and the Soviet Union was Iraq's largest weapon supplier. Israel provided arms to Iran, hoping to bleed both the nations by prolonging the war. At least ten nations sold arms to both warring nations to profit from the conflict.

The United States followed a more duplicitous policy, towards both the warring parties in order to prolong the war and cause maximum damage to both.

The United States followed a more duplicitous policy toward the warring parties to prolong the war and cause maximum damage to both of them. The United States and Iraq restored diplomatic relations in November 1984. Washington extended a $400 million credit guarantee for the export of US goods to Iraq. The CIA established a direct Washington-to-Baghdad link to provide the Iraqis with faster intelligence from US satellites.[51] The satellite data provided to Iraqis was some factual and some misleading information. Casey, the CIA director, was urging Iraqi officials to carry out more attacks on Iran, especially on economic targets.[52]

---

[51] Stephen Engelberg, "Iran and Iraq Got Doctored Data, US Officials Say," *New York Times*, Jan. 12, 1987, A1, A6.

[52] Bob Woodward, *Veil*, 480.

The US policy toward Iran was two faced as it followed two tracks at the same time. On the one hand, the US government carried out a covert program to undermine the government of Iran[53]. Starting in 1982, the CIA provided $100,000 a month to a group in Paris called the Front for the Liberation of Iran, headed by Ali Amini, who had presided over the reversion of Iranian oil to foreign control after the CIA-backed coup in 1953. The United States also provided support to two Iranian paramilitary groups based in Turkey, one of them headed by Gen. Bahram Aryana, the Shah's army chief.[54] The United States also carried out clandestine radio broadcasts into Iran from Egypt, calling for Khomeini's overthrow and urging support for Bakhtiar. Simultaneously, the United States pursued the second track of clandestinely providing arms and intelligence information to Iran in 1985 and 1986. In 1984, Washington launched Operation Staunch in an effort to dry up Iran's sources of arms supplies by pressuring US allies to stop supplying arms to Iran. While Washington was pretending to be neutral in the war and trying to make everyone else stop selling arms to Iran, the United States made secret arms transfers to Iran and encouraged Israel to do the same.[55] The United States provided intelligence to Iranians, which was a mixture of factual and bogus information. The USA did, however, provide full critical data to Iran before its critical victory in the Fao Peninsula in February 1986.

The Iran-Iraq War was not between good and evil. Islam forbids fighting among the Muslims and forbids murder and the taking of life unless it is in the cause of justice. Saddam Hussein launched

---

[53] The Tower Commission, *President's Special Review Board* (Bantam Books, New York), 294–95.

[54] Leslie H. Gelb, "US Said to Aid Iranian Exiles in Combat and Political Units," *New York Times*, March 7, 1982, A1, A12.

[55] Leslie Gelb, "Iran Said to Get Large-Scale Arms from Israel, Soviets and Europeans," *New York Times*, March 8, 1982, A1, A10; Anthony Cordesman, *The Iran-Iraq War*, 31.

a murderous war to regain a few square miles of territory that his country had relinquished freely in 1975 border negotiations. There were one and a half million Muslim casualties in this senseless fraternal war. The war ended in a cease-fire that essentially left prewar borders unchanged. The covenant of Allah not only forbids such an internecine war but also provides a mechanism for dispute resolution. Instead of condemning the aggressor, the Arab states sided with Saddam Hussein, providing him with funds for further bloodletting. Saddam Hussein used banned chemical weapons against fellow Muslims, the Iranians, and Kurds. The eight-year-long war exhausted both countries. The primary responsibility for the prolonged bloodletting must rest with the governments of the two countries, the ruthless military regime of Saddam Hussein and the ruthless clerical regime of Ayatollah Khomeini in Iran. Whatever his religious convictions, Khomeini had no qualms about sending his followers, including young boys, to their deaths for his own greater glory. This callous disregard for human life was no less characteristic of Saddam Hussein.

Saudi Arabia gave $25.7 billion and Kuwait $10 billion to Iraq to fuel the war and the killing of Muslims by Muslims. Saddam Hussein also owed the Soviets, USA, and Europe $40 billion for the purchase of arms. The cost of war to the Iranians was even greater. The rest of the world community sold arms for eight and a half years and watched the bloodletting. The USA sold arms and information to both sides to prolong the war strategically and to profit and gain influence and bases in the Gulf countries. Ayatollah Khomeini, in particular, was a hypocrite in dealing with Israel in secret, especially when his public pronouncements were venomously anti-Israel.

Iran, Iraq, and all the Arab states of the Persian Gulf took Western countries, the Soviet Union, and Israel as their *awliya* in contradiction to the commandments of the covenant. The ayatollah and his clerics should have known and understood their obligations to Allah and to their people as spelled out in Allah's covenant. The uncontrolled Arab-Iranian hostility left a deep, festering wound in the body of the nation of Islam. The West made gains by setting up permanent bases in Saudi Arabia, Oman, the United Arab Emirates, Bahrain, Qatar, and Kuwait. This is the land that Muhammad, the blessed *rasul.* of Allah, freed from the infidels, only to be handed over to infidels by the *Munafiqeen.*

1990 to 2006: Saddam Opens the Gateway of Islam to the *Kafireen:* On August 2, 1990, Saddam Hussein was into mischief again. He invaded and occupied Kuwait. The sheikh of Kuwait and his family fled to Saudi Arabia. A coalition of Arabs, NATO, and many other countries carried a massive bombardment of Baghdad and other parts of Iraq on January 17, 1991, destroying the military installations, industrial units, and civilian infrastructure of Iraq. On February 24, 1991, American-led forces launched a ground offensive into Iraq and defeated the Iraqi Army. A United Nations resolution placed Iraq under an embargo till Iraq gave up all its biological and chemical weapons and also all nuclear weapon-making material.

After the Kuwait war at the invitation of King Fahd, the USA has continued to maintain large operational army and air force bases and command and control facilities that enable them to monitor all air and sea traffic as well as all civilian and military communications in the Middle East. Bahrain, in the meantime, has become the headquarters of the naval fleet command. Qatar has the longest runways in the Middle East and host to the United Stated Central Command Center. The Middle East, at the beginning of the twenty-first century, is under the absolute military and economic grip of the USA and NATO. The circle of evil—the *Yahudi*, *Salibi*, and *Munafiqeen*—continues to dominate the lives of the Muslims.

1992 to the Present: The American Empire: After Saddam Hussein's Iraq was thoroughly trounced by the United States and its NATO and Arab allies in February 1991, the Western countries used their power in the United Nations Security Council to set up an embargo on Iraq. No food, medicines, or equipment for use in the reconstruction of the destroyed power and water purification plants was allowed into Iraq. Over the following twelve years, over half a million Iraqi children died and five million children suffered from malnutrition and disease. Iraq suffered from depravation and disease created by the United Nations, a world body established to bring about peace and reduce suffering in the world. Eventually, when the UN did start the oil-for-food program, the funds were skimmed by the United Nations to pay for war reparations, and the food aid meant for the victims of the embargo did not always get to them.

The New American Century: Iraq was thoroughly humiliated and defeated in February 1991. This was considered by the Americans to be a magnificent victory. In fact, the war was between a war-weary Iraq, with a population of eighteen million people, and a coalition of the world's most developed countries and the wealthy Arabs. The Arabs supplied over a hundred billion dollars and all the air, land, and naval bases to fight this war. After its humiliating defeat in Vietnam, the USA had avoided any frontal assault on any country till the war on Iraq. Actually, the Americans had been bold enough to attack two mini states, Granada and Panama, which had only parade ground armies and won hands down.

In early 1990s, emboldened with these victories and by the fall of Soviet Russia from internal decay, a group of Republican politicians founded the Project for the New American Century. They planned and conspired to take the White House and the two other branches of government as well. They began to lay on the drawing board their vision about how the United States should move in the world when the time came.

Donald Rumsfeld, Dick Cheney, James Woolsey, Paul Wolfowitz, Richard Perle, Bill Kristol, James Bolton, Zalmay M. Khalilzad, William Bennett, Dan Quayle, and Jeb Bush led the Project for the New American Century. They were representing ideas and ideologies of faceless, influential, wealthy individuals and corporations that helped them set up think tanks and provided them funds to buy up media outlets—newspapers, magazines, TV networks, radio talk shows, and cable channels. Through the inside manipulations of the governor of Florida, Jeb Bush, and through the friendship of Dick Cheney with his fishing pal, justice of the Supreme Court Antonin Scalia, George W. Bush was selected the president of the United States. The new president was a foreign policy novice and described by some as intellectually incurious who had struggled with alcoholism all his life. The Western governments have powerful diplomatic, economic, and military alliance that has an edge over the rest of the world.

The Circle of Evil: Beyond what has been stated, more than the diplomatic, economic, and military strength of their alliance is the power provided to United States, Britain, and Israel by the traitors of Islam. In our age, we have people who think that they can get the best both the worlds by compromising their nations and Islam's interests with the enemy. They constitute the other half of the circle of evil that is destroying Islam. They pretend to be Muslims. They pray, they fast, and they go for the hajj pilgrimage. Their fingers robotically sift through their prayer beads. Allah has bestowed on them so much wealth and power that their next one hundred generations will be able to live lavishly off their wealth. They love the luxury of their private Gulf Stream jets and granite places with silken rugs and gold plumbing fixtures. Dozens of attendants' rush to their raised brow. Are they happy? Moreover, are they in peace with Allah's grace upon them? No. Wealth and power is not enough; they want more of it.

Nine countries collectively have acted as the Muslim part of the circle of evil. They are Egypt, Pakistan, Bahrain, Kuwait, Qatar, United Arab Emirates, Oman, Jordan, and Saudi Arabia. In the Afghanistan and Iraq invasions of 2002–2006, an estimated 260,000 Muslim men, women, and children were killed, and hundreds of thousands injured, and millions made homeless by bombing. Two sovereign Islamic nations have been decimated, their state structure shattered, and economies annihilated. It would take at least thirty years to rebuild these nations and rehabilitate their citizens. The loss was not to the Taliban or to Saddam Hussein. The loss is to the unity of the *ummah*, the unity that has been ordained in the covenant with Allah. Who will assist in the destruction of Islam perpetrated by a secret cabal of *Yahudi-Salibi* conspirators in Washington? In the twenty-first century, treason is hard to hide but hard to explain.

Pakistan: Pakistan's illegitimate dictator Musharraf, who had stolen the government by force of arms, craved for legitimacy. Power corrupts, and absolute power corrupts absolutely. Any power and wealth acquired with *harramma* will continue to be maintained with *harramma*. Those who promote disunity of the *ummah* are promised severe retribution. Disobedience of the covenant of Allah is haram and is cursed. Haram will breed more haram and Allah's wrath. It reminds us of how the scales of Allah's justice, the two hands of Allah—His mercy and His wrath—are reflected in the human domain, where people have been appointed Allah's vicegerents. Deeds of goodness and wholesomeness are associated with mercy, paradise, and the beautiful. Evil and corruption is rewarded with wrath, hell, and the ugly.

The other "Muslims" who perpetrate evil association with the *kafireen* are princes and kings of Arabia, the land of Islam, Allah's blessed prophet, and the holy shrines of Mecca and Medina. Bahrain, Kuwait, Qatar, United Arab Emirates, Jordan, Oman, and Saudi Arabia united with the evil to destroy the lives of 50 million Muslims in Iraq and Afghanistan and the faith of 1.5 billion believers. Although *Bahrain* is a constitutional monarchy, it is run like a family enterprise by the Al Khalifah family. In 1992, the sheikh gave himself the title of king. The king, the crown prince, the commander in chief, the prime minister, the defense minister, housing minister, the interior minister, the oil and development minister, and the foreign ministers are related through blood and marriage, and they all are kith and kin of the Al Khalifah family, afraid to share governance with their 724,000 subjects. This family has carved most of Bahrain's agriculturally fertile land for their own private use. Members of the Al Khalifah family control over 80 percent of the agriculture land in Bahrain. They have allocated themselves virtually all the coastal land. Thirty-three percent of all oil revenue goes to the members of the Al Khalifah family; the instruments of the state are run on the rest. Two percent of the population owns 90 percent of the wealth of the islands. To safeguard the wealth and position of this family, the Al Khalifah clan has secret treaties with the United States to protect the family from their subjects and from their neighbors. They act as the springboard for the United Stated Army, Marines, and Navy in their two invasions of Iraq and Afghanistan and in the ongoing hostilities against Iran. The Al Khalifah family has permitted the American Fifth Fleet to be based in Bahrain. The Fifth Fleet, for over thirty years, has menaced the Persian Gulf and has worked against the freedom of Iran and Iraq.

Kuwait, an oil-rich patch of desert, was carved out of the Basra district of the Ottoman Empire through the connivance of the British to circumvent the German plan to build railways from Berlin through the Ottoman Empire to Kuwait in the Persian Gulf. Kuwait, being the only deep water harbor on the western edge of the Persian Gulf, provided the British with a supply and refueling center for its navy. It has continued to be subservient to the *kafireen* to maintain the Sabah family's power and riches. The Sabah family, like other Arab monarchies, runs their country as a family incorporation, all ministries being run by the family. Most of the country's wealth reverts to the royal family.

2003 to Present: Muslim Complicity in the Invasion of Iraq: Saudi Arabia: Bahrain, Kuwait, Qatar, United Arab Emirates, Oman, Jordan, Pakistan, and Saudi Arabia willingly provided Britain and the United States facilities for overflight, air operations, basing, port facilities, and facilities to preposition equipment for the Iraq invasion. It should come as no surprise to Muslims around the world that the Saudi royal family directly participated in the American invasion of Iraq and the slaughter of about 260,000 Iraqis and in the destruction of Iraq's infrastructure.

The Betrayers of the Covenant of Allah: The Saudis, the Traitors among Us: On Friday, November 15, 2002, the Saudi ambassador Prince Bandar bin Sultan came to the Oval Office to see Pres. George W. Bush. Dick Cheney and Condoleezza Rice were also there. Bandar had been a long-term fixture in Washington, having served during four American presidencies. He had a ready access to American presidents, particularly the first President Bush, and the Bush family regarded him as a member of the family, where the prince had acquired the name Bandar Bush. On the same token, the Saudis had reputedly invested $1.4 billion in the Bush family, and the American president could safely be named George Bush Ibn Sa'ud. In this relationship, the Saudis do the American bidding in the Middle East, and the Americans protect the royal family interests and investments. In spite of this deep relationship and $3 trillion Saudi investment and support to the American economy, the Saudis do not have the resolve and will to use their clout to solve the Palestinian problem.

Bandar handed the president a private letter from Prince Abdullah, the de facto ruler of Saudi Arabia, and provided an English translation of the text. The text, in summary, congratulated the president's victory achieved by the Republican Party under his leadership. It stated that Prince Bandar was authorized to convey and discuss his message to the president face-to-face. As instructed Bandar then said formally, "Since 1994, we have been in constant contact with you at the highest level regarding what needs to be done with Iraq and Iraqi regime. Now, Mr. President, we want hear from you directly on your serious intention regarding this subject so we can adjust and coordinate so we can make right policy decision."

In 1994, King Fahd had proposed to President Clinton a joint US-Saudi covert action to overthrow Saddam, and Crown Prince Abdullah in April 2002 had suggested to Pres. George Bush that they spend up to $1 billion in a joint operation with the CIA. "Every time we meet, we are surprised that the United States asks us to give our impression about what can be done regarding Saddam Hussein," Bandar said, suggesting that the repeated requests caused them to "begin to doubt how serious America is about the issue of regime change. Now tell us what you are going to do."

Bandar read, "If you have a serious intention, we will not hesitate so that our two military people can then implement and discuss in order to support the American military action or campaign. This will make Saudi Arabia a major ally for the United States."

President Bush thanked the ambassador and said that he always appreciated the crown prince's views; he was a good friend and a great ally. Bush added that when he made up his mind on the military option, he would contact the crown prince before his final decision.[56]

On January 11, 2003, Dick Cheney invited Prince Bandar bin Sultan, the Saudi ambassador, to his West Wing. Present on this occasion were Defense Secretary Don Rumsfeld and Joint Chief of Staff

[56] Woodward, *Plan of Attack*, 228–30.

Chairman Gen. Richard Myers. The American defense officials appraised Bandar, a foreigner, of their battle plans against Iraq, even before Colin Powell, the US secretary of state, knew of them. General Meyers unfurled a large map of the area and explained the first part of the battle plan. The plan involved a massive bombing campaign over several days. The United States would drop on Iraq four times the bombs that destroyed it during the forty-two days of the Gulf War. And during those days, Americans dropped more bombs on Iraq than were dropped by all the combatants during the Second World War. Bandar was informed that his fellow Arab and Muslim Iraqis were to be exploded, incinerated, and blown to bits with four times the explosives than had ever been used on this planet previously. Special forces, intelligence teams, and air strikes would be launched through the five-hundred-mile Saudi border with Iraq.

The next day, Bandar met George W. Bush. The Saudis wanted an assurance that, this time, Saddam would be totally finished, and the president reminded the ambassador of his briefings from "Dick, Rummy, and General Meyers," in which they had assured Bandar that, this time, Saddam indeed would be toast.[57] Bandar flew to Riyadh and provided a verbatim report of the battle plan to Crown Prince Abdullah. Abdullah advised Bandar to maintain strict secrecy till they could figure out their next move.

On Friday, March 14, 2003, Bandar was shown into the Oval Office; Cheney, Rice, and Card were there. Bandar was unshaven, he had put on weight, and the buttons on his jacket were straining. He was tired, nervous, and excited. He was sweating profusely. "What's wrong with you?" the president asked Bandar. "Don't you have a razor to shave with?"

"Mr. President," Bandar replied, "I promised myself I would not shave until this war starts."

---

[57] Ibid., 263–68.

"Well, then, you are going to shave very soon."

"I hope so," Bandar said. "By the time this war starts, I will be like bin Laden." He then indicated a long beard of a foot or two.

On Wednesday, March 19, 2003, at 7:30 p.m., Condoleezza Rice told Bandar, "The president has asked me to tell you that we are going to war. At about 9:00 p.m., all hell will break loose."

"Tell him he will be in our prayers and hearts," Bandar said. "God help us all."

Bandar then called Crown Prince Abdullah in a prearranged code in reference to an oasis, Roda outside Riyadh. "Tonight, the forecast is there will be heavy rain in the Roda," Bandar said from his car phone to Saudi Arabia.

Abdullah asked, "Do you know how soon the storm is going to hit?"

Bandar replied, "Sir, I don't know, but watch TV."

The American air campaign against Iraq was essentially managed from inside Saudi Arabia, where American military commanders operated an air command center and launched refueling tankers, F-16 fighter jets, and sophisticated intelligence-gathering flights, according to American officials.[58] Senior officials from both countries told the Associated Press that the royal family permitted widespread military operations to be staged from inside the kingdom during the invasion of Iraq.

Between 250 and 300 air force planes were staged from Saudi Arabia, including AWACS, C-130s, refueling tankers, and F-16 fighter jets, during the height of the war, the officials said. Air and military operations during the war were permitted at the Tabuk air base and the Arar regional airport near the Iraq border. "We operated the

---

[58] "New Details on Saudi Help in Iraq War," Associated Press, April 25, 2004, http://wwwfoxnews.com/story/0,933,118084,00.html.FoxNews.

command center in Saudi Arabia. We operated aero planes out of Saudi Arabia, as well as sensors and tankers," said Gen. T. Michael Moseley, a top air force general who was the architect of the campaign. During the war, US officials held a media briefing about the air war from Qatar although the air command center was in Saudi Arabia—a move designed to prevent inflaming the Saudi public.

When the war started, the Saudis allowed cruise missiles to be fired from navy ships across their airspace into Iraq. The Saudis provided tens of millions of dollars in discounted and free oil, gas, and fuel for American forces. During the war, a stream of oil delivery trucks, at times, stretched for miles outside the Prince Sultan air base, said a senior US military planner. The Saudis were influential in keeping down the world oil prices during the run-up to the Iraq War by pumping 1.5 million barrels a day. The Saudis kept Jordan supplied with cheap oil for its support in the Iraq War. Although King Abdullah of Jordan had met with the leaders of Turkey, Syria, and Egypt and made well-publicized statements against the war on Iraq, he had secretly committed to support the American war effort against Iraq. American troops and intelligence services operated from inside the Jordanian borders in their invasion of Iraq.

Saddam Hussein was a traitor to Islam and a tyrant and deserved humiliation. However, at the eve of the war, he contacted Egypt for asylum. The Egyptians, at the behest of the Americans, refused. Prince Bandar had been informed directly by Hosni Mubarak. Yet Iraqis were attacked, and the country decimated.[59]

The Saudis, Egyptians, and other Arab rulers were aware of the magnitude of the planned air attack on the Iraqi people. The invasion of Iraq ostensibly was to depose Saddam and his regime. Saddam tried to abdicate, leave Iraq, and sought asylum in Egypt. Yet the Arab

---

[59] Woodward, *Plan of Attack*, 312.

rulers let the invasion go unchallenged and, in fact, assisted a *kafir* power to occupy a sovereign Muslim country. They allowed 560,000 Iraqis to be blown to bits and hundreds of thousands of civilians to be maimed. Eighty percent of the population lost their jobs. The country was decimated. The infrastructure had been blown into stone age, and the desert had been poisoned with radioactive waste from spent ammunition for thousands of years to come.

2012–2019: Palestine, Libya, Syria, and Yemen: There are three major conflicts ongoing in the Muslim world. First, the ongoing Israeli occupation of Palestine has mostly been sidelined by Arab states. The Saudis, Egyptians, and Jordanians have abandoned their pledge to the covenant of Allah to protect believers from oppression. Men, women, and children are oppressed, tortured, and murdered daily in Palestine by the Israeli state army. The only Muslims who are fighting the oppression of their brethren are the Iranians, Syrians, Hezbollah, and Hamas. Sadly, the Saudis, Egyptians, and Jordanians are actually colluding openly with the Israelis in this atrocity.

The Koran ordains:

> And why should you not fight in the cause of Allah and for those men, women and children, who are weak, abused and oppressed, those who beseech their Lord to deliver them from their oppressors and those who ask Allah to send for them protectors and helpers. (Qur'an 4:71-75 An Nisa).

> And slay them wherever you catch them and turn them out from where they have turned you out; for Fitnah, tyranny and oppression are worse than slaughter; And fight them on until there is no more Fitnah, tumult or oppression and there prevail

justice and faith in Allah; but if they cease, let there be no hostility except to those who practice oppression. (Al-Baqarah 2:190–93, Koran)

Second, Saudi Arabia prioritizes its rivalry with Iran under the pretext of Shia-Sunni rift; but in reality, it is moved by power politics for regional influence unfolding in Iraq, Lebanon, Syria, Yemen, and the Gulf states.

Finally, there is a Sunni-Sunni rift, with Egypt, Saudi Arabia, and the UAE vying with Qatar and Turkey. Arabs have thousands of years of history of infighting and disunity.

12. The Covenant of Allah: Perseverance and Patience

﴿ يَٰٓأَيُّهَا ٱلَّذِينَ ءَامَنُوا۟ ٱصْبِرُوا۟ وَصَابِرُوا۟ وَرَابِطُوا۟ وَٱتَّقُوا۟ ٱللَّهَ لَعَلَّكُمْ تُفْلِحُونَ ٢٠٠ ﴾

O you who believe! persevere in patience and constancy; vie in such perseverance; strengthen each other; and fear Allah; that you may prosper.

Ṣabr, *ṣābir*, *ṣabbār*, and *ṣābara* denote the quality of patience and steadfastness, self-restraint, forbearance, endurance, and perseverance. One of Allah's ninety-nine names is *al-Ṣabur*, the Patient. It is the one who does not precipitate an act before its time but decides matters according to a specific plan and brings them to fruition in a predefined manner, neither procrastinating nor hastening matters before their time but disposing each matter in its appropriate time in the way of its needs and requirements and doing all that without being subjected to a force opposing Allah's will. *Ṣabr*, *ṣābir*, *ṣabbār*, and *ṣābara* are mentioned in the Koran sixty-nine times. Allah reassures the believers:

Believers be patient and vie you with patience. (Ali 'Imran 3:200, Koran)

- Pray for succor to Allah and be patient. (Al-A'raf 7:128, Koran)
- Be thou patient, Allah will not leave to waste the wage of good doers. (Hud 11:115, Koran)
- Be thou patient, Surely Allah's promise is true. (Ar-Rum 30:60, Koran)
- Bear patiently whatever may befall you. (Luqman 31:17, Koran)
- So, be thou patient with a sweet patience. (Al-Ma'arij 70:5, Koran)
- And be patient unto your Lord. (Al-Muddaththir 74:7, Koran)
- Believers seek you help in patience and prayer. (Al-Anbiyaa 21:153, Koran)
- But come sweet patience. (Yusuf 12:18, 83, Koran)
- Surely Allah is with the is with the patient. (Al-Baqarah 2:153, 249, Koran)
- Allah loves the patient. (Ali 'Imran 3:146, Koran)

For a man and a woman to be patient (*şabr*) requires endurance and discipline to affirm a rational resolve in opposing the impulses of passion or anger. It involves balancing two opposing desires. The believer has to overcome the impulse leading to rashness and haste and at the same time lean toward the inclination to delay the act. To be patient, one has to resolve the conflict between acts, anger and rashness on one hand and procrastination and delay on the other.

The Betrayal of the Covenant of Allah: Lack of *Şabr*: Lack of *şabr*, self-restraint, patience, and self-discipline has overwhelmed the Muslim world at the beginning of the twenty-first century. The Muslim world has been rudderless and leaderless over one hundred years and poorly led during the previous one thousand years. The result is 1.5 billion individuals following their own instincts for the sake of mere survival.

Ṣabr teaches self-restraint in the matters of need and giving precedence to others over oneself in matters of need. Islam teaches that the elders, the sick, the needy, the women, and the children take precedence in matters of care, shelter, and food and that spirituality takes precedence over one's daily needs. Consideration and the well-being of the kin, the neighbor, and the fellow man requires a thought before fulfilling one's own requirements. The state of *ṣabr* in the Muslim world is obvious when one looks at the lineups at the bus and rail stations. People are being trampled at the holy sites. Old men, women, and the disabled were pushed and trampled during the holiest act of circumambulation of the Kaaba, at *Safa* and *Marwa*, and during the ritual stoning of the devil. The same is true in the shopping centers, down the streets, and inside the classrooms.

The extreme desire for immediate gratification of desires and cravings leads to small and major crimes. Lying, theft, and robbery are common acts involved in the impulse of possession of the unreachable. Military revolutions, palace coups, conspiracies, and conquests have brought power and wealth in the hands of people with vast but criminal ambitions. Such people lack perseverance, capacity for hard work, honesty, and *ṣabr.*

> Persevere in patience and constancy; vie in such perseverance; strengthen each other; and be in taqwa of Allah, fear Allah that you may prosper. (Ali 'Imran 3:200, Koran)

13. The Covenant of Allah: Betray Not the Trust of Allah and His *Rasul*: Theft, Deception, Fraud, Dishonesty, and Injustice

> Betray not the trust of Allah and His Rasool. Nor knowingly misappropriate wealth entrusted to you, whether on behalf of an orphan or another

party And do not devour each other's wealth dishonestly, nor use it as bait for the judges, with intent that you may devour dishonestly, and knowingly a little of (other) people's wealth.

Betray not the trust of Allah and His *rasul*. Nor knowingly misappropriate wealth entrusted to you, whether on behalf of an orphan or another party. Be honest in handling property, goods, credit, confidences, and secrets of your fellow men and display integrity and honesty in using your skills and talents. Whenever you give your word, speak truthfully and justly, even if a near relative is concerned. Similarly, the *amri minkum*—those entrusted with the administration of the affairs of the believers—should not betray the trust of Allah, the *rasul*, and the believers and knowingly misappropriate the wealth of the Muslims. The populations of the Islamic lands are akin to the orphans whose land and heritage has been forcibly sequestered by conquest, soon to be redeemed and accounted for from the those who ceased it, who will on the appointed day be asked to account for every grain of sand and every grain of stolen gold. The Arabian Peninsula and other Muslim lands have been the plundering fields of the royal families and their kin for one hundred years in partnership with the circle of evil.

The Betrayal of the Covenant of Allah: The Plunder of the *Ummah*

The rulers of the Arabian Peninsula and their royal relations regularly skim off the top third of the wealth of the *ummah* for their personal benefit. The dictators, the royals, and their circle of sycophants and cheerleaders in all Muslim nation-states have siphoned off the cream of their national wealth. Suharto, Asif Ali Zardari, Benazir Bhutto, Nawaz Shariff, Pakistani generals, Reza Shah of Iran, Saddam Hussein, Anwar Sadat, Hosni Mubarak, kings of Arabian Peninsula, their families, and the inner circle of their regimes have plundered their nation's treasuries of billions of dollars over the years of their prolonged rein on power. However, the greatest pillage and plunder in history took place systematically when the descendants of ten barefoot, camel-herding Bedouins took control of the Arabian Peninsula with the help of British money and arms. In the latter half of the twentieth century, over a short period of forty-five years, they took a heist of $4.5 trillion. In the Arabian Peninsula, in the kingdoms of Oman, Kuwait, the United Arab Emirates, Qatar, Bahrain, and Saudi Arabia, there are now six kings and over two hundred billionaires and thousands of millionaires among this narrow circle of ten clans. Over this short period, these tent dwellers who had never been inside the confines of a dwelling now own hundreds of palaces in Arabia, Europe, and America. Yet the plunder goes on. The total amount of petty cash taken out by the ever-increasing progeny of these Bedouin sheikhs in allowances, salaries, commissions, and expenses is to the tune of $125 billion annually, which is more than the total combined annual budget of nation-states of Pakistan, Afghanistan, Iran, Syria, Turkey, and Jordan, with a population of 300 million people. The cost of security of these "royals" (90,000 troops), personal jets, helicopters, yachts, travel, and private royal air terminals in Jeddah, Riyadh, Dubai, and Doha is an additional $10 billion. At the same time, most of the Arabs and Muslims live in conditions of utter poverty and deprivation.

Two fundamental terms used in the Koran are *haqq* (right and honest means of income) and *batil* (wrongful and dishonest way of making money). The ways of making money approved by the Koran are halal, and those forbidden are haram.

Muslims the world over follow the verses of the Koran about fasting in Sura Al-Baqarah 2:183–87 but very conveniently ignore the following verse 188:

> 'And do not devour each other's wealth
> dishonestly, nor use it as bait for the judges, with

intent that you may devour dishonestly, and
knowingly a little of (other) people's wealth.'

O you who believe! Fasting is prescribed to you as it was prescribed to those before you, that you may (learn) self-restraint,(Fasting) for a fixed number of days; but if any of you is ill, or on a journey, the prescribed number (should be made up) from days later. For those who can do it (with hardship), is a ransom, the feeding of one that is indigent but he that will give more, of his own free will, it is better for him. And it is better for you that you fast, if you only knew.

Ramadan is the (month) in which was sent down the Qur'an, as a guide to mankind, also Clear (Signs) for guidance and judgment (between right and wrong). So, every one of you who is present (at his home) during that month should spend it in fasting, but if anyone is ill, or on a journey, the prescribed period (should be made up) by days later. Allah intends every facility for you; He does not want to put you to difficulties. (He wants you) to complete the prescribed period, and to glorify Him in that He has guided you; and perchance you shall be grateful.

When My servants ask thee concerning Me, I am indeed close (to them): I listen to the prayer of every suppliant when he calls on Me: let them also, with a will, listen to My call, and believe in Me: that they may walk in the right way.

Permitted to you, on the night of the fasts, is the approach to your wives. They are your garments, and

you are their garments. Allah knows what you used to
do secretly among yourselves; but He turned to you
and forgave you; so now associate with them, and seek
what Allah hath ordained for you, and eat and drink
until the white thread of dawn appear to you distinct
from its black thread; then complete your fast till the
night appears; but do not associate with your wives
while you are in retreat in the mosques. Those are
limits (set by) Allah: approach not nigh thereto. Thus,
doth Allah make clear His Signs to men: that they may
learn self-restraint. (Al-Baqarah 2:183–87, Koran)

﴿ وَلَا تَأْكُلُوٓا۟ أَمْوَٰلَكُم بَيْنَكُم بِٱلْبَٰطِلِ وَتُدْلُوا۟ بِهَآ إِلَى ٱلْحُكَّامِ لِتَأْكُلُوا۟ فَرِيقًا مِّنْ أَمْوَٰلِ ٱلنَّاسِ بِٱلْإِثْمِ وَأَنتُمْ تَعْلَمُونَ ﴿١٨٨﴾

And do not devour each other's wealth dishonestly,
nor use it as bait for the judges, with intent that
you may devour dishonestly, and knowingly a little
of (other) people's wealth. (Al-Baqarah 2:188)

There are several dishonest financial practices, cheating, bribery, stealing, embezzlement, hoarding, and swindling, but one mentioned specifically in the Koran is often overlooked. That is the one practiced by the aristocrats, clergy, clerics, and claimants of spiritual leadership all across the world:

﴿ ۞ يَٰٓأَيُّهَا ٱلَّذِينَ ءَامَنُوٓا۟ إِنَّ كَثِيرًا مِّنَ ٱلْأَحْبَارِ وَٱلرُّهْبَانِ لَيَأْكُلُونَ أَمْوَٰلَ ٱلنَّاسِ بِٱلْبَٰطِلِ وَيَصُدُّونَ عَن سَبِيلِ ٱللَّهِ ۗ وَٱلَّذِينَ يَكْنِزُونَ ٱلذَّهَبَ وَٱلْفِضَّةَ وَلَا يُنفِقُونَهَا فِى سَبِيلِ ٱللَّهِ فَبَشِّرْهُم بِعَذَابٍ أَلِيمٍ ﴿٣٤﴾ ﴾

> O you who believe! There are indeed many among the priests and clerics,(leaders) who in falsehood devour the substance of men and hinder (them) from the Way of Allah. And there are those who bury gold and silver and spend it not in the Way of Allah: announce unto them a most grievous penalty. (At-Tawbah 9:34, Koran)

Like the politicians and dictators, these priests and spiritual leaders deceive the unlettered masses with false doctrines and fallacies to keep them entrapped in their web to safeguard their own power over people and wealth.

14. The Covenant of Allah: Obey Allah and His *Rasul* and Those Charged with Authority among You

> Obey Allah and obey the Rasool, and those charged amongst you with authority in the settlement of your affairs. If you differ in anything among yourselves, refer it to Allah and His Rasool (The Qur'an and the Prophet's teachings). If you do believe in Allah and the last Day that is best and the most beautiful conduct in the final determination. (An-Nisa 4:43, Koran)

The Koran teaches that all affairs of the individuals and of the Muslim community should be conducted through mutual consultation (*ijma*) and decisions arrived at through consensus. Furthermore, the Koran proclaims consultation as a principle of government and a method that must be applied in the administration of public affairs. The sovereignty of the Islamic state belongs exclusively to Allah, whose will and command binds the community and state. The dignified designation in the Koran of the community as vicegerent of Allah on the earth makes the Muslim community, the *ummah*, a repository of what is known as "executive sovereignty" of the Islamic state.

The Betrayal of the Covenant of Allah: The Community of Islam Appoints Its Own *Wakil* in Consultation

The community as a whole, after consultation and consensus, grants people among themselves with authority to manage its affairs (*ulil amri minkum*). Those charged with authority act in their capacity as the representative (*wakil*) of the people and are bound by the Koranic mandate to consult the community in public affairs, and consensus is the binding source of the law. The community by consultation and in consensus has the authority to depose any person charged with authority, including the head of state, in the event of gross violation of Allah's law.

وَٱلَّذِينَ ٱسْتَجَابُوا۟ لِرَبِّهِمْ وَأَقَامُوا۟ ٱلصَّلَوٰةَ وَأَمْرُهُمْ شُورَىٰ بَيْنَهُمْ وَمِمَّا رَزَقْنَٰهُمْ يُنفِقُونَ ﴿٣٨﴾ وَٱلَّذِينَ إِذَآ أَصَابَهُمُ ٱلْبَغْىُ هُمْ يَنتَصِرُونَ ﴿٣٩﴾

> Those who hearken to their Lord and establish regular prayer; who (conduct) their affairs by mutual Consultation; who spend out of what We bestow on them for Sustenance; And those who, when an oppressive wrong is inflicted on them do not flinch and courageously defend themselves. (Ash-Shura 42:38–39, Koran)

Islam pursues its social objectives by reforming the individual. The ritual ablution before prayer, the five daily prayers, fasting during the month of Ramadan, and the obligatory giving of charity all encourage punctuality, self-discipline, and concern for the well-being of others. The individual is seen not just as a member of the community and subservient to the community's will but also as a morally autonomous agent who plays a distinctive role in shaping the community's sense of direction and purpose. The Koran has attached to the individual's duty of obedience to the government a right to simultaneously dispute with rulers over government affairs. The individual obeys the ruler on the condition that the ruler obeys the covenant of the Koran and Allah's commandments, which are obligatory to all Muslims regardless of their status in the social hierarchy. This is reflected in the declaration of the blessed *Nabi: "There is no obedience in transgression; obedience is only in the righteousness."*

The citizen is entitled to disobey an oppressive command that is contrary to the covenant of the Koran. The blessed *Nabi,* Allah's emissary, brought His word to the world and disseminated it to the populations of all the continents. Therefore, it is essential to obey and follow what Blessed Nabi Muhammad brought from Allah for mankind.

15. The Covenant of Allah: Freedom of Religion: Let There Be No Compulsion in Religion

The Koranic notion of religious belief (*iman*) is dependent on knowledge that is actualized in practice in the term *islam.* The term *islam* signifies the idea of surrender or submission. Islam is a religion of self-surrender; it is the conscious and rational submission of dependent and limited human will to the absolute and omnipotent will of Allah. The type of surrender Islam requires is a deliberate, conscious, and rational act made by a person who knows with both intellectual certainty and spiritual vision that Allah, who is the subject of Koranic discourse, is reality itself.

The knower of God is a Muslim (fem. *Muslimah*), "one who submits" to the divine truth and whose relationship with God is governed by *taqwa*, the consciousness of humankind's responsibility toward its

Creator. However, consciousness of God alone is not sufficient to make a person a Muslim. Neither is it enough to be merely born a Muslim or to be raised in an Islamic cultural context. The concept of *taqwa* implies that the believer has the added responsibility of acting in a way that is in accordance with three types of knowledge—*ilm al-yaqin, ain al-yaqin* and *haqq al-yaqin* (knowledge of certainty, eye of certainty, and the truth of certainty). The believer must endeavor at all times to maintain himself or herself in a constant state of submission to Allah. By doing so, the believer attains the honored title of "slave of Allah" (*abd Allah,* feminine: *amat Allah*), for he recognizes that all power and all agency belongs to God alone. Allah says to the believers,

> Let there be no compulsion in religion: Truth stands out clear from Error: whoever rejects Evil and believes in Allah hath grasped the most trustworthy handhold that never breaks. And Allah hears and knows all things. (Al-Baqarah 2:254–57, Koran)

Islam (submission) and *iman* (faith) arise out of the communion of a believer with his Maker. According to the Koran, *iman* is not just belief but also, in fact, knowledge. *Iman* is conviction that is based on reason and knowledge. The Koran does not recognize belief that involves blind acceptance. Islam does include acceptance of certain things that cannot be explained by perception through human senses. Our reason and thinking will compel us to recognize the existence of such things. *Iman*, according to the Koran, signifies conviction based on full mental acceptance and intellectual satisfaction. *Iman* gives us inner contentment, a feeling of *amn* (same common root). Thus, *iman* means to believe in something and to testify to its truthfulness, to have confidence in that belief, and to act in accordance with that belief.

There are five fundamental facts stated in the Koran that a believer must accept *iman* in:

1. *Allah:* Belief in Allah means that not only to profess obedience to Him and His covenant but also to show it in one's actions and to be in *taqwa* of Allah.
2. *The law of* mukafat *and the afterlife:* Belief in the law of *mukafat* means to have conviction that every action of man has an inescapable consequence of reward or retribution.
3. *Angels (*malaika*):* Angels are not the winged creatures depicted in children's literature. They are heavenly forces that carry out the laws of Allah governing the universe. They bow to Allah since they follow His orders. They also bow to humans because we are able to study, understand, and manipulate the laws of nature for the benefit of mankind.
4. *The revelations.*

   The Rasul's: Belief in revelations and *Rasul's* implies that human intellect alone cannot safely reach the final destination without divine guidance in the form of *wahiy* (revelation) delivered by the *Rasul's* to mankind. This guidance is to the whole humankind sent through many *Rasul's*. The Muslim tradition began with Ibrahim, our father (Abraham of the Bible). The believers have a belief system and a course of action to be witness over the whole mankind and spread the message to them that began with Nabi Ibrahim and was completed with Nabi Muhammad.

The Betrayal of the Covenant of Allah: *Iman* Is a Conviction That Is Based on Reason and Knowledge

Whereas the message of *wahiy* is divine and universal for all human races, man-made edicts, creed, and dogma directing the believers to beliefs and actions separate the believer in his communion with

God. This is exclusive, and in this relationship, no man can intervene. Therefore, compulsion in matters of religion is only a human fantasy. In the same manner, the message of Hadith collections of the third century is human and therefore subject to error, and so it cannot be equated with the *haqq* of the Koran. Mullahs, scholars, Deobandi priests, Wahabi, Taliban, and ayatollahs who compel believers to conform to their own narrow beliefs assume the rights that are only Allah's prerogative.

16. The Covenant of Allah: *Awliya*: Allah Is the *Waliy*, Protector of Those Who Have Faith: Take Not the Jews and the Christians as Your *Awliya*.

> Take not infidels for Awliya (friends and protectors) in place of believers.

> O you who believe! Allah is the Waliy and the protector of the Believers. Allah commands Believers not to take people outside their ranks in closeness and confidence, who in their loathing for them wish them destruction.

The recurring theme in the Koran extols the believers to stand united. In this unity, all believers are bonded to one another to the exclusion of other men. Just as the bond to Allah is indivisible, all the believers shall stand behind the commitment of the least of them. In this scheme of things, there is no room for unbelievers and wrongdoers in the affairs of the believers.

Allah, in His covenant, reminds the believers repeatedly not to take the *kafirun* (infidels), Jews, and Christians as their *awliya* (friends and protectors) in place of believers. They are friends and protectors unto one another. He who among believers turns to them is one of them. Allah does not guide those who are unjust and evildoers (*zalimun).*

He who among the believers turns to them is among the *kafirun*, *mushrikun*, and the *zalimun*.

Allah is the Waliy, protector of those who have faith. From the depths of darkness, He will lead them forth into light. Of those who reject faith their Waliy (protectors) are the false deities: from light, they will lead them forth into the depths of darkness. They will be Companions of the Fire, to dwell therein (forever). (Al-Baqarah 2:254–57, Koran)

Take not into intimacy those outside your ranks: they will not fail to corrupt you. They only desire your ruin: rank hatred has already appeared from their mouths: what their hearts conceal is far worse. We have made plain to you the Signs, if you have wisdom. (Ali 'Imran 3:118–20, Koran)

If you obey the Unbelievers, (kafaru) they will drive you back on your heels, and you will turn your back to your Faith to your own loss. Allah is your protector, and He is the best of helpers. (Ali 'Imran 3:149–50, Koran)

Take not the Jews and the Christians as your friends and protectors (awliya). They are friends and protectors unto each other. He who amongst you turns to them is one of them. Allah does not guide those who are unjust and evil doers (zalimun). (Al-Ma'idah 5:51, Koran)

Take not for friends and protectors (awliya) those who take your religion for mockery, whether from amongst people of the book or from amongst the kafireen. Be in taqwa of Allah, fear Allah if you have faith indeed. (Al-Ma'idah 5:57, Koran)

Take not for your protectors and friends (awliya) your kin who practice infidelity over faith. Whosoever does that will be amongst the wrong doers. (At-Tawbah 9:23, Koran)

Take not My enemies and yours as awliya (friends and protectors), offering them love and regard, even though they have rejected the Truth bestowed on you. And they have driven out the Rasool and yourselves from your homes, because you believe in Allah as your Rabb (Lord)! You have come out to strive in My Cause and to seek My favor, take them not as friends, holding in secret regard and friendship for them: for I know all that you conceal and all that you reveal. And any of you that do this has strayed from the Straight Path.

If they were to gain an upper hand over you, they would treat you as enemies, and stretch forth their hands and their tongues against you with evil; and they desire that you should reject the Truth. (Al-Mumtahinah 60:1–2, Koran)

Befriend not people who have incurred Allah's wrath. They are already in despair of the Hereafter, just as the Unbelievers are in despair about those in graves. (Al-Mumtahinah 60:13, Koran)

Allah is the Wali protector of those who have faith.
From the depths of darkness, He will lead them
forth into light. (Al-Baqarah 2:254–57, Koran)

Establish regular salaat; give regular charity,
and holdfast to Allah. He is your Mawla,
Protector, the best of Protectors and the
best Helper (Al-Hajj 2:277-78, Koran)

These verses of the Koran often cause confusion among the believers, Christians, and Jews, yet the explanation is quite simple: the Koran recognizes only one true religion—the religion of those who have submitted themselves to the one universal God, have faith in that God, and perform wholesome and beautiful deeds. Allah sent thousands of His *Rasul's* and *Nabiien* with a message to humankind. Some of the *Rasul's* are named in the Koran, while others are not obvious to us. Millions of people who subscribe to the teaching of these *Rasul's*—although they may on the surface be followers of Islam, Hinduism, Buddhism, teachings of Confucius, Christianity, and Judaism—have submitted themselves to one universal God, the Creator. They do His bidding as taught by the *Rasul's*, and they perform beautiful and wholesome deeds in the service of Allah's creation. They seek peace and do not harm any humans. Such people are the believers of God, Allah, and they are *Muslims* according to the Koran.

There are millions of people who call themselves Muslims, Christians, Jews, and others who have not submitted themselves to the will of one God, their Creator; they do not have the same faith in the one universal God. Such people do not have the *nur* of Allah in their hearts; they create evil and mischief on the earth. Such people cause wars, murder whole populations, steal from nations, and profit from famines and destitution. Such are the people Allah warns us about. The believers should not take them as their *awliya*.

It is not only the Koran that makes the believers aware of the tricks of such people. Jesus spoke of them in these terms:

> Beware of false prophets, which come to you in sheep's clothing, but inwardly they are ravenous. You shall know them by their fruits. Do men gather grapes of thorns, or figs of thistles? Even so every good tree brings forth good fruit, but a corrupt tree brings forth evil fruit. "A good tree cannot bring forth evil fruit; neither can a corrupt tree bring forth good fruit." Every tree that brings forth bad fruit is hewn down and cast into the fire. Therefore, by their fruits shall you know them.

The Koran says:

> They have made their oaths a screen for their misdeeds, thus they obstruct men from the Path of Allah: truly evil are their deeds. That is because they believed, then they rejected Faith: so, a seal was set on their hearts: therefore, they understand not. When you look at them, their exteriors please thee; and when they speak, you listen to their words. They are as worthless as rotten pieces of timber propped up, unable to stand on their own. They think that every cry is against them. They are the enemies; so beware of them. The curse of Allah be on them! How are they deluded away from the Truth! (Al-Munafiqun 63:4)

It should become abundantly clear to Muslims that the present world situation is the continuation of the Council of Clermont in 1095 CE when Pope Urban declared a crusade against Islam, a war till its destruction. There are powerful forces in the Euro-Christian world, which for the first time in history is not threatened by the barbarians or by any other force among themselves. The Christian West for the first time is united in NATO and the European Economic Community. The threats to Islam have been ongoing since the beginning of the Crusades and are now being renewed daily very subtly. In this battle, every component of the modern civilization has been harnessed against Islam—intelligence services, armed forces, diplomacy, economics and communications, and organizations such as the United Nations, the World Bank, the IMF, and the World Trade Organization.

The unwritten plan of the fundamentalist Christian, Jewish, and banking and oil interests that work in cohesion is to weaken and degrade the Islamic state and its military and economic infrastructure in such a way that Muslims will continue to be client states under American and NATO hegemony. Muslim countries will continue to live in ongoing poverty and degradation under the despotic rule of incompetent, dishonest, and self-serving kings and dictators. Muslim and Arab states will be further divided into ministates so they can never be united to present a coherent, united front to the West. Iraq will break down into three fragments—Shiite, Sunni, and Kurdish. Saudi Arabia will be divided into the eastern Shia oil sheikhdom and the western Sunni religious kingdom centered on Mecca and Medina. Afghanistan will break down into Pashtun and Farsi components. Iran and Turkey will be forced to give up their Kurdish territories. Israel will absorb West Bank and Gaza and expel Palestinians to Jordan, which will come to be called a Palestinian state. Sunni Iraq will become the Hashemite kingdom. Sudan will become the Desert Arab republic in the north and oil-rich Christian in the south. Punjab and Sind in Pakistan will be absorbed into India. Baluchi and Pathan areas of Pakistan will join their brethren in Afghanistan. India will further break down into several countries. Indonesia will similarly disintegrate into several states. The wealth of all the new ministates will be administered by the United Nations to be controlled by America and Europe.

This is the plan of the *Yahudi-Salibi* think tanks funded by secret and faceless people and corporations. Several complete groups of *Yahudi* and *Salibi* planners have been embedded in the higher offices of the United States, Britain, Australia, and several European governments. They have been carefully and successfully planted into the NATO headquarters, the United Nations, the World Bank, and the IMF. The best-known example of the complete takeover of the planning for the Iraq War is in the Pentagon, the National Security Council, and the Office of the Vice President of the United States by the agents of the Israeli government and its security apparatus. After several years of covert operation in Washington, this group has sufficient backing that it is emboldened to come out in the open.

The covert and the obvious planning of the *Yahudi-Salibi* conspirators is thorough and detailed. Their agents speak Arabic, Farsi, Turkish, and Urdu fluently. They have been carefully planted in the diplomatic corps, intelligence services, armed forces, NGOs, various aid groups, commercial enterprises, airlines, and shipping and tourism services. Their function is to gather intelligence and to recruit corrupt and willing agents in the Muslim states to enhance the goals of the conspirators. A believer, aware of his history, has to pause and consider the effort and treasure that goes into such planning. This planning not only is worldwide but also dates back to the year 1095 CE, when Pope Urban called on his followers to destroy Islam. The expenditure on war against Islam since the 9/11 plot spent in the name of homeland security, covert and military action in Muslim countries, and war in Afghanistan and Iraq has totaled over a trillion dollars. Such worldwide planning, coordination, and financing could not possibly occur without an office, a full-fledged headquarters with staff and a head. Somewhere in this wide world, perhaps in Europe, in a stately home with boulevards and well-manicured gardens, there is a secret headquarters with a man overseeing the vast apparatus that controls the world's wealth and wants to control it in perpetuity. He has constant contact with his minions executing the policy set forth by an executive of stakeholders of wealth, Zionism, and Euro-Christianity who meet in secrecy.

Efforts by the believers to achieve unity and prosperity continue to be defeated. The average Muslim just cannot understand why the *ummah*'s efforts never come to fruition. As already mentioned, covert plans to defeat the believers' efforts toward unity are constantly formulated, discussed, and implemented.

There is a recurring cycle in Islamic history of destruction and humiliation of Islam by the manipulations of the circle of evil. The story starts sometimes with a scheming Jew who spins a web, meticulously planning to amass the world's wealth, and uses the power and the organization of the strongest Christian monarch by tempting him with acquisition of a world empire and its fabulous wealth. Then meticulous planning starts; the execution of such an expedition may take several years in which intelligence services, diplomats, and armed services play a role, while only the top select echelon is aware of all the moves on the chessboard. A willing victim, a weak Muslim—a *Munafiq*—with propensity toward greed and lust for power and usually endowed with overwhelming vanity and conceit is picked up, trained, and slowly eased into a position of power to be used at the opportune moment. A score of such people descended on Iraq and Afghanistan with the invasion of these countries. Ahmed Chalabi, Zalmay

Khalilzad, Ibrahim al-Ja'fari, and Hamid Karzai were some of them, just to mention a few. Legions of the *Munafiqeen* are now standing in the wings, awaiting their rewards with the coming invasion of Iran.

An article on the subject written by Rowan Scarborough appeared in the *Washington Times* on February 20, 2006, that points to the intentions of the world's greatest military power. Though the article talks of a long war on terrorism, Osama bin Laden's religious ideology, and extremism, the underlying objective of the plan is to fight a long war against Islam. The covenant of Allah specifies each believer's obligation to the cause of Allah and to the unity of the believers. The Western Euro-Christian civilization, however, has yet to achieve the objectives of the one-thousand-year-old crusade called by Pope Urban in 1095 CE to destroy Islam.

The United States Joint Chiefs of Staff planners have produced a twenty-seven-page briefing on the war on terror that seeks to explain how to win the "long war" against the Muslims. The report states that, in this war, Islamic extremists may be supported by twelve million Muslims worldwide. Military planners worry that al-Qaeda could win if the "traditional allies prefer accommodation." The "traditional allies" refer to the traditional traitors of Islam in Egypt, Saudi Arabia, UAE, Kuwait, Jordan, Oman, Qatar, and Pakistan.

Al-Qaeda leader Osama bin Laden, the document states, "is absolutely committed to his cause. His religious ideology successfully attracts recruits. He has sufficient population base from which to protract the conflict. Even support of 1 percent of the Muslim population would equate to over 12 million 'enemies.'"

The unclassified production titled "Fighting the Long War—Military Strategy for the War on Terrorism" is a component of the Pentagon's ongoing campaign to explain that a lengthy struggle requires patience from the American people and Congress. The briefing was prepared for Rear Adm. William D. Sullivan, vice director for strategic plans and policy within the Joint Staff, which is under Marine Corps general Peter Pace, Joint Chiefs of Staff chairman. Admiral Sullivan used it to deliver a lecture in January to a national security study group at Mississippi State University. "It is an effort, when asked, to explain why we are doing what we are doing from a military perspective to fight the long war," said Air Force major Almarah Belk, spokeswoman for General Pace. The same core information is used in briefings by other speakers to explain this protracted planned war.

The Bush administration's effort to explain Iraq and the broader war includes more than briefings. In February 2006, Defense Secretary Donald H. Rumsfeld was in New York, talking to the Council on Foreign Relations, and General Pace addressed the National Press Club in the district. At the same time, President Bush was in Tampa, Florida. speaking on the war.

Bin Laden, the Joint Staff paper says, wants to "expand the Muslim empire to historical significance." And Iraq "has become the focus of the enemy's effort. If they win in Iraq, they have a base from which to expand their terror. Extremists now have an Emirate in Iraq that serves as a base of operations from which they can revive the Caliphate [Islamic rule]. . . . Baghdad becomes the capital of the Caliphate. The revived Caliphate now turns its attention to the destruction of Israel."

Admiral Sullivan's briefing contains a map that shows the bin Laden–style caliphate conquering North and East Africa, the entire Middle East, and Central and South Asia. This dire scenario can only happen if the United States is defeated in Iraq and Afghanistan. "The United States cannot be defeated militarily," the briefing claims, "the enemy knows this. But consider terror attacks weaken the world economy. Continued casualties weaken national resolve. Traditional allies prefer accommodation." The enemy has "inherent weaknesses," including "no military capacity to expand their fight beyond terrorist tactics."

"Americans will commit to a 'long war' if they are confident our leaders know what they are doing." This twenty-seven-page briefing clearly states, "Marginalizing an ideology requires patience and promoting reform from within. We cannot discredit all of Islam as we did with communism. It is a divine religion. We can only discredit the violent extremist[60]." Clearly, any believer reading this briefing will understand that any reference to bin Laden, extremists, and terrorism really points to mainstream Islam and the dangers posed to the *ummah.*

In this game, on one side of the chessboard are men with an attention span going back a thousand years to the Council of Clermont in 1095 CE, when Pope Urban declared a crusade against Islam. Their commitment and passion are fueled by a thousand years of pent-up hatred stored in Europe's political and ecumenical history. The ideologues are intellectuals with accumulated knowledge and information of Islamic history, the fault lines of the Muslim psyche. The players are in full control of the economics and the mercenary armed forces of the Muslim states. They are backed by wealth, intelligence services, and absolute military power of the West. At their beck and call are all the major players in the world of Islam. These "Muslim" *Munafiqeen* have been bribed, bought, or intimidated into subservience and service. Most of them are the descendants of the first-generation *Munafiqeen* who helped the West dismember the Ottoman Empire and establish Western control over the Middle East, Iran, Afghanistan, and Muslim India.

---

[60] Rowan Scarborough, "Military Plots a 'Long War' on Terror," *Washington Times*, February 20, 2006.

On the other side of the chessboard are the Muslim and Arab rulers whose attention span is constricted to one day at a time, devoted to staying in power and holding on to their ill-gotten wealth. In some, the attention span flickers from one alcoholic binge to the next, while others like King Fu'ad submerged in drinking and gambling. Kings, sheikhs, and presidents are virtually unaware of the demands of their *din* regarding their obligation to the *ummah*. Those in charge are oblivious to the dangers that lie ahead that will destroy their nations and their *din*. They are insensitive to the requirements of statecraft necessary to protect the world of Islam from the plots against it. In most cases, Muslim rulers themselves are a part of the conspiracy to destroy Islam. They form a part of the circle of evil—the circle of the *Yahudi*, *Salibi*, and *Munafiq* coalition out to destroy Islam.

The uninformed politico-military generals are confident that their parade ground skills are adequate to run the business of state and the *din* all across the Islamic world through Indonesia, Bangladesh, Pakistan, Afghanistan, Iraq, Syria, Turkey, Egypt, Libya, Algeria, and a host of West African countries; this curse of Islam has played havoc with the world of believers. The generals puff around in their fancy bemedaled uniforms like peacocks trying to dazzle their subjects with their shiny buttons. Islam has lost in this war time and again during the last two hundred years and will continue to do so unless the Muslims begin to take heed of their covenant with Allah and learn from their history. Allah addresses the believers repeatedly to emphasize the importance of unity among them. He repeatedly admonishes them not to take pagans, Christians, and Jews as their *awliya* in place of believers.

The plan to destabilize the Ottoman Empire was hatched by the Jewish Rothschild cousins in Berlin, Paris, and London. Each branch of the family collaborated with their favorite governments in each city. The German chancellor von Bethmann-Hollweg, a Jew, and a Rothschild cousin won the day, and the Kaiser began to make overtures to the Young Turks and assisted their revolution against the sultan. Enver Pasha was the Turkish *Munafiq* who joined the circle of evil— the *Yahudi*, *Salibi*, and *Munafiq* coalition. Talat, Cemal, and Enver *presided* over the dissolution of the Ottoman Empire, subjugating the Middle East to the West for the next one hundred years.

The history of the creation of the state of Israel tells us that Theodor Herzl and Chaim Weizmann were the founding fathers of Israel. The hidden hand that helped create the Jewish state is seldom mentioned.

The actual creators of Israel were a group of English and Jewish conspirators in the British cabinet. David Lloyd George appointed Alfred Milner, a Jew, to his war cabinet in 1916 as secretary of war. After becoming the secretary of war, he brought in Leo Amery, another Jew, albeit a secret one, as secretary of the war cabinet. Milner had close contacts with the Rothschilds; in 1912, he had helped Natty Rothschild unify the divided Jewish community of London under one spiritual head, Chief Rabbi Joseph Herman Hertz.[61]

Another Jew, a cabinet minister, Herbert Samuel, convinced the cabinet in 1915—when Palestine was still a Turkish possession—that Palestine should become a British protectorate, "into which the scattered Jews in time swarm back from all quarters of the globe, in due course obtain home rule and form a Jewish Commonwealth like that of Canada and Australia." Lord Walter Rothschild, as the leader of the British Jews, twisted the ears of the prime minister Lloyd George and his foreign secretary for a declaration about Palestine. Lloyd George had previously served as the legal counsel for the British Zionist Federation. Balfour suggested that "they submit a declaration for the cabinet to consider." The declaration was written by Milner and revised several times. The final version was drafted by Leo Amery, which read,

---

[61] Niall Ferguson, *The House of Rothschild* (Penguin Books), 259.

His Majesty's Government view with favor the establishment in Palestine a national home for the Jewish people, and will use their best endeavors to facilitate the achievement of this object, it being clearly understood that nothing shall be done which may prejudice the civil and religious rights of existing non-Jewish communities in Palestine, or the rights and political status enjoyed in any other country.

This declaration was approved by the British cabinet and was addressed to Lord Walter Rothschild and signed by the foreign secretary Balfour. The Balfour Declaration—as this Jewish Magna Carta came to be known, the document that gave the illegitimate birth to the state of Israel—was written by Lord Alfred Milner, a Jew, revised and finalized by Leo Amery, another Jew, at the behest of and addressed to Lord Walter Rothschild, the leader of the Jews in London, for the purpose of the creation of a Jewish state in the name of the British government on a land that did not belong to either the Jews or the British. In fact, this was an agreement among a group of conspiring *Yahudi-Salibi* conspirators belonging to a secret organization that had a long history of fraud and extortion to grab the world's wealth.

In this case, the plotters made a full circle in their relationship. Lord George Joachim Goschen, a German Jew, patronized Alfred Milner, another German Jew, and brought him into the English establishment and introduced him to the Rothschilds. Milner, in turn, brought Leo Amery, a secret Jew, into the war cabinet; and together, they wrote the Balfour Declaration for the Lord Rothschild. To complete the circle, George Goschen's daughter Phyllis Evelyn Goschen married Francis Cecil Balfour, Foreign Secretary Balfour's son, on August 31, 1920.

Herbert Samuel was appointed overseer of Palestine to guide and control King Abdullah of Jordan to facilitate the Jewish migration to Palestine. Arthur Hirtzel, a Jew, was appointed as head of the British

India Office, which also controlled the British governance of Iraq and Arabia. Hirtzel, at that time, expressed the need for Ibn Sa'ud to establish himself in Mecca. Rufus Isaacs, Lord Reading, another Jew, was appointed as the British viceroy of India. Isaacs directed the British policy in Iraq, Palestine, and Arabia. He used 'Abd al-'Aziz to remove Sharif Hussein's son Ali from Hejaz. He had a free hand in Arabia and Iraq. He used British Indian troops to quell uprisings in Iraq. Isaacs also facilitated the massacres and repression in At Ta'if, Bureida, and Huda by providing 'Abd al-'Aziz with money, artillery, rifles, ammunition, training, and transport.

From this time onward, Zionists were considered an ally of the British government, and every help and assistance was forthcoming from each government department. Space was provided for the Zionists in Mark Sykes's office with liaison to each government department. The British government provided financial, communication, and travel facilities to those working in the Zionist office. Mark Sykes, who had negotiated the Sykes-Picot Agreement giving Syria to the French, was now working for the Zionists, offering them a part of the same territory.

To complete the circle of evil, Sharif Hussein and his sons—hungry for power, fame, and gold—were the willing recruits of the British to destabilize the Ottoman Empire and carve out a Jewish state in Palestine. Hussein led a revolt against his caliph, sultan, country, and coreligionists under the protection of an alien, *kafir*, colonial, expansionist power under the full knowledge that parts of the Islamic state—including Syria, Lebanon, Palestine, and Iraq—would pass from Islamic rule to an economic and colonial serfdom of a non-Muslim, *kafir* power. While the British set out to expedite the war against the Turks, they also began to lay the groundwork for an indirect postwar British political control of Arabia.

June 1916 was a historical moment when, for the first time in the history of Islam since the Battle of Badr in the first year of hijra, combined forces of the *kafireen* and *Munafiqeen* and British and Hussein's armies attacked the city of the *Nabi* of Islam, though unsuccessfully; this attack introduced the combined evil dominion of the *Mutaffifeen*, *kafireen*, and *Munafiqeen* over the heartlands of Islam for the century to come.

For his treachery, Sharif Hussein received his first reward in gold sovereigns in March 1916, a shipment amounting to £53,000, three months before he announced his revolt. Commencing on August 8, 1916, the official allowance was set at £125,000 a month, a sum that was frequently exceeded on Hussein's demand; for example, in November 1916, £375,000 in gold sovereigns was dispatched to Hussein by the British for hajj expenses. The payments were broken down into five categories representing the four armies under the command of Hussein's sons and an allotment for the upkeep of the mosque at Kaaba and for hajj facilities as well as for the operation of Hussein's government in Mecca and Jeddah. Forty thousand pounds was allotted to Faisal, £30,000 to Abdullah, £20,000 each for Ali and Zeid, and £15,000 for expenses at Mecca and Jeddah.

The year 1916 must have been the lowest point in the history of Islam, when it was surrounded by powerful enemies around the world; and inside, it was being destroyed by self-serving traitors at the very heart of the faith, the Kaaba. For the first time in the history of Islam, the very upkeep of the holy mosque of Mecca and the Kaaba and hajj expenses were being paid for by the *kafireen*, at the behest of the *Munafiqeen*, under the claim of their lineage to the holy prophet. While claiming the bloodline, they forgot the teachings of the Koran and the example of the prophet.

'Abd al-'Aziz was picked as a willing tool by British scouts in around 1902 and was kept on a short leash with small handouts to keep him available and above starvation level. 'Abd al-'Aziz set out to conquer Arabia with the financial and military assistance of the British. Sir Percy Cox, a British resident in the Persian Gulf, wrote, "With Ibn-Saud in Hasa (the Gulf Coast of Arabia) our position is very much strengthened." Percy Cox openly encouraged Ibn Sa'ud to attack the remaining territory of the Ibn Rashid's to divert them from reinforcing Turkish troops against the British. Ibn Sa'ud had constant British financial aid, arms, and advisers, initially William Shakespeare and Percy Cox and later Harry St. John Philby.

After they helped him master eastern Arabia in 1917, the British found another use for Ibn Sa'ud. In 1924, Hussein declared himself caliph of Islam without the consent of the British. Ibn Sa'ud, with British encouragement, started his thrust to Hejaz; although the British ostensibly cut off the arms supplies to both sides, they continued to supply small but crucial amounts of money and arms to Ibn Sa'ud and his merciless Ikhwan. Some of the military equipment used by Ibn Sa'ud was expensive and could only have been obtained from the British and used with the help of British instructors. At the time, statements by British officials did point to the British hand in Ibn Sa'ud's attack on Mecca. Arthur Hirtzel—a Jew, head of the British India Office at that time—expressed the need for Ibn Sa'ud to establish himself in Mecca. The British viceroy of India at that time, another Jew, Rufus Isaacs, Lord Reading, directed the British policy in Arabia. He used 'Abd al-'Aziz to remove Sharif Hussein's son Ali from Hejaz.

The drawing of borders of the new division of the Middle East was also at hand. Jewish personnel were posted to the key positions of control of the Middle East to facilitate such a control. Herbert Samuel, a protagonist of the Jewish state, was appointed as high commissioner to Palestine to promote Jewish immigration and to control Abdullah in Jordan and Faisal in Iraq. Arthur Hirtzel, a Jew, was appointed as head of the British India Office, which also controlled the British governance of Iraq and Arabia. Hirtzel, at that time, expressed the need for Ibn Sa'ud to establish himself in Mecca. Rufus Isaacs, Lord Reading, another Jew, was appointed as the British viceroy of India. Isaacs directed the British policy in Iraq, Palestine, and Arabia. He used 'Abd al-'Aziz to remove Sharif Hussein's son Ali from Hejaz. He had a free hand in Arabia and Iraq. He used British Indian troops to quell uprisings in Iraq. Isaacs also facilitated the massacres and repression in At Ta'if, Bureida, and Huda by providing 'Abd al-'Aziz with money, artillery, rifles, ammunition, training, and transport.

Ibn Sa'ud afforded Britain the comfort of keeping the Arabs and Muslims divided and protected its commercial and political interests, which opposed a unified Muslim state. Sharif Hussein and his sons Faisal and Abdullah continued to be clients and servants of the British. For a few thousand pounds and personal glory, they and their descendants, Faisal, Abdullah, Hussein, and Abdullah sold the honor of Islam for the next one hundred years. 'Abd al-'Aziz's sons inherited their father's debauchery and treason against Islam for their personal gain.

Treason runs deep in the veins of the descendants of Sharif Hussein and 'Abd al-'Aziz. They are *Munafiqeen* who have taken their *awliya* from among the *kafireen*. According to the covenant, they are of the *kafireen*. This circle of evil, the coalition of the *Yahudi*, *Salibi*, and *Munafiqeen* triumphed over Islam for over one hundred years. The Jewish money in London, New York, Berlin, and Paris collaborated with the Christian powers of Europe and America and the *Munafiqeen*—Enver Pasha, Cemal Pasha, Talat Pasha, Sharif Hussein and sons, and Ibn Sa'ud and sons—to defeat the Islamic Empire and fragment it into scores of impoverished mini-client-states for political and economic exploitation by the *Yahudi*, *Salibi*, *Munafiq* coalition.

Anwar Sadat and the Egyptian Army won partial victory over the Jewish state of Israel in 1973. The victory made Sadat a hero in the eyes of many Arabs—if not equal to, then almost comparable to the great Arab hero Gamal Abdel Nasser. Puffed up by success and sycophancy from the likes of Henry Kissinger, Sadat forgot his own roots and began to take advice and comfort from Kissinger and Israeli lobbyists in Washington. Against the advice of his closest advisers and the leaders of other Arab countries, Sadat offered himself as a servant and a tool of the circle of evil, the *Yahudi-Salibi* confederation. He made a trip to Israel and addressed the Knesset, the Israeli Parliament. Under American tutelage and patronage, he abandoned his Arab allies, negotiated, and signed a peace treaty with many secret appendices with Israel at the expense of the Palestinians, Syrians, and Muslims in general.

As a consequence, all Palestine and the Golan Heights are under Israeli occupation. The Arabs are disunited and in disarray. Sadat sold the Egyptian sovereignty, the Islamic nation, and the holy Islamic places in Jerusalem for three billion dollars a year. Sadat took Jews and Christians as *awliya* and willfully disobeyed the covenant that every Muslim has pledged to obey. He also disobeyed the provisions of the covenant of Yathrib and the prophet's teaching:

> Just as the bond to Allah is indivisible, all the believers shall stand behind the commitment of the least of them. All believers are bonded one to another to the exclusion of other men.
>
> This Pax Islamica is one and indivisible. No believer shall enter a separate peace without all other believers whenever there is fighting in the cause of God but will do so only on the basis of equality and justice

> to all others. In every expedition for the cause of God we undertake, all parties to the covenant shall fight shoulder to shoulder as one man. All believers shall avenge the blood of one another when anyone falls fighting in the cause of God.

Once again, the *Yahudi-Salibi* ingenuity used a *Munafiq* to grow the seeds of discord in the Islamic world.

Saddam Hussein replaced al-Bakr as President of Iraq in July 1979. The bloodbath that followed eliminated all potential opposition to him. Saddam was now the master of Iraq with no one around him daring to question his actions. Two actions that he initiated led the Islamic community to disastrous disunity and debt. He attacked fellow Muslims, Iran in 1980 and Kuwait in 1990.

The Iran-Iraq War turned out to be a battle between two egomaniac personalities with a Messiah complex, neither of them willing to call a truce to the hostilities. The result was emaciation and bleeding of both countries to near bankruptcy. The Iraqi troops launched a full-scale invasion of Iran on September 22, 1980. France supplied high-tech weapons to Iraq, and the Soviet Union was Iraq's largest weapon supplier. Israel provided arms to Iran, hoping to bleed both the nations by prolonging the war. At least ten nations sold arms to both the warring nations to profit from the conflict. The United States followed a more duplicitous policy toward both warring parties to prolong the war and cause maximum damage to both of them.

The Iran-Iraq War was not between good and evil. Islam forbids fighting among the Muslims, murder, and taking of life unless it is in the cause of justice. Saddam Hussein launched a murderous war to regain a few square miles of territory that his country had relinquished freely in the 1975 border negotiations. There were one and a half million Muslim casualties in this senseless fraternal war. The war ended in a ceasefire that essentially left prewar borders unchanged. The Covenant of Allah not only forbids such an internecine war but also provides a mechanism for dispute resolution.

Instead of condemning the aggressor, the Arab states sided with Saddam Hussein, providing him with funds for further bloodletting. Saddam Hussein used banned chemical weapons against fellow Muslims, Iranians, and Kurds. The eight-year-long war exhausted both countries. Primary responsibility for the prolonged bloodletting must rest with the governments of the two countries, the ruthless military regime of Saddam Hussein and the ruthless clerical regime of Ayatollah Khomeini in Iran. Whatever his religious convictions were, Khomeini had no qualms about sending his followers, including young boys, to their deaths for his own greater glory. This callous disregard for human life was no less characteristic of Saddam Hussein. Saudi Arabia gave $25.7 billion and Kuwait $10 billion to Iraq to fuel the war and the killings. Saddam also owed the Soviets, the USA, and Europe $40 billion for the purchase of arms. The cost of war to the Iranians was even greater. The world community sold arms for eight and a half years and watched the bloodletting. The USA sold arms and information to both sides to prolong the war strategically and to profit and gain influence and bases in Gulf countries. Ayatollah Khomeini, in particular, was a hypocrite in dealing with Israel in secret when his public pronouncements were venomously anti-Israel.

Iran, Iraq, and all the Arab states of the Persian Gulf took the Western countries, the Soviet Union, and Israel as their *awliya*, in contradiction to the commandments of the covenant. The ayatollah and his clerics should have known and understood their obligations to Allah and to their people as spelled out in Allah's covenant. The uncontrolled Arab-Iranian hostility left a deep, festering wound in the body of the nation of Islam. The West made gains by setting up permanent bases in Saudi Arabia, Oman, the United Arab Emirates, Bahrain, Qatar, and Kuwait. This is the land that Muhammad, the Blessed messenger of Allah, freed from the infidels, only to be handed over to infidels by the *Munafiqeen*.

After the Kuwait war, at the invitation of King Fahd, the USA has continued to maintain large operational army and air force bases and command and control facilities that enable them to monitor air and sea traffic and civilian and military communications in the Middle East. Bahrain became the headquarters of a US naval fleet. The Middle East, at the beginning of the twenty-first century, is under the absolute military and economic control of the USA and NATO. The circle of evil—the *Yahudi*, *Salibi*, and *Munafiqeen*—continue to dominate the lives of Muslims.

17. The Covenant of Allah: Jihad: Proclaim Jihad to Fight against Fitnah, Tyranny, and Oppression.

> Fight the infidel until there is no more treachery and oppression and there prevails Justice and Faith in Allah altogether and everywhere. If they cease, then Allah is seer of what they do. If they refuse, be sure that Allah is your Protector, the Best to protect and the Best to help. And why should you not fight in the cause of Allah and for those men, women and children, who are weak, abused and oppressed, those who beseech their Lord to deliver protectors and helpers.

The Koranic use of the term *jihad* means "struggle." The Koran commonly uses the verb along with the expression *in the path of Allah*. The path of Allah, of course, is the path of right conduct that Allah has set down in the Koran. Jihad is simply the complement to *islam*, the surrender to the will of Allah. The surrender takes place in Allah's will, which people struggle with in His path. Hence, submission and surrender to Allah's will demands struggle in His path. Submission to Allah's command requires the believers to struggle against all negative tendencies in themselves and in the society that draw them away from Allah's path. Salat, zakat, fasting, and hajj are all struggles in the path of Allah. The greatest obstacles that people face in submitting themselves to Allah are their laziness, lack of imagination, and currents of contemporary opinion. These weaknesses and events carry them along without resisting. It takes an enormous struggle to submit to an authority that breaks one's likes and dislikes of current trends and pressures of society to conform to the crowd.

The jihad, which is normally a daily struggle within oneself against temptations and evil, will sometimes take an outward form against the enemies of Islam. Such a war is permitted strictly in the path of Allah in today's contemporary world to enforce truth, justice, and freedom.

> And why should you not fight in the cause of
> Allah and for those men, women and children,
> who are weak, abused and oppressed, those who
> beseech their Lord to deliver them from their
> oppressors and those who ask Allah to send for them
> protectors and helpers. (An-Nisa 4:71–75, Koran)

The oft-repeated phrase in the Koran to proclaim jihad is to fight *fitnah*, tyranny, and oppression. Yet most of the wars in the Muslim world were civil wars, with Muslims killing Muslims for the sake of territory, wealth, and power.

Life is a chain of emotions, intentions, and actions. Before each deed, the human stops to intend an action. Each intention is the product of an emotion that acts on the human's self, the *nafs*. The *nafs* may intend to act on its animal instincts of craving and lust, or in situations where the self is sufficiently refined with *taqwa* of Allah, the human will follow His path as commanded by the covenant. The self is in a continuous battle whether to follow its base cravings or to perform wholesome deeds. Such ongoing fluctuation of intent between the base and the honorable is stressful. Such stress leads to anxiety, anger, and depression, which in the end will cause an emotional turmoil and breakdown. When the human intends to do his deeds with the knowledge that Allah is with him, that Allah is aware of his intent, and that Allah guides him to the right objective and action, there is peace and satisfaction.

When the believer is in *taqwa* of Allah, the *nur* of Allah cleans his *nafs* and aids him in obeying His covenant. Jihad is this struggle that prepares the believer in following and obeying Allah's commandments without question. Jihad is the struggle of the human from the path of ignorance to the path of Allah. The human hears Allah's call amid the noise and commotion of the world and, through the eye of his soul, lets the *nur* of Allah into the niche of his heart. Allah's call is about obedience, goodness, and selflessness. The human bows down his head on the earth in submission to his Lord and in humility. The Lord guides, and the believer follows; the believer has faith in Allah, and Allah holds his hand. Allah shows His believer the way to goodness, and the believer performs wholesome deeds. The *nur* of Allah glows in the believer's heart, and the believer accepts Allah in his heart.

This communion between the believer and Allah becomes exclusive. Submission establishes a link between the believer and Allah. Allah commands, and the believer follows. The believer asks, and Allah gives. The believer loves Allah, and Allah loves him in return. The believer asks for the straight path, and Allah shows him the way. The believer praises Allah, and Allah showers His mercy and grace upon him. The believer remembers Allah, and Allah responds to those who praise Him.

The *nafs*, unlike the Freudian ego, is capable of both good and bad. The *nuqta* of the *nafs*, when magnified a million times, becomes visible as a shiny disk, a mirror. The inherent nature (*fitra*) of the *nafs* is to shine like a mirror with Allah's *nur.* When the human walks the path of Allah in *taqwa* of Him with the knowledge that Allah is with him, watching him and guiding him, Allah's *nur* shines on the *nafs*, keeping it pure and safe. However, when the human's desires, cravings, and ego overpower his love and obedience of Allah, the shiny mirror of his *nafs* becomes obscured by the dirt and smoke of his desires, and he loses sight of the *nur* of Allah and trips into error and decadence.

The effort required to keep focusing on Allah's *nur* and *taqwa* of Him is the inner jihad. And this jihad is obedience to Allah's commandments when He calls on His believers with the words,

يَـٰٓأَيُّهَا ٱلَّذِينَ ءَامَنُوا۟

O you who Believe.

And He commands them to do acts of faith and goodness in the *seventy-five* verses of the Koran. Obedience to every such command is jihad. Jihad is the struggle to fulfill the commandments of Allah in the covenant. *Taqwa* of Allah shines His light (*nur*) into core of the human, in the self (*nafs*), that clears the smoke of evil and temptation from the *nafs*, allowing the human to follow God.

Once the believer has purified himself with Allah's *nur*, he has prepared himself for the external jihad. When the believer has purified his own *nafs* and soul with submission to Allah (*islam*) and faith (*iman*) in the only reality, the Lord, and by performing wholesome deeds in the name of Allah, he is ready for the outer struggle for his *din*, to fight the *fitnah* of tyranny and oppression.

The blessed *Nabi* of Allah wrote the following covenant in the first year of hijra in Medina. This is the essential constitution of the whole *ummah*. This is a covenant given by Muhammad to the believers.

1. They constitute one *ummah* to the exclusion of all other men.
2. The believers shall leave none of their members in destitution without giving him in kindness and liberty what he needs.
3. No believer shall slay a believer in retaliation for an unbeliever, nor shall he assist an unbeliever against a believer.
4. All believers shall rise as one against anyone who seeks to commit injustice, aggression, or crime or spread mutual enmity among the Muslims, even if such a person is their kin.
5. Just as the bond to Allah is indivisible, all the believers shall stand behind the commitment of the least of them. All believers are bonded to one another to the exclusion of other men.
6. This Pax Islamica is one and indivisible. No believer shall enter a separate peace without all other believers whenever there is fighting in the cause of God except on the basis of equality and justice to all others. In every expedition for the cause of God we undertake, all parties to the covenant shall fight shoulder to shoulder as one man. All believers shall avenge the blood of one another when anyone falls fighting in the way of Allah.
7. The pious believers follow the best and the most upright guidance. Whoever is convicted of killing a believer deliberatively but without righteous cause shall be liable to the relatives of the killed. Until the latter are satisfied, the killer shall be subject to retaliation by each and every believer.

Allah speaks to the believers thus about the struggle in His way:

﴿ وَقَٰتِلُواْ فِي سَبِيلِ ٱللَّهِ ٱلَّذِينَ يُقَٰتِلُونَكُمۡ وَلَا تَعۡتَدُوٓاْۚ إِنَّ ٱللَّهَ لَا يُحِبُّ ٱلۡمُعۡتَدِينَ ١٩٠ ﴾

Fight in the cause of Allah those who fight you, but do not transgress limits; for Allah loves not transgressors.

﴿ وَٱقۡتُلُوهُمۡ حَيۡثُ ثَقِفۡتُمُوهُمۡ وَأَخۡرِجُوهُم مِّنۡ حَيۡثُ أَخۡرَجُوكُمۡۚ وَٱلۡفِتۡنَةُ أَشَدُّ مِنَ ٱلۡقَتۡلِۚ وَلَا تُقَٰتِلُوهُمۡ عِندَ ٱلۡمَسۡجِدِ ٱلۡحَرَامِ حَتَّىٰ
يُقَٰتِلُوكُمۡ فِيهِۖ فَإِن قَٰتَلُوكُمۡ فَٱقۡتُلُوهُمۡۗ كَذَٰلِكَ جَزَآءُ ٱلۡكَٰفِرِينَ ١٩١ ﴾

And slay them wherever you catch them and turn them out from where they have turned you out; for Fitnah, tumult and oppression are worse than slaughter; but fight them not at the Sacred Mosque, unless they fight you there first ; but if they fight you, slay them. Such is the reward of those who suppress faith.

﴿ فَإِنِ ٱنتَهَوۡاْ فَإِنَّ ٱللَّهَ غَفُورٞ رَّحِيمٞ ١٩٢ ﴾

But if they cease, Allah is Oft-Forgiving, Most Merciful.

﴿ وَقَٰتِلُوهُمۡ حَتَّىٰ لَا تَكُونَ فِتۡنَةٞ وَيَكُونَ ٱلدِّينُ لِلَّهِۖ فَإِنِ ٱنتَهَوۡاْ فَلَا عُدۡوَٰنَ إِلَّا عَلَى ٱلظَّٰلِمِينَ ١٩٣

And fight them on until there is no more Fitnah, tumult or oppression and there prevail justice and faith in Allah; but if they cease, let there be no hostility except to those who practice oppression. (Al-Baqarah 2:190–93, Koran)

وَمَا لَكُمْ لَا تُقَٰتِلُونَ فِى سَبِيلِ ٱللَّهِ وَٱلْمُسْتَضْعَفِينَ مِنَ ٱلرِّجَالِ وَٱلنِّسَآءِ وَٱلْوِلْدَٰنِ ٱلَّذِينَ يَقُولُونَ رَبَّنَآ أَخْرِجْنَا مِنْ هَٰذِهِ ٱلْقَرْيَةِ

ٱلظَّالِمِ أَهْلُهَا وَٱجْعَل لَّنَا مِن لَّدُنكَ وَلِيًّا وَٱجْعَل لَّنَا مِن لَّدُنكَ نَصِيرًا ﴿٧٥﴾ ﴾

"And why should you not fight in the cause of Allah and for those men, women and children, who are weak, abused and oppressed, those who beseech their Lord to deliver them from their oppressors and those who ask Allah to send for them protectors and helpers."

﴿ ٱلَّذِينَ ءَامَنُوا۟ يُقَٰتِلُونَ فِى سَبِيلِ ٱللَّهِ ۖ وَٱلَّذِينَ كَفَرُوا۟ يُقَٰتِلُونَ فِى سَبِيلِ ٱلطَّٰغُوتِ فَقَٰتِلُوٓا۟ أَوْلِيَآءَ ٱلشَّيْطَٰنِ ۖ إِنَّ كَيْدَ ٱلشَّيْطَٰنِ كَانَ

ضَعِيفًا ﴿٧٦﴾ ﴾

Those who believe fight in the cause of Allah and those who reject Faith fight in the cause of Evil: so, fight you against the friends of Satan: feeble indeed is the cunning of Satan. (An-Nisa 4:75-76, Koran)

﴿ وَلَا تَهِنُوا۟ فِى ٱبْتِغَآءِ ٱلْقَوْمِ ۖ إِن تَكُونُوا۟ تَأْلَمُونَ فَإِنَّهُمْ يَأْلَمُونَ كَمَا تَأْلَمُونَ ۖ وَتَرْجُونَ مِنَ ٱللَّهِ مَا لَا يَرْجُونَ ۗ وَكَانَ ٱللَّهُ

عَلِيمًا حَكِيمًا ﴿١٠٤﴾ ﴾

And slacken not in following up the enemy; if you are suffering hardships, they are suffering similar hardships; but you have hope from Allah, while they have none. And Allah is full of Knowledge and Wisdom. (An-Nisa 4:104, Koran)

﴿ إِن يَنصُرْكُمُ ٱللَّهُ فَلَا غَالِبَ لَكُمْ ۖ وَإِن يَخْذُلْكُمْ فَمَن ذَا ٱلَّذِى يَنصُرُكُم مِّنۢ بَعْدِهِۦ ۗ وَعَلَى ٱللَّهِ فَلْيَتَوَكَّلِ ٱلْمُؤْمِنُونَ

If Allah helps you none can overcome you:
if He forsakes you, who is there, after that,
that can help you? In Allah, then, let Believers
put their trust. (Ali 'Imran 3:160, Koran)

﴿ وَلَقَدْ أَرْسَلْنَا مِن قَبْلِكَ رُسُلًا إِلَىٰ قَوْمِهِمْ فَجَآءُوهُم بِٱلْبَيِّنَٰتِ فَٱنتَقَمْنَا مِنَ ٱلَّذِينَ أَجْرَمُوا۟ ۖ وَكَانَ حَقًّا عَلَيْنَا نَصْرُ ٱلْمُؤْمِنِينَ ﴿٤٧﴾ ﴾

We did indeed send, before you Rasools to their
respective peoples, with Clear Signs: To those who
transgressed, We meted out Retribution: and as
a right those who earned from us, We helped
those who believed. (Ar-Rum 30:47, Koran)

﴿ هَٰذَا بَيَانٌ لِّلنَّاسِ وَهُدًى وَمَوْعِظَةٌ لِّلْمُتَّقِينَ ﴿١٣٨﴾ ﴾

Here is a declaration to the human, a guidance and
advice to those who live in awareness, Taqwa of Allah!

﴿ وَلَا تَهِنُوا۟ وَلَا تَحْزَنُوا۟ وَأَنتُمُ ٱلْأَعْلَوْنَ إِن كُنتُم مُّؤْمِنِينَ ﴿١٣٩﴾ ﴾

So, lose not hope nor shall you despair, for you
shall achieve supremacy, if you are true in Faith.

إِن يَمْسَسْكُمْ قَرْحٌ فَقَدْ مَسَّ ٱلْقَوْمَ قَرْحٌ مِّثْلُهُۥ ۚ وَتِلْكَ ٱلْأَيَّامُ نُدَاوِلُهَا بَيْنَ ٱلنَّاسِ وَلِيَعْلَمَ ٱللَّهُ ٱلَّذِينَ ءَامَنُوا۟ وَيَتَّخِذَ مِنكُمْ شُهَدَآءَ

وَٱللَّهُ لَا يُحِبُّ ٱلظَّٰلِمِينَ ﴿ ۝ ﴾

If you have suffered a setback, verily a setback
has been there for the other party too. We make
such days of adversity go around amongst the
humans so that Allah may distinguish those who
believe and choose His witnesses from amongst
them. And Allah loves not the evil doers.

﴿ وَلِيُمَحِّصَ ٱللَّهُ ٱلَّذِينَ ءَامَنُوا۟ وَيَمْحَقَ ٱلْكَٰفِرِينَ ﴾ ﴿ ۝ ﴾

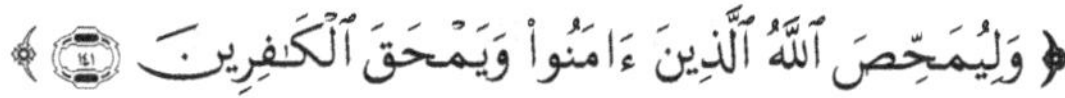

Allah's objective is to distinguish the True
Believers from those who reject Faith.
(Ali 'Imran 3:138–41, Koran)

Wars and slaughter are abhorrent to Allah. Allah says:

If anyone slew a person, unless it is in retribution for
murder or for spreading mischief, fasaad in the land
it would be as if he slew the whole people. And if
anyone saved a life, it would be as if he saved the life
of the whole people. Take not life, which Allah has
made sacred, except by the way of justice or law. This
He commands you, that you may learn wisdom.

And then Allah declares to the believers that *fitnah*, treachery, and
oppression are worse than slaughter and taking of life. *Fitnah*, treason,
and oppression are so vile and repugnant to Allah that He commands
the believers to fight those who assail them and inflict oppression:

> "And slay them wherever you catch them and turn them out from where they have turned you out; for Fitnah, tyranny and oppression are worse than slaughter; And fight them on until there is no more Fitnah, tumult or oppression and there prevail justice and faith in Allah; but if they cease, let there be no hostility except to those who practice Oppression. (Al-Baqarah 2:190–93, Koran)

Allah's command to fight *fitnah*, however, is conditional:

> If the oppressors cease, let there be no further hostility except to those who practice oppression. Do not transgress limits. Allah does not love transgressors. (Al-Baqarah 2:190–93, Koran)

> When the Believers fight against Fitnah and oppression, they fight in the cause of Allah. Those who reject faith in Allah, they fight in the cause of evil. (An-Nisa 4:75–76, Koran)

Fitnah: Allah has granted each believer a right to freedom; right to practice his and her *din* in accordance with his and her beliefs since, in Islam, there is no compulsion in matters of religion; right to life, which includes mental, physical, and emotional well-being; right safeguard to one's property; right to intellectual endeavors, acquisition of knowledge, and education; right to make a living; and right to free speech and action to enjoin good and forbid evil. In enjoying his freedoms, the individual ensures that his activities do not impinge on the similar rights of others. Oppression and tyranny—which deprives an individual believer, a community of believers, or their nation (the *ummah*) of their God-given right to such a freedom—is *fitnah* as described in the Koran. The perpetrators of such tyranny and oppression cannot belong to the fellowship of Allah, the fellowship of His covenant, nor the fellowship of the blessed Nabi*ien* of Allah.

In the above *ayahs*, Allah commands the believers to fight such infidels until there is no more *fitnah*, treachery, and oppression and there prevails justice and faith in Allah everywhere. He orders them to slay them wherever they catch them and turn them out from where they have turned them out, for *fitnah*, tumult, and oppression are worse than slaughter. Allah has forbidden the taking of life. "Take not life, which Allah has made sacred, except by the way of justice or law." *Fitnah*, tyranny, and oppression are so vile and repugnant that Allah commands the believers to fight those who assail them and inflict oppression. "Go forth, advance! Whether equipped well or lightly, perform *jihad* strive your utmost and struggle with your wealth and your persons in the cause of Allah." Allah loves those who fight in His cause in unison and solidarity. *Fitnah*, treachery, and oppression not only afflict those who perpetrate it but also affect everyone, guilty and innocent alike. Allah's command to fight *fitnah* is conditional, however: if the oppressors cease, let there be no further hostility except to those who practice *fitnah*. Do not transgress limits. Allah does not love transgressors.

In the twenty-first century, weakness, poverty, disunity, and fragmentation of the *ummah* arise from its lack of appreciation of the immense store of understanding and knowledge that is in the Koran. Muslims look at the word of Allah but do not see it. They listen to the word but do not hear it. Allah's *nur*, His light, is with them, but they do not let it enter their hearts. The mirror of their *nafs* is covered with the smoke of their greed and craving of worldly wealth. They cannot see Allah's *nur* through the smoky darkness in their heart. *Fitnah*, treachery, and oppression are by-products of darkened hearts, causing blindness to the *nur* of Allah. Without His *nur*, there cannot be *taqwa* of Allah; and in the absence of the consciousness of the reality of Allah, the darkened soul is open to the evil haunts of Satan.

Muslim societies have been plagued by *fitnah* and oppression since the death of the blessed *Nabi.* In Muslim countries, *fitnah* is the result of the combination of internal and external forces. Although the perpetrators of *fitnah* often proclaim Allah as their Savior, their actions always belie their faith in Him.

Most believers, men and women, are not aware that Allah has granted each believer rights and freedom. Most do not know that when the blessed Muhammad died, every believer inherited the Koran, Allah's covenant, His *din*, and the Dar es Salaam. Every believer became the successor, inheritor, and the custodian of the blessed *Nabi's* legacy till the end of time. Consequently, in the twenty-first century, majority of believers are unaware of their rights granted by Allah. They are unaware that Allah commands them to fight the *fitnah* of tyranny and oppression perpetrated by their self-appointed rulers, kings, military dictators, and infidel *awliya*, their Euro-Christian patrons.

The Betrayal of the Covenant of Allah: The *Fitnah* and *Fasaad*

Internal *Fitnah*: Hundreds of years of rule of sultans and later of Western colonial masters produced three unique sources of internal *fitnah* that rules the roost in our day.

1. Priesthood. There is no priesthood in Islam; the believer has a highly personal and exclusive relationship with Allah. Such relationship does not permit the intervention of another human being. When the blessed Muhammad was taken up by Allah, the priests and clerics of Islam assumed the legacy of the pagan priesthood and began to speak on behalf of Allah. Through distortion and misrepresentation of the word of Allah and the pronouncements of His *Nabi,* over the last fourteen hundred

years, the priests and imams of Islam have created divisions and schisms in Islam to generate hundreds of self-righteous sects and subsects among the Muslims. Each sect is the enemy of the other. Every group has the dagger in the back of the other. This gradually smoldering *fitnah* of the priesthood is slowly consuming the body of the *ummah*.

2. Mercenary Armies of Islam. The blessed *Nabi* said,

> All believers shall rise as one man against anyone who seeks to commit injustice, aggression, crime, or spread mutual enmity amongst the Muslims. All believers are bonded one to another to the exclusion of other men. The believers shall leave none of their members in destitution without giving him in kindness that he needs by the way of his liberty.

However, this fight for unity, equality, and justice did not occur in the lands of Islam; the army of God and of Islam did not arise to fight in the cause of Allah to defend against *fitnah*, tyranny, and oppression and to seek retribution against injustice. The absolute loyalty of the army of Islam is to God, the Koran, and the *ummah*. The army of Islam defends the believers, their faith, their land, their wealth, and their honor and fights only against *fitnah* for truth and justice. In case of injury to the believers, their faith, their land, their wealth, and their honor, the believers are obliged to exact retribution. No believer shall side with an unbeliever against a believer. Whosoever is convicted of killing a believer without a righteous cause shall be liable to the relatives of the killed. The killers shall be subject to retaliation by each believer until the relatives of the victim are satisfied with the retribution.

Had the Muslim communities stood united as one to avenge the blood of every fallen Muslim and rejected a separate peace with the pagans without all the Muslims participating in it, there would have been no *fitnah* and massacres in Algeria, Palestine, India, Afghanistan, Iraq, Bosnia, Chechnya, Kosovo, and Darfur. This unity demands revenge, retribution, and reprisal for every act of murder and injury in Dayr Yasin, Sabra, Shatila, Srebrenica, Janin, Sarajevo, Fallujah, Kosovo, Chechnya, Gujarat, Kashmir, Iraq, Guantanamo Bay, and Abu Ghraib. Had the Muslims stood up for one another and fought those who perpetrated the *fitnah*, they would not have been groveling in the dustheap of humanity today.

Contrary to the stipulations of the covenant of Allah, the present six-million-man mercenary armies of Muslim states serve to bolster illegal regimes of *Munafiqeen, the* traitors to the cause of Islam. Instead of relieving the believers of *fitnah* and oppression, they cause them. They are the source of dichotomy and division in Islam; they are the defenders of the foreign hegemony over Islam. The armies of the sultans of the previous centuries and the rulers of modern times are the perpetrators of *fitnah* and the enemies of Islam. They are the defenders of the borders created by the Western colonial powers that divide Islam today. They are the *fitnah*.

3. **Rulers of Islam**. Islam is a religion of voluntary submission of a human to the will of Allah after a considered conviction that Allah is the only reality and that everything else springs out of that reality. Allah has given every human the freedom of choice to submit or not to His will. There is no compulsion in matters of the *din*. And yet there are humans who, by force of arms, compel other humans to submit to their will. They demand obedience through imprisonment, torture, and murder. Every Muslim state in this day is a police state. Every Muslim ruler abuses his authority to plunder and debase the lands of Islam. Every Muslim state today is the source of *fitnah* that is eating into the heart and the soul of Islam.

The rulers of Islamic societies and the ruling bureaucracy must be bound by their covenant with Allah, *taqwa* of Allah, and *furqan*, the criterion to judge between right and wrong. This should include the ability and knowledge of their job and accountability, prerequisite wisdom, sense of justice, ability to champion the good, ability to maintain fellowship with others, generosity, capacity for empathy for the suffering, capacity for forgiving, absolute truthfulness, politeness, honesty, charitableness, courageousness, and virtue that champions the cause of righteousness.

Unfortunately, and sadly, most of Islamic rulers today are corrupt, dishonest, greedy, unjust, and ruthless. For fourteen centuries, they have not obeyed the guidance of the covenant of the Koran. Their quest has been power, loot, plunder, and self-aggrandizement.

4. The External *Fitnah* of the Circle of Evil. Two hundred years ago, the circle of evil began its control of the world's wealth through conspiracy, subterfuge, and secrecy by undermining the stability of countries through war, strife, and discord and by undermining governments through the creation of confusion in the financial markets. The Western armies and intelligence services are the foot soldiers of the circle of evil, and the rulers both of the East and the West are their pawns and puppets to be manipulated at will for the purpose of control of the power and wealth of the world.

The circle of evil is the external *fitnah* whose intent is to destroy Islam. Its intent has always been to corrupt, divide, and control the wealth of the Islamic land through the manipulation of its rulers who were initially placed in positions of power by the circle with the help of Western armies, intelligence, and diplomacy. The weakness of the nation-state mercenary armies of the modern Islamic states clearly arises from the nonfulfillment of Allah's injunctions in the covenant. Faith in Allah's promise and His power, unity of the *ummah*, justice, and struggle to end *fitnah* and tyranny are essential actions ordained in the covenant. When an individual believer reneges in the fulfillment of his covenant with Allah, he only does it to the detriment to his own soul. However, such an action on the part of the community and its appointed leaders leads to the undermining, enslavement, and impoverishment of the whole Islamic community for many generations.

The foundation of the regimes of the imperial families of the Arabian Peninsula, Jordan, Brunei, and Morocco and the imperial occupation governments of Hosni Mubarak of Egypt and the generals of Pakistan are supported by the external *fitnah*—the British, US, and NATO armed forces, intelligence, and diplomatic services in opposition to the aspirations of their own people. In return, these regimes provide services to the circle of evil to subvert, undermine, and weaken the neighboring Islamic and Arab countries of Iran, Afghanistan, Iraq, Syria, Libya, Algeria, Sudan, and Mauritania. The *ummah* is saddled with the curse and the *fitnah* of priesthood, mercenary armies of Muslim states, and their corrupt rulers.

Imagine a country with the largest land base, with coasts rimmed by thousands of miles of blue water oceans, with a vast number of rivers flowing from hundreds of snowcapped mountains through its deserts, grasslands, fertile valleys, and plains into rich deltas, lakes, and oceans bursting with marine life and other resources—a land blessed by Allah with resources never equaled in history, peopled with devout, hardworking populations who know how to utilize such resources in the service of Allah and His creatures. Again, see in your mind's eye an army, the largest in history of mankind, keeping this land, its borders and resources, its oceans and skies, its people and wealth secure from marauders who have traditionally raided other lands for their resources.

These defense forces compose of an army of six million men in about 300 infantry and mechanized divisions equipped with 30,000 tanks and armored vehicles, an air force of 3,580 aircraft of varying vintage, and a naval force equipped with 230 coastal and oceangoing ships equipped with armaments bought from the West and Russia. There are also 60 submarines in the armada. These armed forces are also equipped with short- and medium-range missiles tipped with about 100 nuclear bombs. The country has a budding arms-manufacturing industry producing low- and medium-technology weapons. The annual budget of the combined forces is a hundred billion dollars, of which fifty billion dollars annually goes to Western countries to purchase their discarded and obsolete weaponry. The West then uses these funds to refurbish its own arsenal with the latest high-tech weapons.

You might have guessed that we are talking about the combined might of the Islamic world at the beginning of the twenty-first century. This army has never won any battle of significance since the war for the Gallipoli Peninsula about a century ago. These armed forces have not defended in any significant manner the Islamic world since the disintegration of the Ottoman Empire. The wars of independence of Islamic lands from the colonial rule in India, Iran, Iraq, Syria, Egypt, Morocco, and Algeria were fought by the masses with civil disobedience and jihadi guerrilla warfare. The largest army in the world, the state-organized mercenary army of Islam, has failed to safeguard the freedom of the people of Palestine, Iraq, Kashmir, Sinkiang, Iraq, Kosovo, Bosnia, Mindanao, Chechnya, and Russia.

What went wrong? The Muslim army of the twentieth and twenty-first centuries has its guns pointed inward toward its own people, whereas the external borders of Islam are guarded and patrolled by the naval fleets of America and United Europe. The Muslim state armies should be fighting the *fitnah*, treachery, and oppression by enemies of Allah and

Islam—the *kafirun*, the *mushrikun*, the *Munafiqeen*, and the *zalimun*, who have usurped and plundered the resources of the believers for the last two hundred years. Instead, the Muslim armies and security forces are themselves the source of *fitnah*, oppression, and treachery to the *muttaqeen*, resisting the tyranny of the circle of evil of the *Munafiqeen* and the *Mutaffifeen*. Clear examples are the armed and security forces of Reza Shah Pahlavi of Iran, the mullahs of Iran, Saddam Hussein of Iraq, the Taliban, the Pakistani governments, the Saudi family of Arabia, Suharto, the Assad's of Syria, Anwar Sadat, Hosni Mubarak, Gaddhafi, the Algerian military, and Morocco's royalty. This is a clear testimony that the believers of the covenant of Allah and those who control the so-called armies of Islam have not surrendered to the will of the same Allah and do not strive in the His path.

The obligations assigned to the individual believer in the covenant of Allah are the same for the community of Islam and for the leaders whom the believers have appointed to look after and protect their individual and communal interests. The covenant is specific in pointing out the responsibilities of the individual, the community, and its appointed leaders.

Jihad is the internal struggle of the believer to cleanse oneself of the temptations of the evil that surrounds him or her. It is also a constant external struggle to rid the community of the treachery and oppression by the enemy of the covenant and *din*. The enemy may be obvious, visible, and easily overpowered. The web of intrigues and conspiracies of the *kafaru*, *mushrikun*, *Munafiqeen*, and *zalimun* is hard to detect and overcome. The deception may come from familiar people working from within the community for the circle of evil whose motive is to tempt you away from Allah's path and also take control of your land and wealth, enslaving you in the process. The following four principles should guide the believers in their striving for Allah's cause.

a) Faith in Allah's Covenant and Promise. Join not anything in worship with Him. Allah is the *Waliy* (Friend and Defender) of the believers who obey His covenant. Allah promises His strength and power (*al-qawiyy al-Aziz*) to aid the believer and promises victory in his striving for Allah's *din*. Therefore, the believer shall maintain his faith in Allah's promise always. Trust in Allah's promise endows the believer with the greatest strength from Allah's might in his determination to struggle and fight for Allah's cause. All strength belongs to Allah. All physical, worldly, political, and cosmic strength is nothing before the infinite strength of Allah.

إِنَّ رَبَّكَ هُوَ ٱلْقَوِىُّ ٱلْعَزِيزُ ﴿٦٦﴾

Allah is the All-powerful the Almighty, Al-qawiyy al-Aziz. (Hud 11:66, Koran)

لَا قُوَّةَ إِلَّا بِٱللَّهِ

There is no Power except in Allah. (Al-Kahf 18:39, Koran)

﴿ كَتَبَ ٱللَّهُ لَأَغْلِبَنَّ أَنَا۠ وَرُسُلِىٓ ۚ إِنَّ ٱللَّهَ قَوِىٌّ عَزِيزٌ ﴿٢١﴾

Verily it is I and My Messengers who will be victorious Verily Allah is All-powerful, All-mighty. (Al-Mujadila 58:21, Koran)

b) Unity. The believers constitute one *ummah* to the exclusion of all other men. Just as the bond with Allah is indivisible, all believers shall stand in commitment with the least of them. All believers are bonded to one another to the exclusion of other men. The believers shall leave none of their members in destitution and give them in kindness and liberty what they need. The pious believers follow the best and the most upright guidance of Allah's covenant.

c) Jihad. All believers shall rise as one against anyone who seeks to commit injustice, aggression, or crime or spread mutual enmity among the Muslims. This Pax Islamica is one and indivisible. No believer shall enter a separate peace without all other believers whenever there is fighting in the cause of Allah but will do so only on the basis of equality and justice to all others. In every expedition for the cause of Allah, all parties to the covenant shall fight shoulder to shoulder as one man. All believers shall avenge the blood of one another when anyone falls while fighting for the cause of Allah.

d) Murder. No believer shall slay a believer in retaliation for an unbeliever, nor shall he assist an unbeliever against a believer. Whoever is convicted of killing a believer deliberately but without righteous cause shall be liable to the relatives of the killed. Until the latter are satisfied, the killer shall be subject to retaliation by each and every believer.

Justice. Justice (*'adl*) is a divine attribute defined as "putting in the right place." The opposite of *'adl* is *zulm*, which in Koranic terms means "wrongdoing." Wrongdoing is a human attribute defined as "putting things in the wrong place." *Zulm* (wrongdoing) is one of the common terms used in the Koran to refer to the negative acts employed by human beings. Wrongdoing is the opposite of justice, putting everything in its right place, and every act of humans as prescribed by Allah. Wrongdoing is to put things where they do not belong. Hence, wrongdoing is injustice, for example, associating others with Allah; others do not belong in the place for the divine. It is to place false words in place of the truth and to put someone else's property in place of your own. Other examples are taking a life against the divine commandments, replacing people's liberty with oppression, waging war instead of peace, and usurping people's right to govern themselves. The Koran repeatedly stigmatizes men of wrongdoing.

The Koran, when it points out who is harmed by injustice and wrongdoing, always mentions the word *nafs* (self). People cannot harm Allah. By being unjust or by putting things in the wrong place, people harm themselves. They distort their own natures, and they lead themselves astray. Who can one wrong? It is impossible to wrong or do injustice against Allah since all things are His creatures and do His work. Hence, wrongdoing and injustice is an activity against people and Allah's creation. Allah had prescribed His covenant to the humans for the good of human beings. People, tribes, and nations are being helped since Allah leads them into accord, harmony, and justice, which in turn create peace in the world. Allah has laid out all the basic principles for justice in His covenant for the humans to live in harmony. Those who refuse to follow His commandments are therefore ungrateful and hence *kafirs*. Thus, they are wrongdoers (*zalimun*) and only harm themselves. Therefore, there can be no jihad unless it is for justice and against wrongdoing.

There is a clear reason for the glaring weakness of the state-run armies of the Muslim nation-states. The Muslim states are governed by self-appointed kings, dictators, and politicians who are divorced from their *din* and their people. They belong to and serve the interests of the circle of evil.

Two hundred years ago, the circle of evil began its control of the world's wealth through conspiracy, subterfuge, and secrecy by undermining the stability of countries through war, strife, and discord and by weakening governments through creation of confusion in financial markets. The Western armies and intelligence services are the foot soldiers of the circle of evil, and the rulers of both the East and the West are their pawns and puppets to be manipulated at will to control the power and wealth of the world. The circle of evil is the external *fitnah* whose intent is to destroy Islam. It has always been its intention to corrupt, divide, and control the wealth of the Islamic land through the manipulation of its rulers, who were initially placed in positions of power by the circle with the help of the Western armies, intelligence, and diplomacy.

The foundation of the regimes of the imperial families of the Arabian Peninsula, Jordan, Brunei, and Morocco and the imperial government of Hosni Mubarak and al-Sisi of Egypt are supported by the British and American armed forces, intelligence, and diplomatic services in opposition to the aspirations of their own people. In return, these regimes provide services to the circle of Evil to subvert, undermine, and weaken the neighboring Islamic and Arab countries of Iran, Afghanistan, Iraq, Syria, Libya, Algeria, Sudan, and Mauritania. Turkey and Pakistan are also puppets of the circle of evil; the asking price for the subservience for Turkey is seventeen billion dollars and for the Pakistani dictator a paltry couple of billion dollars in debt relief tagged to some minor trade concessions.

The weakness of the nation-state mercenary armies of the modern Islamic states clearly arises from the nonfulfillment of Allah's injunctions in the covenant. Faith in Allah's promise and His power, unity of the *ummah*, justice, and struggle to end oppression and tyranny are essential actions ordained in the covenant. When an individual believer reneges in the fulfillment of his covenant with Allah, he only does it to the detriment to his own soul. However, such an action on the part of the community and its appointed leaders leads to the undermining, enslavement, and impoverishment of the whole Islamic community for many generations.

Make careful preparations and take precautions. Then go forth in groups or all together to the endeavor.

There amongst you is he who will linger behind, if misfortune befalls you, he will say, "Allah did favor him as he was not with you." When good fortune comes to you from Allah, he would wish that he had been with you.

Those who swap the life of this world for the hereafter let them fight in the cause of Allah. Whosoever fights in the cause of Allah, whether he is slain, or he is victorious, there is a great award for him from Allah.

And why should you not fight in the cause of Allah and for those men, women and children, who are weak, abused and oppressed, those who beseech their Lord to deliver them from their oppressors and those who ask Allah to send for them protectors and helpers. (An-Nisa 4:71-75, Koran)

Remember Allah's blessings on you. When a people planned to stretch out their hands against you and Allah did hold back their hands from you to protect you from your enemies. Be in taqwa of Allah, fear Allah and place your trust in Allah. (Al-Ma'idah 5:11, Koran)

Be in taqwa of Allah, fear Allah. Perform Jihad and strive your utmost in Allah's Cause and approach Him so that you may prosper. (Al-Ma'idah 3:35, Koran)

If any among you turn back on his faith Allah will bring a people whom He loves and who love Him and who are humble towards the believers and stern towards unbelievers, who perform jihad and strive in the cause of Allah and fear not reproaches of any blamer. Such is the Grace of Allah that He bestows on whom He wills. Allah is All-Sufficient for His Creatures and all Knowing. (Al-Ma'idah 5:54, Koran)

When you meet the infidels rank upon rank, in conflict never turn your backs to them. (Al-Anfal 8:15, Koran)

Respond to Allah and His Rasool when He calls you to that gives you life. And know that Allah intervenes in the tussle between man and his heart, and it is to Allah that you shall return. Fear treachery or oppression that afflicts not only those who perpetrate it but affects guilty and innocent alike. Know that Allah is strict in punishment. (Al-Anfal 8:24-25, Koran)

Fight the infidel until there is no more treachery and oppression and there prevails Justice and Faith in Allah altogether and everywhere. If they cease, then Allah is seer of what they do. If they refuse, be sure that Allah is your Protector, the Best to protect and the Best to help. (Al-Anfal 8:39-40, Koran)

When you meet the enemy force, stand steadfast against them and remember the name of Allah much, so that you may be successful. And obey Allah and His Messenger and do not dispute with one another lest you lose courage and your strength departs and be patient. Allah is with those who patiently persevere. (Al-Anfal 8:45–46, Koran)

Whether you do or do not help Allah's Messenger, your leader, Allah strengthens him with His Peace and with forces that you do not see. The words of the infidels He humbled into the dirt, but Allah's word is Exalted, High. Allah is Mighty, Wise. Go forth, advance! Whether equipped well or lightly, perform jihad strive your utmost and struggle with your wealth and your persons in the cause of Allah. That is best for you, if you knew. (At-Tawbah 9:38–41, Koran)

Fight the unbelievers who surround you. Let them find you firm and know Allah is always with those who have taqwa, who are Allah-wary. (At-Tawbah 9:123, Koran)

Remember the Grace of Allah, bestowed upon you, when there came down hordes to overpower you: We sent against them a hurricane and forces that that you did not see but Allah sees all that ye do.

Behold! They came on you from above you and from below you, your eyes became dim and the hearts gaped up to the throats and you imagined various vain thoughts about Allah! (Al-Ahzab 33:9, Koran)

If ye will aid (the cause of) Allah, He will aid you and make your foothold firm. But those who reject Allah, for them is destruction and Allah will render their deeds vain. That is because they hate the Revelation of Allah; so, He has made their deeds fruitless. Do they not travel through the earth and see what was the end of those before their times, who did evil? Allah brought utter destruction on them and similar fates await those who reject Allah. That is because Allah is the Protector of those who believe, but those who reject Allah have no protector. (Muhammad 47:7–11, Koran)

Be not weak and ask for peace, while you are having an upper hand: for Allah is with you and will never decrease the reward of your good deeds.

The life of this world is but play and amusement: and if ye believe, fear Allah and guard against evil, He will grant you your recompense and will not ask you (to give up) your possessions.

Behold, you are those invited to spend of your wealth in the Way of Allah: but among you are some that are parsimonious. But any who are miserly are so at the expense of their own souls. But Allah is free of all wants and it is ye that are needy. If ye turn back (from the Path), He will substitute in your stead another people; then they would not be like you! (Muhammad 47:33–38, Koran)

When ye are told to make room in the assemblies, spread out and make room: ample room will Allah provide for you. And when ye are told to rise up, for prayers, Jihad or other good deeds rise up: Allah will exalt in rank those of you who believe and who have been granted Knowledge. And Allah is well acquainted with all you do. (Al-Mujadila 58:11, Koran)

Why do you promise what you do not carry out? Hateful is indeed to Allah that you say what you do not act upon. Allah loves those who fight in His cause in array of unison and solidarity. (As-Saf 61:2–4, Koran)

Shall I guide you to a bargain that will save you from a painful torment? That you believe in Allah and His Messenger and that you perform Jihad (strive to your utmost) in the way of Allah, with all that you own and in all earnestness: that will be best for you, if you but knew! He will forgive you your sins and admit you to Gardens beneath which rivers flow and to beautiful dwellings in Jannat of adn (Gardens of Eternity): that is indeed the supreme blessing. And another favor will He bestow, which you will cherish; help from Allah and a speedy victory. So, give the glad tidings to the believers. (As-Saf 61:10–13, Koran)

18. The Covenant of Allah: Forgiveness: Be Quick in the Race for Forgiveness from Your Lord, Restrain Anger, and Pardon All Humans.

O you who believe! Be quick in the race for forgiveness from your Lord. Those who give freely whether in prosperity, or in adversity, those who restrain anger and pardon all humans, for Allah loves those who do beautiful deeds. Fear the Fire, which is prepared for those who reject Faith; And obey Allah and the

Messenger; that ye may obtain mercy. Be quick in
the race for forgiveness from your Lord and for a
Garden whose measurement is that of the heavens
and of the earth, prepared for the righteous.

Those who give freely whether in prosperity,
or in adversity, those who restrain anger and
pardon all humans, for Allah loves those who do
beautiful deeds. (Ali 'Imran 3:130–34, Koran)

Among Allah's names are *ar-Rahman* (the Beneficent), *ar-Rahim* (the Merciful), and *al-Ghafoor* (the Forgiving). His mercy overtakes His punishment and anger.

﴿ ۞ قُلْ يَـٰعِبَادِىَ ٱلَّذِينَ أَسْرَفُوا۟ عَلَىٰٓ أَنفُسِهِمْ لَا تَقْنَطُوا۟ مِن رَّحْمَةِ ٱللَّهِ ۚ إِنَّ ٱللَّهَ يَغْفِرُ ٱلذُّنُوبَ جَمِيعًا ۚ إِنَّهُۥ هُوَ ٱلْغَفُورُ ٱلرَّحِيمُ ﴿٥٣﴾ ﴾

Say: "O my Servants who have transgressed against
their souls! Despair not of the Mercy of Allah: for Allah
forgives all sins: for He is Oft-Forgiving, Most Merciful.

Every human action in daily life reaches back into the divine reality that everything in the universe is governed by tawhid, yet Allah has granted humans a freedom of choice, which can upset the balance in the creation, balance of justice, and balance of atmospheric elements and of environmental pollution and cause destruction of animal species and of populations, cities, and agriculture through human actions. The covenant tells people why they should be Allah's servants and explains which path they should follow to become His vicegerents. It makes clear that human activity is deeply rooted in the Real, and this has everlasting repercussions in this world and in the hereafter.

The wholesome (*salihun*) are the ones who live in harmony with the Real (*Haqq*) and establish wholesomeness (*saalihaat*) through their words and deeds throughout the world. In contrast, the corrupt (*mufsidun*) destroy the proper balance and relationship with Allah and His creation. *Fasid* are the corrupt, the evil, and those who do wrong.

Allah measures out good and evil, the wholesome and the corrupt. Humans have enough freedom to make their own choices; if they make the choice to do beautiful and wholesome deeds(*saalihaat*) motivated by faith (*iman*) and god-wariness (*taqwa*), they please Allah and bring harmony and wholesomeness to the world, resulting in peace, justice, mercy, compassion, honor, equity, well-being, freedom, and many other gifts through Allah's grace. Others choose to do evil and work with corruption (*mufsidun*), destroying the right relationship among the creation, causing hunger, disease, oppression, pollution, and other afflictions. In the universal order, corruption is the prerogative of humans, and vicegerency gives them the freedom to work against the Creator and His creation. Only the misapplied trust can explain how moral evil can appear in the world. When humans choose wrong and corrupt actions, they displease Allah. Allah loves those who do what is beautiful, not those who do what is ugly:

وَإِذَا تَوَلَّىٰ سَعَىٰ فِي ٱلْأَرْضِ لِيُفْسِدَ فِيهَا وَيُهْلِكَ ٱلْحَرْثَ وَٱلنَّسْلَ ۗ وَٱللَّهُ لَا يُحِبُّ ٱلْفَسَادَ ﴿٢٠٥﴾

When he turns his back, he hurries about the
earth to work corruption there and destroy
the tillage and the stock. Allah loves not
corruption. (Al-Baqarah 2:205, Koran)

Allah loves doing what is beautiful and because of His
love for those who do the beautiful, He brings them
near to Himself and His nearness is called Allah's mercy:

وَلَا تُفْسِدُوا۟ فِى ٱلْأَرْضِ بَعْدَ إِصْلَـٰحِهَا وَٱدْعُوهُ خَوْفًا وَطَمَعًا ۚ إِنَّ رَحْمَتَ ٱللَّهِ قَرِيبٌ مِّنَ ٱلْمُحْسِنِينَ ﴿٥٦﴾

Work not corruption in this world after it has made wholesome and call upon Allah in fear and hope. Surely the mercy of Allah is near to those who do what is beautiful. (Al-A'raf 7:56, Koran)

The covenant of the Koran presents us with the scope of the freedom of choice that humans have in doing what is wholesome and beautiful or what is corrupt and ugly and in the human role among the creation that distinguishes right activity, right thought, and right intention from their opposites. It reminds us of how the scales of Allah's justice, the two hands of Allah—His mercy and His wrath—are reflected in the human domain, where people have been appointed Allah's vicegerents. Deeds of goodness and wholesomeness are associated with mercy, paradise, and the beautiful. Evil and corruption is rewarded with wrath, hell, and the ugly.

To err is human. Allah is most forgiving to those who have erred and repented. Above all, Allah's mercy knows no bounds. The Koran and the teachings of the blessed *Nabi* guide those who seek the path of Allah. Allah says:

"O my Servants who have transgressed against their souls! Despair not of the Mercy of Allah: for Allah forgives all sins: for He is Oft-Forgiving, Most Merciful.

"Turn ye to your Lord (in repentance) and bow to His (Will), before the Penalty comes on you: after that ye shall not be helped. (Az-Zumar 39:53, Koran)

Allah, in His Mercy, has laid down guidelines for the punishment of transgressors. For transgressors and sinners, there is Allah's wrath with life constricted in this world and the next. If they repent, Allah forgives them. The Koran constantly emphasizes repentance and reform of the individual and Allah's mercy and grace. Allah's mercy knows no bounds. Justice (*'adl*) is a divine attribute defined as "putting every object in the right place." When the transgressor repents and mends his ways and does not repeat the wrongdoing and the wrong and evil has been put in the right place and replaced with good, Allah bestows His mercy. The community's obligation is to pardon and help educate and reform the individual. Allah advises every individual to restrain from anger and resentment. Anger is a smoldering volcano quietly burning the human from the inside, robbing his tranquility and peace. Forgiveness restores peace and brings nearness to Allah.

For the unrepentant transgressor, the penalty is prescribed in the Koran. Never is the gate to Allah's mercy closed. The key to this gate is repentance and a walk in Allah's straight path.

19. The Covenant of Allah: Allah Forbids the Taking of Life

> If anyone slew a person, it would be as if he slew
> the whole people: and if anyone saved a life, it
> would be as if he saved the life of all the people.

Life is sacred. Allah forbids the taking of life unless it is by way of justice (jihad against tyranny and oppression) or when ordained by the law of equality or punishment for murder, in which case the Koran recommends clemency. As the covenant forbids the believers and the community of Islam to take a life and murder, the same injunction applies to the ruler or the *amri minkum* appointed by the believers. War against Muslims and others for acquisition of territory and wealth is forbidden, and anyone waging such a war blatantly disobeys Allah's covenant and is not of the believers. Persecution, punishment, imprisonment, and murder of the citizens of the Islamic state who strive for the cause of Allah is a heinous crime. Rulers and their bureaucracy responsible for such crimes are unfit to discharge their responsibility and liable for punishment for their crime according to the law of the Koran.

> If anyone slew a person - unless it be for murder or for spreading mischief in the land - it would be as if he slew the whole people: and if anyone saved a life, it would be as if he saved the life of the whole people. (Al-Ma'idah 5:32, Koran)

> Take not life, which Allah hath made sacred, except by the way of justice or law: This He commands you, that you may learn wisdom. (Al-An'am 6:151–53, Koran)

20. The Covenant of Allah: Usury and Hoarding of Wealth: Devour Not Usury, Doubled and Multiplied; Be in *Taqwa* of Allah (Fear Allah) That Ye May Prosper

Forbidden is the practice of usury to the Muslims. Also forbidden is making money from money. Money in its present form is only a medium of exchange, a way of defining the value of an item, but in itself has no value and therefore should not give rise to more money by earning interest through deposit in a bank or loaning it to someone else. The human endeavor, initiative, and risk involved in a productive venture are much more important than the money used to finance it. Money deposited in a bank or hoarded is potential capital rather than capital. Money becomes capital only when it is invested in a venture.

Accordingly, money loaned to a business is regarded as a debt and is not capital; and as such, it is not entitled to any return, such as interest.

Muslims are encouraged to spend (purchase necessities or spend in the way of Allah) or invest their money and are discouraged from keeping their money idle. Hoarding money is unacceptable. Allah's commandments in His covenant with the believers in the following three *ayahs* exhort Muslims to (a) spend in charity after their needs are met, (b) devour not in usury, and (c) hoard not gold and silver.

ۗ وَيَسْـَٔلُونَكَ مَاذَا يُنفِقُونَ قُلِ ٱلْعَفْوَ ۗ كَذَٰلِكَ يُبَيِّنُ ٱللَّهُ لَكُمُ ٱلْءَايَٰتِ لَعَلَّكُمْ تَتَفَكَّرُونَ

They ask thee how much they are to spend (in charity); say: "What is beyond your needs." Thus doth Allah make clear to you His Signs: in order that ye may consider. (Al-Baqarah 2:222, Koran)

يَمْحَقُ ٱللَّهُ ٱلرِّبَوٰا۟ وَيُرْبِى ٱلصَّدَقَٰتِ ۗ وَٱللَّهُ لَا يُحِبُّ كُلَّ كَفَّارٍ أَثِيمٍ ﴿٢٧٦﴾

Allah will deprive usury of all blessing but will give increase for deeds of charity; for He loves not creatures ungrateful and wicked. (Al-Baqarah 2:275-76, Koran)

ٱللَّهِ ۗ وَٱلَّذِينَ يَكْنِزُونَ ٱلذَّهَبَ وَٱلْفِضَّةَ وَلَا يُنفِقُونَهَا فِى سَبِيلِ ٱللَّهِ فَبَشِّرْهُم بِعَذَابٍ أَلِيمٍ ﴿٣٤﴾

And there are those who hoard gold and silver and spend it not in the Way of Allah: announce unto them a most grievous penalty. (Al-A'raf 9:34, Koran)

Gharar (uncertainty, risk, or speculation) is forbidden. Any transaction entered into should be free from uncertainty, risk, and speculation. The parties cannot predetermine a granted profit, and this does not allow an undertaking from the borrower or the customer to repay the borrowed principal, plus an amount to consider inflation. Therefore, options and futures are regarded as un-Islamic; so are foreign exchange transactions because rates are determined by interest differentials.

The Betrayal of the Covenant of Allah: Modern Economics, Banking, Usury, and Fiat Money

An Islamic government is forbidden to lend or borrow money from institutions such as international banks, the World Bank, or the International Monetary Fund on interest as both usury and interest are expressly forbidden. Banking based on fiat money is also forbidden. The value of money is diluted by the creation of new money out of nothing; the property rights of savers and those who have been promised future payments, such as pensioners, are violated. This is stealing. The trappings of the money and banking system have been compared to that of a cult; only those who profit from it understand its inner workings. They work hard to keep it that way. The central banks print notes adorned with signatures, seals, and pictures of a president or that of a queen; counterfeiters are severely punished; governments pay their expenses with them; and populations are forced to accept them. They are printed like newspapers in such vast quantity, representing an equal worth to all the treasures of this world, all the resources above and under the ground, all assets of populations, and their work and labor to fabricate every item that has ever been manufactured. And yet these notes cost nothing to make. In truth, this has been the greatest hoax, the worst crime against humanity, a swindle of proportions never seen by humanity before.

As we have found, the Koran forbids usury, gambling, speculation, and hoarding of gold and silver. The Koran does advocate trade; spending on good things in life, kith, and kin; and giving wealth for the cause of Allah. The modern economic system is entirely alien to the teachings of the Koran and full of pitfalls and trappings laid down by Satan. The Dar es Salaam has slid downhill, submerged into the quicksand of make-believe economy. Every successful businessman and trader is forced to operate in the pagan, sinful system of economy. Here is the solution for a successful economic system as laid down in the covenant of the Koran:

1. Elimination of usury and interest in Dar es Salaam.
2. Elimination of fiat money and of banking based on money created out of nothing with a printing press. There will be no more creation and lending of capital nine times that of the bank deposits. It is dishonest and forbidden because it is based on institutionalized theft, supported by the state and international institutions.
3. Creation of a single currency for the united Islamic state, such as gold dinars and silver dirhams based on the measures established by Umar ibn al-Khattab, the second caliph. A currency bureau, an arm of the state of Dar es Salaam, will supervise the minting and circulation of the currency.
4. Drastic changes to Dar es Salaam's trading relations with the rest of the world. All goods utilized within the state—whether industrial, agricultural, manufactured, or raw—will be produced within the country so that the *ummah* is self-sufficient and independent of foreign trading systems. The goods for export—oil, minerals, raw and manufactured goods—shall be sold against gold and gold-based currency as well as barter. Paper and printed money will not be acceptable.

Pricing for international trade will use an index of equal value to human labor internationally.

Those that spend of their goods in charity
by night and by day, in secret and in public,
have their reward with their Lord: on them
shall be no fear, nor shall they grieve.

Those who devour usury will not stand except
stands the one whom the Satan by his touch has
driven to madness. That is because they say: "Trade
is like usury," but Allah hath permitted trade
and forbidden usury. Those who after receiving
direction from their Lord, desist, shall be pardoned
for the past; their case is for Allah to judge; but
those who repeat (the offence) are Companions
of the Fire; they will abide therein (forever).

Allah will deprive usury of all blessing but
will give increase for deeds of charity; for
He does not love ungrateful and wicked
creatures. (Al-Baqarah 2:274–76, Koran)

Those who believe and perform wholesome
deeds, establish regular prayers and regular
charity have rewards with their Lord. On them
shall be no fear, nor shall they grieve.

Fear Allah and give up what remains of your demand
for usury, if you are indeed believers. If you, do it not,
take notice of war from Allah and His Messenger: but
if you turn back, you will still have your capital sums.

Deal not unjustly and ye shall not be dealt with unjustly.

If the debtor is in a difficulty, grant him time until it is easy for him to repay. But if ye remit it by way of charity, that is best for you. (Al-Baqarah 2:277–80, Koran)

Devour not usury, doubled and multiplied; Be in taqwa of Allah (fear Allah) that ye may prosper.

Fear the Fire, which is prepared for those who reject Faith; and obey Allah and the Messenger; that ye may obtain mercy.

Be quick in the race for forgiveness from your Lord and for a Garden whose measurement is that of the heavens and of the earth, prepared for the righteous.

Those who give freely whether in prosperity, or in adversity; those who restrain anger and pardon all humans; for Allah loves those who do beautiful deeds (Al -Muhsinun). (Ali 'Imran 3:130–34, Koran)

There are indeed many among the priests and clerics who in falsehood devour the substance of men and hinder them from the way of Allah. And there are those who bury gold and silver and spend it not in the way of Allah: announce unto them a most grievous penalty.

On the Day when heat will be produced out of that wealth in the fire of Hell and with it will be branded their foreheads, their flanks and their backs, "This is the treasure which you buried for yourselves: taste then, the treasures which you buried!" (At-Tawbah 9:34–35, Koran)

21. The Covenant of Allah: Be Good to Your Parents; Allah Forbids Infanticide and Abortion

The Koran repeatedly commands the believers to do what is beautiful to be brought under the sway of Allah's gentle, merciful, and beautiful names. Human qualities gain their reality from the most beautiful divine qualities. When humans turn to Allah, their beautiful qualities become indistinguishable from Allah's own.

﴿ وَلِلَّهِ مَا فِي ٱلسَّمَٰوَٰتِ وَمَا فِي ٱلْأَرْضِ لِيَجْزِيَ ٱلَّذِينَ أَسَٰٓـُٔواْ بِمَا عَمِلُواْ وَيَجْزِيَ ٱلَّذِينَ أَحْسَنُواْ بِٱلْحُسْنَى ٣١ ﴾

To Allah belongs all that is in the heavens and on earth; so that He rewards those who do ugly, according for what they have done, and He rewards those who do beautiful with the most beautiful. (An-Najm 53:31, Koran)

The first beautiful act that believers perform after tawhid is to do what is beautiful and do good to their parents, those who brought them into existence. It is parents who provide means that Allah employs in creating people, nurturing, educating, and making them beautiful and God fearing. Allah takes credit for His creation, which is the requirement of tawhid. Allah expects his creatures to act appropriately toward His intermediaries of creation. Only in this manner can humans expect other creatures, including their own children, to act beautifully toward them.

The Betrayal of the Covenant of Allah: Respect for Parents and Sanctity of Life

Respect and care for the parents is the fundamental act in the Islamic society to maintain the cohesion of the family structure. The family is the underlying unit of the community that forms the support group for children, adults, the elderly, the relatives, the neighborhood, the kin, and the communal structure around the mosque and schools.

Infanticide and its modern version, abortion, and the taking of life of both humans and animals are forbidden by the Koran. Allah has made life sacred. And avoid *Fahasha*, the shameful deeds that set the human down a slippery slope of the ugly and evil. The breakdown of the family structure in modern society, abandonment of elderly parents, and infanticide are caused by the loss of *iman* and hope in Allah' s mercy and grace. Allah assures the believers:

> Be good to your parents; kill not your
> children on a plea of want - We provide
> sustenance for you and for them.

لَا تَعْبُدُونَ إِلَّا ٱللَّهَ وَبِٱلْوَٰلِدَيْنِ إِحْسَانًا وَذِى ٱلْقُرْبَىٰ وَٱلْيَتَـٰمَىٰ وَٱلْمَسَـٰكِينِ وَقُولُوا۟ لِلنَّاسِ حُسْنًا وَأَقِيمُوا۟ ٱلصَّلَوٰةَ وَءَاتُوا۟ ٱلزَّكَوٰةَ

> Worship none but Allah; treat with kindness your
> parents and kindred and orphans and those in need;
> speak fair to the people; be steadfast in prayer; And
> practice regular charity. (Al-Baqarah 2:82, Koran)

﴿ ۞ قُلْ تَعَالَوْا۟ أَتْلُ مَا حَرَّمَ رَبُّكُمْ عَلَيْكُمْ ۖ أَلَّا تُشْرِكُوا۟ بِهِۦ شَيْـًٔا ۖ وَبِٱلْوَٰلِدَيْنِ إِحْسَـٰنًا ۖ وَلَا تَقْتُلُوٓا۟ أَوْلَـٰدَكُم مِّنْ إِمْلَـٰقٍ ۖ نَّحْنُ
نَرْزُقُكُمْ وَإِيَّاهُمْ ۖ وَلَا تَقْرَبُوا۟ ٱلْفَوَٰحِشَ مَا ظَهَرَ مِنْهَا وَمَا بَطَنَ ۖ وَلَا تَقْتُلُوا۟ ٱلنَّفْسَ ٱلَّتِى حَرَّمَ ٱللَّهُ إِلَّا بِٱلْحَقِّ ۚ ذَٰلِكُمْ وَصَّىٰكُم بِهِۦ لَعَلَّكُمْ
تَعْقِلُونَ ﴿١٥١﴾

Say: "Come, I will rehearse what Allah hath (really) prohibited you from": join not anything as equal with Him; be good to your parents; kill not your children on a plea of want - We provide sustenance for you and for them - come not nigh to shameful deeds, whether open or secret; take not life, which Allah hath made sacred, except by way of justice and law: thus doth He command you, that ye may learn wisdom. (Al-An'am 6:151, Koran)

﴿ لَّا تَجْعَلْ مَعَ ٱللَّهِ إِلَـٰهًا ءَاخَرَ فَتَقْعُدَ مَذْمُومًا مَّخْذُولًا ﴿٢٢﴾ ۞ وَقَضَىٰ رَبُّكَ أَلَّا تَعْبُدُوٓا۟ إِلَّآ إِيَّاهُ وَبِٱلْوَٰلِدَيْنِ إِحْسَـٰنًا ۚ إِمَّا يَبْلُغَنَّ عِندَكَ
ٱلْكِبَرَ أَحَدُهُمَآ أَوْ كِلَاهُمَا فَلَا تَقُل لَّهُمَآ أُفٍّ وَلَا تَنْهَرْهُمَا وَقُل لَّهُمَا قَوْلًا كَرِيمًا ﴿٢٣﴾ وَٱخْفِضْ لَهُمَا جَنَاحَ ٱلذُّلِّ مِنَ ٱلرَّحْمَةِ وَقُل رَّبِّ
ٱرْحَمْهُمَا كَمَا رَبَّيَانِى صَغِيرًا ﴿٢٤﴾ ﴾

Take not with Allah another object of worship; or thou wilt sit in disgrace and destitution Thy Lord hath decreed that ye worship none but Him and that ye be kind to parents. Whether one or both of them attain old age in thy life, say not to them a word of contempt, nor repel them, but address them in terms of honor. And out of kindness, lower to them the wing of humility and say: "My Lord! Bestow on them thy Mercy even as they cherished me in childhood." (Al-Isra 17:22, 24, Koran)

﴿ وَوَصَّيْنَا ٱلْإِنسَٰنَ بِوَٰلِدَيْهِ إِحْسَٰنًا ۖ حَمَلَتْهُ أُمُّهُۥ كُرْهًا وَوَضَعَتْهُ كُرْهًا ۖ وَحَمْلُهُۥ وَفِصَٰلُهُۥ ثَلَٰثُونَ شَهْرًا ۚ حَتَّىٰٓ إِذَا بَلَغَ أَشُدَّهُۥ وَبَلَغَ أَرْبَعِينَ سَنَةً قَالَ رَبِّ أَوْزِعْنِىٓ أَنْ أَشْكُرَ نِعْمَتَكَ ٱلَّتِىٓ أَنْعَمْتَ عَلَىَّ وَعَلَىٰ وَٰلِدَىَّ وَأَنْ أَعْمَلَ صَٰلِحًا تَرْضَىٰهُ وَأَصْلِحْ لِى فِى ذُرِّيَّتِىٓ ۖ إِنِّى تُبْتُ إِلَيْكَ وَإِنِّى مِنَ ٱلْمُسْلِمِينَ ﴿١٥﴾ ﴾

We have enjoined on man kindness to his parents: in pain did his mother bear him and in pain did she give him birth. The carrying of the (child) to his weaning is (a period of) thirty months. At length, when he reaches the age of full strength and attains forty years, he says: "O my Lord! grant me that I may be grateful for Thy favor which Thou hast bestowed upon me and upon both my parents and that I may work righteousness such as Thou may approve; and be gracious to me in my issue. Truly have I turned to Thee and truly do I bow (to Thee) in Islam." (Al-Ahqaf 46:15, Koran)

22. The Covenant of Allah: Equality of Men and Women: Mistreatment of Women by Muslims

You are forbidden to take women against their will. Nor should you treat them with harshness, on the contrary treat them with them on a footing of equality kindness and honor.

The Betrayal of the Covenant of Allah: Mistreatment of Women by Muslims

Fifty percent of the population of the believers, the women, has been excluded from the mainstream Islam by the mullahs, jurist-scholars, and the Hadith scholars against the commandments of the Koran. Women were regarded as inferior beings in most pre-Islamic cultures, including among the Arabs, Persians, Greeks, and Romans as well as the Hindus. Their status was not any higher among the Turkish and the Mongol tribes of Central Asia. In Judaism, women were forbidden from the inner sanctuary of the temple; and in the early Pauline Christianity, their position was relegated to the entrance of or outside the church at prayer time.

Islam brought dignity and grace to the status of women—the mothers, wives, and daughters. Women had their rights established and their social status elevated as equal to that of men. They attended prayer services at the Prophet's Mosque; they held regular and frequent discourse with the *Nabi* of Allah on religious, women, and family issues. They participated in battles alongside their men. Women worked outside their homes. The first person to convert to Islam, Khadijah, was a successful international trader and owned an import and export business, dealing goods from India, Persia, Africa, Yemen, and the Byzantine Empire. She employed several men to assist her in her business. Other women memorized the Koran and taught other Muslims. A'ishah gave regular talks and discourses on religious matters. Other women led the ritual prayers and *dhikr-e-Allah* gatherings.

The ulema and other followers of the *Hadith collections* over the last one thousand years have totally excluded women from congregation prayers, businesses, public and social affairs, and most importantly education. The Muslim communities have betrayed Allah and His *Rasul* concerning their obligations to the women—their mothers, wives, sisters, and daughters. Allah's covenant provides equality to every individual within the community, both men and women. Allah has elevated the rank and dignity of the children of Adam, both men and women, with special favors above that of most of His creation, including the angels. The dignity and favors promised by Allah include six special values: faith, life, intellect (education), property, lineage, and freedom of speech and action.

Equality of Men and Women: The Koran addresses men and women who submit to Allah, who believe, who are devout, who speak the truth, who are righteous, who are humble, who are charitable, who fast and deny themselves, who guard their chastity, and who remember Allah and promises them a great reward and forgiveness for their transgressions. In this address, Allah treats men and women equitably with the promise of a similar reward for their good acts. In Allah's eyes, all men and women who do good deeds carry an equal favor with Him.

Allah admonishes believing men and women to lower their gaze and guard their chastity. Allah is well acquainted with what men did. Allah also admonishes women to dress modestly and not display their adornments outside their immediate family environment. Allah commands believers, men and women, to turn *all together* toward Allah so that they may prosper. This can happen only when the believers, men and women, turn to Allah collectively as a community in a mosque as was customary during the lifetime of the *Nabi* of Allah.

According to the Koran, men and women are autonomous and answerable to Allah for their own deeds and actions, and only they as individuals are rewarded or punished for their deeds. In a community, men as a group or the state has no authority from the Koran to enforce any restrictions on the freedom of righteous and believing women. To every man and woman, Allah has bestowed rights to *faith, life, intellect, property, education, and freedom of action and speech.* The authority of a ruler who denies these basic freedoms to men or to women is openly disputable. A person obeys the ruler on the condition that the ruler obeys the Koran and Allah's covenant.

For men and women who surrender unto Allah,

For men and women who believe,

For men and women who are devout

For men and women who speak the truth,

For men and women who persevere in righteousness,

For men and women who are humble,

For men and women who are charitable,

For men and women who fast and deny them selves

For men and women who guard their chastity,

For men and women who remember Allah much,

For them Allah has forgiveness and a great reward.

Say to the

Believing men that they should lower
their gaze and guard their modesty:

That will make for greater purity for them:

And Allah is acquainted with all that they do.

And say to the

Believing women that they should lower
their gaze and guard their modesty;

That they should not display their adornments
except what is ordinarily obvious,

That they should draw a veil over

Their bosom and not display their adornments.

And that they should not strike their feet

In order to draw attention

To their hidden adornments.

and O ye Believers!

Turn ye all together Toward Allah that ye may prosper.

The believer's men and women are
protectors one of another.

They enjoin what is just and forbid what is evil.

They observe regular prayers, practice regular
charity and obey Allah and His messenger.

On them will Allah pour His mercy, for
Allah is exalted in power, wise.

O ye who believe! Guard your souls,

If ye follow [right] guidance,

No hurt can come to you from those who stray.

The goal of you all is to Allah,

It is He who will show you the truth of all that ye do.

The Koran, as in the sura above, addresses men and women equally, subjecting them together to similar obligations of submission to Allah, regular prayer, giving in charity, modesty in dress and behavior, righteousness, humility, chastity, worship, truthfulness, remembrance of Allah, and being kind and just. Allah blessed mankind (*insan*), both men and women, with dignity, justice, and equality. He promised them the same rewards and gave them the same obligations. *Be steadfast in prayer and practice regular charity* is an ongoing and repetitive theme in the Koran. Allah calls those who believe, both men and women, to hasten to the congregation prayer on Friday, the day of assembly.

يَٰٓأَيُّهَا ٱلَّذِينَ ءَامَنُوٓاْ إِذَا نُودِىَ لِلصَّلَوٰةِ مِن يَوْمِ ٱلْجُمُعَةِ فَٱسْعَوْاْ إِلَىٰ ذِكْرِ ٱللَّهِ وَذَرُواْ ٱلْبَيْعَ ۚ ذَٰلِكُمْ خَيْرٌ لَّكُمْ إِن كُنتُمْ تَعْلَمُونَ ﴿٩﴾ فَإِذَا
قُضِيَتِ ٱلصَّلَوٰةُ فَٱنتَشِرُواْ فِى ٱلْأَرْضِ وَٱبْتَغُواْ مِن فَضْلِ ٱللَّهِ وَٱذْكُرُواْ ٱللَّهَ كَثِيرًا لَّعَلَّكُمْ تُفْلِحُونَ ﴿١٠﴾

O ye who believe! (Men and women) When the call is proclaimed to prayer on Friday (the Day of Assembly), hasten earnestly to the Remembrance of Allah and leave off business (and traffic): that is best for you if ye but knew!

and when the Prayer is finished, then may ye disperse through the land and seek of the Bounty of Allah: and celebrate the Praises of Allah often (and without stint): that ye may prosper. (Al-Mumtahanah 62:9–10, Koran)

Women attended obligatory prayers, *jum'ah* prayers, and Eid prayers in the Prophet's Mosque. Whenever the apostle of Allah finished his prayers with *Taslim*, the women would get up first, and he would stay in his place for a while before getting up. The purpose of staying was that the women might leave before the men who had finished their prayer.

Soon after the *Nabi* died, there occurred an enormous expansion of the Islamic domain. Women, for a while, enjoyed their newly won freedom and dignity given by Islam and proclaimed by the blessed *Nabi* Muhammad. Soon afterward, the Arabs reached an unprecedented level of prosperity and began to accumulate large harems of wives, concubines, and female slaves and servants. These women were increasingly confined to their quarters and not allowed to go out unchaperoned. Subsequently, the architecture of the Middle East dwellings changed to suit the new circumstances. The courtyard of the house had high walls, and the only entrance was where the master of the house sat. The master of the harem was so jealous of the chastity of his women that he only employed eunuchs as his servants and guards at his house. The institution of eunuchs was a peculiar Middle Eastern practice related to the institution of the harems of the elite.

The trampling of women's rights was and is a betrayal of the blessed *Nabi* Muhammad's emancipation of women. As more Arabs, Romans, Persians, Hindus, Turks, and Mongols embraced Islam, they brought with them their peculiar bias against women and female infants. The Islamic emancipation of women was ignored; women were confined within their houses, covered head to foot in cloth, denied spiritual growth, and denied access to education and to places of worship. Shamefully, the scholars and the ulema encouraged this state of affairs. Women were gradually discouraged from praying in the mosque and were excluded from congregational worship. Thus, the Muslims for centuries have betrayed the *Nabi* of Allah and disobeyed Allah's covenant.

Pre-Islamic Arab and other cultures regarded women as their chattel and possession. Abduction and rape of opponents' women was a favored pastime of those victorious in battle to humiliate the vanquished. Thus, the birth of a female child was regarded as a matter of shame, which led to the practice of infanticide. This practice was forbidden earlier on during the prophet's mission. However, the primordial masculine instinct resurfaced in the new Muslim. His subconscious shame and embarrassment of the female in his household was sublimated into gentler and more socially acceptable alternative. As the Koran points out, he chose to retain the female child on sufferance and contempt rather than bury her in the dust. And the Koran says, "*What an evil choice they decide on!*" The shame and cultural burden in some of the Muslim societies is so intense that the female infant is buried in the coffin of yashmak (burka) in the confines of her brick house. She is not killed off physically but intellectually and spiritually by withholding the intellectual and spiritual sustenance that Allah had provided for her.

قَدْ خَسِرَ ٱلَّذِينَ قَتَلُوٓا۟ أَوْلَـٰدَهُمْ سَفَهًۢا بِغَيْرِ عِلْمٍ وَحَرَّمُوا۟ مَا رَزَقَهُمُ ٱللَّهُ ٱفْتِرَآءً عَلَى ٱللَّهِ ۚ قَدْ ضَلُّوا۟ وَمَا كَانُوا۟ مُهْتَدِينَ ﴿١٤٠﴾

Indeed, Lost are those who slay their children, foolishly and without knowledge and have forbidden that which Allah has provided for them and inventing lies against Allah. They have indeed gone astray and heeded no guidance. (Al-An' am 6:140, Koran)

وَإِذَا بُشِّرَ أَحَدُهُم بِٱلْأُنثَىٰ ظَلَّ وَجْهُهُۥ مُسْوَدًّا وَهُوَ كَظِيمٌ ﴿٥٨﴾ يَتَوَٰرَىٰ مِنَ ٱلْقَوْمِ مِن سُوٓءِ مَا بُشِّرَ بِهِۦٓ ۚ أَيُمْسِكُهُۥ عَلَىٰ هُونٍ أَمْ
يَدُسُّهُۥ فِى ٱلتُّرَابِ ۗ أَلَا سَآءَ مَا يَحْكُمُونَ ﴿٥٩﴾

When news is brought to one of them, of the birth of a female child, his face darkens and he is filled with inward grief! With shame does he hide himself from his people, because of the bad news he has had! Shall he retain it on sufferance and contempt, or bury it in the dust? Ah! What an evil choice they decide on? (An-Nahl 16:58–59, Koran)

Women have their freedoms, bestowed by the covenant of Allah. Women can achieve their God-given equality and respect only when they stand up to men to demand equality and respect in all the spheres of life in Muslim societies. This will occur only when women have an intellectual awakening to understand and assert their rights. The dignity and favors promised by Allah include six special values: faith, life, intellect (education), property, lineage, and freedom of speech and action.

Until Muslim men do not eliminate their *fitnah* against 50 percent of believers—their mothers, wives, sisters, and daughters—they will continue to be mired in the pit of ignorance, poverty, and *Fahasha*. To arise out of the pit of decadence, they will have to swallow their ego and pride and learn to respect and honor their women.

To every man and to every woman Allah has bestowed
Equal rights to Freedom, Faith, Life, Intellect, Property,
Education and Freedom of Speech and Action,
enjoining what is right and forbidding what is wrong.

You are forbidden to take women against their will.
Nor should you treat them with harshness, so that
you may renounce of the dower you have given
them and that is only permitted where they have
been guilty of open lewdness. On the contrary live
with them on a footing of kindness and honor.
If ye take a dislike to them it may be that you
dislike a thing, through which Allah brings about
a great deal of good. (An-Nisa 4:19, Koran)

Truly, among your wives and your children are some
that are contenders to your obligations so beware!
If ye forgive them and overlook their faults, verily
Allah is Most -Forgiving, Most Merciful. Your
riches and your children may be but a temptation:
Whereas Allah! With Him is an immense reward.

So be in taqwa of Allah and fear Allah as much as
you can; listen and obey; and spend in charity for the
benefit of your own souls. And those saved from
their own greed are the ones that prosper. If ye loan

to Allah a beautiful loan, He will double it for you
and He will forgive you: for Allah is both Appreciative
(Shakoor) and Magnanimous (Haleem), Knower of
what is hidden and what is manifest, Exalted in Might,
Full of Wisdom. (At-Taghabun 64:14–18, Koran)

Those who slander decent women, thoughtless but
believing, are cursed in this life and in the Hereafter: for
them is a grievous Penalty. (An-Nur 24:21–23, Koran)

23. The Covenant of Allah: Equitable Sharing of Wealth

Crave not those things of what Allah has bestowed
His gifts more freely on some than others, men are
assigned what they earn and women that they earn.

Allah created the earth and then bestowed on man His favors to extract sustenance from it. He also created the sun, moon, and stars to create a just equilibrium and harmony in the universe. The sun provides energy for the growth, sustenance, and well-being of humans, plants, and animals. Gradually, man began to extract more than his personal needs from the earth; and the boom of economics, trade, and commerce started, creating cycles of imbalance, disharmony, wars, poverty, and injustice throughout the globe. Not only did this disharmony caused by greed blemish humans but animal life also suffered by the disappearance of whole species. Pollution and contamination of the environment resulted from the race trying to accumulate and hoard the world's wealth in a few hands. Man disobeyed Allah's universal laws and covenant.

In return for all of Allah's favors, Allah commands the following:

- Justice (*al-'adl*). Justice, fairness, honesty, integrity, and evenhanded dealings are a prerequisite of every Muslim's conduct when dealing with others whether socially or in a business transaction.
- Doing what is good and what is beautiful (*ihsan*). This attribute includes every positive quality such as goodness, beauty, and harmony. Human beings have an obligation to do what is wholesome and beautiful in their relationship with Allah and His creatures.
- Providing for those near to you (*qurba*) and kith and kin. Help them with wealth, kindness, compassion, humanity, and sympathy.

Allah forbids *Fahasha*—all evil deeds, lies, false testimony, fornication, selfishness, ingratitude, greed, and false belief. One must fulfill the covenant of Allah, and whosoever does beautiful and righteous deeds will be given a new life and rewarded with greater wages by Allah.

۞ إِنَّ ٱللَّهَ يَأْمُرُ بِٱلْعَدْلِ وَٱلْإِحْسَـٰنِ وَإِيتَآئِ ذِى ٱلْقُرْبَىٰ وَيَنْهَىٰ عَنِ ٱلْفَحْشَآءِ وَٱلْمُنكَرِ وَٱلْبَغْىِ ۚ يَعِظُكُمْ لَعَلَّكُمْ تَذَكَّرُونَ ۝

وَأَوْفُوا۟ بِعَهْدِ ٱللَّهِ إِذَا عَـٰهَدتُّمْ وَلَا تَنقُضُوا۟ ٱلْأَيْمَـٰنَ بَعْدَ تَوْكِيدِهَا وَقَدْ جَعَلْتُمُ ٱللَّهَ عَلَيْكُمْ كَفِيلًا ۚ إِنَّ ٱللَّهَ يَعْلَمُ مَا تَفْعَلُونَ

Allah commands justice, the doing of good
and liberality to kith and kin and He forbids all
shameful deeds and injustice and rebellion: He
instructs you, that ye may receive admonition.

Fulfill the Covenant of Allah when ye have
entered into it and break not your covenants
after ye have confirmed them: indeed, ye
have made Allah your surety; for Allah knows
all that you do. (Koran 16:90–91)

مَنۡ عَمِلَ صَٰلِحٗا مِّن ذَكَرٍ أَوۡ أُنثَىٰ وَهُوَ مُؤۡمِنٞ فَلَنُحۡيِيَنَّهُۥ حَيَوٰةٗ طَيِّبَةٗۖ وَلَنَجۡزِيَنَّهُمۡ أَجۡرَهُم بِأَحۡسَنِ مَا كَانُواْ يَعۡمَلُونَ ٩٧

Whoever works righteousness, man or woman and has Faith, verily, to him will We give a new Life, a life that is good and pure and We will bestow on such their reward according to the best of their actions. (Koran 16:97)

Tawhid, the main pillar of Islam, signifies that man's economic life depends wholly on Allah's laws of the universe and that their relationship to those who believe is through the obedience to the covenant of Allah. Allah maintains in the Koran that there is no creature on the earth whose sustenance is not provided by Allah.

۞وَمَا مِن دَآبَّةٖ فِي ٱلۡأَرۡضِ إِلَّا عَلَى ٱللَّهِ رِزۡقُهَا وَيَعۡلَمُ مُسۡتَقَرَّهَا وَمُسۡتَوۡدَعَهَاۚ كُلّٞ فِي كِتَٰبٖ مُّبِينٖ ٦

No creature crawls on earth that Allah does not nourish. He knows its essential nature and its varying forms; every detail has its place in the obvious plan. (Koran 11:6)

How Are the People in Need Provided for Their Sustenance and Needs Daily?

All wealth belongs to Allah, who bestows it on some people more than others. This wealth is given in trust, whereby the possessor is obliged to give the surplus for Allah's cause, to his kin, to the widows and orphans, and to the needy first in his community and then in the other communities around him. Wealth is to be shared so that not a single individual of the *ummah*, or indeed in the world should go hungry or without education and shelter.

۞ لَّيْسَ ٱلْبِرَّ أَن تُوَلُّوا۟ وُجُوهَكُمْ قِبَلَ ٱلْمَشْرِقِ وَٱلْمَغْرِبِ وَلَٰكِنَّ ٱلْبِرَّ مَنْ ءَامَنَ بِٱللَّهِ وَٱلْيَوْمِ ٱلْءَاخِرِ وَٱلْمَلَٰٓئِكَةِ وَٱلْكِتَٰبِ وَٱلنَّبِيِّـۧنَ وَءَاتَى
ٱلْمَالَ عَلَىٰ حُبِّهِۦ ذَوِى ٱلْقُرْبَىٰ وَٱلْيَتَٰمَىٰ وَٱلْمَسَٰكِينَ وَٱبْنَ ٱلسَّبِيلِ وَٱلسَّآئِلِينَ وَفِى ٱلرِّقَابِ وَأَقَامَ ٱلصَّلَوٰةَ وَءَاتَى ٱلزَّكَوٰةَ وَٱلْمُوفُونَ
بِعَهْدِهِمْ إِذَا عَٰهَدُوا۟ ۖ وَٱلصَّٰبِرِينَ فِى ٱلْبَأْسَآءِ وَٱلضَّرَّآءِ وَحِينَ ٱلْبَأْسِ ۗ أُو۟لَٰٓئِكَ ٱلَّذِينَ صَدَقُوا۟ ۖ وَأُو۟لَٰٓئِكَ هُمُ ٱلْمُتَّقُونَ ١٧٧

It is not righteousness that ye turn your faces towards East or West; but it is righteousness to believe in Allah and the Last Day and the Angels and the Book and the Messengers; to spend of your substance, out of love for Him, for your kin, for orphans, for the needy, for the wayfarer, for those who ask and for the ransom of slaves; to be steadfast in prayer and practice regular charity, to fulfill the contracts which you have made; and to be firm and patient, in pain (or suffering) and adversity and throughout all periods of panic. Such are the people of truth, the God-fearing. (Al-Baqarah 2:177, Koran)

وَإِذَا قِيلَ لَهُمْ أَنفِقُوا۟ مِمَّا رَزَقَكُمُ ٱللَّهُ قَالَ ٱلَّذِينَ كَفَرُوا۟ لِلَّذِينَ ءَامَنُوٓا۟ أَنُطْعِمُ مَن لَّوْ يَشَآءُ ٱللَّهُ أَطْعَمَهُۥٓ إِنْ أَنتُمْ إِلَّا فِى ضَلَٰلٍ مُّبِينٍ

And when they are told, "Spend you of (the bounties) with which Allah has provided you," The Unbelievers say to those who believe: "Shall we then feed those whom, if Allah had so willed, He would have fed, Himself? Ye are in nothing but manifest error. (Koran 36:47)

۞ إِنَّمَا ٱلصَّدَقَٰتُ لِلْفُقَرَآءِ وَٱلْمَسَٰكِينِ وَٱلْعَٰمِلِينَ عَلَيْهَا وَٱلْمُؤَلَّفَةِ قُلُوبُهُمْ وَفِى ٱلرِّقَابِ وَٱلْغَٰرِمِينَ وَفِى سَبِيلِ ٱللَّهِ وَٱبْنِ ٱلسَّبِيلِ ۖ

فَرِيضَةً مِّنَ ٱللَّهِ ۗ وَٱللَّهُ عَلِيمٌ حَكِيمٌ ﴿٦٠﴾

Alms are for the poor and the needy and those employed to administer the funds; for those whose hearts have been (recently) reconciled (to the truth); for those in bondage and in debt; in the cause of Allah; and for the wayfarer: (thus is it) ordained by Allah and Allah is full of knowledge and wisdom. (At-Tawbah 9:60, Koran)

In the above two verses, the clear indication is that man is given bounty by Allah. In return, his obligation is to distribute the surplus after his needs have been met to the needy. The Koran specifies that the charities be disbursed to the *fuqara* (the poor who ask), to *al masakin* (the poor and the needy who do not ask), to zakat administrators, to those who spread the light of Islam to those inclined, for the freedom of those in bondage, to those in debt, for the cause of Allah, and for the wayfarer who treads the path in Allah's service.

In the covenant between the individual believer and Allah, the individual surrenders to Allah his life and belongings in return for His guidance, a place in paradise in the hereafter, and peace with prosperity in this world. Every believer according to his or her covenant with Allah has the obligation to extend the benefits that Allah has provided them to those who did not receive the same benefits. Such acts of generosity will be rewarded by Allah with a place in *Jannat* (place of peace and plenty) in the afterlife. Life of *Jannat* is to be attained in this world also, provided the compact with Allah is adhered to. The believer is Allah's instrument who will fulfill His promise to Adam that, none will remain without food or clothes, and none will suffer from heat or thirst. (Koran 20:118)

In the verses below, Allah has promised those who believe and obey His Covenant that, as the reward for their acts of charity, He will double the harvest of their labors, forgive their sins, and provide them of His bounties; nor shall they have fear or grieve. Fear and grief arise from misfortunes, which cause anxiety and depression. Allah's promise, therefore, is to safeguard the believers from misfortunes. And to those devouring usury, Allah will deprive them of all blessings. Obeying of Allah's covenant provides *Jannat* in the hereafter and in this world. It also brings balance, harmony, and stability to the economic life of the world in that it meets the necessities of each person and eliminates unnecessary suffering.

يَـٰٓأَيُّهَا ٱلَّذِينَ ءَامَنُوا۟ لَا تُبْطِلُوا۟ صَدَقَـٰتِكُم بِٱلْمَنِّ وَٱلْأَذَىٰ كَٱلَّذِى يُنفِقُ مَالَهُۥ رِئَآءَ ٱلنَّاسِ وَلَا يُؤْمِنُ بِٱللَّهِ وَٱلْيَوْمِ ٱلْـَٔاخِرِ ۖ فَمَثَلُهُۥ كَمَثَلِ صَفْوَانٍ عَلَيْهِ تُرَابٌ فَأَصَابَهُۥ وَابِلٌ فَتَرَكَهُۥ صَلْدًا ۖ لَّا يَقْدِرُونَ عَلَىٰ شَىْءٍ مِّمَّا كَسَبُوا۟ ۗ وَٱللَّهُ لَا يَهْدِى ٱلْقَوْمَ ٱلْكَـٰفِرِينَ ﴿٢٦٤﴾ وَمَثَلُ ٱلَّذِينَ يُنفِقُونَ أَمْوَٰلَهُمُ ٱبْتِغَآءَ مَرْضَاتِ ٱللَّهِ وَتَثْبِيتًا مِّنْ أَنفُسِهِمْ كَمَثَلِ جَنَّةٍۭ بِرَبْوَةٍ أَصَابَهَا وَابِلٌ فَـَٔاتَتْ أُكُلَهَا ضِعْفَيْنِ فَإِن لَّمْ يُصِبْهَا وَابِلٌ فَطَلٌّ ۗ وَٱللَّهُ بِمَا تَعْمَلُونَ بَصِيرٌ ﴿٢٦٥﴾

O you who believe! Do no render in vain your charity by reminders of your generosity or by injury, like him who spends his wealth to be seen of men, but he does not believe in Allah nor in the Last Day. His likeness is the likeness of a smooth rock on which is a little soil; on it falls heavy rain, which leaves it bare. They will not be able to do anything with what they have earned. And Allah does not guide the disbelieving people.

And the likeness of those who spend their substance, seeking to please Allah and to strengthen their souls, is as a garden, high and fertile; heavy rain falls on it but makes it yield a double increase of harvest and if it receives not heavy rain, light moisture suffices it. And Allah is seer of what you do. (Al-Baqarah 2:264–65, Koran)

يَٰٓأَيُّهَا ٱلَّذِينَ ءَامَنُوٓاْ أَنفِقُواْ مِن طَيِّبَٰتِ مَا كَسَبْتُمْ وَمِمَّآ أَخْرَجْنَا لَكُم مِّنَ ٱلْأَرْضِ ۖ وَلَا تَيَمَّمُواْ ٱلْخَبِيثَ مِنْهُ تُنفِقُونَ وَلَسْتُم
بِـَٔاخِذِيهِ إِلَّآ أَن تُغْمِضُواْ فِيهِ ۚ وَٱعْلَمُوٓاْ أَنَّ ٱللَّهَ غَنِىٌّ حَمِيدٌ ﴿٢٦٧﴾ ٱلشَّيْطَٰنُ يَعِدُكُمُ ٱلْفَقْرَ وَيَأْمُرُكُم بِٱلْفَحْشَآءِ ۖ وَٱللَّهُ يَعِدُكُم مَّغْفِرَةً مِّنْهُ
وَفَضْلًا ۗ وَٱللَّهُ وَٰسِعٌ عَلِيمٌ ﴿٢٦٨﴾ يُؤْتِى ٱلْحِكْمَةَ مَن يَشَآءُ ۚ وَمَن يُؤْتَ ٱلْحِكْمَةَ فَقَدْ أُوتِىَ خَيْرًا كَثِيرًا ۗ وَمَا يَذَّكَّرُ إِلَّآ أُوْلُواْ ٱلْأَلْبَٰبِ ﴿٢٦٩﴾
وَمَآ أَنفَقْتُم مِّن نَّفَقَةٍ أَوْ نَذَرْتُم مِّن نَّذْرٍ فَإِنَّ ٱللَّهَ يَعْلَمُهُۥ ۗ وَمَا لِلظَّٰلِمِينَ مِنْ أَنصَارٍ ﴿٢٧٠﴾

O ye who believe! Give of the good things that ye have (honorably) earned and of the fruits of the earth that We have produced for you and do not even aim at getting anything which is bad, in order that out of it ye may give away something, when ye yourselves would not receive it except with closed eyes. And know that Allah is free of all wants and worthy of all praise.

The Evil One threatens you with poverty and bids you to conduct unseemly. Allah promises you His forgiveness and bounties. And Allah cares for all and He knows all things.

He grants wisdom to whom He pleases; and he to whom wisdom is granted receives indeed a benefit overflowing; but none will grasp the Message but men of understanding.

And whatever ye spend in charity or devotion, be sure Allah knows it all. But the wrongdoers have no helpers. (Al-Baqarah 2:267–70, Koran)

ٱلَّذِينَ يُنفِقُونَ أَمۡوَٰلَهُم بِٱلَّيۡلِ وَٱلنَّهَارِ سِرّٗا وَعَلَانِيَةٗ فَلَهُمۡ أَجۡرُهُمۡ عِندَ رَبِّهِمۡ وَلَا خَوۡفٌ عَلَيۡهِمۡ وَلَا هُمۡ يَحۡزَنُونَ ﴿٢٧٤﴾
ٱلَّذِينَ يَأۡكُلُونَ ٱلرِّبَوٰاْ لَا يَقُومُونَ إِلَّا كَمَا يَقُومُ ٱلَّذِي يَتَخَبَّطُهُ ٱلشَّيۡطَٰنُ مِنَ ٱلۡمَسِّۚ ذَٰلِكَ بِأَنَّهُمۡ قَالُوٓاْ إِنَّمَا ٱلۡبَيۡعُ مِثۡلُ ٱلرِّبَوٰاْۗ وَأَحَلَّ
ٱللَّهُ ٱلۡبَيۡعَ وَحَرَّمَ ٱلرِّبَوٰاْۚ فَمَن جَآءَهُۥ مَوۡعِظَةٞ مِّن رَّبِّهِۦ فَٱنتَهَىٰ فَلَهُۥ مَا سَلَفَ وَأَمۡرُهُۥٓ إِلَى ٱللَّهِۖ وَمَنۡ عَادَ فَأُوْلَٰٓئِكَ أَصۡحَٰبُ ٱلنَّارِۖ هُمۡ فِيهَا
خَٰلِدُونَ ﴿٢٧٥﴾ يَمۡحَقُ ٱللَّهُ ٱلرِّبَوٰاْ وَيُرۡبِي ٱلصَّدَقَٰتِۗ وَٱللَّهُ لَا يُحِبُّ كُلَّ كَفَّارٍ أَثِيمٍ ﴿٢٧٦﴾

Those who (in charity) spend of their goods by night and by day, in secret and in public, have their reward with their Lord: on them shall be no fear, nor shall they grieve.

Those who devour usury will not stand except as stands one whom the Satan by his touch hath driven to madness. That is because they say: "Trade is like usury," but Allah hath permitted trade and forbidden usury. Those who after receiving direction from their Lord, desist, shall be pardoned for the past; their case is for Allah (to judge); but those who repeat (the offence) are Companions of the Fire; they will abide therein (forever.)

Allah will deprive usury of all blessing but will give increase for deeds of charity; for He loves not creatures ungrateful and wicked. (Al-Baqarah 2:274–76, Koran)

Economic Principles of the Covenant of Allah

The covenant of Allah in the Koran has laid down principles and guidelines for the well-being of the economic life of the believers. Obeying the principles will bring peace, harmony, spiritual enlightenment, and economic prosperity. Disobeying means misery, ruin, and Allah's wrath.

First Principle: Land and sources of production are not the personal property of individuals. *Ardh* is the source of life and means of sustenance and production of food and resources and therefore must remain available to the community, the *ummah*.

Allah created *Ardh* and *sama* and has power over everything in and between them. To Allah belong the heaven and the earth and what is in between them. *Sama* in the Koran signifies the universe and *ardh* man's domain on the earth pertaining to his social and economic world. Allah is the Lord of the heavens and the earth. The divine laws under which the universe functions so meticulously and smoothly should also apply to the economic life of man so that he might achieve a balanced, predictable, equitable, and just financial life. *Sama* is the source of Allah's benevolence to mankind and of His universal laws that govern the human subsistence and sustenance on the earth (*ardh*), controlling man's economic life. Allah's kingdom over the heavens and the earth sustains man's economic life and directly affects man's conduct and his obedience to Allah's covenant.

Ayahs in Sura An-Nahl are explicit. Allah created the heavens and the earth for just ends—to bring peace, harmony, equilibrium, and justice to the universe. He is Allah, the One, Lord of creation. He sends water from the heavens for the sustenance of life on the earth—humans, plants, and animals. Allah sends sunshine to the earth to provide warmth and light to sustain human, plant, and animal life. Allah created the moon and the stars to create equilibrium in the universe, with every object in its intended place revolving in its fixed orbit in perfect harmony and balance. Allah has the secrets and mysteries of the heavens and the earth, the so-called sciences, and the knowledge of particles, elements, cells, mitochondria, chromosomes, gravity, and black holes, only an infinitesimal portion of which he revealed to man.

In other *ayahs* of Sura An-Nahl, Allah clearly mentions all the comforts He has provided man for the sustenance of life and for his economic well-being. Allah created cattle for humans for warmth, food, and transport and horses, mules, and donkeys for riding and to show. With the moisture from the skies, He produces for man corn, olives, date palms, grapes, and every type of fruit. Allah made good things for humans in different colors and quantities so that man can celebrate and praise Allah in gratitude. Allah made the sea subject to humans so that they may eat fresh and tender seafood, obtain beautiful ornaments from the ocean, sail their ships, and plow the oceans around the world. From the cattle, Allah produces milk, pure and wholesome to drink; and from the fruit of the date palm and vine, you get food and drink. And from the bees, there is honey of varying colors that heals ailments.

Historically, land was there for man and the beasts to roam around freely and spread through the world. Later, tribes and communities laid claims on pieces of land they needed for their needs with some extra surrounding area for their security. At the beginning of the Islamic era, productive land and water resources were owned by tribes for the use of their clan members. After the message of the Koran was established, the clans, tribes, former kingdoms, and nations amalgamated to form the community of Islam, the *ummah*, which in principle owned the title to the land and resources with theoretical tenancy. The owner ship of land by the *ummah* began to change with the downfall of the Abbasid caliphate.

From 1040 to 1200, with the collapse of the central authority, there were many regional power struggles that allowed for the breakdown of the eastern Iranian frontiers against nomadic invasions. Central Asian nomads searching for pasturage in the tenth, eleventh, and the twelfth centuries spilled over into the region north of the Aral Sea and into Transoxania and Afghanistan. From contact with settled peoples, trade, and the activities of the missionaries, these Turkish peoples began to convert to Islam. Their chieftains became acquainted in the ways of agriculture, trade, city administration, and imperial conception of rule and order. Most of the useful land in the Islamic states was taken over by the Turkish chiefs and soldiers for their own use and for the advancement of their own political power.

The Seljuk decline opened the way for the third phase in the history of the region from 1150 to 1350. This was a period of further nomadic invasion from inner Asia, culminating in the devastating Mongol invasions and the establishment of Mongol regimes over most of the Middle East. With every change of the ruling class, the land and resources shifted from the peasantry to the tribal chiefs and the soldiery. To the west, the slave military forces in Egypt and Syria consolidated the Mamluk regime, with land being distributed among the new elite.

The final phase was the Timurid period, 1400–1500. The Mongol period was succeeded by new times of troubles and conquest by Timur, also known as Tamerlane. This era of repeated nomadic invasions brought demographic changes in the ethnic and religious identity of populations. A new Turkic-speaking population migrated into Transoxania, the Hindu Kush mountain range, Iran, the Caucasus, Anatolia, and Mesopotamia. Turkish settlement led to the Islamization of northeastern Iran, Armenia, and Anatolia both by settlement of newcomers and by the conversion of existing populations.

To consolidate their power, control of provinces was delegated to the family members and the nomadic chieftains. *Iqtas* lands were assigned to the military leaders. The result was usurpation of power at both the provincial and local levels, with the formation of micro regimes funded by the resources of the land and heavy taxation of the peasants.

The Ottoman cavalry were recruited from among Turkish warriors. They were not garrisoned as a regular army, but they were provided with land grants and timars (Arabic equivalent of *iqt'at*) throughout the empire. The timar holders provided local security and served in Ottoman campaigns. The timar system was based on an old-fashioned feudal pattern. The Ottomans also used the resources of the land to maintain their control over the empire and toward their new conquests. The timar holders exploited the peasants and the subject population.

The subject population belonged to a lesser order of existence. All commoners, Muslim and non-Muslim, were considered the *reava* (flocks) to be shorn in the interests of the political elite. The Ottomans operated on the principle that the subjects should serve the interests of the state; the economy was organized to ensure the flow of tax revenues, goods in kind, and the services needed by the government and the elites. The populace was systematically taxed by maintaining a record of the population, households, property, and livestock.

All the lands in the empire were owned by the ruler; some lands (*tapulu*) were on perpetual lease to the peasants who had the right to assign that right to their male descendants, and *mukatalu* lands were leased to a tax collector in return for a fixed payment for a lease. In the fifteenth century, the Ottomans had conceded to Turkish military rulers and Muslim religious rulers the ownership right to the land. In the course of the next century and a half, the sultans dispossessed the local notables and reassigned the tax rights to the timar holders appointed by the sultan. Ottoman policies were inimical to accumulation of private property. Large private fortunes were regularly confiscated by the state. The Ottoman economic policy on taxation and trade was based on fiscalism that was aimed at accumulation of as much bullion as possible in the state treasury, which was primarily used for the expenditure of running the Topkapi court and the ongoing wars in the West.

The ownership of land in the Islamic world is not owned or distributed according to the covenant of the Koran, causing the present unequal distribution of wealth, poverty, deprivation, and degradation of a large part of the Islamic society. Land, therefore, belongs to Allah, who bestowed it to man and woman, His regents on the earth. The covenant expects man to take care of the land for all of Allah's creatures—men and beasts—as well as conserve its resources for future generations. Whatever is left over after his own needs are met goes to the necessities of the rest of humanity, starting with his *qurba* (near and dear) and then his community, followed by the surrounding communities. The land does not belong to the states, governments, tribal chiefs, military, aristocracy, timars, or *iqt'at.* Land cannot be owned by individuals or families nor inherited.

Men and women live in small communities. These form a fellowship and a brotherhood that looks after its own who are in need, and such a need may be of sustenance, clothing, shelter, knowledge, well-being, spirituality, understanding, protection, justice, or simple reassurance. And such assistance is extended to the surrounding communities till it reaches the far-flung communities of the *ummah.* Each basic community owns the land in its surrounds, tilled and administered by the community as a whole for its well-being in justice and harmony according to the covenant of Allah. The Islamic economic system is based on capitalism in the production of wealth and communism in its expenditure, with the difference being that individuals are free and able to make wealth but are responsible for the needs of kith and kin and their neighbor. The state has little role in the welfare system. The land owned by the community may be assigned to individuals or may be tilled communally for the mutual benefit of the whole community, producing food and paying for schools, hospitals, roadways, municipal services, and so. on. The community is meant to be self-sufficient economically and responsible for each and every individual's welfare, health, schooling, and old-age pensions.

Second principle: **All surplus money and resources should not remain with individuals.** How much is enough for one's needs? A hundred? A thousand? A hundred thousand? A million? A billion? How much is enough? After accumulation of a certain amount of money, any further hoarding becomes an act of obscenity and evil. All surplus money and resources shall be used for the benefit and uplift of the community and humanity.

وَيَسْـَٔلُونَكَ مَاذَا يُنفِقُونَ قُلِ ٱلْعَفْوَ ۗ كَذَٰلِكَ يُبَيِّنُ ٱللَّهُ لَكُمُ ٱلْءَايَٰتِ لَعَلَّكُمْ تَتَفَكَّرُونَ ۝

They ask thee how much they are to spend (in charity); say: "What is beyond your needs". Thus doth Allah make clear to you His Signs: in order that ye may consider. (Al-Baqarah 2:222, Koran)

Third Principle: Wealth and commodities should not be hoarded. Surplus wealth is to be spent for the needs of the community as prescribed by Allah.

۞ يَٰٓأَيُّهَا ٱلَّذِينَ ءَامَنُوٓا۟ إِنَّ كَثِيرًا مِّنَ ٱلْأَحْبَارِ وَٱلرُّهْبَانِ لَيَأْكُلُونَ أَمْوَٰلَ ٱلنَّاسِ بِٱلْبَٰطِلِ وَيَصُدُّونَ عَن سَبِيلِ ٱللَّهِ ۗ وَٱلَّذِينَ
يَكْنِزُونَ ٱلذَّهَبَ وَٱلْفِضَّةَ وَلَا يُنفِقُونَهَا فِى سَبِيلِ ٱللَّهِ فَبَشِّرْهُم بِعَذَابٍ أَلِيمٍ ﴿٣٤﴾

O you who believe! There are indeed many among the priests and anchorites, who in falsehood devour the substance of men and hinder (them) from the Way of

Allah. And there are those who bury gold and silver and
spend it not in the Way of Allah: announce unto them
a most grievous penalty. (At-Tawbah 9:34, Koran)

Fourth Principle: Wealth shall be spread throughout the community, the *ummah*, and shall not be impounded, stolen, and looted by conquerors, tribes, rulers, classes, and the *Mutaffifeen* (dealers in fraud) as practiced in un-Koranic societies, Muslim and Non-Muslim.

مَّآ أَفَآءَ ٱللَّهُ عَلَىٰ رَسُولِهِۦ مِنْ أَهْلِ ٱلْقُرَىٰ فَلِلَّهِ وَلِلرَّسُولِ وَلِذِى ٱلْقُرْبَىٰ وَٱلْيَتَـٰمَىٰ وَٱلْمَسَـٰكِينِ وَٱبْنِ ٱلسَّبِيلِ كَىْ لَا يَكُونَ دُولَةًۢ بَيْنَ
ٱلْأَغْنِيَآءِ مِنكُمْ ۚ وَمَآ ءَاتَىٰكُمُ ٱلرَّسُولُ فَخُذُوهُ وَمَا نَهَىٰكُمْ عَنْهُ فَٱنتَهُوا۟ ۚ وَٱتَّقُوا۟ ٱللَّهَ ۖ إِنَّ ٱللَّهَ شَدِيدُ ٱلْعِقَابِ ﴿٧﴾

What Allah has bestowed on His Rasool from
the people of the townships, belongs to Allah, to
His Rasool and to the near of kin and orphans,
the poor and the homeless, in order that it
may not (merely) make a circuit between the
wealthy among you. So, take what the Rasool
assigns to you and deny yourselves that which he
withholds from you. And fear Allah, for Allah is
strict in Punishment. (Al-Hashr 59:7, Koran)

Fifth Principle: No one shall subsist on the earnings of another, and except for those who are incapacitated, everyone shall work. Everyone—man and woman—shall also contribute their labor and sweat toward community well-being.

The Koran calls the people who stint *Mutaffifeen*, those who get the full measure from others but stint when measuring for others. They lead an easy life from the earnings of others. The Koran mentions three such groups. One group consists of people who "take with an even balance and give less than what is due."

وَيْلٌ لِّلْمُطَفِّفِينَ ﴿١﴾ ٱلَّذِينَ إِذَا ٱكْتَالُوا۟ عَلَى ٱلنَّاسِ يَسْتَوْفُونَ ﴿٢﴾ وَإِذَا كَالُوهُمْ أَو وَّزَنُوهُمْ يُخْسِرُونَ ﴿٣﴾ أَلَا يَظُنُّ أُو۟لَٰٓئِكَ أَنَّهُم مَّبْعُوثُونَ
لِيَوْمٍ عَظِيمٍ ﴿٤﴾ يَوْمَ يَقُومُ ٱلنَّاسُ لِرَبِّ ٱلْعَٰلَمِينَ ﴿٥﴾

Woe to those that deal in fraud, those
who, from others exact full measure,

But when measuring or weighing for
others, give less than due.

Do they not think that they will be called
to account, on a Mighty Day,

A Day when (all) mankind will stand before the
Lord of the Worlds? (Mutaffifeen 83:1–6, Koran)

Another group comprises those who inherit money, land, and property, and they use that wealth to accumulate more and more without ever giving back to the needy. The third group gobbles up the earnings of others:

۞ يَٰٓأَيُّهَا ٱلَّذِينَ ءَامَنُوٓا۟ إِنَّ كَثِيرًا مِّنَ ٱلْأَحْبَارِ وَٱلرُّهْبَانِ لَيَأْكُلُونَ أَمْوَٰلَ ٱلنَّاسِ بِٱلْبَٰطِلِ وَيَصُدُّونَ عَن سَبِيلِ ٱللَّهِ ۗ وَٱلَّذِينَ
يَكْنِزُونَ ٱلذَّهَبَ وَٱلْفِضَّةَ وَلَا يُنفِقُونَهَا فِى سَبِيلِ ٱللَّهِ فَبَشِّرْهُم بِعَذَابٍ أَلِيمٍ ﴿٣٤﴾

O ye who believe! There are indeed many among
the priests and clerics, who in falsehood devour the
substance of men and hinder (them) from the Way of
Allah. And there are those who bury gold and silver
and spend it not in the Way of Allah: announce unto
them a most grievous penalty. (Qur'an 9:34 Al A'raf).

Squander not your wealth among yourselves in
egotism and conceit: Let there be trade and traffic
amongst you with mutual goodwill nor kill or
destroy yourselves: for verily Allah hath been Most
Merciful to you. If any do that in rancor and injustice,
soon shall We cast them into the fire: and easy it
is for Allah. If you abstain from all the odious and
the forbidden, Allah shall expel out of you all evil
in you and admit you to a Gate of great honor.

And crave not those things of what Allah has
bestowed His gifts more freely on some than
others, men are assigned what they earn and
women that they earn. But ask Allah of His
bounty. Surely Allah is knower of everything.

O you who believe! Let not your riches or your
children divert you from the remembrance of
Allah. If any act thus, the loss is their own.

And spend something (in charity) out of the
substance which We have bestowed on you, before
Death should come to any of you and he should
say, "O my Lord! Why didst Thou not give me
respite for a little while? I should then have given
(largely) in charity and I should have been one of the
doers of good." (Al-Munafiqun 63:9–11, Koran)

The Betrayal of the Covenant of Allah: Unfair Distribution of Wealth

Poverty is a state of existence in which man is deprived of adequate means of subsistence. It creates a state of hopelessness. Although riches and Allah's grace are in abundance, poverty occurs in situations when man is unable to avail the bounty, grace, and guiding hand that Allah offers to His creatures. This state of hopelessness occurs through man's abandonment of Allah's promise and lack of faith in the Creator and the Sustainer. Hope comes when man connects with Allah and lets His guiding light into his heart, and Allah's guiding hand leads man onto His path.

The blessed prophet once said that the span of life is akin to walking under the shade of a tree. Allah reveals to man the pitfalls in the path under shade of the tree of life that humans tread during their life span. With faith in Allah, hopelessness vanishes, and new doorways and pathways open. With the knowledge of Allah, light of hope overcomes the darkness of hopelessness. Greed and ego vanish, and peace overtakes depression. Without faith in Allah, greed gnaws at man, and the itch to acquire eats away into man's flesh. The more man has, the more he wants, and the worse is the world because of his presence.

At the beginning of the twenty-first century, the Muslim world is mired in poverty, hunger, disease, and hopelessness. In the course of the last five hundred years, events of history transformed the existing systems of agriculture, manufacturing, and trade, and this transformation was so rapid that the believers failed to adapt to their new conditions. Yet guidance is in the Koran.

When man began to walk the earth under the shade of the tree of life, Allah's bounty and grace was everywhere, there was abundance, and there was peace. Then some men, of their own accord, concluded that the balance of nature established by Allah was not to their liking, and they assumed the divine prerogative to alter the balance of nature in their world. Since then, the world has been taken over by those who believe that the privilege is their due and that they can assume this right over others. This cabal of privilege, wealth, and acquisition has perfected the art of survival to the point that, after every turmoil and tempest, they end up at the top like a buoy in water. After every trough and crest of the wave, the same people end up with the flag up at the top.

The vast majority of the populations—the simple, hardworking, honest, and devout people—always end up at the bottom. This group is ill prepared, humble, poor, and always suffering. Allah sent thousands of prophets to teach this group the art of goodness and peace. The vast majority are believers of Allah. They are good and devout though weak and poor people who live in communities with vast untapped treasures and reserves of riches. Over hundreds of years, cults from among them have formed international organisms that cooperate with one another to exploit the wealth and the resources of the world. Like chameleons, they merge into their populations and exploit them. Their loyalty is neither to Allah nor to their own people. Their God is their avarice and wealth.

Allah endows every man at birth with a soul and a body. Allah created heaven and earth to endow His creation with sustenance to nurture the body and soul of His creation. He provides for every living being for its life span. Every man arrives in the world without a baggage to walk under the shade of the tree of life and then departs similarly without any possessions. Man's body nourishes and flourishes with the fruits from the tree of life and his soul from those of the tree of knowledge through Allah's grace and bounty. The tree of life yields sufficient provisions for the needs of every living creature; Allah the Creator is also Allah the Provider.

The tree of knowledge endows every living creature with thoughts and ideas of goodness, truth, justice, mercy, compassion for other beings, love, unity, and many other things. However, a small number of humans defy Allah's commandments. Organized groups of such men prevent Allah's grace from reaching down to the common people. As a group, they subtly distort Allah's message to humans and encourage human behavior that makes wealth for themselves, though such actions displease Allah. Men have disrupted the flow of Allah's mercy and beneficence to His creation ever since humans began to walk under the shade of the tree of life.

There are four *curses* that that have plagued Allah's creation walking in the shade of the tree of life. At every stage of human existence, these four curses have subjected the human ego into temptations carefully laid out by the Satan in their path. Over and again, the prophets laid out Allah's commandments to humans for a clean, happy, and contented life. Yet for humans, Satan's lure prove to be too strong. The curses are

1. the cult of money and acquisition,
2. the priesthood,
3. the mercenary and state armies,
4. the rulers.

Allah has endowed the land of Islam with all the ingredients of wealth and prosperity. There should never be poverty, disease, or hunger in the Dar es Salaam.

Islam is founded on tawhid. Adherence to the covenant of Allah reforms the individual. Through *iman* (belief), salat, fasting, and *taqwa* of Allah, man becomes cognizant of *furqan*, the criterion that allows man to distinguish between good and evil and guides him to the straight path of Allah. In doing so, man performs good and wholesome deeds that please Allah. Acts of goodness and charity benefit their parents, their kin, their neighbors, the needy, the sick, and the rest of mankind. Such acts purify the believer. Remembrance of Allah, beseeching His forgiveness, praising His magnificence, and showing gratitude for His grace and mercy are the obligations of every man. Forgiving others for their trespasses cleans anger, grudges, and rancor. Humility wipes out the ego. All actions with the knowledge that Allah is with you and sees you whether you see Him not helps the believer walk the earth in the glow of Allah's love and mercy.

Walking in the straight path of Allah, the believer avoids the temptations and evil that Satan has placed in his path. The believer of Allah surrenders to His will. Such a surrender entails acceptance of the covenant of Allah, which requires a lifetime of service to Allah and His creation.

Islam is a religion of faith, unity, love, truth, peace, justice, equality, and moderation. It emphasizes that humans should love Allah and His people. The believer's love of Allah brings him close to Allah, and acts of goodness toward people generate *humaneness*, love, and kindness toward other humans. *Love and kindness is not any one virtue but is the source of all virtues.* The believer's character literally represents the relationship between people and peoples. It is *co-humanity*, the ability to live together in love, kindness, and humanity. Politeness, courtesy, love, respect, and etiquette of collegiality in salat prayers keep the rituals from becoming hollow and meaningless. This belief, action, and ritual promote the ethical content of the believer that nurtures his inner character and furthers the person's ethical maturation.

Thus, the *outer side* of the believer is conformity and the acceptance of social roles within his community, the *ummah*; the *inner side* is the cultivation of *nafs*, conscience, and character. This cultivation involves broader education and deep reflection of one's motives and actions. It is a lifetime commitment to build, carve, and polish the stone of one's character until it becomes a lustrous gem. It is the lack of will, paucity of conscience, and insincerity of character that leave a person unprepared to accept his fellow human and believer as his brother and sister. When people lack commitment to the fellowship of Allah, it leaves them in the predicament of want, poverty, and hunger. It is the lack of understanding of the concept of unity, equality, and fraternity within the fellowship of believers that has wrecked and weakened the *ummah* to the present day. The Koran is very clear on the subject.

The *ummah* is a community of believers that,

- is united as one people and one nation whose hearts Allah joined in love so that they are brethren to one another,
- enjoins good and forbids evil,
- is committed to truth and administers justice based on truth,
- acts justly to one another and others,
- observes due balance and moderation in all its actions and avoids extremism where men and women are straight and honest in all their dealings.

> I am your Lord and Cherisher: therefore, serve Me and none other. Verily fellowship of yours is a united brotherhood, and hold fast, all together by the Rope, which Allah stretches out for you, and be not divided amongst yourselves. Let there arise out of you a band of people inviting to all that is good, enjoining what is right, and forbidding all that is wrong. You are the best of the peoples evolved from humankind, enjoining what is right, forbidding what is wrong, and believing in Allah. Thus, We have made you an Ummah of the center, that you might be witness over other nations, and the Messenger a witness over yourselves.

Allah affirms to the believers that He is indeed their Lord and Cherisher. He commands the believers to serve Him, to be united in one *ummah*, holding on to the rope of Allah, the covenant, the guidance from Allah. Those who submit to Allah and perform good works have grasped His handhold, the most trustworthy hand.

> The parable of those who spend their wealth in the way of Allah is that of a grain of corn, which grows seven ears, and each ear has a hundred grains. Allah gives plentiful in return to whom He pleases. Those who give generously in the cause of Allah, and do not follow up their gifts with reminders of their generosity are assured of their reward with their Lord. The likeness of those who give generously, seeking to please Allah is as a garden, high and fertile where heavy rain falls on it and makes it yield a double the amount of harvest, and if it receives not heavy rain, light moisture suffices it.

The blessed *Nabi* spoke to the ten thousand believers gathered on Mount Arafat on the ninth day of *Zul-hajj*, 10 hijra:

> All Muslims, (men and women) free or slaves have the same rights and the same responsibilities. None is higher than the other unless he is higher in virtue. All distinctions between the Arabs the non-Arabs, the black, and the white are abolished. All Muslims are brethren. Do Good. Be faithful to your Covenant. Be kind to the orphans. Remember Allah Know that while man being mortal is bound to die, Allah being immortal will live forever.

Summary: All believers unite to form one community, the fellowship of Allah in which every person, man or woman, is independent yet interdependent on one another as all believers grasp on to the same handhold—the rope that Allah has stretched out for them. In this filial tie of independence, interdependence, and bonding, each believer becomes responsible for the welfare of others. In this relationship, every man is a brother and every woman a sister. This relationship of love and bonding creates equality, respect, kindness, and goodness in the family of believers. There is no jealousy or envy among people. Everyone has the same rights and the same responsibilities. None is higher than the other unless he is higher in virtue. No distinctions between race, tribe, caste, and color exist. All Muslims are brethren. Women have rights over men, and men have similar rights over women.

In this fellowship, there should be no oppression. Allah has guaranteed every individual's rights. Every man, woman, and child has a right to freedom and right to practice their faith in accordance with their beliefs as, in Islam, there is no compulsion in matters of religion. Every person has a right to life, which includes mental, physical, and emotional well-being; right to safeguard one's property; right to intellectual endeavors and acquisition of knowledge and education; right to make a living; and right to free speech and action to enjoin good and forbid evil. In enjoying his freedoms, the individual ensures that his activities do not impinge on the similar rights of others. No one individual or group has the right to oppress a believing man or woman nor to usurp their rights endowed by Allah.

Allah created the earth and then bestowed on man His favors to extract sustenance from it. He also created the sun, moon, and stars to create a just equilibrium and harmony in the universe. The sun provides energy for the growth, sustenance, and well-being of humans, plants, and animals. Gradually, man began to extract more than his personal needs from the earth; and the boom of economics, trade, and commerce started, creating cycles of imbalance, disharmony, wars, poverty, and injustice throughout the globe. Not only did this disharmony caused by greed blemish humans but animal life also suffered by the disappearance of whole species. Pollution and contamination of the environment resulted from the race trying to accumulate and hoard the world's wealth in a few hands. Man disobeyed Allah's universal laws and covenant.

Fi Sabilillah: In the Cause of Allah: The ingredients of wealth, prosperity, and human welfare lie in the labor and sweat of man, the natural resources of the land, and the marketing of the products of human sweat and such resources. Allah has provided all these ingredients to humans in every community in abundance. He has, in addition, given the believers the key and the rules for the use of such ingredients in His covenant. It is for the believers to use their labor and Allah's gifts and guidance to create prosperity for the welfare of their communities. While Allah has provided man with the fruit of heavens and earth, *sama* and *Ardh*, it is for man to utilize such gifts for the benefit of his community, the *ummah*. The key lies in the following words:

> Virtue is to spend of one's means out of love of Allah_ for the kin, for the orphans, for the needy, for the wayfarer, for those who ask, and for the ransom of those in bondage. The parable of those who spend their substance in the way of Allah is that of a grain of corn: it grows seven ears, and each ear has a hundred grains.
>
> Allah gives plentiful in return to whom He pleases, Allah cares for all His beings, and He knows all that goes on everywhere. Those who give generously in the cause of Allah,_and do not follow up their gifts with reminders of their generosity or with injury, are assured of their reward with their Lord and on them shall be no fear, nor shall they grieve.
>
> Kind words and the covering of faults are better than charity followed by insult. Allah reminds the Believers, "Void not your charity by boast, conceit, and insult, by reminders of your generosity like those

who want their generosity to be noted by all men but they believe neither in Allah nor in the Last Day.

Theirs is a parable of a hard- barren rock, on which there is a little soil, washed by heavy rain, which leaves it just a bare stone. The likeness of those who give generously, seeking to please Allah and to strengthen their souls, is as a garden, high and fertile where heavy rain falls on it and makes it yield a double the amount of harvest, and if it receives not heavy rain, light moisture suffices it".

Allah calls upon the Believers: "Behold! You are those who are invited to spend of your means in the Way of Allah: but among you are some that are parsimonious. But any who are miserly are so at the expense of their own souls. But Allah is free of all wants, and it is you that are needy".

If you turn back from Allah's Path, Allah will substitute another people in your place who will be in Taqwa of Allah and do Allah's bidding.

And O you Believers! (Men and Women) Turn you all together Toward Allah that you may prosper. The believers, men and women are protectors one of another; they enjoin what is just and forbid what is evil. They observe regular prayers, practice regular charity, and obey Allah and His Messenger. On them will Allah pour His mercy, for Allah is exalted in power, Wise.

Giving and receiving of means, substance, and wealth in the cause of Allah involves two parties among the believers. Those who give and those who receive are both, in effect, endowed with unutilized and unrecognized wealth. Lack of utilization of such wealth is indeed the cause of poverty, want, hunger, and disease in the world. Communists and capitalists have failed to eradicate poverty because both systems lack understanding of God's laws and the ethical and moral use of wealth. Although the "Muslims" in the last 1,400 years achieved spiritual maturity, they failed to recognize the decay of their *nafs* and their obligation to their communities.

The believer's faith in Allah and his commitment to His covenant attains spiritual maturity, which in turn promotes the ethical content in the believer. This ethical content nurtures the believer's inner character and enhances the person's moral maturity. This indeed was the aim of the teachings of all of Allah's prophets throughout the centuries the world over. Only with the achievement of this ethical and moral content in their character will the believers unite to form a community in which every person, man or woman, is independent yet dependent on one another as each one hangs on to the rope that Allah has cast for them.

Fulfillment of the Covenant. Among the 1.5 billion believers around the world, there are about 900 million individuals capable of working. Out of these men and women, about 40 percent are underproductive or unemployed owing to lack of opportunity and social constraints. These men and women have *means and wealth* of 7,920,000 unspent workdays or 1,393,920,000 human hours of work each month that have undergone non- fruition.

In a smaller community of 50,000 men and women, the comparable figures will be 264,000 days' worth of unutilized means and wealth and 2,112,000 human hours of work wasted to the community. In the whole of the Islamic world, the Muslim communities lose over ten billion dollars every month in productivity. A smaller community of 50,000 thus missed over twenty million dollars per month. In fact, the loss to this small community is far, far greater. For instance, if one human hour produces three electric lamps:

> three items (electric lamps) cost $30,
>
> the manufacturer makes a profit of $5 on each lamp ($45),
>
> the intermediary/distributor charges $3,
>
> the retailer makes a profit of $7 on each item ($21),
>
> the transport cost incurred is $2,
>
> 5 percent manufacturer's tax is $3.55, and
>
> sales tax of 10 percent is $7.45.
>
> Total: $82

The total fallout from the manufacture and labor of one human hour benefits the community with $82 plus employment to workers in a factory, wholesale and retail, power, and transport businesses, as well as real estate. When all under- and unemployed workforce of a community of 50,000 donates its available work hours for the benefit of their community in one year, the result is an astounding sum of *over two billion dollars*. Yet this is not the whole picture. The interaction of various trades, professions, and guilds will compound these figures over many folds.

Applying the same incomplete figures of $82 per hour to the lost 1,393,920,000 human hours of work per month, the entire Muslim *ummah* loses the sum total of productivity and wealth amounting to $1,371,616,280,000 every year. In addition, the *ummah* continues to suffer deprivation, poverty, oppression, and humiliation year after year.

Principle No. 1: When a member of a closed fraternal community gains wealth, the fallout of such a gain is to the whole community. Similarly, the loss to one of its members is a loss to the whole community.

Principle No. 2: When community members help one of the members gain wealth, the fallout of this gain helps the whole community.

Principle No. 3: When the whole community helps one another without regard to individual gain, everyone gains materially to a greater and a lesser degree. The gain is material and spiritual and in harmony with Allah's laws of nature.

When the believers in commitment to their *iman* in Allah and to their covenant with Him attain spiritual maturity, their faith, actions, and rituals promote the ethical content in the believer that nurtures inner character and furthers the person's moral maturation. The *ummah* is made up of hundreds of thousands mini-*ummahs* and communities. In a community of 50,000, when the 12,000 unemployed individuals donate their *wealth and means* in the cause of Allah (*fi sabilillah*) in labor and expertise worth 264,000 days or 2,112,000 hours to the community, there will be a tremendous gain to the community. This time is donated to all spheres of life in the community where help is required.

a) A community always requires help in the development of the spiritual, mental, and intellectual bank of the community. The *ummah* had lagged behind in education, knowledge, and technology because those who are empowered to spread education and knowledge to their own children and to their community are selfish and ignorant of their obligations to Islam and Allah's covenant. Everyone who knows must pass on his knowledge and wisdom to those who desire that knowledge. Everyone who has a craft must train others.

Everyone endowed with technology must teach others. The community must set up classes, schools, workshops, and laboratories for every individual to learn and acquire skills. Every man and woman must know their Koran, their three Rs, and computer skills and achieve some aspect of technical skill in manufacturing and building.

b) Unlike the economic systems espoused by capitalism and communism, the Koran proposes a gift economy in the cause of Allah (*fi sabilillah*). People must volunteer their time without expectation of any gain to build the infrastructure of their community. They should construct roads. Every community must have clean and safe running water and sewage systems. The Koran and Islam calls for remembrance of Allah in love, humility, dignity, and decorum. Islam demands cleanliness and orderliness. There are no beggars in Islam. Everyone in need is cared for before he is forced into the street. Submission to Allah obliges the believers to obey the covenant and carry out their duty to their Creator, to their fellow man, and to Allah's creation. Only those who "have faith and do righteous acts" will have success in their earthly lives and in the hereafter. The phrase *amilu al saalihaat* (to perform beautiful acts, to perform wholesome deeds) refers to those who persist in striving to set things right, who restore harmony, peace, and balance. Other acts of good works recognized in the Koran are to show compassion, to be merciful and forgive others, to be just, to protect the weak, to defend the oppressed, to be generous and charitable, to be truthful, to seek knowledge and wisdom, to be kind to others, to be peaceful, to love others, to perform acts of cleanliness, and to perform beautiful deeds.

c)

إِنَّ ٱلَّذِينَ ءَامَنُوا۟ وَعَمِلُوا۟ ٱلصَّٰلِحَٰتِ سَيَجْعَلُ لَهُمُ ٱلرَّحْمَٰنُ وُدًّا ﴿٩٦﴾

On those who believe and do good, will
[Allah] Most Gracious bestow love.

There are fifty verses in the Koran that remind the believers of the rewards of beautiful and righteous deeds. Thus, beautifying and cleaning one's neighborhood, planting trees and gardens, building houses for the homeless, building schools and community workshops, building roads, digging wells, and laying water pipelines are acts of goodness in the cause of Allah.

فِي سَبِيلِ ٱللَّهِ.

d) Acts of goodwill and charity will produce prosperity among the *ummah* only when every person with time on his hand will go to every field, every shop, every home, and every factory to help increase the productivity of that business in the community. Then every barren field will be cultivated, every field with a crop hoed, fertilized, and seeded. Every bare patch of land will be planted with saplings and watered. The orchards will be pruned, fertilized, grafted, and watered. Olive trees, fruit trees, new orchards, and forests will be planted. Irrigation dams, ditches, and canals will be dug. Wells will be dug. Factories will be replenished, repaired, and brought into full production. Cattle, sheep, goats, and poultry will be corralled and managed for the benefit of all. Fish farms will be built to increase food production. Factories will be built to produce consumer goods, machinery, computers, and raw material for the industry. Every derelict home and public building will be repaired or rebuilt. Because of this cooperation and giving of ones *"means and wealth in the cause of Allah,"* the production of land and factories will double and triple within three years. There will be no need to import food and grains into the Dar es Salaam.

e) Those with *means* and those with jobs, professions, businesses, lands, and factories will, in return for the efforts of those who shed their sweat, will donate funds, promissory notes, food, money, clothing, and shelter in the cause of Allah. This is the least any man would and could do.

f) More importantly, they will provide funds, labor, and other means to provide their community with building materials, heavy-duty equipment, and fuel and material for the construction of homes, offices, other buildings, factories, schools, workshops, and clinics. The community, through its means in the cause of Allah, will manufacture its own building material—bricks, stone, cement, wood products, and tools. Initially, this material will be basic; but within five years with experience and import of technology, the optimum standard of manufactured goods will be achieved. Everyone will work to achieve perfection. The material and expertise thus acquired will become the basis of a model Islamic cooperative community, self-sufficient in all essentials. In cooperation, the community will build housing for every family.

g) Every community will set up cooperative industrial, agricultural, and manufacturing plants; technical training institutes; workshops; and laboratories to train every resident in a useful skill. All workers and entrepreneurs will jointly own the community cooperatives.

h) Each community will cooperate with the neighboring communities to share expertise and skills in training, manufacture, and trade.
i) Every community will develop a *social contract* based on the covenant of Allah. It is a contract among
    1. those who provide free labor and services in the cause of Allah,
    2. those who provide the facilities and funds in the cause of Allah, and
    3. the ones who benefit from the labors of the project and give in the cause of Allah.

    This contract will define metered goals, through which by the end of three to five years every member will have a job, education, health care, and a plot to build a home in. All citizens will share in the benefits of this endeavor.
j) The purpose behind the enterprise of sharing work, skills, and enterprise is multifold.

Allah helps those who help themselves. In the present age, 70 percent of the world's wealth is held by fewer than 5 percent of the people. Almost every government of the world is run by people from this group of 5 percent. With the empowerment of the common believer, every man will share the world and, under Allah's covenant, will not suffer from want. The aim, therefore, is

1. to organize united and devout communities that will use their mutual labor, skills, and enterprise to help themselves, the *ummah*, and the rest of humanity for peace, harmony, and prosperity.
2. to enable every man and woman achieve their full potential in their spiritual and material life through education and acquisition of skills.

With the acquisition of common skills required in manufacturing, the communities of the *ummah* will achieve specialization in different fields. All the communities from Indonesia to Mauritania will begin to manufacture products required in the Dar es Salaam. Instead of spending hundreds of millions of dollars to set up mega-factories to manufacture agricultural machinery, communities will set up affordable small units and share the design and fabrication of parts of the equipment. One town may manufacture the chassis of a tractor, the next the transmission, while others share in building the engine, wheels, tires, tanks, hydraulics, and front-end loaders. All such parts will then be shipped and assembled in plants in parts of the Dar es Salaam in Asia, Africa, and Europe where needed. Every community will share in sweat and its fruit.

Automobiles, trucks, aircraft, heavy machinery, and ships will be fabricated in small units. Communities will specialize and subspecialize in different fields of manufacture and share in the manufacture of all machinery. Many communities will share work and its reward. All this will require several central planning, design, and coordination centers staffed by the best skilled people.

To begin with, small factories in the Dar es Salaam will begin to manufacture spare parts for automobiles and trucks used in the land. Some plants will specialize in the fabrication of engines while others build chassis, brakes, carburetors, tires, and so on. After standardization of their manufacturing, they will be able to assemble their own cars and trucks. They will be able to build cheap, durable, and sturdy modular cars and trucks that will withstand rough terrain and hot, dusty climates. Because of their modular design, low price, sturdiness, and cheap spare parts, they will find ready markets in the Dar es Salaam, India, China, South America, and Africa. All such manufactures will find willing buyers among the six billion poor people of the world. Similar cooperation among small communities of the Dar es Salaam in Africa, Middle East, and Central and South Asia will develop local chemical, pharmaceutical, agricultural, industrial, nautical, aeronautical, fisheries, communication, and computer-based industries.

The Dar es Salaam is blessed with Allah's promise of His grace. Muslims have failed to recognize His blessings while the greedy Arab sheikhs and the Western countries are devouring their people's wealth. How could a people with such wealth all around them suffer from such poverty and deprivation? Allah has showered the Dar es Salaam with *means* and wealth:

Commodity	World Percentage	Quantity
Crude oil	45%	10,260,950,000 42-gallon barrels
Petroleum refined products		3,021,250,000 barrels
Natural gas		7,827,540,000,000 cubic meters
Natural gas (dry)	22%	305,951,000,000 cubic meters
Natural gas (liquid)	84%	1,792,339,000 barrels
Nitrogen content ammonia	17%	18,488,100 metric tons
Salt	19%	10,794,287metric tons
Uranium	25%	8,971 metric tons
Potash	6%	1,517,000 metric tons
Bauxite	30%	37,568,923 metric tons
Aluminum metal	74%	16,289,024 metric tons
Cement	12.8%	196,079,300 metric tons
Chromite	34%	4,242,388 metric tons
Anthracite	66%	194,128,325 metric tons
Copper content	13%	1,382,695 metric tons
Refined copper	7%	876,232 metric tons
Gold	20%	2,520,653 kilograms

Diamonds		1,274,000 carats
Gems		156,880 kilograms
Iron ore	10%	52,367,192 metric tons
Steel	15%	112,384,000 metric tons
Lead refined	10%	280,559 metric tons
Manganese	10%	1,535,176 metric tons
Mercury	60%	1,087,060 metric tons
Refined nickel	44%	459,921 metric tons
Tin mine content	33%	64,482 metric tons
Tin refined	39%	94491 metric tons.
Titanium and rutile	11%	663,642 metric tons
Phosphates	29%	39,761,600 metric tons
Granite		54,065,817 cubic meters
Pozzolana		250,000 metric tons
Asbestos		148,500 metric tons
Antimony		21,892 metric tons
Zirconium		10,311 metric tons
Bentonite		208,161 metric tons
Strontium		106,500 metric tons
Vanadium		350,000 metric tons
Marble		1,704,000 cubic meters

The Dar es Salaam produces commodities that are in great demand in the rest of the world; therefore, production and marketing and the prices of the commodities should be regulated by the market forces of supply and demand rather than by political factors where dynasties seek protection by paying with blood money. In spite of depleted petroleum exports from Iraq, the Dar es Salaam exports

- 10,260,950,000 42-gallon barrels of crude oil;
- 3,021,250,000 barrels of refined petroleum products as aviation fuel, automobile petrol, lubrication products, and heating oils;

- 7,827,540,000,000 cubic meters of natural gas;
- 305,951,000,000 cubic meters of dry products of natural gas;
- 1,792,339,000 42-gallon barrels of natural liquid gas such as propane, in addition to plastics and other by-products of the oil industry.

The producing countries are paid at the producing oil wells at prices manipulated by major oil companies. These oil companies also control the economies of the Western world, and the same companies are responsible for all turmoil and conflicts around the Middle East. Such conflicts include the ongoing Iraq wars. The reason for the conflicts is to keep the flow of cheap Middle Eastern oil by keeping the Gulf oil sheikhs and the Saudis on edge constantly, worrying about their thrones, while stealing their money. The Western economy depends on cheap Arab oil that the quarrelsome, ignorant, and greedy Arab sheikhs willingly subsidize.

For over two decades, the price of oil has been artificially priced between $18 and $30. For instance, at $30 to $50 a barrel, the oil companies buy 10,260,950,000 barrels of crude oil at $461,742,750,000 from the Middle East. They ship it in their own tankers, insure it with their own companies, and refine it in their own refineries. The refined by-products of crude oil, petrol, diesel, jet fuel heating oil, propane, asphalt, and chemical products are sold to the motorists, airlines, transport companies, and textile, plastic, sports goods, nylon, pharmaceutical, highway, pesticide, fertilizer, and tire industries in Europe and North America and the Far East for $3.2 trillion, with $1.2 trillion going to the Western governments of G8 in taxes and over $2.0 trillion to the oil companies before paying for the shipping and refining costs to their own companies. That is a profit of over $2.1 trillion, unimaginable in any other industry. No wonder the president of the United States is a functionary of the oil companies, with the CIA as their security force and the American marines their storm troopers.

Overall, if the Dar es Salaam refined and processed its own petroleum products and developed its own chemical and by-products industry, the total gain to its population will be full employment, with every one owning a home in a land with fully developed infrastructure on transport, health care, education, human development, and resource sectors. The petroleum and energy sector alone will provide the Dar es Salaam with over $150 trillion worth of economic benefits in jobs, industrial growth, shipping, insurance, and banking, whereas today only the oil-producing sheikhs receive less than two to three hundred billion dollars. With the world's current economic situation, the realistic value of a barrel of unrefined crude oil is $150. The revenue to the Dar es Salaam for selling only the unrefined crude oil should be over $150 trillion. The world's economic structure is based on Islamic oil exports with systematic transfer of wealth to a handful of industrialized countries.

The Dar es Salaam will need to start the drawing board with the mineral, commodity, and oil industries. The oil companies will need to understand the new realities of doing business with the Dar es Salaam.

1. The Dar es Salaam will refine all its oil for the world.
2. It will also ship oil products in its own ships to the importing ports.
3. It will set up a chemical industry providing raw products to the transport, textile, plastic, sports goods, nylon, pharmaceutical, highway, pesticide, fertilizer, and tire manufacturing industries in the Dar es Salaam and around the world at cheap and competitive rates.
4. The Dar es Salaam oil industry will finance and own 50 to 75 percent share of all distribution to the retail pumps in the consuming countries around the globe. With this understanding, the foreign oil companies will be permitted up to 25 percent share in the refining industry in their own countries and in the Dar es Salaam.

5. As part of the petroleum sales agreement, the consuming countries will be obliged to buy petroleum by-products such as plastics, chemicals, and fertilizers manufactured by industries in the Dar es Salaam.
6. All payments will be in gold and gold coins and the Islamic dinar. No fiat money will be traded in the Dar es Salaam. Goods, however, may be traded with barter and balance of payments adjusted with gold between the countries quarterly. The gold and oil prices will naturally rise to the natural market value as the artificial stimulation of economies through artificial factors of stock market, increased interest rates, and increase of paper notes will disappear from the Dar es Salaam. The price of gold will hit its normal intrinsic value of $2,500–$3,500 per troy ounce.

If one is to estimate the amount of gold hoarded and accumulated in state and private collections in the Islamic world, we will find that during the last few hundred years an average Muslim couple has inherited or purchased about 120 grams of gold in the form of jewelry. Very poor couples do not own any. Rich couples are weighed down by tens of kilograms of gold jewelry, averaging more than 120 grams or about 10 tolas per couple around the Muslim world. This hoard of gold in the Dar es Salaam is estimated to be 52,800 tons of accumulated wealth lying idly, while millions of Muslims starve and go without essentials. At today's prices, this wealth totals more than half a trillion dollars.

In addition, there is a hoard of precious stones worth another one hundred billion dollars. Women own most of the bullion and precious stones. Most of them live in communities where, for hundreds of generations, women and men have lost their independent financial cognitive skills in matters outside the norm of their community.

Women have it in their power to attain equality, respect, and financial independence by attaining skills and knowledge by investing their dormant wealth of gold and precious stones in the agriculture and industrial development of their communities. They will thus control their own and their family's destiny and achieve primacy in their community. The useless symbols of ostentation, pride, and ego will benefit each community of fifty thousand individuals with an investment of about $25 million in agricultural, industrial, and infrastructure projects with a return of 10 percent of $ 2.5 million every year.

The governments of marauding monarchs—whether Muslim, non-Muslim, European, African, Turk, Safavid, or Moguls—were there to rule for their own benefit. Their interest in matters of the *din* or in the welfare of the common man was always subordinate to their accumulation of power and riches. The same is true of this day's governments. No part of the *ummah* can depend on the governments from outside their own community to relieve them of poverty, hardship, or sickness. It must come from within the people. Communities must build their own infrastructure, build their own institutions, and keep peace. *The only institution for such development is the government of the community by the community.* Wise men and women from the community will be just, fair, truthful, and obedient to their covenant. They will run the community's affairs justly. When the communities select evil, dishonest, unjust, and unbelieving people to run their affairs, the communities will have similar unmerited and undeserved consequences. Citizens, believing men and women, must learn their Koran, know their rights, help one another, unite their community, and keep the usurpers and oppressors out of their community.

Islam has teachers, wise men, and holy men, but none of them can claim to be the spokespersons of Allah. There is no priesthood in

Islam. No one has been ordained to speak on behalf of Allah except the prophets. No man, since the days of the prophets, has been ordained to formulate dogma nor creed. Total Koran is the total *din* of Islam. Every believer, man and woman, has inherited the legacy of the blessed prophet, the Koran. Anyone who does not understand a part of the Koran is free to seek the knowledge from the one who knows. One who has the knowledge can only provide his own interpretation. He cannot assume Allah's authority or His prerogative. The recipe for righteousness, peace, and prosperity is in the Koran. People will ignore it at their own peril.

Summary: The knowledge is in the Koran. Salvation and prosperity lies in the practice gained from such knowledge.

24. The Covenant of Allah: Truth and Justice

> Stand firmly for Allah as a witness of fair dealing. Let not the malice of people lead you to iniquity. Be just, that is next to worship. Be with taqwa of Allah, fear Allah. O you who believe! Fear Allah and speak always the truth that He may direct you to righteous deeds and forgive you your sins: he that obeys Allah and His Rasool have already attained the highest achievement. (Al-Ahzab 33:69–73, Koran)

> Stand firm for justice as witness to Allah be it against yourself, your parents, or your family, whether it is against rich or poor, both are nearer to Allah than they are to you. Follow not your caprice lest you distort your testimony. If you prevaricate and evade justice Allah is well aware what you do. (An-Nisa 4:135, Koran)

O you who believe! Stand firmly for Allah as a witness of fair dealing. Let not the malice of people lead you to iniquity. Be just, that is next to worship. Be with taqwa of Allah, fear Allah. Allah is well aware with what you do. (Al-Ma'idah 5:8, Koran)

Betray not the trust of Allah and His Messenger. Nor knowingly misappropriate things entrusted to you. (Al-Anfal 8:27, Koran)

If you have taqwa of Allah and fear Allah, He will grant you a Criterion to judge between right and wrong and remove from you all misfortunes and evil and forgive your sins. Allah is the bestower of grace in abundance. (Al-Anfal 8:29, Koran)

Be in taqwa of Allah, fear Allah and be with those who are true in word and deed. (At-Tawbah 9:119, Koran)

Deal not unjustly and ye shall not be dealt with unjustly. (Al-Baqarah 2:277–80, Koran)

Whenever you give your word speak honestly even if a near relative is concerned. (Al-An'am 6:151–52, Koran)

And come not near the orphan's property, except to improve it, until he attains the age of full strength. Qur'an 6:151-152 Al An 'am

And give full measure and full weight with justice. No burden We place on any soul but that which it can bear. (Al-An'am 6:151–52, Koran)

> If an impostor (fasiq) comes to you with any news, ascertain the truth, lest you harm people unsuspectingly and afterwards become full of remorse for what you have done. And know that amongst you is Allah's Messenger: were he in many matters to follow your desires, you would certainly fall into misfortune: but Allah has bestowed on you the love of iman (faith) and has made it beautiful in your hearts and he has made abhorrent to you disbelief, wickedness and disobedience to Allah: such indeed are those who are righteous (Rashidun). (Al-Hujurat 49:6–10, Koran)

Justice (*'adl*) is a divine attribute defined as "putting all things in the right place." The opposite of *'adl* is *zulm,* which in Koranic terms means "wrongdoing." *Wrongdoing* is a human attribute defined as "putting things in the wrong place." *Zulm* is one of the common terms used in the Koran to refer to the negative acts employed by human beings.

Wrongdoing is the opposite of justice, and justice is to put everything in its right place and every act of the humans to be performed as prescribed by Allah. Hence, wrongdoing is to put things where they do not belong. *Zulm* (injustice) is to, for example, associate others with Allah. Others do not belong in the place for the divine; it is to place false words in place of the truth and to put someone else's property in place of your own. Other examples are taking a life against the divine commandments, replacing people's liberty with oppression, waging war instead of peace, and usurping people's right to govern themselves.

The Koran repeatedly stigmatizes humans of wrongdoing. When it points out who is harmed by injustice, wrongdoing, or *zulm*, the Koran always mentions the word *nafs* or self. People cannot harm Allah. By being unjust or doing wrong or by putting things in the wrong place, people harm themselves. They distort their own natures, and they lead themselves astray. Whom can one wrong? It is impossible to wrong or do injustice against Allah since all things are His creatures and do His work. Hence, wrongdoing and injustice is an activity against people and Allah's creation.

Allah has prescribed His covenant to humans for the good of human beings. People, tribes, and nations are being helped since Allah leads them into accord, harmony, and justice, which in turn create peace in the world. Allah has laid out all the basic principles for justice in His covenant for humans to live in harmony. Those who refuse to follow His commandments are therefore ungrateful and hence *kafirs*. Thus, they are wrongdoers (*zalimun*) and only harm themselves. Of the 250 verses where the Koran mentions *zulm* or *zalimun*, it mentions the object of wrongdoing in only 25 verses. In one verse, the object of wrongdoing are people:

﴿ إِنَّمَا ٱلسَّبِيلُ عَلَى ٱلَّذِينَ يَظْلِمُونَ ٱلنَّاسَ وَيَبْغُونَ فِى ٱلْأَرْضِ بِغَيْرِ ٱلْحَقِّ ۚ أُو۟لَٰٓئِكَ لَهُمْ عَذَابٌ أَلِيمٌ ﴿٤٢﴾ ﴾

The blame is only against those who oppress
men with wrongdoing and insolently transgress
beyond bounds through the land defying right
and justice: for such there will be a Penalty
grievous (Ash-Shura 42:42, Koran)

In a second verse, the object of wrong and injustice is the signs of Allah:

﴿ وَٱلْوَزْنُ يَوْمَئِذٍ ٱلْحَقُّ ۚ فَمَن ثَقُلَتْ مَوَٰزِينُهُۥ فَأُو۟لَٰٓئِكَ هُمُ ٱلْمُفْلِحُونَ ﴿٨﴾ وَمَنْ خَفَّتْ مَوَٰزِينُهُۥ فَأُو۟لَٰٓئِكَ ٱلَّذِينَ خَسِرُوٓا۟ أَنفُسَهُم بِمَا

كَانُوا۟ بِـَٔايَٰتِنَا يَظْلِمُونَ ﴿٩﴾ ﴾

The weighing that day will be true. He whose
scales are heavy, are the prosperous. Those whose

scale are light; they have lost themselves for
wronging Our Signs. (Al-A'raf 7:8–9, Koran)

Allah reveals His signs in nature and in scriptures so that the people may be guided. By disobeying these signs, they wrong only themselves.

In the remaining 23 verses in which the object of wrongdoing is mentioned, the wrongdoers are said to wrong only themselves.

﴿وَظَلَّلْنَا عَلَيْكُمُ ٱلْغَمَامَ وَأَنزَلْنَا عَلَيْكُمُ ٱلْمَنَّ وَٱلسَّلْوَىٰ ۖ كُلُوا۟ مِن طَيِّبَـٰتِ مَا رَزَقْنَـٰكُمْ ۖ وَمَا ظَلَمُونَا وَلَـٰكِن كَانُوٓا۟ أَنفُسَهُمْ يَظْلِمُونَ

﴿٥٧﴾﴾

And We gave you the shade of clouds and sent down
to you Manna and quails, saying: "Eat of the good
things We have provided for you:" (but they rebelled);
to Us they did no harm, but they wronged their own
souls. (Al-Baqarah 2:57, Al-A'raf 7:160, Koran)

﴿إِنَّ ٱللَّهَ لَا يَظْلِمُ ٱلنَّاسَ شَيْـًٔا وَلَـٰكِنَّ ٱلنَّاسَ أَنفُسَهُمْ يَظْلِمُونَ ﴿٤٤﴾﴾

Verily Allah will not deal unjustly with humans
in anything: it is the human who wrongs
his own soul. (Yunus 10:44, Koran)

﴿وَمَا ظَلَمْنَـٰهُمْ وَلَـٰكِن ظَلَمُوٓا۟ أَنفُسَهُمْ ۖ﴾

And We wronged them not, but they
wronged themselves. (Hud 11:101, Koran)

﴿ وَمَن يَعْمَلْ سُوٓءًا أَوْ يَظْلِمْ نَفْسَهُۥ ثُمَّ يَسْتَغْفِرِ ٱللَّهَ يَجِدِ ٱللَّهَ غَفُورًا رَّحِيمًا ﴿١١٠﴾ ﴾

If anyone does evil or wrongs his own soul but afterwards seeks Allah's forgiveness, he will find Allah Oft-Forgiving, Most Merciful. (An-Nisa 4:110, Koran)

The Koran admonishes:

Deal not deal unjustly and you shall not be dealt with unjustly. (Al-Baqarah 2:278, Koran)

25. The Covenant of Allah: Knowledge: O My Lord! Enrich Me in Knowledge

O you who believe! Allah will exalt in rank those of you who believe and who have been granted Knowledge. Proclaim! And thy Lord is Most Bountiful, He Who taught (the use of) the Pen, Taught man that which he knew not. O my Lord! Enrich me in knowledge.

When ye are told to make room in the assemblies, spread out and make room: ample room will Allah provide for you. And when ye are told to rise up, for prayers, Jihad or other good deeds rise up: Allah will exalt in rank those of you who believe and who have been granted Knowledge. And Allah is well acquainted with all you do. (Al-Mujadila 58:11, Koran).

﴿ ٱقْرَأْ بِٱسْمِ رَبِّكَ ٱلَّذِى خَلَقَ ﴿١﴾ خَلَقَ ٱلْإِنسَٰنَ مِنْ عَلَقٍ ﴿٢﴾ ٱقْرَأْ وَرَبُّكَ ٱلْأَكْرَمُ ﴿٣﴾ ٱلَّذِى عَلَّمَ بِٱلْقَلَمِ ﴿٤﴾ عَلَّمَ ٱلْإِنسَٰنَ مَا لَمْ يَعْلَمْ ﴿٥﴾

﴾ Proclaim! In the name of thy Lord and Cherisher, Who created, Created man, out of a (mere) clot of congealed blood: Proclaim! And thy Lord is Most Bountiful, He Who taught (the use of) the Pen, Taught man that which he knew not. (Iqra 96:1–5, Koran)

﴿ وَٱلَّذِى جَآءَ بِٱلصِّدْقِ وَصَدَّقَ بِهِۦٓ ۙ أُو۟لَـٰٓئِكَ هُمُ ٱلْمُتَّقُونَ ٣٣ ﴾

And he who brings the Truth and believes therein, such are the men who do right. (Az-Zumar 39:33, Koran)

﴿ فَتَعَـٰلَى ٱللَّهُ ٱلْمَلِكُ ٱلْحَقُّ ۗ وَلَا تَعْجَلْ بِٱلْقُرْءَانِ مِن قَبْلِ أَن يُقْضَىٰٓ إِلَيْكَ وَحْيُهُۥ ۖ وَقُل رَّبِّ زِدْنِى عِلْمًا

High above all is Allah, the King, and the Truth! Be not in haste with the Qur'an before its revelation to thee is completed, but say, "O my Lord! Enrich me in knowledge." (Taha 20:114, Koran)

﴿ أَمَّنْ هُوَ قَـٰنِتٌ ءَانَآءَ ٱلَّيْلِ سَاجِدًا وَقَآئِمًا يَحْذَرُ ٱلْـَٔاخِرَةَ وَيَرْجُوا۟ رَحْمَةَ رَبِّهِۦ ۗ قُلْ هَلْ يَسْتَوِى ٱلَّذِينَ يَعْلَمُونَ وَٱلَّذِينَ لَا يَعْلَمُونَ ۗ إِنَّمَا
يَتَذَكَّرُ أُو۟لُوا۟ ٱلْأَلْبَـٰبِ ٩ ﴾

Is one who worships devoutly during the hours of the night prostrating himself or standing (in adoration), who takes heed of the Hereafter and who places his hope in the Mercy of his Lord, (like one who does not)? Say: "Are those equal, those who know and those who do not know? It is those who are endued with understanding that receive admonition. (Az-Zumar 39:9, Koran)

Knowledge of God: Humans have always looked at God in two ways:

Emotionally. It is a personal and humanized god that is tribal. This god has favorite children whom he protects and rewards over and above others. He is readily accessible in a temple, shrine, mausoleum, or mosque and has priests in attendance as intermediaries. The priest class formulates dogma, creed, and rituals to appease the god. This god is unpredictable, loving, or demanding, subject to anger and joy in accord with the deeds and sacrifices of his devotees. He has a specially trained class of helpers who acts as cheerleaders and who performs crowd control for him. These helpers include the popes, bishops, priests, ayatollahs, rabbis, imams, ulema, pundits, and various classes of religious police. Proximity to their god provides this class's power over other men and women. This source of power naturally leads to competition and often wars between the devotees. Wars fought in the name of this god leads to injustice and usurpation of the rights of others.

The priest class, scholars, and writers introduced and interjected ideas that made their god dependent on creed and dogma invented by them. Writers of the Old and New Testaments fashioned Yahweh and Jesus according to their own caprice. Muslim scholars produced hadith and interpreted Sharia that made Allah and Muhammad subject to their own fancy and caprice. Such collective manipulations, at first, divided humans and then splintered communities into factions. Marriages of Henry VII fragmented the Christian Europe, and non-succession of Ali split the Muslim world. These mechanizations of men interrupted the message of the God of Abraham that Moses, Jesus, and Muhammad had come to teach. In the fundamental emotional nature of humans, there is an essence of paganism under the surface that wells over in times of stress, grief, and failing belief. The signs of disbelief, mistrust, and *shirk* lies in the faith in astrology, horoscope, saint worship, amulets, and worship of gods of wealth, power, and politics.

Intellectually, humans wholeheartedly accept the concept of God as the Creator of everything that is. He wills, and it is. He is beyond human comprehension, and His divine systems do not conform to human concepts, creed, and dogma. Allah, God the Creator, created the galaxies, worlds, stars, sun, moon, little atoms, protons, neutrons, and tiny particles that show the complexity of His genius. Allah, the Lord of creation, sends water from the heavens for the sustenance of life on the earth. Allah directs sunshine to the earth to provide warmth and light to sustain, human, plant, and animal life. Allah formed the sun, moon, and stars to create equilibrium in the universe, every object in its intended place, revolving in its fixed orbit in perfect harmony and balance. Allah created the secrets and the mysteries of the heavens and the earth, the so-called sciences, and the knowledge of particles, elements, cells, mitochondria, chromosomes, gravity, and black holes, only a minute portion of which he revealed to man. Allah clearly provided humans a mind to wonder at His infinitesimal wisdom. Yet man is conceited and arrogant to believe that God is driven by man-created creed, testament, dogma, Sunna, and Sharia.

Allah does not require a shrine, a temple, a tent, or a talisman to live in. His presence is everywhere. He is present in the smallest particle (*nuqta*) and in the greatest expanse. He is accessible to each and every object He has created. Every object obeys Allah's will except for man. Man has been given free will. The covenant of the Koran presents us with the scope of the freedom of choice that humans have in doing what is wholesome and beautiful or what is corrupt and ugly and in the human role among the creation that distinguishes right activity, right thought, and right intention from their opposites. It reminds us of how the scales of Allah's justice—the two hands of Allah, His mercy and His wrath—are reflected in the human domain, where people have been appointed Allah's vicegerents. Deeds of goodness and wholesomeness are associated with mercy, paradise, and the beautiful. Evil and corruption is rewarded with wrath, hell, and the ugly.

Allah the Divine is open to the most miniscule of beings. From this little particle, the *nuqta*, the connection to Allah, the Cherisher and the Nourisher of the universe, extends into the vastest of expanse. Within this communion of the Divine with the creation passes the Spirit of Allah into His creatures. Man lays his heart and mind open to Allah in submission to receive His Spirit and guidance.

In the space and emptiness of the universe, there flow currents and whispers of wind and energy. These winds of silence, light, and sound carry the divine whisper, and in this sound is Allah's message. This message descends into the believer's receptive heart in peace, silence, and tranquility. When the angels and the Spirit descend with Allah's guidance, the eyes perceive the most beautiful divine light, the ears hear the softest tinkle of the bell, the nose smells the fragrance of a thousand gardens, and the skin feels the most tranquil of the gentle breeze. When this happens, the soul has seen nirvana. The believer is in communion with Allah. This is the knowledge of Allah.

Allah sent thousands of prophets to mankind to teach man precepts and principles to His straight path of unity, truth, and goodness. Over thousands of years, these precepts and principles spread around the world through civilizations till mankind, as a whole, began to comprehend the message of one universal God, the Creator of every particle and every being in the whole universe. Man listened and occasionally regressed into his inherent paganism, greed, selfishness, and egotism. Allah bestowed on man a vicegerency on the earth, a mind, a free will, and a covenant. Allah then announced that there would be no more prophets. The era of prophecy had ended. Man, in stages, had received the knowledge required to live in submission to Allah's will in peace and harmony on the earth in accordance with the divine laws, which were sent down as a guidance to every human community to a life of truth justice, goodness, and peace. Such knowledge consisted of the following:

Unity: There is one absolute Being from which all stems; the universe of galaxies and all the living things in it are all connected to one another and cannot be separated from that absolute Being. Everything alive—humans, animals, plants, and microorganisms—is created by the absolute Being, all nurtured with the same organic matter, all breathing the same air; and in turn, their physical self disintegrates to the same elements that then return to the earth and the universe. In this cycle of creation and disintegration, the only permanence is of the Real, the Absolute. All else is an illusion and a mirage. One moment you are here, and in the next, you are gone. Nothing is left behind—no riches, no honor, no ego, and no pride. What is left, however, is an account of your deeds, on which one day you will be judged.

Mind: Man is bestowed with a mind and free will. The mind has the ability to perceive ideas and knowledge from the Divine and from the signs of Allah. The whisper of the Divine, the rustle of the wind, the light of God, the fragrance of God's creation, and the sensation of the Divine touch all inspire the human mind with an endless stream of ideas and knowledge. Man has been granted the ability to process his thoughts and the knowledge with free will.

The verse of the light encompasses the totality of the message and guidance that God sent to man through His prophets. The pagan in man confused God's message and instead began to worship the *rasul*. With the end of the era of the prophets, man has to open his heart to the light of Allah and learn to recognize the goodness of God within himself, in his own heart.

۞ ٱللَّهُ نُورُ ٱلسَّمَٰوَٰتِ وَٱلْأَرْضِ ۚ مَثَلُ نُورِهِۦ كَمِشْكَوٰةٍ فِيهَا مِصْبَاحٌ ۖ ٱلْمِصْبَاحُ فِى زُجَاجَةٍ ۖ ٱلزُّجَاجَةُ كَأَنَّهَا كَوْكَبٌ دُرِّىٌّ يُوقَدُ مِن
شَجَرَةٍ مُّبَٰرَكَةٍ زَيْتُونَةٍ لَّا شَرْقِيَّةٍ وَلَا غَرْبِيَّةٍ يَكَادُ زَيْتُهَا يُضِىٓءُ وَلَوْ لَمْ تَمْسَسْهُ نَارٌ ۚ نُّورٌ عَلَىٰ نُورٍ ۗ يَهْدِى ٱللَّهُ لِنُورِهِۦ مَن يَشَآءُ ۚ وَيَضْرِبُ ٱللَّهُ
ٱلْأَمْثَٰلَ لِلنَّاسِ ۗ وَٱللَّهُ بِكُلِّ شَىْءٍ عَلِيمٌ ﴿٣٥﴾ فِى بُيُوتٍ أَذِنَ ٱللَّهُ أَن تُرْفَعَ وَيُذْكَرَ فِيهَا ٱسْمُهُۥ يُسَبِّحُ لَهُۥ فِيهَا بِٱلْغُدُوِّ وَٱلْءَاصَالِ

Allah is the Light of the heavens and the earth. The parable of His Light is as if there were a Niche and within it a Lamp: the Lamp enclosed in Glass; the glass as it were a brilliant star: lit from a blessed Tree, an Olive, neither of the East nor of the West, whose Oil is well-nigh luminous, though fire scarce touched it: Light upon Light! Allah doth guide whom He will to His Light: Allah doth set forth Parables for men: and Allah doth know all things. (Lit is such a light) in houses, which Allah hath permitted to be raised to honor; for the celebration, in them, of His name: in them is He glorified in the mornings and in the evenings, (again and again). (An-Nur 24:35–36, Koran)

For mankind, parable of divine light is the fundamental belief in one universal God for the whole humankind. Allah is the light of heavens and the earth. Allah's love, mercy, and grace nurture His creation. The divine light illuminates the depths of the hearts of those who bow down in submission to, love for, and trust in Allah. Aglow is the lamp in their heart with the divine light that shines with the brightness of a star—a star lit from the light of divine wisdom, the tree of knowledge, the knowledge of Allah's signs. For those who believe, Allah is within. The believer is aglow with Allah's radiance—light upon light. The dwellings where Allah's name is praised and glorified in the mornings and evenings are luminous with Allah's light.

The fundamental knowledge is the "knowledge of certainty" (*ilm al-yaqin*, Koran 102:5). This type of certitude refers to knowledge that results from the human capacity for logic and reasoning and the appraisal of what the Koran calls "clear evidence" (*bayyinat*) of Allah's presence in the world. This knowledge also comes through the study of Koran, the teachings of the prophets, and the signs of Allah. The signs of Allah encompass the whole knowledge of the creation; man's scientific and philosophical disciplines include only a miniscule fragment of this knowledge. The knowledge of certainty is rational and discursive, a point that the Koran acknowledges when it admonishes human beings to:

﴿ قُلْ سِيرُوا۟ فِى ٱلْأَرْضِ فَٱنظُرُوا۟ كَيْفَ بَدَأَ ٱلْخَلْقَ ۚ ثُمَّ ٱللَّهُ يُنشِئُ ٱلنَّشْأَةَ ٱلْـَٔاخِرَةَ ۚ إِنَّ ٱللَّهَ عَلَىٰ كُلِّ شَىْءٍ قَدِيرٌ ﴾

Say: "Travel through the earth and see how Allah did originate creation; so, will Allah produce a later creation: for Allah has power over all things. (Al-'Ankabut 29:20, Koran)

﴿ وَهُوَ ٱلَّذِى يُحْىِۦ وَيُمِيتُ وَلَهُ ٱخْتِلَٰفُ ٱلَّيْلِ وَٱلنَّهَارِ ۚ أَفَلَا تَعْقِلُونَ ﴿٨٠﴾ ﴾

It is He Who gives life and death and to Him (is due) the alternation of Night and Day: will ye not then understand? (Al Mu'minun 23:80, Koran)

Over time and under the influence of contemplation and spiritual practice, the knowledge of certitude may be transformed into a higher form of knowledge of Allah, which the Koran calls the "eye of certitude" (*ain al-yaqin*, Koran 102:7). This term refers to the knowledge that is acquired by spiritual intelligence that believers in the East locate metaphorically in the heart. Before attaining this type of knowledge, the heart of the believer must first be "opened to Islam."

﴿ أَفَمَن شَرَحَ ٱللَّهُ صَدْرَهُۥ لِلْإِسْلَـٰمِ فَهُوَ عَلَىٰ نُورٍ مِّن رَّبِّهِۦ ۚ فَوَيْلٌ لِّلْقَـٰسِيَةِ قُلُوبُهُم مِّن ذِكْرِ ٱللَّهِ ۚ أُو۟لَـٰٓئِكَ فِى ضَلَـٰلٍ مُّبِينٍ ﴿٢٢﴾

Is one whose heart Allah has opened to Islam, so that he has received enlightenment from Allah. Woe to those whose hearts are hardened against celebrating the praises of Allah! They are manifestly wandering (in error)! (Az-Zumar 39:22, Koran)

Once opened, the heart receives knowledge as a type of divine light or illumination (*nur*) that leads the believer toward the remembrance of Allah. Just as with the knowledge of certainty, with the eye of certainty, the believer sees Allah's existence through His presence in this world. With the eye of certainty, what lead the believer to the knowledge of Allah are not the arguments to be understood by the rational intellect but by theophanic appearances (*bayyinat*) that strip away the veil of worldly phenomenon to reveal the divine reality underneath.

From the spiritual perspective, the one who perceives reality through the knowledge of Allah is a true "intellectual." Unlike the scholar, who develops his or her skills through years of formal study, the spiritual intellectual does not need book learning to understand the divine light. A spiritual intellectual can be anyone, scholarly or otherwise, whose knowledge extends both outward to take in the physical world and upward to realize his or her ultimate transcendence of the world through his or her link with the absolute. Without such a vertical dimension of spirit, the scholar's knowledge, whatever its extent may be in academic terms, is of little worth.

The third and most advanced type of knowledge builds on transcendent nature of knowledge itself. The highest level of consciousness is called the "truth of certitude" (*haqq al-yaqin*).

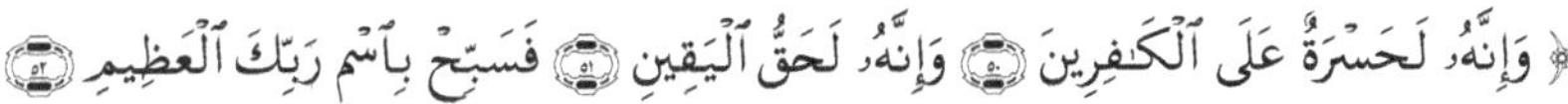

But truly (Revelation) is a cause of sorrow for the Unbelievers. But verily it is Truth of assured certainty. So, glorify the name of thy Lord Most High. (Al-Haqqah 69:50–52, Koran)

It is also known as *ilm ladduni* (knowledge "by presence"). This form of knowledge partakes directly of the divine reality and leaps off directly across the synapses of human mind to transcend both cognitive reasoning and intellectual vision at the same time. The "truth of certainty" refers to a state of consciousness in which a person knows the Real through direct participation in it without resorting to logical proofs. This type of knowledge characterizes God's prophets and messengers, whose consciousness of the truth is both immediate and participatory as what it is based on comes from direct inspiration.

According to both the word of Allah as expressed in the Koran and the tradition of the blessed *Nabi* Muhammad, faith in Islam has as much to do with theoretical and empirical knowledge as it does with simple belief. This multidimensional conception of knowledge comprehends a reality that lies hidden within the unique world yet can be revealed by the human mind and the vision of the spiritual intellect through the signs of Allah that are present in the world itself. In the Koran, Allah calls humanity:

﴿ فَلَآ أُقۡسِمُ بِمَا تُبۡصِرُونَ ٣٨ ﴾

So I do call to witness what you see

﴿ وَمَا لَا تُبۡصِرُونَ ٣٩ ﴾

And what you see not,

﴿ تَنزِيلٞ مِّن رَّبِّ ٱلۡعَٰلَمِينَ ٤٣ ﴾

(This is) a Message sent down from
the Lord of the Worlds.

﴿ وَإِنَّهُۥ لَحَقُّ ٱلۡيَقِينِ ٥١ ﴾

But verily it is Truth of assured certainty.
(Al-Haqqah 69:38–39, 43, 51)

أَلۡهَىٰكُمُ ٱلتَّكَاثُرُ ١ حَتَّىٰ زُرۡتُمُ ٱلۡمَقَابِرَ ٢ كَلَّا سَوۡفَ تَعۡلَمُونَ ٣ ثُمَّ كَلَّا سَوۡفَ تَعۡلَمُونَ ٤ كَلَّا لَوۡ تَعۡلَمُونَ عِلۡمَ ٱلۡيَقِينِ ٥

لَتَرَوُنَّ ٱلۡجَحِيمَ ٦ ثُمَّ لَتَرَوُنَّهَا عَيۡنَ ٱلۡيَقِينِ ٧ ثُمَّ لَتُسۡـَٔلُنَّ يَوۡمَئِذٍ عَنِ ٱلنَّعِيمِ ٨

The lure of abundance beguiles you, Until you reach the graves. But in the end, you will know. Soon you shall know! Nay were you to know with the knowledge of certainty. That you shall surely see the flaming fire. You shall see it with the eye of certainty. Then, you will be questioned on that Day about the pleasures you indulged in. (At-Takathur 102:1–8)

26. The Covenant of Allah: Inviting to All That Is Good and Right and Forbidding What Is Wrong

> Let there arise out of you a band of people inviting to all that is good, enjoining what is right and forbidding what is wrong: they are the ones to attain happiness. (Ali 'Imran 3:103–5, Koran)

The Koranic principle of enjoining what is good and forbidding what is evil is supportive of the moral autonomy of the person, man and woman. This principle authorizes a person to act according to his or her best judgment in situations in which his or her intervention will advance a good purpose. The following saying of the blessed *Nabi* also supports individual action by a believer:

> *If any one of you sees an evil, let him change it by his hand and if he is unable to do that, let him change by his words and if he is still unable to do that let him denounce it in his heart, but this is the weakest form of belief.*

This principle assigns to the individual an active role in the community in which he or she lives. *The Koran annunciated the principle of free speech fourteen hundred years ago.* Believing men and women are reminded that they are the best of people, a witness over other nations. Such a responsibility carries with it a moral burden of an exemplary conduct of one who submits to the divine truth and whose relationship with Allah is governed is by *taqwa*, the consciousness of humankind's responsibility toward its Creator. The believer has the responsibility of acting in accordance with the three types of knowledge—the knowledge of certitude (*ilm al–yaqin*), the eye of certitude (*ain al-yaqin*), and the truth of certitude (*haqq al-yaqin*). With that knowledge and faith, the believer is well equipped to approach others to enjoin what is right and forbid what is wrong. This moral autonomy of the individual, when bound together with the will of the community, formulates the doctrine of infallibility of the collective will of the *ummah*, which is the doctrinal basis of consensus.

27. The Covenant of Allah: Do Not Say to Another Muslim, "You Are Not a Believer"

Islam is a religion of self-surrender; it is the conscious and rational submission of a dependent and limited human will to the absolute and omnipotent will of Allah. The type of surrender Islam requires is a deliberate, conscious, and rational act made by a person who knows with both intellectual certainty and spiritual vision that Allah, who is the subject of Koranic discourse, is reality itself.

> When you go forth in the cause of Allah be careful to discriminate and say not to the one who greets you with alaikum o salaam, "Though art not a believer". Would you covet perishable goods of this life when there are immeasurable treasures with Allah? You were like the person who offered you salutation, before Allah conferred on you His favors. Therefore, carefully investigate for Allah is well aware of all that you do. (An-Nisa 4:94, Koran)

Every believer's journey into Islam cannot be the same and uniform. A lot depends on the cultural background, education, and intellectual biases of the person. The first principle of faith is tawhid, the assertion that God is one, that there is only a single worthy object of worship, Allah. All other objects of worship are false. To serve anything else is to fall into error, misguidance, and sin of *shirk*. The Koranic notion of religious belief (*iman*) as dependent on knowledge is actualized in practice in the term *islam*. The term *islam* signifies the idea of surrender or submission. Islam is a religion of self-surrender; it is the conscious and rational submission of a dependent and limited human will to the absolute and omnipotent will of Allah. The type of surrender Islam requires is a deliberate, conscious, and rational act made by a person who knows with both intellectual certainty and spiritual vision that Allah, who is the subject of Koranic discourse, is reality itself. The knower of God is a Muslim (fem. *Muslimah*), "one who submits" to the divine truth and whose relationship with God is governed by *taqwa*, the consciousness of humankind's responsibility toward its Creator.

However, consciousness of God alone is not sufficient to make a person a Muslim. Neither is it enough to be merely born a Muslim or to be raised in an Islamic cultural context. The believer must endeavor at all times to maintain himself or herself in a constant state of submission to Allah. By doing so, the believer attains the honored title of "slave of Allah" (*abd Allah*, feminine: *amat Allah*), for he recognizes that all power and agency belongs to God alone. After submission to the will of Allah, observation of the five pillars opens the way for the believer to understand *ihsan* and perform good deeds for humanity:

إِنَّ ٱلَّذِينَ ءَامَنُواْ وَعَمِلُواْ ٱلصَّٰلِحَٰتِ وَأَقَامُواْ ٱلصَّلَوٰةَ وَءَاتَوُاْ ٱلزَّكَوٰةَ لَهُمۡ أَجۡرُهُمۡ عِندَ رَبِّهِمۡ وَلَا خَوۡفٌ عَلَيۡهِمۡ وَلَا هُمۡ يَحۡزَنُونَ

٢٧٧

Those who believe, do deeds of righteousness, and establish regular prayers and regular charity, will have their reward with their Lord: on them shall be no fear, nor shall they grieve. (Al-Baqarah 2:277, Koran)

Every individual is at a different stage of their life's journey. Only Allah is the judge and the knower of the hidden and the manifest. Only He knows what is in a person's heart.

28. The Covenant of Allah: Suspicion and Lack of Trust

> Avoid suspicion, for suspicion in some cases is sin; and spy not on each other, nor speak ill of each other behind their backs. Would any of you eat the flesh of his dead brother? No, you would abhor it. Be in taqwa of Allah, fear Allah: for Allah is Forgiving, Most Merciful. (Al-Hujurat 49:12–13, Koran)

Allah gave humans the trust of vicegerency over the earth with the stipulation that they acknowledge Him as their Lord and worship and thank Him for His benevolence. As part of that trust, people are free to make their choices about their actions. Allah does not force them to make the correct choices without taking the trust away from them, and if He took the trust away, they no longer are humans.

With the abuse of vicegerency came selfish acquisition of wealth, land, and women. Acquisition of wealth breeds greed, covetousness, and hoarding of wealth. The prospect of loss of such acquisitions produces insecurity and constant watchfulness. Such paranoia in humans has had a forceful impact on the society of man that leads to assumptions, suspicions, and suppositions that result in quarrels among people and wars between nations, thus a breakdown of the world order. Suspicion among nations has produced expensive and intricate security and intelligence systems that use spying equipment on the ground, in the air, and in space to obtain information on other nations. People and police spy on other people; cities are full of cameras tracking the movement of citizens. Big Brother watches everyone. Mistrust and suspicion prevails over the world, suggesting sickness in society. The same insecurity in people's psyche gives rise to resentment, jealousy, anger, and mistrust, leading to feuds and social disruption.

29. The Covenant of Allah: Do Not Ridicule Other Believers or Revile One Another with Wicked Names

> Let not some folk among you ridicule others: it may be that they are better than you are: nor let some women mock others: it may be that the others are better than them: nor defame or revile each other by offensive names: ill-seeming is wicked name calling for the one who has believed; and those who do not desist are indeed wrong-doers. (Al-Hujurat 49:11, Koran)

The covenant of Allah forbids suspicion, spying on each other, backbiting, and ridiculing other believers. The heart is like a shining mirror. Troublesome deeds are like smoke that will cover the mirror; you will not be able to see yourself, and you will be veiled from the reality of Allah. To understand the reality of Allah, you have to uncover ignorance and darkness so as to see the light and the reality. Some traits of this darkness are arrogance, ego, pride, envy, vengeance, lying, gossiping, backbiting, and other unwholesome characteristics. To be rid of these evils and odious traits, one has to clean and shine the mirror of the heart. This cleansing of the heart is done by acquiring knowledge and acting upon it to fight against one's ego by ridding oneself of multiplicity of being through unity. When the heart becomes alive with the light and *nur* of unity, the eye of the clean heart will see the reality of Allah's attributes.

30. The Covenant of Allah: Secret Counsels and Pacts

> When you hold secret counsel, do it not for iniquity and hostility and disobedience to the Messenger; but do it for righteousness and self-restraint; and fear Allah, to Whom ye shall be brought back.

Secret counsels are only inspired by the Satan,
in order that he may cause grief to the Believers;
but he cannot harm them in the least, except
as Allah permits; and on Allah let the Believers
put their trust. (Al-Mujadila 58:9–10, Koran)

No believer, individual, community, or ruler shall make a compact on behalf of the *ummah* or part of it in secret with the unbelievers. Islam regards secret pacts with enemies and hostile actions against one's own people as treason. When the *Nabi* was in Medina, there were some people who professed Islam but at the same time conspired with the enemy, the *kafirun,* against fellow Muslims. The Koran has the following description of the fate of the *Munafiqeen*.

وَمِنَ ٱلنَّاسِ مَن يَقُولُ ءَامَنَّا بِٱللَّهِ وَبِٱلْيَوْمِ ٱلْءَاخِرِ وَمَا هُم بِمُؤْمِنِينَ ﴿٨﴾ يُخَـٰدِعُونَ ٱللَّهَ وَٱلَّذِينَ ءَامَنُوا۟ وَمَا يَخْدَعُونَ إِلَّآ أَنفُسَهُمْ
وَمَا يَشْعُرُونَ ﴿٩﴾ فِى قُلُوبِهِم مَّرَضٌ فَزَادَهُمُ ٱللَّهُ مَرَضًا ۖ وَلَهُمْ عَذَابٌ أَلِيمٌۢ بِمَا كَانُوا۟ يَكْذِبُونَ ﴿١٠﴾ وَإِذَا قِيلَ لَهُمْ لَا تُفْسِدُوا۟ فِى ٱلْأَرْضِ قَالُوٓا۟ إِنَّمَا
نَحْنُ مُصْلِحُونَ ﴿١١﴾ أَلَآ إِنَّهُمْ هُمُ ٱلْمُفْسِدُونَ وَلَـٰكِن لَّا يَشْعُرُونَ ﴿١٢﴾

Of the people there are some who say: "We believe in
Allah and the Last Day;" but they do not really believe.

Fain would they deceive Allah and those who believe,
but they only deceive themselves and realize it not!

In their hearts is a disease; and Allah has increased
their disease: and grievous is the penalty they
incur, because they are false to themselves.

When it is said to them: "Make not mischief on the
earth," they say: "Why, we only want to make peace!"

Of a surety, they are the ones who make mischief, but
they realize (it) not. (Al-Baqarah 2:8–12, Koran)

ٱللَّهُ يَسْتَهْزِئُ بِهِمْ وَيَمُدُّهُمْ فِى طُغْيَٰنِهِمْ يَعْمَهُونَ ﴿١٥﴾ أُو۟لَٰٓئِكَ ٱلَّذِينَ ٱشْتَرَوُا۟ ٱلضَّلَٰلَةَ بِٱلْهُدَىٰ فَمَا رَبِحَت تِّجَٰرَتُهُمْ وَمَا كَانُوا۟ مُهْتَدِينَ ﴿١٦﴾
مَثَلُهُمْ كَمَثَلِ ٱلَّذِى ٱسْتَوْقَدَ نَارًا فَلَمَّآ أَضَآءَتْ مَا حَوْلَهُۥ ذَهَبَ ٱللَّهُ بِنُورِهِمْ وَتَرَكَهُمْ فِى ظُلُمَٰتٍ لَّا يُبْصِرُونَ ﴿١٧﴾ صُمٌّۢ بُكْمٌ عُمْىٌ فَهُمْ لَا
يَرْجِعُونَ ﴿١٨﴾

Allah will throw back their mockery on them
and give them rope in their trespasses; so they
will wander like blind ones to and fro.

These are they who have bartered guidance
for error: but their traffic is profitless
and they have lost true direction.

Their similitude is that of a man who kindled a fire;
when it lighted all around him, Allah took away
their light and left them in utter darkness. So, they
could not see. Deaf, dumb and blind, they will not
return to the path. (Al-Baqarah 2:15–18, Koran)

In our age, we have people who think that they can get the best of both worlds by compromising their nations and Islam's interests with the enemy. King Abdullah of Transjordan secretly met with Zionist leaders from 1922 onward, merely a year after the creation of Transjordan. These meetings continued during the Palestinian disturbances in 1932 and 1936. The amity between the two conspiring sides was so total that, in a meeting, Abdullah and the Jewish envoy discussed ways of eliminating the mufti of Jerusalem, the leader of

Palestinians, and the enemy of both sides[62]. He secretly conspired with Chaim Weizmann for the partition of Palestine in 1947.

Abdullah's grandson Hussein started his secret contacts with Israeli leaders in 1957, and by 1963, meetings with the leaders became a regular occurrence. In 1963, Hussein made a secret visit to Tel Aviv[63]. In the period preceding 1967, Hussein performed several treasonable acts that were openly anti-Arab. In response to the creation of PLO, which wanted to replace him as the Palestinian representative, Hussein's intelligence service provided the names and location of the Palestinian fighters infiltrating and battling the Israelis[64]. Hussein did not stop here. His intelligence service also provided the Israelis information about other Arab countries[65]. From 1970 onward, there were several secret meetings between Hussein and the Israeli defense minister Moshe Dayan and with Israeli prime minister Golda Meir[66]. This extensive period of secret Jordanian-Israeli cooperation produced the most treasonable act of Hussein's life, informing Israel of the impending Egyptian-Syrian attack on October 1973[67].

The rulers of Islam who work against their own faith and their own people have a disease in their hearts. They make mischief on the earth against their own faith and nation in secret collusion with the enemies in return for personal gain, power, and wealth. Allah promises a grievous penalty for them because they are false to themselves and do not realize it. Every Muslim today is enslaved by an infidel international diplomatic and financial system run through a network

---

[62] Avi Shlaim, *The Politics of Partition*, 203.

[63] Dan Raviv and Yossi Melman, *Every Spy a Prince*, 213.

[64] Ian Black and Benny Morris, *Israel's Secret Wars*, 238.

[65] Raviv and Melman, *Every Spy*, 214.

[66] *Secret Channels*, Mohamed Heikal, 310.

[67] Morris and Black, *Israel's Secret Wars*, 265.

of secretive and deceitful treaties and clauses. Every Muslim carries the burden of four monkeys that direct his daily life. The monkeys of secret international finance, diplomacy, crime, and intelligence syndicates sit on the back of every Muslim through the connivance and ignorance of Muslim rulers, mercenary armies, and religious leaders.

31. The Covenant of Allah: Intoxicants and Gambling: Forbidden to You Are Intoxicants and Gambling

> Intoxicants and gambling, dedication of stones and divination by arrows are an abomination and Satan's handiwork; they hinder you from prayer and remembrance of Allah and place enmity and hatred amongst you. Abstain from them so that you may prosper. (Al-Ma'idah 5:90–91)

Today the world is bedeviled with evils that consume people and deprive them of self-control and motivation to lead a life of purpose and usefulness for themselves, their families, and their fellow humans. The urge for immediate gratification and relief from the stresses of daily life sends people scurrying to alcohol and drugs. In the Western world, a tenth of the adult population is addicted to alcohol or drugs, and another half are habitual users of intoxicants. One in every three families carries the burden of an addicted dear one. In the Muslim world, although alcohol is the lesser substance of abuse, marijuana, cocaine, hashish, and khat use is rampant. Tobacco, a substance of extreme addiction but of mild intoxicant properties, is the weed of popular use. A fifth of the world's workforce is underproductive and disabled physically and intellectually because of intoxication and addiction.

The covenant of the Koran fourteen hundred years ago forbade humans from the use of intoxicants in an effort to save mankind from self-destruction. Gambling in all forms—including lotteries, slot machines, betting, card playing, and entertainment in casinos—is forbidden. The covenant says,

> These are an abomination and Satan's handiwork; they hinder you from prayer and remembrance of Allah and place enmity and hatred amongst you. Abstain from them so that you may prosper. (Al-Ma'idah 5:90–91, Koran)

32. The Covenant of Allah: Forbidden to You Are the Carrion, Blood, and Flesh of Swine and Any Other Food on Which Any Name Besides That of Allah Has Been Invoked

> Eat of good things provided to you by Allah and show your gratitude in worship of Him. Forbidden to you are the carrion, blood and flesh of swine and on any other food on which any name besides that of Allah has been invoked. If forced by necessity, without willful disobedience or transgressing due limits, one is guilt less. Allah is Most Forgiving and Most Merciful. (Al-Baqarah 2:172–73, Koran)

Allah, in His mercy, has permitted the believers to eat of all good things provided by Him. Expressly forbidden is to eat unclean food, which constitutes four things: carrion, blood, flesh of swine, and animals slaughtered in the name of any other than Allah.

During the last millennium, science has discovered harmful parasites and bacteria in the flesh of diseased animals, swine, and the blood of animals. Fourteen hundred years before the establishment of veterinary and pathological sciences and public health regulations, the Koran had made a clear distinction between food that was clean and good and what was bad and harmful for humans.

33. The Covenant of Allah: Make Not Unlawful the Good Things That Allah Hath Made Lawful to You

> Make not unlawful the good things, which Allah hath made lawful to you. Commit no excess; Allah loves not people given to excess. Eat of things that Allah has provided for you, lawful and good. Be in taqwa of Allah, fear Allah in whom you believe. (Al-Ma'idah 5:87–88, Koran)

Allah has, in very explicit words, laid out in His covenant the acts forbidden to the believers:

1. *Shirk*: Join not anything as equal with Him. (Worship Allah and do not associate others with Him.)
2. Mistreatment of parents: Be good to your parents.
3. Infanticide and abortion: Kill not your children on a plea of want. We provide sustenance for you and for them.
4. *Fahasha*: Come not near shameful deeds, whether open or in secret.
5. Taking of life: Take not life, which Allah hath made sacred, except by way of justice and law.
6. Stealing: Come not near to the orphan's property, except to improve it, until he attains the age of full strength. The term *orphan* may also include other helpless citizens who may be subject to oppression.
7. Cheating: And give measure and weight with justice; (do not cheat) no burden do we place on any soul but that which it can bear.

8. Lying and falsification: Whenever you speak, speak the truth, even if a near relative is concerned.
9. Violation of Allah's Covenant: Fulfill the covenant of Allah: "Thus, does He command you that ye may remember. Verily, this is My Way leading straight: follow it; follow not other paths: they will scatter you about from His Path; thus, doth He command you, that ye may be righteous" (Al-An'am 6:151–53, Koran).
10. Intoxicants.
11. Gambling.
12. Dedication of stones.
13. Divination by arrows: "These are an abomination and Satan's handiwork; they hinder you from prayer and remembrance of Allah and place enmity and hatred amongst you. Abstain from them so that you may prosper" (Al-Ma'idah 5:90–91, Koran).
14. Carrion.
15. Blood.
16. Flesh of swine.
17. "Any other food on which any name besides that of Allah has been invoked" (Al-Baqarah 2:172–73, Koran).
18. Usury (*riba*): "Devour not usury double and multiplied: Be in taqwa of Allah, that you may prosper" (Ali 'Imran 3:130, Koran).
19. Disrespect toward women: "It is not lawful for you to take women against their will, nor should you treat them with harshness. On the contrary treat then with honor and kindness" (An-Nisa 4:19, Koran).
20. Any actions that infringe on the unity of the *ummah* and the nation of Islam: "And hold fast, all together, by the Rope which Allah stretches out for you and be not divided among yourselves. You were enemies and He joined your hearts

> in love, so that by His Grace, you became brethren and a community. Thus, does Allah makes His Signs clear to you that you may be guided. Be not like those who are divided amongst themselves and fall into disputations after receiving clear signs; for them is a dreadful penalty."

These twenty actions have been forbidden (haram) by the covenant of Allah. At the same time, Allah commands:

> Make not unlawful the good things, which Allah hath made lawful to you. Commit no excess; Allah loves not people given to excess. Eat of things that Allah has provided for you, lawful and good. Be in taqwa of Allah, fear Allah in whom you believe. (Al-Ma'idah 5:57, Koran)

Islamic scholar-jurists frequently quote various Hadith and proclaim many aspects of the daily life of pious and observant believers as haram. Such actions include listening to music, women's education, women's role in congregational prayers, and other mundane activities such as kite flying, tourism, pursuit of Western education, and use of modern technology. Those are the personal views of the mullahs and do not have the divine sanction of the covenant between Allah and His believers.

Music: Music is part of the human soul. Every child, when happy, springs up to a melody and dance to the rhythm. When the blessed *Nabi* received the revelation from Allah, at times, it appeared in the form of a tinkle or the chimes of a bell, and the words of the revelation blossomed in Blessed Muhammad's mind. The Koran, when recited in rhythmic Arabic, produces a heavenly song of Allah's revelation. Singing Allah's *dhikr* with or without instrument or music has a powerful and profound effect on the listener's soul, which reflects divine beauty. Listening to mere wind chimes makes one aware of the divine origin of the sounds of the wind, the rustle of trees, and the sound of running water in rivers, falls, and oceans. Allah gave the human the ability to produce the most beautiful sounds in His remembrance, to celebrate life and happiness, and to enjoy Allah's other provisions to mankind.

Observation of Allah's covenant bestows peace and tranquility to the soul and hence happiness and contentment on the believer. Islam is not a religion of gloom, sorrow, and melancholia but that of celebration of Allah's blessings and of doing beautiful deeds. To show contentment, peace, harmony, happiness, and proper balance of things in life is to express *shukr*, gratitude to Allah for His mercy and grace. The human is asked to use all his senses—sight, hearing, smell, taste, and touch—to recognize Allah's truth and signs. They signify the perception of Allah's *nur* (light), resonance of the sound of Allah's harmonious music in nature, the fragrance of Allah's garden, the flavor of Allah's bounty, and the feel of Allah's creation around us. Allah does not forbid against His divine gift of harmony and song; on the contrary, He urged the recitation of the Koran in slow, rhythmic tones and the celebration and praising of Allah often, glorifying Him in the morning and at night. It is Allah and His angels who also send their blessings on the believers so "He may lead the Believers you out of the depths of darkness into light." Celebration of Allah's praises and glorifying Him means to rejoice, to be happy, and to be joyous. The word *celebrate*, therefore, has the connotation of a happy occasion, which includes song and music.

Confinement of believing and devout women: Confinement of believing and devout women Believers is not a mandate of Allah's covenant nor is covering women from head to toe.

Acquisition of knowledge: Education is Allah's gift to humanity and is incumbent on every believer, man or woman. Scholars of Islam ignore the Koranic admonition.

> Make not unlawful the good things, which Allah
> hath made lawful to you. Commit no excess;
> Allah loves not people given to excess.

34. The Covenant of Allah: Contracts and Agreements

> When you make a transaction involving future obligations, write it down in presence of witnesses, or let a scribe write it down faithfully. Let the party incurring the liability dictate truthfully in the presence of two witnesses from among your own men and if two men are not available then a man and two women, so that if one of them errs then the other one, can remind him. Disregard not to put your contract in writing, whether it be small or large, it is more suitable in the eyes of Allah, more suitable as evidence and more convenient to prevent doubts in the future amongst you. (Al-Baqarah 2:282–83, Koran)

Fourteen hundred years ago, the Koran laid out the basis of the modern legal system of written and witnessed agreements. Muslim jurists have used this *ayah* to curtail the rights of women as witnesses in the modern court system, where they consider the testimony of two women equivalent to the testimony of one man. The mullahs imply that women have an inferior memory and intellectual capacity. Although the Koran is silent on the reason for the need for two women witnesses, it is obvious that women carry the burden and the responsibilities of nurturing and taking care of their infants and families. Women are Allah's instruments of creation and the nurturer of mankind. The act of creation and nurture has precedence over worldly affairs of commerce. Women cannot neglect their divine obligation of creation to attend to the communal affairs as witnesses in the transactions of this world. The need for a second woman witness becomes necessary when one of them becomes preoccupied with her obligations of procreation and upbringing of a family.

There is abundant of scientific evidence that the intellectual capacity of both men and women is unique in their development. This uniqueness complements the intellect and memory of men and women in the functioning of mankind. This uniqueness is a gift of Allah to humankind.

The human memory is affected by the inbuilt nature and development of the brain and its environment. Adolescent brain development is different in boys and girls. Male's aged six to seventeen years display more prominent age-related reduction in gray matter (the part of the brain that allows us to think) and increases in white matter (which transfers information between distant regions) than females. These changes in brain composition are linked to developmental processes in which nerve cell connections are "pruned" in gray matter and made more efficient (myelinated) in white matter. The more dramatic changes seen in males may be related to the different effects of estrogen and testosterone on the brain[68]. Women have smaller brains than men and have smaller bodies; women have more gray matter, and men have more white matter. This finding may help explain why women are typically better than men at verbal tasks, while men are typically better than women at spatial tasks, as well as why the sexes perform equally well on intelligence tests in spite of males having larger brains [69].

[68] De Bellis, MD, et al., "Sex Differences."

[69] Gur et al., "Sex Differences."

Several studies have evaluated sex differences in the histology of the cerebral cortex. One study in humans detected higher neuronal density in the female cortex compared with males[70]. In contrast, other studies have shown that the number of neurons in the cerebral cortex is greater in males than in females. Studies by Rabinowicz et al. demonstrated that males have 15 percent more cortical neurons and 13 percent greater neuronal density than females[71]. Similarly, Pakkenberg et al. showed a 16 percent higher neuronal number in males, but sex differences in neuronal density were not present[72]. Although women have fewer neocortical neurons, certain anatomical and histological characteristics of female brains may allow for more extensive dendritic arborization and more neuronal connections among nerve cells[73]. Certain diseases that cause neuronal loss in the cerebral cortex may be more detrimental to women due to their lower number of cortical neurons compared with men[74].

The cerebellum, an area of the brain important for posture and balance, and the pons, a brain structure linked to the cerebellum that helps control consciousness, are larger in men than in women[75]. As the brain ages, the amount of tissue mass declines, and the amount of fluid increases. This effect is less severe in women than in men, suggesting that women are somewhat less vulnerable to age-related changes in mental abilities[76]–[77]. However, women are more prone to dementia

---

70 Haug, "Brain Sizes."

71 Rabinowicz et al., "Gender Differences."

72 Pakkenberg and Gundersen, "Neocortical Neuron Number."

73 de Courten-Myers, "Human Cerebral Cortex."

74 Rabinowicz et al., "Structure of the Cerebral Cortex."

75 Raz et al., "Age and Sex Differences."

76 Gur et al., "Gender Differences."

77 Witelson, "Sex Differences."

than men perhaps because of the potentially greater susceptibility to loss of neurons and neuronal connections.

Language Differences. Although men and women have been shown to process some language tasks similarly, in other aspects of language processing, there are significant sex differences[78]. Imaging studies of the living brain show that in women neurons on both sides of the brain are activated when they are listening, while in men neurons on only one side of the brain are activated. Men and women appear to process single words similarly, but in the interpretation of whole sentences, women use both sides of the brain, while men use one side[79]. Boys have a higher incidence than girls of developmental language disorders, such as developmental dyslexia. Despite these differences during childhood, it is not clear whether adult women have better verbal skills than men.

Spatial Information Differences. Men and women process spatial information differently[80]. When negotiating a virtual reality maze, both men and women use the right hippocampus to figure out how to exit. However, men also use the left hippocampus for this task, while women do not. Women also use the right prefrontal cortex, while men do not[81]. In an imaging study, men were found to activate a distributed system of different brain regions on both sides of the brain while performing a spatial task. Women, however, activated these regions on only the right side of the brain. Women appear to rely on landmarks to navigate their environments, whereas men tend to use compass directions[82].

---

[78] Ibid.

[79] Kansaku and Kitazawa, "Imaging Studies."

[80] Ragland et al., "Sex Differences."

[81] Gron et al., "Brain Activation."

[82] Saucier et al., "Are Sex Differences in Navigation?"

Memory Differences. Some functions of memory appear to be different in males and females[83]. Higher rates of blood flow in certain portions of the brain are associated with increased memory of verbal tasks in women but not in men [84]. Compared with men, women have been shown to be better at remembering faces[85]. A key part of the brain involved in processing emotionally influenced memories acts differently in men and women.

The amygdala, an almond-shaped structure found on both sides of the brain, behaves very differently in males and females while the subjects are at rest. In men, the right amygdala is more active and shows more connections with other regions of the brain. Conversely, in women, the left amygdala is more connected with other regions of the brain. In addition, the regions of the brain with which the amygdala communicates while a subject is at rest are different in men and women. These findings suggest that the brain is wired differently in men and women. In men, the right-hemisphere amygdala showed more connectivity with brain regions such as the visual cortex and the striatum. In contrast, the left amygdala in women was more connected to regions such as the insular cortex and the hypothalamus.

Many brain areas communicating with the amygdala in men are engaged with and responding to the external environment. For example, the visual cortex is responsible for vision, while the striatum coordinates motor actions. Conversely, many regions connected to the left-hemisphere amygdala in women control aspects of the environment within the body. Both the insular cortex and the hypothalamus, for example, receive strong input from the sensors inside the body.

Throughout evolution, women have had to deal with a number of internal stressors, such as childbirth, that men have not had to

---

[83] Duff and Hampson, "Sex Difference."

[84] Ragland et al., "Sex Differences."

[85] Gur et al., "Computerized Neurocognitive Scanning."

experience. The brain seems to have evolved to be in tune with those different stressors. One of the brain areas communicating with the amygdala in women is implicated in disorders such as depression and irritable bowel syndrome, which predominantly affect women.

The sexes use different sides of their brains to process and store long-term memories. Another study in 2002 demonstrated how a particular drug, propranolol, can block memory differently in men and women. Differences between men and women in cognitive pattern are now well established. On average, men outperform women on a variety of spatial tasks, with the largest difference occurring on tests of spatial rotation and manipulation, where an object must be identified in an altered orientation, or after certain imaginary manipulations such as folding. Men also excel at tests of mathematical reasoning, with the differences between sexes especially marked at the higher end of the distribution. Women, in contrast, are generally better able to recall the spatial layout of an array of objects, to scan perceptual arrays quickly to find matching objects, and to recall verbal material, whether word lists or meaningful paragraphs.

Some of these differences are found early in development and last throughout the life span. The sex differences in verbal memory, spatial orientation, and mathematical reasoning have been found across cultures. These differences are due to our long evolutionary history as hunter-gatherers, in which the division of labor between men and women was quite marked. Men more often traveled farther from the home base during hunting and scavenging, whereas women gathered food nearer home. In parallel with nonhuman studies, this would tend to show different navigational strategies, with men, for example, relying more on geometric cues and women more on landmark cues.

Summary: At present, when men and women have begun to perform similar tasks, each sex has certain specialization that, on the whole, complements the other sex's abilities. None is better, and none is inferior to the other. Mullahs will continue with their age-old prejudices to maintain women's lower status. Allah, in His infinitesimal wisdom, has bestowed on men and women unique strengths that complement each other for the benefit of humanity.

We digressed from the main topic of the written agreements because of an ongoing controversy in certain legal, scholastic Muslim circles about women's capacity as witnesses in the modern court system. This controversy about women's witnessing needed to be addressed in an informed and scientific manner. It is hoped that the above discussion will go a long way to contradict those mullahs who claim to be privy to Allah's intentions.

35. The Covenant of Allah: Respect Other People's Privacy

> Enter not houses other than yours until you have
> asked permission and invoked peace upon those
> in them. If you find none in the house whom
> you seek enter not unless permission is granted.
> If you asked to leave go back, it is best for you
> that makes for greater purity for you. Allah knows
> all that you do. (An-Nur 24:27, Koran)

The four walls of every person's home are his circle of privacy, within the confines of which he or she has freedom from intrusion by outsiders, be it the neighbor or the state. The residents of the home are protected from physical intrusion or intrusion with electronic devices. This dwelling is the basic autonomous unit of the Islamic state that amalgamates with other such units to form a community. The communities, with some complexity, join other communities to form the state. What is important is that the residents of each dwelling have their seclusion protected by the mandate of the covenant of the Koran. Importantly, each of the adult residents has a voice in the administration of the common affairs of the community. Each family is an independent, autonomous, basic unit of the *ummah*.

36. The Covenant of Allah: This Day I Have Perfected Your Religion for You

This Day I have perfected your religion for you. We have made the (Qur'an) easy in your own tongue, that with it you may give glad tidings to the righteous and warnings to people given to contention. Therein is proclaimed every wise decree, by command from Our Presence, for We are ever sending revelations, as a Mercy from your Lord. We have explained in detail in this Qur'an, for the benefit of mankind, every kind of similitude.

This day have those who reject faith (kafaru) given up all hope of compromising your faith, fear them not but only fear Me. This day have I perfected your religion for you, bestowed on you with My blessings and decreed Islam as your religion. (Al-Ma'idah 5:3, Koran)

Ha Mim. By the Book that makes matters lucid; We revealed it during the blessed night, verily We are always warning against Evil. Therein is proclaimed every wise decree, by command from Our Presence, for We are ever sending revelations, as a Mercy from your Lord: for He is the hearer and knower. The Lord of the heavens and the earth and all that is in between them, if you have an assured faith. There is no god but He: it is He who gives life and death, the Lord and Cherisher, your Lord and Lord of your forefathers. (Ad-Dukhan 44:1-8, Koran)

So, have We made the (Qur'an) easy in your own tongue,
that with it you may give glad tidings to the righteous and
warnings to people given to contention. But how many
(countless) generations before them have We destroyed?
Canst, thou find a single one of them (now) or hear
(so much as) a whisper of them? (Taha 19:97, Koran)

We have explained in detail in this Qur'an, for
the benefit of mankind, every kind of similitude:
but man is, in most things, contentious. And
what is there to keep back men from believing,
now that guidance has come to them, nor from
praying for forgiveness from their Lord, but
that (they ask that) the ways of the ancients be
repeated with them, or the Wrath be brought to
them face to face? (Al-Kahf 18:54–55, Koran)

The blessed *Nabi* of Allah, Muhammad, proclaimed to the world on the mount of Arafat Allah's *wahiy* (message) on the last Friday, the ninth day, of *Zul-hajj* in the tenth year of hijra (631CE).

This day have I perfected your religion for you.

ٱلْيَوْمَ يَئِسَ ٱلَّذِينَ كَفَرُوا۟ مِن دِينِكُمْ فَلَا تَخْشَوْهُمْ وَٱخْشَوْنِ ۚ ٱلْيَوْمَ أَكْمَلْتُ لَكُمْ دِينَكُمْ وَأَتْمَمْتُ عَلَيْكُمْ نِعْمَتِى

وَرَضِيتُ لَكُمُ ٱلْإِسْلَٰمَ دِينًا

This day have those who reject faith (kafaru) given up
all hope of compromising your faith, fear them not but
only fear Me. This day have I perfected your religion for
you, bestowed on you with My blessings and decreed
Islam as your religion. (Al-Ma'idah 5:3, Koran)

On that day, the *din* of Islam was complete, and all man-made innovations after that were just novelties; anyone indulging in such innovations was making a sport of his religion. Those believers who fulfill the commandments of the Koran, Allah's covenant, are the *muttaqeen.* From that day on, men and women who obey and keep their covenant with Allah are the believers (*muttaqeen*) of Allah and the Koran, the word that Allah revealed to the blessed *Nabi,* Muhammad. The Believers who follow the Qur'an and fulfill the Covenant of Allah, for their din Allah is the only Reality and He only suffices them. They follow Islam. They are Muslims. They are not Shia or Sunni nor any other sect.

The Koran establishes a universal order based on the divinely ordained values of life. Were every human to fulfill the covenant of the Koran, the world shall be at peace forever, and justice will prevail. By following the *Hadith collections* of the third-century hijra, *Muslims* have relegated their faith from a divinely ordained order to a human set of values, misleading themselves and deviating others from Allah's path. According to the Koran, *iman* is not just belief but also, in fact, knowledge. *Iman* is the conviction that is based on reason and knowledge. The Koran does not recognize belief that involves blind acceptance. Islam does include acceptance of certain things that cannot be explained by perception through human senses. Our reason and thinking will compel us to recognize the existence of such things. *Iman*, according to the Koran, signifies conviction based on full mental acceptance and intellectual satisfaction. *Iman* gives a person inner contentment, a feeling of *amn* (same common root). Thus, *iman* means to believe in something and to testify to its truthfulness, to have confidence in that belief, and to bow down in obedience.

There are five fundamental facts stated in the Koran that a believer must accept: *iman* in Allah, the law of *mukafat* and the afterlife, angels (*malaika*), the revelations, and the messengers. Belief in Allah means not only to profess obedience to Him and His Covenant but also to show it in one's actions and to be always in *taqwa* of Allah. Belief in the law of *mukafat* means to have conviction that every action of the human has an inescapable consequence of reward or retribution. Angels are not the winged creatures depicted in children's literature. They are heavenly forces that carry out laws of Allah governing the universe. They bow to Allah since they follow his orders. They also bow to the humans because we are able to study, understand, and manipulate the laws of nature for the benefit of mankind. Belief in revelations and messengers implies that human intellect alone cannot safely reach the final destination without the divine guidance in the form of *wahiy*, revelation delivered by the messengers to mankind. This guidance is to whole humankind sent through many messengers. The Muslim tradition began with *Ibrahim*, our father (Abraham of the Bible). The believers have a belief system and a course of action to witness over and spread the message to mankind that began with *Ibrahim* and was completed with *Muhammad*. Whereas the message of *wahiy* is divine and universal for all human races, the message of Hadith collections of the third century are human and therefore subject to error and cannot be equated with the Koran.

37. The Covenant of Allah: Those Who Believe and Perform Beautiful Deeds Are Companions of the Garden, Where They hall Abide Forever

After his submission to the will and mercy of Allah, the believer is obliged to obey and fulfill the covenant he has made with Allah as part of the compact of submission and has to perform wholesome and good deeds.

The covenant of the Koran is a total belief system of an individual based upon total submersion of one's personality with Allah with total awareness and *taqwa* of Him at all times through observance of the thirty-seven commandments of Allah's covenant. This communion is not only with Allah but also, through Him, with other humans and Allah's creation, both alive and inanimate. The phrase *amilu al saalihaat* (to do good, to perform wholesome deeds) refers to those who persist in striving to set things right, who restore harmony, peace, and balance. Other acts of good works recognized in the covenant of the Koran are to show compassion, to be merciful and forgive others, to be just, to protect the weak, to defend the oppressed, to be generous and charitable, to be truthful, to seek knowledge and wisdom, to be kind, to be peaceful, to love others, and to perform beautiful deeds.

إِنَّ ٱلَّذِينَ ءَامَنُوا۟ وَعَمِلُوا۟ ٱلصَّـٰلِحَـٰتِ سَيَجْعَلُ لَهُمُ ٱلرَّحْمَـٰنُ وُدًّا ﴿٩٦﴾

On those who believe and do good, will
[Allah] Most Gracious bestow love.

There are fifty such verses in the Koran that remind the believers of the rewards of righteous deeds. The following are some of the *ayahs* in the Koran mentioning the righteous deeds.

Alladhina aaminu wa 'amilu al saalihaat.[86]

ٱلَّذِينَ ءَامَنُوا۟ وَعَمِلُوا۟ ٱلصَّـٰلِحَـٰتِ

وَٱلَّذِينَ ءَامَنُوا۟ وَعَمِلُوا۟ ٱلصَّـٰلِحَـٰتِ أُو۟لَـٰٓئِكَ أَصْحَـٰبُ ٱلْجَنَّةِ ۖ هُمْ فِيهَا خَـٰلِدُونَ

But those who believe and work righteousness.
They are Companions of the Garden: therein shall
they abide (forever). (Al-Baqarah 2:82, Koran)

[86] Koran 2:25; 2:82, 277; 4:57, 122; 5:5; 7:42; 10:9; 11:23; 13:29; 14:23; 18:2, 88, 107; 19:60, 96; 20:75, 82, 112; 21:94; 22:14; 23:50, 56; 24:55; 25:70–71; 26:67; 28:80; 29:7, 9, 58; 30:15, 45; 31:8; 32:19; 34:4, 37; 38:24; 41:8; 42:22–23, 26; 45:21, 30; 47:2, 12; 48:29; 64:9; 65:11; 84:25; 85:11; 95:6; 98:7; 103:3.

إِنَّ ٱلَّذِينَ ءَامَنُوا۟ وَعَمِلُوا۟ ٱلصَّٰلِحَٰتِ وَأَقَامُوا۟ ٱلصَّلَوٰةَ وَءَاتَوُا۟ ٱلزَّكَوٰةَ لَهُمْ أَجْرُهُمْ عِندَ رَبِّهِمْ وَلَا خَوْفٌ عَلَيْهِمْ وَلَا هُمْ يَحْزَنُونَ

﴿٢٧٧﴾

Those who believe, do deeds of righteousness and
establish regular prayers and regular charity, will have
their reward with their Lord: on them shall be no fear,
nor shall they grieve. (Al-Baqarah 2:277, Koran)

وَأَمَّا ٱلَّذِينَ ءَامَنُوا۟ وَعَمِلُوا۟ ٱلصَّٰلِحَٰتِ فَيُوَفِّيهِمْ أُجُورَهُمْ ۗ وَٱللَّهُ لَا يُحِبُّ ٱلظَّٰلِمِينَ ﴿٥٧﴾

As to those who believe and work righteousness,
Allah will pay them in full their reward;
but Allah loves not those who do wrong
(zalimeen). (Ali 'Imran 3:57, Koran)

وَٱلَّذِينَ ءَامَنُوا۟ وَعَمِلُوا۟ ٱلصَّٰلِحَٰتِ سَنُدْخِلُهُمْ جَنَّٰتٍ تَجْرِى مِن تَحْتِهَا ٱلْأَنْهَٰرُ خَٰلِدِينَ فِيهَآ أَبَدًا ۖ لَّهُمْ فِيهَآ أَزْوَٰجٌ مُّطَهَّرَةٌ ۖ وَنُدْخِلُهُمْ ظِلًّا

ظَلِيلًا ﴿٥٧﴾

But those who believe and do deeds of righteousness,
We shall soon admit to Gardens, with rivers flowing
beneath, their eternal home and therein shall they have
companions pure and holy: We shall admit them to
shades, cool and ever deepening. (An-Nisa 4:57, Koran)

وَٱلَّذِينَ ءَامَنُوا۟ وَعَمِلُوا۟ ٱلصَّٰلِحَٰتِ سَنُدْخِلُهُمْ جَنَّٰتٍ تَجْرِى مِن تَحْتِهَا ٱلْأَنْهَٰرُ خَٰلِدِينَ فِيهَآ أَبَدًا ۖ وَعْدَ ٱللَّهِ حَقًّا ۚ وَمَنْ أَصْدَقُ مِنَ ٱللَّهِ

قِيلًا ﴿١٢٢﴾

But those who believe and do deeds of righteousness,
We shall soon admit them to Gardens – with

rivers flowing beneath – to dwell therein forever. Allah's promise is the truth and whose word can be truer than Allah's? (An-Nisa 4:122, Koran)

وَمَن يَعْمَلْ مِنَ ٱلصَّٰلِحَٰتِ مِن ذَكَرٍ أَوْ أُنثَىٰ وَهُوَ مُؤْمِنٌ فَأُو۟لَٰٓئِكَ يَدْخُلُونَ ٱلْجَنَّةَ وَلَا يُظْلَمُونَ نَقِيرًا

If any do deeds of righteousness, be they male or female and have faith, they will enter Heaven and not the least injustice will be done to them. (An-Nisa 4:124, Koran)

فَأَمَّا ٱلَّذِينَ ءَامَنُوا۟ وَعَمِلُوا۟ ٱلصَّٰلِحَٰتِ فَيُوَفِّيهِمْ أُجُورَهُمْ وَيَزِيدُهُم مِّن فَضْلِهِۦ ۖ وَأَمَّا ٱلَّذِينَ ٱسْتَنكَفُوا۟ وَٱسْتَكْبَرُوا۟ فَيُعَذِّبُهُمْ عَذَابًا

أَلِيمًا وَلَا يَجِدُونَ لَهُم مِّن دُونِ ٱللَّهِ وَلِيًّا وَلَا نَصِيرًا ﴿١٧٣﴾

But to those who believe and do deeds of righteousness, He will give their due rewards and more, out of His bounty: but those who are disdainful and arrogant, He will not punish with a grievous penalty; nor will they find, besides Allah, any to protect or help them. (An-Nisa 4:173, Koran)

وَعَدَ ٱللَّهُ ٱلَّذِينَ ءَامَنُوا۟ وَعَمِلُوا۟ ٱلصَّٰلِحَٰتِ لَهُم مَّغْفِرَةٌ وَأَجْرٌ عَظِيمٌ ﴿٩﴾

To those who believe and do deeds of righteousness hath Allah promised forgiveness and a great reward. (Al-Ma'idah 5:9, Koran)

لَيْسَ عَلَى ٱلَّذِينَ ءَامَنُوا۟ وَعَمِلُوا۟ ٱلصَّٰلِحَٰتِ جُنَاحٌ فِيمَا طَعِمُوٓا۟ إِذَا مَا ٱتَّقَوا۟ وَّءَامَنُوا۟ وَعَمِلُوا۟ ٱلصَّٰلِحَٰتِ ثُمَّ ٱتَّقَوا۟ وَّءَامَنُوا۟ ثُمَّ ٱتَّقَوا۟
وَّأَحْسَنُوا۟ ۗ وَٱللَّهُ يُحِبُّ ٱلْمُحْسِنِينَ ﴿٩٣﴾

On those who believe and do deeds of righteousness there is no blame for what they ate (in the past), when they guard themselves from evil and believe and do deeds of righteousness - (or) again, guard themselves from evil and believe,(or) again, guard themselves from evil and do good. For Allah loves those who do good. (Al Ma'idah 5:93, Koran)

وَٱلَّذِينَ ءَامَنُوا۟ وَعَمِلُوا۟ ٱلصَّٰلِحَٰتِ لَا نُكَلِّفُ نَفْسًا إِلَّا وُسْعَهَآ أُو۟لَٰٓئِكَ أَصْحَٰبُ ٱلْجَنَّةِ ۖ هُمْ فِيهَا خَٰلِدُونَ ﴿٤٢﴾

But those who believe and work righteousness - no burden do We place on any soul, but that which it can bear - they will be Companions of the Garden, therein to dwell (forever). (Al-A'raf 7:42, Koran)

إِلَيْهِ مَرْجِعُكُمْ جَمِيعًا ۖ وَعْدَ ٱللَّهِ حَقًّا ۚ إِنَّهُۥ يَبْدَؤُا۟ ٱلْخَلْقَ ثُمَّ يُعِيدُهُۥ لِيَجْزِىَ ٱلَّذِينَ ءَامَنُوا۟ وَعَمِلُوا۟ ٱلصَّٰلِحَٰتِ بِٱلْقِسْطِ ۚ وَٱلَّذِينَ كَفَرُوا۟
لَهُمْ شَرَابٌ مِّنْ حَمِيمٍ وَعَذَابٌ أَلِيمٌۢ بِمَا كَانُوا۟ يَكْفُرُونَ ﴿٤﴾

To Him will be your return, of all of you. The promise of Allah is true and sure. It is He Who began the Creation and its cycle, that He may reward with justice those who believe and work righteousness; but those who reject Him will have draughts of boiling fluids and a Penalty grievous, because they did reject Him. (Yunus 10:4, Koran)

إِنَّ ٱلَّذِينَ ءَامَنُوا۟ وَعَمِلُوا۟ ٱلصَّٰلِحَٰتِ يَهْدِيهِمْ رَبُّهُم بِإِيمَٰنِهِمْ ۖ تَجْرِى مِن تَحْتِهِمُ ٱلْأَنْهَٰرُ فِى جَنَّٰتِ ٱلنَّعِيمِ ﴿٩﴾

Those who believe and work righteousness, their Lord
will guide them because of their Faith: beneath them
will flow rivers in Gardens of Bliss. (Yunus 10:9, Koran)

إِنَّ ٱلَّذِينَ ءَامَنُوا۟ وَعَمِلُوا۟ ٱلصَّٰلِحَٰتِ وَأَخْبَتُوٓا۟ إِلَىٰ رَبِّهِمْ أُو۟لَٰٓئِكَ أَصْحَٰبُ ٱلْجَنَّةِ ۖ هُمْ فِيهَا خَٰلِدُونَ ﴿٢٣﴾

But those who believe and work righteousness
and humble themselves before their Lord,
they will be Companions of the Garden, to
dwell therein forever! (Hud 11:23, Koran)

ٱلَّذِينَ ءَامَنُوا۟ وَعَمِلُوا۟ ٱلصَّٰلِحَٰتِ طُوبَىٰ لَهُمْ وَحُسْنُ مَـَٔابٍ ﴿٢٩﴾

For those who believe and work righteousness
is every blessedness and a beautiful place of
(final) return. (Ar-Ra'd 13:29, Koran)

Islam is concerned with everyday activities of the believer, differentiating right from wrong and guiding the individual along the correct path. It defines *sin* as "breaking the commandments of Allah" and *good works* as "following Allah's instructions and the prophet's teachings."

Iman adds a dimension to the understanding of human activity in that every human action in daily life reaches back into the divine reality that everything in the universe is governed by tawhid, yet Allah has granted humans a freedom of choice, which can upset the balance in the creation, the balance of justice, and the balance of atmospheric elements and of environmental pollution and lead to the destruction of animal species, populations, cities, and agriculture through human actions. It tells people why they should be Allah's servants and explains which path they should follow to become His vicegerents. It makes clear that human activity is deeply rooted in the Real, and this has everlasting repercussions in this world and in the hereafter.

Ihsan adds to *islam* and *iman* a focus on people's intention to perform good and wholesome deeds on the basis of awareness of Allah's presence in all things. According to the Koran, doing wholesome deeds, along with faith, will yield paradise.

وَمَنْ عَمِلَ صَٰلِحًا مِّن ذَكَرٍ أَوْ أُنثَىٰ وَهُوَ مُؤْمِنٌ فَأُو۟لَٰٓئِكَ يَدْخُلُونَ ٱلْجَنَّةَ يُرْزَقُونَ فِيهَا بِغَيْرِ حِسَابٍ

Whoso does wholesome deeds, be it male or female
and has faith, shall enter the garden, therein provided
for without reckoning. (Ghafir 40:40, Koran)

وَٱلَّذِينَ ءَامَنُوا۟ وَعَمِلُوا۟ ٱلصَّٰلِحَٰتِ سَنُدْخِلُهُمْ جَنَّٰتٍ تَجْرِى مِن تَحْتِهَا ٱلْأَنْهَٰرُ خَٰلِدِينَ فِيهَآ أَبَدًا ۖ لَّهُمْ فِيهَآ أَزْوَٰجٌ مُّطَهَّرَةٌ ۖ وَنُدْخِلُهُمْ ظِلًّا

ظَلِيلًا ﴿٥٧﴾

Those who have faith and do wholesome deeds,
them we shall admit to gardens through which
rivers flow. (An-Nisa 4:57, 122, Koran)

Another fifty verses in the Koran mention that people who perform beautiful deeds and have faith shall inherit the garden. The Koran uses the word *saalihaat* for beautiful and wholesome deeds and the word *salihun* for wholesome people. The root word for both *saalihaat* and *salihun* means "to be beautiful, sound, wholesome, right, proper, and good." Another word used in the Koran about thirty times is *islah*, which means "establishing wholesomeness." In modern times, the word *islah* has been used to mean "reform." The word *sulh* is used in the Koran once to mean "peace and harmony in family relationships." In modern times, the word *sulh* has come to mean "peace in the political sense." While the Koran calls the wholesome people as *salihun*, it employs the opposite, *fasid*, for the corrupt, ruined, evil, and wrong. The wholesome are the ones who live in harmony with the Real (*Haqq*) and establish wholesomeness through their words and deeds throughout the world. In contrast, the corrupt (*mufsidun*) destroy the proper balance and relationship with Allah and His creation. *Fasid* means "corrupt, evil, and wrong."

Allah measures out good and evil, the wholesome and the corrupt. Humans have enough freedom to make their own choices; if they make the choice to do beautiful and wholesome deeds (*saalihaat*) motivated by faith (*iman*)) and god-wariness (*taqwa*), they please Allah and bring harmony and wholesomeness to the world, resulting in peace, justice, mercy, compassion, honor, equity, well-being, freedom, and many other gifts through Allah's grace. Others choose to do evil and work with corruption (*mufsidun*), destroying the right relationship among the creation, causing hunger, disease, oppression, pollution, and other afflictions. In the universal order, corruption is the prerogative of humans, and vicegerency gives humans the freedom to work against the Creator and His creation. Only misapplied trust can explain how moral evil can appear in the world. Modern technology; scientific advancement; nuclear, chemical, and biological weapons of mass destruction; genetic engineering of plants, animals, and humans; and exploitation of nonrenewable resources of the earth have made destruction of the human race and all life on the planet a distinct and imminent possibility.

ظَهَرَ ٱلْفَسَادُ فِى ٱلْبَرِّ وَٱلْبَحْرِ بِمَا كَسَبَتْ أَيْدِى ٱلنَّاسِ لِيُذِيقَهُم بَعْضَ ٱلَّذِى عَمِلُوا۟ لَعَلَّهُمْ يَرْجِعُونَ ﴿٤١﴾

Corruption has appeared on the land and
in the sea because what people's hands have
earned, so that He may let them taste some of
their deeds, in order that they may turn back
from their evils. (Ar-Rum 30:41, Koran)

When humans choose wrong and corrupt actions, they displease Allah. Allah loves those who do what is beautiful, not those who do what is ugly:

وَإِذَا تَوَلَّىٰ سَعَىٰ فِى ٱلْأَرْضِ لِيُفْسِدَ فِيهَا وَيُهْلِكَ ٱلْحَرْثَ وَٱلنَّسْلَ ۗ وَٱللَّهُ لَا يُحِبُّ ٱلْفَسَادَ ﴿٢٠٥﴾

When he turns his back, he hurries about the
earth to work corruption there and destroy
the tillage and the stock. Allah loves not
corruption. (Al-Baqarah 2:205, Koran)

Allah loves doing what is beautiful, and because of His love for those who do the beautiful, He brings them near Him, and His nearness is called Allah's mercy:

وَلَا تُفْسِدُوا۟ فِى ٱلْأَرْضِ بَعْدَ إِصْلَٰحِهَا وَٱدْعُوهُ خَوْفًا وَطَمَعًا ۚ إِنَّ رَحْمَتَ ٱللَّهِ قَرِيبٌ مِّنَ ٱلْمُحْسِنِينَ

Work not corruption in this world after it has
made wholesome and call upon Allah in fear and
hope. Surely the mercy of Allah is near to those
who do what is beautiful. (Al-A'raf 7:56, Koran)

The covenant of the Koran presents us the scope of the freedom of choice that humans have in doing what is wholesome and beautiful or what is corrupt or ugly. The human's role among the creation distinguishes right activity, right thought, and right intention from their opposites. It reminds us of how the scales of Allah's justice, the two hands of Allah—His mercy and His wrath—are reflected in the human domain, where people have been appointed Allah's vicegerents. Deeds of goodness and wholesomeness are associated with mercy, paradise, and the beautiful. Evil and corruption is rewarded with wrath, hell, and the ugly.

Chapter Eight

The Plunder of the World's Wealth through Deceit

Allah is the Master of His universe, the King, the Knower and Wise. Fourteen hundred years had passed by since Allah commanded Angel Jibraeel to reveal the message of His mercy to the blessed Muhammad for humankind. What had transpired in those years, and how did those who embraced Allah's Message fare in their quest? Were the angel Jibraeel to return to see for himself the state of *din* of Allah, what would he find?

The earth is shrouded in a veil, and this veil is woven of filaments as in a net that covers the whole expanse of the world. Beneath this veil is the world—the world that Allah has bequeathed to His vicegerent, human. These veils are of secrecy and concealment made up of filaments of connections between the conspiring groups that have taken over the control of the economy of the human world. The earth has not much changed in appearance except that most of the forests have gone. The earth is studded with sprawling cities, spewing smoke, and pollution. The oceans and the earth are covered with human waste and garbage.

The earth now has been divided into vast network of enclosures or *kraals* called countries. Each Muslim kraal is fenced in, and there are over a sixty of them. Every kraal has a name, and each has a million to several hundred million humans living within its fenced domain.

All adult humans work, some independently, and others carry out assigned chores daily by others. After each day's work, they go to their dwellings to sleep for six to seven hours and then return to their assigned place the next day. People seem to work and work, and very seldom do they sit down to play, meditate, or socialize. At the end of their work period, each worker receives a paper called "money" that has a value or a denomination. This paper pays for the people's needs such as food, clothing, and services such as health care.

People are confined to their kraal. Each kraal has huge dimensions, and people do not realize that they are confined, even though they cannot leave or enter their kraal without a special "permission" called *passport*, which is checked electronically to determine the passport holder's recent whereabouts. The kraal people are constantly scrutinized by armed gendarme called "police" for their own safety. Each person in the kraal is indoctrinated into a prescribed behavior, and those who conform to this requirement are called the *law-abiding citizens* of the land.

Jibraeel will notice that each kraal or country has a regime of rulers that govern its people. The regimes are made up of kings, dictators, presidents, prime ministers, and other politicians. They are called establishments, administrations, and governments. The angel Jibraeel will not have failed to notice that members of these regimes—the kings, the conquerors, and their ministers—through the history of the kraals of empires and political countries began their careers as brigands, crooks, and criminals. They began by enlisting warriors in hundreds or thousands to attack and capture lands, populations, wealth, and resources. These lands became their empires. These marauders became kings and emperors, and the people became their subjects to be shorn of their labor, wealth, and honor.

The rulers are served by standing armies of several hundred thousand soldiers. The armies protect the regimes from their subjects and from the armies of other kraals. Armies are equipped with threatening weapons to intimidate and scare their own citizens and those of other kraals.

Regimes aim to preserve their power over their people. Armies guard and protect the establishments. They employ secret intelligence services to seek and destroy their opponents. There is a soft side to their dealings with their citizens too. It is the propaganda. News media, television, and radio—the instruments of brainwashing—are controlled or influenced by the governments. In this mode of brainwashing, the kraal people are called "the free society," and the repressive regime becomes "the free democracy" or "*the society of ijma*," the repressive army "*the defense force*," and the government propaganda "*the free press*."

The people of the American and European kraals subscribe to the Christian faith. Sixty or so kraals in South Asia, Middle East, and Africa are Muslims. Kraals in India are mostly Hindu.

Each kraal has God-given wealth of natural resources. All resources of minerals, rich land, agriculture, and food products are commandeered by the elite of the regime. Armies of rich kraals invade the weaker kraals and rob them of their resources by capturing their land, harbors, and sea-lanes. With such resource grab, 80 percent of the world's wealth is in the hands of 2 percent of the world's people. The wealth is in the hands of secret cartels and cabals that control the regimes of the world, their elite, universities, and religions through their priests and mullahs.

Angel Jibraeel will also notice that the precious metals from all the world, through the acquiescence of the rulers and politicians, are centralized in the hands of cartels in secret underground vaults. Eighty percent of the world's diamonds are hoarded in an underground vault under London, England, and fifteen thousand tons of gold is stored in London and Switzerland. All the world's oil is traded in paper money printed in the United States, and the profit of the mining and distribution of the world's hydrocarbons ends up in the hands of the same 2 percent of the people.

Angel Jibraeel recited the passage of prohibition of usury to the blessed Nabi Muhammad. He will be utterly amazed to find that deception, usury, and fakery runs the engine of the world's economy. Satan has out maneuvered the forces of good. Through extraordinarily smart maneuvering, several thousand families who all know one another have outsmarted the kraal people of the world. While the people of the world have been confined to their kraals, ignorant of their immediate neighborhood, a small group of people have managed the greatest hoax in the history of the world.

Money: People have traded with one another since time immemorial. Before the imposition of the kraal system, there was widespread use of money; trading involved the simplest use of commercial transaction—barter, which is the exchange of two or more products of roughly equal value. Gold and silver became accepted as money nearly five thousand years ago in most cultures. The earliest gold coins were found in the ruins of Sumer, minted nearly five thousand years ago. Coins of measured value have been routinely minted from precious metals in most cultures. The value of such coins was equal to the labor required to produce any other item that this treasure could buy. Over thousands of years, gold has been regarded as money, known as commodity money.

In the Islamic monetary system, gold and silver coins were minted at the command of the sovereign and used as legal tender in trade and commerce. The value of gold over the centuries continued to be stable among trading nations. Gold and silver coins were traded in exchange for commodities, services, and government expenditure. Soldiers were paid in gold or silver coins, and meritorious services rendered were rewarded with titles to estates owned by the state. Wars were expensive and therefore, by necessity, short. State revenue was collected through taxation of the populace in gold or commodities. In just societies, the subjects were protected with justice, and education, health, and social services were provided through voluntary donation of zakat by the population. Warfare was only defensive. All the offensive wars perpetrated by Muslim rulers against one another were for self-aggrandizement, conquest, and plunder and all strictly forbidden by the Koran. History of such rulers showed that most were gangsters who, along with a few armed followers, took control of the centers of power and terrorized their subjects and neighboring states.

Fraud: From the beginning, coveting an increased amount of money supply led to fraudulent practices that, in turn, caused destruction to honest trade and commerce. Unscrupulous merchants began to shave a tiny portion of each coin they received and then melted it down into new coins. Before long, the king's treasury started doing the same to the coins it received in taxes. In this way, money supply was increased, but the amount of gold was not. This subterfuge initially succeeded, but the end result was what always happens when money supply is artificially expanded—there was inflation. Whereas one coin previously would buy twelve sheep, now it was accepted for only ten. The total amount of gold needed for twelve sheep never really changed. Everyone knew that one coin did not contain the same amount of gold.

The governments became bolder in their plans to exploit their subjects. They began to dilute the amount of gold and silver content in the coins by adding base metals in the coins; thus, the coins appeared to be of the same size and color. People wisely discounted the coins, and the real value of goods and services and gold stayed the same.

Governments do not like to be thwarted in their plans to exploit people. So they found a way to force people to accept these tokens of money. This led to the first legal tender laws. By royal decree, the *coin of the realm* was declared legal for the settlement of debts and payment of taxes. Anyone who refused it at face value was subject to fine or imprisonment.

The business of banking began in Europe in the fourteenth century. Its function was to evaluate exchange and safeguard people's coins. In the beginning, there were notable examples of totally honest banks that operated with remarkable efficiency considering the vast variety of coins they handled. They also issued paper receipts that were so dependable that they freely circulated as money and cheated no one in the process. But there was more demand for money and loans, and the temptation soon caused the bankers to seek easier paths. They began lending out pieces of paper that *said* that they were receipts but, in effect, were counterfeit. The public could not tell one from the other and accepted both of them as money. From that point forward, the receipts in circulation exceeded the gold held in reserve, and the age of *fractional reserve banking* had dawned. This led immediately to what would become the unbroken record from then to the present—a record of inflation, booms and busts, suspension of payments, bank failures, repudiation of currencies, and recurring spasms of economic chaos.

The Bank of England was set up in 1694 to institutionalize fractional reserve banking. As the world's first central bank, it introduced the concept of partnership between bankers and politicians. The politicians would receive spendable money (created out of nothing by the bankers) without having to raise taxes. In return, the bankers would receive a commission on the transaction deceptively called *interest*, which would continue in perpetuity. Since it all seemed to be wrapped up in mysterious rituals of banking that the common man was not expected to understand, there was practically no opposition to the scheme. The arrangement proved to be so profitable to the participants that it soon spread to so many other countries in Europe and eventually to the United States[87].

The First and Second World Wars greatly weakened the old imperial countries' economy as almost all their gold had been traded for war

[87] G. Edward Griffin, The Creature from Jekyll Island (American Media), 183.

material, purchased from the United States. Having lost their gold reserves, the imperial European powers kept on printing money to continue their wars of acquisition. Their colonial populations were drained of their resources with a systematic pillage of their wealth through subtle trading maneuvers. Colonial produce from India, Africa, and the Middle East was first bought with printed paper money. A million-pound sterling note—which cost less than twenty pounds to print, money created out of nothing—was used to purchase cotton, rubber, oil, and metal ore, among other items, and exported directly to Britain or to the United States of America.

During the second half of the nineteenth century and the twentieth century, there was a systematic transfer of wealth from the third world countries to the West. The Western countries through their monopolies in shipping, insurance, banking, and manufacturing industries further multiplied their acquired wealth a hundredfold.

Banking: Among the first bankers in the Western world were the Knights Templar after their return from their Crusades against the Muslims. They had accumulated an immense amount of wealth; they were given enormous riches by the Christians supporting the Crusades against Islam by bestowing legacies, hoping to buy their place in heaven. The Knights Templar also obtained an enormous amount of wealth through loot and plunder of Christian gold and treasures of Constantinople on their way to the Holy Land. More gold and riches were accumulated by them during the rape and plunder of the Muslim lands of Syria and Palestine. The Knights Templar set up their temples in Paris and London and turned them from sleepy hamlets into great financial centers. King Phillip IV of France, in league with Pope Clement V, destroyed the Knights Templar and stole their fortune. The Order of the Knights Templar then went underground to work and plot secretly within other organizations. The world had a strict ban on usury, and as the time passed, this was forgotten, and banking began to develop, which now holds a tight clutch on humanity.

Gold as Currency: The currency at that time was gold and silver, and for safety reasons, the owners began to deposit their wealth with the goldsmiths, who had suitable strong rooms for storage and safekeeping. The goldsmiths issued paper receipts for gold and silver deposited with them. The depositors would pay their debts and expenses by withdrawing a portion of their gold and silver deposits, as necessary. It was obviously a cumbersome process to move all the precious metals, and paper receipts slowly became accepted as currency. Gold and silver were rarely moved, but the ownership changed with the issuing of receipts to pay the debts. Goldsmiths charged storage fee and transaction charges for each receipt. In the same manner today, vast fortunes are made by simply moving numbers between one computer file to another.

The Road to Haram: The goldsmiths and other owners of the strong rooms began to realize that, at any one time, only a fraction of gold and silver was being withdrawn by the owners. So they began to issue notes (money) to people who did not own gold and silver and charge them interest on the notes. The only way their dishonesty would be discovered was if they issued too many notes and if every one of the gold and silver depositors tried to withdraw it at the same time. They began to issue notes for the ownership of the gold and silver greatly more than what they had deposited in their vaults. They began to issue an increasing number of notes depending on the gold and silver that the *"banks" did not even have in their vaults.* And they earned interest on the fictitious gold that did not exist. They could issue lots of bits and pieces of paper for gold and silver that did not exist and charge interest in doing so. In other words, a trick was perpetrated by lending gold and silver that did not exist and that they did not own. And profit was made out of nothing. This whole system of transactions was based on fraud and deceit. *In summary, this is the description of modern banking and the world's financial system.*

In the eighteenth century, there was a major leap in the banking system's influence over world finance. This occurred with the emergence and rapid rise of dominance of one Jewish family, the house of Rothschild. Mayer Amschel Bauer was born in 1743 in Frankfurt, Germany. He worked briefly for the Oppenheimer Bank in Hanover and later became a moneylender. He acted as an agent for William IX, landgrave of Hesse-Kassel. Williams's family made a fortune by hiring out troops to Britain to fight in the American War of Independence. The Rothschild Empire was built on money embezzled by Mayer Amschel from William, who in turn had stolen it from the soldiers he had hired out to the British. The money, said to have been around three million dollars, was paid by the British government to William to be paid to the soldiers but was kept by William for himself.[88] William gave the money to Mayer Amschel Bauer to hide it from Napoleon's armies, but instead, Bauer sent it to England hidden in casks of wine with his son Nathan to establish a London branch of the family empire.

Nathan used the money to buy vast quantities of gold looted by the East India Company from India (Battle of Plassey) and used this gold to finance the Duke of Wellington's military adventures. Nathan was able to brag later that, in the five years he had been in England, he increased his original investment given by his father by 2500 times to 50 million pounds, comparable to purchasing power of billions of dollars today. It was around the time of Nathan's arrival in London that Mayer Bauer changed his name to Rothschild after the red shield emblem on the ghetto home of his ancestors to avoid anti-Semitism, prevalent in Europe in those days.

[88] George Armstrong, *Rothschild Money Trust* (1940), 22.

Mayer and his eldest son, Amschel, supervised the family banking business from their Frankfurt bank, son Nathan Mayer established the London branch in 1804, and the youngest son joined the Paris banking circles in 1811 while son Solomon started operating in Vienna and Karl in Naples. To prevent prying eyes, the family wrote all correspondence in *Judendeutch*, German written in Hebrew characters.

According to the *New Encyclopedia Britannica*, "Mayer set a pattern that his family was to follow so successfully, to do business with reigning houses by preference and to father as many sons as possible who could take care of the family's many business affairs abroad."

"From the earliest days, the Rothschild appreciated the importance of proximity to politicians, the men who determined not only the extent of budget deficit but also the domestic and foreign policies," wrote biographer Niall Fergusson. "Rothschild influence extended to royalty as well. Nathan first came into contact with British royalty thanks to his father's purchase of outstanding debts owed by George, Prince Regent, Later King George IV and his brothers."[89]

Ferguson traced the Rothschilds' influence through British royalty to Queen Victoria's consort, Prince Albert, and his son. The Rothschilds were quite close to most prominent British politicians such as Lord John Russell, Lord William Gladstone, Benjamin Disraeli, Arthur Balfour, Joseph Chamberlain, Lord Randolph Churchill, and his son Winston Churchill. The Rothschilds ingratiated themselves with the British politicians financially, and in return, most subtly influenced British foreign and fiscal policies. The Churchill family had a long-standing relationship with the Rothschilds. Winston Churchill's father, Randolph Churchill, was funded by the house of Rothschild while he was the British chancellor of the exchequer in the mid-1800s. Randolph died owing sixty-five thousand pounds to the Rothschilds

[89] Niall Ferguson, *The House of Rothschild* (New York: Viking, 1998), 9.

when, in comparison, the total British government annual revenue was only ten million pounds.[90] Not only was the loan forgiven but more funds were also advanced to his son Winston by his good friend Lord Victor Rothschild. In return, Lord Victor Rothschild was granted full run of the British intelligence during the Second World War.[91]

The Rothschilds lent money that did not exist to finance wars, lending money to the opposing sides of the war, making immense profits from the interest. They also owned and controlled the armament industries from which the warring countries purchased weapons of destruction. The profits of war continued to multiply with the interest on the loans, commissions, sale of weapons, training of troops, and transport of weapons to the battlegrounds in Rothschild ships. When the warring countries have devastated each other with the help of money and weapons supplied by the bankers, the same banks then lent more money that did not exist to rebuild their shattered nations and economies. The reconstruction produced even greater profit than the sale of weapons of destruction. And through debt, the bankers controlled those countries' governments and their commerce and economy. The Rothschild Empire became highly skilled in such manipulations as did those in America, such as JPMorgan, and many others in Europe. Behind the smokescreen of the global banking empires, armament industries, oil companies, and global corporations conspiring to gain control of the world's wealth are the same few families and individuals. There is evidence to suggest that the house of Rothschild was behind the resurgence of both the great American banking empires, the Morgan's and the Rockefellers.

When Nathan Rothschild died, his eldest son, Lionel, became the head of the London Rothschilds. He advanced massive loans to the British

---

90 *The Churchills*, Independent Television, May 1995.

91 *Secret Societies*, 208.

and American governments as well as to the Egyptians. He lent eighty million pounds to the British government to finance the Crimean War, in which the Ottomans fought the Russians. Interestingly, he also acted as an agent to the Russian government for twenty years and loaned Russia the money to fight the Turks and the British during the Crimean War. The Ottomans received armaments and military assistance from the British in the Crimean War, which was engineered by Russia, France, and Britain in a dispute over which of the Christian churches would administer the holy Christian sites in Jerusalem. The Turkish populace paid for fifty years in gold and commodities, many times multiplied, the money lent by the Rothschilds in the Western-engineered war in which thousands perished. As a result, Egypt was occupied by the British on the pretext of nonpayment of this loan at the instigation of the Rothschilds. Turkey was drained of its lifeblood over usurious loans, the benefits of which never touched the population; the wars imposed caused suffering, poverty, humiliation, and in the end disintegration of the Ottoman Empire.

Lionel Rothschild was succeeded by his son Nathan Mayer, who became the first Lord Rothschild when he was raised to the peerage by Queen Victoria in 1885. He went on to become the governor of the Bank of England with untold power to influence the world's financial system. The Bank of England has always been an arm of the global elite who plotted and conspired to seize the wealth and territories of the world. The Rothschild representatives around the world continued to manipulate world events to expand their power and achieve world domination.

Al-Mutaffifeen: The Purveyors of Fraud

A group of global elite bankers created a network of central banks in each country working together to manipulate the financial system across Europe and the United States. These bankers—*al-Mutaffifeen*, dealers in fraud—have been described in the Koran:

﴿ وَيْلٌ لِّلْمُطَفِّفِينَ ۝١ ٱلَّذِينَ إِذَا ٱكْتَالُوا۟ عَلَى ٱلنَّاسِ يَسْتَوْفُونَ ۝٢ وَإِذَا كَالُوهُمْ أَو وَّزَنُوهُمْ يُخْسِرُونَ ۝٣ أَلَا يَظُنُّ أُو۟لَـٰٓئِكَ
أَنَّهُم مَّبْعُوثُونَ ۝٤ لِيَوْمٍ عَظِيمٍ ۝٥ يَوْمَ يَقُومُ ٱلنَّاسُ لِرَبِّ ٱلْعَـٰلَمِينَ ۝٦ كَلَّآ إِنَّ كِتَـٰبَ ٱلْفُجَّارِ لَفِى سِجِّينٍ ۝٧

Woe to those that deal in fraud, those who, when they have to receive by measure, from men, exact full measure, but when they have to give by measure or weight to men, give less than due. Do they not think that they will be called to account? On a Mighty Day, a Day when (all) mankind will stand before the Lord of the Worlds? Nay! Surely the Record of the Wicked is (preserved) in Sijjin. (Mutaffifeen 83:1-7, Koran)

Usury in Europe: A central bank in each country was an idea of the *Mutaffifeen*, the purveyors of fraud. The earlier central banks were opened in Amsterdam and Hamburg. The Bank of England soon followed. This bank, owned privately by the *Mutaffifeen*, started by lending money to the British government. The owners of the bank made fantastic profits, which came from the pockets of the common man, through income tax and the exploitation of the poor people of the British Empire. This was the beginning of the national debt, when nations began to be indebted to moneylenders who owned the banks.

The kings and politicians did not understand the workings of money. Therefore, the minting of money was given over to a committee that also had the authority to base the country's wealth on gold that was controlled and held by the *Mutaffifeen* bankers. The aristocrats and merchants who created the Bank of England and the East India Company also began to control the country's wealth. With this wealth, they rapidly created a merchant fleet and a private army. The trading corporations expanded their mercantile empires and began to control whole countries in South Asia and the Far East for the European kings and aristocracy. In time, these empires of the *Mutaffifeen* merchant bankers became the greatest drug operations the world has ever seen.

The *Mutaffifeen*—usurious, thieving drug barons—plundered gold, silver, and jewels from India, Burma, Ceylon, Indochina, China, Indonesia, Malaya, and the Philippines and used their ill-gotten wealth to influence world events. The *Mutaffifeen* bankers were involved in the American Civil War, in which they financed both sides. The London Rothschilds funded the North, and the Paris Rothschilds funded the South.

Usury in America: In the earlier part of the twentieth century, these bankers began planning the takeover of the world's largest economy, that of the United States. They wanted two things, a new central bank like the Bank of England to control the American nation's borrowing and the introduction of a federal income tax to give them control over the government's finances. There was serious opposition to this, but in classic *Mutaffifeen* fashion, in a clearly well-planned strategy, they duped the American Congress and the public. First, the *Mutaffifeen* bankers supported the election of Pres. Woodrow Wilson in 1909. He was a front man and a political puppet. The real power of the Wilson administration was in the hands of a man called Col. Edward Mandell House. Mandell House got the instructions from the banking conspirators, and he, in turn, instructed Woodrow Wilson, who did as he was told.

In 1902, the Rothschilds sent one of their agents, Paul Warburg, to America with his brother Felix to rearrange US banking to suit the Rothschilds and the *Mutaffifeen* interests. Another brother, Max Warburg, stayed at home in Frankfurt to run the family banking business there. Upon arrival in the United States, Paul Warburg married Nina Loeb of the Rothschild-controlled Kuhn, Loeb & Co. while Felix married Frieda Schiff, the daughter of Jacob Schiff, the head of Kuhn, Loeb & Co. Both brothers became partners in the company, and Paul was given a salary of half a million dollars. When Jacob Schiff arrived in America to join Kuhn, Loeb & Co., he married the daughter of Solomon Loeb. Schiff was to become the manipulator of American banking for over half a century. Schiff and the Rothschild family had shared the same house in Frankfurt in the days of Mayer Amschel.

The conspiring bankers met at a place called Jekyll Island in Georgia in greatest secrecy to put together the bill for the introduction of the new US central bank, the Federal Reserve System. For years, those who participated denied that such a gathering ever took place. The time of the meeting that supposedly "did not take place" was when the conspiring *Mutaffifeen* bankers took over the US economy and its people with an organization called the Federal Reserve System, which is neither federal nor does it have any reserves.

The secret seven who met in secrecy in Jekyll Island at J. P. Morgan's island resort off the coast of Georgia were Frank A. Vanderlip, Abraham Piatt Andrew, Henry P. Davison, Charles Norton, Benjamin Strong, Paul Warburg, and Sen. Nelson Aldrich. Frank A. Vanderlip represented William Rockefeller and Jacob Schiff's investment firm of Kuhn, Loeb & Co. Vanderlip later was to become the president of New York's National City Bank; Abraham Piatt Andrews the assistant secretary of the United States Treasury; Henry P. Davison a senior partner of J. P. Morgan and Company; Charles Norton the president of First National Bank of New York(a JPMorgan company); Benjamin Strong a Morgan lieutenant; Paul Warburg a partner of Kuhn, Loeb & Co.; and Rhode Island Republican senator Nelson Aldrich the chairman of the National Monetary Commission, the only nonbanker in the group. Aldrich was an associate of banker J. P. Morgan and father-in-law of John D. Rockefeller Jr. Warburg, a representative of the European Rothschilds, was brother to Max Warburg, chief of the M. M. Warburg & Co. banking consortium in Germany and the Netherlands.[92]

The conspirators representing the houses of Morgan, Rockefeller, and Rothschild came up with a plan to take control of the US banking system. These seven men, under the guidance of Paul Warburg, concluded not to have one central bank in the United States but several. They agreed that no one was to utter the words *central* or *bank*. Most importantly, they decided that their creation would be made to look like an official agency of the US government. This proposal came to be known as the Aldrich plan. From the beginning, the plan was ill fated and seen as a transparent attempt to create a system of bankers by the bankers and for the bankers. The proposal never got off the committee stage, and the bill was doomed.

A new tactic was then used by the banking *Mutaffifeen*. Congressman Carter Glass of Virginia was given the task of writing a new bill. Glass attacked the Aldrich plan and stated that it lacked government control and created a banking monopoly in the hands of the New York bankers; it opened the door to inflation. Glass then said that what the country needed was an entirely fresh approach, a genuine reform bill that was not written by the agents of the money trust. He then went on to draft an alternative, the Federal Reserve Act, which in every aspect was an exact image of the Aldrich plan.

Vanderlip and Aldrich spoke venomously against the Glass bill, even though Glass had cleverly incorporated entire sections of the Aldrich plan. It was clearly an effort to garner public support for the Glass bill by the appearance of banker opposition. President Wilson signed the Federal Reserve Act on December 23, 1913, just two days before Christmas, with some of the congressmen already home for the holidays and the average citizen's attention clearly elsewhere.

---

[92] Jim Marrs, *Rule by Secrecy* (HarperCollins), 70.

"Congress was outflanked, outfoxed and outclassed by a deceptive, but brilliant psycho-political attack," commented author Griffin in his well-researched book about the most blatant scam in history, the creation of the Federal Reserve System[93].

The Federal Reserve System is composed of twelve Federal Reserve banks, each serving a section of the United States, but each dominated by the New York Federal Reserve bank. The Federal Reserve System is such a pivotal force in the world economic system that financial experts in every nation pay close attention to any action it takes. Even the slightest interest rate change it makes can shake markets and create or destroy millions of jobs. It is important to know who controls the Fed. By using a central bank to create alternate periods of inflation and deflation and thus squeezing the public for vast profits, it has been worked out by international bankers into an exact science.

An examination of the major stockholders of New York banks shows clearly that a few families related by blood, marriage, or business interests still control New York City banks and, in turn, hold the controlling stock of the Federal Reserve Bank of New York. Eustace Mullins, in his 1983 book, *The Secrets of the Federal Reserve*, presented charts connecting the Federal Reserve Bank of New York and its member banks to the families of the Rothschilds, Morgan's, Rockefellers, Warburg's, and others. The private control of the Federal Reserve continues till today. The Federal Reserve Bank of New York completely dominates the other eleven branches through stock ownership, control, and influence by having the only permanent voting seat in the Federal Open Marketing Committee and handling all open market bond transactions. Two banks, Chase Manhattan Bank (merged with the Chemical Bank) and Citibank, own 53 percent of shares. These facts point to the reality that a handful of determined families control the economies of America and the world.

---

[93] Griffin, *Creature.*

Usury Takes over the World Economy: International Banking: The international banking system is based on the system developed in Europe over the last two hundred years and then grafted into the American economy. At the end of the Second World War, the economies of both the victors and the defeated in Europe and Japan were devastated and depleted of all gold reserves. The plans for a new international economic system were worked out by delegates from forty-four countries at the White Mountain Resort of Bretton Woods, New Hampshire, in 1944. No sovereign Islamic states were present.

The new economic system was the product of the collaboration between John Maynard Keynes, representing Britain, and Harry White of the US Treasury. Instead of an international economy where each nation's economy was backed by its stock of gold, the new system made the US dollar the centerpiece of the new structure. The dollar was supported by 75 percent of the world's stock of monetary gold. The US economy had been boosted by 30 percent during the Second World War, while the economies of Europe, Russia, China, Japan, and the colonial world had been thoroughly devastated. While rearming the allies and the conquest of the enemies, most of the world's monetary gold was transferred to the United States through arms sales and as rewards of the conqueror.

The Bretton Woods arrangements provided that the United States would be the only nation with a currency freely convertible into gold at a fixed value. Before this conference, currencies were exchanged in terms of their gold value, and the arrangement was called the "gold exchange standard," determined by how much gold they could buy in the open market. The Bretton Woods arrangements sought to recapture the advantage of gold standard while minimizing the pain imposed by the gold standard on countries that were buying too much, selling too little, and losing gold. The method by which it was to be accomplished was the same as the method devised in Jekyll Island to allow American banks to create money out of nothing without paying the penalty of having their currencies devalued by other banks. It was the establishment of a world central bank that would create common fiat money based on the dollar for all nations and then require them to inflate together at the same rate. There was to be a kind of common insurance fund that would rush that fiat money to any nation that temporarily needed to face down a run on its currency.

Secrecy: Throughout the history of man, the route to power and control of people and their riches has been through a maze of secrecy, deceitful manipulation, subterfuge, and conspiracy. During and after the European Crusades into the Islamic heartland, various Christian organizations from diverse lands of Europe began to band together into secret organizations to achieve different agendas. In time, they began to control and influence the ruling houses of Europe, the papacy and the church, and the centers that controlled commerce and wealth. Wars between the kingdoms of Europe rarely had to do with the interest of people, justice, freedom, or human rights. Wars were fought to promote the interests of these secret organizations, which were the power behind the kings and the church.

All royal dynasties of the world originated from a band of robbers who invaded a land and came to control the centers of power and wealth. Their first act of governance was to eliminate all opposition (execution, massacres), control the population through brute force (army and secret services), and control the wealth of the land (rob the previous holders of their gold, precious stones, mansions, and estates through taxation of peasants and merchants). The rulers put on fancy garb and sat on a raised platform. The collaborators were given gaudy robes, high-sounding titles, and estates. To perpetuate the largesse from the rulers, the hangers-on supported the prolongation of the dynasty. Such was the beginning of the "establishment," a system of control of instruments of political and military power and acquisition of wealth in the hand of a select few.

With new invaders and the turnover of dynasties, the hangers-on, the courtiers, and the conspirators, the power behind the new rulers never changed. The clans behind the throne, the elite, the parasites, and the leeches honed their skills through greed and lechery, programmed their genes through marriage and social connections, and kept their power through secret organizations and conspiracy. The British Empire and the European royalty are a clear example of this inherited and aristocratic control lasting over a thousand years. The sovereigns of Europe sent their armies to the East and the West to loot and rob. The marauding armies presented the monarch with the pick of the robbed gold, diamonds, and treasures that had been hoarded by generations of Indians and other Asians over thousands of years. In return, the grateful sovereign rewarded his thugs with knighthoods, lordships, and earldoms of the realm. Thugs were ennobled over the meaner subjects to create nobility that would be the backbone of the dynasty. The nobility was presented with charters to fleece Her Majesty's loyal subjects around the world through constitutional pillage by taxation and unjust monopolistic trading practices.

After the Second World War, with the total economic ruin of European colonial powers, there occurred involuntary emancipation of the colonial subjects. The European heartland was in total ruins; with no military might to control the world's wealth, Europe faced further economic and industrial disaster. Nations of Europe and the United States then got together to establish a world order to maintain their hegemony over the rest of the world. The United Nations was created on the corrupted foundation of the League of Nations. Through a carefully crafted world order and a preordained power structure, the United States, Russia, Britain, and France—through a veto power over the rest of the world—reigned supreme. The Security Council became the instrument of the big four to control the world. At that time, the only Islamic countries totally independent of foreign domination were Turkey and Afghanistan. Saudi Arabia, Iraq, Iran, Jordan, and Egypt were beholden to the British apron strings.

Other arrangements of control—the Bretton Woods Agreement, the International Monetary Fund, and the World Bank—were established to strengthen the Western grip over the world's resources. Toward the same end, the American Marshall Plan was inaugurated to rebuild and establish a united Europe with a single unified army, currency, and purpose meant for world domination. Such immaculate and secretive planning, coordination, and cooperation gave birth to the organization of the so-called G8 nations. The United States, Canada, Russia, Britain, France, Italy, Germany, and Japan formed the G8, a grouping of countries with a population of seven hundred million people dominating the world through superior technology, military power, economics, industrial manufacturing, trade, education, and transport. These countries are resource poor, and their economies will crumble if their access to cheap resources of the underdeveloped world is severed.

The greatest threat to the international and Islamic economy is the fiscal system designed at Bretton Woods that made the United States dollar the kingpin of the world's monetary order whereby the world has to acquire the dollar or the currency of G8 countries to buy the West's industrial goods or pay their debts. When Richard Nixon severed the link between gold and the dollar, the G8 countries began a bonanza of printing paper money twenty times their 1971 economic base. The United States Federal Reserve System, a privately owned banking system, was set up in the image of Bank of England to control the country's fiscal system. The USA, being the world's largest economy, influences the world's commercial base. The money supply of the USA and G8 countries is based on consumer demand. The money is printed by the Treasury and handed over to the central bank, or the Federal Reserve service, which in turn lends these notes created out of ink and paper at an interest rate determined by the Federal Reserve service. The commercial banks then loan out this "money made out of nothing" to the consumers at an additional interest rate generally calculated at prime rate fixed by the federal bank plus 1 to 5 percent, making a huge profit. The paper note printed by the treasury becomes *money* only when it is lent out to someone as the principal to be paid back with interest.

Almost all Western governments conduct business on deficit basis, meaning that they spent far greater money than they receive in revenue. The United States government had, by 1999, borrowed and accumulated a debt of $5.7 trillion. By 1997, the US government was paying out $350 billion in interest payments, amounting to the total revenues collected through personal income tax. The current US government debt is *$24 trillion* and growing by the minute. The debt of the American people is another $33 trillion when the total wealth of the whole world is estimated to be $330 trillion. With the printing of additional currency, the purchasing power of the dollar has continued to devalue by 5 percent each year since 1973. Therefore, the 2002 dollar has only 20 percent purchasing power of the 1972 dollar. In 2005, the third world farmers and workers had to labor fifteen hours to purchase industrial products produced by a European or American worker in one hour. In the same vein, the populations of the third world have to work five to seven times longer to service their international debt compared with what they did thirty years ago.

Islam and International Finance:

- The world's richest 2 percent of adults own more than half of the global household wealth, while half the world's population own only 1 percent, a UN report published in December 2006 showed.

- The study finds wealth to be more unequally distributed than income across countries, Anthony Shorrocks, director of the Helsinki-based UNU-WIDER that published the report, said at a press conference.
- The report, entitled "The World Distribution of Household Wealth," found that assets of $2,200 or more placed a household in the top half of world wealth distribution in 2000.
- To be among the most affluent 10 percent of adults required $61,000 in assets, while over $500,000 was needed to belong to the richest 1 percent. *This group of the most well off was made up of 37 million people.*
- Of these most well-off people, *9.25 million* live in the USA, *7.5 million* in Japan, *3.7 million* in Germany, *2.6 million* in Italy, *2.2 million* in Britain, and *1.5 million* each in France and Spain. *Eight million* are dispersed in the rest of the world.
- The concentration of wealth within countries was also found to vary significantly.
  "The share of the top 10 per cent (of wealth) ranges from around 40 per cent in China to 70 per cent in the United States, and higher still in other countries," the report authors said.
- In 2000, the year the data for the survey was collected, there were 499 dollar billionaires and 13 million millionaires throughout the world. These numbers were set to "rise fast in the next decade," the report said.
- These figures become distorted by the day and month.

From the above report it is clear that *2 percent* of the world's population owns more than 50 percent of world's wealth. More than 90 percent of these rich people live in the United States, Japan, Italy, Germany, Britain, Spain, France, and other parts of the West. More than 50 percent of the people of the world own less than 1 percent of the world's wealth.

The total wealth of the world is estimated to be *$330 trillion*. Of this, thirteen million individuals own *$14 trillion*. The world has three economic systems:

1. The international monetary system is based on usury and fake paper money. This system provides money for public, government, and commercial transactions. Its hub is the money printed by central banks, and it finances government expenditure, stocks and shares, commerce, industry, drug trade, currency transactions, and wars. Public and government debts are financed through this system. Most, if not all, real estate transactions are funded by debt; therefore, such wealth is illusory. The estimated fifty trillion debt accumulated by governments and people generates several layers of interest payments. The interest on the illusory wealth of debt everyday siphons into secret caches that constitute real wealth. This system is haram.
2. A secret and concealed economic system is outside the jurisdiction of all the world's people and governments and outside the public glare. Every year three trillion dollars from gains of usury, a trillion dollars from drug trade, and other trillions in profits from the world's gas and minerals go to the purchase of a hoard of gold, diamonds, other precious minerals, mines, agricultural lands, and other resources by a secret group of people. There is no accounting nor any disclosure of such hidden treasure. A few thousand families and secret societies hold this cache as a hedge against the day when all paper money and its illusory wealth will disappear with the shift of the decimal to the left, and its black ciphers will fade into red, and the paper will disintegrate into ashes, only to be blown into oblivion as if it never existed. This system is based on covetousness and greed.

3. The largest economy of the world involves four billion inhabitants of the world's poorest population. It is the *gift* economy that has existed since man began his journey on the earth. Land and resources belong to Allah and will continue to belong to Him. The gift of knowledge and material things is passed on from one human to the next, generation after generation. Every man is connected to the other through their connection with Allah. Everyone helps the other till there is no need, no hunger, and no suffering. This system has been in existence for thousands of years till man, in his greed and covetousness, invaded other lands for more and destroyed the balance that Allah had established. Humans trade goods and services at a mutually agreed value system. Goods in barter or precious metal represent the value of the transaction. And other transactions are in the way of Allah (*fi sabilillah*) when goods and services are exchanged without any expectation of gain. They are merely given to please Allah.

The Ongoing Grabbing of the World's Resources: Angel Jibraeel will have, by now, seen the success of Satan's master plan. It is the control of people and their economies by exploitation of the evil in men. It is the control of the world by a few covetous and evil people. Nineteenth and twentieth centuries brought the evil of greed and exploitation through manipulation and systemic introduction of usury in the world of finance.

The G8 summitry and its move for globalization of the world's trade and economy aims to perpetuate the control of the resources and labor of the third world and the Islamic nations. The aim of the G8 and their elite who dictate their policies of the West is to prevent the unification of the Islamic world through internal subversion, military coups, and creation of discord among Muslim nations (Iran and Iraq,

Iraq and Kuwait) and through the perpetuation of the Palestinian-Israeli conflict. Western support of incompetent and corrupt leaders of the Middle East—Reza Shah, Anwar Sadat, Hosni Mubarak, King Hussein of Jordan, Saddam Hussein, Fahd and Abdullah, and the current Saudi royalty—has muzzled the voice of the believer for the last three generations. For the price of a bit of flattery, a subtle threat, and a pocketful of money, Muslim generals, politicians, and princes have sold their countries' interests to the West. Musharraf put up for sale the sovereignty of Pakistan, Afghanistan, Central Asia, and Iraq to the Americans, renewing Western control over the resources and sovereignty of Islam for another century. Leaders of Islamic nations are watched for their vanity, submissiveness, megalomania, corruption, and lack of principles. Their weaknesses are scrutinized and analyzed. Accordingly, they are pampered with flattery, cash, and gifts and occasionally with blackmail and subtle threats till they singly or collectively become thoroughly emasculated, reminiscent of eunuchs prostrating in the presence of the king of the West in Washington. Before they know it, they have sold out their people's unity, sovereignty, resources, and dignity. All this does not occur accidentally. It is planned with care for years and executed by skillful players who have carefully studied the psyche and weaknesses of the Middle Eastern upstarts.

Conspiracy and intrigue for power and wealth has been with us since prehistoric times. Modern history is woven with the thread of intricate secrecy and planning that has affected the life of every person on this planet for the benefit of the few who control the wealth of the world. Cecil Rhodes, a fabulously wealthy Englishman, exploited the continent and peoples of Africa through gold and diamond mines in southern Africa. Rhodes, as a student at Oxford University, came under the influence of John Ruskin. Ruskin, a professor of fine arts, created a revolution in the thinking of the privileged undergraduates of Oxford and Cambridge Universities. Most of these students, upon graduation, went on to administer and govern far-flung colonies of the British Empire. For the rest of his life, Rhodes remained obsessed with Ruskin's philosophy of the creation of a world government centered on Britain.

As Rhodes's wealth grew with the exploitation of South African gold and diamonds, he established companies like De Beers Consolidated Mines and Consolidated Gold Fields. He became the prime minister of the Cape Colony and used his wealth to influence the parliamentary seats in Britain and South Africa. By the 1890s, he had a yearly income of a million pounds (when Britain's annual revenue was ten million pounds), most of which went to furthering his aims of a world government centered on Britain.

Rhodes planned and set up a secret society that would manipulate events in a way that led to the introduction of a centralized global control in the hands of a few select elite. The society came to be known by several names; one of them was the Round Table and another the Committee of Three Hundred. The society was structured on Illuminati and Freemasonic lines. There was an inner circle, the Society of the Elect, that knew exactly what the game and aim was; and the outer circle of friends, made up of influential people, could help the cause but did not always know the full implications or the ambitions of the Round Table. The Round Table's real manipulators were mostly those with real power rather than those with the *appearance* of power. Their names were not recorded in history like those of the famous politicians and generals, but they controlled the events far more than those documented by history books.

Such secret groups continue to control the world's economy. Ten Arabian clans have guaranteed the sale of all Muslim oil internationally against the worthless American paper dollar in return for protection of their thrones from the *ummah*. This economic slavery continues to impoverish the Muslims of the world to the present day.

Chapter Nine

Creating Prosperity through Allah's Covenant

Poverty creates hopelessness. Poverty is a state of existence in which man is deprived of adequate means of subsistence. Although riches and Allah's grace are in abundance, poverty comes about in situations when man is unable to avail the bounty, grace, and guiding hand that Allah offers to His creatures. Such a state of hopelessness occurs through abandonment of Allah's promise and lack of faith in the Creator and the Sustainer. Hope comes when man connects with Allah and lets His guiding light into his heart, and Allah's guiding hand leads man onto His path.

The blessed prophet once said that the span of life is akin to walking under the shade of a tree. Allah reveals to man the pitfalls in the path under shade of the tree of life that man treads during his life from the beginning to the end. With faith in Allah, hopelessness vanishes, and new doorways and pathways open. With the knowledge of Allah, light of hope overcomes the darkness of hopelessness. Greed and ego vanish, and peace overtakes depression. Without faith in Allah, greed gnaws at man, and the itch to acquire eats away into man's flesh. The more man has, the more he wants, and the worse is the world because of his presence.

At the beginning of the twenty-first century, the Muslim world is mired in poverty, hunger, disease, and hopelessness. It has not always been so. The state of affairs began to deteriorate after the sixteenth century, and it has gone downhill since then.

Muslim populations consisted of agriculturists, pastoralists, and artisans. And there were the merchants, who traded the products of the cultivators, pastoralists, and artisans of the countryside to the city folk. The city folk were dependent on manufacturing and trade, and they also procured food and services for other citizens. The city people became the backbone of the administrations of the cities and empires.

In the course of the last five hundred years, the events transformed the existing systems of agriculture, manufacturing, and trade, and this transformation was so rapid that the believers have not been able to adapt to their new conditions. Yet guidance is in the Koran.

When man began to walk the earth under the shade of the tree of life, Allah's bounty and grace was everywhere, there was abundance, and there was peace. Then some men, of their own accord, concluded that the balance of nature established by Allah was not to their liking, and they assumed the divine prerogative to alter the balance of things in the world. Since that time, the world has been taken over by those who believe that the privilege is their due and that they can assume this right over others. This cabal of privilege, wealth, and acquisition has perfected the art of survival to the point that, after every turmoil and tempest, they end up at the top like a buoy in water. After every trough and crest of the wave, the same people end up with the flag up at the top.

The other group of the vast majority constitutes 90 percent of the populations; the simple hardworking, honest, and devout people always end up at the bottom. This group is ill prepared, humble, poor, and always suffering. Allah sent thousands of prophets to teach this group the art of goodness and peace. The vast majority are believers of Allah; among them are Jews, Christians, Muslims, Hindus, Buddhists, and others. They are good and devout though weak and poor people who live in small communities with vast untapped treasures and reserves of riches. Over hundreds of years, cults from among them have formed international organisms that cooperate with one another to exploit the wealth and the resources of the world. Like chameleons, they merge into their populations and exploit them. Their loyalty is neither to Allah nor to their own people. Their God is their avarice and wealth.

Allah endows every man at birth with a soul and a body. Allah created heaven and earth to endow His creation with sustenance to nurture the body and soul of His creation. He provides for every living being for its life span. Every man arrives in the world without a baggage to walk under the shade of the tree of life and then departs similarly without any possessions. Man's body nourishes and flourishes with the fruits from the tree of life and his soul from those of the tree of knowledge through Allah's grace and bounty. The tree of life yields sufficient provisions for the needs of every living creature; Allah the Creator is also Allah the Provider.

The tree of knowledge endows every living creature with thoughts and ideas of goodness, truth, justice, mercy, compassion for other beings, love, unity, and many other things. However, a small number of humans defy Allah's commandments. Organized groups of such men prevent Allah's grace from reaching down to the common people. As a group, they subtly distort Allah's message to humans and encourage human behavior that makes wealth for themselves, though such actions displease Allah. Men have disrupted the flow of Allah's mercy and beneficence to His creation ever since humans began to walk under the shade of the tree of life.

There are four *curses* that that have plagued Allah's creation walking in the shade of the tree of life. At every stage of human existence, these four curses have subjected the human ego into temptations carefully laid out by the Satan in their path. Over and again, the prophets laid out Allah's commandments to humans for a clean, happy, and contented life. Yet for humans, Satan's lure prove to be too strong.

1. The cult of money and acquisition.
2. The priesthood.
3. The mercenary and state armies.
4. The rulers.

Allah has endowed the land of Islam with all the ingredients of wealth and prosperity. There should never be poverty, disease, or hunger in the Dar es Salaam.

Islam is founded on tawhid. Adherence to the covenant of Allah reforms the individual. Through *iman* (belief), salat, fasting, and *taqwa* of Allah, man becomes cognizant of *furqan*, the criterion that allows man to distinguish between good and evil and guides him to the straight path of Allah. In doing so, man performs good and wholesome deeds that please Allah. Acts of goodness and charity benefit their parents, their kin, their neighbors, the needy, the sick, and the rest of mankind. Such acts purify the believer. Remembrance of Allah, beseeching His forgiveness, praising His magnificence, and showing gratitude for His grace and mercy are the obligations of every man. Forgiving others for their trespasses cleans anger, grudges, and rancor. Humility wipes out the ego. All actions with the knowledge that Allah is with you and sees you whether you see Him not helps the believer walk the earth in the glow of Allah's love and mercy.

Walking in the straight path of Allah, the believer avoids the temptations and evil that Satan has placed in his path. The believer of Allah surrenders to His will. Such a surrender entails acceptance of the covenant of Allah, which requires a lifetime of service to Allah, and that entails performance of deeds of goodness in His cause.

Islam is a religion of faith, unity, love, truth, peace, justice, equality, and moderation. It emphasizes that humans should love Allah and His people. The believer's love of Allah brings him close to Allah, and acts of goodness toward people generate *humaneness*, love, and kindness toward other humans. Love and kindness is not any one virtue but is the source of all virtues. The believer's character literally represents the relationship between people and peoples. It is *co humanity*, the ability to live together in love, kindness, and humanity. Politeness, courtesy, love, respect, and etiquette of collegiality in salat prayers keep the rituals from becoming hollow and meaningless. This belief, action, and ritual promote the ethical content of the believer that nurtures his inner character and furthers the person's ethical maturation.

Thus, the *outer side* of the believer is conformity and the acceptance of social roles within his community, the *ummah*; the *inner side* is the cultivation of *nafs*, conscience, and character. This cultivation involves broader education and deep reflection of one's motives and actions. It is a lifetime commitment to build, carve, and polish the stone of one's character until it becomes a lustrous gem. It is the lack of will, paucity of conscience, and insincerity of character that leave a person unprepared to accept his fellow human and believer as his brother and sister. When people lack commitment to the fellowship of Allah, it leaves them in the predicament of want, poverty, and hunger. It is the lack of understanding of the concept of unity, equality, and fraternity within the fellowship of believers that has wrecked and weakened the *ummah* to the present day. The Koran is very clear on the subject.

The *ummah* is a community of believers that

- is united as one people and one nation whose hearts Allah joined in love so that they are brethren to one another,
- enjoins good and forbids evil,
- is committed to truth and administers justice based on truth,
- acts justly to one another and others,

- observes due balance and moderation in all its actions and avoids extremism where men and women are straight and honest in all their dealings.

The Islamic society

- maintains itself in a permanent state of surrender to Allah.
- is united in a single brotherhood, not to be divided into sects, schisms, principalities, states, or kingdoms as Allah has promised *Azabu azeem*, a dreadful penalty, to those causing divisions among the *ummah*;
- looks after its own members in peace, tribulation, and adversity and in times of stress.

The Islamic society as envisioned in the Koran and the tradition is moral and just. It is a society in which every individual—man and woman, from the highest to the lowest, from the first to the last—has equal, unimpeded, and unquestionable.

- right to freedom.
- right to practice his or her faith in accordance with their beliefs as, in Islam, there is no compulsion in matters of religion.
- right to life, which includes mental, physical, and emotional well-being.
- right to safeguard one's property.
- right to intellectual endeavors, acquisition of knowledge, and education;
- right to make a living.
- right to freedom of speech and action, to enjoin good and forbid evil.

In enjoying his freedoms, the individual ensures that his activities do not impinge on the similar rights of others.

All wealth belongs to Allah, who bestows it on some people more than others. This wealth is given in trust, whereby the possessor is obliged to give the surplus for Allah's cause, to his kin, to the widows and orphans, and to the needy first in his community and then in the other communities around him. Wealth is to be shared so that not a single individual of the *ummah*, or indeed in the world, should go hungry or be without education and shelter or left untreated against illness.

In the communities of the world, rules for living and sharing were established through usage over thousands of years. However, the Koran abolished some rules and established new ones, which essentially became the social fabric of Islam. Muslim societies have stuck diligently to rituals and conventions regarding prayer and worship and have paid lip service only to activities involving community matters and human relations. Such disregard of the Koranic teachings has created a disastrous effect on the social fabric of Islam.

The Koran and the blessed *Nabi* have imprinted a clear message into the hearts and the psyche of the believer:

I am your Lord and Cherisher: therefore, serve Me and none other. Verily fellowship of yours is a united brotherhood, and hold fast, all together by the Rope, which Allah stretches out for you, and be not divided amongst yourselves. Let there arise out of you a band of people inviting to all that is good, enjoining what is right, and forbidding all that is wrong. You are the best of the peoples evolved from humankind, enjoining what is right, forbidding what is wrong, and believing in Allah. Thus, We have made you an Ummah of the center, that you might be witness over other nations, and the Messenger a witness over yourselves.

Allah affirms to the believers that He is indeed their Lord and Cherisher. He commands the believers to serve Him, to be united in one *ummah*, holding on to the rope of Allah, the covenant, the guidance from Allah. Those who submit to Allah and perform good works have grasped His handhold, the most trustworthy hand.

> The parable of those who spend their wealth in the way of Allah is that of a grain of corn, which grows seven ears, and each ear has a hundred grains. Allah gives plentiful in return to whom He pleases. Those who give generously in the cause of Allah, and do not follow up their gifts with reminders of their generosity are assured of their reward with their Lord. The likeness of those who give generously, seeking to please Allah is as a garden, high and fertile where heavy rain falls on it and makes it yield a double the amount of harvest, and if it receives not heavy rain, light moisture suffices it.

The blessed *Nabi* spoke to the ten thousand believers gathered on Mount Arafat on the ninth day of *Zul-hajj*, 10 hijra:

> All Muslims, (men and women) free or slaves have the same rights and the same responsibilities. None is higher than the other unless he is higher in virtue. All distinctions between the Arabs the non-Arabs, the black, and the white are abolished. All Muslims are brethren. Do Good. Be faithful to your Covenant. Be kind to the orphans. Remember Allah Know that while man being mortal is bound to die, Allah being immortal will live forever.

All believers of God unite to form one community, the fellowship of Allah in which every person, man or woman, is independent yet interdependent on one another as all believers grasp on to the same handhold—the rope that Allah has stretched out for them. In this filial tie of independence, interdependence, and bonding, each believer becomes responsible for the welfare of others. In this relationship, every man is a brother and every woman a sister. This relationship of love and bonding creates equality, respect, kindness, and goodness in the family of believers. There is no jealousy or envy among people. Everyone has the same rights and the same responsibilities. None is higher than the other unless he is higher in virtue. No distinctions between race, tribe, caste, and color exist. All Muslims are brethren. Women have rights over men, and men have similar rights over women.

In this fellowship, there should be no oppression. Allah has guaranteed every individual's rights. Every man, woman, and child has a right to freedom and right to practice their faith in accordance with their beliefs as, in Islam, there is no compulsion in matters of religion. Every person has a right to life, which includes mental, physical, and emotional well-being; right to safeguard one's property; right to intellectual endeavors and acquisition of knowledge and education; right to make a living; and right to free speech and action to enjoin good and forbid evil. In enjoying his freedoms, the individual ensures that his activities do not impinge on the similar rights of others. No one individual or group has the right to oppress a believing man or woman nor to usurp their rights endowed by Allah.

The covenant of Allah symbolizes the relationship between humans, among Allah's creatures, and between man and the rest of His creation. They all share in one Allah, one set of guidance and commandments, the same submission and obedience to Him, and the same set of expectations in accordance with His promises. They all can therefore trust one another since they all have similar obligations and expectations. In view of the Koran, humans, communities, nations, and civilizations will continue to live in harmony and peace so long as they continue to fulfill Allah's covenant.

Economics plays a significant role in the social structure of Islam, so significant that Allah did not leave the economic aspect of life to be solely determined by human intellect, experience, caprice, and lust.

Allah made it subject to revelation. Thus, Muslims prosper when they follow Allah's laws and subject themselves to scarcity when they turn to human systems. The Koran promises peace and plenty for those who obey their covenant with Him, and for those who turn away from Allah's covenant, the Koran portends a life of need, scarcity, and want.

وَمَنْ أَعْرَضَ عَن ذِكْرِى فَإِنَّ لَهُۥ مَعِيشَةً ضَنكًا وَنَحْشُرُهُۥ يَوْمَ ٱلْقِيَـٰمَةِ أَعْمَىٰ ﴿١٢٤﴾ وَكَذَٰلِكَ نَجْزِى مَنْ أَسْرَفَ وَلَمْ يُؤْمِنۢ بِـَٔايَـٰتِ رَبِّهِۦ ۚ

وَلَعَذَابُ ٱلْـَٔاخِرَةِ أَشَدُّ وَأَبْقَىٰٓ ﴿١٢٧﴾ أَفَلَمْ يَهْدِ لَهُمْ كَمْ أَهْلَكْنَا قَبْلَهُم مِّنَ ٱلْقُرُونِ يَمْشُونَ فِى مَسَـٰكِنِهِمْ ۗ إِنَّ فِى ذَٰلِكَ لَـَٔايَـٰتٍ لِّأُو۟لِى ٱلنُّهَىٰ ﴿١٢٨﴾

"But whosoever turns away from My Message, verily for him is a life narrowed down, and We shall raise him up blind on the Day of Judgment."

Thus, do We recompense him who transgresses beyond bounds and believes not in the Signs of his Lord: and the Penalty of the Hereafter is far more grievous and more enduring.

It is not a warning to such men (to call to mind) how many generations before them We destroyed, in whose haunts they (now) move? Verily, in this are Signs for men endued with understanding. (Taha 20:124, 127–28, Koran)

In the above *ayah* of the Koran, the word *ma'eeshat* comes from the word *ma'ashiyyat,* which is the recognized meaning of the word *economics.* The consequences of rejection of Allah's covenant and guidance are clearly portrayed. A life narrowed down or constricted is a miserable one, one of need, scarcity, unhappiness, poverty, hunger, disease, pestilence, and famine all at the same time or separately.

The Koran's covenant does not put off the realization of the fruits of obeying or ignoring Allah's guidance until after death, nor does it hide it in spiritual abstractness. Observance of the covenant makes life on the earth economically, physically, and spiritually rich and happy. Nonobservance of the covenant makes life on the earth economically miserable and physically and spiritually depressing. In fact, the economic, physical, and spiritual condition of a people provides a pragmatic test of the soundness of the revealed guidance.

Furthermore, the Koran declares that the people who transgress Allah's guidance and are economically deprived in this world will also be worse off in the hereafter.

Verily for him is a life narrowed down, and We
shall raise him up blind on the Day of Judgment.

Sama in the Koran signifies the universe and *Ardh* man's domain on earth pertaining to his social and economic world. Allah is the Lord of the heavens and the earth and all that comes forth from them. The divine laws under which the universe functions so meticulously and smoothly should also apply to the economic life of man so that he might achieve a balanced, predictable, equitable, and just financial life. *Sama* is the source of Allah's benevolence to mankind and of His universal laws that govern human subsistence and sustenance on the earth (*Ardh*), controlling man's economic life in this world. Allah's kingdom over the heavens and the earth sustains man's economic life and directly affects man's conduct and his obedience to Allah's covenant.

Ayahs in Sura An-Nahl explain that Allah created heaven and earth for a just cause—to bring peace, harmony, equilibrium, and justice to the universe. He is Allah the One, Lord of the creation. He sends sunshine and water from the heavens for the sustenance of life on the earth—human, plant, and animal life. Allah fashioned the moon and stars to create equilibrium in the universe, every object in its intended place, revolving in its fixed orbit in perfect harmony and balance. Allah is the Creator of the secrets and mysteries of the heavens and the earth. Of the so-called sciences and the knowledge of particles, elements, cells, mitochondria, chromosomes, gravity, and black holes, only an infinitesimal portion is revealed to man, yet man is arrogant and boastful.

خَلَقَ ٱلسَّمَٰوَٰتِ وَٱلْأَرْضَ بِٱلْحَقِّ ۚ تَعَٰلَىٰ عَمَّا يُشْرِكُونَ ٣

He has created the heavens and the earth for
just ends: far is He above having the partners
they ascribe to Him! (An-Nahl 16:3, Koran)

هُوَ ٱلَّذِىٓ أَنزَلَ مِنَ ٱلسَّمَآءِ مَآءً ۖ لَّكُم مِّنْهُ شَرَابٌ وَمِنْهُ شَجَرٌ فِيهِ تُسِيمُونَ ١٠

It is He Who sends down rain from the sky. From it
you drink and out of it (grows) the vegetation on
which you feed your cattle. (An-Nahl 16: 10, Koran)

وَسَخَّرَ لَكُمُ ٱلَّيْلَ وَٱلنَّهَارَ وَٱلشَّمْسَ وَٱلْقَمَرَ ۖ وَٱلنُّجُومُ مُسَخَّرَٰتٌۢ بِأَمْرِهِۦٓ ۗ إِنَّ فِى ذَٰلِكَ لَءَايَٰتٍ لِّقَوْمٍ يَعْقِلُونَ

He has made subject to you the Night and the
Day; the Sun and the Moon; and the Stars are in
subjection by His Command: verily in this are Signs
for men who are wise. (An-Nahl 16:12, Koran)

وَلِلَّهِ غَيْبُ ٱلسَّمَٰوَٰتِ وَٱلْأَرْضِ ۚ وَمَآ أَمْرُ ٱلسَّاعَةِ إِلَّا كَلَمْحِ ٱلْبَصَرِ أَوْ هُوَ أَقْرَبُ ۚ إِنَّ ٱللَّهَ عَلَىٰ كُلِّ شَىْءٍ قَدِيرٌ

To Allah belongs the mystery of the heavens and the
earth. And the Decision of the Hour (of Judgment) is

as the twinkling of any eye, or even quicker: for Allah
hath power over all things. (An-Nahl 16:77, Koran)

In other *ayahs* of Sura An-Nahl, Allah recounts the bounties and comforts He bestowed on man for the sustenance of life and for his economic well-being. Allah created cattle for humans for warmth, food, and transport and horses, mules, and donkeys for riding and for display. With the moisture from the skies, He produces corn, olives, date palms, grapes, and every type of fruit for man. Allah made good things for humans in different colors and quantities for man to celebrate the praises of Allah in gratitude. Allah made sea subject to man so that he may eat fresh and tender seafood and obtain beautiful ornaments, sail his ships, and plow the oceans around the world. From the cattle, Allah produces milk, pure and wholesome, to drink; and from the fruit of the date palm and vines, one gets food and drink and from the bees honey of varying colors that heals ailments.

وَٱلْأَنْعَٰمَ خَلَقَهَا ۗ لَكُمْ فِيهَا دِفْءٌ وَمَنَٰفِعُ وَمِنْهَا تَأْكُلُونَ ﴿٥﴾ وَلَكُمْ فِيهَا جَمَالٌ حِينَ تُرِيحُونَ وَحِينَ تَسْرَحُونَ ﴿٦﴾ وَتَحْمِلُ
أَثْقَالَكُمْ إِلَىٰ بَلَدٍ لَّمْ تَكُونُوا۟ بَٰلِغِيهِ إِلَّا بِشِقِّ ٱلْأَنفُسِ ۚ إِنَّ رَبَّكُمْ لَرَءُوفٌ رَّحِيمٌ ﴿٧﴾ وَٱلْخَيْلَ وَٱلْبِغَالَ وَٱلْحَمِيرَ لِتَرْكَبُوهَا وَزِينَةً ۚ وَيَخْلُقُ مَا
لَا تَعْلَمُونَ

And cattle He has created for you (humans):
from them ye derive warmth and numerous
benefits and of their (meat) ye eat.

And ye have a sense of pride and beauty in them
as you drive them home in the evening and as
you lead them forth to pasture in the morning.

And they carry your heavy loads to lands
that you could not (otherwise) reach

except with souls distressed: for your Lord
is indeed Most Kind, Most Merciful.

And (He has created) horses, mules and donkeys,
for you to ride and use for show; and He has
created (other) things of which you have no
knowledge. (An-Nahl 16:5–8, Koran)

هُوَ ٱلَّذِىٓ أَنزَلَ مِنَ ٱلسَّمَآءِ مَآءً لَّكُم مِّنْهُ شَرَابٌ وَمِنْهُ شَجَرٌ فِيهِ تُسِيمُونَ ۝ يُنۢبِتُ لَكُم بِهِ ٱلزَّرْعَ وَٱلزَّيْتُونَ وَٱلنَّخِيلَ
وَٱلْأَعْنَـٰبَ وَمِن كُلِّ ٱلثَّمَرَٰتِ ۗ إِنَّ فِى ذَٰلِكَ لَـَٔايَةً لِّقَوْمٍ يَتَفَكَّرُونَ ۝ وَسَخَّرَ لَكُمُ ٱلَّيْلَ وَٱلنَّهَارَ وَٱلشَّمْسَ وَٱلْقَمَرَ ۖ وَٱلنُّجُومُ مُسَخَّرَٰتٌۢ
بِأَمْرِهِۦٓ ۗ إِنَّ فِى ذَٰلِكَ لَـَٔايَـٰتٍ لِّقَوْمٍ يَعْقِلُونَ ۝ وَمَا ذَرَأَ لَكُمْ فِى ٱلْأَرْضِ مُخْتَلِفًا أَلْوَٰنُهُۥٓ ۗ إِنَّ فِى ذَٰلِكَ لَـَٔايَةً لِّقَوْمٍ يَذَّكَّرُونَ
۝ وَهُوَ ٱلَّذِى سَخَّرَ ٱلْبَحْرَ لِتَأْكُلُوا۟ مِنْهُ لَحْمًا طَرِيًّا وَتَسْتَخْرِجُوا۟ مِنْهُ حِلْيَةً تَلْبَسُونَهَا وَتَرَى ٱلْفُلْكَ مَوَاخِرَ فِيهِ وَلِتَبْتَغُوا۟ مِن فَضْلِهِۦ
وَلَعَلَّكُمْ تَشْكُرُونَ ۝ وَأَلْقَىٰ فِى ٱلْأَرْضِ رَوَٰسِىَ أَن تَمِيدَ بِكُمْ وَأَنْهَـٰرًا وَسُبُلًا لَّعَلَّكُمْ تَهْتَدُونَ ۝ وَعَلَـٰمَـٰتٍ ۚ وَبِٱلنَّجْمِ هُمْ يَهْتَدُونَ

It is He Who sends down rain from the sky.
From it ye drink and out of it (grows) the
vegetation on which ye feed your cattle.

With it He produces for you corn, olives, date
palms, grapes and every kind of fruit: verily in
this is a Sign for those who give thought.

He has made subject to you the Night and
the Day; the Sun and the Moon; and the Stars
are in subjection by His Command: verily
in this are Signs for men who are wise.

And the things on this earth which He has multiplied
in varying colors (and qualities): verily in this a Sign for
men who celebrate the praises of Allah (in gratitude).

It is He Who has made the sea subject, that ye
may eat thereof flesh that is fresh and tender and
that you may extract there from ornaments to
wear and you see the ships therein that plough
the waves, that you may seek (thus) of the
bounty of Allah and that you may be grateful.

And He has set up on the earth mountains
standing firm, lest it should shake with you; and
rivers and roads; that ye may guide yourselves.

And marks and signposts; and by the stars (Men)
guide themselves. (An-Nahl 16:10-16, Koran)

وَإِنَّ لَكُمْ فِي ٱلْأَنْعَٰمِ لَعِبْرَةً ۖ نُّسْقِيكُم مِّمَّا فِي بُطُونِهِۦ مِنۢ بَيْنِ فَرْثٍ وَدَمٍ لَّبَنًا خَالِصًا سَآئِغًا لِّلشَّٰرِبِينَ ﴿٦٦﴾ وَمِن ثَمَرَٰتِ ٱلنَّخِيلِ وَٱلْأَعْنَٰبِ
تَتَّخِذُونَ مِنْهُ سَكَرًا وَرِزْقًا حَسَنًا ۗ إِنَّ فِي ذَٰلِكَ لَءَايَةً لِّقَوْمٍ يَعْقِلُونَ ﴿٦٧﴾ وَأَوْحَىٰ رَبُّكَ إِلَى ٱلنَّحْلِ أَنِ ٱتَّخِذِي مِنَ ٱلْجِبَالِ بُيُوتًا وَمِنَ ٱلشَّجَرِ وَمِمَّا
يَعْرِشُونَ ﴿٦٨﴾ ثُمَّ كُلِي مِن كُلِّ ٱلثَّمَرَٰتِ فَٱسْلُكِي سُبُلَ رَبِّكِ ذُلُلًا ۚ يَخْرُجُ مِنۢ بُطُونِهَا شَرَابٌ مُّخْتَلِفٌ أَلْوَٰنُهُۥ فِيهِ شِفَآءٌ لِّلنَّاسِ ۗ إِنَّ فِي ذَٰلِكَ لَءَايَةً
لِّقَوْمٍ يَتَفَكَّرُونَ ﴿٦٩﴾

And verily in cattle (too) will ye find an instructive
Sign. From what is within their bodies, between
excretions and blood, We produce, for your drink,
milk, pure and agreeable to those who drink it.

And from the fruit of the date palm and the vine,
ye get out wholesome drink and food: behold,
in this also is a Sign for those who are wise.

And thy Lord taught the Bee to build its cells
in hills, on trees and in (men's) habitations.

Then to eat of all the produce (of the earth)and find
with skill the spacious paths of its Lord: there issues
from within their bodies a drink of varying colors,
wherein is healing for men: verily in this is a Sign for
those who give thought. (An-Nahl 16:66–69, Koran)

Allah created the earth and then bestowed on man His favors to extract sustenance from it. He also created the sun, moon, and stars to create a just equilibrium and harmony in the universe. The sun provides energy for the growth, sustenance, and well-being of humans, plants, and animals. Gradually, man began to extract more than his personal needs from the earth; and the boom of economics, trade, and commerce started, creating cycles of imbalance, disharmony, wars, poverty, and injustice throughout the globe. Not only did this disharmony caused by greed blemish humans but animal life also suffered by the disappearance of whole species. Pollution and contamination of the environment resulted from the race trying to accumulate and hoard the world's wealth in a few hands. Man disobeyed Allah's universal laws and covenant.

The ingredients of wealth, prosperity, and human welfare lie in the labor and sweat of man, the natural resources of the land, and the marketing of the products of human sweat and such resources. Allah has provided all these ingredients to humans in every community in abundance. He has, in addition, given the believers the key and the rules for the use of such ingredients in His covenant. It is for the believers to use their labor and Allah's gifts and guidance to create prosperity for the welfare of their communities. While Allah has provided man with the fruit of heavens and earth, *sama* and *Ardh,* it is for man to utilize such gifts for the benefit of his community, the *ummah*. The key lies in the following words:

> Virtue is to spend of ones means out of love of Allah for the kin, for the orphans, for the needy, for the wayfarer, for those who ask, and for the ransom of those in bondage. The parable of those who spend their substance in the way of Allah is that of a grain of corn: it grows seven ears, and each ear has a hundred grains. Allah gives plentiful in return to whom He pleases, Allah cares for all His beings, and He knows all that goes on everywhere. Those who give generously in the cause of Allah, and do not follow up their gifts with reminders of their generosity or with injury, are assured of their reward with their Lord and on them shall be no fear, nor shall they grieve. Kind words and the covering of faults are better than charity followed by insult. Allah reminds the Believers, "Void not your charity by boast, conceit, and insult, by reminders of your generosity like those who want their generosity to be noted by all men, but they believe neither in Allah nor in the Last Day. Theirs is a parable of a hard-barren rock, on which there is a little soil, washed by heavy rain, which leaves it just a bare stone. The likeness of those who give generously, seeking to please Allah and to strengthen their souls, is as a garden, high and fertile where heavy rain falls on it and makes it yield a double the amount of harvest, and if it receives not heavy rain, light moisture suffices it". Allah calls upon the Believers: "Behold! You are those who are invited to spend of your means in the Way of Allah: but among you are some that are parsimonious. But any who are miserly are so at the expense of their own

souls. But Allah is free of all wants, and it is you that are needy". If you turn back from Allah's Path, Allah will substitute another people in your place who will be in Taqwa of Allah and do Allah's bidding. And O you Believers! (Men and Women) Turn you all together Toward Allah that you may prosper. The believers, men and women are protectors one of another; they enjoin what is just and forbid what is evil. They observe regular prayers, practice regular charity, and obey Allah and His Messenger. On them will Allah pour His mercy, for Allah is exalted in power, Wise.

Giving and receiving of means, substance, and wealth in the cause of Allah involves two parties among the believers. Those who give and those who receive are both, in effect, endowed with unutilized and unrecognized wealth. Lack of utilization of such wealth is indeed the cause of poverty, want, hunger, and disease in the world. Communists and capitalists have failed to eradicate poverty because both systems lack understanding of God's laws and the ethical and moral use of wealth. Although the "Muslims" in the last 1,400 years achieved spiritual maturity, they failed to recognize the decay of their *nafs* and their obligation to their communities.

The believer's faith in Allah and his commitment to His covenant attains spiritual maturity, which in turn promotes the ethical content in the believer. This ethical content nurtures the believer's inner character and enhances the person's moral maturity. This indeed was the aim of the teachings of all of Allah's prophets throughout the centuries the world over. Only with the achievement of this ethical and moral content in their character will the believers unite to form a community in which every person, man or woman, is independent yet dependent on one another as each one hangs on to the rope that Allah has cast for them.

Fulfillment of the Covenant. Among the 1.5 billion believers around the world, there are about 900 million individuals capable of working. Out of these men and women, about 40 percent are underproductive or unemployed owing to lack of opportunity and social constraints. These men and women have *means and wealth* of 7,920,000 unspent workdays or 1,393,920,000 human hours of work each month that have undergone non fruition.

In a smaller community of 50,000 men and women, the comparable figures will be 264,000 days' worth of unutilized means and wealth and 2,112,000 human hours of work wasted to the community. In the whole of the Islamic world, the Muslim communities lose over ten billion dollars every month in productivity. A smaller community of 50,000 thus missed over twenty million dollars per month. In fact, the loss to this small community is far, far greater. For instance, if one human hour produces three items (i.e., electric lamps):

three electric lamps cost $30,

the manufacturer makes a profit of $5 on each lamp ($45),

the intermediary/distributor charges $3,

the retailer makes a profit of $7 on each item ($21),

the transport cost incurred is $2,

5 percent manufacturer's tax is $3.55, and

sales tax of 10 percent is $7.45.

Total: $82

The total fallout from the manufacture and labor of one human hour benefits the community with $82 plus employment to workers in a factory, wholesale and retail, power and transport businesses, as well as real estate. When all under- and unemployed workforce of a community of 50,000 donates its available work hours for the benefit of their community in one year, the result is an astounding sum of *over two billion dollars*. Yet this is not the whole picture. The interaction of various trades, professions, and guilds will compound these figures over many folds.

Applying the same incomplete figures of $82 per hour to the lost 1,393,920,000 human hours of work per month, the entire Muslim *ummah* loses the sum total of productivity and wealth amounting to $1,371,616,280,000 every year. In addition, the *ummah* continues to suffer deprivation, poverty, oppression, and humiliation year after year.

When a member of a closed fraternal community gains wealth, the fallout of such a gain is to the whole community. Similarly, the loss to one of its members is a loss to the whole community. When community members help one of the members gain wealth, the fallout of this gain helps the whole community. When the whole community helps one another without regard to individual gain, everyone gains materially to a greater and a lesser degree. The gain is material and spiritual and in harmony with Allah's laws of nature.

Summary

When the believers in commitment to their *iman* in Allah and to their covenant with Him attain spiritual maturity, their faith, actions, and rituals promote the ethical content in the believer that nurtures inner character and furthers the person's moral maturation. Thus, the outer self of the believer leads to conformity and acceptance of social roles within his community, the *ummah*; the inner self cultivates his conscience and character. This cultivation involves broader education and deep reflection of one's motives and actions. It is a lifetime commitment to build, carve, and polish the stone of one's character until it becomes a lustrous gem of moral perfection. And this indeed was the aim of the teachings of all of Allah's prophets throughout the centuries the world over. Only with the achievement of this ethical and moral content in their character will the believers unite to form a community in which every person, man or woman, is independent yet dependent on one another as each one clasps the rope that Allah has cast for them.

The *ummah* is made up of hundreds of thousands mini-*ummahs* and communities. In a community of 50,000, when the 12,000 unemployed individuals *donate* their wealth and means of labor and expertise worth 264,000 days or 2,112,000 hours to the community, there will be a tremendous gain to the community. This time is donated to all spheres of life in the community where help is required.

a) A community always requires help in the development of the spiritual, mental, and intellectual bank of the community. The *ummah* had lagged behind in education, knowledge, and technology because those who are empowered to spread education and knowledge to their own children and to their community are selfish and ignorant of their obligations to Islam and Allah's covenant. Everyone who knows must pass on his knowledge and wisdom to those who desire that knowledge. Everyone who has a craft must train others. Everyone endowed with technology must teach others. The community must set up classes, schools, workshops, and laboratories for every individual to learn and acquire skills. Every man and woman must know their Koran, their three Rs, and computer skills and achieve some aspect of technical skill in manufacturing and building.
b) Unlike the economic systems espoused by capitalism and communism, the Koran proposes a gift economy in the cause of Allah. People must volunteer their time without expectation of any gain to build the infrastructure of their community. They should construct roads. Every community

must have clean and safe running water and sewage systems. The first impression of every habitation comes from its smells, appearance, and sounds. A community in which ten *muezzins* proclaim the *adhan* simultaneously over a hundred loudspeakers to the residents of the same little community results in an incoherent racket of competing, screaming mullahs who disgrace the sanctity of Allah's name. In the same street are seen worshippers walking to their mosque, clutching on to their pant legs, tripping over domestic and animal waste, and reeking of raw sewage. Shopkeepers shout from their stalls over the pandemonium of the screaming mullahs, unaware of the garbage around their feet. The starched white garments and the headgear of those passing by attract attention to the care devoted to their personal appearance and attire. Yet at their feet sits a destitute family with their hands stretched, asking for the compassion and mercy of those passing by with little response. For most people, rituals of congregation prayers are the only essentials of Islam. Leaning over to clean his garbage in the street is beneath the average person's dignity. Such tasks are reserved for the poor, the menial, and the women. This is not what Islam is supposed to be. The Koran calls for remembrance of Allah in love, humility, dignity, and decorum. Islam demands cleanliness and orderliness. There are no beggars in Islam. Everyone in need is cared for before he is forced into the street. Submission to Allah obliges the believers to obey the covenant and carry out their duty to their Creator, to their fellow man, and to Allah's creation. Only those who "have faith and do righteous acts" will have success in their earthly lives and in the hereafter. The phrase *amilu al saalihaat* (to perform beautiful acts, to perform wholesome deeds) refers to those who persist in striving to set things right, who restore harmony, peace, and balance. Other acts of good works recognized in the Koran are to show compassion, to be merciful and forgive others, to be just, to protect the weak, to defend the oppressed, to be generous and charitable, to be truthful, to seek knowledge and wisdom, to be kind to others, to be peaceful, to love others, to perform acts of cleanliness, and to perform beautiful deeds.

c)

إِنَّ ٱلَّذِينَ ءَامَنُوا۟ وَعَمِلُوا۟ ٱلصَّٰلِحَٰتِ سَيَجْعَلُ لَهُمُ ٱلرَّحْمَٰنُ وُدًّا ﴿٩٦﴾

On those who believe and do good, will
[Allah] Most Gracious bestow love.

There are fifty verses in the Koran that remind the believers of the rewards of beautiful and righteous deeds. Thus, beautifying and cleaning one's neighborhood, planting trees and gardens, building houses for the homeless, building schools and community workshops, building roads, digging wells, and laying water pipelines are acts of goodness in the cause of Allah.

فِي سَبِيلِ ٱللهِ.

d) Acts of goodwill and charity will produce prosperity among the *ummah* only when every person with time on his hand will go to every field, every shop, every home, and every factory to help increase the productivity of that business in the community. Then every barren field will be cultivated, every field with a crop hoed, fertilized, and seeded. Every bare patch of land will be planted with saplings and watered. The orchards will be pruned, fertilized, grafted, and watered. Olive trees, fruit trees, new orchards, and forests will be planted. Irrigation dams, ditches, and canals will be dug. Wells will be dug. Factories will be replenished, repaired, and brought into full production. Cattle, sheep, goats, and poultry will be corralled and managed for the benefit of all. Fish farms will be built to increase food production. Factories will be built to produce consumer goods, machinery, computers, and raw material for the industry. Every derelict home and public building will be repaired or rebuilt. Because of this cooperation and giving of ones "*means and wealth in the cause of Allah,*" the production of land and factories will double and triple within three years. There will be no need to import food and grains into the Dar es Salaam.

e) Those with *means* and those with jobs, professions, businesses, lands, and factories will, in return for the efforts of those who shed their sweat, will donate funds, promissory notes, food, money, clothing, and shelter. This is the least any human would do.

f) More importantly, they will provide funds, labor, and other means to provide their community with building materials, heavy-duty equipment, and fuel and material for the construction of homes, offices, other buildings, factories, schools, workshops, and clinics. The community, through its means in the cause of Allah, will manufacture its own building material—bricks, stone, cement, wood products, and tools. Initially, this material will be basic; but within five years with experience and import of technology, the optimum standard of manufactured goods will be achieved. Everyone will work to achieve perfection. This material and the expertise thus acquired will become the basis of a model Islamic cooperative community, self-sufficient in all essentials. In cooperation, the community will build housing for every family.

g) Every community will set up cooperative industrial, agricultural, and manufacturing plants; technical training institutes; workshops; and laboratories to train every resident in a useful skill. All workers and entrepreneurs will jointly own the community cooperatives.
h) Each community will cooperate with the neighboring communities to share expertise and skills in training, manufacture, and trade.
i) Every community will develop a social contract based on the covenant of Allah. This contract will define metered goals, through which by the end of three to five years every member will have a job, education, health care, and a plot to build a home in. All citizens will share in the benefits of this endeavor.
j) The purpose behind the enterprise of sharing work, skills, and enterprise is multifold.

Allah helps those who help themselves. In the present age, 70 percent of the world's wealth is held by fewer than 5 percent of the people. Almost every government of the world is run by people from this group of 5 percent. With the empowerment of the common believer, every man will share the world and, under Allah's covenant, will not suffer from want. The aim, therefore, is:

1. to organize united and devout communities that will use their mutual labor, skills, and enterprise to help themselves, the *ummah*, and the rest of humanity for peace, harmony, and prosperity.
2. to enable every man and woman achieve their full potential in their spiritual and material life through education and acquisition of skills.

With the acquisition of common skills required in manufacturing, the communities of the *ummah* will achieve specialization in different fields. All the communities from Indonesia to Mauritania will begin to manufacture products required in the Dar es Salaam. Instead of spending hundreds of millions of dollars to set up mega factories to manufacture agricultural machinery, communities will set up affordable small units and share the design and fabrication of parts of the equipment. One town may manufacture the chassis of a tractor, the next the transmission, while others share in building the engine, wheels, tires, tanks, hydraulics, and front-end loaders. All such parts will then be shipped and assembled in plants in parts of the Dar es Salaam in Asia, Africa, and Europe where needed. Every community will share in sweat and its fruit.

Automobiles, trucks, aircraft, heavy machinery, and ships will be fabricated in small units. Communities will specialize and subspecialize in different fields of manufacture and share in the manufacture of all machinery. Many communities will share work and its reward.

To begin with, small factories in the Dar es Salaam will begin to manufacture spare parts for automobiles and trucks used in the land. Some plants will specialize in the fabrication of engines while others build chassis, brakes, carburetors, tires, and so on. After standardization of their manufacturing, they will be able to assemble their own cars and trucks. They will be able to build cheap, durable, and sturdy modular cars and trucks that will withstand rough terrain and hot, dusty climates. Because of their modular design, low price, sturdiness, and cheap spare parts, they will find ready markets in the Dar es Salaam, India, China, South America, and Africa. All such manufactures will find willing buyers among the six billion poor people of the world. Similar cooperation among small communities of the Dar es Salaam in Africa, Middle East, and Central and South Asia will develop local chemical, pharmaceutical, agricultural, industrial, nautical, aeronautical, fisheries, communication, and computer-based industries.

The Dar es Salaam is blessed with Allah's promise of His grace. Muslims have failed to recognize His blessings while the greedy Arab sheikhs and the Western countries are devouring their people's wealth. How could a people with such wealth all around them suffer from such poverty and deprivation?

The Dar es Salaam produces commodities that are in great demand in the rest of the world; therefore, production and marketing and the prices of the commodities should be regulated by the market forces of supply and demand rather than by political factors where dynasties seek protection by paying with blood money. In spite of depleted petroleum exports from Iraq, the Dar es Salaam exports

- 10,260,950,000 42-gallon barrels of crude oil;
- 3,021,250,000 barrels of refined petroleum products as aviation fuel, automobile petrol, lubrication products, and heating oils;
- 7,827,540,000,000 cubic meters of natural gas;
- 305,951,000,000 cubic meters of dry products of natural gas;
- 1,792,339,000 42-gallon barrels of natural liquid gas such as propane, in addition to plastics and other by-products of the oil industry.

The producing countries are paid at the producing oil wells at prices manipulated by major oil companies. These oil companies also control the economies of the Western world, and the same companies are responsible for all turmoil and conflicts around the Middle East. Such conflicts include the ongoing Iraq wars. The reason for the conflicts is to keep the flow of cheap Middle Eastern oil by keeping the Gulf oil sheikhs and the Saudis on edge constantly, worrying about their thrones, while stealing their money. The Western economy depends on cheap Arab oil that the quarrelsome, ignorant, and greedy Arab sheikhs willingly subsidize.

For over two decades, the price of oil has been artificially priced between $18 and $30. For instance, at $30 a barrel, the oil companies buy 10,260,950,000 barrels of crude oil at $300,260,950,000 from the Middle East. They ship it in their own tankers, insure it with their own companies, and refine it in their own refineries. The refined by-products of crude oil, petrol, diesel, jet fuel heating oil, propane, asphalt, and chemical products are sold to the motorists, airlines, transport companies, and textile, plastic, sports goods, nylon, pharmaceutical, highway, pesticide, fertilizer, and tire industries in Europe and North America and the Far East for $3.2 trillion, with $1.2 trillion going to the Western governments of G8 in taxes and over $2.0 trillion to the oil companies before paying for the shipping and refining costs to their own companies. That is a profit of over $1.7 trillion, unimaginable in any other industry. No wonder the president of the United States is a functionary of the oil companies, with the CIA as their security force and the American marines their storm troopers.

Overall, if the Dar es Salaam refined and processed its own petroleum products and developed its own chemical and by-products industry, the total gain to its population will be full employment, with everyone owning a home in a land with fully developed infrastructure on transport, health care, education, human development, and resource sectors. The petroleum and energy sector alone will provide the Dar es Salaam with over $150 trillion worth of economic benefits in jobs, industrial growth, shipping, insurance, and banking, whereas today only the oil-producing sheikhs receive less than two to three hundred billion dollars. With the world's current economic situation, the realistic value of a barrel of unrefined crude oil is $150. The revenue to the Dar es Salaam for selling only the unrefined crude oil should be $1,500,260,950,000. The world's economic structure is based on Islamic oil exports with systematic transfer of wealth to a handful of industrialized countries.

The Dar es Salaam will need to start the drawing board with the mineral, commodity, and oil industries. The oil companies will need to understand the new realities of doing business with the Dar es Salaam.

1. The Dar es Salaam will refine all its oil for the world.
2. It will also ship oil products in its own ships to the importing ports.
3. It will set up a chemical industry providing raw products to the transport, textile, plastic, sports goods, nylon, pharmaceutical, highway, pesticide, fertilizer, and tire manufacturing industries in the Dar es Salaam and around the world at cheap and competitive rates.
4. The Dar es Salaam oil industry will finance and own 50 to 75 percent share of all distribution to the retail pumps in the consuming countries around the globe. With this understanding, the foreign oil companies will be permitted up to 25 percent share in the refining industry in their own countries and in the Dar es Salaam.
5. As part of the petroleum sales agreement, the consuming countries will be obliged to buy petroleum by-products such as plastics, chemicals, and fertilizers manufactured by industries in the Dar es Salaam.
6. All payments will be in gold and gold coins and the Islamic dinar. No fiat money will be traded in the Dar es Salaam. Goods, however, may be traded with barter and balance of payments adjusted with gold between the countries quarterly. The gold and oil prices will naturally rise to the natural market value as the artificial stimulation of economies through artificial factors of stock market, increased interest rates, and increase of paper notes will disappear from the Dar es Salaam. The price of gold will hit its normal intrinsic value of $2,500–$4,000 per troy ounce.

If one is to estimate the amount of gold hoarded and accumulated in state and private collections in the Islamic world, we will find that during the last few hundred years an average Muslim couple has inherited or purchased about 120 grams of gold in the form of jewelry. Poor couples do not own any. Rich couples are weighed down by tens of kilograms of gold jewelry, averaging more than 120 grams or about 10 *tolas* per couple around the Muslim world. This hoard of gold in the Dar es Salaam is estimated to be 52,800 tons (1,697,559,418.82 troy ounces) of accumulated wealth lying idly, while millions of Muslims starve and go without essentials. At today's prices, this wealth totals more than three and a half trillion dollars.

In addition, there is a hoard of precious stones worth another one hundred billion dollars. Women own most of the bullion and precious stones. Most of them live in communities where, for hundreds of generations, women and men have lost their independent financial cognitive skills in matters outside the norm of their community. Women have it in their power to attain equality, respect, and financial independence by attaining skills and knowledge by investing their dormant wealth of gold and precious stones in the agriculture and industrial development of their communities. They will thus control their own and their family's destiny and achieve primacy in their community. The useless symbols of ostentation, pride, and ego will benefit each community of fifty thousand individuals with an investment of about $25 million in agricultural, industrial, and infrastructure projects with a return of 10 percent of $ 2.5 million every year.

The governments of marauding monarchs—whether Muslim, non-Muslim, European, African, Turk, Safavid, or Moguls—were there to rule for their own benefit. Their interest in matters of the *din* or in the welfare of the common man was always subordinate to their accumulation of power and riches. The same is true of this day's governments. No part of the *ummah* can depend on the governments from outside their own community to relieve them of poverty, hardship, or sickness. It must come from within the people. Communities must build their own infrastructure, build their own institutions, and keep peace. *The only institution for such development is the government of the community by the community.* Wise men and women from the community will be just, fair, truthful, and obedient to their covenant. They will run the community's affairs justly. When the communities select evil, dishonest, unjust, and unbelieving people to run their affairs, the communities will have similar unmerited and undeserved consequences. Citizens, believing men and women, must learn their Koran, know their rights, help one another, unite their community, and keep the usurpers and oppressors out of their community.

Islam has teachers, wise men, and holy men, but none of them can claim to be the spokespersons of Allah. There is no priesthood in Islam. No one has been ordained to speak on behalf of Allah except the prophets. No man, since the days of the prophets, has been ordained to formulate dogma nor creed. Total Koran is the total *din* of Islam. Every believer, man and woman, has inherited the legacy of the blessed prophet, the Koran. Anyone who does not understand a part of the Koran is free to seek the knowledge from the one who knows. One who has the knowledge can only provide his own interpretation. He cannot assume Allah's authority or His prerogative. The recipe for righteousness, peace, and prosperity is in the Koran. People will ignore it at their own peril.

Summary: The knowledge is in the Koran. Salvation and prosperity lies in the practice gained from such knowledge.

Index

C

D

E

F

G

H

N

O

P

R

S

T

U

W

Y